PATRICK HENRY
PRACTICAL REVOLUTIONARY

Clay bust of Patrick Henry. Made by an Italian traveling in Virginia in 1788 and considered "a perfect likeness."

Patrick Henry

PRACTICAL REVOLUTIONARY

BY

Robert Douthat Meade

J. B. LIPPINCOTT COMPANY

Philadelphia and New York

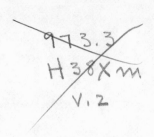

To Lucy Boyd Meade

By Robert Douthat Meade

PATRICK HENRY: PRACTICAL REVOLUTIONARY
PATRICK HENRY: PATRIOT IN THE MAKING
JUDAH P. BENJAMIN: CONFEDERATE STATESMAN

ACKNOWLEDGMENTS

SINCE completing the first volume of this Patrick Henry biography in 1957, I have worked on the second volume in spare hours for over ten years. During this lengthy period I have received invaluable grants-in-aid and other assistance from numerous foundations and interested friends. Often the latter were busy men who gave freely of their own time, and they all, generous corporations' and individuals alike, contributed much to whatever merits the volume possesses.

For this, as well as the first Henry volume, I have endeavored to examine all significant source material, whether located in this country, in England, or in Scotland. Foundations and private individuals who have helped to finance the research and writing for the second volume are the John Simon Guggenheim Memorial Foundation; the American Council of Learned Societies; Eugene B. Casey, Rockville, Md., through the Patrick Henry Memorial Foundation; The Wright and Mariam Tisdale Foundation, Dearborn, Mich.; and the Ford Foundation through Randolph-Macon Woman's College. A number of persons have read and criticized one or more chapters and I wish to make special acknowledgments in this connection to Ralph Ketcham, Syracuse University; Lyman H. Butterfield, Boston, Mass.; Bernhard Knollenberg, Chester, Conn.; Jane Carson, Williamsburg, Va.; Daniel J. Boorstin, University of Chicago; Hugh Lefler, University of North Carolina; the late Judge Leon Bazile, Elmont, Va.; Mrs. P. F. Tuck, a Henry descendant and former staff member of St. John's Episcopal Church, Richmond, Va.; John Fontaine, Paces, Va., another Henry descendant and a fountainhead of information on the Henry family; William M. E. Rachal, Virginia Historical Society; and Robert L. Scribner, *The James Madison Papers*, in care of the Historical Society.

[vii]

ACKNOWLEDGMENTS

For research, clerical assistance, and other valued help, I am particularly indebted to my wife, Lucy Boyd Meade; also to Mrs. Harvey Hoyt of Lynchburg, my principal assistant during the past seven years; the late James Easley, Halifax, Va., when president of the Patrick Henry Memorial Foundation, and D. Quinn Eggleston, Drakes Branch, Va., the current president; Mrs. John Fanfani, Bethesda, Md.; Mrs. Thomas Mayo IV, Hampden-Sydney, Va.; Mrs. Fred Terrell, Jr., Miss Tunstall Collins, and William Dunn, all of Lynchburg, and other persons cited in the Notes for the individual chapters.

I wish to thank the staff members of the Library of Randolph-Macon Woman's College and the Jones Memorial Library, Lynchburg, Va.; the University of Virginia Library; and the Virginia State Library for their efficient help with my many requests; also Randolph-Macon Woman's College, and particularly President William F. Quillian, for giving me leaves of absence from college duties.

Finally, I am very grateful for excellent editing and other encouragement to J. B. Lippincott Company, and especially my chief editor, Miss Tay Hohoff.

CONTENTS

CONTENTS

ILLUSTRATIONS

Grouped in this order following page 244

St. John's Episcopal Church, Richmond, Va.

St. John's interior, setting of "Give Me Liberty" speech

Henry's ivory letter opener, wielded at climax of his famous speech

The Old Capitol, Richmond

Salisbury, near Midlothian. Henry's country home circa 1784-1786

Letter of Governor Henry to Governor Smallwood of Maryland

Patrick Henry's sister, Elizabeth

Dorothea Spotswood Henry, daughter of Patrick Henry

"Attempt at the features" of Patrick Henry

Entries by Henry in the family Bible

The chair in which Patrick Henry died at Red Hill

Red Hill, near Brookneal, Va. Restored house and "law office"

1

⤙✥⤚

The Approaching Convention

The dogmas of the quiet past are inadequate to the stormy present. The occasion is piled high with difficulty, and we must rise with the occasion.——ABRAHAM LINCOLN [1]

Late October, 1774. Henry returns home to Hanover County, Virginia, from the First Continental Congress.

November, 1774. Formation of Hanover County Committee. "Soon afterwards" Henry exhorts the Hanover volunteers.

December 1, 1774. Deadline after which the Americans agreed to import no British goods.

December 15, 1774. Publication of forced recantations by two Hanover County opponents of the Association, the anti-British trade boycott.

January–February–early March, 1775. Call for election of delegates in various Virginia counties. Henry elected a representative from Hanover.

BEFORE LEAVING PHILADELPHIA and the First Continental Congress, Patrick Henry had found ample evidence that a crisis was rapidly approaching in the relations between England and the colonies. On October 12, 1774, the *Pennsylvania Gazette* had carried a New York dispatch of the tenth stating that on that very morning His Majesty's Forty-Seventh Regiment and part of the Royal Irish would embark for Boston. The Tenth and Fifty-Second Regiments, at Halifax, were to hold themselves ready to sail for that disaffected Massachusetts port at an hour's warning.

This grave news, hardly surprising to American leaders such as Henry and the Adamses, was followed within a few weeks by more, of which Henry could appreciate the full import. Even before word reached London of the radical action taken by Congress, the Ministry was initiating "very vigorous measures," the *Gazette* reported. And it added this sentient item: "Some of the principal Gentlemen who distinguished themselves in America in defense of their Charter Rights, are to be brought over [to England] in order for an inquiry to be made into their conduct." [2]

That Patrick Henry would be one of these "principal Gentlemen" there could be little doubt. Had he not stated on the floor of the Philadelphia convention that the American colonies were now in a state of nature, then declared, "The distinctions between Virginians, Pennsylvanians, New Yorkers, and New Englanders, are no more. I am not a Virginian, but an American"? [3] A decade before, in 1763–1765, had he not delivered two speeches of a seditious nature, both evoking cries of "treason, treason" from conservative listeners? [4]

"In the Congress of 1774," so John Adams would write Jefferson, "there was not one member, except Patrick Henry, who appeared to me sensible of the precipice or, rather, the pinnacle, on which he stood, and had candour and courage enough to acknowledge it." [5]

In Philadelphia, concurring with the statement of a Massachusetts patriot, Major Joseph Hawley, read to him by Adams, Henry had stated, "We must fight. By God, I am of that man's mind" (Adams was at pains to explain that Henry intended no irreverence); [6] and back home in Hanover he had reaffirmed his strong position. [7] True, this assertion had been made in a circle of friends, but already the *Edinburgh Advertiser* of October 4 was expressing what was a growing opinion in Great Britain:

> The declaration of the Virginians, that it was lawful to repel force by force in case any measures were taken to carry the Proclamation of General Gage into execution, is looked upon here as an overt act of treason, and implies a rebellious intent. [8]

The reference was to the declaration by the Virginia Convention of August, 1774. For this and other extreme actions in the Old Dominion it was Patrick Henry whom the British government would hold most responsible.

Henry was now standing on "the precipice" to which John Adams alluded. Would he risk the dangers of joint leadership in all-out war with the great power of Britain? To begin with, there was the physical risk, enough to blanch the cheek of all but the bravest man. Would an English judge intone for Henry as one did for some Irish rebels (i.e., unsuccessful patriots) that he was a participant in "a traitorous conspiracy" to overthrow the government which it had pleased "Divine Providence" to establish and, therefore, was to be hanged by the neck . . . but "not until [he] was dead." For there was the last gentle touch with the further religious overtone that

> while you are still living your bodies are to be taken down, your bowels torn out and burned before your faces, your head then cut off, and your bodies divided each into four quarters, and your head and quarters to be then at the King's disposal; and may the Almighty God have Mercy on Your souls! [9]

Such cruel punishments were now less often administered. Yet when John Adams had been ordered in 1777 to proceed to France as an American commissioner, he noted that if he were captured by the British he would be tried for treason and had no doubt that "they would go to the extent of their power, and practice upon me all the cruelties of their punishment of treason." [10] George Washington too described himself as "a man who fights under the weight of a proscription" [11]—as could Henry with almost equal reason. Years later, when a counsel in the British Debts Case, he would dwell on the wholesale confiscations inflicted by the British on the Irish rebels, although they "thought themselves engaged in a laudable cause," and on the gibbets in Scotland after the rebellion of 1745. [12] He might expect equally short shrift as an American rebel leader in 1775.

Then there could be the other consequences of inciting an all-out war. "A desperate and bloody touch it will be," Henry had declared. [13] Wars are not fought with feather dusters, and, if the Americans rebelled, the British could hardly be expected to disdain the aid of the

[3]

savage Indians. Soon after Henry returned from Philadelphia, Pinkney's *Virginia Gazette* ran a detailed account of the fierce battle, with
little quarter given, between the redskins under Cornstalk and the
Virginia back-country men under Andrew Lewis. In the battle, fought
October 10, 1774, at Point Pleasant on the Ohio River, several of
Henry's friends or in-laws were involved, one being desperately
wounded.[14]

Henry doubtless had no regular access to newspapers, other than
the *Virginia Gazettes*. To the lively pages of these journals whose
rival editions were published at Williamsburg, the colonial capital,
he perforce turned for his chief source of political news or inspiration
during the period from his return to Virginia in the early fall until
the meeting of the Virginia Convention in late March and the opening guns the next month at Lexington, Massachusetts. Secluded at
Scotchtown, his plantation in upper Hanover, during nearly all of this
interregnum, he was absorbed with plantation and domestic affairs—
including a crushing personal tragedy. But there was time for further
study of a few valued books,[15] for reflection, and some limited agitation in connection with the public events now fast moving to the
issue of rebellion or abject submission.

On his great sprawling estate, Henry had enough to do keeping an
eye on the work of overseers and slaves, the crops, and other plantation business. By late October, when he returned from Philadelphia,
the corn must have been shocked, but there were the matters of late
shucking or storing, of seeding the winter wheat, of killing hogs after
a sufficient cold spell, and of preparing the tobacco for shipping.
Henry's wheat was sold at his half brother's, John Syme's, mill with
consequent unhappy friction as to amounts and credits, of which we
shall hear more later.[16] Fortunately, this ill feeling did not extend
into the political realm. At this time only one of Henry's relatives is
known to have had pronounced anti-Whig sentiments.[17]

During the early months of 1775, Henry was vitally concerned
with local military preparations and meetings of the Hanover County
freeholders, while we also have some evidence of his wider contacts.
There is a tantalizing assertion that about this time Henry and
Parson Peter Muhlenberg, the future American General of Dunmore

County in the Valley, laid plans of "deep sedition."[18] We are also told that Henry discussed the political situation with his uncle, Anthony Winston of Buckingham, like Muhlenberg a delegate to the impending state Convention.[19] Anthony's indentured servant, Peter Francisco, a young Hercules six feet six inches tall and weighing some 260 pounds, was one of the sturdiest of the sturdy countryfolk who would rise up to support Henry's ideals. Even before Peter entered the American Army, there was a tale of how, when attacked by two bullies in a tavern brawl, that swarthy, dark-eyed giant of mysterious origin had picked up one in each hand and banged them together until they cried for mercy. The rustic joke, of a type Henry savored, was that the officers of the peace could not arrest Peter because he had not struck either of his opponents! [20]

While susceptible Peter Francisco listened, Henry is said to have discussed "the burning issues" of the day not only with his uncle Anthony but with some other leaders of the Piedmont area. What ideas Henry inculcated in these or other influential friends and relatives we do not know. Yet soon after his return from the Philadelphia Congress, or about November, 1774, Henry had confidentially informed some Hanover friends that he believed war with England was inevitable.[21]

At the end of 1774 it had been thirty-four years since Patrick Henry had been born in the Tidewater region of lower Hanover, and almost exactly eleven since he had so startled his audience in the little county courthouse by his first great speech on the Parson's Cause. To Edmund Randolph, son of Sir John, the King's attorney for Virginia, we are indebted for some revealing comments on Henry as he had developed at this time. The handsome, accomplished young Randolph did not join his Tory father in unhappy exile in England; remaining in Williamsburg with his uncle Peyton, speaker of the House of Burgesses, he had a rare opportunity to know the Virginia Revolutionary leaders.

With the approach of war, so Randolph noted in his manuscript history of Virginia, there was a new standard of leadership based on "fitness for the rising exigency. . . . The vanity of pedigree was now justly sunk in the positive force of character." Patrick Henry was due "the first place . . . as being the first who broke the key stone of that aristocracy," Randolph declared.

Henry, Randolph noted, had been unknown until his Stamp Act resolutions, except to those with whom he had "associated in the hardy sports of the field and the avowed neglect of literature." Certainly, he had been little known until his speech in the Parson's Cause of 1763, and then not widely beyond Hanover and neighboring counties. Even before his Stamp Act speech, Randolph continued, Henry

> did not escape notice, as occasionally retiring within himself in silent reflection, and sometimes discanting with peculiar emphasis on the martyrs in the cause of liberty. This enthusiasm was nourished by his partiality for the dissenters from the established church. He often listened to them, while they were waging their steady and finally effectual war against the burdens of that church, and from a repetition of his sympathy with the history of their sufferings, he unlocked the human heart and transferred into civic discussions many of the bold licences, which prevailed in their religions. If he was not a constant hearer and admirer of that stupendous master of human passions, George Whitfield [sic], he was a follower a [sic] devotee of some of his most powerful disciples at least.[22]

Henry did have a significant relationship with Whitefield, Samuel Davies, and other religious Dissenters.[23] But who were the "martyrs" that influenced him before his Stamp Act speech in Williamsburg on May 30, 1765, or during the next decade? Judging from the inventory of his books, which included the two volumes of the Irish-born Thomas Leland's *Demosthenes*, and knowledge of Henry's early reading, he seems to have been best acquainted in this period with the heroes of Greece and Rome and of England.[24]

Henry had won fame through the Stamp Act speech in the old capitol and to a lesser though noteworthy degree through other speeches. Could I rank among the great orators of the age? he must have asked himself by 1775. Little disposed as he may have been to such study, Henry had learned something of the heroes of antiquity. Athens and her allies were disastrously defeated at Chaeronea by Philip of Macedon, father of Alexander the Great. But, as Henry could read in Demosthenes' "Oration on the Crown," the noble feeling by which the Greeks were inspired had saved the battle from being a complete disgrace.

"I maintain," Demosthenes declared, "that if the issues of this struggle had from the outset been manifest to the world, not even then ought Athens to have shrunk from it, if Athens had any regard for her own glory, her past history, or her future reputation." [25]

Inevitably, Demosthenes' speeches lose something in the translation and from the absence of speaker and audience. But in Leland's Preface is a commentary on the techniques of various orators, particularly of ancient times. Leland, like Edmund Burke, another learned graduate of Trinity College, Dublin, was not chary in his praise of British governmental institutions. In Great Britain, he wrote, "a profusion of literary ornament, gay flights of fancy, and figurative eloquence" by no means formed the character of national eloquence. Rather, Leland argued, "simplicity and severity of reasoning, force, and energy eminently" distinguished the speakers of every kind from those of neighboring nations. Leland went on to mention several ancient orators who "like some great and popular actor" had swayed popular audiences: Cicero, Hyperides, Aeschines, but "chiefly" Demosthenes. Byron, a bit inexactly, would term Henry "the forest-born Demosthenes." Already, however, Henry had undergone certain experiences not unlike those of the pre-eminent Greek orator. Demosthenes

> generally acted in scenes of turbulence and public confusion. The speakers of the opposite party had first labored to prepossess the people against the sentiments he was to deliver. . . . In the midst of clamour and commotion the orator arises: his adversaries dread him, and endeavor to drown his remonstrances in tumult. By degrees he gains a patient audience. Opposition is checked, dismayed, and silenced. . . . His countrymen . . . rush enthusiastically forward, to the dangerous field of glory, which he points out to them.[26]

With the revolution now threatening in America, would Henry hold back or urge his countrymen forward to the battlefield?

Leland likewise spoke of Demosthenes' enemies as insinuating

[7]

that he was "more solicitous about rounding a period, than preserving his country." [27] Leland proved the accusation against Demosthenes to be false. He also made much of the point that some countries enjoyed so little liberty that they could not appreciate its values. But that was not true of the Great Britain whence Henry's ancestors had sprung, or of the America where he had his own roots. The people to whom he spoke could understand Leland's additional comment: "Liberty (if we may so speak) hath its own ideas and its own language, whose force cannot always be felt, or even its meaning rightly and thoroughly conceived by strangers." [28]

However much Patrick Henry might study Demosthenes' oratorical methods, might revere him and other martyrs for liberty, he was no doctrinaire; he would not plunge America into a war without preparation. Back home from Philadelphia by October 27, 1774,[29] Henry hardly found time to straighten out his personal affairs after his extended absence before he began organizing what is said to have been the first independent military company formed in Virginia in this prewar period. During November, 1774, a county committee was formed in Hanover and a local company enlisted. Composed of volunteers, it was separate from the regular militia organization of the colony. Soon afterward he sent a notice to the volunteers, who were not yet "embodied," asking them to come to Smith's Tavern, near Hanover Courthouse. There was a matter of great importance he wanted to communicate to them. And since it is the young men who are the most likely to rush into a revolution, it is not surprising that "a considerable number of the younger part" of the rustic organization came to the tavern to hear directly from Henry, their acknowledged champion.[30]

Smith's Tavern, only about a dozen miles north of Richmond, was described in an insurance policy of the 1790's as consisting of a wooden tavern sixty-eight by eighteen feet and one story high, with a long wooden stable, an adjoining shed and carriage house.[31] Conveniently located near the courthouse and the center of the county, the tavern was one of the best known in the area and often visited by Patrick Henry.[32] Perhaps even then it should have borne its later name of

[8]

Merry Oaks, for it was said the hearty people in that section of Hanover "had their time, and thought more of their sports than their spiritual welfare." When the tavern yard was a drill ground for the local militia, we may wonder if their maneuvers, inexpert at best, were affected by the proximity of the bar.[33]

At the First Continental Congress in Philadelphia, which had adjourned late the previous month, Henry had been a leader in the movement for intercolonial unity; for the enactment of the anti-British trade boycott and its enforcement by usually zealous local committees.[34] Now, within a few weeks after his return to Hanover, he came to Smith's Tavern to appeal to the rustic volunteers. Reminiscent of the stirring speech made at the county seat by his uncle, William Winston, during the French War,[35] this was the first of several talks Henry would make to the Virginia soldiers, always with striking effect. Addressing the men in "a very animated manner," Henry pointed out the necessity of a recourse to arms in the defense of their rights and recommended in strong terms that they should immediately form themselves into a volunteer company. A number of the men at once enrolled. When enough of them had enlisted to form a company, they elected their commanding officers.[36] Such was the beginning of the Hanover volunteers, which some six months later would attract widespread attention by marching to recover gunpowder seized by Lord Dunmore.

It is significant that they acted without dangerous opposition from older, comfortably placed citizens. In Virginia the American cause attracted the upper classes, as well as the lower, and most of the experienced leaders. Some of the prominent planters were loath to move as fast as Henry, but, impelled by the unrelenting logic of events, the great majority would close ranks and advance under the patriot banner.[37]

During winter and the Christmas season, there was a slackening of work at Scotchtown. But with Henry's wife critically ill it was a bleak Christmastide, though there must have been some festivity for the family and slaves. Then came the new year—1775—the first year of the Revolution. The editor of the Poet's Corner in Dixon and

Hunter's *Virginia Gazette*[38] was not to be caught napping and came forth with a jingle:

> SEVENTEEN HUNDRED SEVENTY-FOUR
> Is now forever past;
> Seventeen Hundred Seventy-Five
> Will fly away as fast. . . .

Catering as usual to its social-minded readers, this *Gazette* also reported the festivities on the Queen's birthday (January 19, 1775). The Royal Governor, His Excellency the Earl of Dunmore, had given "a ball and elegant entertainment" at the Palace in Williamsburg for a numerous company of ladies and gentlemen; and the same day His Lordship's youngest daughter had been baptized with the name of Virginia.[39] However, for many Virginians it was too late for such flattery. Staunchly backing their Whig brethren in Massachusetts, Henry and his supporters were not pacified by news from England such as was brought into the Potomac about February 1, 1775, by the ship *Caroline*, six weeks from London. In his "most gracious speech" at the opening of Parliament on November 30, George III had said that he had taken the measures which he deemed "most effectual" for executing the laws passed by the last Parliament for protecting commerce and preserving peace and order in Massachusetts Bay.[40] Moreover, the troop movements to America indicated the seriousness of his purpose.

But workaday life had to go on. Henry could read in Pinkney's *Virginia Gazette* how his uncle, Anthony Winston, was offering for sale "very cheap" his large Buckingham plantation "Huntington," northward of present Farmville: land that could bring tobacco for five or six years "without dung" and was near a point on the Appomattox River whence during the dry November two canoe loads of wheat had been sent down to Petersburg.[41] Was Winston battening down his hatches for stormy political weather? Ominous also, for uncle and nephew, was the notice in Dixon and Hunter's *Gazette* from Peyton Randolph "Moderator" requesting the various Virginia counties and corporations to elect representatives to the extralegal convention at Richmond, Monday, March 20, 1775.[42]

At the Virginia Convention the previous August, 1774, when

[10]

Henry and the other delegates were elected to the Continental Congress, provision was made for Peyton Randolph, President of the Convention, to call another convention when he deemed it advisable.[43] The call may well have been made after Randolph got in touch with Henry. In any case, Henry had reason to believe that defense of the colony would be an important item on the Convention agenda. And he was disturbed by reports of the British troops at Boston: in late January, 1775, they totaled, according to a dispatch in Dixon and Hunter's *Gazette*, fourteen regiments, exclusive of artillery and Massachusetts Tories.[44]

More political news came in a significant letter from Wethersfield, Connecticut, on January 2. Silas Deane, who had known Henry at the First Continental Congress, wrote him that the New England patriots were standing firm but obviously needed help from other colonies. Deane, born in 1737, the year after Henry, was a comfortably situated Connecticut lawyer who nevertheless served as a Whig leader. In his lengthy letter, Deane extolled the firmness and patience of the Boston people under the British penal measures and declared their militia, and indeed that of all the New England colonies, would be on "a very respectable footing" by spring. Between 20,000 and 30,000 men could be assembled at Boston in two days.

Deane, after including a statement of the provisions by which the New England colonies had been confederated in 1643, then added:

> I need not mention to you, what would have been the Consequences, had this Confederation been continued until now, and the other Colonies, early acceded to it, it is not, I trust, too late to form such an one, that will suit our present circumstances, and, which being varied, as future contingencies arise, may last forever; something of this kind, appears to me most absolutely necessary, let us turn which way we will, if a reconciliation with G. Britain takes place, it will be obtained on the best Terms, by the Colonies being United, and be the more likely to be preserved on just and equall Terms,—if no reconciliation is to be had, without a Confederation, we are ruined, to all intents and purposes. United we stand, divided we fall, is our Motto, and must be. One general Congress has brought the Colonies to be acquainted with each other, and I am in hopes another may effect

a lasting Confederation which will need nothing, perhaps, but
Time, to mature it, into a compleat and perfect American Constitution, the only proper one for us. . . .[45]

Throughout history, revolutions have usually been the work of determined minorities. Rarely has the leadership come from the lowest class.
There is no more formidable organizer of revolution than an aristocrat, or at least a man of the middle class with some education and
the character to help him cling to a principle; witness Julius Caesar
or Oliver Cromwell, and now Patrick Henry. On his secluded plantation during that winter of 1774–1775, almost crushed by family troubles, Henry could not then carry the ball of revolution as did Samuel
and John Adams. Nor was the British yoke felt as heavily in Virginia;
in Massachusetts, not only was the chief port of Boston closed but the
city was garrisoned and other liberties were suspended. Yet early in
the new year there were signs that Henry's political principles were
still spreading through receptive associates, especially friends and relatives, and that they were contributing to the mounting reaction against
the ministerial policy.

After the concrete action of the First Continental Congress, early
that fall, a flock of other resolutions was passed in various Virginia
counties and Whig sentiments were bandied about through publication
in the *Virginia Gazette*s and by word of mouth. At a meeting in distant Southwest Virginia of the Fincastle freeholders on January 20,
1775, Henry's brother-in-law, Colonel William Christian, was elected
chairman of the committee to see that the boycott of British goods
was properly executed. Other committee members whom Henry
must have influenced, directly or indirectly, included another of his
brothers-in-law, Captain Thomas Madison, and his future brother-in-
law, young Captain William Russell, who had studied under Henry's
father.[46] In a patriotic address the assembled Fincastle men alluded
to their remote situation and the late Indian war in which they had
chastised the "cruel and savage people" who had committed many
"murders and degradations" among them. Directly addressing Peyton
Randolph, Washington, Henry, and the other Virginia delegates to
the Continental Congress, the Fincastle settlers thanked them for

their noble efforts to reconcile the mother country and the colonies on "rational and constitutional principles."

There was a perfunctory expression of love and duty to George III, but these backwoods people did note that many of them and their forefathers had left their native land, which was "subjected to inordinate power, and greatly abridged of its liberties." They had crossed the Atlantic and explored the uncultivated wilderness surrounded by mountains almost inaccessible to any but savages, who had been incessantly committing "barbarities" on them since they first settled the country. They had patiently encountered these "fatigues and dangers," supported by the pleasing hope of enjoying the rights and liberties which had been granted to Virginia and were denied them in their native country. Since many were of Scotch-Irish Presbyterian background, it is not surprising that they "gloried" too in being the loyal subjects of a Protestant prince. And yet if specific measures should be proposed or adopted by Great Britain and their enemies attempt to dragoon them out of "those inestimable privileges" to which they were entitled and to reduce them to a state of slavery, they were "deliberately and resolutely determined never to surrender [these privileges] to any power upon earth, but at the expense of [our lives]." [47]

Henry's beloved brother-in-law, Colonel Christian, is known to have been in Williamsburg just before the Fincastle Resolutions were published on February 10, 1775, in Purdie's *Virginia Gazette*. He had probably brought them on the long trip to the low country. Since Christian was a delegate to the Virginia Convention the next month, there is strong reason to believe that at Scotchtown or elsewhere he talked over with Henry the ominous political events. [48]

Outside the family circle, Henry had few intimates, and there was no group of men who would offer him more staunch advice—or be more receptive to his daring plans—than his frontier kinsmen. It was no coincidence that, after Henry became the first Revolutionary Governor of Virginia in 1776, one of the early military measures was the dispatch of letters to three of his present or future brothers-in-law, Colonel Christian, Colonel Russell, and Thomas Madison. [49] Nor would the future careers of these frontier leaders belie their early promise.

At the approaching Virginia Convention, the conservatives were likely to try more of their conciliatory tactics. But with America on the brink of revolution, the Virginia county resolutions and accompanying elections for the Convention opening on March 20 proved that there would be plenty of stern delegates who might be influenced into forward action. And Patrick Henry was one of the early representatives elected. On February 20, 1775, a month before the opening session, the Hanover freeholders, meeting in the brick courthouse where he had first revealed his talent as an orator, unanimously named him and John Syme their delegates to the Convention.[50] On March 4 at a "fuller" meeting in the little Georgian building, Colonel Syme was requested to extend "in the most respectful manner" the thanks of the colony to the Virginia congressional delegates. (No great task in one instance since the delegate was his half brother!) Accompanying resolutions further indicated that Henry's constituents would support him in a forward policy.[51]

2

The St. John's Church Speech, Introductory

> When Demosthenes was asked what was the first part of oratory, he answered, "Action," and which was the second, he replied, "Action," and which was the third, he still answered, "Action!"——PLUTARCH [1]

"Early" *1775*. Death of Henry's first wife.

March 20, 1775. Opening session of Virginia Convention in St. John's Church, Richmond.

March 22. Edmund Burke's speech in Parliament favoring repeal of repressive American legislation.

March 23. Henry's "Give Me Liberty" speech. Passage of measure for arming the colony.

O N OCTOBER 15, 1774, Henry's sister, Mrs. Anne Christian, had written another sister, in the back country, that their brother Pat had not returned from Philadelphia "yet his Wife is extremely ill." [2] The last illness of a mother with young children is sad enough in any circumstance. In the case of Sarah, the bride of Henry's youth, the tragedy was compounded, for she suffered from a protracted mental illness which led to her confinement at Scotchtown in a basement room close to the family living quarters.

Certain details are lacking, but the convincing family tradition is that several years before her death Sarah developed "a strange antipathy" to her husband and children. Although she was given "every tender loving care," the situation became so heartbreaking that Henry, when only about forty, spoke of himself as "a distraught old man."[3]

We get some idea of the sequence of events from Henry's land transactions in Louisa County, which had to remain on public record. Nearly all the evidence indicates that in the years just before the Revolution Sarah's (Sally's) condition was worsening. But of several deeds preserved at the county courthouse for land sales by Patrick and his wife during this period, only one—the last—is signed by Sarah. Either she then had a lucid interval or the local farmers witnessing to her signature tactfully overlooked her mental condition. On August 22, 1774 (shortly before Henry left for the First Continental Congress), the deed recounts that he and Sarah sold 500 acres of his land on Roundabout and Fork Creeks to Nathaniel Thacker for £20. "Beginning at a Corner pine Tree on Emanuel Even's Entry. Running thence a strait line unto John Thackers Corner Pine," the deed continues, and three witnesses, including Evens, who made his mark, attested that it was signed, sealed, and delivered in their presence. Mercifully, there is no record of what else the Louisa farmers may have seen at Scotchtown that late summer day. At a meeting of the County Court on February 14, 1775, however, Henry's signature to the deed was acknowledged and proven—but not that of Sarah, the joint vendor.[4]

Henry's biographer-grandson, William Wirt Henry, says that she died "early in the year [1775]."[5] Whatever the exact details, it was under dreary circumstances that Patrick Henry had to gird himself for the critical battle on the Convention floor.

Some of the greatest orations in history have been delivered under difficulties that would crush ordinary men: by Pitt the Elder when suffering from debilitating ill health; by Demosthenes and Churchill when the liberties of their countries were in the gravest danger. Henry's Stamp Act speech and his first noteworthy speech, in the Parson's Cause, had both been triumphs over what seemed hopeless odds.[6] It now remained to be seen whether he could rise above his personal sorrow as well as the timidity and caution opposing him in Richmond.

[16]

Fortunately, for those with courage there are always signs of new hope. Even as spring at desolate Scotchtown was beginning to peep out from under its wintry cover, so work was starting there of the practical nature which, Henry believed, was needed to invoke the blessings of the deity. The Henry store account contains an illuminating record of these workaday activities: on the same day that some myrtle wax was purchased, perhaps for burning after Sarah's death, there was an entry for half a bushel of cotton seed; and in the preceding six weeks charges for four pounds of clothier's cards and one pound of wool cards.[7] They were indicative of the home manufacture which made Scotchtown largely self-sustaining—and helped strengthen the boycott of British goods.

Nor were these the only significant entries. Besides various articles for women and children, we note purchases between December 1, 1774, and March, 1775, of a felt hat, two pairs of shoe buckles, another pair of knee buckles, a "Stock Sock" ($\frac{4}{6}$), and $\frac{5}{8}$ yard of coating. This was further evidence that Henry was paying more attention to dress than in his early happy-go-lucky years. When he appeared on the floor of the provisional Convention, he probably would be dressed not ornately but in good, unobtrusive style.[8]

It was fitting in a sense that the scene should be laid in the small town on the James. In that historic area, a century before the founding of Richmond, Nathaniel Bacon had stirred his rustic followers to open revolt against the Royal Governor. Apart from tales repeated by the older people, the memory of this rebellion had been revived by a full front-page account in Purdie and Dixon's *Virginia Gazette* of February 23, 1769; also, a few months before Henry left for the First Continental Congress, in a letter supposedly written by Edmund Burke to the British Prime Minister, Lord North, and quoted in Rind's *Virginia Gazette*.[9] It was fitting, too, that the Convention should be held in the parish church overlooking the town from Church Hill. The cause of human liberty is never more manfully defended than by citizenry inspired by religious influences. The first legislature in America, at Jamestown in 1619, had met in a church— "The most convenient place we could find . . . was the Quire [sic] of the Church"—the members sitting with their hats on after the fashion of the English House of Commons.[10]

St. John's Church, with an addition made shortly before the war, had seats for only the six score delegates and perhaps a few dozen spectators.[11] Nevertheless, it was the largest building in town, a fact evidently considered by the calmly efficient Peyton Randolph, whose influential clan had many associations with Richmond.[12] With an extralegal meeting at Williamsburg again likely to be broken up by Governor Dunmore, Richmond was the only other sizable town convenient for delegates from the four quarters of what was then the largest American colony. Even this location was nearly a week's ride over muddy roads for some delegates; for few, less than a half day's.

For Patrick Henry, Richmond was a small market town, familiar from business and personal associations. It had been laid out in 1737 by debonair William Byrd II, just about the time Henry was born in nearby Hanover, and had purportedly been named for Richmond, England, to which the pleasant site bore a certain resemblance. By 1752 it had become the county seat with the usual appendages, it appears, of stocks and whipping post but, alas! no ducking stool.[13] Moreover, it was showing promise of notable commercial development.

Henry's uncle by marriage, John Coles, was one of the first Richmond merchants, reportedly having as early as 1741 a cargo of wheat valued at £1,500 sterling ready for shipment to England.[14] Henry was a lawyer for several of the Scotch factors and other traders who by 1764–1765 were shipping each year over 20,000 hogsheads of tobacco which had been rolled and floated to Richmond, besides a considerable quantity of wheat, corn, and even some iron.[15]

Located at the falls of the James, where the Tidewater joined the growing Piedmont, Richmond was in a peculiarly fortunate position. Nearly a century and a half after the first English settlement at Jamestown, the city's growing commercial interests could no longer be satisfied by commerce within the British Empire but needed wider trade outlets. And if this was now true to a limited extent in the entire plantation South, how much more did it apply in the middle states and especially in New England, whose seafaring trade partly overshadowed its subsistence agrictulture? American society was developing, becoming complex; it was not merely agrarian and commercial but, as the explorer, Gabriel Archer, had long before prophesied for Richmond, it was beginning to be industrial.[16]

Certainly, the American colonies had thrived under the British mercantile system, but that was in a simpler day when this system was not so strictly enforced. Suppose Great Britain should continue her onerous restrictions on the colonies? Henry could see the problem, with its double-pronged aspects, personified by his half brother. John Syme did not really need to order silks, brocades, and the like from England; he did not have to run up such large debts.[17] Yet there was no doubt that Virginia planters were squeezed in the vise of the English trade laws, that they needed a wider market. Thomas Jefferson estimated the debts of the Virginians in England about 1775 at £2,000,000.[18] Would not these debts have gradually increased under British regulations even if there had been no current crisis? In any event, were the colonies not entitled to become free and develop their own economic and political organization?

It is of course true that every little bit of territory should not become an independent country. But wasn't America a large country with great potential resources? Weren't the colonists numerous enough, homogeneous enough, intelligent and vigorous enough to maintain a separate government if they wanted to do so?

Patrick Henry was neither a profound student nor a theorist; he was a believer in natural rights. From his sturdy Scotch and English ancestors, from ideas spreading from abroad and nurtured in the Virginia Tidewater, from the inspiration, the hard practical concepts, offered in his own semifrontier environment—from all these sources had come a love of liberty, a fierce love that only death could silence. And what might be the future of an America which would dare to seek her own destiny!

At the parish church on the Richmond hilltop, the Virginia delegates assembled that mild March day. The Tidewater and perhaps nearly all of the Piedmont gentlemen were dressed in the conventional knee breeches, silks, and satins, but some of the delegates from Piedmont, as well as those from the western counties, were rough men, smelly, travel-stained. Young William Cabell was a representative of the enterprising planter families now rising to power in the Piedmont. Living on the Upper James, in what is now only a few hours' drive from Richmond, he left his plantation in Amherst County on March 18 and arrived in Richmond sometime on March 20.[19] The home of Henry's brother-in-law, William Christian, in Fincastle County (now Botetourt) was about two hundred miles distant; what with spring rains, boggy roads, and swollen streams, he could hardly have ridden to Richmond in much less than a week. George Washington, favored by better roads and a shorter distance than many of the other delegates, set out from Mount Vernon on March 15 and arrived at Richmond some hundred and twenty miles southward in five days. On the sixteenth he had stopped at Dumfries to review the independent company—concrete evidence of the military activities already developing in the colony. The next day he reached Fredericksburg; on the nineteenth he dined at Bowling Green, which he spelled "Bolling," and lodged at Hanover Courthouse; he did not arrive in Richmond until the next morning.[20]

Fortunately, Henry could usually ride down from Scotchtown in a day, even allowing for adverse weather conditions. Arriving in Richmond, he got the latest news, which was denied him at the plantation. Some of it doubtless came from friends and associates like Richard Henry Lee, in correspondence with his brother, the well-informed William Lee, at London.[21] But also there were the indispensable weekly *Gazettes*; the March 18 copy of the Dixon and Hunter issue reached Richmond from Williamsburg about the time of Henry's arrival.[22]

In the plantation society, it was not surprising that the newspaper devoted more space to the advertisements for fine stallions at stud than to the impending Convention. Thus we read on the front page about the virtues of Nimrod, "chestnut color, fifteen hands and a half high," and the "beautiful high blooded" bay horse, Godolphin, in full perfection standing in Mecklenburg at a guinea a "leap."[23] Also, there were advertisements for runaway slaves, for imported goods such as rum and sugar, and for a vessel wanted on charter for Bristol, "Burthen" about 260 hogsheads.[24] There was obvious need of boats by which to ship tobacco to England while still permissible under the Association.

Turning to the foreign dispatches, Henry would have found little of consequence in the news from Paris and St. Petersburg of late December (the Dixon and Hunter *Gazette* boasted on its masthead: "With the Freshest Advices, Foreign and Domestic"). But in the London dispatches of January 5, 1775, was some important news which must have influenced Henry's course of action at the Convention. The petition from the Philadelphia Congress to George III was reported to have been presented to His Majesty; it would be laid before Parliament at the next meeting. Due to the "alarming situation" of American affairs with the "total stoppage" of commerce to those parts, a "very numerous and respectable" meeting of merchants concerned with American trade had been held in London on January 4. With only a single dissenter, the merchants had ordered a petition to be drawn up and presented immediately to Parliament.[25]

Although the Convention would take action respecting the reported "defection" of the New York colony from the Association,[26] Henry had ample evidence of the damaging effect of the anti-British boycott.[27] But he could hardly have thought that the Ministry would make concessions to America as it did after the Stamp Act agitation; in view of his suppressed desire for American independence, we may well believe that he did not want them to do so. In proof of his conviction that concessions by the Americans were not merely undesirable but even weak truckling, there was a significant item on the front page of the *Gazette*. An American agent in England had had an interview with a "leading person" during which the agent insisted on the necessity of repealing the anti-American acts.

"Hold!" the statesman countered. "I, for my part, will sooner go to the block, than agree that a single clause should be repealed."[28]

It was of a piece with the general impression Henry had gained already from reports of British policy. Stubborn George III said he had taken such steps as necessary to maintain the laws,[29] and to Henry the large British armament at Boston bespoke the King's sincerity.

[21]

The fourteen regiments in the town, the ships of war in the harbor, were hardly for decorative purposes! [30] Only by drastic defensive efforts could the Americans hope to maintain their rights.

Political conventions usually do little more than organize on the opening day, less if the arrival of delegates is subject to many vicissitudes of time and tide. Henry had time to look about, to appraise the delegates likely to aid or oppose him. Among the members—120 if in full attendance [31]—were many of the same men he had come to know at the August Convention and the previous meeting of the Burgesses. Politics then attracted the top ability and character in the colony, and here at St. John's were Virginia's greatest men. Besides Henry, there were Washington, Jefferson, Richard Henry Lee, and others who would prove or further prove their ability on the national scene. The majority were relatively young, many in their thirties and forties. In this and some other respects the Convention resembled the French National Assembly of 1789, which also helped to usher in a revolution.

While there had not been a great many changes among the delegates since the August, 1774, Convention, Henry could take satisfaction in the perceptibly increased liberal sentiment from the Piedmont, Valley, and western counties. [32] Many delegates, however, especially from the more easterly counties, had strong political and economic ties with the mother country, and there was little known sentiment for separation. But the boycott and public advertisement of some open opponents of the Association were effective. British sympathizers, never very numerous in Virginia after 1774, did not need to be reminded further of the dangers confronting them.

Estimating his support for an advanced program, Henry could rely as usual in recent years on his coterie of relatives, friends, and political adherents. Besides his half brother, John Syme, there were present his brother-in-law, Colonel Christian, his uncle, Anthony Winston of Buckingham, and another relative by marriage, John Bowyer from Botetourt. Also, from back-country Albemarle came ardent young Thomas Jefferson, his courage and radical ideas no longer feared so much as in the previous convention; [33] from Charlotte, tall, blue-eyed

Paul Carrington, evoking memories of the Stamp Act debate.[34] Thomas Johnson was from the Louisa family which had stood so staunchly for the liberal cause.[35] Nat Terry of Halifax, a forthright veteran of the French and Indian War, was a local political leader whom Henry had represented in a prewar case, apparently arising from an election affray.[36] The Reverend Peter Muhlenburg was from Dunmore, a county which would be renamed for patriotic reasons. Directly influenced by Henry, so we are told, Muhlenberg would himself soon change his vestments for the uniform of a Revolutionary colonel.

Because of their education, their ability and experience, as well as their privileged position, it is not surprising to find the leading Virginia families well represented, in several instances by more than one delegate. With Sir John Randolph's seat vacant, there were still present Peyton Randolph from Williamsburg; four Lees, two from Westmoreland County, including Richard Henry Lee; and two Cabell brothers from Amherst County. Fortunately for Henry, political competence and a considerable degree of the current type of liberalism were then associated with some prominent names. Among Henry's conservative opponents, however, there were the suave and resourceful Edmund Pendleton, Archibald Cary, and Carter Braxton, and old leaders such as Robert Carter Nicholas, treasurer of the colony, and Richard Bland. There were two of Virginia's ablest soldiers, those tall, powerful veterans, George Washington and Andrew Lewis, the latter wearing the fresh laurels of Point Pleasant. There was Champion Travis of Jamestown Island, which had never been altogether suited for a colonial capital and was now a rotten borough.[37]

Henry passed through the westerly gate in the brick wall surrounding the churchyard and thence into the little wooden building. On the day of his celebrated speech and presumably throughout the session, the church was crowded to the utmost. With spring proclaimed in the budding trees and the grass of the churchyard, the weather—at least on the one epochal day—was balmy enough for the church windows to be open.[38] Wearing when practicable the mantle of the legal House of Burgesses, the delegates agreed to use its parliamentary procedure,

[23]

PATRICK HENRY

and they selected its speaker, Peyton Randolph, as their presiding officer. The unanimous choice was a notable tribute to Randolph's proven capacities, his ability to reconcile moderate and progressive elements. Miles Selden, rector of the church, was then chosen chaplain. A member of the Committee of Safety for Henrico County, his prayers for the Convention would not be hypocritical; indeed, there was more sympathy for the colonial cause among ministers of the Virginia Anglican establishment than is often realized.[39] John Tazewell was selected as clerk,[40] an office which he, like Charles Thomson, clerk of the Continental Congress, might have used to provide more records for future historians.

On the second day, Tuesday, March 21, the organization completed, the Convention discussed the proceedings of the recent Continental Congress. Henry, as a delegate to the Congress, probably took the floor to clarify points raised by members who had not been present in Philadelphia. This discussion was continued on the third day.[41] Henry was gratified that resolutions were then unanimously passed "entirely and cordially" approving the proceedings of the Continental Congress and expressing their "warmest thanks" to the Virginia delegates there.[42] On the whole, the proceedings so far had been relatively moderate, if not innocuous. Pendleton and his supporters might well hope that there would be nothing to seriously disturb the status quo.

3

The St. John's Church Speech, Conclusion

When the Whigs of America are thus multiplied, let the
Princes of the earth tremble in their palaces.

———DR. SAMUEL JOHNSON in 1775 [1]

March 23, 1775. Henry's famous "Give Me Liberty . . ."
speech.

March 24, 25, and 27. Remaining sessions of the Convention.

O N THURSDAY, MARCH 23, came the fateful fourth session.
That day the Convention met at 10 A.M. and was called to order by
the stout, dignified Peyton Randolph.[2] In accordance with the usual
procedure, the Reverend Mr. Selden read the prayer for the King,
which was not without irony. This prayer, still used in revised form
in the American Episcopal Church, began with an invocation to the
"heavenly Father . . . the only ruler of Princes," and besought His
"favour to behold our most gracious Sovereign Lord King George.
. . . Endue him plenteously with Heavenly gifts," and "strengthen
him that he may vanquish and overcome all his enemies, and finally,
after this life, he may attain everlasting joy and felicity. . . ."[3] From
the standpoint of King George, Patrick Henry and his supporters
were among the enemies against whom he most needed divine help.
But the members had learned not to take such forms too seriously,
any more than when in earlier years some had spoken of themselves

[25]

as "his Majesty's most dutiful Subjects" while drawing up a radical petition.[4]

The minutes of the previous day were read and approved. Then the gentleman from Caroline County, Edmund Pendleton, was recognized by the chair and offered a resolution in connection with the petition to Parliament the previous December from the Jamaican Assembly:

> "That the unfeigned thanks and most grateful acknowledgment of this Convention be presented to that very respectable Assembly, for the exceeding generous and affectionate part they have so nobly taken in the unhappy contest between Great Britain and her colonies, and for their truly patriotic endeavors to fix the just claims of the colonists upon the most permanent constitutional principles.
>
> "That the Assembly be assured that it is the most ardent wish of this colony (and we are persuaded of the whole continent of North America) to see a speedy return to those halcyon days when we lived a free and happy people.
>
> "That the President be desired to transmit these resolutions to the Speaker of the Jamaica Assembly by the earliest opportunity." [5]

The Jamaican petition had been published in Purdie and Dixon's *Gazette* on March 11 and, at least in its general nature, was known to many of the delegates. There is strong reason for believing that Henry, the leading member of the liberal party, sniffing for signs of caution or worse in the opposition, was not greatly surprised by Pendleton's resolution. He probably knew not only that the petition would be presented but that it would be the occasion for some moderate resolutions subtly or not so subtly curbing his party. The petition did indeed contain some sentiments in support of the American position to which Henry could not possibly object. But there was much else which was repulsive to him and other less vocal delegates who believed that the Convention had met for a stern purpose and that the time for moderate resolutions was past.[6]

For reasons of strategy as well as principle, Henry revolted from what he deemed halfway measures. In the Virginia of that more primitive day, the convening of a state-wide assembly from the widely

separated counties offered many difficulties at best. From his standpoint, it was extremely important to strike while the iron was hot: to
make preparations for a likely war in a legislative assembly then available for the purpose and while the volunteer companies this assembly
could implement were active and perfervid. A change, or seeming
change, in British policy (of which there was some evidence) might
dangerously weaken his party.[7]

The remote back country, where lay much of its strength, might
be more difficult to unite; the forces already loath to rebel against the
powerful mother country more timorous and time-serving.

In accordance with Pendleton's motion, the Jamaican petition was
read in its entirety of some two thousand words. It was then "maturely considered," [8] which, in the political parlance of the day, probably meant for an hour or more. The pro-American argument in the
petition pleased the members, and some were disposed to consider its
other features as innocuous or unexceptionable. There are limits to
the size of Goliaths even a David can defeat. The representatives of
the little West Indian island with its preponderant slave population
could hardly be blamed for noting that Jamaica could be crushed "at
will" by the British fleet. The petition presented a plausible case too,
with American overtones, when it referred with alarm to "the approaching horrors of an unnatural contest between Great Britain and
her Colonies" and spoke of its "well meant" endeavors to heal dis-
orders which might otherwise terminate in "the destruction of the
Empire." Reluctantly drawn from its internal affairs, the Jamaican
Assembly beheld "with amazement a plan, almost carried into execution, for enslaving the Colonies, founded, as we conceive, on a claim
of Parliament to bind the Colonies in all cases whatsoever." But while
referring to the colonial right, acquired by charter or otherwise, to
enact local legislation, the petitioners could only add that they and
the Americans had this power except when the laws were disallowed
by the King. And the Jamaicans could only appeal to George III to
act as a "mediator" between his European and American subjects.[9]

Obviously, this last portion of the Jamaican petition expressed a
Tory doctrine offensive to Henry and other advanced liberals. They
believed in natural rights, in legislative powers under the British con-

stitution acquired by the colonists and which could not be withdrawn. And, mostly young aggressive men, they saw no good in further "humble" petitions to George III, who was known to be either inspiring or heartily approving the oppressive British policy.

A number of the Convention delegates, however, including the bulk of the conservative forces, saw much good in Pendleton's commendatory resolutions.[10] Indeed, without strong opposition from Henry, the persuasive Caroline lawyer, with his experienced and influential associates, might lull some of Henry's supporters into voting for Pendleton's motion.

Yet Henry was convinced that there was then no point in trying, as the Jamaicans proposed, to fix the colonial claims upon "permanent constitutional principles." To wish, as did Pentdleton's resolution, for "a speedy return to those halcyon days" of British rule was to help lull the people into dangerous inaction.[11] Burning within Henry, though not yet publicly expressed, was the desire for American liberty. Rising from his seat (number 47) facing Peyton Randolph, Henry offered an amendment to Pendleton's motion. Obviously prepared beforehand, this amendment became the overwhelming issue of the debate:

> "*Resolved*, That a well regulated militia, composed of gentlemen and yeomen, is the natural strength and only security of a free government; that such a militia in this colony would for ever render it unnecessary for the mother country to keep among us, for the purpose of our defence, any standing army of mercenary soldiers, always subversive of the quiet, and dangerous to the liberties of the people, and would obviate the pretext of taxing us for their support.
>
> "That the establishment of such a militia is, at this time, peculiarly necessary, by the state of our laws for the protection and defence of the country, some of which have already expired, and others will shortly be so; and that the known remissness of the government in calling us together in legislative capacity, renders it too insecure, in this time of danger and distress, to rely that opportunity will be given of renewing them, in general assembly, or making any provision to secure our inestimable rights and liberties, from those further violations with which they are threatened.

"Resolved, therefore, That this colony be immediately put into a state of defence, and that [names to be filled in if the resolution passed] be a committee to prepare a plan for embodying, arming, and disciplining such a number of men, as may be sufficient for that purpose." [12]

In view of earlier measures for preparing a trained militia passed in Virginia and other colonies, we may wonder why Henry's proposals were followed by such a surcharged debate. Resolutions to prepare the local militia for an emergency had been enacted, copied or recopied, by so many patriot committees as at times to seem almost a stereotype.[13] Apart from those in northern colonies, of which the delegates could have been only partly informed, such resolutions had been passed in Newcastle, Delaware, on December 21, 1774,[14] followed within a few days by the Maryland provincial convention at Annapolis,[15] and the next month by the committee of Fairfax County, across the Potomac River in Virginia. The Fairfax resolutions had been drawn up at a meeting at which George Washington presided, and their author, George Mason, had embodied therein one section of the Maryland resolution. Moreover, the bold Fairfax representatives had declared themselves ready to defend "to the utmost" their just rights and privileges, based on the principles of the British constitution,[16] and these sentiments were echoed by the Augusta County committee at a meeting in Staunton on February 22, 1775, attended by several of Henry's relatives and associates.[17]

On close examination it is seen that the first paragraph of Henry's resolutions on March 23 uses much the same wording as did that of the Marylanders, including the sarcastic byplay. Even in this crisis, the Virginia delegates had not lost their sense of humor; Henry knew they would appreciate the assertion that "a well regulated militia" would render it "unnecessary" for the mother country to maintain in America a standing army and "obviate the pretext of taxing" her for its support.[18] "Unnecessary," yes, the English Ministry might reply, provided we want to give in to the d—— Americans!

Yet Henry in his second resolution went beyond the earlier Delaware, Maryland, and Virginia resolutions. Some of the laws for the Virginia colonial military establishment had expired, he noted, while

[29]

others would soon do so. The Royal Governor was so obviously remiss in calling the Virginia legislative assemblies as to render it doubtful whether in this dangerous period an opportunity would be given of renewing the laws "in general assembly, or making any provision to secure our inestimable rights and liberties, from those further violations with which they are threatened." From Henry's viewpoint the war had actually begun. He would "immediately put" the colony "in a state of defense," and he would let no British blandishments, no delaying or crippling tactics on the part of any opponents, prevent Virginia from being as prepared as was practicable.

His final resolution, for immediately preparing the militia, aroused the strongest opposition from the more conservative delegates. Still clinging to hopes of reconciliation with the mother country, they believed that the petitions from Congress and other opposition might stay the hand of the Royal government. In any event, why call attention so baldly, as did Henry's resolutions, to the Virginia military preparations? [19]

It is doubtful that the resolutions fully explain the alarm of Henry's opponents. Probably many of them, his old conservative antagonists, were fearful of the influence he might gain by passage of his resolutions. Since they understood him, he hardly needed to spell out his belief that the time for words was past. Perhaps, however, he gave some meaningful explanation, now unavailable, of his resolutions when introducing them. There is a significant hint in the report that several of the members opposed the resolutions as "premature"—that is, as pointing toward action which they deemed unnecessary.[20] Now and to a greater degree in his subsequent supporting speech he was moving into war, the dread extreme which they sought anxiously to avoid.

There was an animated debate in which Henry's resolutions were opposed by such influential members as Robert Carter Nicholas, Richard Bland, and perhaps Edmund Pendleton and Benjamin Harrison.[21] These gentlemen were among the older and most influential members of the Convention. The last three could speak with the authority of Virginia representatives to the late Congress; as a group they carried much weight with the Tidewater and even some Piedmont representatives.

"I have not time to give you a history of our proceedings . . . nor am I able to form even a probable conjecture what Parliament will determine on the subject of our dispute," Edmund Pendleton wrote William Preston a week later.[22] Pendleton added that if he did attempt to form such a conjecture, he would "guess that they would not repeal the Acts, or attempt to execute them by Force, but trie who could longest endure the Commercial Struggle, and as we have resolved not to trade with Great Britain, Ireland & West Indies, they will prohibit every other kind of foreign trade."[23]

In some reminiscences, handed down in the Henry family, it is admitted that Henry's appearance was not prepossessing until he spoke and that people were first attracted to his voice. The story is that once, before Henry became famous, he went to the home of the Ayletts, his future in-laws, at Fairfield in Prince William County. Henry made no impression until he spoke. He said, "I tell you, friends, it is a bitter cold night." His voice was so clear and resonant that everyone stopped what he was doing; they were attracted to him from that moment.[24]

After Henry's resolutions were offered, he rose to speak in their defense. One reliable spectator, Judge St. George Tucker, later recalled that Henry was "calm and collected." [25] In the small church any loud tones, any excess of emotion, might have caused an unpleasant reverberation. The distinguished Edmund Randolph declared in his manuscript history that it was a proud day

> to a Virginian, feeling and acting with his country. Demosthenes invigorated the timid, and Cicero charmed the backward. The multitude, many of whom had travelled to church, could not suppress their emotion—Henry was his pure self. Those who had toiled in the artifices of scholastic rhetoric, were involuntarily driven into an inquiry within themselves, whether rules and forms and niceties of elocution would not have choked his native fire. It blazed so as to warm the coldest heart.

There in the sacred meeting place, when Henry "launched forth in solemn tones, various causes of scruples against oppressors," the audience had no difficulty in imagining that "the British King was lying prostrate from the thunder of heaven. Henry was thought in his attitude to resemble St. Paul, while preaching at Athens, and to speak as man was never known to speak before," Randolph continued.

> After every illusion had vanished, a prodigy yet remained. It was Patrick Henry, born in obscurity, poor, and without the advantages of literature, rousing the genius of his country, and binding a band of patriots together to hurl defiance at the tyranny of so formidable a nation as Great Britain. This enchantment was spontaneous obedience to the working of the soul.[26]

Henry's custom was to start his speeches quietly, and he did not always disdain to use a tone of mock humility. On this occasion Judge Tucker has him beginning not only with his invariable self-possession but "with a majesty unusual to him in an exordium." [27] No manuscript of Henry's speech exists, but the text of the traditional account in Wirt shows evidence of impromptu or lately improvised rebuttal; at times he must have used notes at most.

> "No man," he said, "thought more highly than he did of the patriotism, as well as abilities, of the very worthy gentlemen who had just addressed the house. But different men often saw the same subject in different lights; and, therefore, he hoped it would not be thought disrespectful to those gentlemen, if, entertaining, as he did, opinions of a character very opposite to theirs, he should speak forth his sentiments freely, and without reserve. This," he said, "was no time for ceremony. The question before the House was one of awful moment to this country. For his own part, he considered it as nothing less than a question of freedom or slavery. And in proportion to the magnitude of the subject, ought to be the freedom of the debate. It was only in this way that they could hope to arrive at truth, and fulfil the great responsibility which they held to God and their country. Should he keep back his opinions at such a time, through fear of giving offence, he should consider himself guilty of treason toward his country, and of an act of disloyalty toward the majesty of Heaven, which he revered above all earthly kings.

Mr. President, said he, it is natural to man to indulge in the illusions of hope. We are apt to shut our eyes against a painful truth—and listen to the song of that siren, till she transforms us into beasts. Is this, he asked, the part of wise men, engaged in a great and arduous struggle for liberty? Were we disposed to be of the number of those, who having eyes, see not, and having ears, hear not, the things which so nearly concern their temporal salvation? For his part, whatever anguish of spirit it might cost, he was willing to know the whole truth; to know the worst and to provide for it.

He had, he said, but one lamp by which his feet were guided, and that was the lamp of experience. He knew of no way of judging the future but by the past. And judging by the past, he wished to know what there had been in the conduct of the British ministry for the last ten years, to justify those hopes with which gentlemen had been pleased to solace themselves and the house? Is it that insidious smile with which our petition has been lately received? Trust it not, sir; it will prove a snare to your feet. Suffer not yourselves to be betrayed with a kiss. Ask yourselves how this gracious reception of our petition comports with those warlike preparations which cover our waters and darken our land. Are fleets and armies necessary to a work of love and reconciliation? Have we shown ourselves so unwilling to be reconciled, that force must be called in to win back our love? Let us not deceive ourselves. . . . These are the implements of war and subjugation—the last arguments to which kings resort. I ask . . . what means this martial array, if its purpose be not to force us to submission? Can gentlemen assign any other possible motive for it? Has Great Britain any enemy in this quarter of the world, to call for all this accumulation of navies and armies? No, sir, she has none. They are meant for us: they can be meant for no other. They are sent over to bind and rivet upon us those chains which the British ministry have been so long forging.

And what have we to oppose to them? Shall we try argument? . . . We have been trying that for the last ten years. Have we anything new to offer upon the subject? Nothing. We have held the subject up in every light of which it is capable; but it has been all in vain. Shall we resort to entreaty and humble supplication? What terms shall we find, which have not been already exhausted? Let us not, I beseech you, . . . deceive ourselves longer. . . . We have done everything that could be done, to avert the storm which is now coming on. We have petitioned

[33]

—we have remonstrated—we have supplicated—we have pros-
trated ourselves before the throne, and have implored its interposition to arrest the tyrannical hands of the ministry and
parliament. Our petitions have been slighted; our remonstrances
have produced additional violence and insult; our supplications
have been disregarded; and we have been spurned, with contempt, from the foot of the throne. In vain, after these things,
may we indulge the fond hope of peace and reconciliation. There
is no longer any room for hope. If we wish to be free—if we
mean to preserve inviolate those inestimable privileges for which
we have been so long contending—if we mean not basely to
abandon the noble struggle in which we have been so long engaged, and which we have pledged ourselves never to abandon
until the glorious object of our contest shall be obtained—we
must fight! I repeat it, sir, we must fight! An appeal to arms
and to the God of Hosts is all that is left us! [28]

So we come to the peroration, one of the best known in all the long
annals of oratory. Rising to a crescendo, Henry spoke with perhaps
even more intensity, even more dramatic force, than in his Stamp Act
speech. He continued—at least substantially—in the burning words
which have since become so familiar:

They tell us . . . that we are weak—unable to cope with so
formidable an adversary. But when shall we be stronger? Will
it be the next week, or the next year? Will it be when we are
totally disarmed, and when a British guard shall be stationed in
every house? Shall we gather strength by irresolution and inaction? Shall we acquire the means of effectual resistance by
lying supinely on our backs, and hugging the delusive phantom
of hope, until our enemies shall have bound us hand and foot?
Sir, we are not weak, if we make a proper use of those means
which the God of nature hath placed in our power. Three millions of people, armed in the holy cause of liberty, and in such a
country as that which we possess, are invincible by any force
which our enemy can send against us. Besides, sir, we shall not
fight our battles alone. There is a just God who presides over
the destinies of nations, and who will raise up friends to fight our
battles for us. The battle is not to the strong alone; it is to the
vigilant, the active, the brave. We have no election. If we were
base enough to desire it, it is now too late to retire from the contest. There is no retreat, but in submission and slavery! Our

chains are forged; their clanking may be heard on the plains
of Boston! The war is inevitable—and let it come! I repeat . . .
let it come!

It is in vain . . . to extenuate the matter. Gentlemen may cry,
peace, peace—but there is no peace. The war is actually begun!
The next gale that sweeps from the north will bring to our ears
the clash of resounding arms! Our brethren are already in the
field! Why stand we here idle? What is it that gentlemen wish?
What would they have? Is life so dear, or peace so sweet, as to
be purchased at the price of chains and slavery? Forbid it, Almighty God! I know not what course others may take; but as
for me, . . . give me liberty or give me death! [29]

As Henry exclaimed "Give me liberty . . ." he held aloft an ivory
letter opener, letting it sink slowly into his breast at the word "death."
The speech had contained no *ad personam* arguments such as were
used effectively by Cicero and Demosthenes; no profundities, no
humor. Henry's use of the paper cutter was not overly dramatic; it
did not disturb his tone of burning simplicity.[30]

After Henry sat down, the audience remained for a brief time as if
stunned.[31] The church had no great acoustic virtues, but the windows
were open and at least part of the crowd outside could hear him. For
a few minutes, Edmund Randolph declared, Henry's words vibrated
so loudly, if not in the ears, at least in the memory of his audience,
that no other member was venturous enough to interfere with that
voice which had so recently subdued and captivated.[32]

Then, as the audience recovered somewhat, Richard Henry Lee
offered a motion seconding Henry's resolutions. Any speaker following him was likely to suffer by contrast. We should not label Lee as
ineffective because Randolph states that he refreshed with "a gale of
pleasure"; that "artificial oratory fell in copious streams" from his
mouth. Actually, in "elegance" of speech Lee was superior to Henry,
and he used "rules of persuasion" to accomplish everything which
such rules could effect. Yet Randolph declared that "the vessel of
the revolution was still under the impulse of the tempest, which
Henry had created." He "trampled upon rules, and yet triumphed, at
this time perhaps beyond his own expectations." [33]

That rising popular leader, the thirty-two-year-old Thomas Jefferson, also spoke on behalf of Henry's resolutions. While oratory was not one of Jefferson's outstanding talents, Randolph tells us that he argued "closely, profoundly, and warmly on the same side." [34] More support for Henry came from the ardently patriotic Thomas Nelson, Jr. For the first time taking a notable part in such a debate, this wealthy representative of the eastern aristocracy was particularly influential with some moderates who were in a position to make significant contributions of money and talent to the Revolutionary cause.

Young Nelson declared that if any British troops should be landed within the county of which he was the lieutenant, he would "wait for no orders, and would obey none which should forbid him, to summon his militia and repel the invaders at the water edge." And he told the delegates happy in their wealth and ease that to shrink now was "to be dishonored." [35]

No other man could speak as vehemently as Henry—could push for such extreme action, such radical disturbance of the *status quo*—without expecting strong rebuttal. This criticism came, and at intervals in the future would continue, from persons of different political persuasions. In an earlier volume we have noted the effort to discredit the conventional account of Henry's Stamp Act speech, along with the very strong evidences of its substantial accuracy. [36] Nor have hostile critics overlooked Henry's oration at St. John's Church. "You never heard anything more infamously insolent than P. Henry's speech," wrote a Norfolk Tory on April 6, 1775. [37] And in late years, when a guide at St. John's Church told a brash tourist how Patrick Henry had exclaimed, "Give me liberty or give me death," the tourist flippantly asked, "Which did he get?" [38]

Any serious doubts, however, as to the tremendous effect of Henry's speech are easily removed. One discriminating delegate to the Convention, Thomas Marshall, father of the Chief Justice, spoke of the speech "as one of the most bold, vehement, and animated pieces of eloquence that had ever been delivered." [39] Another delegate, Edward Carrington, later an esteemed Revolutionary officer, was unable to find any room in the church. But he secured a place in an easterly window, nearly facing Henry. Carrington declared, "Let me be buried at this spot!" and his wish was carried out after his death in 1810.[40]

Instead of being theatrical and unreal, the earlier part of Henry's speech had been characterized by a moving simplicity. It had been singularly lacking in hollow oratorical devices. When uttering sentiments which "commanded respect for himself," Henry solicited no admiring look from those who surrounded him.[41] When he paused he was not using the timeworn oratorical trick, and he continued with a burning appeal that in its crescendo became one of the great revolutionary declamations of history.

The evidence of another spectator, an old Baptist minister, handed down by Henry S. Randall, an early Jefferson biographer, might be criticized as not literally accurate. The old minister described an assembly of men too terribly intent to regard their attitudes, or their looks, or their dignity in any respect.

> Henry rose with an unearthly fire burning in his eye. He commenced somewhat calmly—but the smothered excitement began more and more to play upon his features and thrill in the tones of his voice. The tendons of his neck stood out white and rigid like whipcords. His voice rose louder and louder, until the walls of the building, and all within them, seemed to shake and rock in its tremendous vibrations. Finally, his pale face and glaring eye became terrible to look upon. Men leaned forward in their seats, with their heads strained forward, their faces pale, and their eyes glaring like the speaker's. His last exclamation—"Give me Liberty or give me death"—was like the shout of the leader which turns back the rout of battle!

To a more cynical generation the old clergyman's description may seem a little overdrawn. Yet we can accept his statement that he felt "sick with excitement. Every eye yet gazed entranced on Henry. It seemed as if a word from him would have led to any wild explosion of violence. Men looked beside themselves." [42]

The effect of Henry's speech on back-country soldiers like Andrew Lewis is easy to imagine; even the taciturn George Washington is described as "prominent though silent."

[37]

His looks bespoke a mind absorbed in meditation on his country's fate; but a positive concert between him and Henry could not more effectually have exhibited him to view, than when Henry with indignation ridiculed the idea of peace "when there was no peace," and enlarged on the duty of preparing for war.[43]

While there is no doubt as to the general effect of Henry's speech, questions as to its actual wording are not so easily disposed of. Not only is there no manuscript copy of the oration, there is no stenographic report. Nor do we get any more clue to the wording from the *Gazette*s and the contemporary writings of Henry's auditors. Of the Convention at St. John's Church, Dixon and Hunter's *Gazette* carried only a brief mention of the first three sessions.[44] Moreover, searching for reference to Henry's speech in the diary of the reticent George Washington, we find this gem of information: "[March] 23. Dined at Mr. Patrick Coote's and lodged where I had done the Night before." [45]

The surviving writings of the other delegates just after Henry's speech are equally disappointing. It was not until some forty years later that William Wirt first reprinted a reconstruction of Henry's oration. In the absence of contemporary written information, it is not surprising that so friendly a critic as Hugh Blair Grigsby should state a half century after publication of Wirt's biography that "much" of Wirt's text for the speech was "apocryphal." [46] And, a century after Grigsby, Dr. Douglas Freeman found it a "thankless duty" not to give credence to much of the conventional evidence as to Henry's exact words.[47]

The answers to such criticisms can be obtained only by meticulous examination of all the available data. Even then, in certain instances the conclusions must be more suggestive than categorical. To begin with, while William Wirt did not publish the first edition of his Henry biography until November, 1817, he collected much of his information for the book over a decade earlier when many of Henry's auditors at St. John's were still in their clear-minded fifties or sixties.[48] In 1807, Nathaniel Pope wrote Wirt, "You have already received in detail" Henry's speech at St. John's Church.[49] Wirt speaks of Pope as being "indefatigable in collecting information" not only in Hanover

County but from "every quarter," [50] and there is further evidence of the variety and accuracy of his sources.[51]

Precisely who gave Wirt his chief information (whether or not through Pope) as to the wording of the speech? We know that Wirt got much of this data from an intelligent and reliable auditor, John Tyler,[52] and that there is some specific verification of Tyler's account. Wirt likewise got some details of the wording from another reliable source, Judge St. George Tucker, who, as a young man of twenty-three, had been present at St. John's Church.[53] Other information from such a helpful person as Edmund Randolph relates chiefly to the general lines and effect of the speech.[54] The evidence of the Baptist preacher has been discounted as given over fifty years after Henry spoke. Yet William Wirt Henry only offered the preacher's recollections of the effect of Henry's oration,[55] and there is ample evidence to prove that some men in their eighties or even later do have valuable reminiscences.

Knowing Thomas Jefferson's life and writings, would one claim that he was not clear-minded in 1817? Wirt had asked him to criticize the manuscript of the Henry biography which he was about to publish. In a letter to Wirt after returning the section containing his reconstruction of Henry's St. John's Church speech, Jefferson had no scruples about making severe criticisms of Henry; he had not buried their old enmity. Yet Jefferson did not suggest a single change in Wirt's reconstruction of the speech and called Henry the greatest orator that ever lived.[56]

The subject can become tedious. It is safe to say that Wirt's text was based on a few very helpful sources plus many bits of information. He had ample proof for certain burning phrases especially in the last part of Henry's speech, and for its general substance. Moreover, a close analysis proves that the speech has a remarkable resemblance to Henry's other speeches during this period. To a notable degree it conforms to their oratorical style and technique, even in the use of Biblical quotations or analogies. Of course Wirt may have used fragments from Henry's earlier speeches in reconstructing the style and general tone of his St. John's oration. Yet the information on the text as a whole is more precise than for many other great speeches of history.[57]

It is not surprising that Henry's speech overshadowed the remaining proceedings of the Virginia Convention; indeed, the latter are omitted in at least one published account. His resolutions were carried by a vote of 65 to 60, according to James Parker, a Norfolk merchant.[58] Apparently, the margin was almost as narrow as in the passage of his Stamp Act resolutions a decade earlier. The influence of his epochal orations, however, on the St. John's delegates was shown in the strong committee appointed to prepare the plans for arming the colony: Patrick Henry was of course appointed chairman, followed by Richard Henry Lee, who had seconded his motion, while the other members included Andrew Lewis and Henry's brother-in-law, William Christian, who had served with Lewis in the French and Indian War; Thomas Jefferson, Adam Stephen, and Isaac Zane, with Robert Carter Nicholas, Benjamin Harrison, Edmund Pendleton, and Lemuel Riddick from the more conservative faction. The Committee appeared to be dominated by the liberals and fighting men, and if it had had its way Virginia might have been involved in active fighting several months earlier than actually happened.[59]

Still under the influence of Henry's speech, the Committee was ready on Saturday, March 25, with a detailed plan for embodying, arming, and disciplining the militia, which, after amendment, was unanimously accepted. The details indicate considerable work on the part of Henry and his fellow committeemen, even though a number of the recommendations were standard procedure. The colony was to put into execution the militia law passed in the year 1738, and the counties were each to form one or more volunteer companies of infantry and cavalry, which were to be in constant training and readiness to act in any emergency. The resolutions, like those of the Maryland Convention, called for the formation of infantry companies of sixty-eight privates, a captain, and the usual officers. The lack of adequate arms was unhappily indicated by the provision that each man be provided with a good rifle "if to be had" or otherwise a common firelock. The frontier influence was seen in the provision for each infantryman to be armed with a tomahawk and clothed in a hunting shirt. It was hopefully added that each of these recruits endeavor "as soon as possible" to become acquainted with the military exercise provided for infantry appointed by King George III in 1764. A characteristic stipulation also in Virginia was that the Tidewater and certain Piedmont counties each provide one or more cavalry troops. By the latter part of the war the Virginia cavalry would be particularly distinguished; the only regret was that more were not available. Incidentally, it did not take a cavalryman to appreciate the importance of the provision that the mounts be trained "to stand the discharge of firearms." Until more ample arrangements could be made, the county committees were enjoined to collect money for the purchase of ammunition and to store it in places of safety.[60]

On the whole, Henry's plan for arming the militia was as practical a proposal as he could hope to carry with the strong opposition, and it certainly did not lack boldness. But the coming war would reveal the limitations of ill-trained militia called out for relatively short terms of service. With some exceptions, Washington's regular troops, or Continentals, would prove far superior to the state militias. The experienced Robert Carter Nicholas, like a number of "older patriots" in the Convention, was opposed to open resistance to the British at that time yet was a firm supporter of the American revolutionary principles. Recognizing the inadequacy of Henry's proposal, Nicholas moved to change the system and, instead of arming the militia, to raise 10,000 regular troops for the war. Not surprisingly, his motion was defeated.[61]

Henry was appointed to another strong committee, with Nicholas as chairman, to prepare a plan for the encouragement of arts and manufactures in the colony. Along with Peyton Randolph and the other Virginia delegates to the Continental Congress of 1774, he was re-elected to serve at the second Congress to meet in Philadelphia on May 10. On Sunday, March 26, there was an interlude when the Reverend Mr. Selden held divine service at St. John's, including a "seasonable and excellent sermon." [62] By Monday the committee for encouragement of arts and manufactures had prepared a proposal for the Convention which was somewhat like that of the Maryland Convention but much more detailed. Woolen, cotton, and linen manufacture was to be encouraged, especially if adaptable for military purposes; the cultivation of flax, hemp, and cotton promoted, as well as the manufacture of salt and saltpeter, gunpowder, steel, paper, and other articles—all apparently indicating that the colony would be grimly though insufficiently preparing for war.[63]

Meantime, on March 21, Lord Dunmore had issued a proclamation in accordance with the Royal orders, declaring that all vacant lands in the colony should be put up for sale to the highest bidders, subject to a reservation for annual quitrents. Since this procedure was contrary to the established usage for granting lands in the colony, Henry was appointed chairman of yet another powerful committee, to inquire into the matter and report to the next General Assembly or Convention.[64]

Before adjourning, the Convention elected Thomas Jefferson to represent the colony at the Congress in place of Peyton Randolph if he could not serve because of his duties as chairman of the next Virginia Convention.[65] The delegates were to apply to their constituencies for £15 each as expense money for the Virginia congressmen.[66]

The reported five-vote margin favoring Henry's motion to arm the colony was about what was to be expected considering the size of the opposition party, especially in the more conservative Tidewater. Curiously, no funds for arming the colony were provided by the Convention. The committee to which the motion was referred could not agree upon "the ways and means" for its support, James Parker asserted in his letter of April 6, 1776, to his Scotch friend. "What flattened them all down was a hint of a Plea to be presented by P. Henry, no less than the taking of Government into their hands, appointing Magistrates, and levying money. The Treasurer, Col. B. Harrison, Bland, and Col. Ridduck [Riddick] saw into this and formed an opposition . . . which overset the scheme. . . ."[67]

Significantly, James Parker, who had time to get some news from conservatives back from the Convention, gives this account of Henry's speech:

> You never heard anything more infamously insolent. . . . He
> called the K—— a Tyrant, a fool, a puppet and a tool to the

ministry. Said there was no Englishmen, no Scots, no Britons, but a set of wretches sunk in Luxury, they had lost their native courage and [were] unable to look the brave Americans in the face. . . . This Creature is so infatuated, that he goes about I am told, praying and preaching amongst the common people.[68]

Parker, as a Tory merchant likely to lose heavily from an armed rebellion, evidently wrote from a biased viewpoint. His last accusation, as to Henry's subsequent praying and preaching, is unsubstantiated gossip. But what is more in character is Henry, warmed to his theme and arousing an audience until it was past polite protests. And so he could be moved to some expressions akin to those which Parker excoriated. If we are to believe him, the speech stands as a somewhat rawer and stronger utterance than Wirt indicated. It was more in keeping with the hortatory style of some earlier Henry speeches, especially where he singled out the British King during the Stamp Act speech. And, unlike many of the celebrated speeches of history, it still reads well. At times the lines seem to march as in great heroic poetry.

The main point is not the exact wording but the result of the speech. As to its effect on its audience, including seven signers of the Declaration of Independence, with other influential Virginians, there could be no question. It was seen in some Virginia volunteers going off to war with "Liberty or Death" emblazoned on their shirt fronts, and a far larger number who had the motto emblazoned in their minds and hearts. It became a battle cry in a fight for freedom which would extend far beyond American shores.

Except for Lincoln's Gettysburg Address, no speech by an American is better known.

4

The Gunpowder Episode

The people I want to hear about are the people who take risks.
————ROBERT FROST [1]

April 19, 1775. Battle of Lexington, Mass.

April 20. Seizure on order of Lord Dunmore of gunpowder in Williamsburg.

May 2–4. Henry leads Hanover volunteers in expedition to secure reparation for the stolen powder.

May 6. Lord Dunmore denounces Henry as a rebel.

AT ST. JOHN'S CHURCH, Patrick Henry had proved that he believed in striking while the iron was hot, or, as he might have said with Ben Franklin, "Look before or you will find yourself behind." [2] Six weeks later there was a significant incident, when Henry had to prove that he could put his courage to the test of responsibility. Similar crises would crowd upon him in the following months.

Efforts to encourage the Americans to make gunpowder had called forth from Lord Dartmouth a circular letter on October 19, 1774, to the American Governors in which he informed them of an order by King and Council forbidding the export from Great Britain of gunpowder or any kind of arms and ammunition. [3] The Governors were ordered to prevent the importation of the munitions into their colonies, and by late spring the British Army and Navy were being used to enforce the mandate.[4]

It was the attempt of General Gage to destroy military stores at Lexington on April 19, 1775, which led to the shot "heard 'round the world," the opening battle of the Revolution. At about the same time in Virginia, Lord Dunmore ordered the captain of the armed schooner *Magdalen* lying at Burwell's Bay on the James River below Williamsburg to remove—"steal," the colonials termed it—the twenty kegs of powder stored in the public magazine at Williamsburg and load it on the schooner.

Late in the night of April 20, when the good citizens of Williamsburg were deep in slumber, a detachment of marines from *Magdalen* seized the gunpowder in the magazine and carried it off in "his Excellency the Governour's waggon." After news of the maneuver "took wind," there was an uproar in the town. A number of exasperated citizens armed themselves and prepared to force the restoration of the powder, which they deemed to have been deposited in the magazine for the defense of the colony. But cooler heads prevailed. The city council presented a respectful memorial to Dunmore, which, however, emphasized that the magazine had been erected at the public expense of the colony and utilized for the safekeeping of such ammunition as should be lodged there for its protection. The memorialists also noted that they had "reason to believe that some wicked and designing persons have instilled the most diabolical notions into the minds of our slaves, and that therefore the utmost attention to our internal security is become the more necessary." They inquired why the powder had been "carried off in such a manner," and entreated that it "be immediately returned."[5]

Lord Dunmore gave an unsatisfactory oral answer that infuriated the people still further. He referred to what proved to be a false report of an insurrection in a neighboring county and said he had removed the powder to a place of "perfect security" and that upon his "word and honour" it would be returned in half an hour in the event of an insurrection. The gunpowder had been removed at night to prevent "alarm." His Lordship was "surprised to hear that the people were under arms on this occasion" and declared that he did not deem it prudent to put powder into their hands in such a situation.[6]

Although the reply was not straightforward, it was accepted as Lord Dunmore's promise to return the powder when needed; Peyton Randolph, Robert Carter Nicholas, and other influential citizens were able to quiet the people. But the next day the inept Dunmore sent word that if any injury or insult was offered to him, to his secretary, Captain Foy, or to Captain Collins, commander of the marines who removed the gunpowder, he would free the slaves and reduce Williamsburg to ashes.[7]

Just how irritating was this irresponsible threat is not difficult to understand. In Fredericksburg, some fifty miles north of Scotchtown, several companies of armed volunteers assembled near the end of April for a march on Williamsburg. Before they could set forth, a letter from Peyton Randolph informed them that the gunpowder incident was being satisfactorily settled. But the angry men dispersed only after protracted debate and pressure from several leading patriots. Moreover, representatives of the volunteer companies signed an address agreeing that the men would reassemble when needed to defend their liberties. In a bitter parody of the Governor's customary conclusion to the Royal proclamations—"God Save the King"—the address ended with "God Save the Liberties of America." [8]

Having presumably quieted the hotheads, the moderate leaders could now proceed with their interrupted plans. They involved, in the case of that eminent lawyer, Edmund Pendleton, not only attendance at the Philadelphia Congress but the routine matter of an attachment he had instituted in the General Court against Henry's half brother, John Syme, for over £7,000 sterling allegedly belonging to Richard Ford & Co. of London.[9]

It remained for Henry to take the violent course from which the Fredericksburg troops had been so narrowly averted. After learning that Dunmore had removed the powder from the magazine, he immediately sent express riders to the Hanover volunteers in various parts of the county asking them to assemble on May 2 at Newcastle. Also, in order to give more dignity and authority to the meeting, he convoked the Hanover County Committee at the same place.[10]

Newcastle, now little more than some cultivated fields, was in 1775 still a considerable river port in the lower county. It was only a few miles from Henry's birthplace and an even shorter distance westward over the flat Pamunkey River lowlands from the present Richmond–Tappahannock highway bridge. The neighborhood had been the scene of one of his early business failures; [11] it was now a setting for the dynamic action which helped to get him outlawed by the Royal Governor. At Newcastle where the shallow-draft vessels from England came near the head of navigation on the Pamunkey, roads converged from the back country, from the north, and from Williamsburg. At this convenient river point Henry proposed to assemble the volunteers and to march them down to the capital to recover or obtain compensation for the gunpowder.

As a result of his summons, the members of the Hanover Company appeared at Newcastle on horseback, armed with such guns as they had available. The county committee, or enough of it for executive action, also convened there. Henry's plan was hardly weakened by the fact that the committee included his half brother, his cousin George Dabney, and Richard Morris, congenial spirits to whom he had already confided his desire for American independence. [12] Furthermore, about the time the volunteers assembled they appear to have learned of open hostilities in beleaguered Massachusetts. [13] On April 19, 1775, a British expedition had attempted to seize the American arms stored at Concord; they had fired on and killed militiamen opposing them at Lexington and had themselves lost heavily in the subsequent fighting at Concord and during their harassed retreat to Boston. Over a month before, at St. John's Church, Henry had declared that war had actually begun and had taken steps to arm the colony. Now it was obvious, or so he believed, that the war could be won only by drastic action. The intentions of the Ministry could no longer be in doubt.

Lord Dunmore's removal of the gunpowder and the fighting in Massachusetts provided the material Henry needed to arouse the people. "The intelligence of the bloodshed at Lexington changed the figure of Great Britain from an unrelenting parent into that of a merciless enemy." [14]

Henry again gave evidence that he was looking beyond immediate events. "From the *commencement of the Revolution,*" George Dabney wrote William Wirt on May 14, 1805, "it was [Henry's] opinion that an eternal Seperation would take place between Brittain & the United States. Indeed it appears that as a politician he saw further into the consequences than all others at that day."

Dabney went on to mention a conversation which he and Colonel Richard Morris had had with Henry while they were riding together to Newcastle. Henry's proposal to recover the gunpowder had evidently become known to a number of leading Virginians, for Dabney spoke of Henry's proposed action as being "generally condemned" by most of them as "imprudent & impolitic." Yet Dabney said that Henry's "views extended further" than recovery of the arms and ammunition in the magazine. Henry told his riding companions that Dunmore's seizure of the gunpowder "was a fortunate circumstance, which would rouse the people from North to South. You may in vain mention the Duties to them upon Tea & these things they will say do not effect [sic] them. But tell them of the Robery of the Magazine, and that the next Step will be to disarm them, and they will be then ready to fly to Arms to defend themselves." [15]

Looking ahead, Henry privately told a trusted young associate, Parke Goodall, that all the colonies should enter into a confederation against Great Britain. Henry was satisfied that if the southern states were so "pusillanimous" as to desert the northern colonies, the latter would alone enter the war. He was "positive and sanguine," however, that a general confederation of the American states would be formed. If America's own exertions were then insufficient to establish her independence, she should effect it with foreign aid. [16]

For the greater part of that spring day, Tuesday, May 2, the volunteers remained at Newcastle awaiting the decision of the committeemen regarding Henry's proposal. [17] With the volunteers was Dr. Thomas Hinde, Henry's family physician, who more than any other man understood "the many mental and personal afflictions" which Henry had to rise above at this critical period. [18]

There was some disagreement among committee members, the troops were told; nor was this very surprising in view of Henry's radical plan. Late in the evening the committee rose. Henry was informed that they approved his decision; [19] he could march his force to Williamsburg and secure adequate reparation for the loss of the gunpowder. The volunteers being assembled, and doubtless refreshed at neighboring taverns and houses, Henry addressed them in a manner similar to his earlier appeal at Smith's Tavern and, indeed, with "all the powers of his eloquence."

We have a topical summary of this speech, sufficient to give an accurate impression of its fiery contents. Henry began by "laying open" the plan through which the British Ministry had decided to reduce the colonies to subjection by robbing them of all the means of defending their rights. He spread before the men an image in vivid colors of the fields at Lexington and Concord still "floating with the blood of their countrymen, gloriously shed in the general cause," and he showed them that "the recent plunder of the magazine in Williamsburg was nothing more than a part of the general system of subjugation."

Continuing in even stronger terms, he declared that

the moment was now come in which they were called upon to decide, whether they chose to live free, and hand down the noble inheritance to their children, or to become hewers of wood, and drawers of water to those lordlings, who were themselves the tools of a corrupt and tyrannical ministry—he painted the country in a state of subjugation, and drew such pictures of wretched debasement and abject vassalage, as filled their souls with horror and indignation—on the other hand, he carried them, by the powers of his eloquence, to an eminence like Mount Pisgah; showed them the land of promise, which was to be won by their valour, under the support and guidance of Heaven; and sketched a vision of America, enjoying the smiles of liberty and peace, the rich productions of her agriculture waving on every field, her commerce whitening every sea, in teints [sic] so bright, so strong, so glowing, as set the souls of his hearers on fire. He had no doubt, he said, that that God, who in former ages had hardened Pharaoh's heart, that he might show forth his power and glory in the redemption of his chosen people, had, for similar purposes, permitted the flagrant outrages which had occurred in Williamsburg, and throughout the continent." [20]

The scene might have been laid a generation before when the Reverend Samuel Davies exhorted the Hanover troops leaving for the French War.[21] Certainly Henry, who had often heard Davies, used much the same style.

William Wirt, who was able to get information thirty years later from several of Henry's associates in the gunpowder incident, wisely forebore to give more than the "colouring" of Henry's speech. But Wirt did go on to say that the coloring was Henry's own and "beyond the power of any man's imitation." And the effect, not surprisingly, "was equal to his wishes." The meeting was "in a flame," the decision "immediately taken" that the powder be recovered or there would be adequate reprisal.[22]

Once revolutions are started, it is often difficult to control their momentum. Perhaps even Henry himself was a bit surprised when his loyal brother-in-law, Captain Samuel Meredith, resigned his command of the Hanover independent company and Henry was at once put in command. Meredith was made lieutenant, and the ensign's post was given to Parke Goodall, with whom Henry was "in the habits of the greatest friendship and intimacy." During his long public career, there would be some who actively disliked Henry, more who admired and respected him. But there were few described as being as close to him as was young Goodall at this time. With Goodall "he unbosm'd himself more freely than to any other man in the Country," William Wirt was reliably informed.[23]

Having secured what he deemed adequate authorization and military support, Henry now proceeded with his bold plan. While he moved with his main force toward Williamsburg, Goodall was given secret instructions to make a detour with sixteen volunteers to the residence of Colonel Richard Corbin, Receiver-General of the colony, at Laneville in nearby King William County. There he was to obtain from Corbin £330 as compensation for the powder. In case of non-payment of the money, Goodall was ordered to take Corbin prisoner and send an express messenger to Henry, who would be waiting at Doncastle Ordinary, fifteen miles from Williamsburg. To these dangerous commands the staunch Goodall did not demur; he only asked for and received a written order from Henry. Goodall then set forth, and Henry followed along the direct route to the capital. En route his company was swelled by recruits from New Kent and King William counties to some hundred and fifty or more men. Moreover, they were "all well accoutred" and "presented a very martial appearance," according to Purdie's *Gazette,* though that might not have been the verdict of a professional soldier.[24]

Late in the evening of May 2, Goodall's detachment arrived at Colonel Corbin's residence on the Mattaponi River, opposite present West Point.[25] The former glories of Laneville, Corbin's mansion, are still indicated by traces of the extensive foundations near the riverbank. They were said to have been 285 feet across, long enough to help bolster a remarkable story about this worthy and his wife. This highly placed couple reportedly maintained only formal relations, he living at one end of the house, she at the other; once a year Corbin would enter his coach and four and "in full regalia" be driven to the other end of the house to make his wife a formal call.

Sic transit gloria mundi. Years ago the influential Corbin had procured for George Washington his first commission as an officer in the Virginia militia.[26] Now, in May, 1776, Henry's armed emissaries would force Corbin to give restitution for gunpowder removed by his overlord, the Royal Governor. Goodall, finding Corbin not at home, joined Henry at Doncastle Ordinary (Barhamsville), a hamlet in the flat country on the Williamsburg road a few miles south of West Point. Here he learned that his commander had already been successful in getting compensation for the powder—this after some crowded events not without an element of the comic. When Lord Dunmore had learned that Henry was moving on Williamsburg, that descendant of the royal Stuarts worked himself into a pitch of excitement, if not terror. After arming a few Indians and slaves, he planted cannon on the Palace grounds and slipped a small force of sailors and marines into the town. Then he vainly sought to have the Williamsburg officials call out the militia and sent "messenger after messenger" to Henry urging him to stop his march. Henry detained Dunmore's messengers and continued his advance, until he was only about a dozen miles from the capital. Finally, through the intercession of Corbin's son-in-law, Carter Braxton, Corbin offered Henry a bill of exchange for £330 in compensation for the powder. After Henry had secured the approval of his men, he accepted the offer, giving the following receipt:

> Received from the Honourable Richard Corbin, Esq., His Majesty's Receiver-General, £330, as a compensation for the Gunpowder lately taken out of the public Magazine by the Governour's order; which money I promise to convey to the Virginia Delegates at the General Congress, to be under their direction laid out in Gunpowder for the Colony's use, and to be stored as they shall direct, until the next Colony Convention, or General Assembly, unless it shall be necessary, in the mean time to use the same in defence of this Colony. It is agreed, that in case the next Convention shall determine that any part of the said money ought to be returned to His Majesty's Receiver-General, that the same shall be done accordingly.
>
> Patrick Henry, Junior [27]

At a meeting of the Hanover Committee on May 9, reported in Purdie's *Virginia Gazette,* the members thanked Henry and his volunteers, noting how they had avoided "all violence, injury, and insult" to private persons. But Lord Dunmore in a dispatch to the Ministry reported that all the colony was in a state of anarchy, and that Patrick Henry, "a man in desperate circumstances," had extorted £330 of the King's revenue.[28]

If Henry had any lingering doubt as to the wisdom of his gunpowder expedition, he was encouraged by addresses and resolutions from various counties strongly approving his conduct and giving assurances of military support. Leaving Hanover for Philadelphia on May 11, he was escorted by some of the Hanover volunteers as far as Mrs. Hooe's Ferry on the Potomac River. Henry's journey from Hanover to the river crossing was much delayed by the large number of communications sent him by express riders from various county committees. Thus in a letter from Port Royal, on the Rappahannock River, he expressed to James Madison, Sr. (father of the future President), chairman of the Orange County Committee, his gratification that the "Reprizal we have made for the purpose of compensating the Colony for the loss of the Powder from the Magazine, has met with the approbation of your Committee. Give me leave to assure you, Sir, that nothing called us further upon that Occasion, but Zeal for the public good." [29]

With Henry and his command no longer an immediate threat to Williamsburg, the Governor braced himself to issue a proclamation of virtual outlawry against Patrick Henry. No such manifesto had been issued against a leading Virginian since Bacon's Rebellion a century before. Henry had indeed crossed the Rubicon, whence there was little chance of returning to his former ease and safety.

The proclamation began:

> Virginia, to wit:
>
> Whereas, I have been informed, from undoubted authority, that a certain Patrick Henry, of the county of Hanover, and a number of his deluded followers, have taken up arms and styling themselves an Independent Company, have marched out of their County, encamped, and put themselves in a posture for war. . . .

Dunmore followed with a reference to Henry and his companions who had ridden to various parts of the country "exciting the people to join in these outrageous and rebellious practices, to the great terror of all His Majesty's faithful subjects"; also to "other acts of violence, particularly in extorting from His Majesty's Receiver-General £330" so that there was "no longer the least security for the life and property of any man."

With the advice of His Majesty's Council and in His Majesty's name, Dunmore therefore issued this mandate:

> . . . strictly charging all persons, upon their allegiance, not to aid, abet, or give countenance to the said Patrick Henry, or any other persons concerned in such unwarrantable combinations, but on the contrary to oppose them and their designs by every means; which designs must, otherwise, inevitably involve the whole Country in the most direful calamity, as they will call for the vengeance of offended Majesty and the insulted laws to be exerted here, to vindicate the constitutional authority of Government.
>
> Given under my hand and seal of the Colony, at Williamsburg, this 6th day of May, 1775, and in the fifteenth year of His Majesty's reign.
>
> Dunmore

God save the King. [30]

A vital problem confronting Henry during the next few years would be to effect his advanced objectives without alienating too much of the moderate or conservative opposition. After giving the receipt for the money paid by the Governor in compensation for the gunpowder, Henry was at pains to address a tactful letter to Robert Carter Nicholas, the treasurer of the colony. Henry stated that the powder incident was "now settled so as to produce satisfaction" to him and, so he earnestly wished, "to the colony in general." His command had it "in charge from the Hanover Committee, to tender their services" to Nicholas for the purpose of moving the public treasury to a location "where the money would be judged more safe than in the City of Williamsburg." While asserting that the "reprisal" by the Hanover volunteers had been "accomplished in a manner least liable to the imputation of violent extremity," Henry admitted it could possibly cause "future injury to the Treasury."

To this letter, sent "With great regard," Nicholas stiffly replied that he had "no apprehension of the necessity or propriety of the proffered service." [31] The Williamsburg citizens, too, were now less disturbed for fear of drastic action by Dunmore. Henry's men were dismissed to return to their homes, and he went back to Scotchtown to arrange for a belated start to the Continental Congress at Philadelphia.

Not merely the reactionary Governor's Council but a number of leading men in the Tidewater opposed Henry's action in the gunpowder incident. They did not believe war was inevitable but that it might be provoked by what they deemed his "rash and ill-advised" move.[32] Fearing harmful attacks upon him at the approaching Virginia Convention while he was absent in Philadelphia, Henry, before leaving for the city, also wrote his friend, Francis Lightfoot Lee, a lengthy explanation of his conduct.[33]

The letters which Henry wrote Nicholas and Francis Lightfoot Lee are among the few instances in which Henry is known to have looked backward to assuage or to placate after taking a decisive course. But he was merely strengthening his position after the *fait accompli*, not hesitating at a critical moment. It was becoming obvious that he possessed that quality of decisiveness needed by the great revolutionary orator. Asked what were the three parts of oratory, Demosthenes had answered, "Action, action, action!" When Cicero had finished speaking, the people said, "How well he spoke," but when Demosthenes had finished, they said, "Let us march." Henry possessed that same sureness, that same dynamic quality.[34]

The man and the times had met. While it was prudent for Henry to mollify some of the conservative opposition, he had reason to hope that he could rely on a wide popular support. More than five thousand volunteers are said to have been en route to join him in his expedition toward Williamsburg.[35] Although they had returned home after learning of its success, they offered notable encouragement for continuation of his strong policy during the Second Continental Congress. He could blithely ignore another blustering manifesto from Lord Dunmore, this seeking to prevent his attendance at the Continental Congress.

On March 28, the day after the adjournment of the Virginia Convention, Lord Dunmore had issued a proclamation calling attention to the fact that "certain persons, styling themselves delegates" had presumed to assemble in Philadelphia without His Majesty's authority the previous September and planned to meet there again in May, and ordering all magistrates and other officers "to use their utmost endeavours" to prevent the meeting. This proclamation had only irritated the people;[36] Henry was not disturbed in his preparations for departure.

Arriving at Mrs. Hooe's Ferry on the Potomac, Henry and his escort "were most hospitably and kindly entertained" by the worthy lady and "provided with boats and hands." Most of the company took leave of Henry at the Virginia shore line, "saluting him with two platoons and repeated huzzas." A guard accompanied him, however, to the Maryland side of the river, where according to the contemporary account they committed him to the "wise Disposer of all human events" to protect him "while contending for a restitution of our dearest rights and liberties."[37] Obviously, the military escort had been more than ceremonial. In a letter to the Ministry in London,

Lord Dunmore labeled Henry as "a man of desperate circumstances, who had been very active in encouraging disobedience and inciting a spirit of revolt among the people for many years past."[38] It is clear that the Governor sought Henry's arrest.

5

The Second Continental Congress

I believe every man of candour will agree with me in opinion, that, let the event be what it may, the rashness and rebellious conduct of the Provincials on this occasion evince the necessity, and will manifest to all the world the justice of the measures which the King had adopted for supporting the Constitution, and in which His Majesty will firmly persevere.

———Letter from LORD DARTMOUTH to General Gage, London, July 1, 1775 [1]

. . . it has been with difficulty that we have carried another humble petition to the crown, to give Britain one more chance, one opportunity more, of recovering the friendship of the colonies; which, however, I think she has not sense enough to embrace, and so I conclude she has lost them for ever.

———Letter from BENJAMIN FRANKLIN to Dr. Joseph Priestley, in England, Philadelphia, July 7, 1775 [2]

May 10, 1775. Second Continental Congress meets in Philadelphia.

May 10. Americans capture Fort Ticonderoga.

June–July. Congress organizes Continental Army and issues a declaration of causes for taking up arms along with other addresses.

June 15. George Washington appointed commander of Continental Army.

June 17. British win costly victory at Bunker Hill.

August 2. Congress, "after the fatigue of many days," [3] adjourns until September 5, 1775.

O<small>N THURSDAY</small>, May 18, 1775, Patrick Henry took his seat
in the Second Continental Congress at Philadelphia.[4] Although the
opening session had been held more than a week earlier, the delegates
had not accomplished much beyond routine preliminaries. "The
Congress did little more the first week than form themselves," Silas
Deane, a Connecticut delegate, wrote his wife on May 21.[5] Not that
there was any lack of problems with which Congress had to come to
grips. In the weekly *Pennsylvania Gazettes*, now again available to
Henry, the commercial news was in the same pattern as during his
visit the previous fall but much else had radically changed. There
were the usual notices of sloops, brigs, and schooners entering or
leaving through the Custom House. One Pennsylvanian was offering
£3 reward for a dark brown mare, strayed or stolen; another, a lesser
reward for a runaway Irish servant. Owen Biddle was offering to sell
the "Time" (between three and four years) remaining on the inden-
ture of an Irish servant girl; Charles Wharton at his store next to
the drawbridge was advertising sweet oil in quarter casks and half
boxes, Jamaican spirit sugar, old Lisbon wine "of an excellent quality," and brimstone by the hogshead.[6]

But of far more interest to Henry were the affidavits and deposi-
tions from Massachusetts, now spread in the *Journals of Congress*, to
prove that the British had been responsible for starting the "late
hostilities" in Massachusetts. John Robins, "being of lawful age," did
"Testify and say" that on April 19 he was in Captain Parker's company drawn up on the village green at Lexington when, after they
were dispersing according to the British order, a King's officer commanded his soldiers to "fire, by God, fire!" Several of Parker's men
were then shot dead, none of the company, so Robins believed, "having then fired a gun." The house of Hannah Bradish, who was in her
bedchamber with her infant child, was riddled by British bullets, and
various family possessions were missing, "verily" believed to have
been taken by the King's troops: a rich brocade gown, "called a negli-
gée," a white quilt, and three shirts. And so on from numerous resi-
dents of Lexington or nearby.[7]

For Henry the documents offered a foretaste of many atrocity stories, not models of impartiality, which would be spread by both Americans and British during the war. The next year he himself would be one of the victims of a forged letter originating from a pro-British source.[8]

Meantime, at the Second Congress, Henry, with his simple back-country tastes, was not disturbed to miss the fanfare, the military escort and band, which had greeted some New England and middle states delegates arriving before the initial meeting.[9] Yet the bold orator of St. John's Church, the revolutionary leader of the gun-powder episode whom Lord Dunmore had outlawed, found his role in this new Congress something of an anticlimax. For him, as well as for John Adams and other liberal delegates, the session was in many respects a depressing experience, aggravated by summer heat and flies. At least, however, they got some valuable knowledge of the obstacles to colonial unity. And by the last weeks of the protracted two-month session, the tide was definitely turning in their favor. Even though some important measures were carried by only narrow majorities, the Congress did courageously assume control of a united war effort which would somehow tide over the situation until sentiment was ripe for further change.

While Henry's work in the Second Congress cannot be dismissed as inconsequential, it is significant to note the extent to which he and the other Whig leaders, John and Samuel Adams and Richard Henry Lee, were curbed by the more conservative and calculating opposition. After arriving in Philadelphia, Henry found that news of his armed expedition against Lord Dunmore—an overt military action regarded with proper horror by conservatives—had reached the city. Spread over a column and a half of the *Pennsylvania Gazette* issued about the time of his arrival was an account from Williamsburg of the gunpowder expedition led by "Patrick Henry Esq.," with an address by Governor Dunmore to the Council regarding "COMMOTIONS and insurrections . . . suddenly excited among the people, which threaten the very existence of his Majesty's government in this colony . . ."[10] The *Pennsylvania Evening Post* also had published on April 29 the proceedings of the Virginia Convention of 1775, with its indication of Henry's aggressive role. All the New Englanders were not of the Adams breed, and some were disturbed by the report in the Salem, Massachusetts, *Essex Gazette* of Henry's march on Williamsburg, even though his followers were described as "all men of property" and "Gentlemen." [11]

Henry's rash speeches and actions have "lost him the Confidence and Esteem of most sensible moderate men," wrote the Quaker, Edward Stabler, to one of his brethren in Philadelphia.[12] Moreover, Edmund Pendleton, now in Congress, advised a Virginia supporter in a letter of May 30 that the variety of opinions on the subject of Henry's recent march with the Hanover volunteers made it "prudent" to have the incident agitated as little as possible. Otherwise, differences of opinion might be "wrought into dissentions, very injurious to the common Cause." [13]

The same sort of opposition was encountered in greater degree by the Adamses. As late as June 10, that advance organizer of revolution, the grimly determined Sam Adams, was writing of his endeavor to act in Congress with "prudence," [14] while his younger cousin, John, wrote on the seventeenth that this Congress was like the last: the sentiments of the New England and especially Massachusetts delegates were heard "with great caution, and seemed to make but little impression." [15] The force of conservative or time-serving opinion was seen in the committee appointments. When on June 3 the slow-moving Congress got around to naming members of some key committees, the conciliationist leader, personable, socially prominent John Dickinson of Pennsylvania, was made chairman of a key committee to draw up a petition to the King; John Adams had to content himself with being chairman of the committee to draw up a petition to Ireland and to serve on minor committees—to prepare a resolve for a day of fasting and prayer [16] and to help decide what to do about a luckless British officer, the new commander at Fort Ticonderoga. Arriving at Philadelphia en route to his post, the officer, Major Skene, found that the strategic fort, with its valuable artillery train, had been captured by the Americans on the very day Congress opened.[17]

As for Patrick Henry, he was given no committee appointments at all for a month after his arrival. This may be explained in part by his late arrival. But it is significant that the most influential of the southern popular leaders, the most persuasive of the contemporary American orators, was not put on a single committee until June 16. He was then appointed ranking member, after the wealthy and experienced Schuyler of New York, of a middling-important committee to report on measures necessary to secure and preserve the friendship of the Indian nations.[18]

In selecting Henry, the Congress was undoubtedly being influenced by his speaking ability, which Deane, during the previous session, had described as "the completest" he had ever heard.

> If his future speeches are equal to the small samples he has hitherto given us, they will be worth preserving, but in a letter I can give you no idea of the music of his voice, or the high-wrought yet natural elegance of his style and manner.[19]

When Congress met on Wednesday, May 10, 1775, there had been deceptive signs of unanimity among the members. Silas Deane wrote his wife of the sentiment voiced by three Virginia delegates with whom he had spent the previous evening: Colonel George Washington ("a fine figure and of a most easy and agreeable address"), Richard Henry Lee, and "Col." Harrison. Deane "could not perceive the least disposition" among his companions "to accommodate matters" with the British. Moreover, Lee wrote to William Lee on May 10 that "all the old Provinces" were determined "to resist by all ways and to every extremity."[20] Even the more pessimistic John Adams was then hopeful of such action.

Yet Adams soon noted a mounting conservative opposition in the Congress. This movement centered, so he thought, in Pennsylvania among gentlemen who owed their wealth and honors to the proprietary interests and among the great body of the Quakers. It had an influential leader in John Dickinson, the quondam liberal of the Pennsylvania Farmer letters. For Dickinson, however, Adams had a note of pity. He quoted Charles Thomson as saying that the Quakers had intimidated Dickinson's mother and wife and that the latter were continually distressing him with their remonstrances.

"Johnny, you will be hanged; your estate will be forfeited and confiscated; you will leave your excellent wife a widow, and your charming children orphans, beggars, and infamous," so Mrs. Dickinson importuned him, according to Adams' severe appraisal.[21]

Moreover, Adams intimated that "the Proprietary Gentlemen," Israel Pemberton and other principal Quakers, used their insinuations, their social connections, on all the delegates they could influence. A South Carolina delegate, Arthur Middleton, had brought his sister and brother to the city: they "were invited to all Parties and were visited perpetually."[22] But while a number of delegates were susceptible to such pressures, the scheming Philadelphians could not—or did not—attempt to convert another South Carolina delegate, Christopher Gadsden, the advanced liberal from Stamp Act days. Now fifty-one and with his long Charleston wharf susceptible to the losses from all-out war, he remained courageous and optimistic.[23]

The Charlestonian Gadsden apart, there was much about some of the South Carolina delegates to remind Henry of the conservative Tidewater representatives whom he had fought in Virginia. Indeed, John Dickinson was of much the same ilk—this low-country protagonist with his brick mansion below Dover, and its fertile, slave-tilled fields stretching over the flat miles to Delaware Bay.[24] We leave Henry's opinion of the conciliationists to reasonable surmise; certainly he never lacked strong convictions. There is no evidence that the conservatives at Philadelphia wasted time in trying to influence him despite his Quaker ties.

The meetings of the Second Continental Congress were held at the Pennsylvania State House on Chestnut Street between Fifth and Sixth. This was in the old part of Philadelphia where the streets had been named for famous men, but William Penn, opposing such "man-worship," had renamed them with numbers or for trees and flowers:

High, Mulberry, Sassafras, Vine;
Chestnut, Walnut, Spruce, and Pine.

The State House, now famous Independence Hall, is a red-brick Georgian edifice. Congress met in the rectangular east room on the first floor. The building was less than two blocks from Carpenters' Hall, where Henry and the delegates had met the previous fall, and they again resided chiefly in the nearby streets.[25]

Essentially an adjourned session of the First Continental Congress, the Second Congress provided for the same parliamentary rules and injunctions of secrecy, to be upheld "under the strongest obligations of honour." [26] (John Adams revealed some of the proceedings to his wife "under the rose.") [27] The suave Peyton Randolph was again chosen president, and Charles Thomson secretary. The members could claim to speak to a degree for all thirteen colonies, since a Georgia delegate had now arrived. But while he had been elected from only one parish in his thinly settled state, this was hardly the phenomenon that it appeared: a number of the delegates had been hand picked by a small electorate with the opposition inactive or suppressed, as a Tory newspaper would be at pains to point out.[28]

Forty-eight delegates were on hand on the opening day, and sixty on Thursday, May 18, when Henry took his seat. That morning Congress met at nine o'clock, and the second item in the *Journal* was a notation of the presence of the Honorable Stephen Hopkins of Rhode Island and Patrick Henry, Esq., of Virginia.[29] Henry could not, like the veteran Rhode Island legislator, boast of having been present at every intercolonial congress beginning with the Albany Congress of 1756. But he had been a leader of the First Continental Congress and with the passing weeks became increasingly important in the Second. Six days after his arrival, on May 24, Peyton Randolph having left for what he deemed more pressing duties as speaker of the Virginia House of Burgesses, the wealthy Boston merchant (and smuggler, as the British had it) John Hancock was unanimously elected president of the convention.[30] Randolph's absence meant the loss of a moderate influence in the Virginia delegation, and the liberal element there and in the Congress as a whole was strengthened by the arrival on June 21 of Randolph's replacement, the dedicated Thomas Jefferson.[31]

As in so many revolutionary gatherings, Henry would find the boldest leaders were usually the young, or at most, middle-aged men. The notable exception was a new Pennsylvania member, the famous Dr. Benjamin Franklin, now sixty-nine. The best known and most influential American in Europe, the canny Franklin had much more impact than was indicated by his often silent, almost somnolent role. While Joseph Galloway of Pennsylvania, a conservative bulwark in the last Congress, was fleeing to unhappy exile in England,[32] Franklin returned from there to offer his wisdom and experience to the radical movement. With his remarkable youthfulness of spirit, he was the outstanding liberal delegate from the Middle States, not out of place with Sam Adams in his early fifties, John Adams and Patrick Henry in their late thirties, or Thomas Jefferson, a bare thirty-two.

Again, as in the preceding Congress, over a third of the delegates were lawyers, and they were predominantly of British descent. Among those of Scotch ancestry, Henry, himself descended from an Aberdeenshire family, had certain congenial ties with the thirty-three-year-old James Wilson, a rising Pennsylvanian. Wilson, born in Scotland near the University of St. Andrews and educated there and at Edinburgh, had early emigrated to America and like Henry had become a highly successful country lawyer. Henry must have noted Wilson's manuscript, which cogently argued that Parliament had no authority over the colonies, since the paper was distributed to members of the First Continental Congress. But Wilson soon turned more to the right.[33]

Altogether, the Second Continental Congress comprised one of the ablest groups of men ever assembled in America. With public opinion continuing to press for more dynamic action, the Congress would become enshrined the next year as the Signers of the American Declaration of Independence.

If there was any possible doubt as to the alarming condition of public affairs, it was dispelled by early communications to Congress. The motion of Lord Chatham to withdraw the troops from Boston had been defeated in Parliament, and the formidable British force in the city was being strengthened. The Massachusetts Congress, deeply alarmed by the threatening armament, called on the Philadelphia delegates for active support. A powerful army raised by the Continental Congress was "the only medium left to stem" the ministerial forces.[34]

Encouraging to Henry at this critical time was the impression reaching him from newspapers, letters, or word of mouth as to the firm stand of the Virginia populace. On May 15 Captain Montague had taken his British marines (the "boiled crabs") back from Williamsburg to H.M.S. *Fowey*,[35] and in early June they had been followed aboard by Lord Dunmore and his Lady.[36]

The *Virginia Gazette*s continued to publish county resolutions strongly approving Captain Henry's conduct in the gunpowder expedition, along with news of further warlike preparations in the colony. In a Williamsburg dispatch of June 2 to the then Whiggish *London Chronicle* of July 21, the public was assured "on undoubted authority" that 1,300 barrels of gunpowder were safely landed at Baltimore. America "will be well supplied with that commodity, so necessary for the preservation of its liberties," it was optimistically claimed. When the House of Burgesses met in early June, every member was reported to be clothed in homespun and to have "Liberty or Death" sewed or painted on the breast of his coat.[37]

Shortly after Henry's arrival in Philadelphia, there was some abortive sentiment in Congress for removal to Hartford or another northerly place. It was "a very delicate point," especially since the proposed location would be so far removed from the South and would probably cause too much preoccupation with New England affairs. Fortunately, the overworked members did not suffer, as in the previous Congress, from a superabundance of food and drink supplied by generous Philadelphians.

"Great frugality and great industry are now become fashionable here," Benjamin Franklin wrote on July 7 to his learned English friend, Dr. Joseph Priestley. "Gentlemen, who used to entertain with two or three courses, pride themselves now in treating with simple beef and pudding."[38]

It took Henry but a short time to be briefed on the few important matters already disposed of, the others being slowly, often hesitatingly, considered under the pressures of a popular legislative body faced with grave decisions. Transcendent were the twin problems of maintaining a provisional government and army and fighting an undeclared war—a war which Congress might lose through timidity and vacillation. Could the fighting be contained without critical danger to the American cause? With most Americans not yet ready to attempt a final severance of British ties, some temporizing was inevitable. In New York State where an early British attack was feared, Congress ordered several strategic points to be armed. Troops were to be placed in New York City so as to protect the people from "insult" by any soldiers that might land there.

John Adams later complained in his diary of that "Measure of Imbecility"—a second petition to the King—which "embarrassed every exertion of Congress." In a letter to his wife nearly three months after he had left her in Massachusetts, he said that if he had given her a complete account of the behavior of his fellow delegates, "no mortal tale" could "equal it . . . the fidgets, the whims, the *caprice*, the *vanity*, the superstition, the irritability of some of us is enough to ———." [39]

Yet these private outpourings were not to be taken too seriously. The petition to the King was something of a final propitiatory gesture to the Dickinson faction. Meantime, in late June a war chest of two million dollars had been appropriated. During the month significant measures had been taken to organize and supply a Continental Army, to maintain the provisional government, and to influence public opinion, with Henry's name now frequently cited in the official proceedings. A critical issue had faced the members when the Massachusetts patriots specifically asked Congress to assume control of the provisional government there. "We tremble at having an army . . . without a civil power to provide for the control of them." The Massachusetts authorities would readily submit to a "general plan" for the colonies and proposed that Congress take charge of the army now besieging Boston.

In a not too equivocal reply on June 9, Congress stated that the Massachusetts people should choose governing bodies which would exercise their powers until a government of His Majesty's appointment would consent to govern according to its charter. And that would not be soon! During the next week some helpful provisions were made to secure gunpowder, and six companies of "expert rifle-men" were authorized for service before Boston. Two of these companies, marksmen of almost fabulous skill, were recruited from the Virginia back country. Soon these Virginians would march to Boston in record time, one of their captains in whom Henry would take special interest, a powerful ex-teamster and farmer, being the future General, Daniel Morgan. The captains were to be paid only $20 per month and the privates only $6⅔, and apparently all were "to find their own arms and cloaths." [40]

On Friday, June 16, the same day that Henry was appointed to the Committee on Indian Affairs, President Hancock informed George Washington that Congress had by unanimous consent chosen him to be General and commander in chief of the forces raised in defense of American liberty. From the official journal we learn that Washington, standing in his place, accepted the offer with a modest disclaimer of requisite ability. But the journal does not reveal the difficulties under which the appointment was offered and received.

Although George Washington had won deserved distinction in the French and Indian War, there were available officers with much greater military experience. The appointment was largely made through the "politicking" of the Adamses, who felt the need of promoting colonial unity by appointing a Southerner with Washington's prestige. Curiously, John Adams had found opposition to Washington's appointment even among the Virginia delegates. "The apostolical reasonings among themselves, which should be greatest, were not less energetic among the saints of the ancient dominion than they were among us of New England," Adams sarcastically recollected. He found that more than one Virginia delegate was "very cool" toward Washington's candidacy and that Edmund Pendleton in particular was "very clear and full against it."

Deeply disturbed by the disputes and daily fearing bad news from Boston, Adams walked with his cousin, Sam Adams, in the State House yard, where he represented to him the various dangers that encompassed them. John Adams declared that he was determined to take a step which would compel the members of Congress to declare themselves "for or against something."

"I am determined this morning to make a direct motion that congress should adopt the army before Boston, and appoint Colonel Washington commander of it," Adams said.

John Hancock had hoped for the appointment and, so John Adams roguishly noted, his "Physiognomy" did not "soften" when Sam Adams seconded Washington's nomination. In the ensuing debate several delegates opposed Washington, not because of any personal objections but because the army before Boston was from New England, appeared satisfied with Artemas Ward, its New England general, and "had proved themselves able to shut up the British in Boston," all that was "expected or desired at that time." Edmund Pendleton and Roger Sherman of Connecticut were "very explicit in declaring this opinion," several others "more faintly" so. Pendleton's opposition to the high appointments for his fellow Virginian may seem difficult to understand. Surely no ill feeling had cropped up between the long-time friends and political associates; a few days before, Washington had told Pendleton to prepare his will. A Pendleton biographer, David Mays, suggests that Pendleton may have felt that Washington's selection "would have committed Virginia irrevocably to the defense of Boston and a radical course." Mays argues that Pendleton seems to have convinced the rest of the Virginia delegation, and that they and others sharing their opinion had to be won over before Washington was unanimously elected the next day. But Henry and Richard Henry Lee would have been out of character in opposing Washington for such a reason. Washington's reported comment to Henry after his election as commander in chief gives no indication of anything having disturbed their friendly relationship. Washington told Henry that he was unequal to the station in which the country had placed him.

"Remember Mr. Henry what I now tell you—from the day I enter upon the command of the American armies, I date my fall and the ruin of my reputation." [41]

Henry helped to secure another appointment which he later deplored—that of General Charles Lee. He was a former British officer with what to many Americans was a dazzling background of military experience and study. An old friend in field and camp of well-placed British military men, Lee appeared to be a vociferous exponent of American liberty. There were complications, however, which threatened to prevent the appointment. Many delegates argued that Lee could not be expected to rank under any one but Washington. He must be "aut secundus, aut nullus." Also, before this highly touted gentleman would accept his general's commission, he wanted Congress to guarantee that he would be indemnified for any loss thereby to his personal estate. Henry was a member of a committee which, after conferring with Lee, reported to Congress on the delicate matter. Its members then agreed to compensate Lee for any loss of property from his American service. There were almost no available officers with experience in higher command; Henry knew that his committee could not be too particular. Yet he must have begun to doubt an officer who set such a price upon his fight for liberty. Lee's conduct was in shabby contrast with that of George Washington. Risking life and fortune as military leader of a desperate cause, Washington would accept no compensation except for actual expenses.[42]

Washington wrote his brother on June 20, "I am imbarked on a wide Ocean, boundless in its prospect and from whence, perhaps, no safe harbour is to be found."[43] Resolutely, he set out a few days later to take command of the army before Boston, having already heard an incomplete report of a bloody battle there.[44]

After the skirmish at Lexington on April 19, 1775, the British troops had proceeded to Concord to seize American supplies. They had aroused a swarm of militia and soon were encircled at Boston by an army of men from all over New England. It was not until June 17, 1775, that the British commander, the darkly handsome and cautious Lord Howe, ventured a frontal attack, in close order, on the American position at Bunker Hill (actually Breed's Hill) opposite Boston. Patrick Henry was probably among the hundred gentlemen flocking to John Adams' lodgings in Philadelphia on Saturday night, June 23, to get first news of the resulting battle. The British had driven the New Englanders from the sweltering hillside, but only after three desperate attacks and after the raw Yankee militia had run out of powder. "The . . . rebels are not the despicable rabble too many have supposed them to be," General Gage wrote Lord Dartmouth.

Within a few hours after receiving the express from Massachusetts, the Adamses and Hancock started a large shipment of powder to the army. Readily supplied by the Philadelphia Committee, it was symptomatic of the enthusiasm and determination engendered by Bunker Hill.

Now the war had come to a bloody pass. The proud British could be expected to strike back in force. The Adamses, Henry, and other liberal delegates could point to the futility of further conciliatory measures. Indeed, the dragging preliminaries of the Congress were already ended. It was embarked on a forward-looking, though still measured, program which gave an opportunity for the lately curbed radical members.

Henry's purported opinion on one aspect of the battle is noted in a memorial written later by Dr. Benjamin Rush of Philadelphia. Henry, whom Dr. Rush described as amiable in his manners, had been Rush's patient when inoculated for smallpox while attending the first Congress. After the battle of Bunker Hill, Henry "exulted" in the death there of the American General Warren, so Rush asserted.

"I rejoice to hear it. His death will do a great deal of good. We wanted some breaches made upon our affections to awaken our patriotism and to prepare us for war."

Henry was also said to have disapproved of an American expedition to Canada for the purpose of inciting an insurrection against the British. "Men would never revolt against their ancient rulers, while they enjoyed peace and plenty." [45]

Dr. Rush, who would have reason to be prejudiced against Henry, may have had him sound too cold-blooded in his patriotic program. Yet Henry had already welcomed the battle of Lexington as bringing matters to a head; his remarks after Bunker Hill do not seem entirely out of character.

On June 21, 1775, Henry rose in his seat to state that George Washington "had put into his hands sundry queries." The disposition of these queries respecting Washington's course in the war was of vital importance. An able and forceful committee was required, and Congress now moved forward to appoint such a one with a strong liberal membership: Silas Deane, chairman, Patrick Henry, Sam Adams, and Richard Henry Lee, who would outweigh the more conservative John Rutledge.[46]

In July, Congress passed the Petition to the King. John Dickinson, who had become the leader of the conciliationist party in Congress, was appointed to write the Petition. After being debated "by paragraph," it was accepted on July 5 in the "politic" form which Dickinson proposed.[47] But while from the liberal viewpoint there was much reason for believing that the petition was futile if not demeaning, even John Adams came to be more appreciative of Dickinson. His writings, though not as inspiring as Jefferson's, would lead some to term him "The Penman of the Revolution." Henry would support the Articles of Confederation among subsequent products of the Dickinson pen.

Early the same month Congress approved a "Declaration on Taking Arms." Written in spirited terms by Thomas Jefferson, it had not been denatured through changes proposed by Dickinson. With the liberals getting a more receptive ear, Henry must now have taken a more effective part in the debates.

Five days after signing the Petition to the King, Congress made Henry a member of a committee in connection with some Indian goods, then on the thirteenth a commissioner of Indians for the Middle Department. An uneasy peace lay over the frontier, and the Indians might easily be aroused by British agents. On June 30, 1775, the Committee on Indian Affairs had been asked to prepare talks to secure the Indian friendship. Two weeks later their speech for the Indians was debated by paragraphs, passed, and ordered to be delivered with a token of friendship:

. . . "When our fathers crossed the great water," the king of England assured them that the fields and possessions which they acquired should remain as their own. . . .

"BROTHERS AND FRIENDS, OPEN A KIND EAR!" Many of King George's counsellors are "proud and wicked men. They persuaded the king to break the covenant chain. . . ."[48]

Not everything in Philadelphia was heat, flies, and wearisome meetings. There was opportunity for occasional horseback rides to pleasant homes in the outlying town and countryside. There was military display, some inspiriting sermons, intervals of refreshing weather. Yet as John Adams wrote on July 24, "We are lost in the extensiveness of our field of business. . . ."[49]

Henry was more accustomed than Adams to the hot weather, if not the lengthy sessions, often preceded or followed by committee meetings. But with the malarial season approaching and the Virginia Convention in session, he had every reason to welcome a recess. On August 1 Congress adjourned to meet in September. With many of the delegates needed to buttress the war efforts in their individual states, perhaps it had met long enough. As early as June 3 Silas Deane had preferred to spend an hour with two young ladies, "neither of them very handsome," to four hours in Congress with all its "formality." By the eighteenth he was complaining of the "extreme" heat at a nine-to-five session, and by July 14 he had lost a guinea to a fellow delegate when he couldn't find one "handsome face" among a vast crowd of Philadelphia girls (or so he wrote his wife).[50]

On July 31 Henry was appointed a member of a committee to make an urgently needed inquiry in all the colonies as to their supply of virgin lead and leaden ore along with the best methods of collecting and refining it; also the most practical methods of procuring salt. This committee, composed of only one member in each colony, was to serve during the recess of Congress. The quality of the members is indicated by the appointment of such delegates as John Langdon for New Hampshire, John Adams for Massachusetts, Christopher Gadsden for South Carolina, and Benjamin Franklin for Pennsylvania, along with Henry for Virginia.[51]

The past month had seen a Continental Army organized, the *de facto* government stabilized, a war of arms and propaganda launched. Altogether, it was about as much as could reasonably be expected under the circumstances.

6

Henry as Colonel

We both seem to be steering opposite Courses; the Success of
either lies in the Womb of Time.——JOHN RANDOLPH [1]
We Selebrated the Independence of America the howl army
parraded . . . the artilery Discharged thirteen Cannon we gave
three Chears &c. At Night his Excelency and the gentlemen
and Ladys had a Bawl at Head Quarters with grate Pompe.
——Elijah Fisher's Diary [2]

August 5, 1775–February 28, 1776. Henry serves, under the
severely restrictive direction of the Committee of Safety, as
colonel of the First Regiment and commander of the Virginia
regular forces.

1775–1776. Fall and winter. British Army inactive at Boston.

December 9, 1775. Colonel Woodford defeats British at Great
Bridge near Norfolk.

January 1, 1776. Failure of American assault on Quebec.

February 27, 1776. British defeat at Moore's Creek, North
Carolina.

March 17, 1776. British begin evacuation of Boston.

IN JULY, 1775, the new Virginia Convention had ordered two
regiments to be raised, and by the end of the year seven more were
authorized. This would complete the quota of nine regiments assigned
by Congress.[3] From August, 1775, to February, 1776, Henry was
colonel of the First Regiment and commander in chief of her regular

forces, serving to the satisfaction of his men but not of certain members of the Committee of Safety, with their supporters. He became involved in controversies that have been rehashed to this day and raise significant questions as to the wisdom of his ever accepting this military rank and the possible sequel if he had assumed the colonelcy available to him in Washington's army.

The voting on Henry's appointment reveals much about the available military ability—and the political undercurrents—in Virginia at that critical period. With George Washington serving in command of the rustic volunteers in front of Boston, Andrew Lewis, now of Botetourt County, appeared on the record to be the ablest soldier in Virginia. It was less than a year since Lewis, coolly smoking his pipe, had pressed the fight at Point Pleasant while the Virginia frontiersmen in their deerskins and moccasins had fallen around him, among them his own brother, Charles.[4] Andrew Lewis' Scotch-Irish sensitiveness to individual rights, never undeveloped, had been heightened by the events of the following months, not least of which had been Henry's speech at St. John's Church, where Lewis had sat as a delegate.[5] A powerful, downright man, six feet tall, under whom "the earth seemed to tremble," [6] Lewis was needed by George Washington for his Continental Army.[7] Moreover, Lewis hardly carried enough influence to be chosen over Henry in a convention dominated by Tidewater and Piedmont delegates.

The election was held on August 5, before Henry had returned from Philadelphia. Four gentlemen were nominated as colonel of the first regiment: Patrick Henry, Hugh Mercer of Fredericksburg, Thomas Nelson of Yorktown, and William Woodford of Caroline County near Fredericksburg.[8] Of the four-member committee appointed to examine the ballot box, three were members of the Tidewater aristocracy: Robert Carter Nicholas; his cousin, Charles Carter of Lancaster; and Bartholomew Dandridge of New Kent.[9] Yet under the impetus of the Revolution the balance of power was moving to the more westerly counties. Of the officers nominated, only one, Nelson, was from the Tidewater counties or the old aristocracy (as "old" was understood in Virginia social circles).

As the debate developed, it was obvious that Henry and Hugh Mercer were the leading candidates, Mercer apparently having the support of the conservative forces, along with those members who were fearful of Henry's military inexperience. By a coincidence Mercer was born in Aberdeen, Scotland, in 1725, just about the time that Patrick's scholarly father, John Henry, left there for Virginia. A graduate in medicine at Edinburgh, he had fought under Bonnie Prince Charlie at Culloden, where he made effective use of moss on wounds; then, emigrating to Virginia, he had won distinction and been desperately wounded in the French and Indian War.[10]

There is enough evidence to indicate the general thread of the arguments for and against the election of Henry and Mercer. Henry's studies had been directed to civil and not military affairs, it was stated. He was totally unacquainted with the art of war and had no knowledge of military discipline. Such a person was unfit to be at the head of troops who were likely to be engaged against a well-disciplined army commanded by experienced and able generals. These arguments were answered by one delegate who said that Mr. Henry solicited the appointment, which he supposed he would not have done if he did not think himself qualified to command.

Against Mercer the objection was made that he was a North Briton. But in reply it was argued that he had come early to America, had been a warm friend to her rights, and above all possessed "great military as well as literary abilities." [11]

The ballots having been duly counted, the committee reported 41 votes for Mercer, 40 for Henry, 8 for Nelson, and 1 for William Woodford, who had been a young officer in the French and Indian War.[12]

To add to the difficulties of the Henry adherents, both of the other nominees declared themselves in favor of Mercer. Thomas Nelson announced that he would not oppose him and expressed hope that he (Nelson) would not be voted for.[13] William Woodford, an old friend and associate of Edmund Pendleton, was not then a member of the Convention, but he "spoke very largely out-of-doors" in favor of Mercer and expressed his willingness to serve under him since he knew him to be a fine officer.[14] Woodford, a strong character with pronounced opinions, looked upon Henry as a mere civilian. Already there were signs that certain veteran officers nursed understandable objections to those who had not won their spurs.

In view of Mercer's and Woodford's military experience and ability, Henry's election was all the more remarkable. On a second ballot, between him and Mercer, the two highest candidates, Henry was chosen colonel of the first regiment.[15] But the "form" of his commission was not approved by the Convention until August 26, the day of adjournment. And while the wording is somewhat equivocal, he could hardly have realized the unhappy situation it would help to create.

> Whereas the Convention had resolved, so the commission read, that Henry should be "Colonel of the First Regiment of Regulars and Commander-in-Chief of all the Forces" to be raised for the defence of the colony, the Committee of Safety therefore commissioned him Colonel of the First Regiment and commander-in-chief of all such forces as the Convention or Committee may direct "to act in conjunction with them." He was to exercise the office of "Colonel and Commander-in-Chief of the Forces" subject to the orders of the Convention of Committee; "to perform and execute the power and authority aforesaid, and all other things which are truly and of right incidental" during the pleasure of the Convention. And all officers and soldiers concerned were to obey and assist him "in all things touching the due execution" of the commission.[16]

Narrowly speaking, the Committee might direct other troops than the First Regiment independently of Henry. But this could make a farce of his position as commander in chief, and such a purpose is not indicated in the proceedings of the Convention.

On August 9, four days after his election as colonel, Henry took his seat in the new Virginia Convention at Richmond, his substitute delegate from Hanover County retiring in his favor.[17] Nor is there any evidence that he previously exerted any influence on the Convention session except to make known that he wanted the military office.[18] While he was absent in Philadelphia, there was nothing to show that he had lost any of his power over the great body of the Virginia populace, but two letters published by the *Gazette* in mid-July did indicate a lingering antipathy to him in conservative circles.

The new Virginia Convention had met in Richmond on Monday, July 17. As usual, several of Henry's relatives were present, along with many of his other followers, especially from the back country. But, on the whole, the liberal and conservative forces were almost equally divided, as the close vote on Henry's election as colonel helped to indicate. Moreover, later in the session, there would be a significant, though temporary, shift in favor of the conservatives.

In his St. John's Church speech, Henry had supported his resolution that the colony be "immediately" put in a state of defense; but the March Convention, while passing his measure, apparently by a close vote, did not provide taxes to implement it. The provisional government in the colony was still leaning on a thin reed—the militia and volunteer companies.

On the third day of the July Convention a motion similar to Henry's was passed, the members now voting in Committee of the Whole "that a sufficient Armed Force be immediately raised and embodied, under proper officers, for the defence and protection of this colony." [19] Henry's election as colonel followed in early August but only after Mercer had received one higher vote in the first balloting, and Henry's brother-in-law, Colonel William Christian, had been defeated 44 to 36 by William Woodford as colonel of the proposed second regiment.

The first weeks of the Convention had augured ill for its success. During this period, so George Mason wrote Washington,

> parties ran so high that we had frequently no other way of preventing improper measures, but by procrastination, urging the previous question, and giving men time to reflect. However, after some weeks the babblers were pretty well silenced, a few weighty members began to take the lead, several wholesome regulations were made, and, if the Convention had continued to sit for a few days longer, I think the public safety would have been as well provided for as our present circumstances permit. [20]

Obviously, the Convention lacked "weighty members"; much of the best Virginia character and ability was embodied in her delegation at Philadelphia. As late as August 5, when he spoke of the Convention as nominating "our Commander in chief Pat. Henry," one observer was "greatly disgusted" with the proceedings. "We are of as many different opinions as we are men." [21] It was more than coincidence that the Convention took new life after Henry, Pendleton, Jefferson, and Harrison appeared in their seats on Wednesday, August 9, followed within a few days by Richard Henry Lee and Richard Bland.

On August 11 the Convention expressed its unanimous thanks to three members of Congress who were unable to remain in office. Henry and Pendleton, who were present on the floor, received the commendation in person from President Peyton Randolph, and they in turn expressed the "great pleasure they received" from "the distinguished testimony of their Country's approbation.[22]

While serving as a delegate to Congress, Henry had been foresighted enough to purchase some powder for the use of the colony, and on August 10 the Convention requested that the powder be immediately sent for and employed in such a manner as the delegates to Congress deemed best.[23] Two days later Henry was put on a committee to report on an offer for some rifles and gunpowder and a more important committee to bring in an ordinance to encourage the manufacture of saltpeter, gunpowder, lead, the refining of sulphur, and providing arms for the use of the colony.[24] The committee would thus further the recent resolution of Congress in which Henry was appointed the Virginia representative to accelerate such activities.

The Convention was now making notable progress. Within a period of ten days in late August the delegates enacted significant legislation to help prepare the colony for expected hostilities. By the twenty-sixth, the ordinance for providing arms and ammunition had been passed.[25] This ordinance contained provisions for the purchase of arms and gun locks and the acquisition of gun flints and cartridge paper by the Committee of Safety; for the purchase of saltpeter and sulphur and for securing lead from the mines in Fincastle County.[26] Still another provision called for the establishment of a state "manufactory" of arms at or near Fredericksburg. Fielding Lewis, George Washington's brother-in-law, whose classic mansion still stands near the Rappahannock there, was one of the commissioners appointed to superintend the new enterprise, which would render notable service to the American cause.[27]

The portraits by Wollaston of Fielding Lewis and his wife, Betty Washington, now hanging at Kenmore do more credit to the beauty of their costumes than to some other aspects. Lewis, like his brother-in-law, was not the man to count the cost of patriotism. And yet, when accepting his position with the manufactory, he could not have known that he would make sacrifices that would wreck his private fortune.

Nor could Henry, serving on the committee in the Convention to count the votes for a state Committee of Safety, have realized the unhappy effect it would have on his own career. When the votes were tabulated, it was found that Edmund Pendleton had 77, followed by George Mason with 72, John Page with 70, and so on down to John Tabb, the twelfth and last member, who had 36. The majority of the members were conservatives, chiefly representative of the Tidewater and lower Piedmont aristocracy. Because of his top vote and capabilities, Henry's old opponent, Pendleton, was soon elected president of the Committee.

Ominously for Henry's success as colonel and commander in chief, the Committee of Safety was given power to carry into execution all the ordinances and resolutions of the Convention. Unless overruled when the Convention was in session, the Committee could control the organization and movement of troops and the acquisition and disposal of military supplies—authority which, if unwisely used, could have curbed a Napoleon or a Marlborough.

When the vote was taken on August 26, 1775, as to where the next Convention should be held, the Tidewater interests were still strong enough to muster 22 votes for Williamsburg, as compared with 25 for Richmond. Later that day, the Convention adjourned after passing some lengthy ordinances which, among other provisions for the direction of the colony until its next session, spelled out some details of Henry's powers and duties as a military commander.

Taking the oath required of the colonel of the First Regiment and commander in chief of the Virginia regular forces, Henry swore to serve the colony and dominion of Virginia to the "utmost" of his power and to obey such orders as he should receive from the Convention "or other authorities by them appointed." [28] Within the next few months it became increasingly clear that these authorities were concentrated in Edmund Pendleton and his conservative supporters on the Committee of Safety. Although some members of the Convention were doubtless fearful of the use Henry would make of extensive military power, there appears to have been no general intent to control him to a drastic degree. During the subsequent months, however, George Mason, an influential liberal who might have been a counterpoise to Edmund Pendleton, was frequently absent from the committee sessions, while Richard Bland was by now too old and infirm to exert strong influence.

Moreover, after Henry became preoccupied with military affairs, and Jefferson and Richard Henry Lee returned to Congress in Philadelphia, there was a deficiency for some months in the liberal leadership of the colony. It was mustered in greater strength during meetings of the Convention, which had ultimate control over the Committee of Safety, but the Convention met only at intervals and was often bogged down in details. Thus, until the independent state government was established the following July, executive control of the colony usually rested in the hands of the Committee and President Pendleton, the more so since a quorum of only six was required for its legal sessions.[29] Considering the lack of trained troops and military supplies, perhaps it was just as well that the executive control lay with able men who were avoiding precipitate action.

Leaving the Convention about August 25, Henry returned to Scotchtown for needed rest and attention to his private affairs. When his wife had died some six months before, she had left him with six children: Martha, Anne, Elizabeth, John, William, and Edward. Of them only Martha, Henry's beloved "Patsy," was married, and the youngest child was about five years old. Arrangements were made to care for the large plantation, and "Patsy," Mrs. John Fontaine, took charge of the younger children.[30] About September 18 Henry started back to Williamsburg to take up his command.

Some effort was made to give the new colonel and his men the proper military furbishings. As colonel and commander in chief,

Henry was allotted the munificent sum of 25 shillings per day, a secretary at 4 shillings per day, a tent, and several horses. The ordinances made no mention of his uniform, but Henry's orders on the military store at Williamsburg during the next month indicate that he had at least secured plenty of material for a blue coat, besides "2 Sticks twist" (hairpins) and a piece of "Scarlet Gartering." Two drummers and seven fifers were assigned to each of his companies, but it is doubtful if many were able to fill their full complements. The green shirts of many riflemen also did not meet the usual professional standards. These rough shirts, however, were less likely to attract the attention of the enemy than more showy uniforms.

Setting about his new duties, Henry soon found grave deficiencies with which he often had little or no means to cope. The First Regiment was to include 544 men and the usual officers. With volunteers then plentiful, it would be an easy matter to fill the complement of eight companies, including the two of expert riflemen to serve as light infantry. But in addition to all the problems of training raw or half-disciplined troops, there was an appalling lack of arms and ammunition. The expert riflemen had to be ordered to bring their own rifles, and, for the main body of the troops, the Convention could only provide that where muskets were not available the men were to be supplied with the best guns "of any sort."

Even when the colony could recruit, train, and equip two regiments, with some others planned, they would all be pitifully inadequate to defend the state in the event of a formidable invasion. This problem of manpower would soon become more difficult, if not insoluble, when Congress issued an urgent call for troops to reinforce Washington's army. The Convention did provide that certain portions of the Virginia militia were to be enlisted as minutemen and more strictly trained and equipped, but it would take weeks to muster some of the companies and march them to distant points in a state as large as Scotland and Wales.

It is true that the so-called "regulars" now being assembled in Henry's First Regiment were hardy men, usually brave and zealous, and including many excellent marksmen. Yet despite some augmented training for the militia and volunteer companies during the months just passed, these "regulars" were still in sad need of further discipline. Many of them—if not their colonel—would be guilty of military gaucheries which would disgust a trained officer. It could have been Virginia, not Massachusetts militia, who when marching to the training field had sometimes broken ranks "to engage in the chivalrous pastime of frightening young women" by firing their muskets.[31]

Fortunately, Henry's men were pleased with him. He did have a little military experience during his gunpowder expedition, and they were not bothered about military niceties. As their political champion, he enjoyed a prestige not then surpassed by any Virginia soldier. He was courageous and energetic, as proved in the gunpowder expedition and elsewhere, and his lieutenant colonel, William Christian, could advise him on military matters while he was gaining experience.

Altogether, Henry's qualifications for the command would have been scoffed at by a King's officer and indeed were doubted by some high-placed Virginians. But they were about as good as those of many men who would obtain distinction in the American service during the following years.

When Henry left for Williamsburg, there were troops already quartered in the capital. And they were not finding life too onerous, if we may judge from the account of one cheerful young volunteer, his cousin, John Coles. John's company was "Commodiously lodged" in three large rooms of the capitol, and he assured his anxious wife, Beckey, that he was not in "the least danger." A ship which Lord Dunmore sent for the remainder of his bodyguard had returned without a man, John declared. In consequence, "the Norfolk gentlemen" had "picked up spirit" and called several of the Scotchmen before the local Committee. Some they forced to "ask pardon upon their horses"; some they beat. "Poor little Shaw got beat very much."

Coles, who was apparently sleeping on the capitol floor, didn't find "the least disadvantage from laying hard." He reported having dined with George Wythe, who was setting out the next day for Congress, and added a little gossip about Lord Dunmore. His Lordship was said to have used a tender to sail up a creek behind Williamsburg for a dalliance with "Miss ———," instead of employing it to intercept a powder shipment.

Altogether, the war was as yet a rather pleasant affair for young volunteers such as Coles. But what of Colonel Henry, especially if his new, woefully ill-prepared levies had to meet a serious British attack?

Losing no time after his arrival in Williamsburg, Henry published notices in Purdie's *Gazette* for September 22, 1775, and the two subsequent issues for his various captains whose companies were completed to march to a point near the city and await further orders. Meantime, he had issued directions for picking a camp site; by the twenty-ninth it had been marked out "behind" William and Mary College, and tents and other equipage were being prepared "with the utmost expedition." The encampment was situated near the present Jamestown highway in an area now largely filled with college buildings and private residences. Country roads through the quiet Tidewater woods led within some ten miles to the ruins of Jamestown and to Greenspring, where proud Governor Berkeley had once hanged several of Bacon's rebels.

Before the end of the month one company had arrived at the camp from Chesterfield County near Richmond, a "set of hearty, clever, young men" so Purdie's *Gazette* proclaimed. Within two weeks they were joined by eight more companies of regular troops and a battalion of Culpeper Minutemen, while some 350 more Minutemen were encamped in Northern Virginia.

Among the Culpeper Minutemen, with their deadly rifles and their hunting shirts with "Liberty or Death" sewn on the breast, was a tall, dark-complexioned, back-country lad, the future chief justice, John Marshall; also, several nephews of Edmund Pendleton.[32] As these minutemen marched toward Williamsburg in their green shirts, with bucktails in their hats and carrying their scalping knives and tomahawks, they frightened some people along the road almost as much as if they were British regulars.[33]

By the middle of October upwards of a thousand volunteers had arrived or were soon expected in Williamsburg, about enough to fill the two regiments, while many more recruits were available—if only they could be armed and supplied. "Had we arms and ammunition, it would give vigor to our measures," Edmund Pendleton wrote on October 15 to Richard Henry Lee in Philadelphia. "We hourly hoped to hear of the arrival of the necessaries, but now fear we shall be defeated." A "villain" had given Governor Dunmore information about an anticipated cargo boat and he had six or seven tenders searching for it near the Capes. "What can a parricide deserve?"[34]

In order to secure vitally needed saltpeter, the Committee of Safety was even urging planters to preserve their tobacco suckers, stalks, and sweepings. The Committee had been working valiantly without a recess for a month in spite of sickness and absences,[35] and it was receiving some helpful assistance. With supplies from abroad being cut off, Thomas Bullitt, adjutant general, was attempting to secure blankets and other articles but, alas! had to advise some soldiers meanwhile to provide themselves with "necessary" clothing.[36]

Among other officials upon whom Henry was depending, his old associate, John Hawkins of Hanover, now commissary of provisions for the two regiments, was seeking beef, pork, and flour, with stalled beef for delivery at intervals until June.[37] Also, a state commissary officer, William Aylett, was advertising for a long list of articles: kettles, ducking, Russia drab for tents, Osnaburg for hunting shirts, blankets, coarse stockings, canteens, spades, shovels, etc., with ready money for any quantity of saltpeter, sulphur, and lead.[38]

It was to be expected that the new recruits under Colonel Henry would be derided by British and Tory critics. Captain John Smyth of the Queen's Rangers, en route to Norfolk with his servants and baggage, was seized at Surry Courthouse by what he described as "a very dirty crew." They would have carried him to "the rebel general," Patrick Henry, at Williamsburg had he not plied them with punch and ridden off at "full speed." James Parker, the Norfolk merchant, who encountered some of "the shirt men" with their tomahawks and scalping knives, said that "they look like a band of Assassins and it is my opinion if they fight at all it will be in that way."[39]

Yet these rough men made excellent soldiers when sufficiently trained, and that Patrick Henry had a peculiar ability to appeal to them is revealed in an incident told by Philip Mazzei, an Italian then living in Albemarle County. An independent company from Albemarle, including Mazzei, was called out by a British alarm at Hampton, so he wrote. The company could boast of only three blankets, had to use hunting pieces instead of rifles, and had a form to make their own bullets, but their enthusiasm partly compensated for their lack of regular military training. Crossing the boundary from Albemarle into Orange County, they met a little private, twenty-one years old, in the local company—James Madison, the future President. Then, marching toward Williamsburg, they learned that the British who had landed at Hampton had re-embarked and that the campaign was terminated. This information came to them from a militia officer—Colonel Patrick Henry—"a man who has no superior in eloquence or patriotism." [40]

Henry, with his own companies drawn up in formation opposite Mazzei's, delivered them "an eloquent speech of thanks" for their volunteer service. With the skillful politician's touch, he was tactful enough to mention the three native Tuscans who had enlisted with Mazzei. One of them, Vincenso, who was near Mazzei and noted that Henry was speaking to them, asked Mazzei what he was saying.

"When I explained to him, his radiant face showed that he would not change his place with that of a millionaire," Mazzei recalled. [41]

With his manifold duties Henry was obviously in need of staff officers, and he was given an "aide-du-camp" [sic], Captain Alexander Spottswood Dandridge. Later, Henry spoke of Dandridge, son of Colonel West Dandridge, as having "lived with him several years at the beginning of the war"; he knew "from long and intimate knowledge" that Dandridge despised a "mean action." Thus Henry not only had the assistance of an ardent and well-connected young patriot but also an opportunity to form closer ties with the family of his old Hanover neighbors, including his aide's attractive young sister, now of marriageable age. [42]

Since there would later be criticism of Henry as a military disciplinarian, it is significant to note correspondence which he had with Mayor William Pasteur of Williamsburg. By the end of October all the men in the temporary encampment were quartered in public buildings or private homes in Williamsburg. With so many soldiers crowded into the little town, a military order was issued on November 19, 1775, enjoining the officers and men to remember that their profession was "to defend and protect the citizens, and all others who are in the American interest. A modest respectful behaviour toward our friends, it is hoped, will characterise all our troops, and that no condition, age, or sex, will justly charge them with licentiousness or immorality." [43] Henry sent Pasteur a copy of the order to the troops, and on December 11 the mayor, in the name of the citizens, returned to Colonel Henry his "most unfeigned and sincere thanks for the care and vigilance shewn by him to keep up the most precise order and discipline among the troops now quartered here under his command, the good effects whereof we have already abundantly experienced. . . ." [44]

The war was now beginning to come closer home. In early November firing was heard from Jamestown, one of several posts being maintained to meet possible enemy attacks. Two British tenders had slipped up the James River, but their bombardments did little damage. [45] Had there been serious fighting, not only Colonel Henry but his son, John, a young volunteer, and Henry's brother-in-law, Colonel Christian, would probably have become involved. [46]

When William Christian came down from his frontier home to serve as lieutenant colonel of the First Regiment, he brought with him his wife, Henry's sister, Anne, and she took charge of Henry's household. Anne was soon joined by another sister, Elizabeth. Now twenty-six, it is likely that this spirited girl had remained unmarried more because no suitor met her approval than from any lack of feminine charm. She is described as of medium height, with soft, grayish-blue eyes and a face full of character. Certainly, there could be no question of her force and intellect. In her personal characteristics, she bore a striking resemblance to her brother, Patrick.

It is not surprising that Elizabeth became "a toast" among the young officers at Williamsburg. Returning to Scotchtown, she was married in April, 1776, to one worthy of her mettle, Captain William Campbell, from the Holston settlement in Fincastle County, who had served with Colonel Christian in Dunmore's Indian expedition. According to one family tradition, Colonel Henry came from Williamsburg for the wedding, and it was then that he fell in love with young Dorothea Dandridge, his future wife.

Six feet two, with a splendid physique, Captain Campbell had martial qualities befitting his appearance. Undaunted by dangers from Indians and Tories or the primitive life, Elizabeth would follow her husband to his home, "Aspenvale," at Seven Mile Ford in Southwest Virginia. There, they would settle in a rude house, at first only a two-room log cabin with a dog trot in between, but overlooking the fertile valley of the Holston River (South Fork). Meantime, while waiting until he could join his wife, he wrote to her in August from Williamsburg the news he had received from his frontier home. A fort had been built there in which about four hundred people had found shelter.

Eighteen of our men, two or three women, and some children, have been killed. Our people have scalped twenty-seven Indians, and it is thought that many more have been killed, from the large quantities of blood that flowed from those who were wounded and ran away.

. . . I most heartily thank you, my dear, for your attention, for providing me such necessaries as I stand in need of. I fear you are too solicitous and give yourself too much trouble. You bring to my mind Solomon's excellent description of a good wife. "She seeketh wool, and flax, and worketh willingly with her hands. She layeth her hands to the spindle, and her hands hold the distaff. She maketh herself coverings of tapestry; her clothing is silk and purple. Her husband is known in the gates, when he sitteth among the elders of the land." Such is my dearest Betsy. Her worth I esteem far above rubies.[47]

Later, William and Betsy would have careers worthy of their promise, he as the General William Campbell of King's Mountain fame and she as one of the outstanding Virginia matrons of her time.[48]

On September 29 Purdie's *Virginia Gazette* published a note that "the Hon. COMMITTEE OF SAFETY" had adjourned from Hanovertown to Williamsburg for convenience in transacting "the important business committed to their charge."[49] Within the next two months it would become obvious that, while Henry was the purported commander of the Virginia forces, the Committee would make major decisions of military policy. Edmund Pendleton, John Page, Thomas

Ludwell Lee, and the Committee members generally had no more military experience than Henry. It remained to be seen whether their somewhat cautious policy would be properly adjusted to coming emergencies.

Henry's authority was being curtailed at the very time the Committee was considering stronger action against Lord Dunmore. His Lordship had collected a small fleet with which he was raiding the coastal counties, plundering plantations for provisions, stopping boats and molesting their passengers, and carrying off slaves. His depredations were especially damaging in the Norfolk area, where there was a strong Tory element disposed to submit to his authority.

In late October the Committee of Safety did decide to make a positive move. Passing over Henry, they ordered Woodford with his Second Regiment and the Culpeper battalion from the First Regiment to march to the Norfolk area. Woodford was thus given an independent command. In specific instructions from the Committee he was ordered to report to them and to "the commanding Officer here [Henry, in Williamsburg]" such matters as "shall appear necessary to be communicated." [50]

In superseding Henry, the most popular man in the colony, the Committee had created a tense situation. It needed to be handled with great delicacy. Yet Pendleton on October 25 explained the Committee action to Henry in this one-sentence letter:

> I have the Honour to inclose you the resolution of Yesterday for forming an encampment near Norfolk, which you'll please to give the necessary orders for the Execution of: As on the one hand the distresses of the people there require that all unnecessary delay should be avoided, so on the other due regard should be paid to the comfort and Security of the Troops in their March.[51]

It was not the first time that Pendleton in writing Henry had disregarded his military title.

Soon afterward a British attack on Hampton was repulsed with the help of a company under Woodford. When Henry sought some information and instructions from the Committee as to the troop movements, Pendleton replied with what his biographer, David

Mays, describes as "one of the most casual letters ever sent by the head of government to his military chief."[52]

> It being inconvenient to Assemble a full committee this Evening, which the Gentlemen here did not think absolutely necessary, I send you the Sentiments of 4. It was mentioned this day in Committee that the Companys ready had better get over the [James] River & Rendezvoux on the other side 'til the others could be properly prepared to pass & join them. The March therefore of the two Companies tomorrow in the morning & afternoon, is agreeable to that Inclination. The Amunition & provisions those Companies should carry for their support 'til the Compleat junction, you will judge of, Afterwards Mr. Hawkins, I doubt not, will provide for feeding the whole, & the Committee will further consider as to the Amunition, & mention their determination to you. The Committee wish the Companies who March to be furnished with Tents & Kettles; those who remain here will be provided with winter Quarters as soon as Possible & Potts will suit them we suppose as well as Kettles. any other Necessarys they may want, I imagine they will be supplied with from Mr. Aylett's Store, upon your Order. I have the honour to be
>
> Sir Your most Obedient
> Edmd. Pendleton [53]

The popular rumblings of discontent at the Committee's treatment of Henry now became too strong to be ignored. On November 4 John Page wrote him a propitiatory letter on order of the Council.[54] Two days later, however, the Committee limited his activity by ordering him to prepare winter quarters for his regiment at Williamsburg.

The Committee of Safety can easily be criticized too severely. Besides a desire on the part of its conservative members to contain Henry and the military operations, there was a sincere feeling that he lacked the proper training for his command. This was no less so when Dunmore took a rash step which convinced many timid and wavering members of the need for strong action.

While personally sincere and courageous, the governor had not lost any of his obtuseness. On November 6 from a ship off Norfolk Harbor he issued a proclamation declaring martial law in the colony. Every person in Virginia capable of bearing arms was required to resort to His Majesty's standard or be looked upon as a traitor, liable to the resulting legal penalties "such as forfeiture of life and confiscation of land, etc." All slaves and indentured servants were to be freed if able and willing to bear arms in the King's service.[55] The proclamation is to be interpreted at least partly in terms of that period, when nearly all the Virginia slaves were illiterate and many not long removed from Africa. To Tidewater planters, outnumbered by slaves on the scattered plantations, Dunmore was inviting all the horrors of an insurrection.

When the Convention met in December there would be a strong reply. Meantime, an unidentified writer to one of the *Gazette*s stated that the Americans had taken up arms as their "undoubted right" in the defense of the British constitution and pointedly asserted that Dunmore's father had been involved in two rebellions.[56]

At Great Bridge on December 9, Woodford met Dunmore's improvised force in the first significant battle of the war on Virginia soil. Woodford's command had now been increased by 700 men from the First Regiment; the remainder were Minutemen. There was a report of a cold reception given by his troops to those detached from Henry's regiment. The deadly rifles of his men, however, fired from a vantage point out of range of the British muskets, played a vital part in the subsequent American victory.

The battle was fought in the flat, swampy country near Norfolk. Woodford, closely conforming to cautious orders of the Committee of Safety, took a position behind earthworks approachable only by a narrow causeway. The attacking British could muster only 500 men, of which 200 were regulars and the remainder untrained Negroes and Tories serving "chiefly to swell the array." With the blind courage which the redcoats had shown at Bunker Hill, Captain Fordyce advanced across the causeway with 120 of the regulars until he was struck down by a dozen balls; nearly all these regulars were killed or wounded. The American victory was partly due to inept British leadership, but Woodford deserves credit for sound strategy. Any serious threat from Lord Dunmore's force was now ended. Woodford won laurels which made it the more difficult for Henry to assert what he deemed his proper authority as commander in chief.[57]

For a time Henry had borne his supersession with considerable patience. On December 6, 1775, however, he wrote Woodford from Williamsburg that he hadn't heard "of any dispatch" from him for a long time and stated that he could "no longer forbear sending to know your situation and what has occurred." He continued:

> Every one, as well as myself, is vastly anxious to hear how all stands with you. In case you think any thing could be done to aid and forward the enterprise you have in hand, please to write it. But I wish to know your situation particularly, with that of the enemy, that the whole may be laid before the convention now here. The number and designs of the enemy, as you collect it, might open some prospects to us, that might enable us to form some diversion in your favor. The bearer has orders to lose no time, and to return with all possible haste.[58]

In his reply the following day, Woodford, after saying that he understood Henry was "out of town," referred him to a letter which he had addressed to the Convention, giving particulars of his and the enemy's "situation." Whenever the Convention was in session, he would address further correspondence to them and they would communicate to Henry "as commanding officer of the troops at Williamsburg." Woodford would esteem himself immediately under Henry's command when "joined," but he was now in charge of a separate body of troops under the Committee of Safety, or Convention when sitting, and considered it his "indispensable duty to address [his] intelligence to them, as the supreme power in this colony." [59]

That Woodford realized he was on dangerous ground was indicated by his following comment that if he was wrong he hoped the Convention would set him right, and that he wished "to keep up the greatest harmony" with Henry. Woodford anxiously consulted Joseph Jones, a Pendleton supporter and a delegate to the August Convention. In reply Jones asserted that the members there drawing up Henry's commission made it stronger than the Convention intended. On the other hand, it was extremely doubtful that the Convention, when disassociating from Henry's command troops employed in a different part of the state, intended to separate those operating as close as Woodford's. A few days after the battle of Great Bridge, Woodford was joined by several hundred troops under Colonel Robert Howe of North Carolina. Woodford agreed that Howe, whose commission antedated his own, should assume command of the united force. Thus, Henry was superseded not only by Woodford but also by a colonel from another colony.[60]

On Friday, December 1, 1775, the Virginia Convention met again in Richmond with Henry's brother-in-law, Samuel Meredith, taking his place as a delegate from Hanover County. In October, Peyton Randolph had died unexpectedly while a delegate to the Continental Congress. Edmund Pendleton, "a gentleman in every respect qualified,"[61] was elected to fill Randolph's place as President of the Convention, and it soon adjourned to meet in Williamsburg. Since Henry's headquarters were in the town, he was in an ideal position to influence his numerous supporters among the delegates.

Just what pressures Henry or his lieutenants may have exerted, we do not know. The perturbed Joseph Jones, however, after a talk with Colonel Henry, reported that Henry felt he had been "ill-treated." He insisted that officers under his command should submit to his orders, and he took up the whole matter with the Committee.[62] Shortly afterward, the Convention administered a direct rebuke to the Pendleton forces. When a vote was taken on December 16 for the new members of the Committee of Safety, Henry's friend, Dudley Digges, received 74 votes, followed by John Page with 73, and Paul Carrington with 72. Edmund Pendleton, with 65, got only a few more than James Mercer and Thomas Ludwell Lee. Among the eleven members chosen, Joseph Jones was near the bottom with 48.[63]

When the new Committee of Safety met it passed a compromise resolution which the members hoped would alleviate the explosive situation. By unanimous vote it resolved

> that Colonel Woodford, although acting under a separate and detached command, ought to correspond with Colonel Henry, and make returns to him at proper times, of the state and condition of the forces under his command; and also that he is subject

to his orders, when the convention, or the committee of safety, is not sitting, but that while either of those bodies are sitting, he is to receive his orders from one of them.[64]

Henry attempted to adjust himself to the new order, although there would be extended periods when Woodford was not under his command.

As for the overworked Pendleton, he was not able to view the situation with his usual equanimity. Convinced of Henry's military incapacity, the resourceful head of the Committee of Safety had another plan to circumvent him. "Believe me, sir," Pendleton wrote Woodford on Christmas Eve, "the unlucky step of calling that gentleman [Henry] from our councils, where he was useful, into the field, in an important station, the duties of which he must, in the nature of things, be an entire stranger to, has given me many an anxious and uneasy moment." [65]

The Virginia regular regiments were expected to be incorporated into the Continental Army, with each of their field officers named by the colony and recommended to Congress. Pendleton next commented on this anticipated action. "A General Officer will be chosen there I doubt not & sent Us," he continued. "With that matter, I hope we shall not intermeddle, lest it should be thought propriety requires our calling, or rather recommending our present First Officer to that station. . . ." [66]

On January 20, 1776, the Convention adjourned, not to meet again until a May session when it would take up the momentous issue of colonial independence. Shortly before the adjournment, Henry, as "The commanding Officer of the Forces raised for the protection and defense" of the colony, was called upon to lay before the Convention a statement of the forces under his command and of their "several stations"—a request with which he complied the same day.[67] The conservatives scored a point when the Convention elected Carter Braxton to Congress to succeed the late Peyton Randolph. But that Henry was being treated with more circumspection is indicated by John Page's statement to Richard Henry Lee in February: "I have been always of your opinion with respect to our present commander in chief. All orders do pass through him, and we really wish to be in perfect harmony with him." [68]

[93]

As Pendleton had expected, Congress, on February 13, 1776, incorporated the First and Second Virginia into the six state regiments to be included in the Continental service and appointed their field officers. These officers for the various regiments were the same as in the Virginia service, thus annulling the officers' commissions from the state. Moreover, Colonel Robert Howe and Colonel Andrew Lewis were appointed brigadier generals.

Patrick Henry was thus reappointed colonel of the First Virginia Regiment. But he could no longer even make a claim to being commander in chief of the Virginia forces. His command was confined to the First Regiment, and two officers whom he had outranked were promoted over him to be brigadier generals. It was about this time that Philip Mazzei is said to have urged Henry that he resign his commission and return to the civil duties for which he was so badly needed.[69]

It is easy to imagine the suppressed feeling that must have actuated Henry and Pendleton when the Committee of Safety sent for Henry on February 28 to offer him the commission as colonel of the Continental Army. The *Journal* of the Committee is a masterpiece of understatement: "Patrick Henry, Esquire, appeared in consequence of the letter wrote to him, and being offered his commission received from the Continental Congress to be colonel of the 1st Battalion, declared he could not accept of the same."[70]

Upon news of Henry's resignation, a great many officers and men from various regiments joined in a remarkable tribute to his ability and character. The soldiers in the capital were especially strong in their protest. When they heard that their commander in chief was about to leave them, Purdie's *Gazette* reported, they went into deep mourning. Then, "being under arms," they proceeded to Henry's lodgings, where they delivered to him a moving address. His withdrawal from the service filled them with "the most poignant sorrow," since it deprived them "of our father and General, yet, as gentlemen," they were compelled "to applaud your spirited resentment to the most glaring indignity. May your merit shine as conspicuous to the world in general as it hath done to us, and may Heaven shower its choicest blessings on you."[71]

Moreover, Henry received a memorial from about ninety officers of the First, Second, Third, Fourth, and Fifth regiments and of the Minutemen. These officers comprised nearly the entire officer personnel of the commands cited—probably excepting Colonel Woodford and a few other supporters of the Committee. "Deeply concerned with the good" of their country, the memorialists "sincerely lamented the unhappy necessity" of Henry's resignation. Whatever may have given rise to "the indignity lately offered him," they joined "with the general voice of the people" and deemed it their duty "to make this public declaration" of their "high respect" for his "distinguished merit." Then, in the warmest tones they spoke of how Henry had "first pointed out" to them "the destructive ministerial measures" and led them forward to resist them. They praised his "firmness, candour and politeness" as their commander and trusted that justice would prevail so that he could again conduct their councils and "hazard his life" in defense of his country.[72]

After the officers had received Henry's reply to their address, they insisted that he dine with them at the Raleigh Tavern. A number of them then proposed to escort him out of town but were deterred from doing so by "some uneasiness" among the soldiers. Assembling "in a tumultuous manner," they demanded their discharge, declaring that they were unwilling to serve under any other commander. It was a real test of Henry's patriotism. Feeling deeply wronged, he might have succumbed to a natural desire for vengeance and left his opponents to struggle out of their difficulties. Instead, he only busied himself to pacify the men. It was necessary for him to stay a night longer in Williamsburg and to spend the time visiting the various barracks and using every argument in his power to make them remain in the service.

Henry told the soldiers that he had resigned "from motives in which his honor, alone, was concerned." Although he was "prevented from serving his country in a military capacity," his utmost ability "would ever be exerted in support of the glorious cause." Colonel Christian and the other officers present likewise made "extraordinary exertions" to dissuade the men from leaving the army. The soldiers reluctantly agreed to remain in the service and were reported as "pretty well reconciled."[73]

7

Independence: The Virginia Resolutions

The spark of liberty in the mind and spirit of man cannot be long extinguished; it will break into flames that will destroy every coercion which seems to limit it.——HERBERT HOOVER [1]

Headquarters, New York, May 2, 1776. Parole, Granby, Countersign, Wilkes. General court-martial, Col. Baldwin, president. Cpl. J—— W—— found guilty of "getting drunk when on duty." Sentenced to be reduced to ranks, and whipped thirty lashes on his bare back.

S—— L—— and A—— F—— tried for "desertion." Found guilty and each sentenced to receive thirty lashes on his bare back. The General approved of the sentences and ordered their execution the next morning at guard mounting.

——*American Archives* [2]

March 17, 1776. British begin evacuation of Boston.

May 6–July 5, 1776. Meeting of Virginia Convention with Henry as prominent delegate.

May 15, 1776. Convention instructs Virginia delegates in Congress to move adoption of an American declaration of independence.

June 7, 1776. Richard Henry Lee moves in Congress that the colonies be declared "free and independent states" and that they take steps to form a confederation.

June 28, 1776. British fleet fails to capture Charleston, S.C.

Among the advertisements in Purdie's *Virginia Gazette* for May 10, 1776, was one by Jacob Hall for a light brown horse "about 14 hands high, a natural pacer" which had strayed from Scotchtown. For the greater part of a year, Henry had not been able to devote much personal attention to the plantation, indeed to many of his domestic affairs, and Hall was obviously a Henry agent or overseer. To such men he would have to entrust much of his private business during the next three years and for considerable periods thereafter. Returning to Hanover after resigning his military commission, he hardly had time to inspect the preparations for early spring planting when he became involved in an important election. On April 19, 1776, Purdie's *Gazette* carried the news that Patrick Henry and John Syme had been chosen as the Hanover delegates to the May Convention in Williamsburg.

The results of the state-wide elections were more significant than indicated by the routine announcements. The highly connected Carter Braxton, suspected of lukewarm Whiggism, was defeated in King and Queen County; George Mason, a modest genius, was returned "with great difficulty" in Fairfax, while in several counties there were spirited contests.[3] Yet there is no evidence that Henry and his half brother had any difficulty in their staunch bailiwick, or indeed that Henry had lost any great popularity throughout the state because of his resignation from the military service. John Page, who believed that Virginia could then make only a poor resistance to an enemy attack, listed among the adverse factors the bad condition of her provisional army and discontent in certain quarters because of Henry's resignation.[4] It was fortunate for the country that Henry did not sulk in his tent.

Critical issues of the war were coming to a head. In Virginia much would depend on Henry and the other liberal leaders. In late March, after he had returned to Scotchtown, news of the departure of the British troops from Boston reached Virginia. On the seventeenth, St. Patrick's Day ("happily" for future generations of Boston Irish![5]), the British commander, Lord Howe, began the evacuation of the city.

[97]

The lackadaisical Howe did not prevent Washington from placing his artillery in a position to shell the port effectively, but there was little to indicate that the British Army would not land again at a more vulnerable point.

In Virginia the issue of American independence was becoming paramount, and Henry could read a letter by "Rationalis" in Dixon's *Gazette* for March 23 opposing this except as a last resort. It was better to get "an advantageous accommodation" with Great Britain than a free constitution, so ran the die-hard argument.

Yet such sentiments were now mere flotsam against a rising tide, especially in view of the obdurate British position. As early as the previous October, 1775, George III had informed Parliament that the Americans should be treated as rebels, and that compliant body had dutifully followed with an act interdicting certain trade in war matériel with the colonies so long as they were in rebellion.[6] After the first of the year, the publication of Tom Paine's *Common Sense* had powerfully reinforced arguments for independence, already becoming manifest from the logic of events. To many thoughtful Americans it seemed foolish to make further protestations of loyalty to a country which for a year they had been openly fighting. Henry was soon vitally concerned with a corollary matter—the effect of independence, if properly timed, on securing aid from foreign powers.

On April 12, 1776, the North Carolina Provincial Congress, assembled at the little town of Halifax, passed resolutions calling on her delegates in Congress to support a joint declaration of independence by the American colonies. It may have been over two weeks before Henry learned of the bold North Carolina action, though Halifax was on the Roanoke, near the Virginia border.[7] But that spring in the *Virginia Gazette*s he found a steadily increasing number of letters and articles favoring independence, with news of encouraging sentiment in some other states. On the very day of the North Carolina resolutions, John Page, reporting from Williamsburg, optimistically asserted that almost every man in Virginia except the treasurer (Nicholas) was willing to declare for independence.[8] Henry had reason to believe that the sentiment was on a particularly firm basis in the back country, as indicated by provocative instructions to the Convention delegates from two Piedmont counties.

Meeting on April 22 in the old courthouse at Deep Creek, the Cumberland County Committee boldly instructed their two delegates to the Convention to work for "an Independency," a "goodnight forever" to George III. One of the two delegates from the Piedmont county was William Fleming, son of the John Fleming who had so strongly supported Henry in the Stamp Act debate. When kneeling at the wooden benches in their simple little churches, the Cumberland Episcopalians felt themselves to be "rank Hypocrites" in beseeching the Almighty God to give the British King strength to vanquish all his enemies. In their instructions they recommended a change in the Anglican liturgy, which was later adopted by the Convention. But, more important from Henry's viewpoint, the Cumberland delegates were instructed to help secure foreign aid and such commercial connections as they deemed prudent.[9]

Moreover, the Cumberland resolutions were reinforced the next day, April 23, 1776, by those of Charlotte County, a little to the southward. The Charlotte delegates were told to use their best endeavors to make the Virginia congressmen press not only for an immediate declaration of independence but for a commercial alliance with any friendly nation. Paul Carrington, Henry's stalwart supporter in the Stamp Act debate, was one of the Charlotte delegates who was so instructed for the Convention sessions. Indeed, the Carrington influence was spreading over the county line, for Paul's brothers in Cumberland, the family seat, were among the ablest and most dedicated patriots in the Piedmont.

In phrases not softened by the war, the Charlotte instructions reminded their delegates of how the British had been endeavoring to enforce their arbitrary rule "by fire and sword"; they explained why one could no longer doubt the British intentions to persist in their "hellish designs." And they declared the Charlotte citizens would risk their "lives and fortunes" to the utmost "of their abilities" to support their delegates, their state, and their sister colonies in the glorious cause.[10]

For at least eighteen months Henry had been looking toward American independence. Although he had much evidence that it was assured of popular support, he was not at all certain that it was best to move for separation before securing foreign aid. Some powerful but as yet not conclusive arguments for independence as the initial step now came to him in a letter from Richard Henry Lee. Written from Philadelphia on April 20, 1776, the letter probably reached Henry about the time he was preparing to leave Scotchtown for Williamsburg. Lee, a leading Virginia delegate to Congress, referred Henry to a letter he had written him in care of General Charles Lee, then invited Henry's attention to "the most important concerns" of the approaching Virginia Convention: "Ages yet unborn, and millions existing at present, must rue or bless that Assembly, on which their happiness or misery will so eminently depend." After pointedly noting that "Virginia has hitherto taken the lead in great affairs, and many now look to her with anxious expectation," Lee mentioned some recent events, among them the capture of a letter from the British secretary of state to Governor Eden of Maryland, as proof of the British design "to enslave America after having destroyed its best Members." Bespeaking the need for Virginia to form a separate government immediately and for America to seek foreign alliance, Lee wrote that

> no State in Europe will either Treat or Trade with us so long as we consider ourselves Subjects of G.B. Honor, dignity, and the customs of states forbid them until we take rank as an independant people. The war cannot long be prosecuted without Trade, nor can Taxes be paid until we are enabled to sell our produce, which cannot be the case without the help of foreign ships, whilst our enemy's navy is so superior to ours. . . . Our clearest interest therefore, our very existance as freemen, requires that we take decisive steps now, whilst we may, for the security of America.

In conclusion, Lee commended to Henry, with certain changes, a "sensible" plan for state government drawn up by their friend, John Adams, and he quoted from Shakespeare's familiar lines:

> "There is a Tide in the Affairs of Men
> Which taken at the Flood leads on to Fortune. . . ." [11]

One hundred and thirty delegates to the Convention at Williamsburg had been chosen from the various counties and corporations. Unlike a number of political assemblies which Henry had attended, there were enough delegates present to effect a formal organization on the first day, May 6. This was accomplished a little more easily since on that Monday an appreciable number of Convention delegates were also present at the decease of the old House of Burgesses. In his speech at St. John's Church, Henry had denounced the frequent failure to convene that popular assembly. Now unfortunately associated with the former Royal regime, it had mustered only 37 members in October, 1775; had been adjourned to March, 1776, when there were 32, then to May 6, as indicated in the *Journal:*

> Several Members met, but did not proceed to Business, nor adjourn, as a House of Burgesses.
>
> FINIS.

The once-honored body had not been finally dissolved, it had merely shrunken and died. But Henry and other leading members of the Convention who had used it as a legislative training ground adopted its rules of order for the Convention sessions.[12]

With the machinery of government under the Crown now completely broken down, it was urgent that the Convention proceed with its work of replacement. When nominations for President were called for, Richard Bland proposed the experienced Edmund Pendleton and was seconded by Archibald Cary. The matter is disputed, but there is reason to believe that Henry, by a vigorous opposition, might have prevented the election of his long-time rival. Henry may well have decided that it was more important to unite dissident factions in the common cause. His old associate, however, fiery Thomas Johnson of Louisa, doubtless resenting the treatment of Henry by the Committee of Safety, nominated Thomas Ludwell Lee and was seconded by Bartholomew Dandridge. But Pendleton was elected, obviously with the aid of conservative and some moderate or liberal votes.[13]

Conducted to the chair, Pendleton made a brief, practical address such as might have been expected from this conservative revolutionist. His speech contained no reference to the strong demand for American independence. Only by careful management could Henry and his liberal associates hope to secure a united front on this and other important measures.[14]

From the start of the session on May 6, Henry began to assume his position as the head of the popular party. With Richard Henry Lee in Congress, there was no one to challenge his leadership. George Mason would work mightily with his pen, but he never rivaled Henry's skill as a political manager. Experienced and influential, Henry was appointed the opening day as a member of the Committee of Privileges and Elections; the next day as a member of a committee to encourage the manufacture of three vitally needed products—salt, saltpeter, and gunpowder; and, on May 8, first ranking member, after Treasurer Nicholas, of the Committee of Propositions and Grievances.[15] This was followed a week later by his appointment to still another key committee, to draw up a Declaration of Rights. After further assignments, in late May and June, he served on nearly every committee of the Convention.[16]

There could be no doubt as to the nature of the work which lay ahead. Apart from the transcendent questions of independence, of the framework of the state and national governments, there were appalling needs in Virginia, especially in the military establishment. One unhappy example, relatively small yet portentous, was revealed during the session. When there was an anticipated British attack on North Carolina, a detachment of 1,300 Virginia troops under Henry's brother-in-law, Colonel Meredith, was ordered to her aid. But many of the militiamen and minutemen called out had no tents or blankets.[17]

During the first week of the Convention, a great deal of Henry's time was taken up with petitions, committee sessions, and reports. Much of this tedious labor had to be done before or after the regular sessions, which began at ten every weekday, not excepting Saturdays. In order to allow all the work to be started with the divine blessing, the delegates, on the second Monday, ordered their chaplain, the Reverend Mr. Thomas Price, to begin reading prayers every morning at seven instead of nine. And to give a further religious overtone, he was requested to officiate at "the Church"—Bruton—in Williamsburg on May 17, the day set apart by Congress for a public fast.[18]

It was of the utmost importance for the Convention not to lose sight of the forest for the trees, not to get bogged down, as have so many legislative meetings, in petty routine. Henry's thoughts on several important issues are revealed in two candid letters by the eccentric General Charles Lee, a former British officer whom the Americans were now exalting with undue haste. Lee, placed by Congress in command of the Southern Department, established his headquarters in Williamsburg. Here, believing that the enemy might attack in either Virginia or South Carolina, he described himself as in "a damned whimsical situation . . . like a dog in a dancing school." Intent on immediate American independence, he said that Edmund Pendleton, while a man of sense, advanced arguments against immediate separation which would have disgraced "an old midwife drunk with bohea tea and gin." Yet Lee, while he wrote Washington on May 10 that he was disturbed by the vulnerability of Virginia to attack through various navigable waterways, said he was satisfied with his officers and men ("some Irish rascals excepted"). The troops included some grenadier companies armed with rifles and spears "thirteen feet long." Moreover, he was even more pleased with the Convention. It was possessed "of a noble spirit," the members "almost unanimous for independence," though differing "in their sentiments about the mode; two days will decide it."

Lee urged immediate independence upon Henry in a conversation on May 6; then, dissatisfied with his attitude, took the opportunity to press him further in a letter the next day. After flattering comment on Henry's character, his liberal thought, and his "great influence" due to his "transcendent abilities," Lee again laid on about the need for immediate independence. America ought not to declare independence without first having felt the pulse of France and Spain, he quoted Henry as saying the previous day "with great justice." But Lee was "almost confident" that this had been done; at least he could assert upon "recollection" that some of the Committee of Secrecy (of Congress) had assured him that the sentiment of both the French and Spanish courts or their agents had been sounded and were found to be as favorable as could be wished.

Henry had argued, so Lee intimated, that the British might prevent

a Franco-American alliance by an offer to the French of British territory. But Lee now wrote Henry that the French "would be wretched
politicians" indeed if they preferred the uncertain acquisition and precarious and expensive possession of one or two provinces to the greater
part of the commerce of the whole. He was convinced that the French
would immediately assist the colonials if independence were declared;
by procrastination, ruin was inevitable.

If it were now determined to await the result of a formal negotiation with France, "a whole year must pass over our heads" before we
could be acquainted with the result, Lee urged, and meantime the
Americans would have to struggle through the campaign without
arms, ammunition, or any other necessities of war. Disgrace and defeat would infallibly ensue and the soldiers become so disappointed
that they would abandon the colors and probably never be persuaded
to make another effort.

It was a case of now or never, Lee in effect wrote Henry. The spirit
of the people cried out for the declaration of independence; the military in particular were "outrageous" on the subject, and a man of
Henry's discernment need not be told how dangerous it would be in
the present circumstances to dally with the spirit or disappoint the
expectations of the bulk of the people. "May not despair, anarchy,
and finally submission, be the bitter fruits?"

Lee's information on the favorable attitude of the French court toward the American cause is believed to have been derived from a
secret agent of the French minister, Vergennes, who had given assurances to the secret committee of Congress in Philadelphia the previous
January. The committee had also received assurances from Spain.
Lee's cheering news is said to have been the first Henry received to
this effect and to have removed from his mind "a burden of anxiety,"
especially since it was an assurance that his early prediction of assistance from these nations would be verified.[19] Nevertheless, while he
now supported a resolution calling for Congress to declare independence, Henry was still concerned with the timing of the foreign
assistance.

Once certain enough in his own mind, at least of his immediate
course, Henry moved ahead with a precision and discretion which

excited the admiration of Edmund Randolph, who, with another young man of great potential powers, James Madison, was first trying his wings in an important political assembly. When Henry felt certain of the disposition of the people as indicated by the delegates, he formulated a plan for the aristocratic Thomas Nelson, Jr., to introduce the question of independence and for Henry himself to follow with the support of his oratorical guns, so Randolph later explained.

As in the convention at St. John's, Nelson took no counsel of his fears. In Randolph's words, Nelson urged the declaration of independence upon what were for him "incontrovertible grounds": that the Americans were "oppressed, had humbly supplicated a redress of grievances which had been refused with insult; and that to return from battle against the sovereign with the cordiality of subjects was absurd."

There was now every reason to believe that the motion to call for independence would be passed. Yet for a considerable time Henry "talked of the subject as critical" but did not commit himself to a precise position. He was convinced that "a course which put at stake the lives and fortunes of the people should appear to be their own act." He believed that "he ought not to place upon the responsibility of his eloquence, a revolution of which the people might be wearied after the present stimulus should cease to operate."

Henry was aroused "by the now apparent spirit of the people. As a pillar of fire, which notwithstanding the darkness of the prospect would lead to the promised land, he inflamed, and was followed by, the convention," Randolph later wrote. "His eloquence unlocked the secret springs of the human heart, robbed danger of all its terror, and broke the keystone in the arch of royal power." [20]

Randolph's impression of the speech might seem incredible were there not so much other evidence of Henry's oratorical powers. A more prosaic account of the proceedings is contained in a letter of May 18 by John Augustine Washington to Richard Henry Lee. This younger brother of George enclosed a resolve of the Convention on the subject of setting up a government, and instructions to the Virginia delegates in Congress to declare the united colonies free and independent. The resolve was "not so full as some would have wished it," young Washington declared, but he hoped it would answer the purpose. What particularly pleased him was that the resolve was made "by a Very full house and without a decenting [sic] voice." [21] The *Journal* confirms that the resolution passed unanimously with 112 members present, though it does not indicate the earlier opposition.

We have much information on the actual resolutions for independence. Three sets were proposed, representing various opinions as to the future course of the revolution. The first was credited to Meriwether Smith of Essex County in the Tidewater, the second somewhat doubtfully to Edmund Pendleton, and the third to Patrick Henry.

The resolutions of Colonel ("Fiddlehead") Smith represented the viewpoint of an eastern Virginia planter in a conservative area peculiarly vulnerable to British attack. They were confined to two brief, simply phrased paragraphs. First they called attention to how Lord Dunmore had suspended "by proclamation the laws of this colony, [a measure] supported by a late act of Parliament, declaring the colonies . . . in actual rebellion," confiscating their property "where ever found on the water," and legalizing the British "robbery and rapine." Then the resolutions stated that the government of Virginia "as hitherto exercised under the Crown" should "be dissolved, and that a committee be appointed to prepare a Declaration of Rights, and such a plan of government as shall be judged most proper to maintain Peace and Order in this colony, and secure substantial and equal liberty to the people." [22] These resolutions, if adopted, could have meant that Virginia would dissolve only the present plan of British government in the colony. Furthermore, they made no reference to intercolonial unity.

Edmund Pendleton's resolutions were almost as brief as Smith's but less cautiously worded. After alluding to "the many tyrannical acts" of the British, they declared that King George had "jointly with the ministry and Parliament" pursued "a barbarous war" against the colonies in violation of all their civil and religious rights. "The union that has hitherto subsisted between Great Britain and the colonies is thereby totally dissolved," and the inhabitants of Virginia discharged from any allegiance to the British Crown. [23] These resolutions show some evidence of collaboration with Smith and, like his, do not propose any intercolonial action.

Henry's resolutions were not only longer but more drastic and comprehensive. They were later found in the capital at Richmond, with those of Smith and Pendleton, labeled "Rough Resolutions Independence." It was thus evident that Henry's resolutions did not have the final polishing by a committee or larger body that have improved some great historical documents.

> As the humble petitions of the continental Congress have been rejected and treated with contempt; as the parliament of G.B. so far from showing any disposition to redress our grievances, have lately passed an act approving of the ravages that have been committed upon our coasts, and obliging the unhappy men who shall be made captives to bear arms against their families, kindred, friends, and country; and after being plundered themselves, to become accomplices in plundering their brethren, a compulsion not practiced on prisoners of war except among pirates, the outlaws and enemies of human society. As they are not only making every preparation to crush us, which the internal strength of the nation and its alliances with foreign powers afford them, but are using every art to draw the savage Indians upon our frontiers, and are even encouraging insurrection among our slaves, many of whom are now actually in arms against us. And as the King of G.B. by a long series of oppressive acts has proved himself the tyrant instead of the protector of his people.

Henry then continued without a paragraph break:

> We, the representatives of the colony of Virginia do declare, that we hold ourselves absolved of our allegiance to the crown of G.B. and obliged by the eternal laws of self-preservation to pursue such measures as may conduce to the good and happiness of the united colonies; and as a full declaration of Independency appears to us to be the only honourable means under Heaven of obtaining that happiness, and of restoring us again to a tranquil and prosperous situation;

And finally this stern mandate:

> Resolved, That our delegates in Congress be enjoined in the strongest and most positive manner to exert their ability in pro-

curing an immediate, clear, and full Declaration of Independency.[24]

On the whole, Henry's resolution, while hardly distinguished for smooth phrasing, is indicative of his opinion as to the causes and objectives of the war. Smith would move forward cautiously to independence, leaving the back door open; Pendleton would declare the Virginians absolved from any allegiance to the Crown. But Henry, the advanced revolutionist, would take further steps: he would deem Virginia "obliged by the eternal laws of self-preservation to pursue such measures as may conduce to the good and happiness of the *united* colonies [italics mine]," and, above all, would enjoin the Virginia delegates in Congress to take the strongest possible action to procure "an immediate, clear, and full Declaration of Independency." [25]

When the debate opened on May 14, various viewpoints had to be considered, including the lingering opposition to independence on the part of the respected Robert Carter Nicholas. Edmund Pendleton employed his gifts for conciliation and compromise to prepare some revised resolutions which combined features of the various drafts and finally won even Nicholas' vote to assure the unanimous approval. In several instances, the wording shows the direct influence of Henry's draft. The resolutions conclude with these words:

> Resolved unanimously, That the delegates appointed to represent this colony in General Congress be instructed to propose to that respectable body to declare the United Colonies freed and independent states, absolved from all allegiance to, or dependence upon, the crown or parliament of Great Britain; and that they give the assent of this colony to such declaration, and to whatever measures may be thought proper and necessary by the Congress for forming foreign alliances, and a confederation of the colonies, at such time, and in the manner, as to them shall seem best; Provided, that the power of forming government for, and the regulations of the internal concerns of each colony, be left to the respective colonial legislatures.[26]

Thus the Pendleton resolutions concurred with Henry's opinion as to the need for foreign alliances. The delegates, however, would not necessarily wait to secure them before issuing a declaration of independence, and Henry now agreed. A confederation of the colonies was called for; the Convention left the regulation of their "internal concerns" to their own legislatures.

"I put up with it [the resolution] in the present form for the sake of unanimity. 'Tis not quite so pointed as I could wish," Henry wrote John Adams on May 20. Yet it was perhaps more effective in the moderate form.

Left for the Convention were the vital matters of preparing a declaration of rights and of setting up a new state government. So Pendleton's revised resolutions also contained these provisions:

> Resolved unanimously, That a committee be appointed to prepare a DECLARATION OF RIGHTS, and such a plan of government as will be most likely to maintain peace and order in this colony, and secure substantial and equal liberty to the people.[27]

Once the Virginia delegates had decided to take the final step of separation, they did not hesitate about the means. A month before, when sentiment for independence had not been quite so strong, North Carolina had called upon her delegates to Congress "to concur" with those from the other colonies "in declaring Independency and forming foreign alliances." [28] Rhode Island had taken a similar action, as had a number of Massachusetts towns. Virginia now took an even more drastic course—she positively ordered her delegates in Congress to propose independency with a colonial confederation.

It was an epochal action, and in Williamsburg the event was dramatically symbolized. No sooner had word spread of the resolutions for independence than the Union Jack was lowered from the capitol and a "Continental" flag raised in its place. Purdie's *Virginia Gazette* for May 18 laid on a bit heavily when it stated that the resolutions were "universally regarded as the only door which will lead to safety and prosperity," but there is no doubt about the enthusiasm with which they were greeted in Williamsburg. Several gentlemen were moved to make a "handsome collation" with which to treat the soldiers, and the next day Henry and the other delegates got a welcome respite from their labors to attend the celebration in the capital.

The resolutions were read aloud; toasts were proposed to the accompaniment of small-arms and artillery fire and the acclamation of the spectators. The following Sunday, May 18, the day of fasting and prayer proclaimed by Congress, the delegates went as a body to Bruton Church, where they heard an appropriate sermon from the text in II Chronicles, chapter 20, verse 15: "Hearken ye, all Judah, and ye inhabitants of Jerusalem, and thou King Jehoshaphat, thus saith the Lord unto you, Be not afraid, nor dismayed, by reason of this great multitude, for the battle is not yours, but God's." [29]

After the adoption of the Virginia resolutions, Thomas Nelson, Jr., at once carried them to Philadelphia, where they were presented to Congress on May 27. On June 7, 1776, Richard Henry Lee, in accordance with the mandate of the Convention, made a formal motion in Congress for independence. This memorable resolution, in essentially the same words of the Virginia prototype, also provided that measures be taken to secure foreign alliances and that a plan of confederation be prepared and transmitted to the respective colonies for consideration.

Lee's resolution was seconded by John Adams; there was some opposition from the same faction that Henry had opposed in Philadelphia. Had he been in Congress he would have found more occasions for his oratory. But the conservative party in Congress was now weakened. A declaration of independence, written by Thomas Jefferson, was reported from committee on June 28, and on July 4 it was adopted by Congress.

Henry could take deep satisfaction in all that he had done, in this and earlier years, to prepare the way for united action. On a lesser issue, though important to the success of the war, Congress now disappointed him. In his May letter to John Adams, Henry had urged that a confederation

> must precede an open declaration of independency and foreign alliances. Would it not be sufficient to confine it [the confederacy], for the present, to the objects of offensive and defensive nature, and a guaranty of the respective colonial rights? If a minute arrangement of things is attempted, such as equal

representation, &c., &c., you may split and divide; certainly will delay the French alliance, which with me is every thing.[30]

Yet "split and divide" is just what Congress did. Richard Henry Lee's resolution, when approved by Congress, did call for a confederation as proposed by the Virginia Convention. But Henry could find little comfort in the work of the committee appointed to present a plan for union. On July 12 this committee offered to Congress a number of detailed articles which were written by John Dickinson and raised delicate questions of interstate relationships. Jealous as the new states were at times of their individual rights, parochial as were many of their congressmen, these states could hardly be persuaded into a minimal unity. It is not surprising that Congress did not approve a plan for confederation until 1778 and that it was not ratified by the last state until February, 1781.

8

A Pilot Declaration of Rights and
a State Constitution

> History, to be above evasion or dispute, must stand on documents, not on opinions.——LORD ACTON [1]
>
> . . . to judge them fairly. . . . We must take the point of view afforded by the civilization of their time.
> ——WILLIAM H. PRESCOTT [2]

June, 1776. Final weeks of the Virginia Convention.

June 29, 1776. Adoption of the constitution for an independent commonwealth, with Patrick Henry as first governor.

IN HIS CORRESPONDENCE during May, 1776, there was further evidence that Henry was not shrinking from drastic action for the Revolutionary cause. Besides certain inducements in his letter to Richard Henry Lee on May 20 for a French alliance, he had even suggested "a general confiscation of Royal and British property. . . . The Fruits would be great, and the measure in its utmost latitude warranted by the late act of Parliament." [3] These measures, however, were not on the current agenda of the Convention, and he became absorbed for several weeks in the deliberations on the proposed bill of rights and state constitution.

"Our Convention is now employed in the great work of forming a constitution," Henry noted in another letter of May 20, this to John

[112]

Adams. Adams, in his reply two weeks later, was fulsome in his compliments. After stating that the subject of the new Virginia constitution was "of infinite moment, and perhaps more than adequate to the abilities of any man in America," he added, "Happy Virginia, whose Constitution is to be framed by so masterly a builder! Whether the plan of the pamphlet is not too popular, whether the elections are not too frequent for your colony, I know not." [4]

The pamphlet to which Adams referred was a copy of a plan for state government which he had written at the request of George Wythe. Henry had commended the Adams constitution and had predicted that the Convention sessions would be "very long, during which I cannot count upon one coadjutor of talents equal to the task. Would to God you and your Sam Adams were here!" [5]

It is not surprising that the Bostonian did not recognize the talents of George Mason, not yet acclaimed as the author of the Virginia Bill of Rights and most of her constitution. But more might have been expected of Henry. Mason was a delegate to the Convention, and Henry had already learned something of his abilities. And yet it was true that Mason's full powers had not become manifest. Elected by a close vote of his Northern Virginia constituency, he had been delayed in reaching Williamsburg by an attack of the gout. He was not appointed to the drafting committee until Saturday, May 18, and it is doubtful if he had attended any of the sessions when Henry wrote Adams.

Besides Mason and Henry, the large committee for preparing the declaration of rights and the constitution finally contained thirty-two delegates. When this committee began its deliberations, it was "overcharged with useless members," so Mason pessimistically wrote Richard Henry Lee. "We shall, in all probability, have a thousand ridiculous and impractical proposals, and of course a plan formed of heterogeneous, jarring and unintelligible ingredients. This can be prevented only by a few men of integrity and abilities, whose country's interest lies next their hearts, undertaking this business and defending it ably through every stage of opposition." [6]

In addition to his other legislative duties, Henry was heavily involved in late May and early June with the committee to prepare the

Declaration of Rights. But it was a draft prepared by George Mason which was reported out of the committee and, after detailed discussion on the floor, was unanimously adopted on June 15 by the Convention.

What part Henry took in this formal debate, with the "button-holing" of delegates "out-of-doors," we can only surmise. But a Mason biographer has properly called attention to "the amazing extent" to which the final draft of the declaration conformed to Mason's original. It is no disparagement of Mason to note how much he drew, sometimes in almost identical words, upon earlier sources, not merely his own address to the Fairfax Independent Company in June, 1775, and other writings but also great English historical documents such as the Petition of Rights.[7]

Beginning with the eloquent phrases, "That all men are by nature equally free and independent, and have certain inherent rights," the declaration goes on boldly to proclaim a compact of basic truths to govern future society. As such it was drawn upon by Jefferson in writing the Declaration of Independence and by numerous American states in preparing their constitutions and statements of fundamental principles. The French Déclaration des Droits de L'Homme in 1789 is partly based upon it—"Men are born and remain free and equal in rights"—as are the first ten amendments to the American Constitution, adopted partly through Henry's influence.

Liberal as were Mason, Henry, and their supporters in the Convention, they could not overlook the omnipresent matter of political expediency. They had to write not only for future ages but for current propaganda. And yet, if considered as a political manifesto, the declaration still carried revolutionary implications, not merely for the conduct of the war but for Virginia's internal government. Its final adoption by unanimous consent does not indicate the bitter struggle in the Convention.

An impression of this little-known conflict is given by both Ludwell Lee and Edmund Randolph. In a letter to his brother, Richard Henry Lee, on June 1, Ludwell Lee sent him a copy of the declaration almost as it came through the committee, then sententiously noted:

> It has since been reported to the Convention, and we have ever since been stumbling at the threshold. In short, we find such

difficulty in laying the foundation stone, that I very much fear for that Temple to Liberty which was proposed to be erected thereon.

"But laying aside figure," Ludwell Lee continued,

> I will tell you plainly that a certain set of Aristocrats—for we have such monsters here—finding that their execrable system cannot be reared on such foundations, have to this time kept us at bay on the first line, which declares all men to be born free and independent. A number of absurd or unmeaning alterations have been proposed. The words as they stand are approved by a very great majority, yet by a thousand masterly fetches and stratagems the business has been so delayed, that the first clause stands yet unassented to by the Convention.[8]

To this Edmund Randolph added the illuminating fact that the proposition in the first article, stating "all men are by nature equally free and independent, was opposed by Robert Carter Nicholas." Again prominent in the opposition to liberal proposals, Nicholas argued against the statement as "being the forerunner or pretext of civil convulsion." Nicholas was answered on practical lines, so Randolph put it, "not without inconsistency, that with arms in our hands, asserting the general rights of man, we [Virginians] ought not to be too nice and too much restricted in the delineation of them; but that slaves, not being constituent members of society, could never pretend to any benefit from such a maxim." [9]

As a result of the subsequent proceedings, Mason's draft of the declaration was increased from fourteen to sixteen articles and there were some verbal changes. Reflecting the opposition on the floor to the initial statement that "all men are created equally free and independent" was a revised wording that "all men are born equally free" and the final phrasing that "all men are by nature equally free." The statement in an early or final form was widely copied in the American colonies and elsewhere. It was used by Thomas Jefferson when he wrote in the Declaration of Independence that "all men are created equal." During the next decade the declaration in the Massachusetts constitution of 1780 that "all men are free and equal" was used by a Negro a few years later in a court proceeding which secured his freedom. In the census of 1790, Massachusetts was the only state which reported "no slaves"; apparently Henry would have approved, while noting the vastly greater difficulties of emancipation in Virginia.[10]

So much for the far-flung results of the idealistic pronunciamento on human rights as drafted by Mason and supported by Henry and some liberal followers. That George Mason wrote the first fourteen of the sixteen articles in the final draft of the declaration is now virtually unquestioned. But there has been a controversy as to the authorship of the last two articles which has remained unsettled to the present day. In his *Manuscript History*, Edmund Randolph wrote that Henry proposed these final articles, only to have any implication as to his authorship challenged later by Mason and Madison biographers. The disputed fifteenth article is as follows:

> That no free government, or the blessing of liberty, can be preserved to any people but by a firm adherence to justice, moderation, temperance, frugality, and virtue, and by frequent recurrence to fundamental principles.[11]

As proof that this article, too, was written by Mason, a Madison biographer notes the similarity of wording to Mason's Fairfax Resolutions. It is true that where Mason refers in these resolutions to "the indispensable duty of all the gentlemen and men of fortune to set examples of temperance, fortitude, frugality, and industry," the fifteenth article of the Declaration of Rights says, "No free Government . . . can be preserved to any people but by firm adherence to justice, moderation, frugality and virtue."[12] Also, in his address to the Fairfax Independent Company early in 1775, Mason stated that "no institution can be long preserved but by frequent recurrence to those maxims on which it was formed," and the fifteenth article calls for "frequent recurrence to fundamental principles."[13]

Henry, a fellow member of the drafting committee with Mason, may well have been influenced not only by his writings but by his oral discussion in or out of the committee sessions. Although Randolph had been a member of the drafting committee, when he wrote his *Manuscript History* a generation later, he may have been confused by Henry's strong advocacy of the article into mistakenly recalling that he had actually written it. Yet, Randolph does not state that Henry actually wrote the article but only that he "proposed" it. The evidence as to the extent of Henry's authorship is incomplete. There is every reason, however, to believe that he and his liberal supporters used their great influence to help secure its enactment.

Possibly Randolph's memory was again inaccurate and he confused Henry's earnest advocacy of the sixteenth article with his authorship. This article states that "all men are equally entitled to the free exercise of religion." However, Randolph gives further evidence. He notes that a question was raised in the Convention as to whether Henry designed his article as a prelude to an attack on the established church. In this case, the proposal would have met with almost certain defeat by the Episcopalians, who then dominated the Convention; Henry disclaimed such an intention. Madison moved on the Convention floor an amended resolution which, while allowing religious toleration, would prevent disestablishment of the Anglican Church without legislative sanction.

The Virginia Declaration of Rights has remained one of the influential political documents of modern times. It has not disappointed the hopes of its ardent proponents that it would be "a perpetual standard . . . around which the people might rally," and that through it they would remain "forever admonished to be watchful firm and virtuous." [14]

The declaration had not been substantially altered on the Convention floor, and as much could be said for the pioneer written constitution later adopted by the delegates. In view of the proud localism still lingering among the colonies, it is remarkable how much this constitution was based on suggestions contained in the pamphlet copy of an outline for a constitution sent to Henry by John Adams. The outline called for a lower house annually elected by the people, a council or senate annually elected by the lower house, and a governor chosen annually by the two houses. Of particular importance to Henry's subsequent career, the governor would have a privy council and veto and pardoning powers and would serve as commander in chief of the state forces. Moreover, he would appoint state judges with the consent of the upper house or by joint or concurrent power of both houses.

Henry is the only Virginian known to have received the copy of Adams' plan for a state government. There is strong reason to believe that Henry had a hand in the publication of a plan for the Virginia government published by Purdie's *Gazette* on May 10. It called for an elective lower house which would select the members of the upper house; and for the two houses to choose the governor, the governor's council, and the judges, the latter serving during good behavior. The proposal in the *Gazette* appears to contain a few changes offered by Richard Henry Lee. But in general it is much like the Adams plan.[15]

If, as seems unlikely, Henry did not propose the *Gazette* plan, he at least favored it over the aristocratic plan recommended by Carter Braxton. That constitution did provide for a lower house elected by the people, with the members to serve for three-year terms. Yet the lower house would not only select an upper house, a governor, and a treasurer, but all of them were to continue in office during good behavior. The Braxton plan probably had more influential support than appeared on the surface. If only the proposal for gubernatorial tenure were adopted, it could be a serious blow to the liberal cause.[16] There were the best reasons, from Henry's viewpoint, for offering suitable alternatives. He now actively supported a constitution along the general lines suggested by John Adams.

"I own my self a Democrat on the plan of our admired friend, J. Adams, whose pamphlet I read with great pleasure," Henry wrote Lee.[17] And he wrote Adams that he was not without hope that his pamphlet "may produce good here, where there is among most of our opulent families a strong bias to aristocracy. I tell my friends you are the author [of the pamphlet]," Henry continued, adding, "The sentiments are precisely the same I have long since taken up, and they come recommended by you."[18]

Adams' reply, written on June 3, 1776, probably reached Henry before the Convention had made some of its most important decisions respecting the new constitution. The New Englander modestly wrote that the task of writing the constitution was perhaps beyond "the abilities of any man in America," although he praised Henry's qualifications. Adams was uncertain whether or not his plan was "too popular," the elections "too frequent," for Virginia. "The usages, and genius, and manners of the people must be consulted." [19]

On May 20 Henry had written Adams that "my most esteemed republican form has many and powerful enemies." [20] But within a few days it was evident that the liberal proposals were securing the support of the best speakers. They gathered strength not merely from Henry's staunch followers but also from the great body of the house.

Even so, the road was not smooth. "Many projects of a Bill of Rights and Constitution, discovered the ardour for political notice, rather than a ripeness in political wisdom," wrote Edmund Randolph. But the plan "proposed by George Mason swallowed up all the rest, by fixing the grounds and plan which after great discussion and correction were finally ratified." [21]

As early as May 24, 1776, Edmund Pendleton had written to Thomas Jefferson that the Convention session "would be a long one, and indeed, the importance of our business requires it & we must sweat it out with Fortitude." [22] Besides his heavy work with the drafting committee for the Declaration of Rights and the constitution, Henry reported on May 16 from the committee apparently appointed to consider a petition relating to mining rights near the James River, [23] and in early June from the committee to consider the case of Robert Sheddon, arrested on suspicion of being inimical to the rights of America. In accordance with the committee resolution, Sheddon was found guilty of being associated with Governor Dunmore's military operations, and the convention ordered him to be confined in a prescribed area within Dinwiddie County. [24]

More important was Henry's continued interest in Indian affairs. He was appointed a member of a committee to inquire into a complaint of encroachment on Indian lands and chairman of another committee to prepare an address to be sent back by three Shawnee captives to their Indian nation. [25]

It was remarkable how well not only Henry's committees but the Convention stuck to their last. When Thomas Jefferson urged one of his young friends in the Convention, presumably Edmund Randolph, to oppose a permanent constitution until the people could elect delegates for this special purpose, the proposal was quickly dismissed. Randolph later wrote that it was "communicated" to some of the leaders of the house, such as Henry, Pendleton, and Mason, who "saw no distinction between the conceded power to declare independence, and its necessary consequence, the fencing of society by the institution of government. Nor were they sure that to be backward in this act of sovereignty might not imply a distrust, whether the rule had been wrested from the King." [26]

Another suggestion was that Congress prepare a uniform plan of government for all the states. It takes little imagination to see how much local opposition this proposal would arouse. Evidence indicates that Henry favored the plan for each state to adopt its own constitution, though he must have been pleased to find the extent to which the Virginia features were later copied elsewhere.[27]

Disregarding British precedent, the delegates decided to try the significant experiment of embodying in written form the supreme law of the state. There had been written codes of laws drawn up in ancient times, and some sketchy efforts had been made to draw up constitutions in American colonies. But the Virginia delegates had evolved an ambitious plan for a permanent constitution, expressive of the popular will. Like the Declaration of Rights, it became a model for other states.[28]

After his proposal for a special constitutional convention was rejected, Jefferson offered the Williamsburg delegates a constitution of his own. But it did not reach them until late June. The delegates were then getting enough of "sweating out" the hot summer days; besides, their drafting committee had a constitution almost ready for consideration on the floor. The Convention gave Jefferson's plan short shrift except to place at the beginning of their constitution the preamble which, with minor changes, he soon included in his draft of the the Declaration of Independence.

Designed largely as war propaganda, this preamble, with its catalog of misdeeds attributed to George III alone, could hardly be criticized for understatement. Playing for desperate stakes, Mason, Henry, and the other Virginia leaders saw a propaganda value in making King

George III the *bête noire*. He, not Parliament, the British government, or all of them collectively, was responsible, as the preamble states, for the long category of offenses ranging from dissolving legislative assemblies, quartering "large bodies" of troops in America, and cutting off her trade to all parts of the world to "plundering our seas" and "ravaging our coasts." [29]

The Virginia liberals were now in the saddle, and typical of the influences affecting them was an address from the Piedmont county of Buckingham. The Buckingham freeholders in the instructions to their convention delegates, John Cabell, and Charles Patterson, both Henry supporters, asked for "a full representation" and "free and frequent elections." Inspired by the revolutionary idealism, the Buckingham gentlemen prayed that "under the superintending providence of the Ruler of the Universe, a Government may be established in *America* the most free, happy, and permanent, that human wisdom can contrive, and the perfection of man maintain." [30]

The new government set up, while containing some conservative offsets, was in many respects sensitive, indeed supersensitive, to the prevalent fear of executive tyranny. Written mostly by George Mason, the constitution was based substantially on the democratic forms Henry had favored. It provided for a legislature of two branches to meet once or oftener a year and together to be called the General Assembly of Virginia. The lower house, known as the House of Delegates, was to consist of two representatives from each county; the Senate of twenty-four members chosen from as many electoral districts. Despite the proposals for restricting the suffrage, the members of the House of Delegates were to be elected "as usual—that is, by freeholders of fifty acres of unimproved land, or twenty-five acres on which there was a suitable improvement, or an improved lot within a town.[31] These freeholders would still come to the county or town courthouses on election day to call out the names of their candidates. There was a statutory fine for failing to vote, although the penalty was not rigorously enforced.[32] It would shame many lackadaisical citizens today to know that their ancestors once walked or rode perhaps twenty or thirty miles to fulfill their obligation.

Like the House, the Senate was to be chosen by direct election.

This was in contravention of the tentative Adams proposal. But it was further provided that all laws had to originate in the House of Delegates, to be approved or rejected by the Senate.[33] The Senate in Henry's lifetime remained a much weaker body than the so-called lower house, and Henry when running for the legislature would always select the House for his forum.

The fear of executive tyranny was manifest in the provision that the Governor should be chosen annually by joint ballot of both houses and that he could not continue in office longer than three years successively or be eligible for service again for four years. With memories of Lord Dunmore still fresh, it was provided that the Governor could not prorogue or adjourn the Assembly during their sitting or dissolve them at any time. When exercising the executive powers of government under the state laws he was to seek the advice of the Council of State. Thus the Council, consisting of eight members chosen by joint ballot of the two houses, could be a helpful—or obstructive—influence on him.

Among other constitutional provisions of special interest to Henry, the Governor would have the power of granting reprieves or pardons, with certain exceptions, and of appointing the justices of peace for the counties with the advice of the Council. The state judges and the secretary of the Commonwealth were to be elected by the General Assembly, but in the case of their death, incapacity, or resignation, the Governor, with the advice of the Council, was to appoint their successors, subject to the approval of the Assembly.

Henry now found himself hoist by his own petard. In earlier legislative assemblies he had labored to curb the power of the executive; now he believed that, in at least one particular, this power of the veto needed to be strengthened if the chief executive were to govern effectively in the war period. Probably Henry was already aware that he would be a strong candidate for the governorship. From Edmund Randolph we learn of the strenuous effort that Henry made to give the Governor the veto power over the laws of the Assembly.

"After creating the office of governor, the Convention gave way to their horror of a powerful chief magistrate, without waiting to reflect how much stronger a governor might be made for the benefit of the people, and yet be held with a republican bridle," Randolph explained.[34]

> These were not times of terror, indeed, but every hint of power, which might be stigmatized as being of royal origin, obscured for a time a part of that patriotic splendor with which the movers had before shone. No member but Henry could, with impunity to his popularity, have contended as strenuously as he did for an executive veto on the acts of the two houses of legislation. Those who knew him to be indolent in literary investigations, were astonished at the manner in which he exhausted the topic, unaided as he was believed to be by any of the treatises on government, except Montesquieu. Among other arguments, he averred that a governor would be a mere phantom, unable to defend his office from the usurpation of the legislature, unless he could interpose on a vehement impulse or ferment in that body, and that he would otherwise be ultimately a dependent, instead of a co-ordinate, branch of power.[35]

In the first state constitutions, the veto power was granted the Governor in only three states. But Henry's practical foresight is indicated by the fact that this power was given the American President in the Constitution of 1787 and is now granted the Governors of all but one of our states.

The new constitution was formally adopted on June 29, 1776. The Convention declared that "the Government of this country [Virginia], as formerly exercised under the Crown of Great Britain, is TOTALLY DISSOLVED." [36] Thus Virginia separated from England five days before the American Declaration of Independence. Moreover, in order to "introduce" [37] the new administration, the Convention chose the new Governor. That same Saturday it elected Patrick Henry Governor of the new commonwealth.

9

Governor First Term

The egotism of human nature will seldom allow us to credit a man for one excellence without detracting from him in other respects; if he has genius, we imagine he has not common sense; if he is a poet, we suppose that he is not a logician.

—LORD BROUGHAM [1]

July 4, 1776. Congress adopts the American Declaration of Independence.

July 5–September 16, 1776 (circa). Henry on protracted sick leave.

August 27. Washington defeated by Howe at Long Island.

October 7. Meeting of the first Virginia General Assembly under the new constitution.

FROM JULY, 1776, to July, 1779, Henry served for three one-year terms as Governor of Virginia, then the largest and most populous of the American states. Although his powers were restricted under the new constitution, much depended on the inspirational quality of his leadership and even more upon his daily performance of a difficult, at times almost exhausting, task. During the retreat of the beaten remnant of Washington's army through New Jersey, or while his little force shivered and well nigh starved at Valley Forge, and on other occasions during the earlier years of the Revolution, the cause seemed

[124]

to be hanging by a thread. Especially in view of the weak central authority during the war, much depended upon the work of such men as Henry in gubernatorial posts. These executives could give invaluable support in men and supplies to the grimly struggling Washington and the floundering Congress; they could set precedents and make decisions of lasting importance.

In Henry's case these decisions included not only such colorful episodes as his support of the plans of that empire builder, George Rogers Clark, for conquest of the Northwest Territory, his opposition to the scheme for ousting Washington as commander in chief and the dispatch to him of vitally needed men and supplies, but also a great many other matters, more prosaic but of cumulative effect.

Henry's election as Governor had not been without a contest in which the conservative Thomas Nelson, Sr. (not Jr.), polled a formidable vote. Nor was it surprising to find the strong hand of Edmund Pendleton again evident in the Henry opposition. Whatever one may think of Pendleton's antagonism toward Henry when head of the Committee of Safety and chairman of the late Convention, the tall and dignified representative from Caroline had again proved his competence. By lifting a finger he could have been the conservative candidate for Governor. But, as he told Spencer Roane years later, "he did not think it became those who pushed on the Revolution to get into the first office." It is also likely that the astute Pendleton did not want a position with powers as restricted (at least constitutionally) as those of the Governor and preferred to await his expected election as Speaker of the new House of Delegates, which could be the most powerful offce in the new government.[2]

The opposition concentrated, therefore, on the aging Thomas Nelson, Sr., last president of His Majesty's Council and its long-time secretary. Surely, the conservatives thought, he could be counted on not to rock the boat. Even Henry's ally, Richard Henry Lee, the Westmoreland gentleman with the Roman nose and antique Roman virtues, had been attracted to the wealthy York merchant, planter, and political potentate of the old regime.

"Would it not be well to appoint M[r]. President Nelson the first Governor if he would accept, since he possesses knowledge, experience, and has already been in the dignified station?" Lee had written Pendleton on May 12, 1776, in reference to an action which the latter may have already had in mind.[3] And certainly Nelson could rely on some powerful support.

If the first generations of the Virginia aristocracy had been noted for acquisitiveness, as might be expected in an undeveloped country, the Revolutionary generation was distinguished for public service. The point, illustrated brilliantly in the Randolphs and Lees, was also proved by the Nelsons. William Nelson was the son of Scotch "Tom" Nelson, the Virginia progenitor of the family and a highly successful merchant. A long-time member of the Council, William was serving on that conservative body as far back as 1747, when it had fined Patrick Henry's grandfather, Isaac Winston, for permitting Dissenting religious services to be held in his house,[4] and Henry had known William as Acting Governor in the interregnum before the arrival of Lord Dunmore. It was William's nephew, Thomas Nelson, Jr., who had so strongly supported Henry's resolutions at St. John's Church, and William's brother, Thomas, Sr., who now became Henry's opponent for the governorship.[5] Edmund Randolph later described him as ranking "high in the aristocracy, who propagated with zeal the expediency of accommodating ancient prejudices by electing a man whose pretensions to the chief magistracy were obvious from his being nominally the governor under the old order of things. . . ."[6]

All the evidence indicates that Henry neither offered his name for the governorship nor worked for his election. A hint as to one strong argument is advanced for him in an excerpt from the diary of Colonel Landon Carter, a conservative Tidewater aristocrat but no British supporter. Carter's family seat was at Sabine Hall, the brick mansion which still looks across the low grounds to the Rappahannock River, near present Tappahannock. At the county courthouse, church, or elsewhere, Carter had picked up some late news of the Convention. Evidently the Henry supporters had been working off the Convention floor to bolster their candidate, for Carter heard it was argued that "the late[ly] dignified person [Henry] was the first who opened the breath of liberty" to America.

"But it was with truth replied and proved," Carter asserted, "that the breath was first breathed and supported by a person not then taken notice of [none other than Colonel Carter, he implied]. I know this merit is claimed also by another but I only say I never courted Public applause. . . ." [7] It was indeed true that resolutions opposing the Stamp Act, in which Colonel Carter had a hand, were passed by the Burgesses over six months before Henry's celebrated resolves of 1765. But the earlier resolutions, milder than Henry's, were ignored by the British government.[8]

The majority of the Convention believed that Henry's record in this and other respects entitled him to be chief executive of the new commonwealth. His name appears to have been put before the Convention by George Mason. When the delegates were polled, the vote was 60 in favor of Henry to 45 for Thomas Nelson, Sr., and one vote for John Page.[9] It was more of a majority than Henry had received on several critical votes in the past. The result was especially encouraging for him in that the legislative districts were unfairly apportioned in favor of the more conservative Tidewater. Henry's vote, which Colonel Carter pessimistically described as "a great majority," [10] did put some curb on the Pendleton forces. It may be assumed that the vote came chiefly from the Piedmont and back country, with a few noteworthy additions from the east among Henry's former political associates. Forty-five members, however, as Edmund Randolph noted, "were caught by the device of bringing all parties together, although Mr. Nelson had not been at all prominent in the Revolution. From every period of Henry's life something of a democratic and patriotic cast was collected, so as to accumulate a rate of merit too strong for the last expiring act of aristocracy." [11]

In his letter of thanks to the Convention for his election, Henry spoke of the "tyranny of the British king and Parliament" as kindling a formidable war now raging through the widely extended colony. Such oversimplification of complex issues is to be expected of revolutionary leaders, especially in a desperate war. In words a bit reminiscent of Richard Henry Lee's letter to him of April 20, Henry said that from the events of the war "the lasting happiness or misery of a great proportion of the human species" would finally result.[12]

Henry's election was part of a popular movement in favor of the liberals. The number of Virginia congressmen was reduced to five. Carter Braxton, one of Henry's long-time opponents in the Tidewater, was not re-elected to Congress owing to his conservative stand on the Virginia constitution. This landed magnate, grandson of "King" Carter and first cousin of Landon, was now charged with retaining "British prejudices." But he signed the important patriotic agreements and was a member of successive Revolutionary Conventions in Virginia.[13] The brave and patriotic Benjamin Harrison, a moderate revolutionist, was also not returned to Congress but soon made a comeback. The other conservatives, while their influence was weakened, still retained a stronghold in the eastern counties. And Henry was not without opponents in the Piedmont. As Jefferson's brother-in-law, Francis Eppes, wrote on July 3:

> You have herd no doubt before this that Patrick Henry is our Governour. What a strange infatuation attends our Convention. At a time when men of known integrity and sound understanding are most necessary they are rejected and men of shallow understandings fill the most important posts in our country. What but inevitable ruin can be the consequence of this?[14]

Benjamin Harrison represented a strong group of Tidewater planters who would cooperate with Henry so long as he adhered to a program of winning the war and did not push a radical program in other respects. Landon Carter was typical of the much smaller group who were sulking in their tents. Not then dangerous to Henry, their numbers could easily be increased if he ran into difficulties. On July 3, 1776, Carter, now getting old and somewhat cautious, was bemoaning Henry's selection as Governor, but in his diary rather than in the public prints.

Henry was "electible only 3 yrs. successive, and must be out 4 yrs. before reelection," Carter noted, then added some strong criticism: "I see and condemn but as the Multitude of my city has done it, I say nothing, but cannot admire the choice. I rather mourn its destructive tendency in secret."[15]

On Saturday, July 13, Carter got what he deemed the bad news that his overseer at Ring's Neck (Ringfield) on the York had "turned" a Baptist. But this was overshadowed by tidings of two "glorious events," one the death of Patrick Henry:

> Came here after dinner Mr. John Selden, who told us Capt Burgess Ball wrote from Hampton that Patrick Henry, the late elected Governor, died last tuesday evening, So that being the day of our batterys beginning to Play on Dunmore's gang & they being routed we ought to look on those two joined as two glorious events. Particularly favourable by the hand of Providence.[16]

Doubtless the rumor of the Governor's death which so elated Colonel Carter grew out of an illness which led Henry to take sick leave in Hanover.[17] That he did appear to be seriously ill is indicated by a letter which Lieutenant Governor Page wrote to his friend, Jefferson, from Williamsburg on July 6. He (Page) must "Immediately attend the Governour who is very ill. If he should die before we have qualified and chosen a President the Country [Virginia] will be without any head—every Thing must be in Confusion. But four of our Board are in Town, who cannot chuse a President. . . ."[18]

Thomas Nelson, Sr., was elected a member of the Governor's Council, though by the lowest vote of the successful candidates. He declined to serve, however, on the ground that he was too old, an excuse not offered when he ran against Henry for the far more demanding gubernatorial office. The anti-Henry party was reduced but not crushed.

The conservatives had wealth, education, and governmental experience far out of proportion to their numbers, and they were still entrenched in the Council. The opposition to Henry's election as Governor may seem a tempest in a teapot, but it could swell into a storm under the influence of war nerves, war fatigue, and disillusionment.

Moreover, this opposition could benefit from the handicaps placed by the new constitution on Henry's authority. Now inordinately fearful of executive power, the delegates had not only limited the Governor to three consecutive one-year terms but had placed other serious limitations on his authority. With the advice of a Council of State, he was to exercise the executive power of the government, have certain

[129]

rights of granting pardons and reprieves and of supplying vacancies until filled by the Assembly, and appoint the county justices of the peace. Especially important during the war and again "with advice of the Council," he could suspend militia officers or fill vacancies among them, order courts-martial and embody the militia, at which time they would be under his sole direction, subject to the Virginia laws.[19]

The Council, with whose "advice" Henry had to exercise so many of his constitutional powers, was authorized "to assist in the administration of government." It was to consist of eight members elected by the Assembly, with four sufficient for a quorum.[20] Henry's success as Governor would largely depend upon their ability and cooperation.

He had not fallen into a bed of roses, but there was much to encourage him at the beginning of his term. Among the letters of congratulation was one from his former soldiers declaring that they had once been happy under his command and were hoping "for more extensive blessings" from his civil administration. Other letters came from the Virginia Baptists, whom he had lately defended; from Dr. Benjamin Rush, his Philadelphia friend; and from General Charles Lee. Rush, one of the Pennsylvania signers of the Declaration of Independence, took the opportunity to object to the provision in the Virginia constitution excluding the clergy from the state legislature. The voluble Lee, while addressing Henry as "His Excellency," objected to the high-flown form of address used for notables in a free commonwealth. How much more dignified was the simplicity of address among the Romans—Marcus, Italius, Cicero, Decimo, Bruto, and so on—than "His Excellency, Major General Noodle," or "The Honorable John Doodle!" Of more serious import was Lee's pointed objection to the constitutional provision by which the Virginia Governor could be elected for three successive terms—this although he said the Virginia people could not have made a "happier choice" than Henry.[21]

Henry was sick at Scotchtown for about five weeks, or until the middle of September, 1776. Besides attending to some correspondence, he had time for thought on many matters relating to his future course as Governor of the new commonwealth; indeed, on his place in history. In late July, Dixon and Hunter's *Gazette* ran an account of the debate four months earlier in Parliament upon news of the death before Quebec of the American General, Montgomery. Among the members engaged in the verbal duel were several outspoken Whigs and the Prime Minister, the good-natured and compliant Lord North. Of Lord North, Edmund Burke would later be constrained to write that he "wanted something of the vigilance and spirit of command which the times required." Yet even His Lordship, while censuring the unqualified liberality of the praises bestowed upon "a REBEL" by a few opposition leaders in the Commons, had admitted Montgomery's bravery and humanity. And young Charles James Fox, a courageous and generous-minded Whig champion, had risen a second time to praise the brave "rebel" in terms for which Henry could find personal application.

The term rebel applied by the noble lord to that excellent person (Montgomery) was "no certain mark of disgrace," Fox exclaimed. All the "great asserters of liberty, the saviours of their country, the benefactors of mankind, in all ages had been called REBELS." The members "even owed the constitution, which enabled them to sit in that House, to a REBELLION." [22]

But one swallow never makes a summer. A spate of eulogies from the little Whig minority in Parliament, a modicum of praise from the great government majority, in no sense indicated that the British Ministry was not overwhelmingly committed to the war. Henry might well find himself a leader in an ill-starred cause. While a considerable portion of the British public was showing insufficient zeal for the war to compensate for the red-coated regulars' measly pay, long service, and brutal discipline, Dixon and Hunter's *Virginia Gazette* was reporting that nearly two dozen shiploads of Hessian "hirelings" had sailed from a German port; they should augment the British force off New York almost any day.[23] In his speech to both houses of Parliament on May 23, 1776, George III was reported as declaring that the British were "engaged in a great national cause." The "essential rights and interests of the whole empire" were deeply involved, and no safety or security would be built except on that constitutional "subordination" for which the British forces were contending. The King, as brave—or obstinate—as he was sincere, was convinced that Parliament could not think "any price too high for the preservation of such principles." The British were confident of effecting a junction with Burgoyne in Canada and thus facilitating the subjection of the colonies.

Although Henry took comfort in some early British defeats, he knew the enemy was girding for a greater effort. In a combined operation which only recently had begun to peter out, the British fleet with an accompanying army had attacked Charleston on June 28 while their Indian allies moved into the Southern back country. The Charleston garrison, which held firm, was aided by some Virginia troops under Henry's old political associate, Parson (now Colonel) Peter Muhlenburg. The Cherokees, too, were being chastised in a series of minor battles and maneuvers in which two of Henry's in-laws took leading parts: his sister Susannah's brother-in-law, Thomas Madison, as chief commissary of one punitive expedition; his own brother-in-law, Colonel Christian, in command of another.[24]

Henry was well aware that such events (considerably magnified in the *Virginia Gazette*s) did not remove the worst threat. By August 17 at Williamsburg and doubtless only a few days later at Scotchtown, it was positively known that General Clinton, after abandoning his attempt against Charleston, had arrived in New York, where an attack was expected in a matter of days. Dixon and Hunter's *Gazette*, with the optimism often used by newspapers to stimulate the public in wartime, reported that the American soldiers were "in high spirits" and ready for them. But how much could be expected of ill-trained militia, outnumbered, and, as it soon developed, outmaneuvered by the British Army? If Henry had retained his commission, he would have been marching northward on the fourteenth with the First Regiment to join the imperiled American Army.

There was some consolation in the turn of events at home. On July 8 General Andrew Lewis drove Lord Dunmore and his small force from Gwinn's Island; the Marylanders shortly afterward chased him from St. George's Island, and the deposed Governor soon departed from America forever. In Virginia, the transition from the British colonial administration was being made with a minimum of difficulty. The liberals were much stronger than under the old regime, but otherwise there was no great change either in form of government or personnel. In Louisa County, for example, of the ten justices then serving under the commonwealth, seven had been members of the local Committee of Safety, and in general they represented the old county hierarchy, composed chiefly of the Johnsons and other Henry supporters.[25]

On August 2, Purdie's *Gazette* took pleasure in informing the public that Henry was so far recovered from "his late severe indisposition" that he was walking out daily at his seat in Hanover. It was hoped that he would soon be able to return to Williamsburg. But he must have had a relapse, for he did not return to the capital for nearly a month and apparently had a later setback. It was during his protracted illness or convalescence that one of the remarkable figures of the Revolution stopped over to see him at his plantation.

About August 20 there appeared at Scotchtown a weatherworn traveler from distant Kentucky, the twenty-three-year-old George Rogers Clark. A powerful six-foot frontiersman, red-haired, with piercing hazel eyes, Clark had already proved his ability to thrive in the wild Ohio River country, hunting, girdling trees, and burning brushwood on land he marked for settlement. Becoming a leader in the new country, Clark was elected a delegate from Kentucky to the Virginia Convention. Delayed in the long journey through the wilderness, he finally reached Botetourt County, only to learn that the Convention had adjourned. But he doggedly pushed on toward Williamsburg, where he hoped to secure vitally needed powder, if not other military assistance, for the isolated Kentucky settlements.

Learning that Henry was at Scotchtown, Clark stopped there and presented the need for the powder, no doubt in moving terms. There were only a few scattered settlements in Kentucky, and they were menaced by greatly superior forces of the savage redskins, now incited by British agents. Henry, as Governor of the state and with a special interest in the western country, needed little persuasion. This was all the more true now that much of Kentucky was claimed by a

[133]

land company which disputed the Virginia claim to the fertile region. Judge Richard Henderson, a Hanover County native who had won office and influence in North Carolina, had sent out Daniel Boone to explore the Kentucky country. Henderson had later made a treaty with the Indians which gave him all the large territory between the Kentucky and Ohio rivers for a land venture, the Transylvania Company. This land was in territory claimed by Virginia under its charter and would directly or indirectly affect Henry's own grants in the western country.

After securing a favorable letter from Henry, Clark proceeded to Williamsburg. There he appeared before the Council and requested five hundred pounds of powder to be sent to Kentucky as an immediate supply. The Council hesitated. Henry was still absent from its sessions; the members were not at all sure of the action of the legislature in regard to Kentucky and the Henderson claim. They would only agree to furnish the powder if Clark would become answerable for it in case the Assembly disapproved of their action. Clark was informed that "they could venture no farther." On this condition an order was handed him upon the keeper of the magazine. But he returned it with a letter stating that he lacked the power to convey the stores at his own expense such a distance through an enemy's country.

"We should have to seek protection else whare which I did not doubt of getting that if a Cuntry was not worth protecting, it is not worth having," Clark wrote in his crude but vigorous style. And, slapping his sword on the table, he hinted that some other country might think Kentucky worth more attention.

Clark started back for the frontier. Some miles out of Williamsburg he was overtaken by a courier with a message from the discomfited Council. They relented. Twenty-five kegs of powder were to be forwarded to Pittsburg at the state's expense. And Kentuckians picking up the kegs there could put them to good use.

George Rogers Clark was a shrewd backwoodsman, adept at bluffing to gain his ends. A patriotic American, with strong Virginia connections, he would hardly have sought to bring Kentucky under a foreign yoke. But the beleaguered Kentuckians, already familiar enough with the horrors of Indian warfare, might well have set up a separate state or come under the control of the Transylvania Company. In an extremity they might have sought aid from Spain, now endeavoring to get a foothold on the east bank of the Mississippi River. Some months would pass, however, before Clark would proceed with his cherished plan to attack the vast British territory to the northward, and Henry would have to decide what men and supplies he could venture with him when they were badly needed elsewhere.[26]

10

Revolution at a Desperate Stage

Luck means the hardships and privations which you have not hesitated to endure; the long nights you have devoted to work.

——MAX O'RELL.

I have still hopes of success. I heard a great man say many months ago, that America would not purchase her freedom at so cheap a rate as was imagined; nor is it proper she should; what costs us a little, we do not value enough.

——Purdie's *Virginia Gazette*, December 13, 1776 [1]

October–November, 1776. Slow but steady British advance across New Jersey.

November 16–20. British capture Fort Washington, Manhattan Island, and Fort Lee, N.J.

December, 1776. Washington's little army—"a receptacle of ragamuffins"—is pushed across the Delaware River into Pennsylvania. To many the American cause seems hopeless. Virginia legislature augments Henry's executive powers.

December 25, 1776–January 3, 1777. Washington recrosses Delaware and defeats British at Trenton and Princeton.

"I HAVE SAID that Mr. Henry could adapt himself to all men in a remarkable manner," his son-in-law, Judge Roane, recalled. "He was also well acquainted with the transactions of life, or, in other words, was a man of business. He could buy or sell a horse or a Negro as well as anybody, and was peculiarly a judge of the value and

[136]

quality of land. He made several excellent bargains for lands in the latter part of his life, owing to his foresight and judgment." [2]

As a war Governor, Henry's business acumen would be tested in transactions involving far more important matters than the "pints" of a horse or the true value of a back-country farm. During Henry's lengthy sick leave, thirty-three-year-old Lieutenant Governor Page attended to the gubernatorial duties in a manner which indicated his growing competence. Yet that slender aristocrat was too lacking in experience and influence to bear the whole burden of the wartime governorship.[3] When Henry returned to the capital, he became engrossed in highly responsible work, testing his abilities not as an orator or political doctrinaire but as a key executive in difficult, at times almost impossible, circumstances. Moreover, his policy decisions —however wise—usually had to be approved by the Council, which in turn was responsible to the Assembly.

With the stresses and strains of wartime, the new Governor would need extraordinary qualities of courage, intelligence, and single-mindedness. And also another quality which many did not even know he possessed: that of the successful conciliator of dissident men and factions. He would have to keep on good terms with individual Councilors and state legislators, and direct local measures of preparedness and defense, while endeavoring to meet the urgent requisitions of the central government and attend to social and minor administrative duties.

For six weeks during Henry's absence, the Council worked under severe handicaps. The military situation was deteriorating, the public business well nigh overwhelming.[4] On Wednesday, September 11, the Board, as it was familiarly termed, wrote Henry a letter urging the necessity of his immediate attendance for the dispatch of public business. By Tuesday, September 17, he was back in Williamsburg and presiding at their meeting.[5]

The reason for the almost peremptory call for Henry's return was doubtless the grave news from the North. As so often in wartime, the *Virginia Gazette*s had tried to sugar-coat it. On September 14, Dixon and Hunter's *Gazette* published the "agreeable intelligence" that George Washington had effected the safe retreat of his army from Long Island, despite "the great numbers" in Howe's army.[6] The hard facts of which Henry and the Council soon got more than an inkling were these: the strategy of the inexperienced Washington had been faulty; only the masterly retreat which he directed and a friendly fog had prevented a portion of his army from being cut off; the Americans, with no fleet or adequate army, at best could hardly hold New York City, at worst would lose the army and with it the principal buttress of their independent government. By September 8, Washington was writing President Hancock of Congress in favor of a defensive war with avoidance of decisive engagements unless "compelled by a necessity,"[7] while Richard Henry Lee in a letter to Henry a week later would offer little more encouragement. Although striving to remain optimistic, Lee had to state that the British design to land their army above the American forces in New York City could be prevented, provided "the large frequent desertions of the militia do not weaken us too much."[8]

Despite his obligation to consult with the Council, Henry was already becoming the key figure in the state government. At times the physical burden alone of his work would be almost more than he could bear. Apart from any spiritual sustenance derived from his deep religious faith, to whom could he turn for private advice and comfort? One of Henry's outstanding characteristics was his strong self-reliance. It is true that he had popularized some ideas of statesmen such as Richard Bland,[9] as he apparently would those of Richard Henry Lee and George Mason. But the great decisions of his life had been usually his own. A rare instance to the contrary was when he "unbosom'd" his plans in the gunpowder incident to his Hanover friend, Parke Goodall. Another was his relationship with Dr. Thomas Hinde. How often during Sarah's period of mental stress must messengers from Scotchtown have ridden up the hill near the South Anna River to summon help!

While Henry was on the friendliest terms with several of his relatives, including William Christian, there is no one except Dr. Thomas Hinde to whom he is known to have unburdened himself of his deep grief and discouragement. An English-born gentleman of about

Henry's age, Dr. Hinde had served as a British army surgeon at the capture of Quebec and later settled near Henry in upper Hanover County, where he became the Henry family physician.

"Henry was poor, and the cries of family afflictions were exceedingly heavy," wrote Dr. Hinde's son. The "family affliction was oppressing him to the Earth (his first companion being then deranged and confined under my father's medical care), yet with all these afflictions he maintained equally with Washington . . . in the cause of his country."

Partly through Henry's influence, Dr. Hinde developed republican sympathies, and he marched, as noted, with Henry in the gunpowder expedition. Later, Dr. Hinde was appointed a surgeon of Virginia troops and appears to have spent some time in the Williamsburg area while inoculating the soldiers. But there is no further record of any association with Henry except that in his last years he helped the doctor to secure a large land grant in Kentucky, where he practiced medicine.[10]

Henry's sister, Anne Christian, soon assisted by her younger sister, Elizabeth, served as hostess at the former Governor's Palace where Henry was now ensconced.[11] We may be sure that his sisters cared properly for Henry's young children and helped him as best they could. In his lonely vigil his thoughts turned more and more to remarriage but, meantime, he had to adjust to a difficult situation.

Soon Henry was settled in the routine which he would follow for his entire wartime governorship. Leaving his commodious quarters in the Palace, he would cross the Palace Green and proceed eastward down Duke of Gloucester Street to the Capitol, his old legislative battleground. Then moving up the stairs in the west wing and turning to the right, he would join the Councilors around the long table in their ornate chamber. The meetings usually began at 10 A.M. and continued for lengthy periods, often on Saturdays and into what normally would have been vacation periods. They were quite informal, and Henry might take time during the proceedings to write letters or issue orders, as instructed by the members, and to have informal conferences.

[139]

Sometimes there would be several dozen items of business attended to daily. They consisted largely of the issuance of warrants—when approved—for disbursements to various military officers and civilians for salaries, supplies, and miscellaneous charges on the state. But there was also the constant stream of more serious problems relating to the dire needs of Washington's army, the protection of the long Virginia coastline and frontier, and threatened invasions of the state.[12]

Meeting with "His Excellency" upon his return to the capital were several Councilors with whom he would be intimately associated. All Tidewater planters, chosen largely because they lived in or convenient to Williamsburg, they were John Page, Dudley Digges, John Blair, Bartholomew Dandridge, and Benjamin Harrison of Brandon. During Henry's wartime governorship, resignations and new elections would not alter the "Board's" somewhat conservative make-up. Whatever the constitutional changes might be in Virginia then and long afterward, old names and faces always seemed to bob up. When Benjamin Harrison of Brandon (a cousin of Congressman Benjamin Harrison from across the James at Berkeley) resigned from the Council on November 6 he was replaced by Nathaniel Harrison of Brandon.[13] Throughout the Revolution, Nelsons, Pages, Harrisons, Randolphs, or their relatives appeared in responsible positions. Even that advanced liberal, Mr. Jefferson, had a Randolph mother.

Henry was fortunate in being supported by these capable plantation masters, vigorous out-of-door men who could stand up under the strain of long hours of work. Whatever the defects of the Virginia oligarchic system, it produced gentlemen who were used to command. And the Councilors, while somewhat conservative, were mostly Henry supporters. Genial, hearty men, usually of good rather than brilliant ability, they would give him invaluable help so long as he adhered to the main purpose of winning a moderate revolution and did not offer too many radical proposals.

On September 15, 1776, about the time Henry started back from Scotchtown, the British General Howe landed his army on Manhattan Island and an opposing militia force ran ingloriously. Washington, after retreating to Harlem Heights, chased back an enemy advance party—a fillip for the discouraged Americans, as he noted in a letter to Governor Henry. Some Virginia troops were distinguished in the skirmish, rifle companies under the command of the quondam Fredericksburg innkeeper, "Joe Gourd" (General George) Weedon, with whom Henry had recently served. Nevertheless, Washington's army remained in the greatest danger, a fact confirmed by Richard Henry Lee in a letter to Henry. The British Army was now reported to number some 24,000 troops, giving it a dangerous superiority, especially in trained men.

Moreover, Lee told Henry that the conduct of the militia had been so "insufferably bad" that the war could not be supported with them: "a powerful army of regular troops must be obtained, or all will be lost." [14] It was a key point for which Henry would find further support in Washington's reply on October 5 to his own letter of September 20. [15]

Soon after his return to Williamsburg, Henry had written the commander in chief seeking his advice on some of his new military problems. Probably he knew that Washington had not favored his own retention in the colonelcy; [16] nevertheless, neither he nor Washington wanted to nurse old differences. After warmly congratulating Henry upon his appointment as Governor and recovery from illness, Washington expressed his satisfaction in establishing the proposed correspondence with him and said he would take pleasure in writing him whenever possible. The retreat from Long Island he defended as an act of "prudence and necessity," and the evacuation of New York City as a necessary consequence. He also had a good word for the Virginia militia, especially from the frontier, in Indian campaigns. But when fighting the British he urged Henry to depend only upon the regular troops with good officers. With the military spirit running high in Virginia, he believed "a very proper choice may be made." [17]

Washington also alluded to another matter with which Henry would be vitally concerned: the requisition by Congress for further regulars from Virginia and other states. With the principal American Army in jeopardy, Congress had on September 16 called upon the states for eighty-eight battalions to serve for the duration of the war. Of these battalions, Virginia and Massachusetts were each to supply fifteen, Pennsylvania twelve, and the other states in smaller numbers according to their white population, down to Georgia and Delaware with one battalion each. Monetary bounties and land grants were to be given to the officers and men who enlisted for the regular service.[18]

In view of the "present naked and defenseless situation" of Virginia as the regular troops were dispatched northward, the Council, with Henry presiding, took further measures to protect the state. With the assistance of the Navy Board established by the Convention, they continued to build or improvise a useful Virginia navy for purposes of defense and trade, even though the small boats could easily be brushed aside by the larger British warships.[19] Twenty-six companies of the militia in the Tidewater and lower Piedmont were ordered to march forthwith to Williamsburg, among them one company each from Hanover and Louisa.[20] Thus many of Henry's old friends and associates were assembled in the city and added variety to the limited social life for which he and his family found opportunity.

We have noted the constitutional provision requiring that major gubernatorial decisions usually be made with the consent of the Council. If Henry did not work well with that aristocratic body, he might easily become a weak Governor, impotent in matters of major policy. The issue was put to the test soon after his election and became settled in his favor before the end of his first one-year term. But two years later he still complained of a limitation on his authority.[21]

On Saturday, October 30, 1776, the Speaker had laid before the House of Delegates a letter from Henry stating that illness prevented him from attending to the duties of his office, and his physician recommended that he retire to the country until he recovered his strength. The disturbed House could only assent, but, after several days' consideration, they passed a bill to provide, if necessary, for his successor. In case of the death, inability, or necessary absence of the Governor and Lieutenant Governor, the eldest Councilor was to perform their executive duties.[22]

Autumn was tingeing the Tidewater woods with its bright hues, but in the works of neither man nor nature was there much to cheer the ailing Governor. On October 12 the dilatory Howe made a further advance against Washington's army, and after another delay of over a month he captured Fort Washington on upper Manhattan Island, taking nearly 3,000 prisoners. It was a serious loss to the small American Army. General Washington, his force still further depleted by desertions and expiration of enlistments, retreated southward to New Jersey.[23]

For two weeks during a critical stage of the war, Henry was absent from the capital. During his earlier illness after he assumed office, when much initial business had to be transacted, young Lieutenant Governor Page had exerted considerable authority. But during Henry's second sick leave, Page and his fellow Councilors did not take a strong hand. During much of Henry's absence, there were only two or three members present at Council sessions, and the items dealt with were hardly world-shaking: issuance of warrants for payment of a messenger and for purchase of military supplies, authorization of a pardon for a Negro slave sentenced to death for felony, and so on. But after Henry's return the amount of business transacted at the meetings increased both in quantity and significance, and by playing a careful hand he could usually guide the major policy.

In early October, Dixon and Hunter's *Gazette*, trying pathetically to put the best face on the war news, had felt constrained finally to report the evacuation of New York City, but the newspaper quoted a letter from Harlem, seven miles distant, as saying New York "never was tenable, and the holding of it obliged us to divide our army into many weak parts." Moreover, as the *Gazette* noted elsewhere, "His Excellency" General Charles Lee (was he becoming reconciled to titles?) had passed above Williamsburg a few days ago "in the greatest haste for New York—to meet General Clinton, and give him another drubbing."[24] Actually, Colonel William Moultrie and other South Carolinians deserved some of the credit for the "drubbing" given Clinton near Charleston. And events would soon prove how much of a drag Lee would be upon Washington's army.

On Monday, November 18, 1776, Henry was back in the capital and in attendance at the meeting of the Council. He had hardly settled again into the interviews, correspondence, long sessions with the Council, and other routine work when he had to deal with another emergency. On the twenty-first the Council was informed that Henry had received an express advising that upwards of one hundred sailing vessels had moved from New York City and were headed southward. Life as a war Governor was a matter of crisis after crisis, of exhausting effort to hurry the plodders, to unify the scattered, to attempt much with little. Henry took measures to meet a possible attack, calling out militia from nearby counties. The House of Delegates, which was now meeting, approved his action in a specific resolution.[25]

Emergency or no emergency, however, under the new governmental setup his time and that of the Council continued to be largely absorbed with petty details. On December 4 and 5 alone, when the Governor and Councilors needed to strain every nerve to help Washington's floundering army, they attended to such momentous matters as paying Miss Moorcock of Williamsburg for a few barrels of corn, a doctor for services to prisoners, and various men for guns, wagonage, provisions, etc.[26] Valuable administrative assistance came from Henry's old associate, the slave trader John Hawkins, who had been appointed Commissary of Provisions,[27] while the Navy Board attended to some of the state's maritime business. But, still overwhelmed with unnecessary routine, on December 6 Henry wrote Edmund Pendleton, Speaker of the current House, that the accounts took up so much time he found it impossible to attend to many matters of consequence to the safety of the state.[28] Two weeks later, the Council appointed an assistant, John Beckley. Even so, Henry still had to devote much of his time to trivial matters when he needed to bend every effort to meet the military crisis.

Howe's great flotilla did not attack Virginia. But in late November Howe stirred himself enough to push southward through New Jersey. Washington, greatly outnumbered, his militia quitting him in droves, could only retreat before the exultant redcoats. Philadelphia was now in danger, the American cause at low ebb. By December 5 even the legislature was sufficiently alarmed to send the Virginia cavalry to reinforce Washington.[29] A few days later Henry was empowered, with the advice of the Council, to prohibit or lay a temporary embargo upon the exportation of beef, pork, and bacon from the Commonwealth.[30] On the thirteenth the public powder on the Eastern Shore was ordered to be moved to the Williamsburg magazine, and a week later the Commissary of Stores was directed to keep a wagon with a good team in readiness to remove the public treasury of the state if found necessary.[31]

On Friday, December 20, graver news stirred the slow-moving Assembly into emergency action. Henry could get no war dispatches from the Philadelphia papers; the printers had fled the city. From private letters, it was learned that a portion of Howe's army was at Burlington, New Jersey, another at Trenton, and still another had crossed the Delaware above Trenton into Pennsylvania. The whole force was between 12,000 and 15,000 men, against which Washington could muster only a pitiful 6,000 troops, including raw militia. General Charles Lee was northward on the flank of the enemy with about 5,000 men, but they also included untrained troops. According to a late report, Philadelphia was being fortified; Congress was preparing to remove to Baltimore.

There would be times when the Tidewater Virginians would seem too complacent, too unconcerned. But perhaps it was just as well that among their other outstanding characteristics was a large blend of gaiety and courage. Despite the omnipresent soldiers on the streets, Williamsburg was trying to preserve some amenities. In Dixon and Hunter's *Gazette* for December 20, 1776, William Dawson was offering a reward for a valued possession left near the capitol: "An elegant ToothPick Case, lately imported from *Paris*, with a Smelling Bottle and Gold Stopper at one End." [32] And there was the acrostic, based on the fictional beauty contest won by Venus, in which a contributor to the *Gazette* sang the praises of Sally, the daughter of Archibald Cary:

> So was the Queen of Sapho's isle
> Among her Graces seen to smile,
> Lovely, divine, genteel in mien,
> Lest other goddess should be Queen:
> Young Paris, had he this maid seen,

"Combin'd o' Graces," would have said,
"Attend this blooming, rival maid,
Respectful to her brighter eyes,
Yield to her worth the golden prize." [33]

This pleasing trivia, however, could not overwhelm the numerous newspaper items relating to the war, such as the advertisement by Hunter's iron factory at Fredericksburg for workmen to help manufacture small arms.

When the news came of the dire danger to Philadelphia and Washington's army, the legislature—fully aroused—met in Committee of the Whole to consider "the state of America." Just how momentous was this secret meeting can be surmised from the extraordinary powers given Henry on the next day, Saturday, December 21. He was "fully authorized and empowered" with the consent of the Council

> from henceforward, until ten days next after the first meeting of the General Assembly, to carry into execution such requisitions as may be made to this Commonwealth by the American Congress for the purpose of encountering or repelling the enemy, to order the three battalions on the pay of this Commonwealth to march, if necessary, to join the continental army, or to the assistance of any of our sister States, to call forth any and such greater military force as they shall judge requisite.

The last provision in particular gave Henry broad powers—always, however, with the consent of the Council. Moreover, he was authorized to raise the troops

> either by embodying and arraying companies or regiments of volunteers, or by raising additional battalions, appointing and commissioning the proper officers, and to direct their operations within this Commonwealth, under the command of the continental generals, or other officers according to their respective ranks, or order them to march to join and act in concert with the continental army, or the troops of any of the United American States, and to provide for their pay, supply of provisions, arms, and other necessaries, at the charge of this Commonwealth, by drawing on the Treasurer for the money which may be necessary from time to time.[34]

After consideration in a surcharged debate, the Assembly, upon an amendment from the Senate, changed the words in the resolution providing "The usual forms of government" to "additional powers to be given to the Governour and Council." [35]

The same day Henry presided at a lengthy session of the Council. In a desperate effort to supply more arms and supplies, Colonel William Aylett, the Commissary, was ordered to use his utmost endeavors to obtain the tents, bedding, arms, accouterments, clothes, wagons, and other supplies needed by the troops raised in the state and purchase them on the best possible terms. He was to purchase and export the produce of Virginia to the foreign points where he could best obtain supplies; to procure salt, wool and cotton cards for use in making cloth, and the necessary ships. [36]

Yet Aylett could relieve Henry of only a small portion of duties. In the early part of December he had also been empowered by the legislature to take measures for the manufacture of cannon within the state; to lay an emergency embargo (with the advice of Council) upon the export of beef, pork, and bacon; and to make—again with the same advice—"Immediate and ample provision for the comfortable subsistence and accommodation" of the Virginia soldiers and sailors. No small order, this was to apply "in sickness as in health." [37]

It was out of this background and particularly the action of the Assembly on December 21 that there developed the persistent story of a plot to make Patrick Henry a dictator, a scheme in which Henry himself, according to the extremist view, was a *particeps criminis*. Thomas Jefferson, neither very accurate nor generous-minded when writing reminiscences of Henry, had much to do with the circulation of the tale. In his *Notes on Virginia*, Jefferson stated that in December, 1776, the American "circumstances being much distressed, it was proposed, in the House of Delegates, to create a Dictator, invested with every power, legislative, executive and judiciary, civil and military, of life and of death, over our persons and over our properties." This statement is repeated in Girardin's continuation of Burk's *History of Virginia*, a volume which Jefferson had the opportunity to correct. Girardin said specifically that several members of the House "proposed and advocated the measure." He also added that it appeared from concurring reports that "this dictatorial scheme produced in the Legislature unusual heat and violence," and the members who favored the measure and those who opposed it walked on opposite sides of the street.[38]

The statement about the dictatorship is also repeated by William Wirt in his early life of Henry. Wirt, a personal friend of Jefferson and obligated to him by numerous ties, had secured Jefferson's correction of his manuscript. While Jefferson did seem loath to make any drastic changes, he was likely to have requested the removal of the statement about the dictatorship if he had found it objectionable.[39] But, probably with Jefferson's approval, Wirt did repeat the statement and added: "That Mr. Henry was thought of for this office has been alleged, and is highly probable; but that the project was suggested by him, or even received his countenance, I have met with no one who will venture to affirm." Wirt repeated the tradition that it was Colonel Archibald Cary, the Speaker of the Senate, who was chiefly responsible for defeating the project. The story continues that the fiery Cary, meeting John Syme, Henry's half brother, in the lobby of the House, accosted him in violent terms.

"I am told your brother wishes to be dictator; tell him from me, that the day of his appointment shall be the day of his death—for he shall feel my dagger in his heart before the sunset of that day," Cary thundered.

John Syme, so the story continues, became greatly agitated and declared that if there was such a proposal, "his brother had no hand in it, for that nothing could be more foreign to him, than to countenance any office which could endanger in the most distant manner the liberties of his country." [40] It was in character for Archibald Cary to make such a violent threat against Henry. A blunt, outspoken little aristocrat, his ill will against Henry dated back to the liberal-conservative struggles in the House of Burgesses and probably to Henry's defense of some Baptist ministers whom Cary was persecuting. There is, however, no adequate proof of Henry's connection with any plan for dictatorship. The charge was consistently denied by Henry and his friends and, while repeated for generations, has never been proved.[41]

A clue to the truth of the story may be found in the parlance of the times. Words used in connection with the debate on the temporary increase of Henry's executive powers may well have been misconstrued by the excitable Cary. The bill increasing Henry's powers came when Washington's army was in the gravest danger. The Assembly, disturbed by the necessity for strong action, changed the bill so as to restrict somewhat the authority given the Governor and Council. Here was a delicate situation likely to explode pent-up emotions. A bill was also passed requesting Congress to give additional authority to George Washington. The situation could easily cause misunderstandings, whatever the basic facts.[42]

On Saturday, December 21, and the following Monday, the Council, with Henry presiding, disposed of a long agenda of military items.[43] Among them was this resolution calling for a committee of the Council to prepare for feeding the militia of the state if they received an early call to active service:

> Pursuant to an Act of the General Assembly directing the purchase of Provisions for ten thousand Men—It is Ordered that Dudley Digges, John Blair, Thomas Walker and David Jameson Esquires or any two of them be a Committee to contract for the purpose.[44]

The Governor and the Council were not timid men. Having taken necessary measures, they held only a short session on Christmas Eve and then adjourned until the twenty-sixth, when Henry was considering with the Council further reports on the desperate plight of the Continental Army. In view of "the critical Situation of American Affairs," the Council resolved that he should issue a proclamation "exhorting and requiring the several County Lieutenants and other Officers of the Militia within this Commonwealth and all other Subjects of the same forthwith, to use their utmost Endeavours to associate Volunteer Companies as the most speedy Method of putting an end to the cruel Ravages of a haughty and inveterate Enemy and to inform his Excellency of their Proceedings therein."[45] Some days

[149]

went by before Henry learned of the victory by Washington's army at Trenton on December 26, which at least temporarily rolled back the British tide. Followed by another successful battle on January 3, 1777, it augured well for the future.

As a general, George Washington had been distinguished more for personal rectitude, for courage and persistence, than for any brilliant strategy. Indeed, while trying to hammer his raw militia into some kind of military discipline, he could not often venture the kind of risky maneuvers that were to be conducted so successfully by a Napoleon or a Robert E. Lee. But leading a force of ill-clad and shivering men across the Delaware River on Christmas night, Washington had surprised and defeated the forces of the drunken Hessian commander at Trenton and a week later another British detachment at Princeton. The cocky Lord Cornwallis to the contrary, the British did not have "the fox in the bag." Washington's twin victories offered encouragement desperately needed by the Americans but included some sad news for the Virginians: the brave General Hugh Mercer had been mortally wounded—that same transplanted Scotsman who had been in competition with Henry for a colonelcy.[46]

On January 9, 1777, Henry, after congratulating Richard Henry Lee on "our well timed success," continued with a realistic discussion of his own efforts to support the cause. The Virginia levies went on "pretty well in many places," but in others they were retarded by the great lack of necessary clothing and blankets. Orders were being issued that very day for the officers and men to be ready to march by companies and parts of companies, and "in a little time they'll go off, but in want of every thing." He continued:

> I observe our people (a few excepted) are firm & not to be shaken. A great number of volunteers may be had. I hope all the enlistments may be filled, but doubt if it can soon be done. I am endeavoring at vigorus [sic] measures. Languor seems to have been diffused thro' the Naval department. However I hope it will mend. The Cherokees are humbled, but I fear hostility about Pittsburg in the spring, & have provided ammunition and provisions in that quarter, & shall be able to muster a formidable militia thereabouts. The powder is not yet sent, but I

wait only for the result of a council of war where to deposit it. Our sea coasts are defenceless almost. Arms & woolens are wanted here most extremely. We are making efforts to secure them.

As for Lee, busy with the anxious Congress in Baltimore, Henry said that he pitied him.

I know how much you detest the spirit of indecision and luke-warmness that has exposed our country to so much peril. Let me tell you that altho' your fatigue is almost too much to bear, yet you must hold out a little longer. Many people pretend they perceive errors in Congress, & some wicked ones are greatly pleased at the hopes of seeing the respect due to that assembly succeeded by contempt.

Henry also sent his affectionate greetings to Col. Frank (Francis Lightfoot) Lee, another Virginia congressman. "Has he forgot me?" Henry asked, and continued, "Indeed he may ask me the same. Tell him that from morning till night I have not a minute from business. I wish it may all do, for there are a thousand things to mend, to begin." [47]

Some days later Washington's army was believed to number about 12,000 men and to be in high spirits.[48] The need for trained troops was still urgent, but especially because of the winter season there was no pressing danger from the cautious Howe. Henry could get a needed respite and took the opportunity to attend to business at Scotchtown before the start of the new planting season.

In addition to his relatives already in the military service, on January 13, 1777, Henry's son John was recommended to Congress as a proper person for first lieutenant. John was to serve in the Virginia regiment of artillery then being raised for the Continental service. Henry could take satisfaction in the service being rendered by his entire family.[49] But there were nagging difficulties of another kind with John Syme. On his brief visits home Henry did not have time to check adequately on such plantation affairs as his account with his half brother. The store and mill account with Syme, which contained records of numerous personal articles bought by the Henry family in the early 1770's, began tapering off with the advent of the war and the Henrys' absence in Williamsburg. In May, 1776, Henry had sold Syme some 390 bushels of wheat for about £50. The following March 15, 1777, shortly after Henry's visit to Scotchtown, he was credited with about £15, apparently for farm produce, and in May for 178 bushels of wheat or £26.14. After 1774 there are only two charges against Henry: £1.5 for bran and about £16 for his blacksmith's account. But the balance which Henry owed was stated to be about £135, and on the outside of the last large sheet in the neat script is this strong exception in Henry's handwriting:

> On this account I observe most gross Errors in Crediting my Crops Wheat every one of which since 1771 to 1778 were deliver'd Col^o Syme at Rocky Mill not one half the Quantity of which are credited. This I do attest.
>
> NB   I am informed it was not Col^o Syme's Custom to give Credit for the Wheat rec^d. Credit for my acco^t is not given.
>
> P. HENRY

Syme's answer to this notation is not available, but Henry would continue to have difficulties with his half brother during periods when he already had troubles enough.[50]

11

Bitter Discouragement but Another

Gubernatorial Term

. . . though they seem to be ignorant of the precision, order
and even of the principles by which large bodies are moved,
yet they possess some of the requisites for making good troops,
such as extreme cunning, great industry in moving ground and
felling of wood, activity and a spirit of enterprise upon any
advantage. Having said thus much, I have no occasion to add
that though it was once the ton [sic] of this army to treat
them in the most contemptible light, they are now become a
formidable enemy. . . .

———From the diary of an officer in Howe's army [1]

March–April, 1777. Another crisis in the Continental Army
organization.

May 27, 1777. Henry re-elected Governor without opposition.

June 14. Congress adopts stars and stripes.

July 6. British General Burgoyne captures Ticonderoga.

September 11, 1777. British victory at Brandywine, followed
on September 26 by their occupation of Philadelphia.

September 15–28 (circa). Henry on his third vacation or
sick leave since early June.

October 9. Henry marries Dorothea Dandridge.

October–December. Henry, besides other pressing duties,
seeks Spanish aid and cooperates with plans of George Rogers
Clark for capture of Kaskaskia.

AFTER HIS unexpected failures at Trenton and Princeton, Howe retired to New York for the remainder of the winter, and Washington hung on his flank at Morristown in the New Jersey highlands. The Americans now had a breathing spell, but despite all the strenuous efforts to recruit Washington's army he had only 4,000 men. The burden that lay on Henry and the Council is indicated by the stream of items dealt with in the *Journal* and his correspondence. Some were petty but time-consuming civil matters; others indicated the endless efforts to recruit enough men and supplies from inadequate resources. On March 10, 1777, Henry was writing the lieutenant of Montgomery County that he could not supply the men requested to protect the isolated Kentucky settlers, and two days later, in a letter to Governor Thomas Johnson of Maryland, he was stressing the importance of cooperation between Maryland and Virginia in defense of the Eastern Shore; Henry was ready to help but he enumerated the difficulties. Not unduly diverted from his main problem, on February 25 he had ordered Colonel Charles Lewis to march his battalion to join Washington without waiting for full companies, and again on March 15 he addressed Lewis, saying that "there was more pressing necessity for your aid than you are acquainted with" or that Henry could, with propriety, explain in detail. Lewis was enjoined to surmount any obstacle and "lose not a Moment less America receive a Wound that may prove mortal."

On Wednesday, March 19, Henry was indisposed and the Council lacked a quorum, so that it adjourned until the next morning at ten o'clock. On that day Henry poured out his feelings in a letter to Richard Henry Lee. Henry was using every possible method to hasten the march of the new troops to join Washington but was sorry to observe a remissness among the Virginia officers over whom he as the Governor could exercise no command "in the opinion of most people." Although the officers did have "a want of necessaries to struggle with," Henry believed that they did not in general exert themselves as they should. Twice he had sent expresses to each colonel, besides repeated notices in the newspapers, but all of this was not enough. The colonels were still remiss. He estimated, however, that two thirds of the Continental recruits had been enlisted, although in broken quotas. The three new Virginia battalions were more than half full. Henry believed that the enlistments of Virginia troops for use in Georgia, permitted against his advice by the Assembly, had greatly hurt the Virginia effort to reinforce Washington. In another letter to Lee a week later he added, "The Terrors of the smallpox, added to the lies of deserters, and the want of necessarys, are fatal objections to the continental Service." [2]

In early April, 1777, George Washington wrote from his New Jersey headquarters to one of his brigadiers, "The campaign is opening, and we have no men for the field." Except for a few hundred troops from New Jersey, Pennsylvania, and Virginia, Washington had to confess that he had not yet received "a Man of the new Continental Levies." [3]

For several days during the middle of April, 1777, as his first term drew toward a close, Henry was absent from the Council sessions. Apparently, he went to Hanover after receiving news of the death of his uncle, the Reverend Patrick Henry. He was the last of Henry's immediate relatives in America on the paternal side and had served as an Episcopal minister for over fifty years. [4]

The British were now evolving one of their major strategic plans of the Revolution. General John ("Gentleman Johnny") Burgoyne, moving downward with an army from Canada, was to combine with another British force moving upward from New York City. Thus New England, a focal point of the Revolution, would be cut off from the middle colonies and the war soon brought to an end. In view of the narrow escape from disaster by Washington's army the previous year, and the inadequate efforts to strengthen his forces, the chances of British success were only too probable. After the Virginia Assembly convened again in May, 1777, the House passed a resolution which called for a reckoning on Henry's work as war Governor during the critical ten months since his appointment. Henry was requested to make a report on his efforts to augment the Continental Army since the last Assembly and also on the troops ordered to be raised for the immediate defense of Virginia.

The end of the one-year term for the chief executive officers of Virginia was now approaching. On Wednesday, May 28, 1777, the House of Delegates proceeded with the nomination of candidates for Governor, members of the Privy Council, and Attorney General. At a joint meeting of the House and Senate the following day, Henry was re-elected Governor, without opposition, a notable tribute to the success of his first term. Henry Lee, a cousin of Richard Henry and "Light-Horse Harry," was a leader in securing his re-election—indicative of Henry's support in the more liberal aristocracy.[5] His conservative opposition was discouraged and diminished; the purported fears of his seeking a dictatorship were now inconsequential. By a coincidence the twenty-ninth was his forty-first birthday and the anniversary of his introduction of the Stamp Act resolves.

Edmund Randolph, the Attorney General, was also re-elected unanimously, and after "extended balloting" John Page, the Lieutenant Governor; Dudley Digges, John Blair, Bartholomew Dandridge, Thomas Walker, Nathaniel Harrison, Thomas Nelson, Jr., and David Jameson were chosen members of the Council. The only new Councilor elected was young Thomas Nelson, Jr., who had already displayed a high patriotism combined with noteworthy civil and military capacity. Nelson, however, declined the office, and Thomas Adams of Richmond was selected in his place.[6]

Life in Virginia's wartime capital did not often lack for variety, and the week of Henry's birthday and re-election as Governor was further enlivened by the visit to Williamsburg of a number of Cherokee chiefs and warriors. In a letter to George Wythe, now Speaker of the House, Henry explained that the Indians had come to the town for the purpose of ratifying a treaty of peace which had been formulated by the Indian commissioners. He tactfully added that if the Assembly wished to give him directions for conducting the negotiations, he would pay "due regard" to them. But, he noted, "The affairs of these Indians will not permit them to remain here but a short Time."[7]

After several conferences with the Indians, Henry wrote on June 3,

1777, a detailed letter of instruction to the Virginia commissioners, including his brother-in-law, Colonel Christian. Henry hoped that the North Carolina commissioners would join with those from Virginia in ratifying the treaty. But if not, the Virginians were to agree with the Indians upon a line between their territory and Virginia "in the best manner you can for the Interest of the Frontier Inhabitants so that you at the same time do strict Justice to the Indians."

There were also various stipulations indicating Henry's knowledge of the Indians and of the Indian lands, which he may have touched upon during his earlier search for his own tracts in the Holston country. He urged that the Indian territory given Virginia should include Cumberland Gap as a needed outlet into Kentucky; if this was not secured, the commissioners should stipulate the right of free travel through this historic passageway. The Indians were to be supplied with the needed bread, also tobacco, ammunition, salt, whisky, and various other goods. The use of whisky—firewater—in the Indian trade was hardly to be commended. But the alternative to placating them was more raiding, scalping, and burning.

In view of Henry's own land speculation in the past and his political position, there were ethical questions which he deemed worthy of explanation. On June 4, 1777, he swore to a deposition respecting the Indian lands in the presence of John Prentis, a recent judge of the Court of Admiralty, and R. Kellon. Soon after his arrival at the First Congress in Philadelphia, Henry had been informed of numerous purchases of Indian land, in all or most of which he was offered shares. But for a number of reasons he refused to accept them: "the enormity of extent" to which the boundaries of the land were carried, the disputes which had arisen regarding the purchases, and the fact that as a member of the Congress and the Convention he thought it improper to be involved in any of the partnerships on which it was probable he might have to serve as a judge. Above all, Henry was determined not to be involved in any Indian purchase whatsoever now that the war would probably lead to the states claiming the right of disposal of the land. He freely discussed the matter with William Byrd III. "The Scheme drop^t," so Henry deposed, and later it was not revived.[8]

An idea of the pressures that were now being put upon Henry is conveyed by his further statement that he received a great number of messages from the Richard Henderson Company, inviting him to be a partner. Henderson and his partner, Allen Jones, a brother of the North Carolina political leader, Willie Jones, both applied to Henry to join in their plan. But Henry said he uniformly refused and "plainly Declared" his "Strongest Disapprobation of their whole proceedings . . . the People of Virginia had a right to the back Country, derived from their Charter & the Blood and Treasure they Expended on that account.

"The deponent says that he is not now nor ever has been Concern'd directly or indirectly in any Indian Purchase of Lands & that he knoweth no thing of Mr Hendersons Contract," Henry continued. He also knew of no application by Byrd or his associates to the legislature or Crown for purchase of the Cherokee lands. The only proposal to the Indians he knew of was to learn if they would treat on the subject, and "further saith not," Henry concluded in the kind of archaic legal phraseology which Thomas Jefferson was now striving to change.[9]

It appears that Henry leaned over backwards to avoid any conduct prejudicial to his official position.

Every few days Henry was given assignments taxing his energy and ability. On June 3, 1777, the House requested him, with the advice of the Council, to employ proper persons to purchase "at a generous price" all the salt imported into Virginia in the next twelve months and to be stored and distributed among the inhabitants as needed. The next day Henry and the Council were requested to lay before the House an estimate of the probable expense of the Virginia army during the ensuing year, a difficult order with which they complied in seven days.[10]

After all the crises of the past year, it was fortunate for Henry that there was a lull in the British military movements during the summer of 1777 insofar as they affected Virginia. In June, Burgoyne did march southward from Canada with a formidable army, but he was slowed down by natural obstacles and American delaying tactics, and a detachment of his army sent to Bennington, Vermont, to capture supplies and pacify the countryside was badly defeated. Not until July 30 did Burgoyne reach the Hudson River at Fort Edward, and in September he was still far from the projected meeting with Howe. Moreover, Howe had not even learned until mid-August that he was supposed to cooperate with Burgoyne, and most of Howe's force was then in Chesapeake Bay. Moving down the Bay, the British again alarmed the Virginians and Marylanders, but for them the summer was relatively quiet as compared with the campaigns of the previous year.

On Saturday, June 28, 1777, the Assembly adjourned after an inconsequential session of about seven weeks. Feeling somewhat secure, the Senate on June 12 had agreed to resolutions of the House directing the treasurer to procure proper robes for the Speaker and gowns for the clerks of the two Houses. There was also to be a mace for the use of the Senate, and each of its doorkeepers was to be furnished with "a decent suit of clothes." [11]

On June 21, John Page had presided at a meeting of the Council, and he continued to do so until July 2, when Henry was back in his seat and his oath of office for his new term was administered by the "first four" members of the new Council. Henry had been taking a leave in Hanover to attend to some "private matters." It was during this vacation, according to his grandson, that he "addressed" (proposed marriage to) Miss Dorothea (Dolly) Dandridge, daughter of his neighbor and old friend, Colonel West Dandridge. A while earlier Henry might have met opposition from another suitor—a Scotsman in his late twenties with unusual charm for women despite his obscure birth and somewhat stormy past—for the lively young girl. But John Paul Jones, future naval hero, soon ended his brief connection with upper Hanover. To Colonel Dandridge, with his social prestige and pecuniary embarrassments, surely Governor Henry was the better match, and probably the dutiful daughter now needed little or no persuading. A letter from Henry's brother-in-law, Colonel Christian, on August 12, 1777, referred to the marriage to Dolly as soon to occur. [12]

During the remainder of the hot summer, in addition to the duties already outlined, there were all the conferences, inspections, receptions, or other entertainments expected of the chief executive. Although he wasted little time on unessentials, he carried on certain correspondence which he might have turned over to John Page. Some administrative details, however, which would now be delegated by a state Governor, were part of Henry's constitutional duties. Among lesser items, on August 8 he wrote a lengthy letter to the Virginia delegates in Congress, taking vigorous exception to the meddling of Lieutenant Colonel Edward Carrington with promotions in the Virginia artillery regiment.[13]

On about August 9 Henry was again in Hanover, probably strengthening the plans for his marriage to Dolly Dandridge. In his absence, August 15, the Council, with John Page presiding, was informed that a large British fleet was off the Virginia coast. In the emergency, the Council asserted itself to call out some militia from the eastern and lower Piedmont counties, with other troops to be held in readiness. But the Council was at pains to send word to Henry, and he was back at its session the following Monday.[14] By then it was obvious that the Governor had become the dominant figure at the Council sessions. There was no member to oppose him seriously so long as he did not offer measures to undermine the settled policy.

When Henry was absent from one winter session of the Council early the next year, the *Council Journal* contained this startling information:

Saturday, February 14, 1778

Present

Dudley Digges Esquire	Lieutenant Governor John Page Jr.
John Blair	David Jameson &
Nathaniel Harrison	James Madison jr.
	esquires

The Lieutenant Governor with the Advice of the Council, recommends it to the Navy Board to Station one Galley at New Port News, it being judged Necessary for the protection of James River.

Present John Page Esqr.

Adjourned til Monday 10 Oclock.

Not a great deal more was done in Henry's absence at a number of later cabinet meetings, for instance in June and September, 1778.

These were somewhat extreme instances, but in general, during Henry's terms as war Governor, the Council remained a patriotic, hard-working body, compliant—as was the Assembly—with his firm yet tactful leadership.

But to return to the reported enemy invasion of the previous August, 1777, state business then became paramount. No more trysts now for the bride-to-be! Back in the capital by August 18, Henry soon found that the British troops carried through the Capes were landed in Maryland. But there was enough business to keep him occupied for another month.

On Saturday, September 13, the Council met for a virtually full session, with the first recorded item of business that of two convicted Negroes. Henry, as usual in such matters, asked the advice of the Council in the case of Will and Lewis, two Negro slaves under sentence of death for murder and recommended to the Governor by the Stafford court as proper objects of mercy. The Council was informed that the dead Negro had been killed "in the course of a mutual fighting" and after giving "provocation of the highest nature." It advised Henry to extend clemency to the slaves, and he ordered pardons to be issued.[15]

New troubles were always brewing, and a letter arrived from General Nelson stating that he had the strongest reason to expect an attack upon Yorktown from several ships then lying at the nearby mouth of the river. The sorely tried Council ordered Henry to postpone his order for disbanding the militia except for three battalions, and, as in many such instances, he complied the same day.[16]

Alarms and alarms, crises and crises. Back in Williamsburg on Monday, September 29, 1777, Henry was confronted by complaints about the excessive zeal of the military guard in the capital. Yet the Council, while putting some restraint on the ill-treated soldiers, still ordered the streets to be guarded from 10 P.M. to reveille. Disorderly persons were locked up and, reminiscent of Lord Dunmore's threatened emancipation of slaves, no Negroes or other servants were permitted to pass the patrols except on errands for their masters or mistresses.

On Tuesday, October 7, Henry was present for what was apparently a brief session of the Council. The next day John Page presided; Henry did not return to the meetings until Wednesday, October 15.

Nature has its ways of compensating for death and destruction. The war does not appear to have caused any great slackening in the business of marriage and procreation in Virginia. Young people, and indeed many older ones, were uncertain of the future and believed it best to make hay while the sun shone. From early October, 1777, to early April, 1778, William Pollard, Clerk of Hanover County, collected £30 and an unexplained one pence in money from the tax on marriage licenses at the stipulated rate of £2 per couple. This was not a poor record, considering the small population of the county. On October 6, 1777, Pollard was paid £2 as license tax for the marriage of one couple; then two days later, there was this entry:

8th   To His Excellency Patrick Henry Esqr.
Miss Dorothea Dandridge,   £2.-.- [17]

Since the Declaration of Independence, the Anglican Church had remained the established church in Virginia, and in any event Patrick and Dolly as Episcopalians would have wanted to be married by a minister of their denomination. In accordance with the colonial practice, the vestry for St. Paul's Parish in lower Hanover had on June 10, 1777, imposed the usual levy of sixteen thousand pounds of tobacco for the salary of the Reverend Patrick Henry the past year. But this was by way of post-mortem compensation, Henry's uncle having departed this world.[18] Moreover, the Reverend Mr. Douglas, who had performed a number of churchly ministrations for the Henry and Dandridge family connections, is described by an authority as a "howling Tory," a brother of the cloth who "refused to take the oath of allegiance to the Commonwealth of Virginia, and threw the dust of Goochland County to the winds." [19] By the process of elimination, it seems likely, therefore, that the ceremony was performed by the Reverend Robert Barrett of St. Martin's Parish, whom Patrick and

Dolly had often heard preach at that simple old brick building, the still surviving Fork Church.[20]

Henry could not spare much time from his official duties. No fee had to be paid for a marriage license provided there was publication of the banns, but the required announcement of the proposed wedding in church on three successive Sundays [21] was now inconvenient for Patrick and Dolly. In return for the fee of £2, the law permitted a marriage to be performed at the convenience of the contracting parties.[22] Since Henry was present at the Council meeting on October 7 and got his license in Hanover on October 8, it might be argued that he did some phenomenal traveling even for an eager bridegroom. And yet by leaving Williamsburg on the morning of the seventh he could have reached the clerk's office some sixty-odd miles distant in lower Hanover the next afternoon, October 8 (that is, if he obtained the license in person). Probably, after picking it up en route he was married on October 9 to the vivacious young girl.[23]

Considering the bad Virginia roads, Henry had ridden hard to cover the nearly one hundred miles from Williamsburg to upper Hanover in two days. The Governor, now forty-one, may have been taking no chances with the vagaries of a bride not much older than his eldest daughter. Possibly he recalled the lines from Vergil: "Varium et mutabile semper femina est." Young maids were often skittish in matters of love. But the women with whom he had been thrown most closely, his mother, sisters, even his first wife, were not creatures of "whim and caprice." And it was the eighteenth century: if Dolly still cherished any errant thoughts of young John Paul Jones or other suitors, there remained hard practicality, with the parental discipline, to keep her in line. And had not the great Mr. Henry reportedly talked to her of liberty? [24]

The *Virginia Gazette*s were still running notices of prominent marriages in the state, but curiously, no mention was made of the Governor's marriage.

In France, John Paul Jones, struggling with the vexations and disappointments of a captain in the new American Navy, received a letter from a Virginia friend with some bad news. "You tell me you are under some expectation of purchasing a Virginia estate, but some more agreeable idea will I fear call you off and deprive us of you, Miss Dandridge is no more, that is, she a few months ago gave herself into the arms of Patrick Henry.[25] It is likely, however, that Jones, who was to know great fame and many loves, soon found consolation.

By October 15 Henry was back in Williamsburg and present at the morning session of the Council.[26] The wedding arrangements, travel and all, had taken only a week. And yet there must have been some of the features associated with such Virginia weddings: the broad toasts, perhaps somewhat toned down for the marriage of a Governor, the mountains of food, the lavish supply of drinks for guests and family slaves, the gathering of the family clans—the Henry-Winston connection from Hanover, Louisa, and Fluvanna; the Dandridges and their aristocratic kinfolk from Hanover, Goochland, and New Kent. Representatives of approving (and calculating?) officialdom would certainly have attended if time permitted; possibly a few guests, with powdered hair and knee pants or military regalia, from as far away as Williamsburg.

Marriage to Dolly inevitably caused difficulties, even though young girls were more subservient to their husbands than in a later day. The problem of equable relations among the children of the two Henry wives would never be settled altogether satisfactorily. And there was the immediate question of how successfully the youthful Dolly would handle the triple duties of wife, stepmother, and hostess at the Palace. Certainly, she could relieve the harassed Henry of many family cares, while she bid fair to strengthen his social and political influence.

The descendant of a brother of a Virginia Governor, Lord Delaware, and of an Acting Governor, Alexander Spotswood, and the daughter of Martha Washington's first cousin, Dolly brought Henry powerful connections with the lowland aristocracy.[27] Moreover, the Dandridges, while conservative in some respects, were no hidebound Tories. With the exception of one contrary-minded aunt, now estranged from Dolly's mother, they were a bulwark for the Revolutionary cause. In a letter the next June, Dolly's mother spoke of "our sister" Mrs. Bernard Moore of King William County, above Richmond, as staying at home and enjoying her own thoughts. "I wish she could alter them," Mrs. Dandridge sadly continued. "I think she must be unhappy to differ in sentiment with almost all the country." Although the two sisters lived only some fifty miles apart, Mrs. Dandridge wrote she had not seen Mrs. Moore "these six years." [28]

Mrs. Moore stood out like a sore thumb in a family of strong American sympathies. Bartholomew Dandridge, George Washington's brother-in-law, was a staunch supporter of Henry in the Council; Dolly's uncle (and Henry's protégé), Alexander Spotswood Dandridge, would marry a daughter of General Stephen; the Dandridge family as a whole prided themselves on Martha Dandridge Custis' marriage to George Washington. Thus Henry's marriage would strengthen him with aristocratic elements favorable to the Revolution. But would the alliance be a force pushing him toward conservatism in other respects, both now and later? A number of such questions could not be answered for years and then not always categorically.

In addition to his personal charm and prestige, Henry brought to the marriage his large landed properties, including his Scotchtown estate, two farms in Botetourt County, and ten thousand acres of undeveloped land in Kentucky. He had thirty slaves, to which were now added twelve as his wife's marriage portion.[29] The couple, endowed with enough worldly goods to help compensate for any lack in the Governor's salary and allowances, established themselves at the Palace together with Henry's unmarried children by Sarah Shelton. Henry, his private life on a happier basis, could return with fresh zeal to his duties as war Governor.

12

A More Hopeful Interlude

This Army—it is Sir the Bullwork of America and should be
nursed and cherished as the salvator of her Liberties. The
Troops that compose it are not more than mortal, and cannot
work Maricles.——GENERAL GEORGE WEEDON [1]

September 11, 1777. British defeat Americans at Brandywine
and,

September 26, occupy Philadelphia.

October 17, 1777. Surrender of Burgoyne's British army at
Saratoga, N.Y.

BACK AT THE CAPITAL, Henry found a letter of October 8,
from Richard Henry Lee at York, Pennsylvania, bearing some important news. At the little market town whither Congress had fled
from the enveloping British, the members were swamped in a sea of
difficulties, but the overworked Lee did find time to send Henry
another full and optimistic report, which the Governor could round
out from other sources.

On September 11 Washington's little army, outnumbered and outmaneuvered, had been defeated at Brandywine, near Philadelphia,
and two weeks later the British had occupied the city. Henry took
what comfort he could from Lee's good report of the Virginia troops
in the battle.[2] Next, at Germantown on October 4, the Americans
bravely assaulted the British, only to have a fog lead them into con-

[166]

fusion and delay, followed by retreat. Lee, while giving Henry details of the victory snatched from their grasp, declared that the army was in high spirits and "satisfied they can beat the enemy." [3]

The news of the repulse at Germantown had reached Henry about the time of his return from his brief honeymoon. Then, as crisp October days spelled the end of the malaria season, the month was crowned with news of a great victory, perhaps with decisive implications. On October 31, Dixon and Hunter's *Virginia Gazette* gave an authentic account, just arrived, of the surrender at Saratoga, New York, of the British army of General Burgoyne, with over 5,000 officers and men. Beginning at 3 P.M. that afternoon and continuing into the night, there was a "feu de joy" in Williamsburg with a military parade, artillery salutes, "3 Huzzas from all present," bell-ringing, and illuminations, all no less happy in that Henry had ordered a gill of rum to be issued each soldier in token of his "hearty congratulations."

Not forgetting in the wild rejoicing the obligations of a Christian people, Henry also issued a proclamation calling for a day of Thanksgiving in the Virginia churches for the great victory. While expressing "pious joy" over the surrender, Virginians should not in their own strength be led to forget the hand of Heaven whose assistance they had so often implored in times of distress.[4] Henry had good cause to be realistic: he knew the weakness of Washington's army and the power of the aroused British. On the following February 6, 1778, France did sign a treaty of alliance with the fledgling United States, and there were other hopeful events. But for Henry they were mostly overshadowed by another personal tragedy, by some irksome executive problems, and by depressing news from Washington's army, which would barely survive the winter at Valley Forge.

Now in his early twenties, Henry's son, John, had been promoted to captain in the American Army and, so we are told, had particularly distinguished himself at Saratoga. At the close of the action, however, he walked over the battlefield, occasionally pausing to recognize those among "the fallen" whom he knew. Then he drew his sword from its scabbard and, snapping it into pieces, dashed it on the ground and went "raving mad."

To add poignancy to the story, Henry was said to have learned that John had been in love with Dorothea Dandridge when she married his father. Patrick was "terribly upset," so we are informed by the historian, Charles Campbell. He said that he had the facts from "an undisputed family source," and there is some confirmation from other quarters.

Whatever the exact details, the reticent George Washington did not dwell upon them in his official correspondence. In a letter to Henry of September 13, 1778, from the army headquarters at White Plains, Washington wrote:

> "I have been honoured with yours of the 21st Augt inclosing a letter for Capt Henry, whose ill state of Health obliged him to quit the service about three months past. I therefore return you the letter." [5]

When Henry returned to Williamsburg on October 15, 1778, he found a number of letters and papers concerning some twenty Pennsylvanians, nearly all Quakers, who had recently been incarcerated at Winchester, Virginia. Congress, exasperated by the neutralist or Tory sympathies of the Quakers, had ordered them confined in Virginia at a safe distance from the British Army. The problem was particularly awkward for Henry because of his earlier relationship with the Friends, not only in Virginia but Philadelphia. His conscience had already been tried through gentle prodding on the slavery issue by a member of that sect.[6] On March 28, 1777, the Quaker, Robert Pleasants, appealed to Henry again on the same general issue. Pleasants, writing from Curles (Neck), Virginia, said that he and some of the Friends had been induced to embrace the cause at "the present favourable juncture, when the representatives of the people have Nobly declared All men equally free." While praising the new Virginia Declaration of Rights, Pleasants advanced a proposal for gradual emancipation of the slaves. Henry could not have been happy with the Quaker's mild importunity: the Declaration was "indeed Noble, and I can but wish and hope, thy great abilities & interest may be exerted toward a full & clear explanation and confirmation thereof." [7] Henry's answer is not known.

Besides Quakers such as Pleasants, there were humane masters who were disturbed by the cruelties of the slavery system. For instance, Nelson Berkeley, Henry's Hanover neighbor, when advertising some valuable slaves for sale that December, specified that they were to be disposed of only "in Families." [8] Yet Henry knew that there was then no possible hope of carrying an antislavery measure through the legislature.

The Philadelphia Quakers were characterized by an industry and progressivism, a thrift and piety, that made them leaders in the development of Pennsylvania. The suffering which the Friends endured in the Revolution because of their refusal to bear arms or pay war taxes deserves genuine sympathy. Yet some Pennsylvania Quakers were more than neutral observers of the desperate war; they were active British sympathizers. When confiding to her diary that she wanted Philadelphia to be captured by Howe's army, Sarah Fisher, a well-connected Quaker, was expressing the not-always-secret wish of numerous Friends. When would they be freed from the "violent people [the Whigs]?" she wrote. And she declared that George III was "the best of kings." [9] There was some fear that the alleged treasonable proclivities of the Philadelphia Quakers had been extended to Virginia. But when the obdurate Friends were confined in Winchester, Henry, with the advice of the Council, used his influence to secure humane treatment for them. [10]

War, like politics, makes strange bedfellows. Due to the wartime exigency, Henry now found himself striving to get into the good graces of the late American enemy, Spain, with her still potent colonial empire. Under the benevolent despot, Charles III (1759–1788), and his able ministers, Spain was temporarily arresting her decline. She was curbing some of her benighted influences, strengthening her trade, and building a formidable navy; indeed, reaching "the highest point" she had attained since the sixteenth century. [11]

Henry could have been only imperfectly informed of conditions in the Hispanic empire, even in her North American possessions. But he and the Council did envisage in Spain a potential ally. In early October, 1777, he took steps as the Council instructed to arrange for the speedy shipment of Spanish goods being held for Virginia in New Orleans, and, more important, he opened negotiations looking toward a Spanish alliance. In flattering letters to the Governors of Cuba and New Orleans, replete with references to "the grandeur of the Spanish nation" and its "Honour, Spirit and Generosity," Henry offered a proposal for a definite *quid pro quo*—livestock, flour, staves, fur, hemp, and, it appears, military cooperation in return for Spanish aid.[12] He even suggested the return to Spain of their former Florida territory acquired by the British in 1763.

Once the Spanish were in possession of Pensacola and St. Augustine, Henry argued, they could enjoy a great part of the trade with the American states. And if the Governor of New Orleans thought it worth the attention of the Spanish court to cultivate a correspondence with the United States via the Mississippi River, they would establish a post at the mouth of the Ohio to facilitate the necessary intercourse. Already a Virginia agent had been told to apply for some of the stores which Henry understood the Spanish had lodged there for the American use, and a boat had been ordered down the Mississippi for the remainder of the stores at New Orleans.[13]

Henry was pursuing a policy well calculated to secure the help of the more progressive Spanish officials. Like her former Bourbon ally, France, Spain was still smarting from her defeats by the British in the Seven Years' War and earlier conflicts and was anxious to avenge herself insofar as this could be done without undue risk. If the United States won independence, the Spanish felt that they offered less of a threat to her than would a victorious Great Britain. A letter written in May, 1776, by General Charles Lee, on behalf of the Virginia Committee of Safety,[14] had led by July of the next year to the deposit at New Orleans—subject to Virginia orders—of 2,000 barrels of gunpowder, considerable lead, and clothing.[15]

Now, in January, 1778, Henry asked the New Orleans Governor, the energetic young Don Bernardo de Galvez, for a loan of some 150,000 pistoles. What compensation could Virginia give, Henry asked rhetorically? "The thanks of this free and independent country, trade in one or all of its rich products, and the friendship of its brave inhabitants." This letter was written just about the time George Rogers Clark started his expedition to conquer British territory in the

Northwest, including the site of a proposed fort to facilitate the Spanish trade. Unfortunately, Galvez lacked the money to make the loan because of funds already supplied Oliver Pollock, a Virginia agent in New Orleans, but the Louisiana Governor did submit Henry's proposal to his government.[16]

On the whole, Spain proved more reluctant than France "to embrace the cause of rebellion against Monarchy"[17] despite the efforts of American emissaries at Madrid. But she did give the Americans some significant help with money and supplies, then entered the war on the side of the United States and France. During 1776–1779, Spanish subsidies to the Americans amounted to some $397,230, and loans during 1778–1782 to $248,098. Of these loans nearly a third came through Pollock and Willing, American agents in New Orleans. Moreover, in late 1778 and early 1779, the capable Pollock sent shipments of powder and other supplies to George Rogers Clark. Although the total amount of money and supplies seems small, it was of great importance to the American military expeditions in the West.[18]

Besides Spain, America had another curious ally in the Revolution —France, also her late enemy in the Seven Years' War. Surreptitious French munitions sent through the playwright Beaumarchais had provided indispensable help for Washington's army in some of his early campaigns, and a leading diplomatic historian, Samuel F. Bemis, has doubted if Saratoga could have been won without this aid.[19] Virginia, while seeking loans from Spain on the state account, could hardly overlook the far richer source offered by France. On March 3, 1778, Henry sought the aid of Benjamin Franklin, then the most influential American envoy in France, in behalf of a Virginia agent, Captain Lemaire, sent to obtain some vitally needed military articles.

After all the "signal services" which Franklin had rendered Virginia "in common with America," Henry asked pardon for seeking one more favor of him. Large quantities of Virginia tobacco were already on board vessels bound to Nantes and other French ports and could now serve to open commerce with France. Would Franklin assist with his influence in the application of efforts to obtain the arms and stores, "the want of which may be fatal to Virginia"?

Normally, the tobacco would be shipped out of Chesapeake Bay, but the Bay was now guarded by an English 64-gun ship and four 36-gun frigates, which "lord it here at present." To oppose them Virginia had only some galleys. He did not expect to cope with the British power successfully without the help of France, whose "interposition" would secure the Virginia trade.[20]

Captain Lemaire, with Franklin's help, did accomplish some useful work, but he was handicapped by the interference of Arthur Lee, one of the American emissaries to France. It was fortunate that Henry appointed another state agent in a more favorable position to work with Lee—namely, Lee's brother, William. William Lee, who had been living in England, where he was made an alderman of London, was appointed commercial agent of the United States in France, Prussia, and Austria.[21] About December 1, 1777, Henry, with the advice of Council, also commissioned Lee a Virginia agent, and the following April he sent Lee the authority to borrow two million livres in France to be laid out in military stores. Lee, with the help of his brother Arthur, secured from the French Ministry cannon, mortars, balls, bombs, and so forth, to the amount of £219,489. Also, Arthur Lee advanced the money for the purchase of swords, pickaxes, and hatchets, which with Lemaire's and other expenses amounted to about £45,000, while William Lee also made a contract at Nantes for several thousand stands of arms and other articles.[22] Arrangements were made to ship the military matériel to Virginia, and despite the British blockade it arrived in at least very helpful quantity.

In February, 1778, France entered the war, followed the next year by Spain with her powerful fleet. When Holland also joined the allies, Great Britain was opposed by three of the leading maritime nations. She was forced to retain considerable military and naval forces in Europe which otherwise would have been sent to America. Thus were fulfilled almost to the letter Henry's predictions to Colonel Overton on the eve of the war: that France, then Spain and Holland, would join with America once they were satisfied of her "serious opposition" to Britain.[23]

Besides the Spanish and French negotiations in late 1777 and early 1778, Henry also gave measured support for that saga of frontier courage and endurance, the George Rogers Clark expedition to the Northwest Territory.

It had now been over a year since young Clark, first securing the assistance of Henry at Scotchtown, had obtained from the Council powder for the beleaguered Kentucky settlements. Clark had remained in Williamsburg long enough to help assure that the Kentucky lands of the Transylvania Company would be incorporated into Virginia. Then, returning to Kentucky, he had endured the hazards of the year 1777, the Bloody Year when life in the lonely settlements was a long chronicle of murder, torture, and rapine. With the white settlers constantly encroaching on their hunting grounds, it was almost inevitable that the Indians would break the fragile peace after Point Pleasant and join the British in the new war. A final straw was the unprovoked murder by renegade whites of the eloquent Chief Cornstalk and some companions. Henry tried unsuccessfully to have the culprits punished.[24]

On December 10, 1777, after another long journey from Kentucky, Clark proposed to Henry and the Council an expedition to what Clark in his diary termed the "FC" (French Country). After the cession of the Old Northwest by the French fourteen years earlier, the British had thinly garrisoned several forts in the area, including their base at Detroit. The scattered white people of the country were chiefly French habitants, happy-go-lucky and improvident and never deeply beholden to the Union Jack. Now seeking to invade their wild country, Clark carefully developed his case, noting in Williamsburg everything he saw or heard which would lead him "to the knowledge of the disposition of those in power."[25]

Henry had already been somewhat prepared for the interview with Clark. In a letter to the Governor Clark gave an account of the situation in the Illinois country, based on the accurate report of two spies, and his plan of action against "Kuskuskies" (Kaskaskia). From Kaskaskia as a center, Clark wrote, the British were able to maintain control of the Indian tribes and dispatch them against the Kentucky settlements. Also, from this focal point the redcoats could control the navigation of both the Mississippi and the Ohio rivers and prevent the Americans from obtaining Spanish goods for use in the Indian trade.

"[We must] either take the town . . . or in less than a twelve-month send an army against the Indians on Wabash, which will cost ten times as much and not be of half the service," Clark urged.[26]

Henry, hard pressed to meet the demands of Washington's army and other commitments, had some misgivings even after the persuasive Clark presented his arguments in person. At first Clark thought Henry was very "fond" of his plan; then Henry hesitated. To detach a party for so great a distance might lead to service of "great utility" yet appeared to be "Daring Hazardous" (so Clark reported Henry's reasoning). Nothing but secrecy would give "sucksess" to the expedition. It would be dangerous to lay the matter before the Assembly, since it would thus be soon known throughout the frontier. Probably through the capture of one of Clark's men it would reach the Indians.

Henry and the Council moved only after due deliberation. An inquiry was made into the proposed plan of operations. There was particular concern over Clark's statement that in case of misfortune he intended to cross the Mississippi into Spanish territory. Thomas Jefferson, George Mason, and George Wythe were consulted and approved the plan. As an encouragement to those who would engage in Clark's service, a paper was signed whereby these gentlemen proposed to use their influence to secure from the Assembly three hundred acres of land for each venturer—in case of success.[27]

Clark's proposed expedition is the only subject treated in the *Council Journal* on January 2, 1778. Climbing the familiar stairs in the capitol, Henry met with an almost full array of Councilors: John Page, Dudley Digges, John Blair, Nathaniel Harrison, and David Jameson. He told them he had had some conversation with several gentlemen who were well acquainted with the western frontier of Virginia and the situation at Kaskaskia. Although there were many cannon there and a considerable number of military stores, he was informed that the post was then held by "a very weak Garrison." This induced him to believe that an expedition against the town might be successful, but he wished the advice of the Council.[28]

The Council thereupon advised Henry to launch the expedition with as little delay and "as much Secrecy as possible." He was to issue a treasury warrant to Clark for £1,200, for which he was to give bond and security. This slender amount, in depreciated currency, was all that the Council would risk from the impoverished Virginia treasury, and it was publicly earmarked for the defense of Kentucky.[29]

Henry was to draw up two sets of instructions for Colonel Clark. One set, which was intended for the public (including any British spies), authorized Clark to "Proceed to Kentucky and there to obey such orders" as Henry would give him. The second and much lengthier letter contained secret instructions to capture Kaskaskia—this with Henry's general orders for carrying out the difficult mission.[30]

In light of the difficulties which Clark later encountered, Henry has been criticized for making the secret instructions too general.[31] But Clark himself states, on the basis of his conversation with Henry, that the Governor did not wish "implicit attention" to his instructions to prevent Clark from accomplishing "anything that would manifestly attend to the good of the public." [32]

Clark was to proceed with all convenient speed to raise seven companies of fifty men each, which, properly armed, were to attack "Kaskasky." He was to apply to the commanding officer at Fort Pitt for boats to transport the expedition down the Ohio, and "during the whole transaction" he was to "take a special Care to keep the True destination" of his force secret. "The success of the expedition depended upon this," Henry enjoined.

In further instructions Henry urged Clark to show humanity to enemy subjects falling in his hands. If the white inhabitants of the Kaskaskia neighborhood gave undoubted evidence of their attachment to Virginia, they were to be treated as fellow citizens. Clark was to make every effort to see that their commerce was beneficial, "the fairest prospects being open" for trade with France and Spain. Henry then spoke of a contemplated post near the mouth of the Ohio, and he told Clark to apply to General Hand, in command at Pittsburg, for the necessary powder and lead. "If he cant supply it, the person who has that which Captain Lynn brought from Orleans can." [33]

That same day Henry got off a short letter to young General Hand, emphasizing Henry's interest in further Spanish aid and the relationship thereto of the Clark expedition. "A good understanding with New Orleans" was one of "the consequential benefits" if Clark's expedition were successful. Henry's letter seeking aid from the Spanish Governor was to be delivered by a Virginia agent, Colonel David Rogers,[34] who was to bring back from Louisiana some goods for Virginia which Henry was expecting, as well as answers to Henry's overtures. Alas, Rogers was killed by the Indians and Clark's men faced grave danger of a like fate from redcoats as well as roving savages.[35]

But nothing could daunt the backwoodsman. Indeed, Clark was so sure of success that he entered into a partnership with Henry for a tract of land in the Illinois country.[36] No one is positively known to have been informed that after taking Kaskaskia Clark planned to move against the main British base in the Northwest at Detroit, but this was permitted in Henry's instructions to him.[37]

Largely because of recruiting difficulties, it was not until May 12, 1778, that Clark was able to set out from Redstone on the Monongahela. After receiving liberal assistance from General Hand, doubtless including some Spanish supplies from New Orleans, Clark's little flotilla moved slowly down the Ohio, watching anxiously for Indian war parties on its lonely shores. Near the end of the month they reached the falls of the river, at the site of Louisville. They now seem to have lost touch with Governor Henry until the next year. Meantime, he had plenty of troubles to occupy him.[38]

13

Still More Crises

It snows—I'm Sick—eat nothing—No Whiskey—No Forage
—Lord—Lord—Lord—" ——from diary of Dr. Albigence
Waldo, written with "Numb fingers" on December 12, 1777 [1]

At bottom, the issue was not that of supplanting Washington
but that of supplying him. . . ."
——DOUGLAS SOUTHALL FREEMAN [2]

Winter, 1777–1778. Washington's army at Valley Forge, Pa.
Conway Cabal; Henry's staunch support of Washington.

May 29, 1778. Henry elected Governor for a third term.

B Y LATE DECEMBER, 1777, George Washington had gone into
uneasy winter quarters at Valley Forge, Pennsylvania. The little village had been selected for reasons largely beyond Washington's control.[3] Here, some twenty miles northwestward of Philadelphia, he
was supposed to be hovering close enough to harass and threaten the
British Army, now based in the city, yet not so close as to be in grave
danger from its forays.[4] And indeed Valley Forge had a real value
in this respect. But Washington's difficulties with supply alone were
enough to overwhelm a less resolute general, and they had a special
significance for Henry.

At the end of October, Henry, disturbed by the various and contradictory reports from the American camp, had written Washington for

[177]

any helpful information that Henry might pass on to the Assembly, now again in session. And he had a clearer idea of legislation needed after two letters from Washington of November 13. Because of the "disaffected and lukewarm" in Pennsylvania, and the failure of that state and Maryland to supply an adequate number of militia, Washington said he had been left to fight two battles with an inferior force in the effort to defend Philadelphia. A main theme of the letters was the necessity of recruiting the Continental battalions, with re-enlistment of as many as possible of the "seasoned" men from the nine old Virginia regiments whose time would expire in February and April.

Washington considered clothing his troops just as important as raising them. Because of the enemy blockade, he could count upon hardly any shipments from abroad, and the domestic supply was nearly exhausted. "Great collections" of clothing had been made in Pennsylvania, and he called upon the Governors of several states, including Henry, for aid. Would he recommend warmly to the Assembly that they lay "a very moderate assessment" for clothing upon the counties?

"I look with the greatest concern, upon the sufferings of the soldiers for the remainder of this year; and as for the next I view them as naked" unless some relief measures were taken, Washington explained. Just how grave the military situation would soon become in this and other respects even the commanding general could not fully envision, nor how important would be the support that could come from Henry.

The problem of feeding and clothing the troops, serious enough already in the invaded country, was now accentuated by a variety of factors. Washington's army was stationed in a part of Pennsylvania already swept by British and Continental quartermasters and with much of the population lukewarm or Tory in sympathy. The supply problems were aggravated by the blunders of Congress, by its lack of adequate control of the states, and by the slow means of communication and transportation. The offices of Quartermaster General and Commissary General, administered through Congress, came vacant about the same time,[5] and there was extraordinary incompetence or worse among the lower officers in these departments. Local farmers, even under threat of heavy penalty, often preferred to sell provisions for British gold rather than depreciated Continental currency.

The army had hardly begun to build their rude winter shelters at Valley Forge when Washington found himself in a desperate plight. Just before Christmas on December 23, 1777, he wrote the President of Congress to warn of imminent disaster to his army because of the supply crisis. "Unless some great and capital change" took place in the commissariat he was convinced that his army "must inevitably be reduced to one or other of these three things: Starve, dissolve, or disperse in order to obtain subsistence in the best manner they can." [6]

If the commissary officers had been more foresighted, if they had been under firmer direction, they might have arranged in time for meat, grain, salt, and other provisions to be transported to Pennsylvania from Virginia, the Carolinas, New England, or other distant points. But the situation was allowed to get out of hand. Not until the last of December, 1777, could Henry have learned the full extent of the crisis, although recent letters from Washington and Richard Henry Lee had warned him of mounting troubles. Incredible as it may seem, Washington wrote the President of Congress from Valley Forge on December 23, 1777, that he had received "no assistance" from the Quartermaster General, Thomas Mifflin, since the previous July. To this failure, the Commissary General, Joseph Trumbull, charged a great part to his own deficiency. Despite Washington's standing and often repeated order that the troops should have two days' provisions by them in the event of a "sudden call," there had been hardly an opportunity to take advantage of the enemy that had not been "either totally obstructed, or greatly impeded" by the lack of ready rations. And that, "the great and crying evil," was not all, for few of his men had more than one shirt, many only "the Moiety of one, and Some none at all"; no less than 2,898, more than a third of his total force, were that day unfit for duty because of "being barefoot and otherwise naked." [7]

There are few more important officers in an army than the prosaic chiefs of the commissary and quartermaster departments, and they failed Washington at a critical time. His Commissary General in nearly all the early campaigns had been the dedicated Joseph Trumbull of Connecticut. A forty-one-year-old Harvard graduate, Trumbull was a member of a mercantile family which was making a contribution to the Revolutionary cause not greatly inferior to that of the Adamses and Lees. His father, Governor Jonathan Trumbull, has been termed the state executive from whom Washington "always had the best hope of succor in every emergency, whether the desperate need was of men or of meat." For his successful work, Joseph Trumbull also won the respect of Washington, but he resigned his office after Congress had blunderingly divided its responsibilities. After serving briefly on the Board of War, by appointment of Congress, he died from illness brought on by his exhausting labors and frustrations in the commissary department.[8] So Peyton Randolph appears to have died from overwork in the cause; Henry and Richard Henry Lee had their warning signals.

While Joseph Trumbull's work had certain "blemishes," he seemed for some time irreplaceable and left a weakness in the army administration which was compounded by troubles with the Quartermaster General. When Henry was in Philadelphia for the Continental Congresses, he must have been entertained, along with other important delegates, in the fine mansion of a young Philadelphia merchant, Thomas Mifflin. A handsome, personable gentleman of ardent Whig sympathies, Mifflin had fought bravely as a Revolutionary officer and then in August, 1776, been appointed Quartermaster General. In this onerous position he had at first served efficiently, but his work had come under stiff criticism, and in the summer of 1777 the sensitive Mifflin had gone home "pleading illness." Congress, overwhelmed with problems, had urged him to continue temporarily in his position, and this he did, "complaining and malcontent." But there was neglect and "gross confusion" in his department until his successor was appointed in March, 1778. Meantime, too, this cultivated Pennsylvanian, a harsh critic of Washington's so-called "Fabian tactics," was one of the officers who seemed likely to join the embryonic movement to replace the commander in chief.

So, while the story had not yet fully developed, it is not surprising to find one of Washington's officers writing on December 13, 1777, the thanksgiving day set aside by Congress for Saratoga, "God knows we have very little to keep it with, this being the third day we have been without flour or bread." On the whole, all he and his fellow soldiers had to be thankful for was that they were alive and "not in the grave with many of our friends." [9]

Even worse from one viewpoint, the situation was avoidable. In a letter to Washington on November 20, 1777, Richard Henry Lee informed him that a committee had been appointed by Congress to confer with the Commissary General and see what could be done about the evil in that department. "That there should be a want of flour amazes me and proves great want of attention in the Commissary Gen. because I well know that any quantity might have been got in Virginia at a reasonable price." [10] A few months later Henry added his own informed statement as to the quantity of provisions available in Virginia and not being utilized by the army.

Moreover, the crisis in supply was only one phase of the desperate situation. In his letter of November 20, Lee spoke unhappily of the weakness and division in Pennsylvania, with Delaware "still worse," and "the ill condition of our finances." In the spring Howe's army, much reinforced, "may effect purposes dangerous to America."

> In order to support the credit of [the American] money, the several states must of necessity impose large and immediate Taxes. This is the most delicate and difficult of all government operations even in old and undisturbed States. Yet it is unavoidable, and Congress have pressingly requested that it may be quickly and extensively entered upon.[11]

Lee would have bad news when he saw Henry in Williamsburg late the next month. This was the period, at the end of 1777 and in early 1778, when Washington's army was reduced to some 6,000 active troops, when his Virginia regiments, like the other Continental units, seemed almost hollow shells, and when the effort was made to remove him from command of the Continental Army, with Henry receiving a key letter in the effort to secure his cooperation.

While not absolving Henry from his own responsibilities, we must now determine how much the Virginia General Assembly, comprised chiefly of planters struggling with their own wartime troubles, co-operated with him in meeting the military crisis.

Although summoned to meet in late October, the Assembly required two weeks to secure a quorum. Beverley Randolph, Charles Porter, John Syme, and another Henry relative were among the legislators who were able to give satisfactory reasons for their tardiness—family and wartime troubles, the dismal state of the roads, or what not. It always takes time for popular assemblies to get into full operation, but as late as December 18 Henry noted that "not one law of importance is passed." [12] He had heard, however, that the members had resolved not to adjourn until Christmas and would remain in session until their business was finished. In his need he asked Richard Henry Lee, at home to recover his health, if he would come to Williamsburg; and on March 1 Lee wrote Samuel Adams that he had been busy there in the "public councils." [13] Besides briefing Henry further on the situation to the northward, Lee certainly gave some needed prods to leaders of the Assembly. At any rate, its work during the session, while hardly brilliant, was in the end more fruitful than Henry had pessimistically feared. In mid-November they had made an appointment which Henry doubtless welcomed, and by December the members were beginning to come to grips with a few of the critical—and politically dangerous—problems.

On November 13 the House elected the brilliant and hard-working James Madison, Jr., of Orange as a member of the Council. A scholarly young man, Class of 1772 at Princeton, "little Jeemie" Madison had not yet won his reputation as Jefferson's principal lieutenant for his reform movement in Virginia. But Madison could be counted upon to bring to problems on the Council agenda a deep learning combined with industry and dedication to the popular cause. Unfortunately, he did not assume office until mid-January, 1778, too late to have helped Henry with his crop of troubles of the previous two months.

In early December, 1777, the Assembly took a notable step in approving the Articles of Confederation. Henry, in a letter of December 18 to Lee, noted that the vote was "nem. con." (unanimous) although the action was opposed by some members who were against "Independency." [14] This statement seems to indicate that Henry favored the measure; indeed, it is inconceivable that it would have been unanimous if he had thrown his powerful influence into the counterstream.

The American Congress, which was little more than "an assembly of ambassadors from sovereign states," had proved woefully lacking in power to conduct an efficient war. But a "confederation of equal states was better than no confederation," [15] and on November 17, 1777, Congress took a step toward colonial unity by adopting the Articles of Confederation. The Articles, which were printed in full in Dixon and Hunter's *Virginia Gazette*, [16] gave to Congress the power to conduct foreign affairs, to declare war, to maintain a navy and an army composed of troops provided by the states, to borrow money, and to issue bills of credit. Yet Henry, reading the long list of Articles, was assured at the outset as to states' rights, a topic on which he would be so sensitive a few years later. Each state was to retain its "sovereignty"; the Congress could not pass most important measures without the consent of a majority of the states and could obtain revenues only by requisitions on them.

The Articles were not to go into effect until ratified by all the states; they were forwarded with a strong exhortation for early action.

"In this great business Sir we must yield a little to each other, and not rigidly insist on having everything correspond to the partial views of every State. On such terms we can never confederate," Lee wrote Henry. The loose union, which was not offered to the states until some eighteen months after it was originally proposed in Congress, was about as strong a central government as jealous, provincial-minded states were then willing to consider seriously. But the power of taxation, so vital in a desperate war, remained with the states, and Congress had recommended to them extensive taxation along with "sinking" the provincial currency and regulating prices. [17] Unhappily, the Articles, weak as they were, did not go into operation until 1781, when finally approved by all the states; meantime, the latter were unable or unwilling to face many of their responsibilities.

Even when ineffectual, the Virginia legislative sessions always meant much work for Henry, and this had been accentuated as the Fall Assembly increased its tempo. In October Congress had recommended that the individual states supply their own troops with sufficient clothing. Because of the dire need, Henry was empowered to seize for the use of Washington's army all "proper" woolens, linens, shoes, and stockings which were found in the possession of any person who had purchased them for sale in any parts of the United States. He was also to have the lieutenants or commanding officers of each county request the inhabitants to provide a pair of shoes, stockings, gloves, or mittens for each soldier raised by the county and serving in the Continental Army, a desperate expedient which he reinforced with public appeal. The articles collected were to be conveyed "with the greatest expedition" to General Washington.[18]

Another matter in which Henry busied himself was re-enlistment of the Virginia Continentals. Because of the meager pay, the frequently almost unendurable living conditions, the stiff discipline, and the requirement of re-enlistment for the war, many soldiers were leaving the army. Henry had appointed General Stephen to secure the re-enlistment of the Virginia Continentals. But Stephen was now removed from command after charges of drunkenness, and, in order that the re-enlistments might not be "totally stopped," Henry wrote to Woodford, Scott, Weedon, and Muhlenberg, the Virginia generals with Washington, to finish Stephen's task.[19] It remained to be seen, however, whether sufficient men would ever reach Washington—and, if so, whether they could be clothed and fed. That Henry had even limited success with the emergency relief measures was largely due to his extreme tact in dealing with the Assembly.

As the winter dragged on, the situation at Valley Forge worsened. By mid-January the army was getting all under roof, though chiefly in rude huts with earthen floors.[20] A former Prussian officer, Friedrich von Steuben, arriving in late February, 1778, began to accomplish wonders in training the troops so that they could hold their own with British veterans. Yet to the horrors of cold and hunger were added those of disease and death. Nearly a thousand sick and dying soldiers were crowded into one improvised hospital hardly big enough to hold two hundred and fifty. Of the Virginia volunteers in the fine regiment which John Marshall joined, forty were jammed into a hospital run by some pitying Moravians and only three came out alive.[21]

With the Americans defeated at Brandywine and Germantown and the British occupying Philadelphia, it was natural that there would be bitter criticism of the conduct of the war, even before the debacle at Valley Forge. And it was inevitable that this criticism would extend to George Washington. Historians now know that there was never a "Conway Cabal" as in the sense that a number of generals and other highly placed Americans joined in a formal conspiracy to remove Washington from command. Yet in the light of later years and his final achievements, it is easy to misunderstand the viewpoint of contemporary critics who, seeing events only in their immediate perspective, lacked faith in Washington's ultimate success. Although some of these men were in truth jealous and bitter-minded, others stand convicted only of an understandable lack of judgment. One of the severest critics, General Thomas Conway, an Irish-born officer formerly in the French service, would resign from the American Army and apologize to Washington after being wounded in a duel by one of Washington's devoted officers; another and less candid opponent, the highly touted General Horatio Gates, would see his laurels fade at the battle of Camden.

Another well-placed malcontent was Henry's Philadelphia friend, Dr. Benjamin Rush. On October 21, 1777, after the American Army, then under Horatio Gates, had defeated Burgoyne, Rush had written John Adams, "I am more convinced than ever of the necessity of discipline and system in the management of our affairs. I have heard several officers who have served under General Gates compare his army to a well-regulated family. The same gentlemen have compared Gen'l Washington's imitation of an army to an unformed mob."[22]

As early as December 18, 1777, there was talk in Williamsburg of a plot against Washington, but we have no positive evidence to indicate that rumors of it had reached Henry. On January 6, 1778, Dr. James Craik, Washington's old friend, warned him of a "strong Faction . . . forming Against you with the New board of War and in the Congress" and which alarmed Craik "exceedingly." At the bottom of the plot, gossip put "R.H.L., G—l M—n, and G—s" (Richard Henry Lee, General Mifflin, and General Gates), and Craik warned Washington to "have an Eye toward these Men."[23]

In mid-February, 1778, when Henry was struggling to get desperately needed food and supplies to Valley Forge, he received a remarkable letter from the temporary capital at York, dated January 12, 1778. Even allowing for the terrible winter roads, the letter should have arrived by the end of January; the delay seems to indicate that the dangerous missive was mulled over and perhaps shown to several persons before being finally dispatched. The letter was also unsigned, though this may not be as insidious as it appears. Beginning with the formal "Dear Sir," it continued as follows:

> The common danger of our country first brought you and me together. I recollect with pleasure the influence of your conversation and eloquence upon the opinions of this country, in the beginning of the present controversy. You first taught us to shake off our idolatrous attachment to royalty, and to oppose its encroachments upon our liberties, with our very lives. By these means you saved us from ruin. The independence of America is the offspring of that liberal spirit of thinking and acting which followed the destruction of the sceptres of kings, and the mighty power of Great Britain.

"But, Sir, we have only passed the Red Sea," the writer added.

> A dreary wilderness is still before us; and unless a Moses or a Joshua are raised up in our behalf, we must perish before we reach the promised land. We have nothing to fear from our enemies on the way. General Howe, it is true, has taken Philadelphia; but he has only changed his prison. His dominions are bounded on all sides, by his out-sentries. America can only be undone by herself. She looks up to her councils and arms for protection; but alas! what are they? Her representation in Congress dwindled to only twenty-one members, her Adams, her Wilson, her Henry are no more among them. Her councils weak, and partial remedies applied constantly for universal diseases. Her army, what is it? a major-general belonging to it, called it a few days ago, in my hearing, a mob.

The correspondent continued with some extreme criticism, which nevertheless did indicate detailed knowledge of the military and governmental crisis. Discipline in the army, he declared, was unknown or wholly neglected.

> The quarter-master's and commissary's departments filled with idleness, ignorance, and peculation; our hospitals crowded with six thousand sick, but half provided with necessaries or accommodations, and more dying in them in one month, than perished in the field during the whole of the last campaign. The money depreciating, without any effectual measures being taken to raise it; the country distracted with the Don Quixote attempts to regulate the price of provisions; an artificial famine created by it, and a real one dreaded from it; the spirit of the people failing through a more intimate acquaintance with the causes of our misfortunes; many submitting daily to general Howe; and more wishing to do it, only to avoid the calamities which threaten our country. But is our case desperate? By no means. We have wisdom, virtue, and strength enough to save us, if they could be called into action. The northern army has shown us what Americans are capable of doing, with a General at their head. The spirit of the southern army is no way inferior to the spirit of the northern.

After this depressing array of arguments, the anonymous writer gave Henry some hints as to the real point of his letter: he was seeking Henry's cooperation in an embryonic movement to influence public opinion and replace Washington.

> A Gates, a Lee, or a Conway, would in a few weeks render them an irresistible body of men. The last of the above officers has accepted of the new office of inspector-general of our army, in order to reform abuses; but the remedy is only a palliative one. In one of his letters to a friend, he says, "A great and good God hath decreed America to be free, or the [General] . . . and weak counsellors would have ruined her long ago." You may rest assured of each of the facts related in this letter. The author of it is one of your Philadelphia friends. A hint of his name, if found out by the handwriting, must not be mentioned to your most intimate friend. Even the letter must be thrown in the fire. But some of its contents ought to be made public, in order to awaken, enlighten, and alarm our country. I rely upon your prudence, and am dear Sir, with my usual attachment to you and to our beloved independence. . . .

The flattery and the appeal to personal friendship and patriotism were lost on Henry. He is said to have sent the letter "at once" to Washington and in fact could hardly have delayed a day in doing so. Along with the letter from York, he enclosed one which he personally penned to the General.

> Dear Sir: You will no doubt, be surprised at seeing the enclosed letter, in which the encomiums bestowed on me are as undeserved, as the censures aimed at you are unjust. I am sorry there should be one man who counts himself my friend who is not yours.
> Perhaps I give you needless trouble in handing you this paper. The writer of it may be too insignificant to deserve any notice. If I knew this to be the case, I should not have intruded on your time, which is so precious. But there may possibly be some scheme or party forming to your prejudice. The enclosed leads to such a suspicion. Believe me, sir, I have too high a sense of the obligations America has to you, to abet or countenance so unworthy a proceeding. The most exalted merit hath ever been found to attract envy. But I please myself with the hope, that the same fortitude and greatness of mind which have hitherto braved all the difficulties and dangers inseparable from your station, will rise superior to every attempt of the envious partisan.
> I really cannot tell who is the writer of this letter, which not a little perplexes me. The handwriting is altogether strange to me.
> To give you the trouble of this gives me pain. It would suit my inclination better to give you some assistance in the great business of the war. But I will not conceal any thing from you by which you may be affected; for I really think your personal welfare and the happiness of America are intimately connected. I beg you will be assured of that high regard and esteem, with which I am, dear sir, your affectionate friend and very humble servant,
>
> P. Henry

Washington was absorbed with cares and responsibilities which taxed even his great strength and endurance. By March 5, 1778, Henry had not yet received a reply. The situation of the country remained critical. Anxious to hear directly from Washington, Henry now wrote again to tell Washington that he had received the anonymous letter which he hoped had arrived safely. Henry was anxious to hear something which would explain "the strange affair" that he was now informed had been instigated against Washington. From Mr. Custis, who had just paid them a visit, Henry had learned "sundry particulars" regarding General Mifflin which surprised him. "It is very hard to trace the schemes and windings of the enemies to America. I really thought that man its friend: however, I am too far from him to judge of his present temper."

Then Henry gave more assurances of support, adding the religious touch found in a number of his writings:

> While you face the armed enemies of our liberty in the field, and by the favour of God, have been kept unhurt, I trust your country will never harbour in her bosom the miscreant who would ruin her best supporter. I wish not to flatter; but when arts, unworthy honest men, are used to defame and traduce you, I think it not amiss, but a duty, to assure you of that estimation in which the public hold you. Not that I think that any testimony I can bear is necessary for your support, or private satisfaction; for a bare recollection of what is past must give you sufficient pleasure in every circumstance of life. But I cannot help assuring you on this occasion, of the high sense of gratitude which all ranks of men in this your native country bear to you. It will give me sincerest pleasure to manifest my regards, and render my best services to you or yours. I do not like to make a parade of these things, and I know that you are not fond of it, however I hope the occasion will plead my excuse.

Henry continued with some comments, not altogether reassuring, on the supply crisis. The Assembly had "at length" empowered him to provide the Virginia troops with clothes, etc., and he was acting accordingly. The state government was giving every possible assistance to the Continental commissary of provisions, "whose department has not been attended to. It was taken up by me too late to do much. Indeed, the load of business devolved on me is too great to be managed well. . . ."

Already, however, Washington had received Henry's previous letter, as indicated in a letter which Washington wrote him from Valley Forge on March 27. He spoke of Henry's first letter as having been received about eight days past. Although sent by express, it had taken nearly four weeks to reach the commander in chief!

> Your friendship, sir, in transmitting to me the anonymous letter you had received, lays me under the most grateful obligations; and if my acknowledgments can be due for anything more, it is for the polite and delicate terms in which you have been pleased to communicate the matter.
>
> I have ever been happy in supposing that I had a place in your esteem, and the proof of it you have afforded on this occasion makes me peculiarly so. The favorable light in which you hold me is truly flattering; but I should feel much regret, if I thought the happiness of America so intimately connected with my personal welfare, as you so obligingly seem to consider it. All I can say is, that she has ever had, and I trust she ever will have, my honest exertions to promote her interest. I cannot hope that my services have been the best; but my heart tells me they have been the best that I could render.
>
> That I may have erred in using the means in my power for accomplishing the objects of the arduous, exalted station with which I am honored, I cannot doubt; nor do I wish my conduct to be exempted from reprehension farther than it may deserve. Error is the portion of humanity, and to censure it, whether committed by this or that public character, is the prerogative of freemen. However, being intimately acquainted with the man I conceive to be the author of the letter transmitted, and having always received from him the strongest professions of attachment and regard, I am constrained to consider him as not possessing, at least, a great degree of candor and sincerity, though his views in addressing you should have been the result of conviction, and founded in motives of public good. This is not the only secret, insidious attempt, that has been made to wound my reputation. There have been others equally base, cruel and ungenerous, because conducted with as little frankness, and proceeding from views, perhaps, as personally interested. I am, dear sir with great esteem and regard, your much obliged friend, &c.

George Washington

As Washington was completing on March 28 his letter of the previous day, he received Henry's letter of March 5. Washington, usually restrained in expressing personal feeling, told Henry that he could only thank him again in "language of the most undissembled gratitude" for his friendship. The General informed Henry that the anonymous letter was written by Dr. Rush, insofar as he could determine from the handwriting. Washington had had ample opportunity to see examples of Rush's handwriting, for they had been associated together when Washington was in Philadelphia at the Continental Congress and later during the war; Rush was then the medical director of the middle department of the Army. It is now generally admitted that the letter was in fact written by him. We can appreciate that the desire of the gifted Rush to replace Washington in the time of disaster was an error of the heart rather than of the mind. But Washington, burdened with many problems insoluble by any mortal being, could not be expected to see Rush's conduct in any favorable light; he believed that he had been not only antagonistic but hypocritical—"elaborate and studied in his professions of regard"—a particular charge for which there has been no full answer.

In view of their past friendship, we may wonder why Henry did not recognize Rush's handwriting. But their previous correspondence appears to have been very limited, and Henry had since received a flood of correspondence from many people. On the face of it, it seems that Rush did not sign his letter to Henry of January 12 because he did not want to reveal his identity. An authority on the period, however, states that the anonymous letter should more accurately be labeled "unsigned"; Rush, one of the most copious writers of his day, not only made no effort to disguise his well-known handwriting but described himself as one of Henry's Philadelphia friends. If Henry recognized the handwriting, he was not to mention Rush's name when revealing the contents of the letter to others. Rush is declared to have had an idiosyncrasy of sending unsigned letters, as, for example, when General Charles Lee in a letter of August 13, 1778, chaffed him for a "letter of no date, and sign'd with no name."

The charge was long repeated that Richard Henry Lee was a member of the alleged conspiracy against Washington. It was argued that proof would be found when certain of his letters were decoded. But no evidence was uncovered that Lee was ever implicated, although he may have had understandable doubts at the time as to

Washington's capacity—doubts which were shared by some other American leaders.[24]

Another anonymous letter with inferential criticism of Washington was circulated among members of Congress. It was dated the same month as Rush's letter to Henry and contained some of the same general arguments.[25] While there is positive proof that Rush was plotting a conspiracy to remove Washington, there were other men who appeared receptive to the plan if properly supported. Washington was now moved to defend himself and proved no mean polemicist. He got needed support in the Army and Congress. Indeed, the private soldiers and nearly all the officers, knowing his courage and self-sacrifice, had never wavered in their allegiance. There was less desertion at Valley Forge than in the months before.

Yet there were some leaders in Congress and the Army who were murmuring. Although cautiously avoiding overt conspiracy, they might have taken action if Henry had stirred public opinion as Rush suggested.

Had Henry been given to wry humor, he might have said that if it was not one crisis, it was two—or more. He had not completed his strenuous measures to help clothe the Virginia Continentals when in mid-January, 1778, he learned from a Virginia congressman, Francis Lightfoot Lee, that the American Army was also suffering from a grave lack of provisions.[26]

Moving with his usual energy in such emergencies, Henry applied to the Deputy Commissary General for some "Active persons" to secure an instant supply of the needed provisions, only to have that officer reply that he could provide no such persons immediately but would write his deputy to attend to the business. This plan Henry deemed "by no means satisfactory." In the northwestern part of Virginia "in that Deputy's Quarter" Henry found that eight or ten thousand hogs and several thousand fine beeves might have been obtained "very lately" in a few counties which were convenient to the American camp.[27]

Bypassing the Continental commissariat (Henry put it more tactfully), he employed three competent agents to "instantly" purchase

10,000 pounds of beef or pork and deliver it to the Army in the quickest manner. He ordered a Virginia officer to seize 2,000 bushels of salt on the Eastern Shore and had it sent to the "Head of Elk" (present Elkton, Maryland), convenient to Valley Forge. By these measures, with arrangements for some additional salt, Henry said that he was doing the best that he could "in the sudden Exigency." And yet he could not "forbear some Reflections" which he begged "Frank Lee" to lay before Congress. With "the deepest concern" Henry saw the army commissariat fall into "a State of uncertainty & Confusion."[28] Although a great abundance of provisions might have been secured from Virginia, he knew of no criticism that had been made of the conduct of the agents employed to forward them to the Army. He wanted it to be understood that he had no authority over the Continental commissariat, and he added with a moving candor:

> It will indeed be unworthy the Character of a Zealous American to entrench himself within the strict Line of official Duty, & there quietly behold the starving and dispersion of the American Army. The Genius of this Country is not of that Cast.
>
> I do not wish to avoid any Labour which may serve the general Interest and which cannot be executed better by others. But I have the Mortification to know that the present Business I have directed, will be executed with great Loss to the public. The pressing occasion puts the price of meat &c in the power of wicked ava[ri]cious & disaffected men. The Value of Money will be more & more lessened, the means of supporting the public Credit counteracted & defeated. I will not enumerate further the Evils which must follow from suffering Business of this vast import to remain in the Channel where it is now going. Let it suffice to say that this Country abounds with the provisions for which the Army is said to be almost starving, particularly that part of it nearest the Camp.[29]

Henry apologized to the Virginia delegates for writing so freely. After a sop to the sensitive Congress—it "will please to be assured of the most perfect Regard of every Member of the Executive of Virginia"—he concluded:

> But that Body would be wanting in the Duty they owe to the great Council of America & to their Country, if they concealed

any of their Sentiments on a Subject so alarming as the present. The Honour & Credit of that great Council are conceived to be deeply concerned in rectifying what is wrong in these Matters.[30]

Fearing the "fatal results" of the lack of provisions, Henry sought the aid of Governor Johnson of Maryland in protecting the meat he was sending to the Head of Elk. The Virginia naval vessels were also ordered to give every possible assistance in transporting provisions up the Bay or rivers.[31] But in that slow-moving age, the problems of food supply were not to be easily solved. As late as March 31 Henry would lay before the Council letters from Washington and the Virginia congressmen which presented the need for provisions in the "most alarming colours." Upon the advice of the Council, Henry appointed the efficient John Hawkins as a purchasing agent to secure and forward "with the utmost dispatch" as much beef and bacon as the Army required or he could procure.[32] A few days later, when informing the Virginia congressmen of Hawkins' appointment, Henry also directed them to have $20 additional bounty paid to Virginia soldiers who re-enlisted.[33]

Writing to Richard Henry Lee from Williamsburg in April, Henry was "as usual in great hurry" but "seized a moment" to explain Hawkins' appointment. Henry had exerted all his personal influence and with great difficulty got Hawkins to undertake the business.

> He has given one-half his salary, which appears at first view large, to an able hand (R^d Morris) who is a fine accountant & man of Fortune. I am really shocked at the Management of Congress in this Department. John Moore's appointment gave me the most painful feelings. Good God! Our Fate committed to a man utterly unable to perform the task assigned him! Raw, inexperienced, without weight, consequence or acquaintance with men or business; called into action at a time when distinguished talent only can save an army from perishing. I tell you, & I grieve at it, Congress will lose the respect due. . . .[34]
> I am really so harrassed by the great load of continental Business thrown on me lately, that I am ready to sink under my Burden, & have thoughts of taking that rest that will I doubt soon become necessary. For my strength will not suffice.[35]

Fortunately, the military situation became more hopeful. The army was augmented by new recruits, and the discipline greatly improved, thanks to the unremitting efforts of General von Steuben. The Commissariat was put under more efficient management—one of the appointments with which Washington was pleased being that of John Hawkins as the Virginia purchasing agent. Perhaps not yet knowing how much Henry was responsible for securing Hawkins' services, Washington nevertheless wrote Henry on April 19 that he had "heard so good an account" of Hawkins that he hoped for the most salutary effects. Washington then expressed himself as "infinitely obliged" to the Legislature for their "ready attention" to his representation of the needs of the army, and he added a personal word of thanks to Henry for "the strenuous manner" in which he had recommended to the Virginia people a compliance with his request for fattening cattle.[36]

On May 13, 1778, Henry presented a detailed report to the new legislature, in which he emphasized such matters as his dissatisfaction with the plan adopted by the last Assembly to reinforce the Continental army, his measures to alleviate the crisis in supplies and to secure French aid, and the difficulty arising from the "great Emissions of Paper Money."[37] Three days later, when writing Governor Caswell of North Carolina, he spoke of "the great event of the treaty with France. It will most probably bring with it our permanent Independence."[38]

One problem which Henry did not have to face was any weakening of the progressive leadership of the House after he became war Governor. Following his epochal work in Congress, Thomas Jefferson had returned to Virginia and on October 7, 1776, had entered the House of Delegates. Here his quiet courage and unobtrusive talents soon brought him to the forefront. Among other reforms, he endeavored to have the legal code of Virginia adapted to a republican government, "with a single eye to reason, & the good of those for whose government it was formed." So changed, this code would be a model for other states. Only five days after his first appearance in the House, Jefferson introduced a motion for the revision of the outmoded Virginia legal code, and he was made a member of the board of revisors. Their report in June, 1778, would comprise 126 laws, of which the great majority would be enacted in substance. In general, this and other legislation favored by Jefferson during this period would be adopted with the support of the Henry party.[39]

Jefferson was then an admirer of Henry and indebted to him. It is not surprising that when on Friday, May 29, 1778, the Assembly unanimously elected Henry Governor for another year, Jefferson was chairman of the House committee which notified him of his re-election. However, Henry's brief and somewhat perfunctory thanks to the delegates apparently indicated that he entered upon his new term more from a sense of duty than from any enchantment with the honors ahead.[40]

14

Henry as Governor—Third Term

In a word, I think our political system may, be compared to
the mechanism of a Clock; and that our conduct should de-
rive a lesson from it for it answers no good purpose to keep the
smaller Wheels in order if the greater one which is support
and prime mover of the whole is neglected.——GEORGE
WASHINGTON to Benjamin Harrison, December 18, 1778 [1]

"The agricultural population produces the bravest men, the
most valiant soldiers, and a class of citizens least given of all
to evil designs."——CATO

June 18, 1778. British evacuate Philadelphia.

July 4, 1778. George Rogers Clark captures Kaskaskia, followed on Feb. 25, 1779, by his recapture of Vincennes.

July 28, 1778. General Charles Lee prevents hopeful American victory at Monmouth, N.J.

December 29, 1778. British capture Savannah.

HENRY WAS NOW embarked on his third one-year term as
Governor, the last he would serve in that responsible but often
thankless office until 1784. His new administration was heartened by
only a few glorious events, such as the British evacuation of Philadelphia, George Rogers Clark's capture of Kaskaskia and Vincennes, and
the entrance of Spain into the war (while avoiding a formal alliance
with the "dangerous" new republic). On the other hand, there would

be no very serious defeats, no months so anxious as when Washington's little army was suffering at Valley Forge. The dubious Charles Lee, however, almost precipitated a military disaster at Monmouth, New Jersey, during the first month of the term, and during the last month a British expedition ravaged the Virginia coast, while there were desperate calls for help against a major enemy attack in the lower South.

The French alliance has been called "a marriage of convenience," [2] and it is true that the French were concerned mainly with national prestige and with revenge against Great Britain, who had so recently defeated *la grande nation* in the Seven Years' War, not to speak of earlier conflicts. But the French had to be given credit, too, for a certain generosity and idealism expressed in the liberal treaty terms and, more glamorously, in their volunteers for the war, notably the ardent Marquis de Lafayette. During December, 1777, Henry, in a communication to Washington, enclosed two letters from France to the recently arrived Marquis, one of them, Henry thought, from his "lady. . . . I beg to be presented to him in the most acceptable manner. I greatly revere his person and amiable character." [3] That same month Lafayette was placed in command of the Virginia division of light troops in the Continental Army.

Henry had been re-elected Governor on Friday, May 29, 1778, and by the latter part of the next week he was sick again, probably due to overwork and another attack of his old enemy, malaria.

"The Governor being indisposed," as the *Council Journal* noted, John Page presided over its meetings from Thursday, June 4, until Thursday, June 18, 1778. The condition of Henry's health, along with some nagging—indeed, well nigh insoluble—military and economic problems, do much to explain the discouraging letters that he wrote during the following months. In one addressed to President Laurens of Congress on the day he returned to duty, Henry sadly noted that not one half of the draft of Virginia soldiers to the Continental Army voted by the Assembly had ever reached camp. "I lament this Capital deficiency . . . but no efforts of the Executive have been sufficient to prevent it." [4]

Many of his difficulties stemmed from the increasing issuance of paper money. Throughout his new term Henry was constantly reminded of its shrinking value; "not worth a Continental" would become a familiar expression, and the state money was even less valuable. After a French ship arrived on the Virginia coast in late May, 1778, Congress requested Henry to purchase some of its cargo for the United States "as cheap as he can." But it was specified that he should pay at a rate not over £450 of Virginia money for every £100 sterling.[5] By November, Richard Henry Lee was writing of "the precipice on which we stand with our paper money." The Continental emissions were exceeding seven fold "the sum necessary for medium; the State emissions added, greatly increase the evil."[6] By the spring of 1779 the Continental money could be redeemed only at 16 or 20 to 1 in specie, while expenses of the Continental quartermaster and commissary departments alone had climbed to over $37,000,000 a year in paper money. It was of little comfort that Congress and the states were virtually forced to issue this depreciated currency. And foreign loans were as yet of little help.

Although the Assembly did sometimes get bogged down in rules and procedure, it accomplished much more than would many legislative bodies in peacetime. The legislature in October, 1778, made it a criminal offense to buy country produce for resale, and Henry was empowered to seize all grain and flour bought by such speculators. Bounties and other inducements were offered Continental volunteers. But considering that the pay was $7 per month for the three-year Continental enlistments, and shoes were selling for $20 a pair, potatoes 90 shillings a bushel, a quart of milk for 15 shillings,[7] it is not surprising that many men felt a strong urge to stay at home and support their families. Even when prices were fixed by the county courts, as in Henry's former home county of Louisa, they were exorbitant enough.

It was the fourth year of the Revolution. The British government seemed as determined as ever. In his low spirits Henry could not foresee Britain ever becoming "cordial" with the United States. She would "ever meditate revenge," he wrote Richard Henry Lee. America would "find no safety but in her ruin, or at least in her extreme humiliation, which has not happened, and cannot happen until she is deluged with blood, or thoroughly purged by a revolution, which shall wipe from existence the present king with his connexions, and the present system, with those who aid and abet it." [8]

Within the next ten days there was brighter news. Henry was again able to work steadily, and his correspondence was in a more optimistic vein. Ever vigilant for the safety of the exposed Virginia frontier, he was able to send some needed powder and gunflints there and to spare £1,500 for provisions. In a letter of June 27, 1778, to Colonel William Preston in distant Montgomery County, he praised the spirit of the young men setting out to fight in the enemy country. But, knowing the type of warfare, he had to warn them that if they moved in large bodies after they crossed the Ohio the Indians would easily track them. This and other suggestions in his letter to Preston were only "Hints." Preston, "on the Spot," could "better Judge of the necessary Measures than the Executive, which resides at such a Distance from the Scene of Action." [9]

Besides the laudable zeal of the Virginia frontiersmen, there was good news of the main military operations. Henry was able to send congratulations to President Laurens of Congress "on our reposs [ess] ing philadelphia, & the pleasing Aspect of american affairs." [10] Nevertheless, Henry had to inform Laurens of certain difficulties. Congress and the Board of War were planning an expedition against the strategic post of Detroit, for which Virginia was to provide 2,000 of the militia required, along with ammunition, provisions, horses, clothing, and other supplies. Henry was forced to state that the expedition was "utterly impracticable" at that season of the year because of obstacles, which he noted, to supplying the men and horses. The preparations ought to have been begun the past winter; now, in the "exhausted State of this Country," he did not see how the men could be ready before spring.

Tactfully concealing what must have been his real feelings, Henry spoke of his "perfect reliance on the wisdom of Congress" and told Laurens that he did not want to touch upon any matter that lay within their province. But he went on to speak of how he was deeply affected by the "miseries" of the Virginia people who lived exposed to the Indian assaults; he suggested that if a military expedition was directed against the hostile tribes nearest the Virginia frontier, very good results might follow.[11] A month later Henry learned that Congress had rescinded its plans for the Detroit expedition. In order to protect the frontier, the war was to be carried into such enemy towns as the new western commander, General Lachlan McIntosh, should direct.[12]

But on the long Virginia frontier the Indians, often stirred by British agents, seemed always ready to attack lonely cabins. In July, 1778, Colonel William Fleming wrote Henry that there was panic among the people; many of the settlers had already fled. A Negro belonging to General Andrew Lewis had been shot, and three boys had been scalped only five miles below Cloverdale, the residence of Henry's brother-in-law, Thomas Madison, in Botetourt County. The settlers in other parts of the county were gathering forces, but as usual there was not enough militia to defend all the vulnerable points.[13]

Outside of the capital, life in the state was running according to the usual wartime routine. Fortunately, much governmental business was attended to by fairly competent local officials, leaving Henry and the Council free to concentrate on essential matters. In Spotsylvania County, for example, during late May, 1778, a jury returned presentments in accordance with the usual procedure. Several overseers of roads were indicted for not keeping them in repair, twelve men and women for retailing spiritous liquor without licenses, and one Thomas Estes for absenting himself from public worship.[14]

Despite the war, some venturesome Virginians were moving westward, among them Captain John Donelson, father of the future Mrs. Andrew Jackson, who in 1779 set out from the present Chatham vicinity for the wilds of middle Tennessee.[15]

The Virginia people were still wholeheartedly in favor of the war; the few outspoken opponents were easily suppressed. In Fluvanna County where Henry's brother, William, had settled near the upper James, John Burgess was charged with treason and raising tumult and disorder in the state. On June 4, 1778, he appeared before the County Court, and after the charge was heard he was held not guilty.[16] Toryism would never become as serious a threat in Virginia as in the states to the southward.

Because of the volume of foreign correspondence, especially with France and Spain, on June 30, 1778, Henry administered the oath to Charles Bellini as clerk of foreign correspondence,[17] a position like that which the poet Milton had held under Oliver Cromwell. Later Bellini would hold the chair of modern languages at William and Mary, the first such appointment in an American college.[18]

On Friday, July 31, the Council attended to only two routine items, the recommendation for appointment of a county justice and the issuance of a warrant for expenses of the public hospital. Then the "Board" adjourned, not to meet again until the following Tuesday. The *Journal* gives no reason for the respite, but on Sunday, August 2, 1778, Henry's seventh child, his first by his second wife, was born, a girl named Dorothea Spotswood.[19] This Dorothea, whose reputed beauty is attested in the portrait by Sharples, the English artist, married her cousin, George D. Winston.[20] They had nine children and numerous other descendants, now scattered in many states.[21]

If there are any serious weaknesses in a governmental system, they are likely to be laid bare in war. As the Revolutionary campaigns entered upon their main Southern or final phase, the Virginia government retained certain oligarchic features, but they were less objectionable than those of the British model. Two Lees were signers of the Declaration of Independence, and another was a rising military officer; Nelsons and Randolphs retained much power in the new commonwealth. Yet these Virginia leaders, chosen from the old aristocracy, were men of superior ability, and they added to their ranks, if at times grudgingly, statesmen such as Patrick Henry and soldiers such as Andrew Lewis, George Rogers Clark, and Daniel Morgan.[22]

On the other hand, the British still entrusted their government to a small hierarchy which in some respects lacked the current Virginian and American competence. It was remarkable how many of the British generals and admirals had sprung from a small interrelated class, based largely on birth and privilege. On the whole, the system produced more generals and admirals of good if not brilliant ability than might have been expected. But its high command had not been imaginative enough to meet some of the new conditions in the American war.

After Sir Henry Clinton, the "paunchy and colorless" British commander in chief, had established his base at New York in the summer of 1778, he sent 3,500 men to Georgia. At the end of the year they captured Savannah and, with Southern Tories flocking to their standard, soon drove the weak Continental force into South Carolina. Then in December, 1779, Clinton left New York with some 8,000 men for an attack on Charleston.[23] For the hard-pressed South Carolinians much would depend on the aid sent them by Congress; also, after the return of Clinton to New York the next year, upon how well that cautious nobleman would cooperate with his Southern commander, the dashing Lord Cornwallis.

In the early fall of 1778, the British plans for the new Southern campaign were not fully revealed. But during its earlier phase this operation would be conducted with what, for the ruling military caste, was exceptional ability. Furthermore, the British high command would benefit from the blunders or worse of an American Congress now at a low level of ability. On September 25, Congress called upon Virginia to give all possible aid for Georgia and South Carolina against the anticipated British attack,[24] and Henry would be disturbed by more urgent—and often ill-considered—appeals for help until the end of his term.

After receiving the first call, through President Laurens, Henry took it up with the Council, then the Assembly. That often dilatory body was impressed with his injunction for early action. It agreed, upon "more certain information," to send not over 3,000 men to South Carolina. Henry requisitioned the militia and planned the march, only to suspend it on advice of the Council. "Pretty certain" information had come through Governor Johnson of Maryland that the enemy expedition had actually turned about and headed northward.[25] Alarms and counter alarms! and not always as foolish as they seemed, since enemy ships in Chesapeake Bay or off the Atlantic coast could usually find inviting prey in the ill-protected counties of the Virginia Tidewater.

Near the end of November came still another call, this through the new President of Congress, John Jay, for 1,000 militia to send to Charleston. By now there was no reasonable doubt of the British threat to the lower South. But the requests from Congress were contradictory, if not almost nonsensical. Henry's patience was growing thin. Only a few days earlier Congress had requested several galleys from Virginia for use in a proposed expedition to conquer east Florida. Henry could only hope that these weak craft, really large rowboats (apparently with sails), would not meet British warships. "The Gallies have orders to rendezvous at Charles Town, which I was taught to consider as a place of acknowledged Safety," he wrote Jay. And the Governor begged "leave to observe that there seems some Degree of Inconsistency in marching Militia such a Distance in the Depth of Winter under the Want of Necessaries to defend a place which the former Measure seemed to declare safe." [26]

The Virginia law authorizing such a troop movement, Henry explained, confined the operations to defensive measures for a sister state "of whose Danger, there is certain Information." He had given orders for the thousand men to march as soon as they were furnished with tents, kettles, and wagons. If information was received that their march was "essential to the preservation of either the States of S° Carolina or Georgia," he would not wait for "the Necessaries commonly afforded to Troops even on a Summers march." He requested the earliest possible reply. Yet it was not until January 15, 1779, that Congress took final action. President Jay was then requested to inform Henry that Congress deemed it "necessary to the success" of the East Florida expedition that the troops and galleys requested be sent to Charleston "with all convenient Speed." [27]

Six weeks had already passed since Henry sent his urgent letter to Congress. Meantime, Savannah had been captured, Georgia was being overrun, and the road lay open to adjacent South Carolina and the port of Charleston. Congress did make a further and more serious effort to aid the threatened city. Yet, of the general ineptness—incompetence or worse—of the current Congress, no less a witness than George Washington had already given unhappy testimony. After the battle of Saratoga, he wrote Speaker Harrison in December, 1778, that British commissioners had been sent to offer the United States an olive branch in the form of peace and dominion status. Arriving in America after the French alliance, they had received a cold shoulder and sailed back home; [28] nevertheless, they were "not a little buoyed up" by "distresses" they found in the county.

> What may be the effect of such large and frequent emissions [of currency], of the dissentions, Parties, extravagance, and a general lax of public virtue Heaven alone can tell! I am affraid even to think of It [Washington continued].
>
> [Many persons] removed (some of them) far distant from the scene of action, and seeing, and hearing such publications only as flatter their wishes they conceive that the contest is at an end, and that to regulate the government and police of their own State is all that remains to be done.[29]

Washington hoped that a "sad reverse" of this situation would not fall upon America "like a thunder clap." He did not want to censure individual states and had kind words for some recent changes in Virginia military and civil policy.[30] But after coming to Philadelphia on December 30 he was even more pessimistic than when he had written Speaker Harrison two weeks earlier. American affairs were "in a more distressed, ruinous, and deplorable condition, than they had been since the commencement of the war." Referring specifically to Congress, he asked his "dear Colo. Harrison" to exert himself to rescue the country by sending the "ablest and best" Virginians to Congress. "Where is Mason, Wythe, Jefferson, Nicholas, Pendleton, Nelson, and another I could name?"[31]

Could the unnamed party have been Harrison himself? It would not have been feasible to send Henry to Congress, since he was one of the war Governors upon whom Washington most relied. He could hardly have expected Henry to leave his responsible position in Williamsburg for what doubtful success he could achieve in the weak Congress. As for Jefferson, there was the continued explanation that he felt he could accomplish more by making Virginia a model state for his reform program; while other able Virginians, who no longer lent their influence and ability to Congress, could offer excuses of varying validity.

In November, Henry dealt successfully with a counterfeiting ring which had assumed dangerous proportions, and he helped somewhat to expedite the long-delayed settlement of the Virginia-Pennsylvania boundary dispute. Back in May he had urged the legislature to take action in the matter, saying that he lacked the authority, and on November 27 he wrote a letter to Benjamin Harrison along similar lines.[32]

But after this, he could only express to Colonel Lochrey of the Pennsylvania Rangers his hope that the Virginia Assembly would take immediate action and recommend that Lochrey use his influence to preserve peace between his people and the Virginians. "Consider we have Enemys enough of the British & the Indians, without making Enemys of our own Brethren."[33]

Before Henry left office the following May, the House of Delegates requested him to inform the Pennsylvania boundary commissioners that the Virginia Assembly would proceed to nominate similar emissaries.[34] But it was not until 1784 that the southwest corner of Pennsylvania was fixed by agreement of the two disputing states.[35]

Happily, not all news was bad, not all problems had to be handled piecemeal with inadequate resources. In the middle of November, 1778, Henry sent the Virginia delegates to Congress some glorious tidings: the expedition of Colonel George Rogers Clark into the Illinois country appeared to have been successful. In dispatches just received from Clark, Henry learned that he had not only captured Fort Chartres and its dependencies in the Kaskaskia area but had struck terror into the Indian tribes between that settlement and the lakes. The tribes there which had "received the Hatchet" from the English emissaries were now binding themselves by treaties and promises to be peaceful in the future. Even the British post at Detroit, Clark wrote, was so weakly defended that it might be reduced by something over five hundred men. To improve and secure these advantages, Henry proposed to support Clark with a reinforcement of militia, though he told the congressmen that this would require approval of the Assembly, to whom it had been submitted.[36]

When the Clark expedition had already equaled "the most sanguine expectation," what superlatives could Henry use to describe its further achievements? For it was a heroic episode, comparable, at least in difficulties overcome, to the Greek Anabasis or Napoleon's Passage of the Alps. A month after reaching the Falls of the Ohio, Clark and his Indianlike band of some 178 men with their fringed buckskins, moccasins, and tomahawks had set out in single file through the wilderness country. After six days' march, two without food, Clark's troops had surprised and captured Kaskaskia on July 4, 1778. Within another month they had taken Cahokia and Vincennes; by diplomacy worthy of a Talleyrand Clark had secured the allegiance of the neighboring French inhabitants and Indians.

The full details of Clark's achievement were not yet available to Henry. But on December 12, 1778, he wrote Clark a letter retaining him in command of the troops in the Illinois country. And upon general instructions from the Council he added some admirable instructions for Clark's future conduct in the remote, thinly settled region, so accessible to Indian and British retaliation. Clark was to be reinforced with five companies of militia if they could be raised.[37] He was to spare no pains to conciliate the French and Indians in the area and if necessary could severely discipline his soldiers to attain that purpose. If there was a fair presumption that the people about Detroit were as favorably inclined to the American cause as those along the Illinois and Wabash River country, Henry felt it was possible they could "be brought to expel their British Masters & become fellow Citizens of a free State." [38] John Todd was appointed county lieutenant of the Illinois country with ample civil powers and would have directions to work in concert with Clark wherever possible.[39] Clark was also to cooperate wherever he could with the neighboring Spanish subjects. Henry was aware of the delicacy and difficulty of Clark's situation but did not doubt that he would accomplish the arduous work with distinction. In view of the distance from the Illinois country, Henry said that he could not be consulted, but he gave Clark general discretionary powers where his instructions were silent and the law made no provision.[40]

On December 9, 1778, the Assembly created the vast county of Illinois in Virginia, and three days later Henry issued detailed instructions to John Todd. "The present Crisis rendered so favourable from the good Disposition of the French & Indians may be improved to great purposes. But if unhappily it is lost, a Return of the same Attachments to us may never happen," Henry wrote him. Todd was to cooperate with Clark and was given similar instructions for cultivating the friendship of the French settlers, the English, and Spanish.[41]

The new Illinois administrator benefited from these and other instructions. Todd, nephew of Parson Todd and a relative of the future Mrs. Abraham Lincoln, proved a competent county lieutenant. Todd laid off his so-called county, actually as large as some European countries, into three districts. In each of them a court of justice, elected by the inhabitants, was set up and further measures taken so that the Virginia government there was able to survive the war and remain under American control after the peace treaty.

Meantime, Clark had been able to hold Vincennes with only a nominal garrison; in his absence it was recaptured on December 17 by the British. Then Clark marched his little force across the frozen plains and flooded bottom lands and retook the fort on February 25, 1779. The details of the suffering endured during the march, Clark wrote his friend, George Mason, were "too incredible for any Person to believe except those that are as well acquainted with me as you are or had experienced something similar to it."[42]

After being out of touch with Clark for a long period—too long for that impatient frontiersman—Henry wrote him a not too fulsome letter of congratulations. Henry said he would help Clark secure some land he wanted. Meantime, Henry was "very anxious" to have Clark get him two of the best stallions that could possibly be found in the Illinois country. Clark was "not to scrimp" in the cost of buying and forwarding the two horses, whose specifications were listed in a detailed memorandum. And he was not to mention the matter in their public correspondence.

Henry's letter seems somewhat out of character. Such tradition as has been handed down does not indicate that he was a keen lover or judge of horseflesh. Some of the details given Clark smack of having come from more of a connoisseur, perhaps that inveterate horse breeder, John Syme. On the other hand, Henry would be needing some new sources of income at the end of his governorship. Judging from the numerous advertisements in the *Virginia Gazette*s for blooded sires at stud, it might seem that horse breeding was the most lucrative business left in Virginia. Perhaps Henry intended to breed and sell blooded stock. He had sold Scotchtown some months before,[43] but there was fine grazing land on the great Leatherwood plantation which he soon bought in western Virginia.

An experienced administrator, Henry realized that there were some difficulties which had best be sidestepped—for instance, an imbroglio with certain students and townspeople. The William and Mary students, so one later wrote, and "most of the respectable inhabitants" of the capital prepared a plan for the celebration of Washington's birthday, February 22, 1779. Certain of them first offered the paper to Governor Henry, but he refused his signature. "He could not think of any kind of rejoicing at a time when our country was engaged in war, with such gloomy prospects." Two members of the Council were also waited on by the committee and gave "less courteous denials, and similar excuses." Nevertheless, a ball was given at the Raleigh Tavern, directed by the twenty-five-year-old Colonel James Innes, later a distinguished lawyer and legislator. Two cannon were procured to help with the celebration, but while they were being prepared for firing, a state officer, Captain Ned Digges, tried to stop the proceedings. The Digges emissary, however, "took some punch" and, not having secured the guns, reported to Captain Digges, who in turn sought instructions from Governor Henry. But Henry referred the captain to "his own judgment." There followed a ludicrous scene. Captain Digges, backed by sixty men, demanded the cannon at the point of the bayonet. Innes, a very large man, dubbed "the fat knight" and "Thunderbolt of War," swore that he would cane Digges. It all ended peacefully when charges against Colonel Innes were dismissed in Hustings

Court.[44] And yet it was a potentially difficult situation—which Henry had avoided.

As war Governor, Henry had figured chiefly in the role of the busy executive. In at least one instance he was too preoccupied with the report of a state purchasing agent to extend the usual social amenities. The aggrieved agent, young St. George Tucker, member of a prominent Williamsburg family, wrote some criticism of Henry which gets at the heart of his problems as a wartime state executive.

On February 18, 1777, the Council, with Henry present, had found it "absolutely necessary" in order to secure arms and other military supplies, to arrange for the deposit of a sum of money in the West Indies. Tucker was sent to Charleston, South Carolina, to purchase £10,000 worth of indigo which would be used to pay for the matériel.[45]

After arranging in Charleston to buy the indigo and have it shipped and exchanged for arms, Tucker returned later in the year to Williamsburg, where he sought from the Council a warrant for £500 which he had advanced for the state. When recalling the circumstances in 1805, he thought that he had attended the Council twice before being admitted and that Henry had not asked him to sit down; "I was not thanked for my zeal and expedition, or for advancing my money."

Henry also made a rather abrupt comment about the high price which Tucker had given for the indigo. It was more than the state had paid for it before, he said, and Tucker, in his 1805 letter, declared that this was very true since depreciation had begun. Henry also said that Tucker had been in too much of a hurry to make the purchase. "I felt indignation flash from my eyes, and I feel it at my heart at this moment," Tucker wrote.[46]

On June 6, 1779, Thomas Jefferson had succeeded Henry as Governor, and Tucker seized the opportunity for an attack on Henry when writing Colonel Theodorick Bland. Tucker was highly laudatory of Jefferson but went on to say that if, as Governor,

> he should tread in the steps of his predecessor, there is not much
> to be expected from the brightest talents. Did the enemy know
> how very defenceless we are at present, a very small addition to

their late force would be sufficient to commit the greatest ravages throughout the country. It is a melancholy fact that there were not arms enough to put in the hands of the few militia who were called down on the late occasion; of those which were to be had, a great number were not fit for use. Nor was there by any means a sufficiency of ammunition or camp utensils of any kind. In short, never was a country in a more shabby situation; for our fortifications and marine, on which more than a million have been thrown away, are in no capacity to render any service to us; nor have we any standing force to give the smallest check to an approaching enemy.[47]

For the failure to provide adequately for the defense of the state, a primary responsibility lay with the Virginia Assembly, which did not provide the necessary legislation. The Assembly would not have accomplished as much as they did if Governor Henry had not continued to tactfully prod them. But considering their lack of resources and inexperience with wartime problems, the legislators probably did about as well as could have been expected. To a notable degree Henry got them to appreciate the importance of sacrificing the lesser for the greater; of providing men and supplies for the central armies, however much this might denude the state. Among a number of such instances, Congress on April 13, 1779, a month before Henry ended his third term, asked and secured from Virginia "one thousand stand of arms, for the purpose of arming the forces destined for the defence of South Carolina and Georgia."[48]

In 1792, St. George Tucker, now forty and a judge of the General Court at Richmond, was for the first time thrown in social contact with Henry. Henry's "manners were the perfection of urbanity," Tucker wrote, "his conversation various, entertaining, instructive, and fascinating. I parted from him with infinite regret, and forgot for the whole time I was with him, that I had so many years borne in mind an expression which might not have been intended to wound me, as it did."[49]

Henry could not possibly maintain protective forces for all the vast territory, from the Atlantic to the Mississippi and the Great Lakes, now under his jurisdiction. Like the Confederate Secretaries of War directing a vast military theater from Richmond nearly a century later, Henry had to gamble on the best use of resources available. On the whole, his relations as war Governor with sensitive state agents such as Tucker, and with patriotic but parochial-minded Assemblymen and Councilors, were more amicable than might have been expected of the fiery orator. They were less happy, however, with George Rogers Clark, and particularly with the inept Congress—no small part of the difficulties coming from faulty communication.

When writing Clark on January 12, 1778, Henry had addressed him as "supposed to be at Fort Pitt." [50] Evidently, when the letter reached Pittsburg the Clark expedition had already set out into the wilderness, for after recapturing Vincennes, Clark had testily written the Governor that he had not received so much as "a scrape of paper" from him in a year. But Henry's letters to Congress, directed to York or Philadelphia, did not have to pass through a wild, Indian-infested region, and that lumbering body's inept relations with him added another frustrating note to his last months as war Governor.

15

War Governor—Gladly Resigning

Congress is ex[t]remely thin, which you will discover by a resolve which has or will soon be sent you.——JOHN HENRY, JR., March 17, 1778, to the Speaker of the Maryland House of Delegates [1]

Late winter, 1778-1779, and *spring, 1779.* British overrunning Georgia and threatening Charleston, S.C.

May, 1779. British foray on Virginia coast.

June 1, 1779. Henry retires as Governor; Thomas Jefferson elected to succeed him.

OFTEN THE MOST revealing historical items are buried in a mass of minutiae. On Henry's urgent letter to Congress of November 28, 1778, there is this notation, perhaps by some obscure clerk:

Read Decr 8. 1778
Referred to Marine Com^e. [2]

It was ten days before this letter, seeking "the earliest Intelligence," was turned over to the Marine Committee, and another five weeks before that bureaucratic body brought in a report which Congress implemented the same day with some unsatisfactory resolutions. [3] One might argue that the loss through misdirection of a few row galleys would be of no great moment, yet they comprised much of

[213]

Virginia's little navy, vitally needed to protect ships trading tobacco for foreign munitions.

In its bumbling efforts the Marine Committee had an unhappy resemblance to Congress as a whole. And yet Henry, while deploring the congressional ineptitude, could not fail to sympathize with the troubles of the individual delegates. The Marine Committee was "in a very bad situation" (as were the Treasury and Commercial Affairs committees), one of its most conscientious members, Josiah Bartlett, had written some months before. It was not only that the members could spare little time for the committee business but that they were being constantly changed before they could become familiar with their duties, and new members "totally ignorant of the past transactions" were appointed in their place.

There had been trouble enough when Congress, the British at their heels, had left Philadelphia to meet in the little market town of York, and there was more when the harassed members returned to the Quaker City. With the mounting inflation, Bartlett paid £37 for his own and his waiter's board for six weeks at York and £145 for four months' victuals and lodging after the Congressmen were able to meet again at Philadelphia. These charges were apart from such items as £15 for his expenses when in the country to recover his health; £64 for "horse keeping"; £17 for drink at Mrs. Peart's; and £12 for nursing his waiter while sick in Philadelphia.[4] To this add the "very bad fare" at York which, so Congressman James Lovell of Massachusetts averred, had "torn out the bowells" of many of his countrymen and "driven several delegates home to their native springs."[5] Richard Henry Lee had trouble even in getting to Philadelphia: "I arrived here on the 19th [February 19, 1779], thro the worst roads that I ever travelled over," he wrote Henry.[6]

There were other reasons for Congress' incapacity. When it delayed answering Henry's letter of December 17, 1778, the members were largely occupied with problems of governmental finance. The states frequently answered roll call with one or two delegates, and at one session there was an insufficient number of states represented to proceed with any business at all. Time was wasted in discussion of petty matters of phraseology. Henry's friend, Francis Lightfoot Lee, for instance, required the "yeas" and "nays" on the question of whether to include in a resolution the words "the same having been taken *ex parte*." [7]

Congress was only guilty of the common faults of legislative bodies, but this was wartime. Some members were indeed struggling to keep up with their agenda, as, for example, Meriwether Smith, who in a letter of February 21, 1778, to John Page, which Henry probably read, spoke of the multiplicity of business in Congress and how he had "snatched a Moment" to answer Page's letter. But Smith admitted that the manner in which business was conducted there rendered his task arduous indeed. [8]

Before Henry left the governorship in June, Congress did take steps by which it gained a measure of efficiency. It assigned some of its work to special boards, improved the committee procedure, adopted General von Steuben's regulations for discipline of the Continental troops, and left more authority in military matters to General Washington. [9] In late February, the Virginia delegation was strengthened by the appointment of Thomas Nelson, Jr., to Congress, where he would serve until August 7 and utilize his military experience on the Board of War. His usefulness on the Board, however, was decreased by the usual delays in communication. [10]

There were also delays in Henry's correspondence with Ben Franklin in France. With communication dependent on such sailing vessels as escaped the British blockade, it was not until February 26, 1779, that Franklin replied to Henry's letter of March 3, 1778. The urbane old Ben, from his comfortable establishment at Passy, near Paris, expressed his desire to serve Virginia. He tactfully indicated, however, that all was not well among the American agents; especially Arthur Lee, he might have added. [11] Despite the difficulties, Captain Lemaire—with Franklin's aid—did purchase a considerable quantity of military matériel as noted. But there was trouble about payment. The supplies had not been landed in Virginia when Henry retired from the governorship the following June, and when they came they were sadly inadequate. Richard Henry Lee had already written Henry in February, 1779, that it would take a hundred thousand stand of good arms and more than a hundred cannon to put Virginia in a proper state of defense.[12] Just how insufficient were the state munitions would be shown when the British penetrated deeply into Virginia the next year.

March brought more troubles; they seemed to have a cumulative effect upon Henry. When writing Washington on the thirteenth, he tried to put a cheerful face on the military situation and could note some encouraging news of the western campaigns. But he had to state that South Carolina was now "in great danger" from the advancing British, while Forts Natchez and Morishac were again in enemy hands, ruining trade with the Spanish along the Mississippi.[13]

The same day Henry answered a letter from President Reed of Congress, in which Reed sought his help with a plan to check the enemy's depredation on American trade by laying "a general Embargo." As much as Henry wished to cooperate in an embargo, he had to reply that the Virginia law did not give him the authority to do so; he could only lay the matter before the May Assembly.[14] Also, beyond collecting and dispatching available troops and supplies for the long trip to South Carolina, there was not very much he could do to help Lincoln's army. And this despite a personal appeal on March 29 by an emissary from the General.[15] The emissary, thirty-three-year-old Major Everard Meade, gave the Council a candid account of the "distressed Situation" of the Southern army because of lack of troops. The Council, in Henry's absence, took immediate steps to hurry more militia southward. But, as Henry well knew, it would take some of them over three weeks to march to Charleston, apart from the time needed to assemble and supply them.

Probably ill in both body and spirit, Henry was absent from a number of Council sessions in late March and early April, 1779. Already, on March 27, he had written George Mason one of his most pessimistic letters. Henry viewed matters very differently from people in general "who seemed to think that the contest was at an end, and to make money, and to get places, the only thing now remaining to do." He had "seen without despondency, even for a moment, the hours which America had styled her gloomy ones," but on "no day since the commencement of hostilities" had he "thought her liberties in such imminent danger as at present."

Henry spoke of how friends and foes seemed "now to combine to pull down the goodly fabric we have hitherto been raising at the expense of so much time, blood, and treasure." Unless "the bodies politic" would "exert themselves to bring things back to first principles, correct abuses, and punish our internal foes," he believed ruin must follow. Henry did not wish to cast reflections upon any particular state or its representatives. But he said it was too notorious to be concealed that Congress was "rent by party," that much "business of a trifling nature and personal concern" drew their attention from matters then of great national moment.[16] "Where are our men of abilities?" Henry asked Mason.

> Why do they not come forth to save their country? Let this voice, my dear sir, call upon you, Jefferson and others. Do not, from a mistaken opinion that we are about to sit down under our own vine, and own fig-tree, let our hitherto noble struggle end in ignominy. Believe me when I tell you there is danger of it. I have pretty good reasons for thinking that administration a little while ago, had resolved to give the matter up and negotiate a peace with us upon almost any terms; but I shall be much mistaken if they do not now, from the present state of our currency, dissensions, and other circumstances, push matters to the utmost extremity.[17]

In dire need of men and supplies, Congress had already called for the enlistment of 3,000 Negro slaves to help repel the British invasion. But the proposal was rejected by the South Carolina legislature "with contempt."[18] Moreover, on April 13 Congress requested Virginia to lend to the United States a thousand stand of arms for troops defending South Carolina and Georgia. The federal Board of War was to replace them without delay.[19] To add to the difficulties, Henry wrote the Virginia congressmen on the twenty-third, the guards for the British prisoners at the barracks near Charlottesville were complaining "most bitterly" because of the lack of clothing which Congress had promised them. Henry feared the consequences if the troops were not supplied with the clothes in "the most speedy manner"; already they were beginning to desert.

In April Henry at the request of Congress called on the people of Virginia to observe the first Thursday in May as a day of fasting, humiliation, and prayer.[20] It was hardly a month before he issued another alarming proclamation. This was to announce that a British fleet had arrived on the Virginia coast. The formidable fleet, thirty-five "sail" with a contingent of 2,000 troops, easily overpowered the small Virginia force at Portsmouth, destroying a number of ships in the harbor. Then the British marched to Suffolk, where they burned or plundered valuable supplies. Henry called upon the military officers in the state and especially those in her navigable waters to hold their respective militia in readiness to oppose attempts of the enemy wherever made.

The extent of the Virginia shore line and the necessity of providing troops for both Washington's and Lincoln's armies had left the Hampton Roads area vulnerable to enemy attack. The Assembly called to the coast part of a cavalry regiment stationed at Winchester and also the new Virginia recruits requisitioned for the Continental Army. Henry, not so easily excited, submitted grudgingly to the legislative action. "Would it not disgrace our country to cry for aid against this band of robbers?"[21] If the British invaders had not returned soon to their ships, there might have been a serious delay in the movement of needed Virginia militia to South Carolina.

By early May, 1779, British General Prevost was meeting so little resistance in the lower South that he marched to a point where he threatened Charleston. His advance was halted, however, and Lincoln, with his militia reinforcements, attempted to recover Georgia. But this abortive movement, and the subsequent defeats of the Americans at Charleston and Camden, would occur after Henry's retirement from the governorship. He could hardly be blamed for the resultant losses of Virginia troops.[22]

Henry's third and last term as Governor was now ending: despite the incomplete records we can make some evaluation of his administration. In 1776, partly during his governorship, Virginia is credited with supplying 6,181 men to the Continental Army. The next year she had a larger quota—10,200; and she had 5,741 on the Continental rolls, as well as 5,269 militia. In 1778 her Continental quota was 7,800 men, of which she supplied 5,230, as well as 600 guards for the Saratoga prisoners in the state and 2,000 militia. During 1779, his term ending, Henry served as Governor for only a half year. Enlistments were being affected by the bad conditions of military service, including the pitifully low pay in depreciated paper currency. The Virginia quota this year was 5,742 regulars, of which she is listed as mustering only 3,973. But she then had 4,000 militia and retained 600 prison guards. Altogether, with the troops provided for the Northwest and Indian campaigns, it appears that Virginia supplied more militia for the war than she did Continentals.

If we add the results of Henry's efforts as they carried over into later gubernatorial administrations, it is doubtful if any other Revolutionary Governor made a more impressive record. We must think in terms not only of total numbers of men and supplies but how well the soldiers served—often after re-enlistments in the Continental Army or repeated tours of militia duty. We must consider how well they met their obligations despite discouragements and failures. No man then living in the state did more to enspirit them than Patrick Henry.

As the end of his third term approached there was an effort to re-elect Henry for still another year. He prevented this attempt by writing to the Speaker of the House of Delegates on May 28 that the constitution made him ineligible for office and he intended to retire in four or five days. The same day Thomas Jefferson was added to a committee appointed to bring in a bill for moving the seat of government to Richmond, a somewhat more central location than Williamsburg and less susceptible to enemy raids. But this change would not become effective until after Henry's retirement; Jefferson became the first in a long line of Governors to serve in Richmond. In the election on June 1, 1779, he defeated John Page on the second ballot by a vote of 67 to 61, many of Henry's followers doubtless contributing to the necessary majority.[23]

The House of Delegates requested Henry, as one of his last ceremonial acts, to present "the finest gelding" that could be procured and caparisoned to Brigadier General Charles Scott as a token of its appreciation of his activity in the late invasion. There remained for the Henry family the tedious task of packing up all their belongings accumulated in Williamsburg during the past three years. On the twenty-ninth Henry signed a paper listing some articles that he had purchased for the Palace on the Governor's account: "Five large dishes, two basons, one 'sett' cups and saucers, four y^{ds} Carpeting, etc.," for a total of £44.3.6.[24]

Already in August, 1777, John Syme, on behalf of Henry, had advertised for sale "the pleasant and healthy seat called SCOTCH-TOWN" including 1000 acres of "very good" soil, 400 of them cleared and enclosed for farming; and a "very commodious" dwelling house 88 by 36 ft. "Negroes or money will be accepted in payment. . . ." Henry sold the estate in 1778 to Wilson Miles Cary for £5,000, and the same year he bought of Thomas Lomax a three-fifths undivided interest in a tract of 16,650 acres on Leatherwood Creek in Henry County.[25]

Soon after he retired as Governor he set out with his family for his new plantation in the western Piedmont, well-nigh exhausted by his gubernatorial labors yet encouraged by the plaudits of the two branches of the Assembly: the Senate, which thanked him "nemine contradicente" for "his faithful discharge of that important trust, and his uniform endeavors to promote the true interest of this State, and of all America," and the House in similar vein.[26]

16

Leatherwood and the British

That Virginia has been prodigal of her blood, and of her treasure is generally agreed.——GENERAL NATHANAEL GREENE, October 24, 1782, to Governor Harrison [1]

June, 1779–November, 1784. Henry residing at Leatherwood in Henry County.

May, 1780–November, 1784. Henry again an outstanding member of legislature.

May 12, 1780. British capture Charleston, S.C.

August 16, 1780. Crushing American defeat at Camden, S.C.

October 7, 1780. American victory at King's Mountain, S.C.

May 15, 1781. British Pyrrhic victory at Guilford Courthouse, N.C.

June 4, 1781. British raid on Charlottesville, Va., where legislature was sitting.

October 19, 1781. British surrender at Yorktown, Va.

M OUNT VERNON is associated with George Washington, Monticello with Thomas Jefferson, and Stratford with the Lees. But no country estate is identified only with Patrick Henry until his retirement at Red Hill. Ever with an itching foot until his last years, he moved again, after ending his third gubernatorial term, to his 10,000-acre Leatherwood plantation in Henry County. Here he would reside, except when serving as a leading member of the Assembly, during the final war and first postwar years until late in 1784, when he started his fourth term as Governor.

At Leatherwood Henry was some 220 miles southwest of Williamsburg and 180 miles from Richmond, soon to become the Virginia capital. It would take his Italian friend, Philip Mazzei, five days to travel to Leatherwood from Orange, above Charlottesville; Henry perhaps a week to ride to Richmond, where he would continue to serve in the Assembly.

And yet the distant plantation did not offer the refuge which Henry had expected. Cornwallis' thrust northward in the Carolinas during early 1781 brought Leatherwood uncomfortably close to the fighting zone, and a few months later Henry and the entire legislature were nearly captured at Charlottesville by Tarleton's cavalry. Moreover, that mortifying event helped to incite an unhappy—and long sustained—controversy with Thomas Jefferson. In the war and uneasy aftermath, the Leatherwood period had more effect on Henry's public career than is often appreciated. Not only in the House of Delegates at Richmond but elsewhere he again found himself grappling with difficult military and political problems.

Even in his private life it was a period of adjusting himself to much that was relatively new and strange, as was illustrated by an incident during Mazzei's visit to Leatherwood. Mazzei had arrived at Henry's home in his absence and had been greeted by a lady unknown to the young Italian.

"Who is the lady I had seen?" Mazzei later asked Henry after embracing him.

"The mistress of the house," Henry replied, and went on to tell Mazzei of the loss of his first wife; how he had been obliged to give up everything that recalled her memory, and how two years afterward he had remarried.[2]

The adjustment of the middle-aged Henry to a young wife and their new family was still being made, and it was not yet clear what the effect would be on his public life.

When settling on the large Leatherwood estate in Henry County, Henry was influenced by a number of considerations besides its purportedly sheltered location. It was intriguing at least to move to a new county named in one's honor, and Leatherwood did offer some obvious advantages. Named for Leatherwood Creek, which winds southward through the estate, it was some twenty miles westward of Wynn's Ferry on the Dan River, the present Danville, and a few miles east of the present Martinsville. In October, 1777, Henry's salary had been raised from £1,000 to £1,500, and to £3,000 a year later, but with the rapidly depreciating currency it was never enough to meet expenses. To the shrewd Henry, the Leatherwood tract must have seemed a good investment, and, more important, it would enable him to provide for his increasing domestic establishment, with children by Dolly being added while several by his first wife were still under the parental roof. The bracing air of the Blue Ridge foothills also should help him to recover his shattered health.

In June, 1779, a few days after the close of his third gubernatorial term, the Henrys and their entourage set out on the trek through the summer heat and dust to their new home on the remote Virginia frontier. Besides the large Henry family and slaves, his married daughter, Martha, her young husband, John Fontaine, and their family joined the caravan, which probably totaled some fifty persons. Upon their arrival at Leatherwood, they found a large part of the land occupied by squatters, who were removed only after much difficulty. There was also a gnawing dispute over the title to the property, a dispute which does, however, help to clear Henry of a charge of unconscionable speculation. Thomas Jefferson, after he became inimical to Henry, would be too expansive in asserting that the "valuable" estate was finally paid for "in depreciated paper not worth oak leaves." [3]

Henry County, cut off only three years before from Pittsylvania, was in a newly settled area bordering the North Carolina line. Beginning at a southerly point near present Eden, North Carolina, it extended some twenty miles northward into the Blue Ridge foothills, then stretched westward another fifty miles, embracing the rugged mountains of present Patrick County. Leatherwood is in the eastern part of Henry County, not far from the valley of the Dan River, the lovely country which evoked the admiration of William Byrd. [4]

Still a semifrontier region in 1779, Henry County was settled chiefly by a characteristic breed of small farmers, sturdy and independent but with little formal education. With a few noteworthy exceptions, the early land grants in the county were for a few hundred acres or less, much of this on infertile, hilly land. Thus, in July, 1779, Garrot Birch acquired 412 acres on what was inelegantly described as the "Dung Branch" of Leatherwood Creek, and Susanna Reynolds 38 acres westward on a branch of Mayo River. Three years later there were only 8,479 settlers in the county, including 1,551 slaves, and it was still geared to a wartime economy. There was a sprinkling of what would become profitable plantations, with large acreage and good bottom land. But most of the people could eke out little more than a subsistence with their corn, tobacco, and cattle on little, hilly farms. It is understandable that later some would see no harm in selling some of their corn in the form of more remunerative "mountain dew," or illicit whisky.

Never disturbed by rough living conditions, Henry took up his residence near the old Danville road, about five miles from present Martinsville. The so-called family "mansion" appears to have been a simple two-room brick structure, "a sort of camp," with basement on the ground level. Old men, living long afterward, told of serving as guards for the Henry house, portholes having been made for their guns. "The Torys have been plotting hereabouts as well as over the Mountains," Henry wrote in August, 1780, "but I hope they are pretty well suppressed. We have partys out in pursuit. . . ." [5]

Henry had hardly left Williamsburg for Leatherwood when on June 17 the Assembly elected him a delegate to Congress for the term beginning the following November. An indication of his remoteness from the main political activity was the statement in his letter of declination to Governor Harrison of October 18, 1779, that he did not receive the notice of appointment for "several months." [6] Moreover, when writing to Jefferson on February 15, 1780, Henry said that he had "scarcely heard a word of public matters" since he moved to Leatherwood.

His lack of contact with public affairs, however, was not the full explanation for his refusal to serve in Congress. Until lately he had been too ill to attend to business, he wrote Harrison in the October letter, and he was so "circumstanced" as to make his attendance at Congress "impossible." In those days, matters relating to a lady's accouchment were alluded to by gentlemen with delicacy; the circumstance to which Henry apparently referred was the advanced pregnancy of his young wife, Dorothea. Soon after the first Christmas in their new home, on January 4, 1780, she gave birth to their second and his eighth child, a girl they named Sarah Butler.[7]

Meantime, Henry could hardly avoid some participation in affairs of the developing county. Certainly, that was true after the British moved nearer to Leatherwood from the Carolinas, and the Tories became more active in the Virginia back country. In 1778 commissioners had been appointed to secure bids in the county for a prison, stocks, and a new courthouse of solid logs, 24 by 20 feet, with a bar, benches, and a window and door on each side. The following August, 1779, Patrick Henry, his son-in-law, John Fontaine, and William Letcher were recommended to Governor Jefferson among "proper persons" to serve as county justices. At meetings within the next two years the justices attended to such business as paying the bounty in tobacco for wolves' heads; licensing an ordinary and a member of the Baptist Society to solemnize marriages; arraigning one Isaac Donaldson on charge of high treason; and appointing militia captains, among them George Hairston, of the great county landholding clan, and John Fontaine.

There is no evidence that Henry ever sat on the bench of the County Court, but the seat of William Letcher, an active justice and local Whig leader, soon became vacant under circumstances which horrified the lonely settlers. Letcher, home on furlough from the Southern army, was shot by a Tory raider while his wife lay helpless in a bed nearby. The murderer was caught and executed in summary justice. With women in short supply, the blooming widow soon found solace and protection through marriage to George Hairston (a child born to them was grandmother of the dashing General Jeb Stuart).[8]

In his letter to Jefferson of February 15, 1780, Henry appeared as apprehensive of the fate of Virginia as when writing Mason the previous March. Henry spoke of his "many anxieties for our common-wealth, principally occasioned by the depreciation of our money." Judged by this "pulse of the State," he feared that "our body politic was dangerously sick. God forbid it may not be unto death." The recent increase in prices, he thought, was "in great part owing to a kind of habit which is now of four or five years growth." [9]

These prices, Henry might have added, were sky high, even when regulated by the County Court. By March, 1781, while he was attending the meeting of the legislature in Richmond, inflation had forced the Henry County Court to raise stipulated charges at ordinaries so that they were $13 per gill (not quart) for West Indian rum, $12 per gill for "good" peach brandy, $8 per gill for "good" whisky, $20 for a cold dinner and $10 more when hot, $15 per gallon for corn, and $2 per bundle for fodder. Within two more months the price of a dinner, evidently "warm," had jumped to $40; good rum to $15 per gill. [10]

Besides commiserating with Jefferson about the inflationary prices in Virginia, Henry agreed with him about her "disguised tories." It gave Henry "the utmost pain . . . to see some men, indeed very many, who were thought good whigs, keep company with the miscreants . . . labouring for our destruction." In the low spirits now often associated with his debility, he was satisfied that his health would "never again permit a close application to sedentary business." He even doubted whether he could "remain below long enough" to serve Jefferson in the Assembly. And he expressed to Jefferson his fear of the lack of public spirit; "this more than the British arms" made him "fearful of final success, without a reform." Concluding with a cordiality that would not characterize their correspondence after another year, Henry "most sincerely" wished Jefferson "health and prosperity" and signed himself "your affectionate friend." [11]

Despite his misgivings about his health, Henry did attend the May, 1780, Assembly, though there is no proof that he was present until the eighteenth. The respect with which he was received and the committees with which he was connected indicate that he was the most important member of the House, influential and courageous enough to stand up successfully for that brave and outspoken Cumberland minister, the Reverend Christopher McCrae, in danger of being exiled from the state as an alleged Tory.

When a petition for his banishment was presented, Henry, according to McCrae's daughter, instantly arose and declared that it contained many fictitious names. He knew Mr. McCrae intimately, and if the minister were banished Cumberland would lose one of its best citizens. Henry persuaded the House to wait until he could get "a counter-petition, signed by the most respectable portion of the community," and McCrae was allowed to remain.[12]

At the May, 1779 session, the Assembly had moved the seat of government to Richmond as "more safe and central than any other town situated on navigable water."[13] But Richmond, so familiar to Henry when a Hanover resident, could as yet boast of few pretensions as a state capital. Messrs. Clarkson and Davis, who moved their printing business with the *Virginia Gazette* from Williamsburg to the new capital, were unable to secure a suitable office for some time, despite their "utmost endeavors." The temporary capitol building was a "clumsy" wooden building, so inconspicuous that the British would not bother to burn it during their 1781 invasion. Nearly a decade later, Richmond would still number only three hundred houses, mostly simple wooden structures, a story or two each, with dormer windows, heavy shutters, and chinked chimneys.[14]

"Richmond must one day or other be a great Town," hopefully wrote David Jameson, a Councilor from the Tidewater; ". . . were we in Peace I should think it a proper place for the seat of Government." At present, however, he did not think he could ever "be reconciled to it as a desirable place of residence. half the mornings since I have been here the Town has been covered with Fog." Perhaps this fog and "the thin putrid state of the Air" helped to explain why Henry left the House on June 7, 1780.[15]

Thomas Jefferson had now been Governor for nearly a year, and, like Henry when in the executive office, he continued to drain the state of men and supplies for the American armies. While seeking to meet this basic need, Jefferson could only hope that there would be no critical invasion of Virginia. As yet there had been none, and the genial, sandy-haired young master of Monticello had lost little or none of the influence which he had gained while he was liberal leader of the House. On June 2, 1780, Jefferson was nominated and elected as Governor for a second one-year term. He was supported by Henry, the leading personage in the Assembly, and thus Henry returned the favor Jefferson had rendered in nominating him two years before.[16]

It was the sixth year of the war, and the state was beginning to scrape the bottom of the barrel. Nevertheless, the Assembly, with Henry in key positions, made a strenuous effort to send more men and supplies to the South. Horses and wagons were authorized for the use of Maryland troops moving to South Carolina, and arms were ordered to supply some North Carolina troops. After news of the anticipated capture of Charleston, 2,500 more Virginia militia were called out (including 135 from Hanover County and 108 from Henry County). The desperate state of the wartime finances, to which Jefferson and Henry had alluded, was further revealed in the military pay scale. In accordance with the legislative provision, the militia on the new duty were to be paid chiefly in tobacco as currency: only 8½ pounds of tobacco and 1 ration for a drummer and fifer, and 7½ pounds of tobacco and 1 ration for a private. There was an emergency call by the Assembly for Congress to send "a further speedy and powerful reinforcement" of Continental troops to the South, and also a supply of arms for the North Carolina militia, to whom the Governor of Virginia had already furnished all he could spare.[17]

On June 6 came the expected word of the fall of Charleston, with some 5,683 troops, about half of them Continentals, and valuable stores.[18] Among the Continentals surrounded and captured by the overwhelming British force and marched out, with colors cased, to ground their arms, were almost 1,400 Virginians, including over 900 Continentals from the First, Second, and Third Virginia, with over 50 officers from other Virginia Continental regiments.[19]

On April 6 Henry's old rival, General Woodford, had arrived at Charleston with 750 of the Virginia Continentals, all that were then left in Washington's army. The troops had marched five hundred miles in twenty-eight days but were too few and too late to save the city.[20] Its capture was one of the worst calamities of the war; on the day when the bad tidings reached Richmond, the House passed a measure providing for confiscation of food from private families.[21] There was also a debate on the grave question of finance, Henry and Richard Henry Lee arguing on opposite sides. Congress had now issued over $260,000,000 in paper money, the states at least an equal amount. The Continental money could no longer be relied upon to purchase food for the Army,[22] and on March 18, 1780, Congress in resolutions "dictated by despair" provided that the states should put into the Continental treasury for another year $15,000,000 in paper money each month or the equivalent in specie at 40 to 1; as the old bills were brought in they were to be destroyed and new bills issued for only one twentieth of the amounts. Thus Congress would repudiate its promise to redeem its old money at face value.[23]

Nevertheless, the congressional resolutions were supported in the Virginia legislature by George Mason and Richard Henry Lee. These statesmen believed, so Edmund Randolph wrote, that the resolutions were "the only expedient remaining for the restoration of public credit." But, Randolph said, "Patrick Henry poured forth all his eloquence in opposition." The motion to adopt the Congressional Act of March 18 was defeated. Henry carried a substitute measure which provided that "ample and certain funds" be established for sinking in fifteen years the Virginia quota of the Continental debt; also "certain" funds to furnish Congress with the Virginia quota in support of the war for the current year.[24]

Henry had doubted that his health was sufficiently recovered to enable him to remain in Richmond throughout the session, and the next day, June 7, 1780, he obtained a leave of absence.[25] After he had left his seat, the congressional plan for refinancing was again proposed and now adopted.[26] But a year later the inflation was still rampant. The new Continental notes, writes one authority, were "'viler than the rags' on which they were printed, seldom used in trade, and valued at purely speculative rates of five hundred to one and lower." There was no satisfactory solution for the currency crisis at the time, but Henry's plan might well have been the more satisfactory of the two considered.[27]

Back home at Leatherwood, Henry could reflect upon his fate if he had remained in the military service. Would he have been captured at Charleston, like so many officers from his old First Regiment and other Virginia Continental commands? Would he have died or his health been broken in a British prison? Or suppose he had remained an active militia officer? Would he have been shot or cut down in the rout at Camden?

On June 11 Jefferson had written Washington that he was sending 2,500 men southward. But he did not note that a large portion of the Virginia troops were raw country lads who had never seen a battle, nor did he know that Congress was sending the overestimated General Horatio Gates south to command the new army.[28]

The subsequent debacle was even worse than might have been expected. At Camden on August 16, 1780, Gates' army, ill-led, half-disciplined, debilitated by night marches and rations that included half-cooked meat and molasses which "purged us as well as if we had taken jallap," was routed by a British force under Cornwallis despite the gallant stand of some better-trained troops.

"Come on, men! Don't you know what bayonets are for?" Colonel Stephen called out to his militia in the face of the advancing British. But how could they have known! "They had never had a bayonet in all their lives until the very day before and had never used one, except for a spit on which to roast that last ration of beef."[29]

In September, when Henry was making ready to go down for another session of the legislature, some of the miserable fugitives from the battlefield were still trickling back to their farms.

The Assembly was scheduled to meet on October 16, 1780, but did not convene until a month later, even though the requisite quorum was reduced to fifty. There was considerable excuse, however, for some tardy members, since besides other seasonal or wartime exigencies the British General Leslie with 2,500 men had landed in early October at Portsmouth. Although Leslie sailed away in late November, there was strong reason for fearing that he would reinforce General Cornwallis on his march upward through the Carolinas.

As usual, Henry's influence in the House was indicated by his committee appointments. He was made chairman of the Committees of Propositions and Grievances and of the Courts of Justice. And he served on special committees which dealt with such important matters as the procurement of Virginia's quota for the Continental Army and necessary clothes and provisions, the defense of the frontier, and of the Virginia coast. Other members of the latter committee included Richard Henry Lee and General William Campbell, fresh from his laurels as the American commander at King's Mountain, South Carolina. Henry's stern, red-haired brother-in-law could give a firsthand account of the desperate fight early that October in which the staunch frontiersmen from the Carolinas, Virginia, and the new Watauga settlement had defeated and killed or captured nearly all of Colonel Ferguson's British force—a turning point, as it developed, in the Southern campaign.

Among various resolutions which he offered during the session, Henry proposed that a special Virginia emissary be sent to Congress to explain the condition of the state and devise with the members some plans to drive out the enemy. It was a wise move, for although Leslie did sail away from Virginia he was soon succeeded by more dangerous invaders. Stout, sensible Benjamin Harrison, the experienced representative chosen for the task, persuaded Congress to pass an act providing that all the Continentals from Pennsylvania and the states to the southward be attached to the Southern Army. Moreover, "the boy" Lafayette, as Cornwallis too lightly dubbed him, was ordered to move southward immediately to Virginia with 1,200 Continentals.

Meantime, in December, 1780, General Horatio Gates arrived at Richmond en route to meet with a military court of inquiry. Not a year ago there had been prominent Americans who would have substituted "the hero of Saratoga" for Washington. But now Gates had been defeated grievously, many thought disgracefully, at Camden. The House might have given the cold shoulder to the fallen hero. But a committee of which Henry was chairman magnanimously proposed and the House approved a resolution assuring Gates of "the high regard and esteem" of the delegates. "The remembrance of former glories cannot be obliterated by any reverse of fortune." [30]

After nearly six years the war contained little of the comic even for the more lighthearted Virginians. But popular assemblies are seldom without their humorous element, whether or not intentional. It was about this time that a Virginia legislator is said to have proposed that the state pay her part of the war debt by keeping a sty of pigs. By "figures that cannot lie," this Solon reportedly argued that enough revenue would be derived from the natural increase of the pigs not only to pay the war debt in ten years but to run the government.[31]

In early January, 1781, hogs provided the subject of another amusing incident—but for the British rather than the legislators. On December 28 Henry had proposed the resolution commending General Gates; the legislature soon after adjourned. Had Henry remained in Richmond a few more days he would have seen a curious sight: drunken hogs staggering about the streets. The British, under "the traitor" Arnold, had occupied the city and had broken open some liquor casks, on which the swine regaled themselves.

A year earlier, Richmond had had its first glimpse of the redcoats when some of Burgoyne's captured or paroled officers were housed in the homes of Richmond gentlemen. One of the town's "rougher element," seeing a local physician on the streets with a British officer, had attacked the doctor and gouged out one of his eyes.[32]

In early January, 1781, there were a great many more British on the streets of the new capital. And the humiliating circumstances of its capture would contribute to an explosive legislative inquiry of Jefferson's governorship, with Henry as a co-sponsor. Sailing up the James River, a British force of 1,200 men under General Benedict Arnold, landed at Westover, twenty-five miles below Richmond. Then it marched virtually unopposed into the capital.

Three quarters of a century later a Richmond writer would recall the bitter memory of the feeble resistance mustered by the Jefferson administration. A few hundred militia had come on the ground, "unprepared by possessing good discipline or good officers to meet a well-trained foe." These troops were easily driven back, and that night the redcoats were occupying the capital city, some being quartered even in that "sacred edifice," St. John's Church. "Great credit" was due Thomas Jefferson for his services to the state and nation, the Richmond writer continued, but Jefferson had failed to pay enough heed to a warning from General Washington of an anticipated attack on the state; Richmond had not been properly defended.[33] And yet the disgraceful fiasco was in no sense due to a lack of energy or courage on Jefferson's part. There was something pathetic about his riding around the countryside belatedly seeking the needed officers and men. He had also been inhibited by his constitutional scruples in conscripting slaves to work on a river battery, or, as it was harshly put by Baron von Steuben, then the Continental commander in Virginia, "the executive power [was] so confined" that the Governor lacked the "power to procure 40 Negroes to work at Hood's." [34]

Patrick Henry and later Thomas Nelson, while Governor, would have believed that the emergency justified a stretching of the constitution. On the whole, the episode was not the phase of Jefferson's career which Virginians remembered most happily. A fair-minded Jefferson biographer would later state candidly that "Arnold had caught him off his guard." [35] One should not expect perfection even of the Virginian with the versatility of a da Vinci.

Moreover, a vital point in Jefferson's defense should never be overlooked. While obviously lacking the basic knowledge of a professional soldier, Jefferson did continue to appreciate a cardinal point— that it was necessary to concentrate the Virginia resources at vital places and take a chance on lesser risks. In spite of the heavy losses in Virginia troops as well as supplies at Charleston,[36] Jefferson soon got a force of sorts in the field at Camden, and Virginia troops played a significant part, greater than that of any other state, in the subsequent American victories in the South. Within a few weeks after Arnold's raid on Richmond came news of the glorious victory by "Old Dan'l" Morgan over Tarleton at Cowpens, South Carolina; two thirds of Morgan's force of nearly 1,000 men were Virginia militia, who did much to overcome the disgrace of Camden.[37] Morgan proved himself probably the ablest commander of irregular troops in the war, and Henry later offered a successful motion in the Assembly to honor him.

But, as after King's Mountain, the results of Cowpens were not soon realized. Cornwallis, with a greatly superior force, pursued Greene northward toward the Virginia line. Jefferson, in dire need of funds for military matériel, called a meeting of the Assembly for early March, though apologizing for asking the legislators to leave their families after their recent "long and laborious session" and at a time when the state was invaded.

"Had anything been heard lately from Patrick Henry?" John Syme was writing the Governor on February 26. However, Henry was soon in Richmond and served as chairman of the only standing committee of the House during a productive session before it was terminated by another forward movement of the British Army.[38] On March 26, Arnold, then at Portsmouth, was reinforced by 2,000 men under Phillips, and the combined force, moving up the James River, defeated at Petersburg a smaller detachment of Americans under Henry's old liberal supporter, General Muhlenberg.

To add to the burden confronting the state, Cornwallis with an overwhelming force had now pursued Greene to the Virginia border. By a masterly retreat that resourceful general saved his army, but on February 12, 1781, he had to cross the Dan River at Boyd's Ferry, the present South Boston, Virginia. This was only about forty miles east of Leatherwood, and Henry's plantation helped to provide supplies for the hard-pressed army commissary—a barrel of corn for the use of dragoon horses of Colonel William Washington's legion, 164 bushels of corn for Greene's army, and forage for twenty-eight horses for one night.[39]

"Our force is so inferior, that every exertion in the State of Virginia is necessary to support us. I have taken the liberty to write to Mr. Henry to collect fourteen or fifteen hundred volunteers to aid us," Greene wrote Jefferson on February 10.[40] Precisely what Henry did in response to Greene's appeal we do not know. But troops from Pittsylvania, Halifax, and adjacent counties turned out in large force, among them 300 from Henry County, more than asked for. Not long after Henry left for the special session of the legislature, his son-in-law, Captain John Fontaine, set forth with the men of the Leatherwood area to join the county contingent.[41] They crossed Matrimony Creek (facetiously named by William Byrd), near the North Carolina line, and marched southward along the old Greensboro road in time to join Greene's army before the impending battle.

Altogether, of the 3,650 Americans who fought at Guilford Courthouse that chilly March 15, some 2,481 were Virginians from various counties.[42] And not only the Continentals but many of the Virginia militia, including Colonel William Campbell's riflemen, fought well in the bitterly contested battle. "Virginia has given me every support I could wish," Greene wrote Washington after the battle.[43] Nor did the British, so gallant on many fields of the war, lose their laurels. Although the Americans finally retreated before Cornwallis' smaller force, he won only a Pyrrhic victory. Badly mauled, he turned toward the North Carolina coast, and the hard-working Jefferson and the Virginia Assembly could see some hopeful results from their efforts.

In what later proved to be a brilliant strategic move, Greene, instead of pursuing Cornwallis toward Wilmington and thence into Virginia, turned to attack the British posts in the lower South. For the remainder of the war, some of the best Virginia troops would be involved in that protracted but successful campaign.

Yet within the state there was little respite. On April 24, 1781, Cornwallis arrived in Petersburg from Wilmington. Soon his combined command totaled nearly 7,000 men, twice that of the opposing force under Lafayette. The legislature, meeting on May 7 in nearby Richmond, adjourned to Charlottesville for safety.[44] Letters were sent to the absent members requiring their punctual attendance at the little Albemarle County seat, sixty-five miles westward from the capital.

The people expected decisive measures "to rid them of an implacable enemy that was now roaming at large in the bowels of our capital," Speaker Harrison told the Assembly in his opening message on May 29. Omitting some introductory frills, the House on the second day of the session ordered Harrison to call out "with all sufficient expedition" an adequate number of militia to oppose the enemy effectively. In view of the obvious lack of arms and ammunition, the troops were to bring with them such guns as they could secure—a motley lot, we can well imagine. A strong committee, with John Page chairman and Henry a member, successfully introduced a bill establishing martial law in certain dangerous areas, and Henry was ordered to draw up an appeal for help from Congress. He offered a resolution that post riders keep the Assembly informed of the events

[235]

of the war, a measure which if adopted earlier might have prevented the fiasco when Tarleton surprised the members a few days later.[45] Henry also made several other motions regarding the defense of the state.[46]

War was now having its full effect in Virginia. Of the immense destruction in the state by British raiders and the losses—in military matériel, in the already depleted food supplies, in horses, cattle, slaves captured and mistreated—St. George Tucker, Jefferson, and others have left indignant testimony. In the war fought for American freedom, it was ironical to have slaves emancipated by the purportedly reactionary British. But of the 30,000 Virginia slaves carried off in the various British invasions, the astounding number of 27,000 are said to have died of smallpox or camp fever. Jefferson, who bore with equanimity some of his heavy property losses from the redcoats, was outraged when he learned that on his Elk Hill plantation they cut the throats of horses too young for service, and that twenty-seven of about thirty of his slaves carried off had died. If he had taken the slaves away to give them their freedom, Cornwallis "would have done right," Jefferson wrote, "but it was to consign them to inevitable death from the smallpox and putrid fever then raging in this camp."[47]

From Petersburg, Cornwallis pursued Lafayette, who cleverly eluded him and got as far as upper Hanover. For the first time the war came home to Scotchtown. From his camp nearby, Cornwallis sent Colonel Tarleton with 250 cavalry to Charlottesville in the hope that he would secure one of the biggest prizes of the war: Governor Jefferson, the legislators, and other state officials assembled there.

Near Louisa Courthouse the hard-riding British were espied by Captain Jack Jouett, who rode at night over a back route in time to warn the Governor and the Assembly. At Castle Hill, a few miles east of Charlottesville, Tarleton gave them a further breathing spell by stopping for a hearty breakfast, and it was there that he is reported to have captured John Syme, a state senator. Henry's half brother was at best no Adonis. Brought from his bedroom, undressed and with disheveled hair, Syme is said, according to a traditional account, to have so amused Tarleton that he "threw himself into the attitude of Hamlet upon discovering his father's ghost, and exclaimed:

" 'Angels and ministers of grace, defend us!
  Be thou a spirit of health, or goblin damned?' " [48]

The dragoons then proceeded to Charlottesville, where they missed making their rich haul, Jefferson, Henry, and others. Just how narrow was the escape and how grateful to Jouett were the harassed legislators was indicated by their action the next week in Staunton; they agreed to award him an "elegant sword and a pair of pistols" as a memorial of the "High sense" they entertained of his activity and enterprise. Reading the House Journal for that memorable Monday, one can almost see Tarleton's redcoats as they rode hell for leather up the little streets of the future university town.

Summoned by Jefferson after Jouett's warning, the House declared that fifty would constitute a quorum during "the present dangerous invasion." Then, "having reason to apprehend an immediate incursion of the enemy's cavalry," they adjourned to meet on Thursday at Staunton, forty miles westward. The bedeviled Assemblymen had hardly found time to start toward the little Augusta County seat (seven were captured) when the dragoons rode into Charlottesville. Already some of the redcoats had ascended the mountain to Monticello, where they nearly captured the cool, unhurried Jefferson, and now, their horses foaming and lathering in the early summer heat, they galloped some distance toward Staunton in pursuit of the fleeing legislators.

Probably Henry and his colleagues followed the rough dirt road to Staunton over the Blue Ridge at Rockfish Gap, for it was there that militia and other aroused citizenry assembled to stop any British move toward the town. Ordinarily, Henry would have enjoyed the vistas of the mountains and nestling coves, the luxurious green foliage now studded with rhododendron and seasonal flowers. But the cross-mountain trip was too burdensome, too fraught with worries, for him to give much thought to nature's bounty. Yet joys and sorrows are often curiously mixed; the tragicomic note sounded when the dragoons captured John Syme was repeated as the legislators were chased up the Staunton road. General Edward Stevens, dressed as a farmer and riding a "sorry" horse, was overlooked by some British dragoons, who passed him to chase a more conspicuous figure in a scarlet coat. It was the tall, powerful Jack Jouett, that daring horseman having deliberately enticed them. Perhaps Henry was watching anxiously from a roadside covert as the redcoats galloped by. At any rate, he and his companions were said to have been soon involved in an incident more wryly comic than Syme's capture.

In the little Henry party were his brother-in-law, Colonel Christian, who was an active member of the state Senate, John Tyler, and his Charles City neighbor, Speaker Harrison. Tired and hungry, the men are said to have come after a time to a cabin in a mountain gorge where they asked for "refreshment." But an old woman, so the story runs, the only occupant of the dwelling, wanted to know who they were and whence they came. The dialogue which followed bears the earmarks of literary embellishment, especially in the quoted conversation, but its substance was handed down by the reliable Tyler. In reply to the old woman's queries, Henry told her that he and his companions were members of the legislature who had been compelled to flee because of the approach of the enemy. "Ride on then, you cowardly knaves," the old woman indignantly replied. Henry tried to explain further, and finally Tyler stepped forward.

"What would you say, my good woman, if I were to tell you that Patrick Henry fled with the rest of us?" he demanded.

"Patrick Henry! I would tell ye there wasn't a word of truth in it," she answered angrily. "Patrick Henry would never do such a cowardly thing."

"But this is Mr. Henry," rejoined Mr. Tyler, pointing him out.

The old woman looked astonished. After a moment's consideration and a twitch or two at her apron string, she said, "Well then, if that is Patrick Henry, it must be all right." [49]

After narrowly escaping from Monticello, Jefferson rode to Poplar Forest, his plantation beyond Lynchburg, from which he returned to Monticello in early August. Making all possible allowances for Jefferson, it does appear that he might have done more to bridge the gap until the election of his successor. His term of office had expired on Saturday, June 2, and he had not sought re-election. Not only was there no Governor but also William Fleming, president of the Council, acted as executive head of the government for nearly two weeks. When the House convened at Trinity Church in Staunton on June 7, it was Fleming who laid before the members certain matters for their consideration. The Assembly indemnified him for calling out the militia and other measures deemed essential to good government in the interim before election of the new Governor.[50]

Under ordinary circumstances Henry might have enjoyed another visit to Staunton, with its memories of his early legal practice. Insofar as the war had not interfered, the town was still the trading center of Augusta, a great western county. It was a stopping point on the much-traveled wagon route northward toward Winchester and southward toward the Carolinas or over the Wilderness Trail into Southwest Virginia and Kentucky. In size and physical accommodations the town had not changed greatly from the frontier village where a few decades earlier Henry's McClanahan relative had built his rude log hostelry opposite the new courthouse.

But of immediate concern that hectic June, 1781, was the housing of the legislators, officials, and their entourage. They soon overflowed the few inns and the hospitable private homes, while Trinity, the parish church, the best meeting place available, proved sadly inadequate. When the members moved in with their books, papers, and other effects, there was not enough space for every one to be seated. Fortunately, neighboring people came to the rescue; chairs and settles were put in the aisles and in front of the pulpit so that the session could proceed more comfortably.

The chief concern of the members was of course the military emergency, and there were numerous meetings in Committee of the Whole. Indeed, on June 10, for the first time during the war, the House met on Sunday. In a brief session that day the members agreed to convene the next morning at ten o'clock in Staunton; but if there appeared to be danger from the enemy in so doing, the House was to meet on Thursday at Warm Springs, some forty miles westward in Augusta (present Bath) County. And if a sufficient number of members did not appear there, the Speaker was invested with the power not only to adjourn the session from day to day but in case of necessity to select any other time and place for the meeting that seemed to him advisable.

Happily, the legislators were not so hardened by the war as to lose their sense of humanity. When a petition was presented on behalf of a mulatto Negro slave, Billy, who had been condemned to death for treason by the Prince William County Court, the House declared the sentence illegal on the ground that a slave could not commit treason; Billy had been given a reprieve by the conscientious Jefferson and the final action appears not to have been entirely due to the influence of Billy's mercenary owner.

Among the wild stories about Henry is one of a night alarm at Staunton, of his flying so fast with the other members that he lost one of his boots and "blushed to the roots of his wig" when a Negro ran up to him with the missing footwear. Actually, the troops approaching the town turned out to be Virginians, and the legislature saw no need to adjourn. Even if Tarleton, with considerable reinforcements, had attempted to move to Staunton, it is extremely doubtful that he could have forced the mountain pass, guarded by formidable riflemen, other militia, and neighborhood folk. Some of the last, who were unarmed, were even preparing to roll down great rocks on any assailants.

So the Assembly, its meetings no longer interrupted, proceeded with its vital work. To help alleviate the financial crisis it passed a bill to enable Congress to levy a 5 per cent duty on certain goods and merchandise and all prizes of war. While able legislators such as John Page and Speaker Harrison were making their presence felt, Henry again appears to have been the leading member of the House. Among the bills which he took to the Senate, presumably as sponsor or principal sponsor, was one authorizing Davis Ross, the Virginia commercial agent, to purchase without delay such arms, ammunition, and military stores as the state needed; another empowered General

Lafayette to impress such horses as he required for the public safety.

Indicative of the broad authority asserted, the House on June 21 received a petition requesting the establishment of the town of Lexington in Kentucky. The petition was presented by the lone Kentucky member, Daniel Boone. That famous frontiersman would later serve with Henry on a committee in the October Assembly, and the commonwealth would be presented a bill for his 1,200-mile round trip.

With a relatively small number of members present and no Governor as yet elected, the House bore a strong likeness to the state Committee of Safety in the first year of the war. In the resolution which Henry took to the Senate giving extraordinary powers to Lafayette, he was likewise authorized to deliver public arms and ammunition to "the well affected citizens at large or otherwise" as he deemed most conducive to the public safety. Apparently, Henry would have favored continuance of the war if necessary by irregular or guerrilla operations, more feasible in the rugged back country than in the Tidewater. Henry also drew up a resolution according to order, which provided for filling the state's quota of Continental troops. As it was jocularly said during the last period of the Southern Confederacy, recruits were taken from the cradle to the grave. These Revolutionary soldiers needed to be only five feet four inches, with no age limit. There were provisos, however, that the men should be of "able body" and "sound mind," not subject to "fits," and they should not have been past deserters.

On June 12 General Thomas Nelson was elected Governor by a majority vote. It was an excellent appointment, for the forty-two-year-old General, "alert and lively for his weight," brought to the gubernatorial office not only the remaining wealth and influence of a leading Tidewater family but considerable civil and military experience. Happily, Nelson was not deterred by the difficulties of his task, including the vulnerability of his lower Tidewater estate to enemy raids.

The Council likewise was strengthened by the election of three influential men from the Piedmont or western counties—William Cabell, James McDowell, and Samuel Hardy. Since their homes were not too far from the *de facto* seat of government, there was little likelihood of another critical absence of executive leaders. In another forward step, the House elected able congressional representation—James Madison, Edmund Randolph, Theodorick Bland, and John Blair. It was in happy contrast to the earlier delegation, of which Washington had complained.

Altogether, with Henry and other dedicated war leaders dominating the Assembly, Virginia could be counted upon for strenuous efforts to successfully conclude the protracted war.

17

Mr. Jefferson and Other Difficult Problems

> No man can act a conspicuous part in the public concerns of his country, without making enemies, as well as friends. . . . He can scarcely avoid opposing, in his course, measures which others have found profitable, or have honestly believed salutary, and thus patriotism concurs with rivalry and self-love, to draw down upon him a degree of ill-will, in proportion to the sphere of his activity.——GEORGE TUCKER [1]

1781–1782. Henry in House of Delegates from Henry County.

October 19, 1781. Surrender of Cornwallis' army at Yorktown.

December 12, 1781. Report to the House of legislative committee appointed to investigate Jefferson's conduct as Governor.

THE LEGISLATURE, which met in Staunton during those hectic June days, was a small select group dominated by brave men, grimly determined to take the necessary measures to cope with the enemy invasion. By the nineteenth it was known in Staunton that Lafayette was "nigh Nat Dandridges," Henry's father-in-law's place in upper Hanover, and that the British were in the Richmond area.[2] With Cornwallis still in a position where he might strike a fatal blow, the Assembly, further overcoming their fears of executive tyranny, passed an act enlarging the powers of both the Governor and the Council.[3]

[243]

Henry, who when Governor had complained of the restrictions on his authority, was a member of the committee which proposed the bill, and there is reason to believe that he gave it his powerful support.

The powers given the Governor and Council were not labeled as dictatorial but in effect they were. In order to provide "strenuous opposition" to the enemy and to secure "punctual execution" of laws upon which the "safety and welfare of the commonwealth" depended, Governor Nelson, with the advice of the Council, was empowered to call out "the forces and the resources" of the state for such purposes as might be necessary for the common good. He could secure, by impressment or otherwise, provisions and equipment of all kinds—Negroes as pioneers; horses, wagons, ships, and their crews; and "all other necessaries" needed to supply the troops in the public service. He could seize—and the sternly patriotic Nelson would not avoid any such duty—"disaffected persons" and banish them into the enemy lines, and even declare "civilly dead" persons opposing the laws for calling out the troops. "Civilly dead" was a grim phrase reminiscent of earlier British history and, according to the new statute, meant that the property of persons so punished would descend to their heirs or be distributed among their next of kin. More important, too, from a military viewpoint, the state quartermasters and commissaries could be discontinued and their powers transferred to the Continental staff.[4]

Actually, there had been a movement in the Staunton Assembly to appoint a dictator, so named, for Virginia. George Nicholas proposed that George Washington be chosen, but Nicholas was opposed by Mann Page and some other delegates.

When Nicholas sat down, Henry addressed the chair, so Judge Archibald Stuart recalled nearly two generations later. Henry declared that "it was immaterial with him whether the officer proposed was called a Dictator, or Governor with enlarged powers, or by any other name, yet surely an officer armed with such powers was necessary to restrain the unbridled fury of a licentious enemy." Henry "concluded by seconding the motion," Stuart continued, but "after a lengthy discussion the proposition was negatived."[5]

Instead of accepting Nicholas' proposal, the House resolved that

St. John's Episcopal Church, Richmond, Va., built in 1741.

St. John's Church, interior view. Henry rose from his pew (third from the front, indicated by the open door) to deliver his famous "Give Me Liberty" speech.

Ivory letter opener, slightly reduced in size. Patrick Henry held this letter opener aloft as he cried, "Give me liberty or give me—," then slowly pressed it to his breast as he exclaimed, "Death!" Property of Charles S. Borum, Hendersonville, N.C., a descendant of Henry through his daughter, Elizabeth Aylett.

—*Photo: Barber's Studio, Hendersonville, N.C.*

The Old Capitol which stood at Fourteenth and Cary Sts., in Richmond. It was the scene of the meetings of the General Assembly, 1780–1788, and of the opening session of the Virginia Constitutional Convention in 1788.

—*Courtesy of the Valentine Museum*

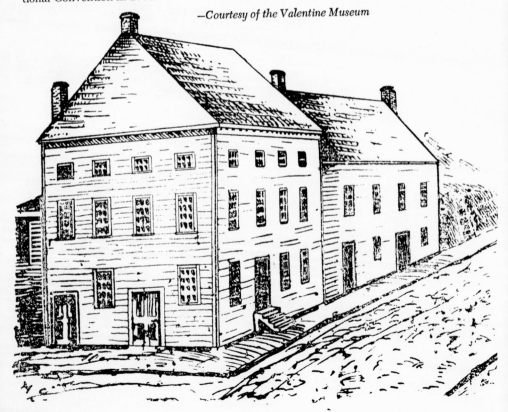

Salisbury, near Midlothian, Va. Henry's country home, circa 1784–1786, while he was Governor for his fourth and fifth terms. The house was destroyed by fire in the early 1900's.

Sir. Richmond May 1st 1786 ———

I should have answered your Excellencys — Favor of March 30th sooner, but for an Indisposition, on account of which I went in to the Country for some some Time — Due Attention shall be paid to the Act of your Legislature, a Copy of which accompany'd your Letter.

The Duty on Salt continues to — be paid in this State —

I beg leave to assure you of the great Regard with which I am

Sir,
Your Excellencys most obedient Servant

P. Henry

His Excellency
Gov: Smallwood

Letter of Governor Henry to Governor Smallwood of Maryland. The letter is dated about the time of year when Henry appears to have been susceptible to his recurrent malaria, and he probably had sought relief for one of the milder attacks at Salisbury, his country place.

Patrick Henry's sister, Elizabeth, from a penciled sketch, made in her later life. She was married first to General William Campbell, then to General William Russell. In intellect and person she was described as much like her brother. Her voice "carried" like his, ringing "as clear as a bell" for 1,100 yards between her own house and her daughter's.

Dorothea Spotswood Henry, daughter of Patrick Henry, who married her cousin, George D. Winston. The portrait by Sharples, the English artist, was painted when she was eighteen.

"Attempt at the features" of Patrick Henry. Tracing by Thomas Crawford, the sculptor, from B. H. Latrobe's sketchbook. The sketches were made when Henry was appearing in the federal court at Richmond, not long before he retired.

P. Henry and Dorothea Dandridge were marry'd — October 9 1777 — the issue of that Marriage are

Dorothea Spotswood Henry born August 2 1778 —
Sarah Butler Henry born January 4 1780 she departed this life 18 December Henry
Martha Catharina born Nov 3 1781 she departed this life May 2 1801
Patrick Henry born August 15 1783 he departed this life September 3 1804
Fayette Henry born October 9 1785 he died March 26 1813
Alexander Spotswood Henry born June 2 1788
Nathaniel Henry born April 7 1790
Richard Henry was born march 27 1792 Died the 20 August 1793
Edward Winston Henry was born January 21 1794 died NB. His name is Edward Winston Henry
John Henry was born February 16 1796 — died 1808
Jane Robertson Henry Born January 15 1799 died 4 days after her Birth —

Dorothea Dandridge Henry Born at Flees Bay January 14 1800 — She Departed this Life Nov 27 1813 she was the daughter of ___ Henry who married Martha Catharine Henry

Entries by Henry in the family Bible. The interlineations were
made by other members of the family after his death.

The chair in which Patrick Henry died at Red Hill. During his last illness he was in less pain when sitting than reclining.

Red Hill, near Brookneal, Va. The restored house is at the right, and Henry's original "law office" in the approach view to the left.

on the following Tuesday, June 12, it would elect a Governor and new members of the Council. In view of the enlargement of the powers of the executive, Henry seems to have been satisfied with the procedure.[6] Thus, we find no proof of any accusations that Henry then attempted to make himself a dictator.

On another occasion, however, during the Staunton session, Henry became involved in a controversy—and with his former liberal ally, Thomas Jefferson—of which there are repercussions to this day. When writing to Jefferson from Staunton on June 19, 1781, Archibald Cary gave him some news of the legislative session there, including one disturbing "peice" about Jefferson himself. George Nicholas, so Cary declared, had offered a motion in the House of Delegates for an inquiry into Jefferson's conduct as Governor—"a catalogue of omissions, and other Misconduct." Cary had not yet seen the particulars but, confident that the inquiry would do Jefferson honor, had seconded the motion. Earlier, Cary said, he had heard some motion of inquiry "was to be brought on the carpit" and that it would give Jefferson "no pain."[7] Was Cary trying to soften the blow? Actually, few events of his lifetime caused Jefferson more pain; we may wonder why he was so deeply affected.

Specifically, Nicholas' motion called for an inquiry at the next session of the Assembly into the conduct of the executive of the state for the past twelve months. A committee was to be appointed to investigate such information on the subject as was presented to them and to report to the House on December 12. During this session of the Assembly "the usual antidote for public distress was resorted to. Two persons were named with acrimony, as delinquent," Edmund Randolph later wrote. They were Baron von Steuben, for not having succeeded in protecting from the British the state military stores in the vicinity of Point of Fork on the James River, and Jefferson, the Governor at the time of Arnold's invasion,

> as not having made some exertions which he might have made for the defence of the country. . . . Colonel George Nicholas and Mr. Patrick Henry were those who charged Mr. Jefferson. They aimed to express themselves with delicacy toward him, without weakening the ground on which they supposed that their

suspicions would be found ultimately to stand. But, probably without design, they wounded by their measured endeavor to avoid the infliction of a wound. Colonel Nicholas moved, however, for an inquiry into the conduct of the governor at the succeeding session. The motion was carried with the concurrence of his friends and his foes; of the former to afford him an opportunity for exculpation, of the latter, who conceived him to be ruined.[8]

Jefferson, obviously disturbed, wrote Nicholas to specify the particular incidents in which he was remiss. Jefferson supposed that the motion "could not be intended just to stab a reputation by a general suggestion under the bare expectation that facts might be afterwards hunted up to boulster it." Nicholas replied with several particulars, the most important being "the total want of opposition to Arnold on his first expedition to Richmond." Among the other charges was one that Jefferson had rejected an offer made by Colonels Campbell, Christian, and McDowell to raise regiments for the Southern service.[9] Since Campbell and Christian, two of Henry's brothers-in-law, were in Staunton at the time of the legislative session, it is likely that they helped to influence him in supporting Nicholas.

Returning from the emergency legislative session, Henry soon found militiamen, including some of his friends and relatives, again leaving their crops at a busy season, again bidding good-by to their anxious families. This time, however, the citizen soldiers were leaving for what developed into the final Revolutionary campaign on Virginia soil. As a military leader, George Washington, like William the Silent, was usually distinguished more for bravery and devotion to duty than for brilliant generalship. But in a masterly combined operation such as we now associate with some later wars, Washington joined his forces with the French army and supporting fleet to surround and capture Cornwallis' army on October 19, 1781, at Yorktown. The 3,000 Virginia militia which Governor Nelson had somehow been able to scrape together for the campaign were not the best troops which Virginia had supplied for the war, but they nevertheless contributed materially to the final victory.

In Richmond, there was a victory ball to celebrate the glorious surrender. But the October Assembly there, interrupted by wartime activities, could not muster a quorum until November 19. Patrick Henry was one of the legislators brought to the House in the custody of the sergeant at arms and admitted to their seats after paying the prescribed fee for lateness. The Assembly seems to have been marking time until the appearance of the old master hand. The day of his arrival Henry was put on two of the most important committees, while the previous day, as if in anticipation of his coming, the House had started to take up the delicate and controversial proposal to inquire into Jefferson's past gubernatorial administration, as called for by the June Assembly.

There was still a large contingent of Virginia troops fighting with Greene to the southward. But with no invading army in the state, the Assembly sat under calmer circumstances than when in Staunton. After a motion had been duly made, the House agreed to inquire into the conduct of "the executive" and a committee was appointed to present on December 12, 1781, such information as was offered to them on the subject. It is noteworthy that Jefferson was not named in the resolution and that it was broadened to include members of the Council. Also, the investigating committee was something less than crusading: the inconsequential John Bannister, chairman; Tyler, Southall, and Morgan. Henry was not a member and neither he, Nicholas, nor anyone else offered any evidence against Jefferson at the committee hearing or on the floor. Since the summer, young Nicholas, a political novice, had thought better of his plan to push the inquiry into the conduct of his distinguished Albemarle neighbor.

At Staunton during the enemy invasion, Nicholas and Henry had found influential support for the inquiry.[10] But with American independence now virtually assured, the Assembly, in an exuberant mood,[11] was disposed to deal more kindly with past errors, and especially any committed by so dedicated a patriot as Thomas Jefferson, author of the Declaration of Independence and a leader of the popular party.

The motion for the inquiry was duly presented, and Jefferson rose to answer the "objections" made earlier by Nicholas.[12] The House then passed a motion which, after being amended by the Senate, ordered "the sincere thanks of the General Assembly" be given Jefferson "for his impartial, upright, and attentive administration *of the powers of the Executive, whilst in office.*" The resolution referred to the "popular rumours," gaining credence by more pointed "Accusations" which had made it necessary to conduct the inquiry, but declared that Jefferson's conduct "having become the object of open scrutiny, tenfold value is added to an approbation founded on a cool and deliberate discussion." [13] The Assembly wished, therefore, to express "in the strongest manner" the high opinion which they entertained of Jefferson's "Ability, Rectitude, and Integrity as chief Magistrate of this Commonwealth, and mean by thus publicly avowing their Opinion, to obviate all future, and to remove all former unmerited Censure." [14]

The Assembly would seek to prevent all unmerited censure, but nothing was said about what might have been merited. The House, with Henry present, passed this resolution unanimously. He evidently felt that he had done all that duty required in the matter. His motives are further interpreted by the well-informed Lyon G. Tyler, a grandson of the John Tyler who was a friend of both Henry and Jefferson:

> This dissatisfaction against Mr. Jefferson was due, in the case of many like Patrick Henry and Col. George Nicholas, to honest feelings, since defeat never fails with the best of us to impair the popularity of a leader, while success, purely the result of accident, converts into a hero the man of most mediocre attainments.

Tyler also quoted the statement of Edmund Randolph that Nicholas and Henry at Staunton "expressed themselves with delicacy" toward Jefferson but "without weakening the ground on which they supposed their suspicions were to be found ultimately to rest. . . . probably without design, they wounded by their measured endeavor to avoid infliction of a wound." [15]

Since harsh measures become the stock in trade during wartime, Jefferson's treatment was perhaps milder than could have reasonably been expected. But he was cruelly hurt. He could never give Henry credit for good intentions in supporting the original inquiry. Perhaps the affair might have been smoothed over if Henry had not been living at distant Leatherwood and he and Jefferson had not pursued different courses. But the breach was not closed.

There was a partial excuse in Jefferson's unhappy personal life. He was distraught by the illness of his beloved wife after the birth of their last daughter in May, 1782. In a letter that month to James Monroe, he spoke despondently of how during his thirteen years of public service his private affairs had "run into great disorder and ruin . . . so far from gaining the affection" of his countrymen by his sacrifices, he had "even lost the small estimation" he had before possessed.[16] In September he was thrown into a deeper depression by his wife's death. Conscious of his great service to his country, he remained acutely sensitive of what he deemed the foul blow struck him in the investigation. He had for some time, however, been willing to discount Nicholas as "a trifling body" who was "below contempt," and as "more an object of pity." Nicholas publicly acknowledged that he had acted hastily, and he and Jefferson later became personal and political friends.[17]

Moreover, the transition was easier in that Jefferson believed Nicholas' "natural ill temper was a tool worked by another hand." It was clear that Jefferson thought this hand was Henry's.

Nearly a year later Jefferson was no less bitter. In a letter from George Rogers Clark which the versatile Jefferson received during August, 1782, Clark stated that he had hoped to secure for Jefferson some "big bones" (elk horns, petrifactions, etc.), and in replying to Clark on November 26 Jefferson told him that he was "not unapprised" that Clark's service to his country had failed to make "due impression on every mind. That you have made enemies you must not doubt, when you reflect that you have made yourself eminent." Jefferson was "not a little surprised, however, to find one person hostile to you as far as he has personal courage to shew hostility to any man. Who he is you will probably have heard, or may know him by this description as being all tongue without either head or heart."[18]

In general, the accusations which Jefferson made against Henry in later years are somewhat less vitriolic. But they indicate that the old wound never entirely healed. Less than a decade before his death Jefferson endorsed the story later published by the historian, Girardin, that Henry wanted the Staunton Assembly to appoint him a dictator. In this and some other instances Jefferson may have been misinformed. But in so quickly crediting derogatory evidence against Henry he did not show his usual judgment.

His attitude toward Henry seems less understandable when we learn that Jefferson himself cast doubts on his own qualifications for war Governor at the time of the British invasion. In a letter to George Washington from Charlottesville just before Jefferson retired from the governorship, he wrote that a few days would bring that "period of relief" which the constitution had "prepared for those oppressed with the labours" of his office. He spoke of his "long declared resolution" to relinquish the office "to abler hands." [19] And in his *Memoirs,* he would declare that he resigned

> from a belief, that under the pressure of the existing invasion, the public would have more confidence in a military chief, and that the military commander being invested with the civil power also, both might be wielded with more energy, promptitude and effect, for the defence of the state.[20]

Few Americans would accomplish as much in a lifetime as did Jefferson. It was a pity that he could not view the inquiry in the Fall Assembly with the detachment shown in these statements.

Among other events during this Assembly, Henry served on a large committee appointed to calculate the true value of the state loan office certificates, and he introduced several money bills which were duly enacted. One broad measure not only imposed a tax of £1 on every hundred pounds value of land, the chief source of income in Virginia, but graduated taxes of two shillings on every horse and mule, three pence a head on cattle, five shillings per wheel on pleasure carriages, £5 on every license to operate an ordinary, and ten shillings capitation on white males above twenty-one and on all slaves. Except for the land tax, payable only in specie, the taxes could be paid partly in agricultural products.[21] The rich and the poor were both to be caught in the net. An additional charge of £50 on every billiard table was almost prohibitory, and it is not surprising that only two billiard tables were listed the next year in a census for the town of Richmond. On the whole, the tax bill may have been as good as could reasonably be secured, but there was soon serious trouble with the collections.

Other bills which Henry introduced and which were passed provided for calling in and funding Virginia paper money and adjusting all debts and contracts entered into between January 1, 1777, and January 1, 1782, payable in paper money. "At the close of the war many of us wished to reopen all accounts which had been paid in depreciated money, and have them settled by the scale of depreciation," Jefferson later wrote William Wirt.[22] "But on this he [Henry] frowned most indignantly, and knowing the general indisposition of the Legislature, it was considered hopeless to attempt it with such an opponent at their head as Henry." [23]

Another action of this legislature was to elect Benjamin Harrison governor in place of General Thomas Nelson, who had resigned, broken in health and fortune after extreme sacrifices for the Revolutionary cause. The now veteran Harrison, with his versatile experience in both the state and national governments, proved a competent chief executive. He was elected for two more terms, the constitutional limit for consecutive service. This was apparently with Henry's support, and there is no evidence of any rift between Henry and his one-time conservative opponent.

On November 21, 1781, Henry received a leave of absence, probably again on account of sickness. After his recent illnesses, Henry was jeopardizing his health by his protracted public service. It should be noted, however, that he had a special reason to hurry back to Leatherwood—the birth of Dorothea's third child, Martha Catharina, on November 3.

At the next legislative session, in May, 1782, Henry was back in his seat and received a flowery letter written on May 10 from General Horatio Gates congratulating him on the "inestimable" blessing of peace and independence. Now Henry could "exult with Cicero, 'Cedant Arma Togae,' & so I hope will all Columbia's Sons. Seven years is long enough for the Sons of Mars to Ravage. Equal Law, Equal Liberty, & General Republicanism, will, I anxiously hope, prevail throughout the Land." [24]

Despite Gates' optimism, the new Assembly was handicapped by the fact that the final peace treaty had not been signed. Nevertheless, some important legislation was enacted. Through a significant law which Henry is believed to have supported, the Assembly permitted a limited manumission of slaves.[25] It also expressed the willingness of Virginia to set off the counties on the western waters of the Ohio River into separate states as soon as circumstances would render this possible. Kentucky, whose population had greatly increased, was divided into three counties and a district court organized. The next year, too, Virginia would cede her great Northwest Territory to the United States.[26] Finally enacted after much interstate squabbling, this generous measure was the most important act of the Harrison administration.

At the October, 1781, session of the Assembly, Henry had fought against further depreciation of the currency; now he took a contrary course. In so doing he laid himself open to a charge of political expediency, but there was an obvious explanation for his action. Because of the hard times and scarcity of specie, it was very difficult to pay the land tax and other hard money exactions required in his tax law. Under Henry's leadership the May, 1782, Assembly passed an act giving a tax commutation so that only half of the state taxes would be due by July 1 and the remainder by November.[27] But even after this abatement there was acute difficulty with the tax collections. From every section of the state came reports to the executive offices indicating a crisis in the state financial system. John Pryor, the state commissary general of military stores, who was making "every effort" to establish shops in various parts of the state for repair of arms, quoted the people as saying that "the money is not in the country" and believing that they would not be paid for their work.[28] From Staunton on July 6, 1782, Thomas Payne wrote requesting an additional stipend because the expense of living at a tavern without the benefit of his ration was "more than the finances of a Continental officer can stand."[29] At the end of the month, Colonel Arthur Campbell wrote to Governor Harrison from Washington County that he could not get powder for Bedford "for want of money to pay the waggoner."[30] In western Pittsylvania, near Leatherwood, in September, John Wilson, the county lieutenant, lacked the means to send six shirts across the mountains to Montgomery Courthouse.[31] And two months later John Robertson, purchaser of provisions for the Army, was "overwhelmed by the importunities of creditors" from whom he bought stores upon promise of payment on November 1.[32] There was even difficulty in arranging for future payment of some records ordered to be bound for the General Court, John Brown, the contractor, declaring that in renting a house for an office in Richmond, he had found the people were "so unwilling to credit the publick" that he agreed to pay the rent and ask the Governor for indemnification.[33]

In the opinion of many creditors, many conservatives, the inflation could be reduced by the increased circulation of hard money. But, obviously, little of this was available. Trade had not recovered from the war. The suffering, tax-burdened small farmers, of a type Henry knew in his home county, would be much on his mind during the next five or six years.

Henry was not present at the Fall, 1782, Assembly. The next legislature, in May, 1783, did not meet until the twelfth, so that he had time to receive a remarkable letter of May 6 from his former liberal associate, George Mason. With none of the Virginia statesmen had Henry been on terms of closer friendship and respect. Mason's letter now came like a breath of fresh air, a salutary change from narrow provincialism. After reflecting "with pleasure" on their former acquaintance, Mason congratulated Henry on the accomplishment of what he knew was "the warmest wish" of Henry's heart—"the establishment of American Independence, and the liberty of our country." America would now "rank among the nations of the world; but whether our Independence shall prove a blessing or a curse, must depend upon our own wisdom or folly, virtue or wickedness." [34]

To a student of Henry's writings the words have a familiar ring. We have seen how characteristic it was of him to pick up ideas from others and popularize or otherwise employ them. Among the papers left after his death was his personal copy of his Stamp Act resolutions, with an inscription in his handwriting on the back explaining how he happened to write the resolutions and adding these lines reminiscent of Mason's letter, in one phrase with similar words:

> Whether this [American Independence] will prove a blessing or a curse, will depend upon the use our people make of the blessings which a gracious God hath bestowed upon us. If they be wise, they will be great and happy. If they are of a contrary character, they will be miserable. Righteousness alone can exalt them as a nation. Reader! whoever thou art, remember this, and in thy sphere practice virtue thyself, and encourage it in others.[35]

Mason said he was anxious "to restore that confidence and reverence in the people for the Legislature, which has been so greatly impaired by a contrary conduct." He brought several matters to Henry's attention, who had it in his power "to do more good and prevent more mischief than any man in this state." The people in Mason's part of the country were made "very uneasy" by reports that the Assembly would make some laws or resolutions regarding British debts which would infringe the articles of the peace treaty under the mistaken idea that Great Britain would not risk a renewal of the war.

> In conversation upon this subject we sometimes hear a very absurd question: "If we are now to pay debts due the British merchants, what have we been fighting for all this while?" Surely not to avoid our just debts, or cheat our creditors; but to rescue our country from the oppression & tyranny of the British Government, and to secure the rights and liberty of ourselves, and our posterity; which we have happily accomplished.

Mason argued that the Americans had obtained better terms of peace than they had cause to expect, "all the great points" being ceded to them; and he thought that "it would be highly dangerous and imprudent" to risk a breach of the treaty.[36]

A letter such as Mason's would be noteworthy at any time, and it was especially significant for Henry in that early May of 1783 when he was entering into one of his most fruitful—and controversial—legislative sessions. Before noting the details, including his action on Mason's proposal for reopening the British trade, we need to portray the Assembly at the end of the war with its new faces, its new manners—and with Henry in a virtually new role still variously interpreted by historians.

18

Postwar Legislator

The farther we get away from the land, the greater our insecurity.——HENRY FORD

It is the peculiarity of some schools of eloquence that they embody and utter, not merely the individual genius and character of the speaker, but a national consciousness—a national era, a mood, a hope, a dread, a despair—in which you listen to the spoken history of the time.——RUFUS CHOATE

1782–1784. Henry, still residing at Leatherwood in Henry County, is an outstanding state legislator.

April 12, 1782. British Admiral Rodney's victory over the French fleet in the West Indies.

September 3, 1783. American peace treaty with Great Britain.

November, 1784. Henry chairman of committee drafting bill for "a moderate assessment" for the Christian religion.

I T IS DIFFICULT, if not impossible, for democracy to match the glamour of aristocracy. For its inelegant legislative hall, the little wooden building at the foot of the Richmond hill, the Virginia Assembly had a good excuse: no better place was available. The members of both the House and Senate, so wrote a German traveler in November, 1783, were permitted on the floor in the same clothes in which they went hunting or attended to their tobacco fields. And while some were still bedecked in the stockings and knee breeches reminiscent of the House of Burgesses, more often they wore boots, trousers or Indian leggings, great coats or "ordinary coats," and perhaps short jackets, all in accord with the members' "caprice or comfort, and all equally honorable."[1]

To the German visitor, Johann Schoepf, with his Old World background, the legislature had other unusual aspects. It was said of the Assembly that "it sits," Schoepf observed, but that was "not a just expression." At a session of the House which he attended, the members showed themselves "in every possible position rather than that of sitting still, with dignity and attention. An Assembly of men whose object was the serious and important one of making laws, should at least observe a certain *decorum*, but independence prevails even here." During Schoepf's visits to the Assembly, the estimable body was "quiet not 5 minutes" altogether. Some members were leaving the hall, others entering, and most were "talking of insignificant or irrelevant matters." To judge from "the indifference and heedlessness of most of their faces" it must have been "a trifling business to make laws."[2]

Moreover, Schoepf was no more complimentary of some other workings of the Virginia popular assembly. A loud-voiced doorkeeper, he noted, was "almost incessantly . . . calling out" various members, while in the anteroom others were chattering about horse races, runaway slaves, "yesterday's play," and, of course, politics. Until very recently the legislators had been paid at the rate of eighteen Virginia shillings or three Spanish dollars per day. Yet during the war, Schoepf added, with nothing but paper money in circulation, they had preferred to receive fifty pounds of tobacco per diem rather than accept Virginia currency. And as for the voting in the House, the Speaker usually judged from "the strength of the noise" whether the affirmative or the negative had carried a measure.[3]

But if Schoepf's description of the contemporary Assembly seems rather harsh,[4] two informed Virginians were even more caustic. In a letter to Edmund Randolph on February 15, 1783, Thomas Jefferson spoke of "the very low state" to which the legislature had been reduced; there was "in it much good intention, but little knowledge of the science" to which the members were called. Another critic was

Joseph Jones, a member of what might now be called the Jefferson-Madison coterie. Jones, who looked to a feminine observer like "a Presbyterian priest,"[5] with his dark complexion and black attire, was now a well-known Virginia legislator. A prolific Madison correspondent, Jones wrote candidly to him on June 14, 1783:

> You cannot well conceive the deranged state of affairs in this Country [Virginia]. There is nothing like system or order. . . . The two great Commanders [presumably Henry and Richard Henry Lee] make excellent harrengues, handsome speeches to their men but they, want executive officers . . . useful men, who do business as well as speak of it. a Pendleton and Jefferson would be valuable acquisitions to this assembly. . . .[6]

Also, in a letter to Jefferson near the end of the year, Jones spoke of the "great and perplexing questions" confronting the next sessions of the Assembly and the "not so promising" outlook for the members to possess the needed moderation and wisdom to deal with them.[7]

Fortunately, however, the wave of idealism, the upsurge of talent from various classes during the Revolution, had not spent itself. There was a good deal of sound ability in the delegates to the early 1780's Assemblies. They were not so small, so jealous-minded, as to reject the leadership of their ablest members, Henry, Lee, Madison, Tyler, and others.[8]

Deserving of serious consideration are the anti-Henry criticisms in the voluminous Jefferson-Madison correspondence of the period, which have been widely published and have definitely influenced later opinion. The ardently patriotic young Madison had sympathized with Jefferson regarding the proposed legislative inquiry into his governorship, and during the next few years a Damon and Pythias relationship developed between the master of Monticello and his scholarly ally in neighboring Orange County. The two statesmen wrote to each other frequently during 1780–1783 while Madison was an overworked and underpaid member of Congress. Jefferson stayed with Madison a month in Philadelphia, while waiting, as he thought, to sail to France as a peace emissary; and Jefferson consoled the thirty-two-year-old Madison on the unhappy ending of a love affair with a young lady half his age—"Firmness of mind and unintermitting occupations will not long leave you in pain." [9] Now out of office for several years, Jefferson found time to correspond brilliantly with Madison on a number of subjects, and the often hard-pressed Madison sometimes managed to reply in kind. When Jefferson commented on Henry, however, we must note the extent to which he varied from his idealistic tone.

In laying bare to Madison some of his innermost thoughts, Jefferson used a secret cypher, which has since been decoded. As evidence of his continued antipathy toward Henry, the letters are especially revealing about the time of the May, 1783, Assembly, which Madison entered after his service, 1780–1782, in Congress. Although one of the youngest members of that body, Madison had been a leader in the effort to strengthen the weak central government. He had been outstanding in efforts to fund the federal debt, to prevent the issuance of further paper money, and to secure additional Continental revenue by a 5 per cent tax on imports.

In accordance with the weak Articles of Confederation, this tax or impost had to be approved by all the states. Although the Virginia legislature first passed the necessary enabling act, it later rescinded the action after finding that another state, Rhode Island, had withheld its consent. With the Philadelphia government in desperate need of funds, a bill again giving Virginia's approval of the tax was expected to be introduced in the May, 1783, Assembly.[10] Jefferson did not like all the features of the bill but, public-spirited as usual, in late April and early May he waited two weeks in the Richmond neighborhood to help line up supporters. After spending the previous day "in associating and conversing" with as many legislators as possible, he wrote Madison on May 7 how the leaders appeared likely to line up on the issue. Not only did he give such predictions for Henry, Richard Henry Lee, General Nelson, Tyler, and Nicholas, but also certain members as yet little known: John Taylor, Thomson Mason, and a "Mr. Stewart [Archibald Stuart], a young man of good talents from the Westward." [11]

Throughout his Madison correspondence, Jefferson wrote freely in a number of respects, but his observations on Henry are particularly sharp-edged (the italicized words are decoded):

[258]

Henry as usual is *involved in mystery:* should the *popular tide run strongly* in either *direction, he* will fall *in with it.* Should it *not,* he will have a *struggle between his enmity to the Lees, and his enmity* to every*thing which may give influence to* Congs.[12]

Actually, Henry did come out in favor of the impost. He was the second-ranking member of the committee which brought the new enabling bill before the House. And though Jefferson noted Henry's friendly attitude toward the measure in a letter to Madison from Monticello on June 17, he added that "when the question came on he [Henry] was utterly silent."[13] With the bill still encountering formidable opposition, the vote was postponed until the fall. Henry may have had justifiable reasons for not speaking at the time. But Jefferson was reluctant to give him credit for good motives. And long afterward a Madison biographer would say that Henry did not want to "face the ignominy of being defeated by underlings" and had reversed himself.[14]

Again, as after his Stamp Act speech and on some other occasions, a question was raised as to how much Henry was governed by expediency. To what extent did he keep his ear to the ground, advocating only measures which he felt would meet with popular approval?

There were three outstanding measures that he championed in the House during the early 1780's. They were to reopen trade with the wartime enemy, the British, as George Mason had just proposed; to permit return of the hated Tories to Virginia; and, perhaps even more counter to popular prejudices, to permit and even subsidize marriages between white Virginians and Indians. Were these measures which would be advocated by an expedient politician, a time-serving conservative? Or was Henry displaying in these—and some other measures—a notable progressivism?

The whole question of his real political principles during the period deserves more than a casual consideration. Perhaps we can evaluate the underlying question of his policy on states' rights, one in which neither he, Jefferson, Madison, nor many of their contemporaries would pursue an undeviating course. And there is another connected matter—that is, how effective was his oratory at this time, especially when facing doubting or hostile audiences?

When the bill removing the penalties on British trade in Virginia came up at the May, 1783, Assembly, there was a memorable battle. During the two sessions of the legislature that year, Henry appears to have been in better health than the previous year, and he attended the meetings much more regularly. An initial item of business on the belated opening day, May 12, was the election of a speaker. Henry and his distinguished liberal colleague, Richard Henry Lee, were rivals for the leadership of the House. Unlike Henry, who was a champion of the poor debtor class, Lee saw a pressing need for deflation of the currency. Reflecting the current Henry-Lee conflict, the House nominated Lee for Speaker, and Henry proposed John Tyler. Henry was seconded by George Nicholas, and Tyler won by a lopsided 60 to 1 majority.

When Henry rose later that day to advocate the bill for removing the restrictions on British commerce, he was not only opposing Tyler, the friend and admirer whom he had just nominated as Speaker, but calling for a measure to which Tyler was strongly hostile. A slightly built, blue-eyed, brownish-red-haired man still in his mid-thirties, the respected Tyler, we may recall, had been one of the party escaping with Henry across the mountains after Tarleton's raid on Charlottesville. While a student at William and Mary College, Tyler had listened to Henry's speech on the Stamp Act and had "caught fire at the sound" of his voice. He had become so strong an opponent of the British government that his father often predicted he would be hanged as a rebel. His feelings had not been softened by the recent British depredations in his native Tidewater. Even in 1813, shortly before his death during the period of the second war with England, Tyler would say that his only regret was "that he could not live long enough to see that proud British nation once more humbled by American arms." [15]

From Tyler's first appearance on "the public stage," Henry had been attracted to him by his "Roman frankness" of manner, along with his decisive character and usually benevolent spirit. [16] While a member of the legislature in Richmond during the last war years,

Henry frequently rode down the Peninsula to visit at Greenway, the Tyler home in Charles City County, and he was reported to have been present at the christening of Tyler's eldest son, Wat Henry Tyler.

"We have named him, sir, after the two greatest British rebels of history, Wat Tyler and Patrick Henry," Mrs. Tyler replied when asked why this name was chosen.[17] A Tyler daughter was later named Maria Henry.

The treaty of peace had still not been signed; many delegates in addition to Tyler had fresh memories of ravaging British forces. Indeed, "the name of 'British Tory' was of itself enough at that period to throw almost any company in Virginia into flames." Philip Mazzei would find that Patrick Henry's overseer at Leatherwood shared such feelings and that Henry had not been entirely devoid of them. Yet Henry was usually not one to nurse enmities. A new day was dawning and Henry, seeing at first hand the suffering caused by interrupted trade, was willing to let bygones be bygones. Like another great orator of the English-speaking people, Winston Churchill, Henry believed that in war there should be resolution, in peace magnanimity.

On the opening day of the Assembly, then, and soon after Tyler's election, Henry proposed a resolution calling for the repeal of the act prohibiting importation of British goods and subjecting them or the persons importing them "to any manner of forfeiture or condemnation."[18] And he aroused the strong opposition of the legislative leader whom he had just nominated.

"I opposed him [Henry] on this ground, that that measure would expel from this country the trade of every other nation, on account of our habits, language, and the manner of conducting business on credit between us and them," Tyler later wrote. To change the current of commerce would be to "drive away all competition, and never perhaps should regain it, (which has literally happened)."[19]

But Henry's reply was "beyond all expression eloquent and sublime," Tyler freely conceded. "After painting the distresses of the people, struggling through a perilous war, cut off from commerce so long that they were naked, and unclothed," Henry concluded with several figures of speech which Tyler could never forget "because, beautiful as they were in themselves, their effect was heightened beyond all description, by the manner in which he acted what he spoke." [20]

> "Why [Henry said] should we fetter commerce? If a man is in chains, he droops and bows to the earth, for his spirits are broken," (looking sorrowfully at his feet:) "but let him twist the fetters from his legs, and he will stand erect,"—straightening himself, and assuming a look of proud defiance.—"Fetter not commerce, sir—let her be as free as air—she will range the whole creation, and return on the wings of the four winds of heaven, to bless the land with plenty." [21]

Another measure implementing his magnanimous British policy was introduced by Henry at the same session.[22] This was a bill to repeal the act denying Tories the right of Virginia citizenship and to permit their return to the state. Because of Henry's sickness, which caused him to leave the House before adjournment, or because of the bitter opposition, the bill was not considered in the Committee of the Whole until the fall. Even then the proposal in behalf of "so odious" a people was received with "the strongest surprise." At first the opposition—which included Speaker Tyler—was "apparently insuperable." [23]

How could Henry, above all men, "think of inviting into his family, an enemy, from whose insults and injuries he had suffered so severely?" Tyler asked him.[24]

"The personal feelings of a politician ought not to be permitted to enter these walls," Tyler would recall Henry as replying. And from Tyler's account, written some twenty years later, we learn that Henry continued with an eloquent exposition of what for him had become a favorite theme: the means for development of the American nation. The question of citizenship for the Tories was a national one, and in deciding it, if the members

> acted wisely, nothing would be regarded but the interest of the nation. On the altar of his country's good he was willing to sacrifice all personal resentments, all private wrongs—and he flattered himself, that he was not the only man in the house who

was capable of making such a sacrifice. We have, sir, an extensive country, *without population*—what can be a more obvious policy than that this country ought to be peopled? [25]

"*People*, sir, form the strength, and constitute the wealth of a nation," Henry exclaimed. "I want to see our vast forests filled up by some process a little more speedy than the ordinary course of nature. I wish to see these states rapidly ascending to that rank which their natural advantages authorize them to hold among the nations of the earth." Henry declared that if America encouraged husband-men, mechanics, and merchants of the Old World to come to "this land of promise," there were those then living "who will see this favoured land amongst the most powerful on earth—able, sir, to take care of herself, without resorting to that policy which is always so dangerous, though sometimes unavoidable, of calling in foreign aid." [26]

Again, noting that the opposing gentlemen had objected "to any accession from Great Britain, and particularly to the return of . . . those deluded people," Henry said that they had "mistaken their own interests" and "suffered the punishment due" their offenses. But the relations Virginia bore to the Tories and to their native country were now changed. Their King had acknowledged American independence; the quarrel was over; peace had returned and found America a free people.

> . . . Let us have the magnanimity, sir, to lay aside our antipathies and prejudices, and consider the subject in a political light. Those are an enterprising, moneyed people—they will be serviceable in taking off the surplus produce of our lands, and supplying us with necessaries, during the infant state of our manufactures. Even if they be inimical to us in point of feeling and principle, I can see no objection, in a political view, in making them tributary to our advantage. And as I have no prejudices to prevent my making this use of them, so, sir, I have no fear of any mischief that they can do us." [27]

Henry then continued with one of his memorable quotations:

> "Afraid of *them!*—what, sir,"—said he, rising to one of his loftiest attitudes [so Tyler continued], and assuming a look of

the most indignant and sovereign contempt,—"shall *we*, who
have laid the proud British *lion* at our feet, now be afraid of his
whelps?" [28]

The force of Henry's figure of speech and the energy with which
it was developed made the House, in Tyler's words, "start simul-
taneously." The oratorical passage continued to be admired years
after his speech was delivered. It was frequently quoted by George
Wythe to his law students at William and Mary College as "a happy
specimen of those valuable figures, which unite the beauty of decora-
tion with the effect of argument." [29]

To another hated people Henry was ready the next year to extend
the hand of friendship—and even marriage. For many Americans of
that period "the only good Injun" was a dead one. Thousands had
fresh memories of scalpings and burnings by the redskins, often incited by their British allies. There were still Indian raids on the frontier, and Henry had his own reasons for understanding some of the
worst features of the Indian character.

But beginning on November 5, 1784, Henry proposed two measures favoring amicable relations with the Indians. The first measure
called on the Governor of Virginia, with the advice of the Council,
to adopt such measures as he found necessary "to avert the dangers of
hostilities with the Indians and to incline them to treat with the commissioners of congress; and for that purpose" he could "draw on
the treasury for any sum of money not exceeding one thousand
pounds." [30]

It would take far more than a treaty with the Indians to remove
the old enmities, particularly since the white men were continuing to
push westward into the Indian hunting grounds. What Henry proposed, therefore, in his second measure, was to encourage marriage
between the whites and the Indians. It was a policy which, as he
stated in the preamble of his bill, could have "great effect in concili-
ating the friendship and confidence of the latter, whereby not only
their civilization may in some degree be finally brought about, but in
the meantime, their hostile inroads be prevented." [31]

Free white male inhabitants marrying Indian women and thereby inducing them to become inhabitants of Virginia were to be paid £10 each; free female Virginians marrying male Indians £10, with £5 for each child and further benefits in tax exemption, in livestock, and in free education for the children in a public seminary "until the age of twenty-one." Moreover, offspring of the mixed marriages were to have the same legal rights and privileges as offspring of free white people. Henry is said to have advocated this bill "with irresistible earnestness and eloquence. . . . Extremely sanguine" as to its utility, he was pleased when the bill passed through two readings and was engrossed for final passage. But soon thereafter he became Governor, and in his absence from the House it was defeated on the third reading.[32]

"We have rejected some [bills] which in my conception would have been advantageous to this country," John Marshall wrote James Monroe in December, 1784. "Among these I rank the bill for encouraging intermarriages with the Indians. Our prejudices, however, oppose themselves to our interests, and operate too powerfully for them." [33] A political veteran like Henry surely knew that his bill would arouse these "prejudices," but he might have carried it if he had remained in the House.

As in his Stamp Act and "Give Me Liberty" speeches, and numerous other occasions throughout his career, the issue was not one to be raised by a time-serving politician. Henry's action offered another example of what Judge Spencer Roane described as Henry's "astonishing portion of political courage." Roane, who had differed strongly from Henry, denied that Henry "always seized and advocated the popular side of the question."

Nothing was less true, Roane declared, than the imputation that

> the man who moved the Stamp Act resolutions, and took up arms to recover the gunpowder, pursued his own course. . . . I take the fact to be that he generally thought like the most of people, because he was a plain, practical man, because he was emphatically one of the people, and because he detested, as a statesman, the projects of theorists and bookworms. His prejudices against statesmen of this character were very strong. He emphatically led the people in promoting and effecting the Revolution.[34]

[265]

It was as a "plain, practical man" or, as some of his opponents would have it, with his ear to the ground, that Henry delivered another notable speech during the Fall, 1784, Assembly—another speech in which his oratory enabled him to cajole a reluctant, if not hostile, House. The speech dealt with the difficult—indeed, then largely insoluble—problem of war finance. It had now been about eighteen months since the *Gazette* had published the proclamation of Congress declaring a cessation of war "as well by sea as by land." But the resulting celebration was somewhat premature, for trade had not yet been fully reopened, the grievous wounds of the war not yet healed. The problem of tax collections, which Henry had tried to remedy with the commutation act the previous year, was still acute. There had been lists in the *Gazette* of persons whose lands would be sold if they did not soon pay overdue taxes. Among the delinquents was Henry's cousin, John Winston, in the toils of debt as before the Revolution: 700 acres of his land (or as much thereof as necessary) was to be auctioned in Charlottesville before Jouett's Tavern to cover his overdue tax of £2.14.6.[35] A more deserving case—but involving the credit of Virginia—was that of Thomas Bentley. In July Bentley was writing from Richmond to urge the payment by the state of his unspecified claim of £4,272.18 "already allowed." Bentley had waited for the money two years at great expense, and he was anxious to return to the Illinois country, where his private affairs were "suffering greatly for his detention."[36] A year later, the state Auditor's Office was noting some unpleasant facts about the failure of the county lieutenants to secure the recruiting tax. Many of the larger counties showed considerable deficits, and judgments had been secured against the lieutenants in the General Court. Altogether, there were forty-seven counties delinquent for various sums totaling £7,515.18.3.[37]

When the Fall, 1784, Assembly met, the finances of the country were still much disarranged and public credit was at a low ebb. The economic situation was all the more frustrating because the return of some foreign ships to Virginia ports after the end of the war pointed to what should be better times. A strong party in the legislature now thought that it was high time to place the character and credit of the state on a more respectable footing by laying taxes commensurate with all the public demands. A bill designed for this effect was brought before the House and referred to the Committee of the Whole, where it was supported by several legislators "of great respectability," according to Judge Archibald Stuart, including John Tyler, Mann Page, William Ronald, Howard Tazewell, "to the best of my recollection Richard Henry Lee," and "perhaps" James Madison.[38]

On the other hand, Patrick Henry thought the effort of the bill's supporters was "premature . . . ; that policy required that the people should have some repose after the fatigues and privations to which they had been subjected, during a long and arduous struggle for independence."[39]

After using "their utmost efforts," the advocates of the bill secured a majority of some thirty, which seemed to assure its passage. When the Committee of the Whole rose, the bill was reported to the House. Henry, "excited and roused by his recent defeat, came forward again in all the majesty of his power." For a time his opponents did not show any recognition of the danger to their cause. As he began to speak, Tyler's face was turned from him, Tazewell was reading a pamphlet, and Page was "more than usually grave," wrote Stuart. But after some time Tyler's countenance began to relax; he would occasionally look at Henry and sometimes smile. Gradually, Tyler's attention became more fixed, Stuart continued, until it "became completely so." He began to appear in good humor; he leaned toward Henry, seemed "charmed and delighted, and finally lost in wonder and amazement."[40]

From Henry's speech we get further proof of the influences in favor of the poor debtor class that were affecting him now that he was living in the remote back country among small farmers who would have had enough difficulty eking out a living even if their distant markets had not been cut off or badly curtailed as a result of the Revolution.

Henry drew, so Stuart also recalled,

> a most affecting picture of the state of poverty and suffering in which the people of the upper counties had been left by the war.

His delineations of their wants and wretchedness was so minute, so full of feeling, and withal so true, that he could scarcely fail to enlist on his side every sympathetic mind. He contrasted the severe toil by which they had to gain their daily subsistence, with the facilities enjoyed by the people of the lower counties.[41]

The advocates of the bill had come mostly from the Tidewater, where, since they lived on salt rivers and creeks, Henry said they could draw their supplies at their pleasure from the waters that flowed by their doors. He drew such a "ludicrous image" of the proponents of the measure, "peeping and peering along the shores of the creeks to pick up their mess of crabs or paddling off to the oyster rocks to rake for *their daily bread*," that the House roared in amusement.

Reading the contemporary accounts of Henry's legislative activity, one may usually suspect a preternatural seriousness and gravity. But, adept at gauging his audiences, he could employ a homely wit with deadly effectiveness. In this instance, we learn that as he continued Tazewell "laid down his pamphlet and shook his sides with laughter"; that Page's "gravity" was affected; that even among the advocates of the bill there was "a corresponding change of countenance . . . and you might discover that they had surrendered their cause." On a division, Henry now got a majority of nearly thirty against the bill.[42]

Clever wit, like brilliant oratory, often has to be heard to be fully appreciated. But Stuart's testimony is reinforced by that of John Tyler. He wrote that he had seen Henry reply to Page, Tazewell, Richard Henry Lee, and others "with such a volume of wit and humour that the house would be in an uproar of laughter, and even set his opponents altogether in a perfect convulsion." But Tyler went on to say that Henry did not often indulge this talent, which he deemed "beneath a statesman." [43]

Among his numerous activities in the Assembly, Henry was now particularly interested in internal improvements and education. At Leatherwood he was living on a tributary of the Roanoke River, and his last plantation home would overlook the fertile low grounds of another such tributary, the Staunton River. As the most important

political leader in the area fed by this large river system, he successfully introduced a bill at the May, 1783, Assembly looking to the
extension of navigation of the Roanoke from its falls upward into its
main tributaries, the Staunton and the Dan. Henry headed a group
of trustees including his cousin, Isaac Coles, Paul Carrington, James
Calloway, and other prominent men of the section who were authorized to take subscriptions to pay for the clearing of portions of these
rivers in Virginia and were permitted to institute lawsuits for recovery
of subscriptions of unpaid money for the enterprise.[44] From this beginning there would develop the Roanoke Navigation Company,
which in later years would cut a canal around the falls of the Roanoke
and do much to facilitate shipping on the river.[45] Also, from another
committee of which Henry was a member came a bill, passed at the
next session, for digging a canal near Suffolk in eastern Virginia. This
would become the Dismal Swamp Canal, still operating in the great
swampy region along the Virginia–North Carolina border. Henry
obtained large landed interests in this or nearby areas—not without
charges of land grabbing and undue influence.

More constructive on the whole was his interest in popular education. His scholarly father, Colonel John Henry, had endeavored to
instill in his son a love of learning of which Patrick in his youth was
not always appreciative. But maturity and particularly the need for
educating the youth of the new democracy, including his own sons,
now led Henry to become prominently identified with various
schemes for developing education in Virginia. When attending the
May, 1783, session of the Assembly, he was a member of a committee
authorized to bring in a bill "for the more general diffusion of knowledge." Evidently, the committee was under the influence of a bill to
that effect which had been introduced earlier by Jefferson. But the
tradition of an aristocratic education applying chiefly to the upper
classes was strongly imbued in the legislature. Nearly two centuries
later there would still be difficulty in persuading some Virginia legislators to vote in favor of generous public school appropriations. At the
end of the Revolution, the state could neither afford—nor was it even
asked—to provide a public school system. It did, however, make a
notable effort to promote institutions for higher education.

[269]

With this movement Henry became prominently identified. Already a trustee of the Hampden-Sydney Academy, he was also active in the movement by which the Academy was incorporated and opened its doors in 1776 as Hampden-Sydney College. This institution, which served especially the needs of the growing Piedmont, would become one of the leading Presbyterian colleges in the United States, with many distinguished alumni. Henry remained one of its trustees until his death. Several of his sons and grandsons would be among the early students attending the little church college at its quiet tree-bowered site.

At the same Assembly which approved the charter for Hampden-Sydney, Henry served on a committee which reported a bill for the incorporation of an academy in Northampton County on the Eastern Shore. He also had special reason for interest in the incorporation by the legislature during 1782–1783 of Liberty Hall Academy in Rockbridge County, the nucleus for the future Washington and Lee University,[46] and of Transylvania Seminary in Kentucky, the future Transylvania University.[47] Recognizing the acute need for educated leaders in the new commonwealth, the act for the incorporation of Liberty Hall provided that professors and students in this and all other seminaries were to be exempted from military duty.

When the Assembly met in October, 1784—the same Assembly that would soon elect Henry as Governor for a fourth one-year term—there was much to indicate that he was still as essentially progressive as in his earlier years. Certainly, his activities during 1780–1784 as a leading advocate of the restoration of Tory citizenship and of British trade, of immigration, of increased internal trade, and of intermarriage with Indians did not connote the hidebound reactionary. One may argue, too, that his successful efforts to ease the individual tax burden actually represented a progressive stand. But, at least privately, by late 1783 and more openly within the next few years, Henry was questioning an increased centralization of governmental powers. In time, Madison and other leaders of the nationalist coterie in the Assembly would consider Henry their principal opponent, and the issue would become of national significance. Curiously, our first intimation of his growing concern with the subject comes from Captain John Paul Jones.

Among the young men who found fame, but not fortune, in the American Revolution was Dolly's former suitor, John Paul Jones. She must have had unusual qualities to attract the greatest orator and the greatest naval hero of the war. By his diehard courage during a battle late in 1779 with a British squadron, and other exploits, that obscure Scotsman had won international fame. His traditional battle cry, "I have just begun to fight," when the *Bon Homme Richard* was sinking would become a patriotic slogan like Henry's "Give Me Liberty." And four years after this battle, Jones, by another turn of fortune, found himself in a significant conversation with Dolly's husband, "His Excellency," Patrick Henry.

The gist of the conversation is found in a memorandum drawn up by Jones in January, 1788, for Thomas Jefferson, then American minister to France. Jones had just come to Paris and offered Jefferson his opinion on the proposed American Constitution of 1787. Jones' observations had an added value in that he had been in Philadelphia shortly before the adoption of the Articles of Confederation and in touch with some participants in the preceding debate.

To Jones' amazement, Patrick Henry contended that even the Articles of Confederation, as they were being interpreted and enforced, conferred too much authority on the central power and stripped the individual states of their rightful sovereignty in many respects.

Jones argued to the contrary, but Henry "rather bluntly" informed him that his conception of government—whatever might be his impulses of patriotism and aspiration for the rights of man—was after all the result of his lifelong experience on quarterdecks. He could not apply the discipline of the ship to the problem of governing a free people.

Vainly, Jones countered that "no government could hope to be respected at home or honored abroad that was not firmly united or capable of presenting an undivided and unbroken front in any emergency." And this "could not be done by any other than a strong and unquestioned central authority.

[271]

"I could not persuade Mr. Henry out of the conviction," Jones concluded, "or, rather, I could not reason him into the admission that the absorption of power by any central government could mean anything but surrender of the rights of communities and the freedom of individuals." [48]

Just how and when did Henry, the fiery revolutionist and some-time nationalist, become the leader of a nascent states' rights party in Virginia? The explanations can too easily be given in black and white, especially when related to the issue of conservatism against liberalism. The states' rights advocate may be called a conservative today, a liberal tomorrow. Indeed, even Henry's advocacy of states' rights can be overstressed. He did not always take the anti-Nationalist viewpoint during the 1780's, and during his last years he would display some distinct Federalist tendencies. On the whole, however, in the last two decades of his life he did become less radical, less the crusading liberal. And this tendency, with the resulting political action, offers a key to his postwar career.

There are a number of possible explanations for Henry's increasing conservatism. In the early 1780's the war was brought to a victorious conclusion and American liberty secured. Henry, now in his late forties, with large property and family responsibilities and an assured position, was under different influences than when, as a little-known young man of twenty-nine, he had introduced the Stamp Act resolutions or when, even a decade later, in 1775, he had made his speech at St. John's Church. In the subsequent years he never lost his crusading zeal for personal liberty. But within a few years after his retirement to Leatherwood, there was a discernible change in his thought pattern. The historian can easily become too categorical in his interpretation of human motives. But at least we need to emphasize the different influences when Henry lived in Henry County as compared with those when he was back in Hanover, Louisa, and Williamsburg (and Philadelphia). We have noted some results of his moving to remote Henry County, largely a milieu of poor, debt-ridden farmers. Other effects of this new environment began to be noticeable at the May, 1784, Assembly, especially when connected with the changing Richmond scene. At the opening of the Assembly he appeared to be in the nationalist camp, but within a few weeks his position was becoming somewhat uncertain.

In a letter to Jefferson from Richmond on May 15, William Short described a significant conversation on the issue which he had had the previous evening with Henry, Madison, and Joseph Jones at "a coffee house," probably Formicola's. This popular hostelry run by the Sicilian, Formicola, another of his family, and some half dozen or more slaves was not unlike many which Henry had known as an itinerant country lawyer. In the unpretentious wooden building below Shockoe Hill, with its two large rooms downstairs and two above, clerks, judges, doctors, military officers, statesmen, or politicians of "every weight and caliber" foregathered during the political assemblies to drink, smoke, sing, or talk "ribaldry." [49]

The occasion for the meeting of the four gentlemen was that Jones and Madison wished to sketch out some proposals for giving greater powers to the federal government—and for Henry to support the plan on the floor of the House. The Confederation was now in a grave plight, with Congress utterly unable to collect requisitions from delinquent states. "It was thought a bold Example set by Virginia would have Influence on the other States," Short wrote his friend Jefferson in Paris. Indeed, Henry declared that this was the only inducement he had for coming to the present Assembly. He saw "ruin inevitable unless something was done to give Congress a compulsory Process for the delinquent States, etc."

In another letter on May 15, Edmund Randolph wrote to inform his cousin, Thomas Jefferson, now Minister Plenipotentiary to France, of the line-up of the new Assembly. "The great leaders of the Assembly" not having arrived, its business was "stagnated." But Henry was in the neighborhood, Randolph continued. And he added, "The increase of new members had introduced some of the children of the Revolution" (Revolutionary veterans), who sought to satisfy themselves and disdained "dependency on the dictum of any individual or faction."

In the previous Assembly there had been three party divisions: one led by Henry, another by Richard Henry Lee, although absent, and a third by Speaker Tyler, "founded on a rivetted opposition to our late enemy, and everything which concerned them." The Henry party had always been numerous and would probably remain so, the Lee party had not "varied a single point for some years," and the Tyler party was "but a temporary buffer, contrived to save the trouble of thinking on a truly national policy." Randolph was somewhat harsh in stating that the Tyler faction was motivated only by such a provincial policy. He was on more solid ground, however, in hoping for an impetus to the nationalistic party from the young Revolutionary officers then in the Assembly.

Randolph suspected that the "new legislative guests" would "want a general to enable them to make head" against members of the opposing factions, who would "not fail to impeach them with an affectation of novelty when they only press the result of liberality and reflection." And this, as Jefferson could happily read, rendered it probable that their "friend of Orange," James Madison, would "step earlier into the heart of battle, than his modesty would otherwise permit, for he is already resorted to, as a general of whom much has been preconceived to his advantage." [50]

With Jefferson in France, his friend Madison was quietly coming to the fore as a leader of the anti-Henry forces. Recalling his impressions after entering the Assembly in May, 1783, Spencer Roane would write that "as an orator, Mr. Henry demolished Madison with as much ease as Sampson did the cords that bound him before he was shorn." [51] But the unobtrusive Madison, learned, logical, persistent, was becoming a more formidable opponent. His liberal and nationalistic arguments had a special appeal for the new members of the House who, as veterans of the Revolution, appreciated the need for a stronger government in a period of crisis.

Later, Madison would state that his chief purpose in entering the legislature was to secure stronger powers for Congress so as to rescue "the Union and the blessings of liberty staked on it from an impending catastrophe." [52] Since Henry was the most influential member of the Assembly, it was extremely important for Madison to secure his cooperation, and they did work well together at this time. With Henry's support the Assembly passed a resolution instructing the Virginia congressional delegates to expedite the settlement of federal-state accounts. If necessary, the amounts owed the United States were to be secured by "distress on the property of the defaulting states or their citizens." After one of Henry's anti-Federalist speeches during the Virginia Constitutional Convention of 1787, George Nicholas would jeeringly accuse Henry of writing these resolutions. "I am sure that the gentleman recognizes his own child." [53]

Yet early in the May, 1784, session Henry had begun to reverse his nationalist stand. A bill was introduced stating that Virginia should pay in 1784 three fourths of the amount it owed Congress in 1781, and the measures passed two readings. But Henry, still sensitive to the plight of the poor debtors, used his oratory effectively, as noted, to make the House reverse its position.

Disgusted by the difficulties in collecting taxes in Virginia and by the confusion in its revenue department, Madison believed that the basic remedy was a revised state constitution. Devoted as he was to this plan, Madison was discouraged into silence by "the adverse temper of the House, and particularly of Mr. Henry." Richard Henry Lee, a proponent, was unwell before the vote, and Henry above all "showed a more violent opposition" than the proponents expected. The Assembly not only defeated the bill but declared that it had no authority to call a convention except when directed by "a majority of all the free people." And this after Madison had pointed out in a speech that the Constitution of 1776 was never authorized by the people and never ratified. [54] Considering the strong opposition aroused by Henry's oratory, it was not surprising that Madison and his nationalist associates were coming to consider Henry their chief stumbling block.

When George Mason, in his letter of May 6, 1783, urged Henry's support for revision of various laws by the Assembly—since American independence would depend on "our own wisdom or folly, virtue or wickedness . . . among us a depravity of . . . morals prevails to the destruction of all confidence between man and man" [55]—Henry needed no reminder of the decline in morals during the war; he had already given voice to his opinion on that unhappy subject when war Governor. Nor had he been inclined to a more optimistic view by his later experiences with some rough backwoodsmen in Henry County. One means by which he was endeavoring to make better citizens of his fellow Virginians was through legislation for more collegiate education; another, legislation to bolster religion and morals.

In contrast to his customary progressivism during the first postwar years, Henry has been labeled an opponent of religious freedom. As usual, the story is written too much in black and white. It is an over-simplification to represent his advocacy in the Fall, 1784, Assembly of the bills to incorporate the Episcopal Church and to impose a tax for the benefit of religious denominations as merely a manifestation of his increasing conservatism since the war. Undoubtedly, however, the war had been a determining factor in the decline of the Virginia established church. The facts were impressed on Henry for various reasons.

That the Virginia Episcopal Church suffered from its Tory taint would be amusingly attested (from a Whig viewpoint!) by one Anglican minister from a Southside area in which Henry would spend his declining years. Accused of "openly" drinking a glass of grog at a local tavern while expressing his hope for the success of the British forces, the Reverend Thomas Johnson, late of Oxford University, received a visitation from the local Committee of Safety and offered an apology which the Committee ordered to be published in the *Virginia Gazette*: ". . . I solemnly declared it was done inadvertently." [56]

The decreasing influence of the Episcopal Church, owing to its weaknesses as a part of the British establishment and the rise of the Dissenting denominations, had been accentuated by the Revolution. Henry, lawyer for anticlerical parties in the Parson's Cause of 1763 and other prewar cases, supported the memorable statement in the Virginia Declaration of Rights of 1776: ". . . all men are equally intitled to the free exercise of Religion according to the dictates of Conscience." [57] Yet for an Episcopalian born and bred such as Henry, the war led to a sad chronicle of ministers resigning, of parishes becoming vacant or barely surviving, of vestrymen resigning, and of Dissenters reluctant to even pay tithes for the support of the poor. [58] A key measure in Thomas Jefferson's legislative reform program was his bill in 1779 for religious freedom. It passed two readings in the Assembly that year, and in December the Assembly repealed a law providing salaries for the now discouraged and often penurious Anglican clergymen.[59]

During the seven years from the negative vote on Jefferson's bill for abolition of the religious establishment until 1786, when this epochal step was finally accomplished, numerous petitions on the religious issue were presented to the Assembly. The demoralizing effect on the churches of the long war had not only aroused Henry's "pious patriotism" but that of the Dissenters, who sought separation of church and state. "The sabbath had been almost forgotten," complained a Presbyterian writer, and a Baptist historian stated, "With some few exceptions, the declension [of religion] was general throughout the State. Iniquity greatly abounded."[60] In the end the petitions seeking removal of the Anglican establishment proved more influential. Jefferson's proposal of the bill for religious freedom would be one of his outstanding achievements, which, at his suggestion, was inscribed on his tombstone.

Henry, the devout Anglican, looked with favor on religious reform of a different type. In a petition to the Assembly at the May, 1784, session, some Powhatan citizens stated that they were "of the opinion a reasonable and moderate contribution for the support of ministers of the Gospel and the Christian religion . . . is essential to the good and prosperity of the Commonwealth." In June a convention of clergymen and laymen was held in Richmond to reorganize the Virginia Episcopal Church. When a bill for the incorporation of the church was offered at the incumbent legislature, it was debated for two days, then postponed until the fall session. Indeed, Madison, who was present, wrote, "Extraordinary as such a project was, it was preserved from a dishonorable death by the talents of Mr. Henry." However, he stated that the friends of a measure to provide a state tax assessment for religious denominations "did not choose to try their strength in the House."[61]

The subject of assessment was brought up at the Fall Assembly on the basis of some strong though not altogether positive support from several religious groups. The Hanover Presbytery affirmed the necessity of the support of religion and concluded that the state might take steps to "preserve the public worship of the Deity, and support institutions for inculcating the great fundamental principles of all religion."

On the basis of the sentiment expressed, the pro-church party felt that they could push their measures, and the House by 47 to 32 voted in favor of "a moderate assessment for the support of the Christian religion." Henry was chairman of the committee to draft the bill. The House also agreed that acts should be passed for the incorporating of Christian religious societies so applying. This action was by a vote of 62 to 23, with Henry appointed a member of the committee to incorporate the clergy of the Protestant Episcopal Church.[62] But with the aid of some political maneuvering, including assistance from the Madison party in removing or elevating Henry to the governorship, his religious bills would never be enacted.

19

Governor for a Fourth and Fifth Term

> *I want you* in the *Virginia Assembly* and also in *Congress*, yet
> we cannot have *you everywhere*. We must therefore be con-
> tented to have *you where you chuse*. THOMAS JEFFERSON in
> Paris to James Madison, March 18, 1785 [1]

November, 1784–November, 1786. Controversy over state religious issue. Passage in 1786 of Jefferson's bill for religious
freedom.

November, 1784–April, 1786. Deaths of Henry's mother and
other relatives.

November 17, 1784. Henry elected Governor for a fourth
one-year term.

November 25, 1785. Henry elected Governor a fifth one-
year term.

January–May, 1786. Virginia Assembly (January) calls for
a national trade convention at Annapolis in May. Upon recommendation of this convention, Congress called for a national
convention at Philadelphia, May, 1787, to revise the Articles
of Confederation.

D URING THE five years since Henry had retired from the
governorship, three incumbents had sat in the seat of the Virginia
chief executive. Thomas Jefferson had chosen to retire at the end of
his second term, and his successor, General Thomas Nelson, had resigned after six months because of ill health. Benjamin Harrison had

then served three one-year terms to the general satisfaction. Since this was the constitutional limit for consecutive terms, the House and Senate, on Wednesday, November 17, 1784, proceeded to the election of a new Governor.

Under the constitutional provision, Henry could not have been a candidate for the office for three years after he had last served. But this period of abstention had ended two years ago. On November 14, 1784, James Madison wrote James Monroe from Richmond that the governorship was at Henry's "option. . . . I fancy he will not decline the service." [2] Indeed, as Madison later informed Jefferson in France, Henry's election was "without competition or opposition." [3] Considering the frequent rivalry in the Assembly, it seemed an astonishingly easy victory. It may, however, be explained by some obvious causes: Henry was the most influential political figure in Virginia, he had served successfully as Governor for the three terms, and he was no longer opposed by the Lee party, including Richard Henry Lee, recently elected to Congress.

But was there still another reason for Henry's election? Was it true that some of his leading opponents wanted him out of the House? Certainly his removal—elevation?—to the governorship contributed materially to the defeat of some important legislation: two religious bills, the bill to encourage marriages with Indians, and at least one other measure frowned upon by some influential delegates.

The Assembly votes on the religious issue are especially significant. On November 14, 1784, Madison wrote Monroe that the House was "still occupied" with the bill for a general assessment for Christian denominations. This bill, based on a resolution introduced by Henry, called for a "moderate tax or contribution" for such a purpose. It had been passed by a vote of 47 to 32 in the House Committee of the Whole and, so it appeared, would be easily carried when it came to the floor for final action. [4] On November 17, probably within an hour or two after Henry's election, the House went again into Committee of the Whole. It then resolved by a vote of 62 to 23 that acts ought to pass for the incorporation by the state of all societies of the Christian religion "which may apply for the same." Along with Henry, still present in the House, the ayes comprised nearly all the leading members, including rising young delegates such as Archibald Stuart and Spencer Roane; James Madison was the only outstanding member listed in the opposition. Henry was also encouraged when the House the same day "gave leave" to bring in his bill to incorporate the clergy of the Protestant Episcopal Church and appointed him to the committee "to prepare and bring in the same."

He could hardly have anticipated the sequel. On the twenty-seventh of November Madison in a lengthy letter to Monroe noted that the bill for the religious assessments had not yet been brought in—that is, considered for final passage. "Mr. Henry, the father of this scheme, has gone up to his Seat for his family & will no more sit in the H. of Delegates, a circumstance very inauspicious to his offspring," Madison added.[5]

On December 4, Madison wrote that the bill had been reported the previous day and would be taken up in the Committee of the Whole the next week. "Its friends are much disheartened at the loss of Mr. Henry. Its fate is I think very uncertain." [6] In fact, the final action on the bill was postponed and with Henry, its principal champion, now Governor, it was never passed. And his bill for incorporation of the Episcopal Church met with the same fate. On December 22, a month after he left the House, this measure was read the third time and passed by only 47 to 38, with Madison voting in the affirmative.[7] The bill was ordered to be carried to the Senate for their concurrence. But it was not passed during the remainder of the session, and the opposition built up until the measure languished and died. In 1786 Jefferson's bill for establishing religious freedom in the state was finally passed.

James Madison was the most influential figure in the measures to arouse the Dissenters and other Virginians who secured the final separation of church and state. In his surviving *Writings* and those of his allies we find no evidence of disappointment at Henry's election as Governor—no adverse comments, even in secret code. Moreover, it is significant to note the membership of the committee appointed by the House to notify Henry of his election as Governor. Normally, at least a majority of the members would be selected from leading House supporters of Henry's candidacy. The committee members chosen were Jones of Prince George, Madison, and Ronald. Altogether, it appears likely that the Madison party worked successfully to help get Henry out of the House.

Why did Henry want to become Governor when it meant the defeat of his favored bills—indeed, loss of prestige as the leading member of the House? Obviously, he was too sure of the final passage of the religious bills; he had not counted on such a large change of the House sentiment in his absence. Also, we should not overlook the influence of his young aristocratic wife and his marriageable daughters by his first wife. When he returned to Leatherwood he could tell his family about some of the exciting events at the capital during the legislative session: the fall races, followed by the ball with General Greene present; the visits to the city of General Washington and young Marquis de Lafayette. Henry himself had been chairman of the committees appointed by the House which drew up laudatory resolutions to be presented to the revered generals, and he reported their replies to the House, including Lafayette's praise for the Virginians in the late war. "Our armed force was obliged to retreat but your patriotic hearts stood unshaken." [8]

To Henry's young wife and his children such events were in glamorous contrast to life on the distant plantation. In Richmond, Henry and Dolly would be living near many old friends and relatives as well as influential political personages. The two marriageable daughters could meet more eligible suitors than in the remote back country; within eighteen months after Henry became Governor they married gentlemen whom they might never have known had the family remained at Leatherwood. On the other hand, there were strong reasons for declining the responsible position. Henry had not forgotten his exhausting labors as war Governor, and physically he was now past his prime. The Virginia Governor still labored under the constitutional restriction by which he could not carry out numerous measures without the consent of the Council.

And yet peace had been declared and trade was being restored. The governorship now promised to be a position of dignity and honor, with fewer administrative burdens. Thanks to Henry's prestige, his tact and experience, he could reasonably hope to secure an ascendancy over the Council just as he had when war Governor.

There is a saying that "Happy is the country that has no history." In a letter to Jefferson on September 10, 1785, Henry would speak of the "present Tranquility" in Virginia as not affording many anecdotes "interesting enough to relate" but as conducive to growth.[9] And indeed the state did need a period of rest and recuperation after the almost insurmountable difficulties of the Revolution. Henry's role was less exciting—and less dangerous—than during the war. But he had a notable opportunity to heal wounds and soften animosities; to pay off or at least postpone pressing debts; to help rebuild and expand trade and agriculture; in short, to accelerate all the activities of a large and productive state.

After Henry's election as Governor on November 17, 1784, it was several days before he could leave on the long journey to bring his family back to Richmond. Not until Tuesday, December 21, did he take his seat as the presiding officer in the Council chamber. Who were the seven gentlemen with whom he would meet there so often during the next two years? Just how should they be classified for their political ideas, their experience and ability? The ranking Councilor and Lieutenant Governor was the forty-year-old Beverley Randolph, a former delegate from Cumberland and a militia colonel in the 1780 campaign. Later, in 1789–1791, Randolph would follow his cousin, Edmund Randolph, as Governor—a Randolph succeeding a Randolph. And yet there would be little or no cry of nepotism and undue influence, for besides his family prestige Beverley possessed a good share of its political competence. There is no evidence that Henry found him unreliable or uncooperative.

The other Councilors, already elected or to be elected within the next few months, included Miles Selden; his in-law, Dr. James McClurg of Richmond; Spencer Roane, now of Richmond, and soon to be Henry's son-in-law; Joseph Jones of Prince George, near Petersburg; General James Wood; and Colonel Sampson Matthews. For sound, practical reasons, the Councilors were thus still largely chosen from experienced gentlemen living convenient to the capital, but

Selden was from Hampton, Wood from Winchester, and Matthews from Staunton.

Probably the most talented—though not along the usual political lines—was Dr. McClurg. Although still under forty, McClurg had become one of the outstanding American physicians. Not only had he graduated from William and Mary College and received his M.D. degree from Edinburgh but he had done postgraduate medical study in Paris and London. Henry was Governor when, in January, 1777, Dr. McClurg was appointed Physician and Director General of the state military hospital at the munificent salary of $4 per day.[10] And to Henry McClurg is said to have chiefly owed his position on the Council. Henry, "very fond of men of genius," became "much attached" to the doctor because of his professional distinction, Spencer Roane recalled, and he "had a great agency in getting him [McClurg] into the Council in May, 1784." Indeed, Roane believed that McClurg would not have been elected had it not been for Henry's speech just before the balloting. As Henry spoke, "many members were seen to tear up their ballots prepared for other candidates," Roane continued. Henry "took the ground for Dr. McClurg that he was a man of great genius and eminence in his profession. At this time party had not thrown our citizens so far asunder."[11]

Undoubtedly, the Council continued the traditions of competence in the Virginia ruling class, the more so since the legislature had recruited some new blood from outside of the now-declining Tidewater. Henry might have some difficulty with Joseph Jones, usually considered a member of the Madison faction, but Jones would contribute valuable experience both in Congress and the legislature. Spencer Roane, the later appellate judge of "stern and forbidding" cast, was already showing some independent qualities. But as a new member of the House he had voted with Henry more often than not,[12] and he now brought to the Council exceptional ability as well as a respect and admiration for Henry not for some years to be marred by political and family differences.

As a whole, the Councilors were bound to Henry by strong ties of patriotic loyalty and personal admiration. They would willingly accept his leadership, provided he paid tactful heed to their advice—and did not advocate extreme measures.[13]

As when war Governor, one of Henry's important and time-consuming duties was the appointment of various state officials. Despite his wide experience in Virginia politics, he could not personally know many of the suitable candidates, especially those in distant places and among the new postwar generation. Advice was needed not merely from the Council but from other responsible persons. Thus, when he had to select county lieutenants and field officers for the militia, the Council, meeting on Saturday, January 22, 1785, advised him to address a letter to some of "the most respectable Characters," excepting those on the western waters, and request the correspondents to nominate for him "the most proper" persons to hold the specified militia offices in the various counties.[14]

Soon after Henry became Governor, an opportunity came to lend a helping hand to the Indians, along with many deserving white settlers—and this from an unexpected source. Selina Hastings, the English Countess of Huntingdon, proposed to establish colonies of worthy European Protestants in or near the Indian country. By the industrious pursuit of their trades and crafts, she believed that these settlers would not only support themselves but also set a valuable example for the neighboring Indians. Lady Huntingdon's plan was endorsed in an accompanying letter from Sir James Jay, brother of John Jay, with whom Henry had served in the Continental Congress.

Almost unique in the England of her day, Lady Huntingdon was a wealthy noblewoman who had embraced the Methodist movement and become a supporter of the two Wesleys and George Whitefield. It was Whitefield who described the Countess as looking like "a good archbishop with his chaplains around him." She had lost £10,000 before the war when a Georgia orphanage burned to the ground,[15] and she was prepared to invest large sums in the projected western settlement.

Lady Huntingdon's proposal struck a responsive chord in Henry. In one of his early manuscripts, he had pointed out that a great evil besetting Virginia was its system of slavery and large plantations. As a remedy he had advocated an influx of free farmers and artisans,[16] and he had later elaborated on some aspects of the theme. Lady Huntingdon now offered a plan not only for bringing desirable emigrants to the unsettled frontier but for improving Indian relations. No wonder Henry wrote the Virginia congressmen on February 3, 1785, that it indicated "a mind well informed, liberal, and generously enlarged." [17] Waxing still more enthusiastic, he declared:

> The civilization and christianizing of the Indians, if indeed they are two things, are matters of high moral and political concern. But when these shall be attended with the acquisition of people from Europe of the description given by the Countess, they form an object so desirable, and so truly great, as deeply to interest the feelings of every good American and good man. [18]

While acknowledging the difficulty of the undertaking, Henry told the congressmen that if it depended on him "a moment would not be lost." But Richard Henry Lee wrote that Congress could not approve the plan since the public lands were deemed pledged for payment of the national debt and it was feared that the settlers would be sympathetic to Great Britain and have a dangerous influence on the Indians. Henry, with the approval of the Council, also took up the matter with the Virginia legislature. But it was all to no avail. In fact, he had already anticipated the likely disapproval of the Assembly when noting that the Virginia lands bordering the Indian country had been "ceded to Congress." [19] Lady Huntingdon's generous proposal deserved a better fate.

Henry also took up the matter of emigration to the western country in a letter of February 4, 1785, to his recent Leatherwood neighbor, Colonel Joseph Martin. Henry told Martin about an offer from a Portuguese gentleman to bring settlers to the area. The scheme would do "as much for the good of the Indians" as the new emigrants. "Old soldiers and tradesmen would be the people he would bring over." If the Indians asked questions about this proposal, Martin was to assure them that Henry was "laboring for their good, by trying to learn them our arts & manufactures, and to encourage good people to go among them, and that our people will be punished if they do them any injury." [20]

Already, on January 6, Henry, with the authorization of the Assembly, had issued a proclamation forbidding until further notice the surveying or acquiring of land northwest of the Ohio and below the mouth of the Tennessee River which had been reserved for soldiers of the Virginia Continental Line and the Illinois regiment.[21] Thus, he hoped to discourage conflicts with Indians in the area. Throughout his governorship, however, there would continue to be a stream of complaints about atrocities by the savage tribesmen, and they were followed by none too gentle retaliation from the western settlers. Indian relations—and other gubernatorial problems—were complicated by the establishment, after Henry became Governor, of "the lost state" of Franklin in the western territory of North Carolina and by a secession movement in Southwest Virginia.

In various respects the events of Henry's two years in the governorship were leading toward the next great crisis of his career—his fight against the ratification of the federal constitution. A long unsettled boundary dispute between Virginia and Maryland had become intensified under the Confederation. During the early 1780's Maryland was asserting the right to impose taxes on Virginia commerce in the Potomac River, and Virginia was retaliating by taxing Maryland trade passing through the mouth of the Chesapeake Bay. It was one of a number of controversies which led statesmen like Madison to feel the need for a strong central government which could settle such difficulties. Largely through his foresight and persistence, a conference to deal with the Maryland-Virginia problem was held at Alexandria in the spring of 1785. Madison then drew up a resolution for a commercial convention of all the states. Introduced by John Tyler in the House of Delegates, the resolution was unanimously adopted on January 1, 1786, and out of the following Annapolis Convention in September came the proposal for the Philadelphia Convention of 1787 which drew up a new American constitution.

In these events prior to the Philadelphia Convention, Henry took no more than an acquiescent role. There had been no question of his strong interest in Virginia commercial development, and the resolution for the Annapolis Convention would hardly have passed unanimously against his opposition. But throughout his governorship various influences, some not readily apparent, were shaping up to increase his fears of a stronger central government.

When the legislature met in October, 1785, four years had elapsed since the surrender at Yorktown. The Assembly had continued to be beset by petitions from poor Revolutionary veterans, wounded or disabled in the service of their country. Yet, at least for a rising new generation, the memory of the war was becoming somewhat less grim. Significant as a sign of better times was the increasing trade, largely in British bottoms. Among a variety of such notices, the *Virginia Gazette or American Advertiser* in late 1784 and early 1785 was announcing the arrival in the James River of such foreign ships as the *Cincinnatus*, two months out of London, and the *Mermaid*, bringing rum, sugar, coffee, etc., from Jamaica and sailing for Glasgow. Connor and Gernon of Richmond were advertising a late shipment of French luxury goods—silk stockings, feathers, hair powder, chocolate, "Coniac brandy seven years old," and the like. The *Gazette or Advertiser* also continued to report numerous sailings at Norfolk to or from New York, the West Indies, and Liverpool. Throughout Henry's governorship there were signs of increasing trade in Virginia. It was an important reason why he would not feel as urgently as some American statesmen the need for a new national constitution which might aid the commercial classes.

Meantime, his personal life was deeply affected by the large number of deaths in his family during his governorship. His correspondence reveals much of the deep religious feeling which impelled him to favor the state subsidy for religous denominations, while one death, as we will see, increased his opposition to the central government which he deemed partly responsible. Such a tragedy would have impelled some of his contemporaries to favor a stronger, a more energetic national government, but Henry became more disgusted with Congress, more willing to rely on the Virginia government until he was fully assured that changes in the Confederation would be for the better.

Henry had hardly begun to serve as Governor in late 1784 when he heard first from his sister, Jane, and then from her husband, Colonel Meredith, news of the death of the elder Mrs. Henry. After

John Henry died in 1773, Mrs. Henry had lived for a number of years with the Merediths in Hanover County. Then in 1780 she accompanied the Meredith caravan when they moved to Winton, the large estate in Amherst County which Colonel Meredith had bought from Joseph Cabell. Here Mrs. Henry remained for the last five years of her life. The Winton mansion has since been greatly renovated. Her upstairs bedroom in the old central portion and the place where she used to sit in the side yard are still pointed out. She died in November, 1784, after an illness of six or seven months, and Colonel Meredith wrote Henry one of the most remarkable tributes ever paid by a man to his wife's mother after she had lived with his family for many years.

During the "upwards of eleven years" that she had been with his family, Colonel Meredith wrote, her life had been "one continued scene of piety and devotion, guided by such a great share of good sense as rendered her amiable and agreeable to all who were so happy as to be acquainted with her. Never did I know a Christian character equal to hers. . . . What an honor it is to all those that claim their descent from such a person." [22] Reportedly at his own request, Colonel Meredith would later be buried by the side of his mother-in-law in the Winton cemetery.

It is often stated that great men are more influenced by their mothers than their fathers. The evidence is hardly conclusive in the cases of George Washington and Thomas Jefferson. But, on the whole, Sarah Henry seemed a stronger character than Patrick's father, Colonel John Henry, and Patrick derived more from her than from his father. In her last years there was no great indication of the sprightliness with which, as a young widow, she had attracted the attention of William Byrd II; she was now especially known for her amiability and Christian qualities. From her Patrick inherited much of his piety, intelligence, and firmness of character. There was also an oratorical strain (as has been noted) in her paternal family, the Winstons, and this was handed down to her distinguished son.

Soon after his mother's death, Henry in a letter to Judge Bartholomew Dandridge (who also would soon die), lamented the death of a Mr. Burbidge, so far as it is rational to lament the exchange of a bad world for one where sorrow never enters. This particular time is remarkable for the deaths of my near connections. My dear and ever honored mother died six or eight weeks ago, my brother William two weeks, and my only surviving aunt ten days. Thus is the last generation clearing the way for us, as we must shortly do for the next.[23]

All these deaths had a cumulative effect on Henry. They strengthened his belief in the Christian religion as a surcease in trouble for himself and others. While Governor, or shortly thereafter, he was so pleased with Soame Jenyns' *View of the Internal Evidence of the Christian Religion* that he had several hundred copies printed and distributed at his own expense. Still surviving is a small hair trunk covered with deerskin which Henry took with him later when as a lawyer he rode the circuit between Prince Edward and New London, a little west of Lynchburg. In the trunk he kept linens, legal papers, and the religious literature he would pass out while traveling and on the courthouse green.[24]

A few months after Henry's mother died, Colonel Christian was killed by Indians in a fight which Henry partly attributed to congressional ineptitude. The death of his beloved brother-in-law, coming at a time when Henry was already disturbed by problems of the western country, increased his dissatisfaction with the central government.

Among letters to Henry giving further information on the western situation was one from John May of Lincoln County, Kentucky, on July 14, 1786. Since the last winter the Americans in Kentucky had been "very much distressed" by the redskins, John May wrote. The difficulties were aggravated by the failure of the British to surrender their forts in the Northwest Territory as required by the peace treaty. Consequently, May was not very surprised that French inhabitants there were not only encouraging the Indian belligerents but had declared that the French were British subjects. He even understood that the British traders with the French had encouraged them to maintain this idea. Since "congress seems to have totally neglected them," May continued, "it is not to be wondered at if they should still think themselves under the British government, especially when they see that the several British posts, which they were told were to be delivered up to the Americans, are still in the possession of the British." [25]

To increase the difficulties, May said that the Wabash Indians and most of the Shawnees were at war with the American settlers in the western country, and "put to death in a most cruel manner all the prisoners who are so unfortunate as to fall into their hands." Since Colonel Logan wrote Henry in April, a great many murders had been committed; every two or three days the settlers heard of a new one.[26]

Added to the troubles with Great Britain and with the Indians since the peace treaty were those with Spain, America's late ally. Spain had been greatly disappointed when she failed to secure Gibraltar and territory in the Mississippi Valley under the terms of the treaty. Since then Spain had not only agreed to supply arms and ammunition to the Indians for use against the western settlements but even declared flatly that she would not consent to American navigation of the Mississippi. Nevertheless, the pioneer emigrants to Kentucky and Tennessee remained undaunted. Before the end of Henry's last gubernatorial term some sixty thousand had settled in the Kentucky-Tennessee territory. When the natural outlet for their trade at the mouth of the Mississippi was cut off by Spain, they threatened to take matters into their own hands, if Congress did not help them, and drive the Spanish from the area. But whether through incompetence or indifference on the part of many Congressmen, little help was forthcoming. There was even reason for fearing that the new American government would not be able to hold some of the western territory granted by the peace treaty. For Henry the matter was particularly distressing because of the large Virginia possessions there. The situation was pointed up by the death of Colonel Christian.

On April 8, 1786, Henry's brother-in-law was mortally wounded while fighting the Indians in the Ohio country. Christian, like Henry, had obtained large land grants in Kentucky and in August, 1785, had moved his family there. Then, disturbed by the constant danger from the Indian raiders and the failure of Congress to provide an adequate defense, he characteristically set an example by leading armed parties to oppose them. While commanding a detachment of twenty men, he pursued some braves across the Ohio River near Louisville into the Wabash country. Without waiting for the remainder of his men he rushed with three companions upon a large group of Indians and was fatally wounded.

Letters from Kentucky gave Henry more details about the loss of a man whom he regarded as his "friend and brother" and greatly increased his anxiety as to the fate of the western country. He was particularly close to Christian's wife, his sister Anne, and in writing to her on May 15, 1786, he had to draw upon all the resources of his religious philosophy.

"Would to God I could say something to give relief to the dearest of women and sisters. My heart has felt in a manner new and strange to me; insomuch that while I am endeavoring to comfort you, I want a comforter myself." He said he forbore to tell Anne how great was his love for her late husband; he adored "with humility the unsearchable ways of that Providence which calls us off this stage of action, at such time and in such manner as its wisdom and goodness directs."

Henry also spoke to Anne of "the many precious lessons of piety given us by our honored parents." And in words which anticipated the scene at his own death, he said that this was "one of the trying scenes, in which the Christian is eminently superior to all others and finds a refuge that no misfortunes can take away. To this refuge let my dearest sister fly with humble resignation." [27]

Colonel Christian left valuable land in Kentucky, part of which has in late years been incorporated into the city of Louisville. Several of his descendants became leading citizens in Kentucky and elsewhere. [28] Added to all his other family burdens, Henry took on those of Anne as her executor; then, after her death in a few years, those of her young son, Johnny. Not surprisingly, his brother-in-law's death spurred Henry to political action. Since becoming Governor, he had been making various efforts to protect the long Virginia frontier. But he was handicapped by inadequate resources and especially by the fact that many of the Indian marauders came from territory north of the Ohio which was under the control of Congress. The small forces which the scattered Kentuckians could muster were not even permitted to pursue the Indians across the Ohio except under limited conditions. Obviously, it was a case where Congress needed to assert itself.

On May 16, 1786, the day after receiving news of Colonel Christian's death, Henry wrote letters to inform the Virginia congressmen and the President of Congress of the harassed condition of the western people and their dire need for aid. He emphasized that, exposed as the Kentuckians were on all sides, it was impossible for them "to defend themselves by the usual method of assembling the militia, and stationing them in or about the settlements." Experience proved that attacking the Indian towns was the only effective means of defense against the hostile tribesmen. An expedition against the Wabash Indians across the Ohio River from Kentucky was necessary, and Henry spoke of how "extremely unjust" it was that such a measure should be at the expense of Virginia. At the same time he was constrained to comment on the seeming neglect or mismanagement of Indian affairs. He emphasized that Virginia, with her vast extent of frontier and the great number of independent Indian tribes scattered over the western country, had perhaps as much or more interest in the Indian Department than all the other states combined.

Henry also stressed the Indian issue in a letter to the Virginia congressmen on July 5. Henry said that he knew it was

> urged by some, & with too much Truth, that our own people are the Aggressors. Admitting the Fact, the residence of proper Agents among the Savages appears more necessary. At present if any Injury is received by an Indian, to whom can he make known his Complaint? To trust his person amongst the people who Committed the Injury would be too hazardous. The Trespasser or his associates would feel an interest in killing him to prevent a discovery of their Villainy.

Henry admitted that the "Character of such Americans as usually frequent the Indian Borders, coming into co-operation with that of the Indians themselves, necessarily produces contention." [29]

In early July, 1786, Henry was informed that Congress was ordering two companies of troops to be sent to Kentucky, and they were intended to cooperate with the local militia. On July 12 Henry wrote to inform the officer commanding the Continental troops that he had ordered the Kentucky county lieutenants to report to him what reinforcements were necessary.[30]

In one of the last letters which Henry wrote as Governor, about November 27, 1786, he informed the Speaker of the House of Delegates that application had been made to him for arms and ammunition to be sent to Kentucky. He regretted to report a lack of money to provide the needed arms but said that they could be purchased if the Assembly so authorized. The "posture of affairs" in Kentucky seemed to require "every possible preparation for defence," yet he felt that he must call on the state legislature, not Congress, for the needed arms.[31]

With occasional exceptions, Henry's correspondence had continued to be mostly that of an efficient business executive. But from this not always sparkling source, and from family letters, memoirs, and other scattered data, we can glean enough to form a clearer picture of his last years as a Virginia Governor. Among other statesmen, present or potential, who visited him when at the Governor's mansion was that brilliant young Swiss, Albert Gallatin, the future Secretary of the Treasury. Gallatin, who spent most of the winters between 1783–1789 in Richmond, would recall "that old proverbial Virginia hospitality" to which he had found no parallel in his travels. He came to know prominent state officials and legislators, and while everyone encouraged him, he particularly cited John Marshall, already a leader of the Richmond bar, and Governor Henry. With Henry's special interest in the back country, it was not surprising that he advised Gallatin to go west, where he might study law, and predicted that he was "intended for a statesman." Henry referred Gallatin to several other sources of personal assistance and gave him a letter of introduction which he used when he settled in western Pennsylvania.[32]

Henry was also placed in a position to perform a pleasing service for his friends, Washington and Lafayette. On January 5, 1785, the Assembly voted unanimously to give Washington one hundred shares in the James River Company and fifty shares in the Potomac Company. But the appreciative Washington nevertheless wrote to say he felt he should decline the generous gift; "my first declaration in Congress after accepting my military appointment [was] that I would not receive anything for such services as I might be able to render the cause in which I had embarked." It was his "fixed determination" to adhere to this principle, but he did not wish to be "disrespectful to the generous intention of my country." Asked by Washington what decision he should make, Henry replied tactfully that for Washington to resign the shares would throw a damper on the worthy enterprise and suggested that he could make alterations in the disposition of the stock given him. The legislature therefore passed an act providing that the stock should be used for "such objects of a public nature" as Washington would direct. The shares were presented to Washington, and he later designated them for Liberty Hall Academy at Lexington, Virginia, the nucleus for the future Washington and Lee University, and for a national university hopefully to be established in the District of Columbia.[33]

During the Revolutionary War, Henry had known more than his share of critical and exhausting executive responsibilities, and in a letter to Lafayette penned in the Council chamber on January 29, 1785, he expressed his "double pleasure" on an occasion when "the duties of office correspond with the feelings of the individual." The Assembly had authorized the erection of marble statues of Washington and Lafayette, the Washington statue to be placed in the capitol square at Richmond and the Lafayette statue in Paris. Called upon to conduct the negotiations, Henry enlisted the aid of Jefferson, the American minister in France. He recommended that the Washington statue be made by Jean Houdon, who had a reputation "unrivaled in Europe." Houdon came to Ameria to study his subject and, after making a plaster cast of the Washington bust, returned to France, where he completed the statue of him now standing in the rotunda of the capitol at Richmond. Houdon also made the Lafayette statue, which was erected in Paris and a copy placed beside that of Washington in Richmond.[34] During the course of these negotiations Henry received the aid of Lewis Littlepage, another Hanover County native, whose career in some respects was as glamorous and certainly more cosmopolitan than his own, with remarkable episodes in the

French army and at the Spanish and Russian courts. Back in Virginia for a time, Littlepage was given a letter of introduction by Henry to Washington: "I have spent some little time in his company very happily, and feel myself interested in his future welfare."[35]

Not to be caught short of military matériel as they had been during the war, the Assembly ordered Henry to spend £10,000 on military supplies from abroad. Henry secured the assistance of Lafayette, who informed him that if America should have any future use for soldiers he hoped she would not leave him off her list.[36]

Among other visitors to Richmond in 1785 was John Fitch, who had developed a plan for a steamboat. Henry did make an effort to help Fitch but it was insufficient. His idea for a steamboat was perfected by Robert Fulton and Fitch committed suicide, never having received from Virginia the funds necessary to construct boats on her waters for which the state had given him an exclusive right.[37]

One of the powers given Henry as Governor was to pardon criminals. Repelled by some provisions of the harsh criminal law, Henry devised a plan for giving pardons in instances where the crime was not too flagrant and with the understanding that the convict would serve a period at hard labor. Henry's proposal coming under criticism, he was specifically authorized by the legislature to grant the pardons except for murder or treason. The plan was later utilized in 1796, when Virginia adopted a penitentiary system.[38]

Henry was fortunate during his last years as Governor in having a generally peaceful and constructive administration. But problems of the southern back country, long of special interest to him, caused him a mounting anxiety. Besides those relating to the Mississsippi navigation, they arose largely in North Carolina and affected western Virginia, causing many complaints to pour into the Governor's office. It was not surprising that disaffected spirits in western North Carolina and Virginia should seek to separate themselves from the remote governmental control of their mother states. Dissatisfied with the treatment accorded them by North Carolina, her counties west of the Alleghenies formed the separate state of Franklin in 1785, which for a few years retained its independence and later in 1796 was incorporated into the new state of Tennessee. In Kentucky there was also

a movement for separation which culminated in 1792 with the formation of a new state, mostly settled by Virginians. In Southwest Virginia, Colonel Arthur Campbell—a cousin of the late General William
Campbell—led a movement to carve out a new state from the Old
Dominion. Arthur Campbell and his followers even attempted to
prevent the operation of some Virginia laws in Washington County,
and excited letters to Henry told of an embryonic rebellion. But he
dealt with the situation coolly and firmly, and the legislature passed
a law making it a treasonable act to establish an independent government within the state except by an act of the Assembly. Henry was
authorized to call out the militia to suppress any such disaffection, but
the collapse of Campbell's movement rendered this unnecessary.[39]

Meantime, on November 25, 1785, Henry had been re-elected
Governor for a fifth term, and he could take comfort in the returning
prosperity.[40] Routine gubernatorial duties became more burdensome
during his last term, though there were the marriages of his daughters
to counteract the deaths in the family circle during his first term.
Colonel Christian's death, however, occurred during the following
spring of 1786, and Henry's final months as Governor were disturbed
by unhappy events on the western frontier, events which, as we have
seen, did not make him more amenable to the call for a Constitutional
Convention to meet at Philadelphia in June, 1787. He could have
doubtless been re-elected Governor for still another term, but he preferred to return to private life. An old war horse scenting battle, he
should not have been surprised that he was soon involved in another
great political struggle.

20

Life in the Richmond Area

My fellow Americans, ask not what your country will do for
you—ask what you can do for your country.
—JOHN F. KENNEDY

1784–1786. Henry lives at the gubernatorial mansion in Richmond and at Salisbury in Chesterfield County.

1785–1788. Laws regarding slavery in Virginia somewhat
modified.

September 5, 1785. Henry draws up a memorandum for his
executors of his personal accounts.

September–October, 1786. Marriage of Anne Henry to Spencer Roane and Betsey Henry to Philip Aylett.

WHEN PATRICK HENRY had attended the last routine meeting of the Council, in the fall of 1786, and ended his fifth and last
term as Governor, he had been in public life for over twenty years.
As the champion of many hard-fought causes, he had made his share
of enemies, some that were left over from the old conservative aristocracy, others that developed from newer men and issues. When he
first appeared before the legislative committee in the disputed Dan-
dridge-Littlepage election of 1764, he had been little known in
Williamsburg. Despite all the impulse he gave to the Revolution
through his Stamp Act resolves and other bold political activities, he

was not—as a person—well known beyond Virginia when he arrived at Philadelphia in 1774 as a delegate to the First Continental Congress. As late as June 12, 1775, only Samuel Adams and John Hancock—their offenses being "of too flagitious a nature"—would be excluded from the British amnesty proclamation.

It is not surprising, then, that we have limited information on the Patrick Henry of the prewar years. Only after much sifting of diverse sources are we able to draw an authentic, though circumscribed, picture of the poor back-country youth; the hard-working attorney riding the rural courthouse circuit; the master of secluded Scotchtown. Even during the most significant periods of his life before 1775, there is far more data to explain Henry's political and legal career than there is to help us understand "the inner man."

Yet by the mid-1780's the Revolution had definitely been won; the American Founding Fathers were in the ascendancy. Henry himself could now muster more power and influence—when he chose to do so—than almost any other American of his day. To Virginians, especially in the Southside, he had become almost a legend in his own time. A large mass of facts on him was accumulating. The problem for the historian becomes one of piercing the veil, of evaluating opinions pro and con, and of placing him in his postwar milieu.

A convenient place to pause for this study is when Henry was living in Richmond during his last gubernatorial terms. Here he resided with his family in the cramped quarters (derisively compared to the former Governor's Palace) which the state provided, escaping when opportunity afforded to his rural Acadia in Chesterfield County. Here in the state capital and nearby countryside he was coming under the related influences of a changing Virginia. For him it was definitely a formative period. Events were moving toward the next high point of his career, his fight against the ratification of the federal constitution.

"Lotts have rise[n] to an enormous price on Shocoe [sic] Hill," so James Currie wrote Thomas Jefferson from Richmond on August 5, 1785. "The number of its respectable inhabitants are not a few for such a plaice as Richmond; the Governor, the Attorney General [Edmund Randolph], the Treasurer, Register, Mr. Pendleton, Mr.

Marshall town Recorder; Mr. Blair . . . Mr. Matthews and a long list more, some of them very respectable. . . ." [1]

Richmond, which Henry in 1779 had spoken of as "very unfit" for the residence of some state military officers, could now boast of a thousand or more people. As early as 1782 the local census had listed over seventy-five tradesmen and professional men, nearly all lately moved to the capital. There were one or more wagoners, chairmakers, tailors, blacksmiths, saddlers, shoemakers, innkeepers, and physicians. A quack dentist was also there, at least for some time during Henry's governorship; the worthy "Doctor" Fendall advertised in *The Virgina Gazette or American Advertiser* for August 3, 1782, that he would clean teeth, extract them, pull them out of one person and affix them in another, and extract "stumps" in the "easiest manner be they ever so deeply situated in the jaw." He could be "spoke with" at Gault's Tavern, and "the sooner gentlemen and ladies applied the better," since his stay in Richmond was "uncertain."

Whatever its growing pains, a leading American state needed an appropriate capitol building, and Virginia had accepted a plan for one offered by the versatile Jefferson, based on the surviving Roman temple at Nîmes, France. This classic monument Jefferson would gaze at "like a lover at his mistress." [2] Although less aesthetic in his taste, Henry, in a letter to Jefferson on September 10, 1785, noted the progress of work on the new capitol and declared that it would be "the most magnificent in the 13 states by far, unless the Design is alter'd, or ill timed Frugality curtails the Execution." [3] The modern visitor, climbing to its upper story and enjoying the panoramic view, may well believe that the building has lived up to his prediction.

Unfortunately, when procrastinating legislators extended themselves during a period of hard times to begin work on the large marble capitol with fluted Corinthian columns, they could hardly be expected to take a similar interest in a home for their Governor. In fact, it would take considerable time to erect many suitable buildings, official or otherwise, in a village struggling to become a fitting capital of a state which extended from the Atlantic to the Mississippi. In May, 1780, the Assembly had provided that a house for the Governor should be located on Shockoe Hill, and two years later the Marquis of Chastellux, while visiting Governor Harrison, had described him as living in "une maison fort simple mais assez spacieuse, qu'on venoit d' accomoder pour lui" (a very plain house, but spacious enough, which had just been fitted up for him). But we may wonder if the good marquis would have deemed the house "assez spacieuse" if he had had to live there with a family as large as Governor Henry's.[4]

Not until 1813 did the state complete the present dignified mansion for her Governors. Meantime, the small wooden house of Henry's day stood on the site in the as yet undeveloped capitol grounds. "Deep dells" with springs provided the only attractive spots in "acres" of chinquapin bushes and jimson weed. There was a ravine between the Henry residence and the capitol which became "a raging torrent" after each rain, while at a nearby street corner there was "a ramshackle wooden guard house" where soldiers' wives raised chickens and hung out the family wash.[5] It was all in ironic contrast with the Governor's Palace at Williamsburg, even when it was recovering from the rough usage by the Virginia soldiery.

During Henry's new governorship, the state did make some effort to improve his residence and environs, for among routine accounts before the Council in 1785 were items for erecting a wooden railing on the Governor's lot for 6 shillings per panel, an outdoor kitchen and a chimney at £91.7.10.[6] But that Henry, or at least Dolly, was not satisfied with the improvements is indicated by the fact that during the year he charged the Commonwealth of Virginia for various items such as £2.7.6 for haircloth for the "passage," 6 shillings to Samuel Ege for mending candlesticks, and 4 shillings to Thomas Terry's Negro for repairing the stable.[7] If Henry was not reimbursed for these and some other expenditures listed (payment for them is not noted in his account book), it speaks ill for the state government. Fortunately, we get a better picture of Richmond life from other contemporary sources.

When Henry wrote Jefferson that September, 1785, about the work on the new capitol, he was back in Richmond and presiding at the Council sessions. Conscious of the dignity of his executive office, Henry did not appear often on the street and "never without a scarlet cloak, black clothes, and a dressed wig." His family was supplied with an excellent coach, one of few in the Richmond area. The Henrys "lived as genteelly, and associated with as polished society, as those of any Governor before or since have ever done," Spencer Roane wrote. Henry's daughter Betsey (Mrs. Aylett) spoke of leading Virginians of the Revolution as coming to their Richmond residence. She saw Albert Gallatin and General Washington in conversation there, Gallatin talking in "very broken English." And Washington in his diary for May 1, 1785, speaks of supping and spending the night at the Governor's house. Coming down from Mount Vernon to the capital, he had intended to stop over at Judge Peter Lyons' in Hanover (Studley, Henry's birthplace). But finding the Lyonses away from home, the General had proceeded to Richmond, where, after arriving about 5 p.m., he felt free to stay with Patrick and Dolly (Washington's in-law).

On the basis of this and perhaps other visits to the Governor's home, Betsey described Washington as "grave"—he "did not laugh." But Henry was "a great laugher." Where his position did not require any show, he retained his simple tastes, often making his own fire. And Betsey tells of his riding horseback to his farm, at times carrying one of his children before and another behind him.[8]

There will be indications that some of Henry's children were brought up without adequate discipline and that the results were unfortunate. Otherwise, however, there is no dissent from Roane's statement that Henry's relations "as a husband, father, master, and neighbour" were "entirely exemplary." [9]

Shortly before Henry brought his family to Richmond, *The Virginia Gazette or American Advertiser* ran an announcement that on Monday, December 20, 1784, there would be auctioned, in front of Gault's Tavern, the Scotchtown mansion and 960 acres, twenty-eight miles from the city, "in a genteel neighborhood" and "remarkably healthy." Whether or not the estate was now too distant, too expensive, or otherwise ill suited to Henry's purpose, we can only surmise. At any rate, he rented Salisbury in upper Chesterfield, only twelve miles from the city. Riding out to this convenient plantation, he could escape from the crowded Governor's residence and from the filth, the heat, the flies, and perhaps the malaria and other diseases which then plagued so many American cities. While at Leatherwood he had somewhat recovered from the stresses and strains of his war governorship; at Salisbury he might secure the rest and recreation which would help him to avoid a similar debility.

For over a century and a quarter after the Henry occupancy, the hip-roofed wooden house survived the hazards of war and peace (it was burned during the 1920's, reportedly in a fire started by a still in an upstairs room). When advertising the place for sale the spring after the Henrys departed, Thomas Mann Randolph lauded the well-built residence with its six rooms on a floor and "spacious passage," the convenient outhouses, the large orchards, and "the remarkably healthy" situation. With the large unfinished attic, there was space for all the young Henrys. Not that this seemed to offer any great problem for Patrick and Dolly; the children could sleep in double or trundle beds or in the attic.[10]

Now a Richmond suburb, the Salisbury estate is in the northwest section of Chesterfield County near the Powhatan, Goochland, and Henrico County lines. From the house site, today on the grounds of a country club, the land in Henry's time spread over some 1,263 acres of gently rolling country three miles south of the James River.[11] From Salisbury he could easily cross the James River to Tuckahoe, the Thomas Mann Randolph mansion, just to the northward, or he could conveniently visit his relatives in Hanover and particularly in adjacent Goochland, where Lucy Henry and her husband, Valentine Wood, a Revolutionary colonel, were continuing the tradition of public service among the descendants of the Henry sisters; a grandson would be General Joseph E. Johnston, C.S.A.[12]

In his account book for 1785, we find Henry charging Mrs. Lucy Wood of Goochland for some carpeting, a girl's hat, and a cask of wine, which he probably secured for her in Richmond, and crediting such items as 50 yards of sheeting at £5 and a small black horse at £6. For reasons of health or otherwise, Henry's son Edward ("poor

Neddy") was a continuing responsibility, and Henry now boarded him for a year with his kindly sister Lucy for £15.[13]

Although at Salisbury Henry was in touch with his Goochland relatives, he was in much closer contact with his Chesterfield neighbors, especially the local Huguenots and Baptists. A surviving copy of a deed in 1760 for land in the Salisbury area contains a reference to the nearby "French line"—that is, the southern boundary of the land grant on the upper James River to the French Huguenots. In proportion to their number, there were perhaps no finer emigrants to colonial America than the persecuted Protestants who fled from France after the revocation of the Edict of Nantes in 1685. Already, Henry's daughter Martha had married one of the Fontaines, and now at Salisbury a number of other Huguenots, the Sublettes, the Ammonettes, the Sallés, and the Trabues, were among his neighbors, with still more living not far distant.[14] Henry, when escaping from the burdens of his official duties, found congenial ties with these intelligent, industrious, and independent-minded people.

Also, through them and other Chesterfield farmers, he renewed his contacts with the local Baptists. With their Calvinistic tradition of congregational government and simple religious rites, it is not surprising that some of the Huguenots were attracted to this Dissenting sect. When a Baptist church was established in Chesterfield County during 1773, there were not only numerous members with English names such as Woolridge and Clay, relatives of the future Henry Clay, but also an Ammonette and two Trabues. "Quaries" (queries) for decision by this congregation included whether the washing of feet was a duty among the brethren and whether a "sister" had the right to vote. (Answer: "We think not, from our present Light.") The church records show that one member was excommunicated for living with a man "unmarried in sin," and several Negroes were baptized.[15]

Undoubtedly, the Baptists, with other Dissenters, offered a formidable challenge to all that was cynical and complacent in Virginia religious life. For the Episcopalian Henry, the Baptist service was too formal, the religious tenets either too strict or too latitudinarian. But

when the Baptists were persecuted before the war, no Virginia statesman had fought harder for their freedom of worship. And renewal
of the contacts with the Chesterfield Baptists, as with the Dissenters
near whom he would soon live in Prince Edward, could only bolster
his belief in individual liberty—and probably anti-Federalism.

With his rural tastes, his dislike of "the bustle" in the capital,
Henry must have slipped away often to Salisbury. It had a particular
appeal during the hot season, and it was there on September 7, 1786,
that his daughter, Anne, was married to that promising young lawyer
and Councilor, Spencer Roane; the Reverend John Buchanan, rector
of St. John's Church, rode out to Salisbury to perform the ceremony.
The marrying fever easily affects the girls of a family, or at least
their aspiring mothers. A month later Betsey Henry was married to
Philip Aylett. Betsey's marriage was not only romantic but gives an
insight into the Henry domestic establishment; Anne's marriage was
more significant for other and less glamorous reasons.

The removal from Leatherwood to the Richmond area had provided Betsey and Anne with what—at least to parental eyes—appeared promising suitors. Dolly Henry ardently promoted the Aylett
match. She had a special interest in the attractive stepdaughter, born
not many years before the girl's mother had become mentally ill.
Indeed, Dolly had been a real mother to Betsey through all her teen-
age years.

The story of Betsey's courtship is especially important for the evidence it gives of the influence that Henry's young wife had acquired
in the family circle. "P. H. was perhaps the best husband in the
world," Colonel Meredith declared. "It is said that he never took an
important step without consulting Dolly, his wife." [16] Dolly's influence was to a degree conservative, and it was certainly directed toward
keeping her daughters in the upper social circle.

By 1786 Betsey Henry was a beautiful girl of seventeen, and her
stepmother was anxious to make a brilliant marriage for her. Philip
Aylett, only nineteen, was the son of an ardent Whig who had done
important work as a state commissary during the Revolution. A member of one of the wealthiest and most influential families in King and

Queen County, Philip had an unimpeachable family background. But like many young gentlemen of the day he was gay and dashing; he played cards and drank.

Philip met Betsey at a ball in Richmond, fell very much in love, and was "crazy" to marry her. Mrs. Henry, too, was "exceedingly anxious for the match." But Betsey was a demure, devout young lady, brought up to read her prayerbook and Bible every day and to attend the Episcopal church. Although attracted to Philip, she continued to consider him "too wild" for her to marry.

The denouement was worthy of a romantic novel: Philip's father had died and his stepfather, anxious to get the difficult lad out of the country, was about to send him to Oxford University. Before leaving, Philip made one last appeal to Betsey. Although she was ill, she came downstairs—upon Dolly's urging—to see him; she again rejected him and fainted from exhaustion. Philip then left the house but Mrs. Henry sent a servant to tell him to return, leaving the impression with him that Betsey had fainted from grief. He did so and pressed his suit with the young lady, who in a "semi-conscious state" now feebly said that she would marry him.

The "wild" young gentleman was not to be curbed immediately, and there is a story that he later made a trip on a cold day in a coach with a white companion and two Negro servants, all of whom had fortified themselves with liquor to a comic degree. But he settled down and became a good husband, while Betsey was "a very loving wife and mother." She survived until 1842 and left some brief but valuable reminiscences of her father. On Patrick Henry's advice, Philip Aylett built his mansion, "Montville," in King William County, some miles back from the river in order to escape malaria. There was an outbuilding on the place where Henry stayed on his visits.[17]

Anne Henry's marriage on September 7, 1786, bears much more resemblance than Betsey's to the eighteenth-century *mariage de convenance*, and the results were less happy. Unfortunately, from a romantic viewpoint, Anne appears to have been more estimable than attractive. Her marriage to Spencer Roane seems to have followed calculating negotiations regarding the dowry. After Henry's death,

Roane would make Dolly Henry the defendant in a lawsuit over Henry's will which was hardly to the credit of one of the outstanding American judges.

But while the marriage had been based on a short courtship, reinforced, so Roane wrote, by some financial inducements, it was not without admiration on his part for and political association with Anne's father. In his reminiscences of Henry, Roane tells how his father, a Burgess for Essex County in the Revolution, came home "in raptures" over Patrick Henry. Spencer Roane himself was a volunteer in the war at the age of thirteen, armed with a short carbine, tomahawk, and a hunting shirt with the words "Liberty or Death" embroidered in capitals over his heart. Roane did not meet Patrick Henry, however, until they both sat in the May, 1783, Assembly. Roane then lodged with Richard Henry Lee for one or two sessions, but he generally found himself voting with Patrick Henry. They formed a friendly relationship which was strengthened while Roane was a Councilor.[18] It does not appear to have been marred after Roane became a judge of the Virginia Court of Appeals, until Henry's last years, and then for political rather than personal reasons.

For certain facts regarding Roane's courtship and marriage we can only quote from his "Complaint" against the will of Patrick Henry in the lawsuit.[19] Addressing the Honorable George Wythe, Judge of the High Court of Chancery, Judge Roane in his own right and as administrator of his lately deceased wife, alleged that sometime in the spring of the year 1786, "your orator was induced to pay his addresses" to Anne Henry and that this was "with the entire consent and approbation" of her father. Roane further wrote that it was "generally understood and stated . . . that [Patrick Henry] intended to make the fortunes of all his Daughters Equal. . . . This intention was expressly and particularly declared by the said Henry to your orator when he gave his permission to address his said daughter as aforesaid." Roane then continued:

> Your orator further charges that finding his addresses likely to prove successful, and apprehending also from his increased acquaintance with the family of the said Patrick Henry that there was considerable Danger of the Children of his first marriage

being unjustly dealt by through the influence of his then wife, the present defendant, Dorothea Henry, which apprehension has since been fully verified to your orator's great loss and injury, he conceived it proper to state to the said Patrick Henry the circumstances of his own private fortune, which was but moderate, by a letter addressed to him, which letter was also calculated to lead him, the said Henry, in a delicate manner, if so he chose, to declare particularly what he meant for the portion of his said Daughter, so that your orator might be under a Certainty of not suffering through the influence aforesaid.

A surviving picture of Judge Roane [20] shows a young man of thirty-five or forty with dark side and chin whiskers. Despite the kindly efforts of the artist, it is obvious that Roane was not a handsome man; there is something dubious about the eyes, and the face is not pleasing.

We may wonder how Anne really felt about entering into the marriage and just how satisfactory were her domestic relations in the following years.[21] At least we know that, not very long after the marriage, Henry felt constrained to write her a letter of fatherly advice. This letter, which is quoted below *in toto*, is remarkable not only as a literary composition but for the insight it gives into Patrick Henry's character and, indeed, the social customs of the time.

My Dear Daughter:

You have just entered into that state which is replete with happiness or misery. The issue depends upon that prudent, amiable, uniform conduct, which wisdom and virtue so strongly recommend on the one hand, or on that imprudence which a want of reflection or passion may prompt on the other.

You are allied to a man of honor, of talents, and of an open, generous disposition. You have, therefore, in your power all the essential ingredients of happiness: it cannot be marred, if you now reflect upon that system of conduct which you ought invariably to pursue—if you now see clearly the path from which you will resolve never to deviate. Our conduct is often the result of whim or caprice—often such as will give us many a pang, unless we see beforehand what is always the most praiseworthy, and the most essential to happiness.

The first maxim which you should impress upon your mind is never to attempt to control your husband, by opposition, by displeasure, or any other mark of anger. A man of sense, of prudence, of warm feelings, can not, and will not, bear an opposition of any kind, which is attended with an angry look or expression. The current of his affections is suddenly stopped; his attachment is weakened; he begins to feel a mortification the most pungent; he is belittled in his own eyes; and be assured the wife who once excites those sentiments in the breast of a husband, will never regain the high ground which she might and ought to have retained. When he marries her, if he be a good man, he expects from her smiles, not frowns; he expects to find her one who is not to control him—not to take from him the freedom of acting as his own judgment shall direct, but one who will place such confidence in him, as to believe that his prudence is his best guide. Little things, that in reality are mere trifles in themselves, often produce bickerings, and even quarrels. Never permit them to be a subject of dispute; yield them with pleasure, with a smile of affection. Be assured one difference outweighs them all a thousand, or ten thousand times. A difference with your husband ought to be considered as the greatest calamity— as one that is to be most studiously guarded against; it is a demon which must never be permitted to enter a habitation where all should be peace, unimpaired confidence, and heartfelt affection. Besides, what can a woman gain by her opposition or her indifference? Nothing. But she loses everything; she loses her husband's respect for her virtues, she loses his love, and with that, all prospect of future happiness. She creates her own misery, and then utters idle and silly complaints, but utters them in vain.

The love of a husband can be retained only by the high opinion which he entertains of his wife's goodness of heart, of her amiable disposition, of the sweetness of her temper, of her prudence, of her devotion to him. Let nothing upon any occasion ever lessen that opinion. On the contrary, it should augment every day; he should have much more reason to admire her for those excellent qualities which will cast a lustre over a virtuous woman, whose personal attractions are no more.

Has your husband stayed out longer than you expected? When he returns, receive him as the partner of your heart. Has he disappointed you in something you expected, whether of ornament, or furniture, or any convenience? Never evince discontent; receive his apology with cheerfulness. Does he, when you are housekeeper, invite company without informing you of it, or bring home with him a friend? Whatever may be your repast, however scanty it may be, however impossible it may be to add to it, receive them with a pleasing countenance, adorn your table with cheerfulness, give to your husband and to your company a hearty welcome; it will more than compensate for every other deficiency; it will evince love to your husband, good sense in yourself, and that politeness of manners which acts as the most powerful charm. It will give to the plainest fare a zest superior to all that luxury can boast. Never be discontented on any occasion of this nature.

In the next place, as your husband's success in his profession will depend upon his popularity, and as the manners of his wife have no little influence in extending or lessening the respect and esteem of others for her husband, you should take care to be affable and polite to the poorest as well as the richest. A reserved haughtiness is a sure indication of a weak mind and an unfeeling heart.

With respect to your servants, teach them to respect and love you, while you expect from them a reasonable discharge of their respective duties. Never tease yourself, or them, by scolding; it has no other effect than to render them discontented and impertinent. Admonish them with a calm firmness.

Cultivate your mind by the perusal of those books which instruct while they amuse. Do not devote much of your time to novels; there are a few which may be useful and improving in giving a higher tone to our moral sensibility; but they tend to vitiate the taste, and to produce a disrelish for substantial intellectual food. Most plays are of the same cast, they are not friendly to the delicacy which is one of the ornaments of the female character. History, geography, poetry, moral essays, biography, travels, sermons, and other well-written religious productions, will not fail to enlarge your understanding, to render you a more agreeable companion, and to exalt your virtue. A woman devoid of rational ideas of religion, has no security for her virtues; it is sacrificed to her passions, whose voice, not that of God, is her only governing principle. Besides, in those hours of calamity to which families must be exposed, where will she find support, if it be not in the just reflections upon that all-ruling Providence which governs the universe, whether inanimate or animate?

Mutual politeness between the most intimate friends, is essential to that harmony which should never be once broken or interrupted. How important, then, is it between man and wife? The more warm the attachment, the less will either party bear to be slighted, or treated with the smallest degree of rudeness or inattention. This politeness, then, if it be not in itself a virtue, is at least the means of giving to real goodness a new lustre; it is the means of preventing discontent and even quarrels; it is the oil of intercourse, it removes asperities, and gives to everything a smooth, an even, and a pleasant movement.

I will only add, that matrimonial happiness does not depend upon wealth; no, it is not to be found in wealth; but in minds properly tempered and united to our respective situations. Competency is necessary. All beyond that point is ideal. Do not suppose, however, that I would not advise your husband to augment his property by all honest and commendable means. I would wish to see him actively engaged in such a pursuit, because engagement, a sedulous employment, in obtaining some laudable end, is essential to happiness. In the attainment of fortune, by honorable means, and particularly by professional exertion, a man derives particular satisfaction, in self-applause, as well as from the increasing estimation in which he is held by those around him.

In the management of your domestic concerns, let prudence and wise economy prevail. Let neatness, order, and judgment be seen in all your different departments. Unite liberality with a just frugality; always reserve something for the hand of charity; and never let your door be closed to the voice of suffering humanity. Your servants, in particular, will have the strongest claim upon your charity; let them be well fed, well clothed, nursed in sickness, and let them never be unjustly treated.[22]

It is unlikely that the Roanes could have had many servants other than slaves. In referring to the slaves, Henry used the less harsh "servants." Slavery was a sensitive topic for Virginians still affected by post-Revolutionary idealism. It was not surprising that a temporary Northern resident of Richmond put his finger on the sore spot. William Ellery Channing, a member of a prominent New England family, was at nineteen a tutor in the family of David Meade Randolph, the Marshal of Virginia. Like Albert Gallatin, Channing was superlative in his praise of Virginia hospitality. The Virginians were freer in their manners, less cold and avaricious, than the New Englanders, he wrote. In Virginia there were "great vices, but greater virtues" than he had left behind him. The Virginians were "more disinterested" than the New Englanders; "their patriotism was not tied to their purse strings. Could I only take from Virginians their sensuality and their slaves I should think them the greatest people in the world." [23]

Precisely what Channing meant by "sensuality" is not clear. He must have observed the heavy drinking only too common among prominent local families, but he was probably referring to the easy sexual access to Negro slave girls. "Sensuality and slavery"—the two words went hand in hand.

Channing also noted that Mrs. Randolph was opposed to slavery. In fact, he might have observed a small but growing sentiment for emancipation in the state. In 1784 Jefferson had proposed the abolition of slavery in the western territories, and by the Northwest Ordinance of 1787 it would be eradicated in those north of the Ohio River. While Henry was Governor, the October, 1785, Assembly prohibited the further importation of slaves into Virginia. Besides Jefferson, Washington, and George Mason, Henry and two of his relatives were among the Virginians who expressed their antipathy to slavery. We have seen that in 1773 Henry, while appreciating the "inconvenience" of living without slaves in an area of large plantations and manual labor, had hoped that "an opp°. [opportunity] will be offered to abolish this lamentable Evil." [24] A generation later Henry's sister, Elizabeth, and her son-in-law were expressing a candid opposition to slavery, but circumstances had made Henry more cautious. In 1795 Elizabeth Henry (now "Madam" Russell), an ardent Methodist, stated eloquently in her will:

> Whereas by the wrongdoing of man it hath been the unfortunate lot of the following negroes to be Slaves for life, to wit, Nina, Adam, Nancy sen^r, Nancy, Kitty and Selah. And whereas believing the same have come unto my possession by the direction of providence, and conceiving from the clearest conviction of my conscience aided by the power of a good and just God, that it is both sinful and unjust, as they are by nature equally free with myself, to continue them in Slavery I do therefore by these presents, under the influence of a duty I not only owe my own conscience, but the just God who made us all, make free the said Negros, hoping while they are free of

man they will faithfully serve their MAKER through the merits of CHRIST.[25]

Moreover, in 1793 Elizabeth's son-in-law, Francis Preston, had freed a Negro formerly belonging to General William Campbell, in accordance with a promise made to that faithful body servant by the General and to promote "a participation of LIBERTY to a fellow creature who by nature is entitled thereto." Liberty, a key word in the Henry family connection, was written in larger, more pronounced letters than the other words.[26]

It is easier to favor reform movements when they are distant in space or time. Why did Henry not express himself more strongly on the slavery issue some years after his private letter to the Quaker, Robert Pleasants, in 1773? Possibly he might have found an occasion to do so while Governor in 1785–1786. In August, 1785, James Currie wrote Thomas Jefferson how the late Joseph Mayo of Powhatan County had "astonished some of our acquaintances by his will giving liberty to all his Slaves, their number from 150 to 170. I believe its report has caused 2 or 3 combats between Slaves and their Owners, now struggling for the liberty to which they conceive themselves entitled." [27] Moreover, Madison when writing to Jefferson the following January spoke of several petitions to the Assembly, chiefly from Methodists, in favor of the gradual abolition of slavery.

Yet these petitions, Madison continued, while not "thrown under the table," had been "treated with all the indignity short of it." For reasons of human cupidity, or fear of too great liberties for a people who had had limited opportunity for advancement, the act of October, 1785, prohibiting further importation of slaves into Virginia contained some restrictive provisions. It prohibited slaves from serving as witnesses in court against white persons and punished "with stripes" or otherwise, at the discretion of the justices of the peace, slaves joining in unlawful assemblies or leaving home without a pass.[28]

To Henry the sentiment of the country obviously indicated that the "opportunity" for abolition of slavery had not come. He would make a calculated appeal to the slave-holding interests in the Virginia Convention of 1788. It is likely, however, that the movement for gradual emancipation would have grown considerably during the next decades had the cotton gin not been invented in 1793. During the following generation it would be found that great profits could be made in the lower South with new lands and slaves (many imported from Virginia and other border states).

After Henry had written his marital advice to Anne, we have nothing more from him on the subject. But, besides his admonitory letter, Anne's marriage probably contributed to what by all odds are the best personal reminiscences of Henry—those of her husband, Spencer Roane. Within a decade after her marriage, Anne Henry Roane bore her husband six children and died some months after the birth of the last daughter. Roane's lawsuit against Henry's widow was tried only a few years later in the appeal court of which he was a member, though he excused himself during the suit. The court awarded Anne Henry Roane's heirs £1,500 and a similar sum to Betsey Henry Aylett.[29]

On behalf of the defendant, Dolly Henry, it is argued that the verdict was unjust since before his death Henry had amply provided for the children of his first marriage. At any rate, Roane's reasons for entering suit, with the implied aspersions on his late wife, were not such as to create family amity. A desire to smooth over this situation, as well as his high professional standards, doubtless influenced Roane to write the full and perceptive Henry Memoir, including the following description of him sometime after Roane first met him during the 1783 Assembly.

Henry, so Roane wrote, was then "rather stoop-shouldered . . . , probably the effect of age." He was "of middling stature," with "no superfluous flesh; his features were distinctly marked, and his complexion rather dark. He was somewhat bald, and always wore a wig in public." Also, as Roane recalled, Henry was "very attentive to his teeth, his beard, and his linen."

Altogether, in Roane's estimation, Henry "was not a handsome man," yet he had "a fine blue eye, and an excellent set of teeth, which, with the aid of a mouth sufficiently wide, enabled him to articulate very distinctly. His voice was strong, harmonious, and clear, and he could modulate it at pleasure." [30]

That fine speaking voice, the more remarkable because Henry was thrown so often with persons who slurred sounds and dropped syllables, remained an important reason for Henry's pre-eminence as an orator.

With so many of his relatives dead and he himself past the normal life expectancy for that period, Henry on September 5, 1785, drew up a memorandum to which he desired his executors to pay "particular Regard." "Seeing a great number of old Debts now demanded from persons with little expectancy and fearing it be the Case against my Estate after my Death," Henry instructed the executors not to pay any British debt charged to him since he knew of none except £7 to one creditor whom he would pay the next month. He enumerated several British mercantile firms which he had paid in full. Undoubtedly, fear that his estate would be encumbered with unjust British debts was a primary reason for writing the memorandum.

He also sought to avoid some other possible claims for which he said his estate was not obligated. The claim against him by the Paul Tillman estate was not proper, since it was "for Treats at Elections" which his friends Colonel Fontaine, Colonel Overton, John Winston, and others paid or engaged to pay. They "gave the Treats" on their own account and not his. It was still customary in Virginia to treat the voters before elections. There had been an early incident in which Henry was known to have offered treats, but none in later years.

In his memorandum Henry also referred to that delicate family issue, his long-unsettled account with John Syme. "I think certainly I owe him nothing," Henry wrote, and he went on to enumerate credits which Syme had omitted for wheat, cash, legal fees, laying off and selling land, etc. "I am willing to be even, but owing nothing." John Syme, as in the years before the Revolution, had a capital of land and debts; he was still hoping to make money from his racing stock. At the Richmond races on May 9, 1786, for example, there was a race for a purse of 100 guineas competed for by four horses, including Colonel Syme's bay mare, but the race was won "with great ease" by Colonel Goode's gray horse.

In his memorandum to his executors, Henry was also concerned with the proof of the amount of land he held in North Carolina. He went into detail regarding his holdings in Richmond and Bladen County there, and in the Dismal Swamp adjoining the Virginia border. After allowing for certain partnerships in the land held by John Fontaine, George Elliot, and Bartholomew Dandridge, Henry stated that he still owned 23,250 acres in North Carolina. With his large land holdings also in the Leatherwood area, in Kentucky, and elsewhere, Henry would appear to have been one of the wealthiest Virginians. But the fact is that, like many Southern planters, he was "land poor." A large part of his land was undeveloped and hard to reach. A full 2,000 acres of his North Carolina land was then worth so little that he planned to pay Judge Dandridge for it with "my Negro frank." [31]

21

A New Home and a New Arena

Some of the outstanding Nationalist leaders like Washington, Madison, and Hamilton have had their letters printed, sometimes in many editions. But we do not have the same easy access to the letters of such men as Patrick Henry, George Mason, Samuel Bryan, George Bryan, and George Clinton.

——MERRILL JENSEN [1]

"We are now vibrating between too much and too little government, and the pendulum will rest finally in the middle."
——THOMAS JEFFERSON from Paris, February 2, 1788, to William S. Smith

1786–1787. Efforts to exclude Americans from the Mississippi navigation; Henry's reaction.

December, 1786 (circa). Henry moves to Prince Edward County.

1787. Henry resumes law practice.

February 13, 1787. Henry declines to become a delegate to the Constitutional Convention in Philadelphia.

May 25–September 17, 1787. Meeting of Philadelphia Convention.

September, 1787–June, 1788. Debates in newspapers, legislatures, and elsewhere on ratification of Constitution.

October, 1787. Henry back in legislature.

May–early June, 1788 (circa). Constitution adopted by eighth state. Henry leaves for Virginia ratification convention.

[317]

O<small>N</small> J<small>ULY</small> 12, 1786, Attorney General Edmund Randolph was about to depart from hot, humid Richmond "to breathe the mountain air" without which he said he could not survive the summer. But he took time to write a letter, thanking Jefferson for his present of books, and added some political news. The apparent scarcity of cash, Randolph reported, had excited "a great clamour for paper money [in the state], an expedient very acceptable to those who are in debt, or are unwilling to purchase the precious metals by labour." The firmness of Madison and Mason, Randolph trusted, would defeat the attempt to emit the paper currency. But Randolph added that Henry intended to resign as Governor and wanted to serve in the next legislature. "His politics are not known, but are supposed not to run vehemently against paper money." [2]

Henry had been a popular and successful Governor, and, with his hold on the Virginia electorate still little diminished, he doubtless could have been easily elected for another or sixth one-year term. But on October 28 he wrote the Speaker of the House requesting for "a variety of circumstances" that his name not be put up for nomination for the ensuing year. He presented his "best acknowledgements" to the Assembly for their past favors and assured the members "that the approbation of my country is the highest reward to which my mind is capable of aspiring." [3]

What were "the variety of circumstances" that impelled Henry not to run again for the office? In the letter to Mrs. Christian from Richmond in October, he said he would resign the governorship in November as he and his wife were "heartily tired of the bustle we live in here." Perhaps only excepting a few years just before the Revolution, he had never been in easy financial circumstances. When Governor in 1784–1786 his salary had not been enough to meet his expenses. Nor had the drain on his pocketbook been much alleviated by the marriages of his two daughters. And Dolly had been presenting him with more children (and would continue to do so for over a decade). Besides the first of these "little stair steps," the girls born to them in 1778, 1780, 1781, there was now Patrick Henry, Jr., born in 1783, and the baby Fayette, born October 9, 1785, near the end of Henry's fifth gubernatorial term.

> "The Belgian hare could nothing to you show,
> Prolific Patrick—what a family man!"

Already Henry had had eleven children by his two wives, of whom at least six, including "Neddy," were still under his care.[4] Moreover, he wanted to provide a college education for the eligible boys. At the age of fifty when he ended his governorship, he needed a much larger income to support his family adequately than that which had been derived from his salary as Governor and from his plantation lands.

Revealing his embryonic plans to Mrs. Christian, Henry said that he had considered moving back to Hanover County on land which he was "like to get" from General Nelson, and that if this negotiation was unsuccessful he would move back toward Leatherwood. There was no doubt of his liking for the Piedmont counties: he ended by settling in Prince Edward, eighty miles southwest of Richmond. Here he lived in a simple wooden house, seven miles from present Farmville and about the same distance north of Hampden-Sydney College. At this plantation, on a hill about a mile south of the Appomattox River, he would make his home for the next six years. He would represent Prince Edward County during the great debates on the ratification of the federal constitution, and life in the county would influence the active stages of his remaining career. The county still contained a large element of back-country farmers, of Presbyterians and other Dissenters, who had supported Henry in the past and would hearken to him again. But Prince Edward, no longer on the frontier, was losing this leveling influence and was affecting Henry by its remoteness, its states' rights particularism, and its increasing conservatism as it became more wedded to the slavery system.

Prince Edward, not cut off from Amelia County until 1783, was in a rolling country with a tobacco and slave economy. The county contained good land, not yet depleted by an exhausting agriculture,

and well watered by the Appomattox River on the northern boundary
as well as by tributary streams. Tobacco, the principal money crop in
the county, could be floated down the Appomattox in bateaux to
Petersburg. For the labor in the tobacco and corn fields, the hoeing,
worming, harvesting, and so on, the planters were heavily dependent
on Negro slaves, and there were about as many Negroes in Prince
Edward as whites. It was a significant fact that would affect the history of the county until the present generation. Prince Edward contained many sturdy and hospitable citizens, some of whom had stood
solidly behind Henry in the Revolution, but by the late 1780's they
were not likely to encourage him in what for them was advanced
political thought.

Not since his early married life had Henry tried to eke out a living
for his family on a small farm, nor would he at this time. In 1787 he
bought from Colonel John Holcomb a large plantation—or, rather,
individual tracts—comprising 1,689½ acres. For this land he agreed
to give what now seems the small price of 25 shillings per acre. After
the heavy expenses of his governorship Henry lacked enough ready
money for the purpose. He did pay for it, however, within a few
years by exchanging a miscellany of land near Richmond, other land,
Negroes, legal services, two horses, and incidentals. Owing to the
wastefulness of the slave system, the distance from markets, and other
considerations, he soon found it necessary to supplement the income
from his plantation. This is clear from his records for the period. In
1785 he had sold only sixteen hogsheads of tobacco from the Leatherwood plantation with a shrinking total of nine in 1786 and four in
1787, for which we know that he received £45. With tobacco his most
important money crop, he could hardly have secured more than a few
hundred pounds' cash income from all his landed holdings in 1786.
It was not surprising that he accepted the suggestion of a friend that
he resume the practice of law. The need for additional income was
acute, now that several of his children had to be educated, and he had
to meet the payments on his new land. During 1787 and early 1788,
however, he was largely absorbed with the task of getting settled in
Prince Edward and of trying to put his plantations there on a profit-

able basis. Not until 1789 would he again become known as a leading Virginia lawyer.[5]

When journeying from Richmond through Southside Virginia in 1790–1791, a young South Carolinian, William Loughton Smith, was on the whole quite favorably impressed with the country and the people. Several counties through which Smith traveled—Powhatan, Amelia, Prince Edward, and Charlotte—he found "generally thickly settled," at least by the standards of the time. Moreover, the inhabitants he met were polite and kind to strangers; there was plenty of fodder for his horses; plenty of bacon, eggs, and cornbread; "tolable rum" for his own fare; and the bills were reasonable.

But Smith did have some immoderate criticism. The dwellings of even the local "gentlemen of property" were mostly out of order for lack of mechanics to repair them. At a tavern he had to borrow some rum from a "neighbour" and "the bugs made a happier supper" on him than he did on his bacon and eggs. The plantation owners had certain "peculiarities." They pronounced "there" as "thar" and "stairs" as "stars." With "their abundant and tolerably fertile land, cultivated in many parts altogether by slaves," the masters spent most of their time on the tavern porches chatting about their "mars" (mares) and geldings and the neighborhood lore.

In Prince Edward not all the white inhabitants whom Smith depicted were anywhere near as prosperous as the slaveowners. As in the hard war years, many were having difficulty in keeping the wolf— or sheriff—from the door. But at least the larger landowners were living a pleasant and, thanks to the slave labor, not too hard-working existence. It was comfortable enough to make Henry have further doubts as to the value of a stronger and more restrictive national government.

More specifically, Smith went on to report that Patrick Henry was then living within six or eight miles of Prince Edward Court House. He was making, as Smith asserted,

> a great deal of money by large fees of £50 or £100 for clearing horse thieves and murderers, which has lost him much of the great reputation he enjoyed in his neighborhood; he has been left

out of the Assembly at the last election; some say because he insisted on not being elected, others that his conduct has given general disgust. I am told that he will travel hundreds of miles for a handsome fee to plead for criminals, and that his powers of oratory are so great he generally succeeds, insomuch, that a man in his neighborhood has been heard to say he should have no apprehension of being detected in horse stealing, for that Governor Henry, or Colonel Henry, as he is sometimes called, would for £50 clear him.

Smith's account of Henry's criminal practice must be accepted with large reservations. The South Carolinian was a strong Federalist and a few years later was even hanged in effigy at Charleston by some political opponents. When he came to Prince Edward it was only a few years after Henry had participated in the bitter debates on the ratification of the constitution. It is likely that Smith was willing enough to repeat inimical stories of Henry told by local Federalists.[6] However, there will be more evidence to indicate that Henry was not squeamish in his choice of criminal cases.

Politically, for the six years that Henry lived in Prince Edward, he was largely absorbed with his great fight first to defeat the proposed American Constitution of 1787, then, after its ratification, to secure amendments thereto. When considering further the events which at the outset of the period were already turning him from a moderate nationalist into a strong states' rights advocate, we may begin with one basic fact. This was his distance except on certain notable occasions from the principal events of the constitutional struggle—indeed, even his lack of adequate knowledge of them.[7] Henry's difficulties in communication with many political leaders, serious enough when he was war Governor, were compounded when he moved to Leatherwood and then to Prince Edward. A letter which Governor Edmund Randolph sent him on December 6, 1786, urging him to become a Virginia delegate to the Constitutional Convention at Philadelphia the following summer, did not reach him for some two months; he stated on February 13 that it had not come to him "until very long after its date."[8] Another letter, written by George Washington at Mount Vernon on September 24, 1787, seeking

Henry's support of the Constitution as "the best that could be obtained at this time," did not reach him for about three weeks.[9]

Riding over his plantation in secluded Prince Edward during 1787 and early 1788, enjoying the leisurely country folks and country ways, relaxing with his close-knit family, Henry built up strength to help him endure the strenuous debates in the Virginia Convention of 1788 that following summer. Even today, walking down the hill from the site of the Henry house to where the Appomattox gently meanders between its sandy banks, one is impressed with the peacefulness—the salubrity—of the scene.

And yet Prince Edward was not the best place for Henry to secure prompt news of the developing legislative struggle or to be stirred to efficient action thereon. In some respects he was in better contact with political sentiment in western Virginia and Kentucky than that in New York or Massachusetts. Except for one important communication on August 12, 1786, from James Monroe in Congress at Philadelphia, there are few surviving letters which Henry wrote or received from political leaders north of the Potomac from the time he received Monroe's letter until June, 1788, when he was a delegate to the Virginia Convention of 1788. His Richmond newspaper, now the *Virginia Independent Chronicle*, was his chief source of outside information while living in Prince Edward, and that newspaper, reaching him perhaps nearly a week after publication, might contain news from other states or distant parts of Virginia that was a month old. After the earlier exposures of the critical weakness of the Confederation, a last straw which impelled many Americans to favor a stronger national government was the uprising in Massachusetts during the fall and winter of 1786–1787 by some poor debt-ridden farmers. For a time this outbreak, led by Daniel Shays, a Revolutionary veteran, assumed alarming proportions, especially since Congress provided no troops to suppress the movement. Henry could learn belatedly from the *Independent Chronicle* of February 7, 1787, that General Lincoln with 2,000 volunteers had marched from Boston to protect the Massachusetts court; then, from the issue for February 28, that Lincoln's force had captured or dispersed the rebels.[10] For many Americans, Shays' Rebellion had provided "an emotional surge . . . toward a new

Federal Constitution." [11] Yet Henry, reading that the revolt had been suppressed, could not have been greatly alarmed. Perhaps he was more concerned with the plight of the poor farmers now crushed by Lincoln's troops.

We need not be surprised that Congress lacked the resources to provide a military force to march to western Massachusetts, for it could not meet even its normal expenses. Not permitted under the Articles of Confederation to raise money through taxation, it had been unable to pay even the interest on the war debt. For the five years from 1781 to 1786, when Henry last retired as Governor, that beleagured body had collected by requisition on the states some $2,500,000. This relatively small sum was insufficient to meet the interest on the foreign debt alone; the credit of the United States was seriously impaired. By 1784 the total debt of the Confederation was $35,000,000 and increasing yearly. Responsible leaders such as Madison, Hamilton, and Washington were gravely concerned. [12]

"Our situation," Madison wrote Edmund Randolph in February, 1787, "is becoming every day more and more critical." He continued with these depressing observations:

> No money comes into the federal treasury; no respect is paid to the federal authority; and people of reflection unanimously agree that the existing Confederacy is tottering to its foundation. Many individuals of weight, particularly in the eastern district, are suspected of leaning toward monarchy. Other individuals predict a partition of the States into two or more confederacies. It is pretty certain that if some radical amendment of the single one cannot be devised and introduced, one or the other of these revolutions, the latter no doubt, will take place. [13]

Suppose Congress had failed to hold together the central government which was bound by such weak strands? Suppose Shays' Rebellion in Massachusetts had spread, as some feared, to other disaffected areas? Many influential Americans had had enough of such anxieties, and it is not surprising that in their desire for a stronger national government they tended to underemphasize one significant fact—a fact that loomed larger for Patrick Henry in the Virginia back country. This was that the dreary postwar depression in America was ending in 1786 and by the following summer there were obvious signs of good times.

"Our husbandmen, who are the bulk of the nation, have plentiful crops, their produce sells at high prices and for ready, hard money. . . . Our working people are all employed," Benjamin Franklin wrote in November, 1786. "Buildings in Philadelphia increase amazingly, besides small towns rising in every quarter of the country." [14] John Adams, back from England in early 1788, found that "the agriculture, fisheries, manufactures, and commerce of the country are very well, much better than I expected to find them." [15] Unwise management of Massachusetts state finances, with inequitable taxation, was a primary cause of Shays' Rebellion. But the improving economy in the country as a whole was reflected in the fiscal reports of some other states. In South Carolina the public debt during 1786 was about the same as the increased debt for Massachusetts the previous year. By 1787 New York State actually had a balance in her treasury of £46,173, and Virginia—thanks in no small degree to the Henry party—had an even better financial record. In 1785–1786, his last year in the governorship, the state recorded tax receipts of £348,805 and had already paid off a considerable portion of her war debt. Moreover, there was a surplus in the treasury of £25,905 the year that Henry retired as Governor and, basically under the same fiscal system, of £122,342 the next year. [16] Improved economic conditions would be one of the arguments against a new constitution offered by anti-Federalists at the Virginia Convention of 1788.

There is strong reason to believe that Henry was in accord. But we find more explicit evidence of his fears that the proposed new government would sacrifice the interest of the agrarian South and West to those of the commercial North. In May, 1784, Madison wrote Jefferson that he found Henry "strenuous for invigorating the federal government, though without any precise plan." And according to another Richmond correspondent, William Short, Henry "saw Ruin inevitable, unless some thing was done to give Congress a compulsory Process on delinquent States"; and he believed that "a bold Example set by Virginia" would influence the other states. [17] Even in December, 1786, Madison was describing Henry to Washington as having "been hitherto the Champion of the Federal cause . . . in the event of an actual sacrifice of the Mississippi by Congress [he] will unquestionably go over to the opposite side." [18] After allowing for other factors, how great was the effect on him of events relating to the western country! In 1784 the Spanish Governor at New Orleans had proclaimed that the Mississippi River would be closed to American trade.[19] Then in the summer of 1785 Don Diego de Gardoqui, the Spanish *chargé d'affaires*, appeared in Washington. After negotiating with Gardoqui, John Jay, Secretary of State under the Confederation, proposed to Congress an agreement with Spain, apparently the best he believed he could secure for the weak American government. In return for what he deemed important commercial concessions to the United States, Jay wished Congress to surrender the navigation of the Mississippi for twenty-five or thirty years. At the end of the period of American exclusion from the Mississippi, so he argued, the United States would be strong enough to force the issue.

Word of Jay's proposal came to Henry in a long and strongly worded letter of August 12, 1786, from James Monroe, in Congress at New York. "The affair" had "come to such a crisis" that Monroe risked writing the letter when he did not have use of a satisfactory "cypher." Monroe declared that Jay had exceeded his instructions from Congress; that he had engaged in intrigue with the eastern states to carry through his plan. Although the Articles of Confederation required approval of treaties by two-thirds or nine of the states, Jay proposed to have the negotiations handled by a special congressional committee with full power to instruct him "on every point relative to the proposed treaty with Spain." The object of the "occlusion" of the Mississippi, Monroe continued, was "to break up so far as this will do it, the settlements on the western waters, prevent any in future, and thereby keep the States southw'd as they now are, or if settlements will take place, that they shall be on such principles as to make it the interest of the people to separate from the Confederacy." He also referred to talk among "the eastern people" of forming a separate government to include in time all the states north of the Potomac.[20]

Evidence of alarm in Virginia at Jay's negotiations soon became evident. Besides protesting to the Virginia congressman, Henry sent a letter of warning to Kentucky, and his influence was doubtless found in unanimous resolutions of protest by the House of Delegates on November 29, 1786, "That the common right of navigating the river Mississippi . . . ought to be considered as the bountiful gift of Nature to the United States." The confederacy had "been formed on the broad basis of equal rights," and the sacrifice of those "of any one part to the supposed or real interest of another part" would be "a direct contravention of the end for which the federal government was instituted. . . ."[21] The Mississippi issue would be of real significance in the impending constitutional struggle.

In accordance with their authorization from Congress of the previous month, the Virginia Assembly on December 4, 1786, elected seven delegates to the Constitutional Convention. As might have been expected, George Washington obtained the highest vote. The next highest, in order, were received by Patrick Henry, Edmund Randolph, John Blair, James Madison, George Mason, and George Wythe.[22] But Henry was deeply disturbed by the Mississippi question. It was already doubtful if he would support the movement for a stronger national government.

"I am entirely convinced, from what I observe here, that unless the project of Congress [for ceding to Spain the Mississippi for twenty-five years] can be reversed, the hopes of carrying this State into a proper federal system will be demolished. Many of our most federal leading men are extremely soured by what has already passed," James Madison wrote Washington from Richmond on December 7, 1786, and went on to explain Henry's antagonistic viewpoint.

Three months later Henry was reported as even more affected by the Mississippi question. Henry, "whose opinions have their usual influence," had been heard to state that "he would rather part with the Confederation than relinquish the navigation of the Mississippi," John Marshall wrote Arthur Lee.[23]

The question would again be raised by Henry and other anti-Federalists at the Virginia Convention of 1788. Henry may now seem unduly alarmed. But even George Washington, more interested in opening communication with the Ohio Valley, had thought that it would be advisable to sacrifice the right of navigation of the lower Mississippi for twenty-five years. When Henry retired to Prince Edward he had good reason to be alarmed by the proposal. If this prevented him from supporting the work of the forthcoming Constitutional Convention, its work might well be rejected in Virginia and her negative example followed by some other key states. When sending Henry official notice of his appointment as delegate to the Convention, Governor Randolph made a particular effort to secure his assent. "From the experience of your late administration," he wrote, "you must be persuaded that every day dawns with perils to the United States. To whom, then, can they resort for assistance with firmer expectation, than to those who first kindled the Revolution?"[24]

On February 13, 1787, Henry responded with a tactful but firm refusal. He declined the appointment "with much concern," adding that he deemed it his duty to answer Randolph by the "first opportunity" so that Randolph could quickly secure a replacement. Evidently Randolph made further efforts to enlist Henry's services, for he wrote Madison that he had "essayed every means" to prevail on Henry to be a delegate.[25] But Henry was now "peremptory in refusing," being "distressed in his private circumstances."[26] Certainly it was true that in the few months since resigning the governorship Henry had not found time to meet his financial obligations. However, Madison offered another and very practical explanation. He feared that Henry had rejected the appointment because of "a wish to leave his conduct unfettered on another theatre, where the result of the Convention will receive its destiny from his omnipotence."[27]

Although there were reports of leading men in various states accepting appointments to the Philadelphia Convention, the situation in Virginia remained ominous. Richard Henry Lee declined to serve, ostensibly because of ill health and conflicting congressional duties.[28] Possibly Lee, like Henry, did not want to commit himself. There was a declination, too, from General Nelson, while Thomas Jefferson, still minister to France, was unavailable. But George Washington was persuaded that it was his duty to serve, and Dr. James McClurg was appointed to take Henry's place, apparently with the approval of James Madison.[29]

During the long summer of 1787 while some of Henry's political associates were attending one of the most important conventions ever held in America, we have to look in his plantation accounts for the chief record of his activities. The proceedings of the Philadelphia Convention were secret, and little news of them reached Prince Edward. Meantime, despite improved economic conditions, Henry was hard pressed to support his family on his new plantation. His difficulties were embarrassingly suggested by a notice in the *Independent Chronicle* for June 20 that his Norfolk County land was to be sold for nonpayment of taxes. As late as the following December he had not been able to arrange more than crude living conditions for his family. Now back in the legislature, he was writing his daughter Betsey from Richmond that he had "been obliged to go up once to try to get some house to winter in." Dolly and all their family were living "at one fire" and did not have "one out-house that [would] assist." [30] Yet there is no evidence that he blamed these or other personal difficulties on the state government or believed that they were ameliorated by the delegates meeting at the Philadelphia Convention.

Despite his absence, and that of Jefferson and Lee, the Virginia delegation had been the most influential on the Convention floor. George Washington, who presided, had the prestige of the former commander in chief, while among the other Virginians the "modest, sweet-tempered" James Madison, as a Georgia delegate described him, blended to a highly successful degree "the profound politician with the scholar." [31] It would be a grave error to underestimate the influence of delegates from other states such as Alexander Hamilton, James Wilson, Gouverneur Morris, Benjamin Franklin, and some less known but solid personages. As a whole, they contributed greatly to a constitution which set up, or would set up after the adoption of the Bill of Rights, "the most complex government yet devised by man, and . . . the most nicely poised and guarded." [32] Yet Madison of Virginia had so much effect on the actual framing of the Constitution that he became known as its "father," and Edmund Randolph offered the Virginia or large state plan by which the states were to be represented in Congress on the basis of population.

It was Governor Randolph who began the significant work of the Convention by offering on May 30 an outline of government through which the Articles of Confederation were to be superseded by "a National government, consisting of a supreme legislature, executive, and judiciary." [33] This proposal, which was accepted and constituted a basic agenda for the Convention, was made with the approval of the Virginia delegation. We wonder whether it would have been secured if Henry—sniffing tyranny—had been present. Also, if he had been at Philadelphia, what would have been the effect of his oratorical ability, not equaled by any of the delegates? And of his ability as a working committeeman, proved as a legislative leader of the Virginia Assembly? [34] As it was, two Virginia delegates, George Mason and Edmund Randolph, did not sign the completed document. On the other hand, the Constitution as finally approved was largely based on a series of compromises smoothing over economic, sectional, and doctrinal differences. If Henry had been thrown into actual contact with the able delegates from various states, he might have been brought to see the wisdom of most of these compromises or at least have concurred with Washington that it was the best constitution which could be secured.

On September 17, the wearisome sessions of the Convention were finally ended and the new Constitution offered to the states for approval or rejection. There now followed a constitutional debate which in the ability of the chief contestants, the importance of the issues, the strength, and at times the bitterness, of the feeling engendered was one of the most significant in American history. Ratification of the proposed system of government was to be secured not by a majority of the votes cast but by the approval of nine states. After the debate fully developed, the anti-Federalists or opponents of the Constitution probably comprised a slight majority of the white population not only in Virginia but in the states as a whole. [35] Yet this advantage was probably compensated for by the fact that the Federalists in some critical areas were wealthier than their opponents and thus better able to meet the state monetary and property qualifications for voting. In a number of Virginia counties where Henry had his strongest support from the poorer classes, about half the adult males were not qualified to vote.[36] This factor, along with the over-representation on a population basis of many eastern counties, had an important influence on the type of delegates elected to the constitutional conventions in various states.

Better led, better organized, the Federalists were soon off to a good start in the ratification battle. They received a powerful impetus from the chief American newspapers which, while publishing much anti-Federalist material, usually made clear their support of the Constitution. Convinced of the vital importance of their cause, they were not above perversion of the facts in their favor or invocation of the deity. Thus, the *New Hampshire Spy* of October 30, 1787, after giving a biased account of the Federalist strength in several states, quoted a clergyman as asking "whether men can be serious in regard to the Christian religion, who object to a government that is calculated to promote the glory of GOD, by establishing peace, order, and justice in our country." The worthy divine continued:

> Would it not be better for such men to renounce the Christian name, and to enter into society with the Shawanese or Mohawk Indians, than to attempt to retain the blessings of religion and civilization, with their licentious ideas of government? [37]

Through pamphlets, newspaper articles, and speechmaking, the anti-Federalists made none too gentle replies, but their media for propaganda were somewhat more limited.

Soon Virginia news was being colored or fabricated for out-of-state consumption. As early as October 17, the *Pennsylvania Journal* was publishing an unproven story that George Mason had been in personal danger from "an enraged populace" at Alexandria because of his failure to sign the constitution. And Patrick Henry was the subject of another fanciful tale. On October 7 the *Pennsylvania Gazette* had Henry working for ratification, and on the thirtieth the *New*

Hampshire Spy repeated a similar falsehood. By December 7 the *Spy* was even telling its readers:

> It is currently reported that there are only two men in Virginia, who are not in debt, to be found among the enemies to the federal constitution. Debtors, speculators in papers, and States demagogues act consistently in opposing it. It will reduce them to a level with their fellow citizens, and prevent their thriving any longer by the distresses of their country.[38]

Another extreme would be reached on April 17, 1788, when the *United States Chronicle* of Providence, Rhode Island, reported that of all the members so far elected to the Virginia Convention *"there are only three or four against the Constitution."* It was "the general opinion, that there will scarcely be found ten men in the whole state, who when they meet here in June, will set their opinions in competition with those of the great and good patriots in America, and thus suffer themselves to be branded with the *odious* and *disgraceful* appelation of antifederalists."

In Virginia, George Washington led off for the Constitution by appealing to Henry and some other leading statesmen. The *Virginia Independent Chronicle* too, while printing a variety of pro- and anti-ratification news from various states, was on balance Federalist in sympathy, as its proprietor would later admit.

It was now nearly two decades since the outbreak of the Revolution. There had been a reaction from some of the radicalism of the war. Federalist chieftains such as George Washington and the more active James Madison in Virginia, James Wilson in Pennsylvania, and Alexander Hamilton were receiving wide support throughout the country. This was becoming especially strong in the cities, among the merchant and shipping interests, the Tidewater conservatives, and even in certain areas of the back country, such as the Valley of Virginia. The Constitution would also receive the backing of the majority of the signers of the Declaration of Independence.[39]

Yet during that fall and winter the Federalists found little comfort in the attitude of other outstanding Founding Fathers. Thus, in Virginia, when responding to Washington's appeal, Benjamin Harrison wrote that unless the condition of America was "very desperate," he feared that the remedies as provided by the Constitution would prove "worse than the disease," and George Mason deplored the absence of a declaration preserving the liberty of the press and trial by jury and protection against the dangers of standing armies in time of peace. Richard Henry Lee, in addition to replying unfavorably to Washington, urged in letters to Samuel Adams and Governor Randolph during October that a bill of rights and other changes should be inserted in the Constitution before adoption.[40] In December, Thomas Jefferson at Paris still remained rather cool toward the Constitution in its present form, though he was being exposed to some strong Federalist arguments from James Madison and other American correspondents.

"I own I am not a friend to a very energetic government. It is always oppressive," Jefferson wrote Madison on December 20. "The late rebellion in Massachusetts has given more alarm than I think it should have. Calculate that one rebellion in thirteen states in the course of 11 years, is but one for each state in a century and a half. No country should be so long without one."

If Jefferson expressed such opinions today he might be put on a subversive list. However, he is not to be taken too seriously: he would hardly have favored revolutions of the catastrophic twentieth-century type, unless as a last resort. Moreover, by April, 1788, he would be enough affected by Federalist arguments to favor adoption of the Constitution by nine states with four holding back, the better to secure amendments. John and Sam Adams also would become reconciled, Sam the more grudgingly. "I stumble on the threshold," that aged Cato said as he entered the Massachusetts convention hall. "I meet with a National government, instead of a Federal Union of Sovereign States."

By the summer of 1787 Henry had lived in Prince Edward considerably less than a year but was elected a member of the House of Delegates from that county. Since Congress had sent the Constitution to the states for consideration, the October legislature had to provide for Virginia's action thereon. In a highly optimistic report at the beginning of the Assembly, a member wrote Washington that the sentiments of his fellow legislators were "infinitely more favorable to the constitution" than its most zealous advocates could have expected. Henry, Washington's informant continued, was reported as opposed, but the legislator could only "conjecture" this from a conversation with him on the subject.[41] Washington, who forwarded the information to James Madison at New York on October 22, would have been less confident if he had seen a letter which Henry wrote his brother-in-law, Colonel Thomas Madison (James' cousin). Colonel Madison, then living at the Salt Works (present Saltville), was near the Wilderness Road, the most important line of communication for the Virginia southwestern and Kentucky counties.

> Such is the warmth of all the Members of Assembly concerning the new Constitution [Henry wrote], that no kind of business can be done 'til that is considered, so far at least as to recommend a Convention of the people. Great divisions are likely to happen, & I am afraid for the consequences. I can never agree to the proposed plan without Amendments, tho' many are willing to swallow it in its present form. Pray how are politics your Way? The Friends of Liberty will expect support from the back people.[42]

Definite information as to how the lines were being formed in the House of Delegates came on October 25 when the members held a final debate on the question of its reception of the Constitution. Henry was disturbed when young Francis Corbin of the conservative Tory family proposed and strongly advocated a resolution calling for ratification of the Constitution by a state convention. At once Henry was in opposition. "No one was more truly federal than himself," he declared. But there were "errors and defects" in the Constitution, and under Corbin's resolution the state convention could not propose amendments as a prior condition to ratification. In the warm debate Corbin was supported by George Nicholas, Henry by George Mason. John Marshall, fearing the effect of Henry's plan on the federal cause, proposed a compromise. Suavely he agreed with Henry that the proposed convention should not be restricted in its action, but he also affirmed, along with Nicholas, that the people should have no reason to suppose that their legislature disapproved of the new Constitution. Marshall, therefore, offered a resolution that the proceedings of the several conventions as transmitted to Congress should be submitted to "a convention of the people for full and free investigation and discussion." [43] This motion Henry did not oppose, and it was adopted unanimously. Indicative of his strength, however, was another measure which he moved and which was carried in the House on November 30. In a bill being introduced to provide for the expenses of the state convention, he secured a provision for paying the expenses of any delegate which the Convention might send to other states to consult with them as to proper amendments to the Constitution; also, of delegates to another federal convention if this was agreed upon. [44]

There is an absence of adequate information from Henry and his allies during this period. For the story of the ratification struggle, we must continue to rely in large part on the correspondence of his Federalist opponents. Early in November, 1787, Madison was relaying to Jefferson a report that, among leading Virginians, Henry, General Nelson, the Cabell family, St. George Tucker, John Taylor of Caroline, and the judges of the General Court, Paul Carrington excepted, were all opposed to the Constitution. By December 9 Madison, again writing Jefferson, said that Henry was the "great adversary" who would render ratification "precarious." As usual, not measuring his words in such personal letters, Madison went on to say that Henry was "working up every possible interest into a spirit of opposition." [45] On the other hand, with Washington believing that he should not take a very active hand, [46] Jefferson by December 15 was seeing Madison as the "main pillar" for the Constitution in Virginia. Yet, "immensely powerful" as was that pillar, Jefferson could not believe that Madison could "bear the weight" of the opposition host. [47]

Busy as Henry was with his regular legislative activities, he had only limited time for anti-Federalist agitation. In addition to his work on the floor, he was chairman of the committee on Courts of Justice and a member of those on Propositions and Grievances, Commerce, and Privileges and Elections. On November 17, 1787, he secured a leave of absence from the House for several days, and on December 22 he was excused for the remainder of the session. In Prince Edward, except for one more brief period, he was now chiefly engaged in plantation affairs until he returned to Richmond in June for the state Constitutional Convention. During the winter and spring of 1787–1788 while the Virginia Federalists were cleverly organizing and propagandizing, Henry was digesting some significant ideas which he would propound on the Convention floor. Yet his opponents, a clever and well-organized minority, were doing much more to muster and indoctrinate their forces.

Henry's first notable speech, his last, and a number of intervening speeches were delivered at courthouses or on courthouse greens. Among them was his noteworthy address at old Prince Edward Courthouse in February, 1788. On the monthly court days, the little Virginia county seats continued to attract the usual throng of visitors, lawyers, clients, trafficking farmers and merchants: the enterprising and ambitious, the idle and the curious. When Henry at the February Prince Edward court announced his candidacy as a delegate to the state Constitutional Convention the following June, it was not surprising that a large crowd turned out to hear him. And here at the former county courthouse, in present Worsham, he held forth—not tepidly, we may be sure—on what he deemed the defects of the proposed Constitution.

His arguments struck a sympathetic chord with many of the countryfolk. He might have been elected and lined up Prince Edward and the surrounding area for the anti-Federalists with little more ado if he had not met with an adversary worthy of his steel. This was a latecomer to Virginia, a native Pennsylvanian and graduate of the distinguished Princeton University class of 1773, the Reverend John Blair Smith, at the time president of Hampden-Sydney College. That Henry and his learned opponent of the fighting Presbyterian breed did not exchange light blows is clear enough, but again it is the Federalist cause that has been more fully presented.

"It was one of his [Smith's] peculiar properties to put out his strength in everything he undertook, and to do nothing by halves," one of his former pupils wrote. Of frail physique, Smith once ruptured a blood vessel when preaching and fell in the pulpit. As a pioneer Presbyterian minister in Prince Edward during the postwar religious lethargy, he had his troubles. It was no easy task to awaken sinners, to arouse "cold professors," and to reclaim backsliders. But the lean, black-haired little man with the pale cheeks and piercing eyes, twenty years Henry's junior, was not to be daunted. He struggled on to become the minister of several Presbyterian churches in the Prince Edward area and an influential teacher at, then president of, Hampden-Sydney College—all this before he locked horns with Henry, a member of the college board.

To Henry's speech when announcing his candidacy there was no immediate reply, and he and General Robert Lawson were elected as delegates from Prince Edward to the Convention. The Reverend John Blair Smith had intended to answer Henry at the courthouse but was unable to be present. The pertinacious minister did, however, send one of his family to take down Henry's speech in shorthand. A few days later there was an exhibition of speechmaking at Hampden-Sydney, with Henry in attendance. To his surprise, one of the speakers delivered Henry's recent speech, and another student followed with one prepared by the Reverend Smith in opposition, specifically replying to Henry's objections to the Constitution. The young man delivering the shorthand account of Henry's speech was described as one of the best student speakers. Yet there was a comic touch. Henry, however modest, was not likely to think that the student offered an adequate substitute for himself. In complaining to the Reverend Smith, Henry complimented the correctness of the stenographer but objected to the "tautness" of the reply and the attempt to ridicule him before a large audience. Smith defended his action and Henry stopped attending his sermons. The incident, along with Smith's outspoken preaching, probably contributed to his resignation from the college presidency in 1788.

Certainly, Smith remained ill disposed toward Henry. By June 12, 1788, he was writing his friend and college mate, James Madison, that Henry had "artfully prepared" the minds of the people against the Constitution so that "all opposition at the election of delegates . . . was in vain." He had "descended to lower artifices and management on the occasion than I thought him capable of. . . . If Mr. Innes has shown you a speech of Mr. Henry to his constituents, which I sent him, you will see something of the method he has taken to diffuse his poison." Smith went on to say that he was grieved that such "great natural talents" were used to such purposes. He spoke of how Henry had written the people in Kentucky and alarmed them with an apprehension that their interests were about to be sacrificed by the Northern states, and how he had found means to make some of the best people in Prince Edward believe that "a religious establishment was in contemplation under the new government." [48]

Actually, in the absence of full documentary evidence, we can only conjecture how far Henry went beyond the limit of fair-minded political debate. Smith's statements were quoted in well-known Federalist writings. By the twentieth century, a brilliant and usually accurate biographer of John Marshall was, on the basis of the Smith letter, declaring that Henry was "feverishly active" and wrote "flaming letters" to Kentucky saying that the Mississippi would be lost if the new government was adopted. The Smith letter was used by certain Madison biographers as evidence that Henry did not hesitate about the arguments he used, provided he found them effective. However, W. W. Henry states that Smith's criticism of Henry's conduct in the election was on its face "baseless," and certainly much of it cannot be verified. [49]

It all depended on whose ox was gored. What were termed slick electioneering tricks when their opponents used them could become noble patriotic efforts when employed by the Federalists, and vice versa. Even George Washington was writing General Lincoln on April 2, 1788, that "every art that could inflame the passions or touch the interests of men have been essayed" by the anti-Federalists. [50] And Richard Henry Lee was asserting in his widely read *Letters of a Federal Farmer* that "by means of taxes, the government may command the whole or any part of the subjects' property." [51]

On April 5, George Nicholas wrote to Madison in Charlottesville that there was a slight majority of Federalists elected to the Virginia Convention but he feared some of the members would be unwilling "to give the best hand" to the Constitution unless the conduct of the other states justified it. Nicholas spoke of Henry as "now almost avowedly an enemy of the union. . . . His real sentiments will be industriously concealed, for so long as he talks only of amendments such of the friends to the union as object to particular parts of the constitution will adhere to him." [52] By the twenty-second Madison was informing Jefferson that some of the Virginia anti-Federalists were opposed to the substance of the constitution and others only to particular modifications. "Mr. H——y is supposed to aim at disunion," Madison continued:

> Col. M——n is growing every day more bitter, and outrageous in his efforts to carry his point, and will probably in the end be thrown by the violence of his passions into the politics of Mr. H——y. The preliminary question will be whether previous alterations shall be insisted on or not? Should this be carried in the affirmative, either a conditional ratification, or a proposal for a new Convention will ensue. In either event, I think the Constitution and the Union will be both endangered.[53]

By April 22 the Virginia elections had ended after much political maneuvering in which the Federalists had played the cleverest hand. Madison believed that they had probably won a majority of the delegates, although the Kentucky vote was not known. On the other hand, George Mason wrote a Maryland friend on May 1 that no man could at present form a judgment as to the decision of the Virginia Convention.[54]

Meantime, by February 6 the Constitution had been adopted by six states, and by May 23 by eight, one less than the nine required for ratification. It was adopted easily in December and January by Delaware, New Jersey, and Connecticut, small states which welcomed the protection of the Constitution and felt that it adequately guaranteed their rights. Frontier Georgia, too, had on January 2 joined without a dissenting vote in a union which would give it stronger military support. Pennsylvania had ratified in December but only after some sharp electioneering, to which Henry would allude during a speech in the Virginia Convention. In one instance a crowd in Philadelphia had dragged two members of the Pennsylvania legislature from their lodgings to the State House—and held them in their seats—in order to secure a quorum and order the Constitutional Convention.[55]

In another large state, Massachusetts, the Federalist strength centered in Boston and other coastal areas. At the last, Sam Adams, whatever his doubts, did not vote against the wishes of the Boston tradesmen.[56] The vote on February 6, 1788, was 187 to 168 in favor of ratification, but the small majority was obtained largely by a recommendation that nine amendments, embodying the principles of a bill of rights, should be urged on Congress by its Massachusetts representatives.[57] The same day of the Massachusetts ratification, Jefferson was writing Alexander Donald from Paris that he wished with all his soul that the first conventions might accept the new Constitution, since this "would secure to us the good it contains," but he equally wished that the four latest conventions, whichever they may be, might refuse to accede to it, till "a declaration of rights be annexed." [58]

On the twenty-sixth of April ratification was easily secured in Maryland, 26 to 11; and on the twenty-eighth of May in South Carolina. Although the New Hampshire Convention had met in February and adjourned until June 21, its ratification was deemed certain, but the actual vote was fairly close—57 to 46.

When Henry left for the meeting of the Virginia Convention in June, eight states had ratified the Constitution. Even if New Hampshire did cast a favorable vote at her approaching convention, Virginia, New York, North Carolina, and Rhode Island could still be left out of the union. And especially since Virginia and North Carolina comprised large adjoining areas, the recalcitrant states could cause great difficulties for a new government. On the other hand, approval by Virginia would certainly provide the ninth state needed for ratification.

We may wonder if Henry had spent as much time preparing for the impending debates as he had for his recent legal cases and his spring crops. The tilt with the Reverend John Blair Smith, the numerous articles on the Constitution in the *Independent Chronicle,* and probably pamphlets such as those containing the widely distributed *Farmer's Letters* of Richard Henry Lee had served to strengthen Henry's opinions on the issue developed at the last legislature. When in Richmond and perhaps elsewhere, he had been in touch with his son-in-law, Spencer Roane, one of the ablest of the younger anti-Federalists. Yet, despite these contrary examples, one is impressed by the paucity of Henry's outside contacts when in Prince Edward. He is known to have had little correspondence while there with leading Federalists or anti-Federalists, to have formulated with the latter few or no plans for an organized opposition to the Constitutionalists' program. In Richmond he and George Mason would develop a belated plan for strategy on the Convention floor. But when Henry set out alone in his gig for Richmond, he would face there—ill-prepared and none too well supported—some of the most formidable opposition in his political career.

22

Convention of 1788

I fear that overwhelming torrent, Patrick Henry.
———GENERAL HENRY KNOX [1]

June 2–June 18, 1788. Sessions of Virginia Convention being
held at Richmond. Henry leading fight on the floor against
ratification without prior amendments of the federal Constitution.

ONE OF HENRY's more prominent supporters, Colonel William Cabell from the upper James in present Nelson County, notes in
his diary that he set out for the Constitutional Convention on Saturday, May 30, 1788, and took his seat on June 2.[2] Henry, riding from
Prince Edward, must have taken nearly as long for the trip. On Sunday, May 31, he was observed riding into town from the Southside
about sunset. He was driving his plain, topless gig, and his clothes,
made on his own loom, were covered with the dust of the dry summer
day. Yet, prematurely old at fifty-two as Henry was, leaning forward
as if worn from the trip, he nevertheless seemed capable of enduring
fatigue.[3] And this he would prove in the impending Convention
debates.

With the swarms of people arriving in the capital, Henry, like
George Mason and Edmund Pendleton, was fortunate in securing
quarters at the Swan. Probably the largest peacetime crowd until then
collected in Richmond, it filled the inns and spare rooms in private

residences. Besides the delegates to the Convention and their entourage, there was a throng of visitors from all over the state. Most were attracted by the nature of the constitutional struggle, with Virginia a crucial battleground, but some had come out of sheer curiosity. It was now over twelve years since Henry had thundered forth at the Convention on Church Hill, and many of the younger generation found their first opportunity to see and hear him and his compeers. The Jockey Club was in session, adding size and variety to the crowd. And in early June the Richmond summer had not yet become too oppressive.[4]

On Monday morning, June 2, the Convention was called to order and Edmund Pendleton was unanimously elected president. In his position as presiding officer, the Judge could give powerful support to the Federalists. But so great was Pendleton's ability and prestige that the anti-Federalists did not deem it expedient to risk likely defeat in opposing his nomination. Because of his crutches and frail health, he was permitted to keep his seat while presiding as chairman.

In a few well-chosen words, Pendleton thanked the Convention for the honor conferred upon him and strongly recommended to the members that they use the utmost moderation and temper in their deliberations on the great and important subject before them. Emphasis on moderation, on calm reasoning instead of emotional oratory, would be a proper tactic of the Federalists, vitally needed to counteract Henry's forensic powers.

Before adjournment for the day, the Federalists scored another point, at least for future history. David Robertson of Petersburg, with an assistant, appeared to take down the proceedings in shorthand. This was unprecedented for Virginia conventions, and Robertson was a Federalist sympathizer. Permission for him to record the debate was granted with some misgivings on the part of the anti-Constitutionalists. Robertson could obtain only what he termed "an ineligible seat," not being allowed to place his table in front of the presiding officer where there was better audibility.

For none of Henry's famous speeches of the past had there been a full manuscript or indeed any stenographic report. Shorthand reporting was not then perfected, and Robertson had his own limitations.

Whatever his personal sympathies, he seems to have striven to report the proceedings correctly. But there were a number of instances when the speakers talked too low or too fast, and Robertson indicates that he was unable to report them. Some of the Federalists later revised Robertson's reports of their speeches, but the opposition disdained to do so, considering him in the Federalist "interest." [5] Thus these anti-Federalists were to a degree cutting their own throats. This was especially true of Henry, for Robertson appears not only to have been unable to follow several of his most stirring passages because of the rapidity of utterance but to have been too moved to take up his pen. We thus get only the substance or hints of it, while losing some of the spirit of Henry's speeches. The omission is the more regrettable in that he was battling, often seemingly alone, against several of the keenest intellects of America and showed frequent flashes of his old form.

Interest was heightened as the strategy of the opening forces began to develop. The anti-Federalists wanted to prolong the discussion in order to give full opportunity for their counterblasts. While they often seemed to be attacking at random, they focused more and more on a few vulnerable points which they would belabor at length through a variety of argumentive devices. The Federalists, on the other hand, were more fearful of delay. They had some brilliant speakers who could ring the emotional changes, but not quite like Henry. Their strategy, as quickly developed by Pendleton, Madison, and their leading associates, emphasized factual discussion of the Constitution clause by clause: calm, logical analysis of the successive questions, then orderly progress to others and convincing summation. When George Mason, an impressive figure with his flowing white hair and black suit, rose early on the third day to offer a motion, he unwittingly fell in with the Federalist strategy. He proposed that the Constitution be discussed in the order written before proposal of "a general previous question." Mason declared that he wanted "the freest discussion, clause by clause," and, after Madison had "blandly" agreed, the motion was adopted. Madison happily wrote George Washington of the successful maneuver. The Federalists would appear not to oppose free discussion, yet could pursue a strategy of limiting the debate. Mason was not as gullible as he appeared; he did favor the Constitution after amendments and believed that an orderly discussion would expose weaknesses which could be remedied before ratification.[6] But while Mason and Henry doutbless burned candles of nights at the Swan planning their strategy, they were not cooperating very effectively.

There was time for further business that first day, and a Federalist speaker, General Henry "Light-Horse Harry" Lee, revealed his party's fear of delay by urging the delegates to begin discussion of the Constitution. If they did not complete their work on June 22, he said, they would be compelled to adjourn, since the Legislature was to meet on the twenty-third. There was no reason for delay, since the Constitution, he believed, was understood by every gentleman present.[7] Nevertheless, the members voted to adjourn until eleven o'clock the next day, when they would meet in Committee of the Whole.[8] They had agreed to change their meeting place from the old capitol to the New Academy, the largest assembly hall in town, but it also proved too small for the crowds listening with anxiety or sheer fascination to the lengthy debates.

By Wednesday, June 4, 1788, nearly all the delegates were present, not merely the leaders but their supporters on each side. Henry was now able to make a shrewd appraisal of the opposing forces, not only en masse but down to the few doubtful members, susceptible to change in the ensuing debate. There was a grand total of 170 delegates, two from each county and one each from Norfolk and Williamsburg boroughs. Inevitably, he noticed the absences of a few personages present at some earlier meetings which he had attended. The suave and courtly John Robinson, leader of the House of Burgesses in 1765, had long since died; so during the past fifteen years had Richard Bland, Peyton Randolph, and Robert Carter Nicholas. Among living statesmen, Thomas Jefferson was in France; Richard Henry Lee had not been elected to the Convention, and George Washington preferred to exert a limited influence from Mount Vernon. Yet these absentees did not materially detract from the brilliance of the assemblage. As the debate developed, Henry was not surprised to find Edmund Pendleton and James Madison active as Federalist chieftains, and they received powerful support from John Marshall, George Nicholas, "Light-Horse Harry" Lee, and Governor Randolph. Among the anti-Federalist leaders Henry learned what he could expect of George Mason, James Monroe, William Grayson, John Tyler, and others; he decided how much, despite their notable support, he ought to take the lead in the debates. For while his party did represent the majority of the Virginia electorate, he obviously realized that the Federalists mustered the larger number of talented and influential delegates. He could hardly hope to sway more than a dozen or two. Who were they and how could they be best approached?

Henry found the Federalist strength concentrated mostly in the Tidewater, Northern Neck, and Valley delegates, the anti-Federalist in those from the Piedmont counties south of the James, with some other sections divided. Seeing some of the Tidewater delegates who had opposed him in earlier battles, it is small wonder that he became so exercised over the threat to liberty. A few members, he unhappily noted, were even scions of well-known Tory families, and one young Tidewater delegate, Francis Corbin, had spent the war years with his Loyalist family in England.

The lines had been shifting, and not to Henry's liking. To be sure, he could again count on a coterie of blood relatives and in-laws,[9] in addition to an almost solid Southside representation. Yet there had been serious defections among his old supporters, not only in the Northern Neck and Valley but in the west. Obviously, Henry would have to reclaim some of the lost sheep. In the close vote he now anticipated, the Kentucky vote was particularly important. As was evident after election of the delegates, Henry's opponents were reaping the results of the inequitable system of representation and the Federalist strategy by which Governor Randolph and several appellate judges now sat in the Convention.

As if the Federalists had not mustered enough strength beyond their popular following, Henry found them aided by two persuasive lobbyists from the North, affable Gouverneur Morris of Pennsylvania and his cousin, Robert Morris, the "financier of the Revolution."[10] On the other hand, Colonel Eleazer Oswald, editor of the Philadelphia *Independent Gazetteer*, was in the city briefly to help the anti-Federalists and was "closeted" a few times with Henry, Mason, and others.[11] Oswald delivered to Henry a letter and three pamphlets from General John Lamb, a gallant though contentious Revolutionary officer and now a leader of the New York anti-Federalists. Sensitive, if not unduly so, to issues of human liberty for which he had struggled, Lamb had become the chairman of an association of Federal Republicans opposed to the ratification of the Constitution. In New York City, the veteran soldier had fortified his house after it was threatened by Federalist mobs; in Virginia he corresponded with Henry, Richard Henry Lee, and William Grayson.

Through these letters Lamb sought to strengthen the interstate relationships of the anti-Federalists. And Henry's reply on June 9, 1788, to a letter from him is especially valuable for Henry's estimate of the current outlook for the Virginia anti-Federalists. After thanking Lamb for the sentiments in his late letter and for several pamphlets, Henry continued with observations from the Virginia vantage point.

"It is a matter of great consolation, to find that the sentiments of a vast majority of Virginians are in unison with those of our northern friends. I am satisfied four-fifths of our inhabitants are opposed to the new scheme of government," Henry asserted optimistically. "Indeed, in the part of this country lying south of James River, I am confident nine-tenths are opposed to it." But Henry then put his finger on a serious obstacle confronting the anti-Federalist forces. He told Lamb that "strange as it may seem, the numbers in the convention appear equal on both sides, so that the majority, which way soever it goes, will be small. The friends and seekers of power, have, with their usual subtilty wriggled themselves into the choice of the people, by assuming shapes as various as the faces of the men they address on such occasions."[12]

If the Federalists carried their point and precluded previous amendments to the Constitution which the anti-Federalists had ready to offer, Henry believed that it would become necessary to form the society which Lamb proposed; indeed, it appeared to him "the only chance to secure a remnant of those invaluable rights which are yielded by the new plan."

Henry declared that George Mason had agreed to act as chairman of the Virginia republican society—"He is every way fit"—and they were sending Lamb a copy of the bill of rights and of the amendments they intended to propose to the Convention. Thus, while the Federalists did have the better of the political maneuvering to date, Henry's party was now seeking to broaden its influence. But eight states had already adopted the Constitution, and, with the difficulties of communication, efforts to prevent approval by the necessary ninth state were most likely to be ineffectual. Moreover, Henry had to tell Lamb that the fate of the bill of rights and amendments in the Convention was uncertain. Belatedly indicating the need of unity among the anti-Constitutionalists, he said that "to assimilate our views . . . is of the last moment" and spoke of their opponents as expecting "much from our dissension."

"I can assure you that North Carolina is more decidedly opposed to the new government than Virginia," Henry added. He also spoke of further anti-Federalist associations that might help to overcome what he realistically termed the "dispersed situation" of his party,[13] but must have realized that his crucial efforts would have to be made on the Convention floor.

On Wednesday, June 4, the disputed elections having been settled, the convention met in the Committee of the Whole.

The veteran George Wythe, signer of the Declaration of Independence, eminent legislator and jurist, took his seat as temporary presiding officer, and Edmund Pendleton was in a position to speak from the floor. Henry, conscious that the Federalists were winning the early maneuvers, called for the clerk to read the act of Assembly appointing deputies to meet at Annapolis to consult with those from some other states on the situation of the commerce of the United States; the act of Assembly appointing deputies to meet at Philadelphia, to revise the Articles of Confederation; and other public papers relative thereto.[14] But Pendleton, rising on his crutches, declared that the purpose of the Convention was not to consider whether the federal

Convention exceeded its powers. It had submitted a new governmental system, and the people had deputed the delegates to consider
it. Henry then withdrew his motion, presumably fearing a test of
strength at this stage.[15]

The clerk read the preamble of the Constitution and the first two
sections of the first article dealing with the powers and responsibilities
of the House of Representatives. The Federalists, not making a
single grave error in their strategy, led off with the first "set" speech
of the Convention—by young George Nicholas.[16] To Henry he
brought disagreeable memories of the abortive Jefferson inquiry. A
squat, corpulent man with "a nose like the caricature of an eagle," [17]
Nicholas' appearance had earlier provoked the mirth of even the
serious-minded Madison.[18] But he was highly connected, courageous,
and a brilliant lawyer and debater who neither asked nor gave quarter. Nicholas was said to have been probably the only man in the
Convention whom Henry feared.[19] He made a forceful, close-
reasoned speech in defense of the constitutional provisions relating to
the House of Representatives, incidentally anticipating some of the
opposing arguments.[20]

Henry apparently realized the error of the anti-Federalists in
letting their opponents start the full-dress debate with such a powerful argument. He now took the floor for his first lengthy speech of
the Convention. The worn veteran of many triumphs and adversities,
he was somewhat stooped and his penetrating blue eyes were a bit
obscured by spectacles. His thinning hair was covered with a wig
which he would nervously push back and forth in the heat of debate.
Ignoring Nicholas, Henry said that "the public mind" as well as his
own was "extremely uneasy at the proposed change of government."
He was one of a number of those who wished to be thoroughly
acquainted with the reasons for "this perilous and uneasy situation"
and why the members were brought to Richmond "to decide on this
great national question.

"I consider myself as a servant of the people of this commonwealth, as a sentinel over their rights, liberty, and happiness," Henry
declared, thus revealing, with no false modesty, what he considered
a principal motif of his political career. Some of the greatest speeches

[349]

in history—by a Demosthenes or a Churchill, by many obscurer figures with more courage than oratorical genius—have been delivered on this theme. Now Henry would speak again on the burning subject. But could he now strike the same spark as of old? Would his opponents prove too formidable, too well organized, for even his oratory?

Henry began on a controversial note. He declared that before the meeting of the late federal Convention there was "a universal tranquillity" in the country, but since that period the people were "exceedingly uneasy and disquieted." It was true that the economic and political conditions of Virginia in particular, and even of the country as a whole, were better than some of Henry's opponents depicted. But surely he knew that the Confederation had been unable to collect needed revenue, that it was faced with some problems which could lead toward anarchy. His opponents would score on this issue.

When Henry sought election as a delegate to the Convention, he continued, his "mind was extremely agitated for the situation of public affairs"; he believed "the republic to be in extreme danger." This condition arose "from a proposal to change our government—a proposal" that means "the utter annihilation of the most solemn engagements of the states, a proposal of establishing nine states into a confederacy, to the eventual exclusion of four states." He emphasized the threat to liberty and asserted that if a wrong step were then made, the republic might be lost forever. Although he praised the sincerity of the "worthy characters" who, at the federal Convention, felt it was necessary to form a consolidated government instead of a confederation, he asked, "What right had they to say . . . *We, the People*, instead of *We, the States?* . . . The people gave them [the delegates] no power to use their name. That they exceeded their power is perfectly clear." [21]

Governor Randolph now took the floor for the Federalists. A leading member of a family which with all its branches was one of the wealthiest and most influential in Virginia, he was, next to Washington and Henry, probably her most popular political personage. In debate he was able to follow Henry without too great disparity in talents. Randolph was in a delicate position in that he had not signed the Constitution, and the anti-Federalists had counted on him as one of their principal proponents. Extremely sensitive to any hints of apostasy, the proud Randolph expatiated on the reason for his change of position. He pleaded for toleration and for a "persuasion that no man has a right to impose his opinions on others." Regardless of allurements to continue as he had begun, he had come to the Convention to repeat his earnest endeavors for a firm, energetic government.[22] He spoke of how the public credit was gone, commerce languishing, produce fallen in value, justice trampled underfoot, America become comtemptible in the eyes of foreign nations. In reply to Henry's question why *We, the People,* he declared that the government was for the people and it was unfortunate that the people had previously had no agency in the government. Was it unfair or unjust to consult the people on the construction of a government by which they were to be bound? Making light of Henry's contention, he declared that this was "one of the least and most trivial objections that will be made to the constitution." [23] Randolph had refused his signature to the Constitution and if the same reasons were operating he said he would still refuse, but since he thought that the eight states which had adopted the Constitution would not secede, he was a friend to the union.

Clearly, the proponents were still carrying the ball despite Henry's speech. The revered George Mason now took up some cardinal points which would become a recurring theme for Henry and other anti-Federalist speakers. Mason said that the provision in Section Two of the Constitution for apportionment of direct taxes among the states created a government which was national and no longer a confederation. He questioned if the people would consent to be taxed by two distinct powers and said he did not believe that one general national government could exist in so extensive a country as America. When amendments were made to secure the great essential rights of the people, he would heartily make concessions in the interest of conciliation and unanimity. Such an indispensable amendment was that Congress should not exercise the power of raising direct taxes until the states had refused to comply with the requisitions of Congress.[24] Thus Mason had brought up several points on which Henry in par-

[351]

ticular would expatiate, probably after discussion outside the new convention hall by the two men.

The Convention had now been meeting three days. On the basis of "good authority" reaching him at Mount Vernon, George Washington thought that Randolph's "declaration" would have "considerable" effect upon wavering delegates, as indeed proved the case. Henry and Mason had "by no means equalled the public expectation" of their speeches, Washington was informed. The anti-Federalist leaders in the Convention appeared "rather chagreened" and hardly decided as to their mode of opposition.[25] The sanguine Federalists, who had counted on a majority of twenty at their first meeting, now believed that this would be greatly increased; more temperate friends of the Constitution spoke less confidently of the size of the majority and were worried about "the arts" that might be used to excite the Kentucky delegates. All Washington's informants, however, agreed that "the beginning" of the Convention had been as "auspicious as could possibly have been expected."

The optimistic reports even led Washington to believe that a few days would "ascertain" the result of the Convention. Certainly, the experienced Henry sensed the growing opposition.

The Federalists were now ready for a change of pace. James Madison was no flaming orator, no exponent of the bold forensic attack, the strong emotional appeal. But the Federalist leaders evidently felt that the Convention was ready for his quiet logic, his unsurpassed knowledge of the subject matter under debate. After beginning on a calm, conciliatory note, Madison declared that the provision for direct taxes was only explanatory of the relation which representation and taxation should bear to one another. Obviously seeking to prevent Henry and his colleagues from launching into a general discussion of the Constitution with emphasis on certain vulnerable points, Madison said that the power of laying direct taxes would be more properly discussed when the Convention came to the part of the Constitution which vests that power in Congress. At present, he must endeavor to reconcile the proceedings to the resolutions calling for the discussion of the sections in the order written. He argued that the Confederation would not be converted into a complete consolidation and that with more attention the Convention would see that Mason was mistaken.[26]

Apparently in accord with the planned strategy, Madison was followed the next morning, Thursday, June 5, by Edmund Pendleton. Beginning suavely with an allusion to his "worthy friend" (Henry), Pendleton immediately got to the heart of the matter. Answering Henry's assertion as to the good condition of the country before the framing of the Constitution, Pendleton stated the general government was totally inadequate to the purpose of its institution and that American commerce was decayed, finances deranged, public and private credit destroyed. Like a number of assertions by debaters from both camps, Pendleton's statement could not be accepted as literally accurate. Again in a sense replying to Henry, he declared that there was no quarrel between government and liberty; the former was a shield and the protector of the latter. The war was between government and licentiousness, faction, turbulence, and other violations of the rules of society to preserve liberty. As for the Philadelphia Convention, its power was very broad and intended to remove all defects in the national government. The question must be between the new government and the Confederation. It was not the latter, he argued, but the common danger and spirit of America which were the bonds that carried her through a dangerous war.[27]

Alluding to Henry's and Mason's argument that the Constitution was a consolidated government annihilating that of the states, Pendleton said he understood a consolidated government to be one which should have the sole and exclusive power, legislative, executive, and judicial, without any limitation; but the national government under the Constitution had powers which extended only to the general purpose of the union. He declared that this government "does not intermeddle with the local particular affairs of the states,"[28] an argument which would some day be greeted with derision by certain proponents of states' rights.

Before concluding, Pendleton made a strong point when he attacked the anti-Federalist contention that the national government should resort to requisitions rather than direct taxes on the states. He spoke of the time that would be lost through requisitions, and argued that resistance to the collectors would be the probable consequence.[29]

Henry Lee of Westmoreland, the dashing "Light-Horse Harry" of the Revolution, then took the floor on behalf of ratification. Still only in his mid-thirties, he was no plodding military figure and he spoke forcefully, not bothered as to whether he hurt the sensibilities of such older statesmen as Henry. "On so important an occasion, and before so respectable a body," Lee had expected a new display of Henry's "powers of oratory; but, instead of proceeding to investigate the merits of the new plan of government," he had appealed to the "fears" of the House. "I trust he is come to judge, and not to alarm. I trust that he, and every other gentleman in this house, comes with a firm resolution coolly and calmly to examine, and fairly and impartially to determine."[30] And Lee reiterated the Federalist arguments with regard to the "imbecility" of the Confederation; he even contended that not "an American bottom [merchantman]" was to be seen. He injected a note of bitterness which had been avoided by Pendleton and Madison.

Henry was of course under the disadvantage of not having been a delegate in Philadelphia and of having been separated from much of the subsequent agitation. This he had now partly compensated for by reading and discussion of the issues, and his numerous historical allusions during the debates drew a courteous recognition even from a Federalist opponent. "The honorable gentleman is possessed of much historical knowledge," Francis Corbin remarked on the Convention floor. "I appeal to that knowledge, therefore."[31] Nevertheless, Henry did not come to the Convention as well prepared as Madison and a few others of his associates. His frequent practice was to play his forensic fiddle by ear: to listen to the opposing arguments, then with his remarkable ability at improvisation to set his bow in motion. The general arguments at least were ones on which he had thought much, and he was nothing if not quick-witted.

Now he was impelled to answer the formidable Federalist arguments with another major speech. Even as abridged by Robertson, it covers twenty pages of *Elliot's Debates* and was his second longest speech of the Convention, requiring perhaps a day for the delivery.

Altogether, of the 652 pages of Elliot's printed debates, 136, or over a fifth, are taken up with Henry's speeches. After the first days of the Convention, he did indeed "bear the brunt" of the Federalist attack. On several days he made three speeches, on another day five, and on another eight. And yet Judge Edmund Winston, an eyewitness, would write that when Henry was speaking "there was a perfect stillness throughout the House, and in the galleries. There was no inattention or appearance of weariness. When any other member spoke the members and the audience would in half an hour be going out or moving from their seats." The full impact of his speeches, as we have noted, cannot be determined by reading the printed version, and as St. George Tucker, no blind admirer of Henry, emphasized, the speeches were taken down in shorthand—not "accurately," he thought.

"At that time it appeared to me that Mr. Henry was sometimes as great" as at the Convention of 1775, wrote Tucker, who had heard him on both occasions. "I recollect the fine image he gave of Virginia seated on an eminence and holding in her hand the balance in which the fate of America was weighing," Tucker continued. "Old General Steven [Adam Stephen] attempted to parodize and burlesque it, but I think he failed." Tucker declared, however, that "the variety of arguments which Mr. Henry generally presented in his speeches, addressed to the capacities, prejudices, and individual interests of his hearers, made his speeches unequal." [32]

Despite the sharp attack on him by Henry Lee, the previous speaker, Henry did not let the soldier lure him into an *ad personam* debate. On the contrary, he began by expressing himself as "much obliged to the very worthy gentleman for his encomium." [33] He then made an impassioned argument in which he continued to avoid discussion of the Constitution, clause by clause, as his opponents desired, and belabored certain specific points in accordance with the strategy which he and Mason had been employing in earlier speeches. The revolution by the formation of the Constitution had been as radical, so Henry asserted, as that which had separated the colonies from Great Britain. It was radical since in this transition American rights and privileges were endangered and the sovereignty of the states relinquished.

> The rights of conscience, trial by jury, liberty of the press, all your immunities and franchises, all pretensions to human rights and privileges are rendered insecure, if not lost, by this change, so loudly talked of by some, and inconsiderately by others. . . . You are not to inquire how your trade may be increased, nor how you are to become a great and powerful people, but how your liberties can be secured; for liberty ought to be the direct end of your government.[34]

Henry followed with a panegyric on liberty—liberty which had been a guiding star through the fierce battles of his political career:

> Liberty, the greatest of all earthly blessings—give us that precious jewel, and you may take every thing else! But I am fearful I have lived long enough to become an old-fashioned fellow. Perhaps an invincible attachment to the dearest rights of man may, in these refined, enlightened days, be deemed old-fashioned; if so, I am contented to be so. . . . Guard with jealous attention the public liberty. Suspect every one who approaches that jewel. Unfortunately, nothing will preserve it but downright force. Whenever you give up that force, you are inevitably ruined.[35]

Henry then offered a tribute to the government under the Articles of Confederation which, though exaggerated, would nevertheless to a limited degree be in accord with future scholarship. The Confederation, this "despised government," merited "the highest encomium," he said. "It carried us through a long and dangerous war; it rendered us victorious in that bloody conflict with a powerful nation; it has secured us a territory greater than any European monarch possesses: and shall a government which has been thus strong and vigorous, be accused of imbecility and abandoned for want of energy?"[36]

Henry offered unrealistic criticism of the provision in the Constitution stating that the number of representatives should not exceed one for every thirty thousand. After declaring with seeming modesty that he was not well versed in history, he asked the delegates whether liberty had been destroyed most often by the licentiousness of the people or by the tyranny of the rulers. He believed that the delegates would find the balance on the side of tyranny. "Happy will you be if you miss the fate of those nations, who, omitting to resist their oppressors, or negligently suffering their liberty to be wrested from them, have groaned under intolerable despotism," he continued.[37] With his omnipresent fear of despotic power, he attacked the plan for giving control of the army to the central government. "Let my beloved Americans guard against that fatal lethargy that has pervaded the universe. Have we the means of resisting disciplined armies, when our only defence, the militia, is put into the hands of congress?"

Henry stressed the point, already advanced by the anti-Federalists, that the Philadelpia Convention had exceeded its powers, and he spoke further as might a statesman with a rightful claim to being a "sentinel of liberty."[38]

"When the American spirit was in its youth, the language of America was different: liberty, sir, was then the primary object. We are descended from a people whose government was founded on liberty: our glorious forefathers of Great Britain made liberty the foundation of everything. That country is become a great, mighty, and splendid nation; not because their government is strong and energetic, but, sir, because liberty is its direct end and foundation. We drew the spirit of liberty from our British ancestors; by that spirit we have triumphed over every difficulty. But now, sir, the American spirit, assisted by the ropes and chains of consolidation, is about to convert this country into a powerful and mighty empire. If you make the citizens of this country agree to become the subjects of one great consolidated empire of America, your government will not have sufficient energy to keep them together. Such a government is incompatible with the genius of republicanism. There will be no checks, no real balances, in this government. . . ."[39]

While Henry was in the midst of his long speech that Thursday, June 5, he recognized a familiar face in the audience. He hesitated a moment, then stooped down: evidently he was in dread of bad news.

"Dawson, I see my son in the hall; take him out," he whispered to a friend, an anti-Federalist, sitting near him. The son had been left to protect the family while Henry was at the Convention; he knew the young man would not come to Richmond unless to bring some important domestic news. But soon Dawson returned to tell Henry that Dolly had given birth to a son, and that both he and the mother were getting along well.[40] Henry's twelfth child and the sixth by Dorothea, he was named Alexander Spotswood for her great-grandfather, the Lieutenant Governor. He would live to marry a daughter of the influential Cabell family and enjoy a full life as a country gentleman, blessed with nine children.[41]

Later in his speech Henry expressed his dread of the effect of the Constitution on the middle and lower classes. Suppose Virginians wanted to alter their government, could the majority of them do so? "No; because they are connected with other men; or, in other words, consolidated with other states." The new Constitution gave the central government unlimited and unbounded power of taxation.[42] Doubtless with memories of his fight against the British Stamp Act, he declared that he would never give up the power of direct taxation except as a "scourge." Many historians would still agree that under the Confederation the system of requisitions on the states instead of direct taxes had often been a grievous failure. To many Americans it now seems axiomatic that the power of direct taxation, within reasonable limits, is essential to a strong central government. Yet Henry's position is more understandable when we read his following declaration that he was "a lover of the American union" and that if Virginia did not make punctual payment of the federal requisitions he would let Congress control Virginia trade until the last farthing, the last soldier, had been supplied. He added:

> "Nay, sir, there is another alternative to which I would consent; even that they should strike us out of the Union, and take away from us all federal privileges, till we comply with federal requisitions: but let it depend upon our own pleasure to pay our money in the most easy manner for our people. Were all the states, more terrible than the mother country, to join against us, I hope Virginia could defend herself; but, sir, the dissolution of the union is most abhorrent to my mind. The first thing I have at heart is American liberty; the second thing is American union; and I hope the people of Virginia will endeavor to preserve that Union." [43]

[358]

Moving toward the end of his lengthy speech, Henry expatiated on the dangers from both state and federal tax gatherers.[44] He declared that the Constitution "squints toward monarchy. . . . Does not this raise indignation in the breast of every true American? . . . Show me that age and country where the rights and liberties of the people were placed on the sole chance of their rulers being good men, without a consequent loss of liberty." [45] The history of Switzerland clearly proved that Virginia could be in amicable alliance with the states which had adopted the Constitution. A confederacy there had stood for upwards of four hundred years despite the immense difficulties confronting it.[46]

Henry questioned whether or not it was "proper to stand by awhile, and see the effect of" adoption of the Constitution in other states. They had "no reason to think from the antecedent conduct of Virginia that she has any intention of seceding from the union, or of being less active to support the general welfare. Would they not therefore acquiesce in our taking time to deliberate?" Deliberate whether the measure is perilous, not only for Virginia but for the adopting states.[47]

The great majority of the people even of the adopting states were averse to the new government. Henry believed that they had been "egregiously misled." Pennsylvania had perhaps been tricked into adoption. If the other states had not been tricked, they had been too much hurried in their action.

> There were very respectable minorities in several of them; and if reports be true, a clear majority of the people are averse to it. If we also accede, and it should prove grievous, the peace and prosperity of our country, which we all love, will be destroyed. This government has not the affection of the people at present. Should it be oppressive, their affection will be totally estranged from it; and, sir, you know that a government, without their affections, can neither be durable nor happy. I speak as one poor individual; but when I speak, I speak the language of thousands. But, sir, I mean not to breathe the spirit, nor utter the language, of secession.[48]

Henry's speech is said to have been one of the two or three during the Convention which changed votes[49] or, rather, the relatively few votes which could be changed. General Posey, a Revolutionary veteran present, and a strong Federalist, declared that Henry's eloquence was so overwhelming that Posey believed the Constitution would ruin our liberties as much as he believed in his own existence. Yet later reflection and the Federalists' arguments caused him to return to their ranks. Another intelligent onlooker, from an eastern county, declared that the vivid description Henry presented of a people enslaved by a federal executive in command of his armed forces was so moving that "he involuntarily felt his wrists to assure himself that the fetters were not already pressing his flesh, and that the gallery in which he sat seemed to become as dark as a dungeon."

Previously Henry had not been known as a lengthy speaker. None of his celebrated orations in the past could have taken much more than an hour; indeed, a Madison biographer describes him as an half-hour speaker.[50] But he had now held forth for a day without losing the attention of his audience. The Federalist leaders were worried about the effect of his speech and irritated by his long deviation from the set order of debate. When he finally sat down, Governor Randolph rose to say that if the Convention went on in this irregular manner, contrary to their resolution, instead of three or six weeks it would take six months to decide the question.

The Federalists did not want Henry to take the floor again the following morning, Friday, June 6, so they began to open up that day with their "big guns," first Randolph, then Madison and Nicholas. Randolph was indeed able to follow Henry without "a painful contrast of talents."[51] Much of what Randolph said was an amplification of previous Federalist arguments, and he seemed most impressive in his lengthy recital of the various delinquencies of the states in meeting the requisitions of the Confederation and the consequent difficulties.[52]

The large, vigorous Randolph was followed by the frail, little Madison. His "exordium," so Robertson wrote, was so low that he could not be distinctly heard.[53] During the Convention Madison always rose as if to express some casual thought. He kept his hat in his hand and his notes in his hat, and the "warmest excitement" of the debate was noticeable in him "only by a more or less rapid and forward seesaw motion of his body." [54] In one of the most close-reasoned speeches during the Convention, Madison now accented the Federalist point that the delegates ought not to address their arguments to "feelings and passions." He spoke from intensive study as well as his experience in the Philadelphia Convention. Alluding to Henry's statement that the Constitution ought to be rejected because it endangered the public liberty, Madison said that the dangers should be clearly pointed out; the delegates should not be satisfied with general assertions. On a candid examination of history they would find that turbulence, violence, and abuse of power by the majority trampling on the rights of the minority had produced factions and commotions, which in republics have more frequently than any other cause led to despotism.

Madison confessed that he had been unable to find Henry's usual consistency in his arguments on this occasion. If everything was in perfect tranquillity, as Henry asserted, why were deputies from all the states sent to the general Convention? Why had complaints of national and international distresses been echoed and re-echoed throughout the country? The power of raising and supporting armies was exclaimed against as dangerous and unnecessary. But ought it to be known to foreign nations that the general government of the United States of America had no power to raise and support an army, even in the utmost danger, when attacked by external enemies? [55] The delegates were flattered with the possibility of obtaining previous amendments. But if amendments were proposed by one state, other states had the same right, and these amendments could not but be dissimilar and opposite in their nature. This diversity of opinion would, without many reciprocal concessions, render a concurrence impossible.[56]

Nicholas, the next speaker, also raised the Federalist point that the debate was not proceeding in an orderly manner. This being so, he himself proceeded to answer various arguments by Henry and other anti-Federalists, especially with regard to the dangers from over-centralization in government. Nicholas made the telling comment that "as there can be no liberty without government, it must be as dangerous to make powers too limited as too great." [57] He was guilty of extremism, however, when he expressed his belief that "a great and decided majority of the people" were in favor of the Constitution.[58]

Francis Corbin, Randolph, and Madison next pierced the anti-Federalist armor in one of its most vulnerable spots. Has not the payment of the debts due by the United States been "shamefully withheld?" Corbin asked, "How long, sir, shall we be able, by fair promises to satisfy these creditors? How long can we amuse by idle words those who are amply possessed of the means of doing themselves justice? . . . Such a plan would destroy the richest country on earth." [59] Referring to the proposal to compel the delinquent states to pay requisitions to Congress, Corbin argued that this system which could be used under the Confederation led directly to civil war and destruction.[60] And he was buttressed by Randolph, who spoke of the credit of the Confederation as being "irretrievably gone," and of how "humiliated and disgraceful" it was to recur to loans.[61] Madison, too, lamented how "ruinous and disgraceful" it was to borrow money even to pay the interest on the Confederation debts.[62]

As a member of the House of Delegates the previous October, Henry could not forget Randolph's lengthy letter to the Speaker explaining his reason for failing to sign the Constitution. Federalist arguments in Richmond and elsewhere had had their influence on the Governor. From an opponent of the Constitution Randolph had become one of its leading proponents. Now in the forefront of the Federalist speakers, he proceeded on the following Saturday, June 7, to answer the objections against the powers of the national government to lay direct taxes. Randolph had no doubt as to his position. Were he "to rise from the dead to declare the expediency" of these powers, he could not be more firmly persuaded of their propriety.[63] He would not have restrained Congress in this case unless "he meant to destroy the government." [64]

To Henry, Randolph was not merely a turncoat but blatantly self-righteous in taking a prominent position in support of a cause which he had once so notably opposed. "That system which was once execrated by the honorable member must now be adopted, let its defects be ever so glaring," Henry acidly commented.[65] It was not surprising that the sensitive Randolph disdained Henry's "aspersions." They were "warranted by no principle of parliamentary decency, nor compatible with the least shadow of friendship," Randolph exclaimed, adding melodramatically that if this "friendship must fall, *let it fall like Lucifer, never to rise again!*" [66]

There was a further explanation of his changed position from Randolph, and an apology from Henry for any unintentional offense to "the honorable gentleman." But Randolph said that if it had not been for the "concession" he would have disclosed certain facts that "would have made some men's hair stand on end." Henry told Randolph that if he had anything to say against him he should do so, and Randolph, after failing to carry out the threat, read part of a letter to his constituents in which he expressed sentiments friendly to union with the other states. Still unappeased, he tauntingly threw the letter on the clerk's table, declaring that it might lie there "for the inspection of the curious and malicious."

However irritating, Randolph's earlier aspersion might have been overlooked by Henry. But the reference to "the curious and malicious" seems needlessly provocative. The code duello had not yet reached its full flower in the South, and, considering the strong political issues which he had supported, Henry's life had been remarkably free of private quarrels. Now, however, he felt that his honor was involved. That night he and his representative, Colonel William Cabell, called on Randolph. While awaiting the result of their conference, the delegates of both parties were disturbed for fear of a duel between two men so respected and of such eminent position as Henry and Governor Randolph. There was a great feeling of relief when it became known that the dispute had been amicably settled. "Mr. Henry acted with great firmness and propriety," Spencer Roane heard Cabell say. Mr. Henry "let Mr. Randolph down, however, pretty easily, owing to the extreme benignity of his disposition." [67]

In a lengthy speech soon afterward, Henry bore down on the theme that Congress, by its powers of taxation, of raising an army, and of regulating the militia, would have control of both the purse and the sword. As the debate gradually extended to the various legislative, executive, and judicial provisions of the Constitution, his arguments seem at times more distinguished for their "ingenuity" [68] and emotional appeal than for their solid reasoning. This is particularly true in comparison with the speeches of such Federalist champions as Madison and Pendleton. But as the debates proceeded, Henry's forceful phrases had a cumulative result. He became more effective, especially when he emphasized a few strong points.

"Patrick Henry gave such reasons for hating the Constitution as were hiccoughed out in the taverns," the historian McMaster asserted.[69] But this was not the judgment of a discriminating Federalist opponent, John Marshall, who heard Henry on the Convention floor. William Wirt's biography did not do full justice to Henry, in Marshall's opinion. Asked what he thought of the biography, Marshall, then Chief Justice, said that the popular idea of Henry derived from Wirt's book was that of a great orator, but Henry was "that and much more, a learned lawyer, a most accurate thinker, and a profound reasoner. . . . If I were called upon to say who of all the men I have known had the greatest power to convince, I should perhaps say Mr. Madison, while Mr. Henry had without doubt the greatest power to persuade." [70]

June 13, so rumor had it, would be a critical day of the Convention. The people began to assemble in the New Academy at an early hour. Reminiscent of Henry's "Give Me Liberty" speech at nearby St. John's, the spectators soon filled the available seats and "an eager crowd" overflowed into the windows and approaches to the hall. When the bell struck ten, every delegate was in his place; the chaplain, the Reverend Abner Waugh, read the collect of the day with "unusual solemnity." [71]

Word was passed that at this Friday meeting the Mississippi issue would be the leading topic for debate. The vital question of free navigation of the great river appealed to the "passions" of both rich and poor, and in no state more than Virginia. The anti-Federalists, led by the audacious Henry, or so it was rumored, might use the Mississippi question as a wedge to seek an immediate vote unfavorable to ratification of the Constitution.

The previous Monday morning, June 9, Henry and Mason had been observed as they arrived at the New Academy arm in arm after walking together from the Swan. There was a rumor then that they had planned some new strategy over the week end. Taking the floor, Henry had, indeed, broached the Mississippi issue. The seven Northern states were determined to relinquish the right to navigation of the river, he said. Was he mistaken in his opinion that federal measures would lose it to America forever? "If a bare majority of Congress can make laws, the situation of our western states is dreadful." Pursuing the subject further on June 12, he followed a line of argument which became a central theme throughout his speeches:

> We are told that, in order to secure the navigation of that river, it was necessary to give it up for twenty-five years to the Spaniards, and that thereafter we should enjoy it forever, without interruption from them. This argument resembles that which recommends adopting first and then amending.[72]

As a veteran in the struggle for human liberty, and as a trial lawyer, Henry had seen the worst features of human nature. The depraved nature of man was "well known" and he had "a natural bias toward his own interest," Henry said. He could not believe that, "after clearing the river, strengthening themselves, and increasing the means of retaining it, the Spaniards will tamely surrender it." [73]

Thousands of frontiersmen, then pouring into what became the large states of Tennessee and Kentucky, deemed navigation of the Mississippi essential to their welfare. It was far too expensive and time consuming for them to send their commercial products back over the mountains. What if Spain could present a strong claim to much of the territory along the riverbanks? The aggressive westerners were not willing to recognize this claim; indeed, some believed that they should have free navigation of the river as a natural right. With his strong Kentucky ties, Henry was particularly sensitive to such opinions, and his arguments on the Mississippi question struck a responsive chord. In reply, the Federalists offered arguments to prove that the river could best be defended under a stronger national government. On the excitedly anticipated thirteenth, despite the Federalist effort to divert the debate, Henry called on the delegates who had been in Congress to communicate to the Convention what they knew about the subject, and two of them, William Grayson and James Monroe, bolstered Henry's position.[74]

The outlook for the Federalists was "less favorable" than on June 8, Madison wrote Washington on the thirteenth. "The business is in the most ticklish state that can be imagined." Madison thought "the majority will certainly be very small," and he dared not encourage much expectation that it would be favorable to the Federalists. A week later he still believed that the majority on either side would be precarious, though he indulged in the belief that the friends of the Constitution had the advantage.[75] He had considered the Mississippi a principal subject for private discussion and public debate and had reason to believe that events might depend on the Kentucky delegates, who seemed to lean against the Constitution.

Stroke and counterstroke, and continuing now into the third week. With their grim sincerity, their perfervid belief that the fruits of the Revolution, the future course of America, were tied up with the ratification issue, the opposing delegates could not be expected always to weigh their words. In extravagant language, the alarmed anti-Federalists were the most conspicuous offenders: Henry, who had never attacked with a feather duster, declared on June 18 that the treaty-making power, "ill guarded" as it was, extended farther than in any other country in the world.[76] Mason gloomily predicted that the Vice-President would be "not only an unnecessary but dangerous officer." [77] On the other hand, Nicholas had asserted that "a great and decided majority of the people" were in favor of the Constitution,[78] while even the factual-minded Madison had optimistically declared that the 160 members of the Virginia House of Delegates, drawn from the people at large, "must ever" possess more influence than the few men who would likely be elected to Congress.[79]

Henry's fears, waved aside by the Federalist debaters, that the national government would become far more centralized, have long since been confirmed. It has long been conceded that our government needs to be strong enough to administer efficiently the great population and territory of the United States and to cope with her domestic and foreign enemies. But precisely how strong this central authority should be, to exert such powers at a given time and place without unduly restricting the states and individual citizens, remains moot. Henry believed that a government with the powers granted or implied under the American Constitution must be limited by definite written guarantees. The subject will require more analysis after we shall have recounted the chief events connected with the adoption of the American Bill of Rights.

23

The Battle for Amendments

In a Democracy, the opposition is not only tolerated as constitutional, but must be maintained because it is indispensable.
————WALTER LIPPMAN

Envy and detraction is a tax which every man of merit pays for being eminent and conspicuous.————JOSEPH ADDISON

June 25, 1788. Virginia Convention ratifies federal constitution, 89 to 79.

July, 1788–1791. Henry a leading advocate of constitutional amendments.

December, 1788–March, 1789. Decius' vitriolic newspaper attacks on Henry.

April, 1789–March, 1797. George Washington first president under the new government.

November, 1791. Henry ends long career in Virginia legislature.

December, 1791. Final ratification by the states of first ten amendments to the Constitution (the federal Bill of Rights); Henry becoming more reconciled to the Constitution.

ALLOWING FOR some *ad personam* argument, some exaggeration and more digression, especially during the first two weeks, the debates had been conducted on a high level. The time allotted for them was drawing to a close. Four factors may be listed as tipping the scales in favor of the anxious Federalists, three relating to the highly placed Edmund Randolph. The first two were his defection from the anti-Federalist ranks and his powerful speeches for the Constitution; the third was his delayed transmission of an important letter from a New York Federalist leader, Governor Clinton. The last was a change in strategy by which the Federalists proposed a series of post-amendments to the Constitution.

In accordance with Henry's legislative resolution the previous fall, Governor Randolph had written letters calling upon the other states to join with Virginia in proposing amendments to the Constitution. New York State was a center of anti-Federalist sentiment, and Henry could hope that her reply would be helpful to his party. Governor Clinton did express the sympathy of the New Yorkers with the Virginia anti-Federalists. He was persuaded that the New York Convention, which would meet on June 17, would hold—with "great cordiality"—communication with any sister state on "the important subject," particularly a state with Virginia's standing. Since the Virginia Convention would take place before that of New York, Clinton presumed that it would initiate "the measures for holding such communication as shall be deemed necessary."[1]

Although delayed for various reasons, Clinton's letter did reach Virginia in ample time for transmission to the state Convention. But Randolph was now a Federalist, and the letter might persuade some Virginia delegates, whose votes his party needed, to favor a delayed decision on ratification until after action of the New York Convention. Whatever his motives, Randolph did not hasten consideration of the letter. Was it a public or private communication? he asked the Council; and he received the rather obvious opinion that it was the former. He therefore sent the letter to the legislature, which was not scheduled to meet until the twenty-third. Before action was taken on it, the Convention had adjourned.[2]

On Monday, June 23, the Convention was moving to its climax—the final vote within the next few days. The shorthand reporter was absent on the twenty-third and the printer endeavored, with the assistance of his notes, to give as full and impartial account of the proceedings "as was practical."[3] During the lively interchange among

[369]

the tense debaters, George Nicholas made an insinuation against Henry's personal character but did not offer proof, as Henry demanded.[4] Scarcely four or five votes separated the fiercely contending parties.[5] To compensate for the dangerous margin, the Federalists expressed their willingness to support suitable amendments after the adoption of the Constitution. They would satisfy some of those who did not "think it prudent to mount a high-blooded, fiery steed without a bridle." On Tuesday, the twenty-fourth, George Wythe rose to offer a momentous motion. It was that the Convention ratify the Constitution and recommend such amendments as were deemed necessary for consideration of the first Congress under the new government. Wythe, who appears to have been quite agitated, spoke so "very low" that his words could not be fully understood.[6] But he argued cogently that the critical situation of America, the extreme danger of dissolving the union, rendered it necessary to ratify the Constitution and then add such amendments as seemed advisable.[7] His words had considerable impact, coming as they did from a revered elder statesman who was acting chairman of the Convention when Pendleton took the floor.

Replying, Henry said that if he understood Wythe rightly, the Speaker admitted the new system was defective. "For immediately after the proposed ratification there comes a declaration" that the Constitution was "not intended to violate any of these three great rights—the liberty of religion, liberty of the press, and the trial by jury." Yet the rights not enumerated were relinquished, and Henry listed a number of other valuable ones which were omitted.[8]

Henry, who had been anticipated by Wythe, offered a resolution containing a declaration of rights, and certain amendments to the most objectionable parts of the Constitution. Designed particularly to prevent any usurpation of power by the central government, the declaration and other amendments were to be given to the states for their consideration prior to the ratification of the Constitution. Judging from their context and other evidence, Henry had probably been in consultation again with his fellow guest at the Swan, George Mason. The declaration, or bill of rights, with its twenty proposed divisions, was essentially an elaboration of Mason's bill of rights of

1776. It spoke of certain natural rights of which men cannot be divested under the social contract, and it provided for such specific rights as freedom of speech, assembly, and religion; for no excessive bail or cruel and unusual punishment; and for keeping the jury system "sacred and inviolable." [9] The twenty amendments likewise spelled out the fears of men who had fought for human freedom. Some of the amendments, however, dealt with subjects that could be handled by ordinary legislation, while others which restricted the term of office for the President and the length of military enlistment are of more present interest and importance. One to which Madison particularly objected limited the power of Congress to collect direct taxes or excises until the individual states had been given the opportunity to provide their quota of the amount due.[10] Madison correctly perceived that the provision could curtail authority needed for a forceful central government.

The final debate and vote was on Wednesday, June 25. The attendance at this meeting was "remarkably full," with only two members absent; Madison thought that the Federalists would win by a "bare majority." During the discussion on the now paramount issue of amendments before or after Virginia ratified the Constitution, Henry emphasized his argument that the prior ones could be secured as easily as the latter.[11] Evidently, Henry feared that his party would lose in the forthcoming vote, for he said that if he were in the minority he would have "those painful sensations which arise from conviction of being overpowered in a good cause." He had already taken the occasion to generously praise a preceding opponent, James Innes, as "endowed with great eloquence—eloquence splendid, magnificent, and sufficient to shake the human mind." [12] Whatever the outcome of the vote, Henry assured the delegates that he would be a "peaceable citizen," and that his head, hand, and heart would "be at liberty to retrieve the loss of liberty and remove the defects of that system in a constitutional way." [13]

The debates were continued until both sides were ready for the decision. A motion was offered to refer the declaration of rights, together with the proposed amendments to "the most exceptional parts" of the Constitution, to the other states. On a roll call proposed by Henry and seconded by Theodorick Bland, his amendment was found to have been defeated 88 to 80. Then a motion for ratification of the Constitution was passed 89 to 79. That same day a committee was appointed to report such amendments to the Convention as the committee deemed necessary. This committee, comprising such leading members as Wythe, chairman, Henry, Randolph, Mason, and Madison, reported on June 27. There had been little time for literary composition, and the declaration of rights and other amendments proposed were almost the same as those which Henry had offered.

Even with the assurance that the Federalists would support subsequent amendments, the ratification had been won by only the "bare majority." Just how much some members still feared governmental concentration was indicated by a later action. A motion to delete the third amendment limiting the powers of Congress to lay direct taxes or excises was defeated by 85 to 65. Edmund Pendleton and Paul Carrington voted with Patrick Henry and George Mason among the majority.[14]

Henry appears to have been more resigned to the decision than George Mason and some of their supporters. But before the vote on ratification, Henry had said that he would wait in hopes that "the spirit which predominated in the revolution was not yet gone."[15] To the battle for a federal bill of rights and concomitant amendments, he would devote himself during no small part of his remaining political career.

"There is no rejoicing on Acct. of the vote of ratification—it would not be prudent to do so . . . the Federalists behave with moderation and do not exult in their Success,"[16] Spencer Roane wrote Philip Aylett from Richmond the day after the vote on ratification.

There were celebrations in various states, but in Virginia, where public sentiment was so bitterly divided, the Federalists usually avoided rubbing salt into the wounds. The *Virginia Independent Chronicle*[17] did publish an account of the festivities in Staunton on July 4, 1788, after receipt of the "pleasing information" that both Virginia and New Hampshire had adopted the Constitution. There were toasts and a bonfire, the newspaper reported; also firing of volleys by Captain Gibson's company "in uniform" and those of Captains Perry and Douthat, no uniforms mentioned; all concluded with a ball at Mrs. Burns'. Yet in the Old Dominion such public celebrations were usually conspicuous by their absence. Fearful of Henry's influence, Madison gloomily predicted on June 27 that Henry's plan would be "to engage two-thirds of the [state] Legislatures to the task of undoing the work" of ratification or to secure a Congress that would "commit suicide on their own Authority." [18] Also, he and Mason were reported as having attempted to get the anti-Federalists in the Convention to sign an address to the people. [19]

New Hampshire had ratified the Constitution on June 21, thus providing the ninth state needed for the inauguration of the new government. She was soon followed by Virginia, as noted, and a month later by New York. But the New York Convention had approved the Constitution reluctantly, by a majority of only three votes, and with a recommendation for amendments, some much like those from Virginia. [20] President George Clinton of the New York Convention was commissioned by that body to send a circular letter to all the states calling for a convention to propose the amendments necessary to allay popular "apprehensions and discontents." [21]

When advancing their cause the anti-Federalists were not overscrupulous. Yet the Federalists would hardly have secured the ratification without the aid of discriminatory suffrage and skillful politicking and propagandizing. Even so, the conventions in Massachusetts, New Hampshire, Virginia, and New York had all recommended specific amendments to the Constitution, while South Carolina had ratified it with certain written reservations. Finally, North Carolina and Rhode Island had as yet failed to ratify at all.

The time was ripe to oppose the new government, and before Henry returned home from Richmond he had to give definite proof that he would indeed do so "in a constitutional way." After the final vote of the Convention, two former Revolutionary officers, Henry's friend William Cabell, and "General" Meade, assembled "the discontents" in the old Senate chamber. The meeting was partly organized, then a deputation was sent inviting Henry to take the chair. Henry acceded to the request. But understanding that the purpose of

[373]

the meeting was to formulate a plan of resistance to the federal government, he addressed the men with his "accustomed animation" on important occasions. He "had done his duty strenuously in opposing the constitution in the proper place," Henry said. "The question had been fully discussed, and settled," and as true Republicans the members of the audience had better go home and give the Constitution fair play. He reproved the "half suppressed factious spirit," and his hearers followed his advice.[22]

At the Virginia Convention the anti-Federalists had eloquently pointed out to the electorate the purported weaknesses of the Constitution. During the following months the anticonstitutional opinion seemed as strong as before the Convention. As late as December, 1788, George Mason referred privately to Edmund Randolph as "the young [Benedict] A——ld."[23] The lingering bitterness was particularly evident in the fall, when a volume of the proceedings of the Convention was published. Some of the Federalists had supervised the correction of their speeches, but Mason stated flatly that the reporter was a Federal "partizan"; he knew some of the anti-Federalist leaders had been privately applied to by the shorthand writer to correct their speeches but had "treated the proposal with contempt."[24] Considering the general reaction to the Constitution in the state, it was not surprising to find the people supporting an anti-Federalist Assembly, with Henry in the driver's seat.

The special June, 1788, session of the legislature had overlapped the Convention for several days. The Assembly was late securing a quorum and never accomplished a great deal. Among its minor activities, Henry had a special interest in the election of the respected Edmund Winston as an appellate judge. He could hardly have imagined Cousin Edmund succeeding him in the role of Dolly's husband!

Returning home in early July, Henry found the outlook good for corn and tobacco. But he had not yet put his lands (with the unprofitable slaves) on a satisfactory paying basis. Management of the new plantation, along with the renewal of his law practice, consumed the major portion of his time until the fall Assembly.[25] He secured some needed cash on October 17 by the sale of his 214-acre tract of land in Henrico County for £700. Shrewd trader as usual, he made a profit of £220½ on the land purchased less than three years earlier.[26] Altogether, this was a prosaic, workaday period, and it would be a mistake, as in some other phases of his remote rural life, to read into it a great deal of feverish political activity. There were several public events, however, from which he could take encouragement, and the fall Assembly would offer his party a prime opportunity.

Besides calling for a bill of rights and other amendments very much like those proposed in Virginia, North Carolina on August 2 rejected the Constitution by about a hundred votes. On the twenty-third Madison wrote Jefferson from New York that the "bold step" was to be ascribed partly to "the influence of the minority in Virginia which lies mostly in the Southern part of the State and to the management of its leader." [27] There was evidence indicating that Henry was in touch with public opinion in North Carolina, and especially in view of his residence in the adjoining Virginia area he doubtless continued to have considerable direct or indirect influence on the Tarheel State.

Meantime, Madison had more cause for worry about Henry's anti-Federalist leadership after the distribution of the New York circular letter calling for amendments to the Constitution. "The great danger in the present crisis is that if another Convention should be soon assembled, it would terminate in discord, or in alterations of the federal system, which would throw back *essential* powers into the State Legislatures." [28]

The Assembly was to meet in regular session on October 20, 1788, and the Federalists had strong reason for fearing that its membership would be as firmly anticonstitutional as when it was elected. Indeed, George Washington was reported as "fully persuaded" that anti-Federalism would be the legislature's "actuating principle . . . great circumspection is necessary to prevent very mischievous efforts from a cooperation in the insidious proposition of New York" (regarding another constitutional convention). Washington was "particularly alarmed" at the prospect of an anti-Federalist majority in the United States Senate. There was a report in Northern Virginia that Patrick Henry and Richard Henry Lee would be pushed as senatorial candidates, and the General was said to be "apprehensive" that the "conjecture" would prove true. Washington had already expressed his fear of the part that the anti-Federalists would play in shipwrecking the state "in sight of the port." But to exclude Henry from the Senate "would be impossible," and Lee, supported by Henry's influence, would be elected unless a Federalist very well established in the confidence of the people could be opposed. Washington favored Madison as his candidate.[29]

That autumn of 1788 was described as "the most uncommon ever known" in Richmond. "Like an Indian summer," it provided a salubrious background for Henry's entrance upon his heavy duties in the Assembly. A member of four standing committees, he was encompassed with routine duties but managed to adhere to his anticonstitutional objective. Certainly, he did not want the persistent Madison to be a stumbling block. It was doubtless more than benevolence which made him help to get Madison out of the Assembly by securing his election to the old Congress sitting in New York.[30] On October 29 Henry is even said to have declared that he would "oppose every measure tending to the organization of the Government, unless accompanied" by others for amendment of the new Constitution. He favored a general convention for this purpose "as soon as practicable." [31] And among other steps, he pushed his own candidates for the United States Senate.

Henry offered resolutions, duly passed, to appoint a committee to prepare a proper application for amendments to Congress, a reply to Governor Clinton's letter as president of the New York Convention, and a circular letter to the other states. In reply, the Federalists offered a milder substitute motion under which Congress would be urged to recommend to the various states that they ratify a bill of rights and certain other amendments proposed by the Virginia Convention.[32] The Federalists' maneuver to prevent another constitutional convention failed, however, by the overwhelming majority of 39 to 85. Henry's resolution in this respect was then carried without division.[33] The letter to Congress, written by him as authorized, is a convincing expression, at some length, of his best literary style. The objections to the Constitution as stated in the Convention and the present legislative resolutions "were not founded in speculative theory, but deduced from principles . . . established by the melancholy example of other nations, in different ages." The sooner the public apprehensions about the government were quieted, "the more salutary will be its operations, and the longer its duration."

"The cause of amendments" the Assembly considered "a common cause" which would "ill admit of delay." And in view of the "slow forms" of congressional action, Henry recommended that Congress immediately call a convention of deputies "from the several states, with full power to take into their consideration the defects of this constitution that have been suggested by the state conventions, and report such amendments thereto, as they shall find best suited to promote our common interests, and secure to ourselves and our latest posterity, the great and unalienable rights of mankind." [34]

That the anti-Federalists under Henry's leadership were then riding high is further shown by an incident—comic, yet with a serious implication—that occurred during the debate on the resolutions. With the opposing leaders so dedicated to the constitutional issue, there had not been much relieving humor during either the June Convention or the October Assembly. But during the debate on the question of calling a constitutional convention, Henry was provoked into offering such byplay, though of the devastating type. It is not altogether surprising that the target for his deadly ridicule was that polished scion of the eastern aristocracy, Francis Corbin. Having had the temerity to debate against Henry in the Convention, young Corbin now essayed another and more dangerous venture. Henry had argued that the speedy adoption of amendments was the only measure which would reconcile the people to the new Constitution. Whatever the individual sentiments of the legislators, they were bound to conform to the popular will. He himself was ready and willing at all times and on all occasions "to bow, with the utmost deference, to the majesty of the people." [35]

It was this last remark which proved too tempting for the cocky

Corbin and led to the passage of arms. Considering the bitter memories of the late war, Henry had been remarkably generous to his Tory
opponents. But never before had one made a studied—and protracted
—effort to ridicule him on the floor of the House. And the attempt
was no less provocative when coming from a man many years Henry's
junior. Shades of Corbin's father, Colonel Richard Corbin, from
whom Henry had forcibly secured restitution for the captured gunpowder! He could hardly have known that a royal commission was
issued Colonel Corbin in 1775 to succeed Lord Dunmore as Lieutenant Governor. But Corbin's son, Francis, represented the apothe-
osis of what Henry had opposed in the long war. No veteran of
Brandywine or Guilford, or of the harassed wartime Assemblies,
Corbin had spent the whole period of the Revolution in England,
where he received the genteel education denied so many colonials
during the war years.

Seizing upon Henry's expression "bow to the majesty of the
people," Corbin set out to beard the lion in his den. In a pleasing
tone, with "easy, sprightly elocution," he denied Henry's argument
with regard to the popular interest in amendments and asserted that
in the Preamble to the Consitution the people had a sufficient guarantee of their rights. And yet, Corbin continued, Henry said that he
bowed "to the majesty of the people." Corbin then proceeded with a
series of arguments to prove that Henry was actually opposing the
will of the people. In each case Corbin employed the same sarcastic
ending, followed by a "profound and graceful bow," thirteen times
in all, according to an eyewitness.

"It was of little importance whether a country was ruled by a
despot with a tiara on his head, or by a demagogue in a red cloak, a
caul-bare wig, . . . although he *should profess on all occasions to* bow
to the *majesty of the people,*" Corbin exclaimed.[36]

To Henry's friends the attack on a statesman of his age and character was "very little short of sacrilege"; to his opponents it brought
a "smothered sort of dubious laugh" which seemed to contain "as
much apprehension as enjoyment." Confident that he had won a
legislative triumph, Corbin complacently went on to the end of his
speech.

Henry raised himself "heavily" and with an "affected awkwardness" from his seat. "I am a plain man," he declared, "and have been educated altogether in Virginia. My whole life has been spent among planters, and other plain men of similar education, who never had the advantage of that polish which a court alone can give." Indeed, Corbin's "employments and mine (in common with the great mass of his countrymen) have been as widely different as our fortunes." Henry then continued with a still more pointed comparison:

> "While that gentleman was availing himself of the opportunity, which a splendid fortune afforded him, of acquiring a foreign education, mixing among the great, attending levees and courts, *basking in the beams of royal favor at St. James'*, and exchanging courtesies with crown heads [here he imitated Mr. Corbin's bows at court, making one elegant, but most obsequious and sycophantick bow], I was engaged in the arduous toils of the revolution; and was probably as far from thinking of acquiring those polite accomplishments, which the gentleman has so successfully cultivated, as that gentleman *then* was from sharing in the toils and dangers in which his *unpolished countrymen* were engaged. I will not therefore presume to vie with the gentleman in those courtly accomplishments, of which he has just given the house so agreeable a specimen; yet such a bow as I can make, shall ever be at the service of the people." [37]

Henry, who could make a very graceful bow, now made one so awkward and ludicrous as to take the members by surprise and to set off a roar of laughter.

> "The gentleman, I hope, will commiserate the disadvantages of education under which I have labored, and will be pleased to remember that I have never been a favorite with that monarch, whose gracious smile he has had the happiness to enjoy." [38]

He pursued this contrasting theme for fifteen or twenty minutes, "without a smile, and without the smallest token of resentment, either in countenance, expression, or manner. . . .

> "You would almost have sworn" [a correspondent wrote Wirt], "that he thought himself making his apology for his own awkwardness, before a full drawing-room at St. James'. I believe there was not a person that heard him, the sufferer himself excepted, who did not feel every risible nerve affected."

[379]

Corbin meantime hung his head and, "sinking lower and lower" in his seat, submitted quietly to the "discipline." [39] Never again was he known to have crossed swords with Henry.

After the passage of Henry's resolutions, the next step was to secure legislators who would act favorably upon them. Certainly the Henry party did not want a Federalist to have either of Virginia's two seats in the Senate, and as expected they frowned upon the candidacy of James Madison. Not only had Madison been one of their most formidable opponents, but they believed that his present advocacy of some constitutional amendments was influenced by his senatorial ambitions. Madison later spoke of his name being brought forward by his supporters for the post, although he "had not allotted [his] pretensions." [40] In any event, he became the only serious Federalist aspirant for the Senate seat, and, whatever the arguments of his friends in the Assembly, he should not have been surprised at the formidable opposition.

Perhaps it was too strong to say that Henry was "omnipotent" in the Assembly, as Madison later bitterly asserted, but there was no doubt that he was the directing force. Two weeks before the election, George Washington reported that Henry himself was talked about for the Senate seat. And while he refused to let his name be offered, he did keep a strong hand on the helm. When the House and Senate met together on October 8 to elect the two Senators, Richard Henry Lee, William Grayson, and James Madison were the principal candidates, and, not unexpectedly, Henry opened up with his oratorical guns. Besides using "the expedients common in such occasions," so Madison wrote, Henry delivered a "public philippic against my federal principles." [41]

From another Federalist account we learn that Henry admitted Madison's "talents and integrity," but only after expatiating in favor of Lee and Grayson. It was unreasonable, Henry argued, to elect a Senator whose Federalist policies were so adverse to the opinions of many members. Madison received support from some zealous friends, but one acknowledged it was doubtful that Madison would obey instructions to vote against direct taxation.

"Thus, gentlemen," Henry replied, "the secret is out, it is doubted whether Mr. Madison will obey his instructions." [42]

"The friends of the system are much displeased that Mr. Madison was left out of the choice. They urged his election most warmly, claiming as a sort of right the admission of one Federal member," Henry wrote Lee on November 15. But Henry said the efforts of Virginia to secure amendments would have been expected to be of "no purpose . . . if one of her senators had been found adverse to that scheme. The universal cry is for amendments, & the Federals are obliged to join in it; but whether to amuse, or to conceal other views seems dubious." [43]

When the senatorial ballots were opened it was found that the veteran Richard Henry Lee had received 98 votes, Grayson 86, and Madison 77. The remaining votes were described as "cast away," with Henry receiving 26. There is strong reason to believe that he would have been elected if he had allowed his name to be placed on the ballot. But there was one compelling reason for not doing so, he explained to Lee: while he was glad to learn that Lee's health and spirits were "enough to decline no exertion," Henry did not believe his own health was equal to "distant" political operations. He did not intend to take part in political deliberations outside Virginia, unless in North Carolina. Living not very far from that state, he wished to be "attentive" to her politics. If Congress did not pass "substantial amendments" he would turn his eyes to North Carolina, with which he might find it necessary to form a connection. Meantime, he was happy with the unanimity which then prevailed in the section of Virginia where he lived. In nearly twenty adjoining counties, he thought at least nineteen-twentieths of the people were anti-Federal, and "this great extent of country" adjoined North Carolina, forming with her "a great mass of opposition not easy to surmount." [44]

This opposition, Henry added, it was "the wish of [his] soul to see wise, firm, temperate." But he believed it would scarcely maintain the latter position longer than Congress would "hold out the hope of forwarding amendments." Henry was convinced that the American union depended "on the success of amendments. God grant I may never see the day when it shall be the duty of whiggish Americans to seek for shelter under any other government than that of the United States." [45]

Besides Lee, Henry also corresponded with William Grayson, the other Virginia Senator-elect. His letters to these anti-Federalist chieftains undoubtedly influenced their policy. Described as "the handsomest man in the convention," the accomplished Grayson had been a gallant Revolutionary colonel and member of the legislature after the war. A "devoted servant" of Henry, he had joined heartily in his anti-Federalist plans. When on November 9 Henry was reported as "putting in agitation" the name of Governor Clinton as Vice-President, Grayson was "warm in such an election." [46]

Under Henry's dominating influence the Assembly passed resolutions providing for the division of Virginia into twelve districts for balloting on presidential electors and ten districts for the election of Congress. A committee of fifteen, including seven Federalists, was appointed to redistrict the state. A bitter controversy arose over the effort to apportion Madison's home district so as to prevent his election to Congress. To Orange County, where Madison lived, the Federalists wished to add certain counties favorable to him, but the anti-Federalist majority on the committee added to Orange counties which they strongly hoped would prevent his election. There were charges, long repeated, that Henry had been responsible for the unfair arrangement of the district. "Gerrymandering was really the invention of Patrick Henry," one Madison biographer asserted. [47] But Henry was not a member of the redistricting committee which endeavored to eliminate Madison, and the charges have to rest chiefly on Henry's general influence in the Assembly.

As we shall see, Madison, after strenuous efforts, would be elected to Congress from the new district. And a switch of five votes could have elected him to the Senate. One Federalist delegate "religiously believed" that if the balloting could have been delayed one day Madison "would have been elected." [48] But Henry remained the most influential statesman in Virginia, and when the Federalists gained strength there, in late 1788 and 1789, it was largely through their conciliatory tactics. An important event in this trend was that Henry, when back in Prince Edward, was cut off from the main battle scene, but there were a number of other factors. These we should note while remembering that Henry himself retained most of his popularity with the Virginia masses.

In striking contrast to the late Richmond Convention, Henry had been aided in his legislative program by the lack of outstanding Federalist leaders in the Assembly. The situation became more pathetic —or ludicrous—after Corbin's crushing failure. None of Henry's strongest opponents in the Convention—Madison, Randolph, Nicholas, and Pendleton—were in the Assembly, while Henry had been bolstered by Benjamin Harrison, Grayson, and Monroe, with other members of a large working majority. When the situation was becoming critical for the Federalists, their strength was augmented by a powerful new recruit, Edmund Randolph. In a letter to Madison on October 12, 1788, Randolph told him he would become a member of the House two days later. "I could not get in sooner, as a vacancy could not be sooner created than today," Randolph wrote, and he spoke of some efforts, "not a little strenuous," which he would make there.[49] Within a few days his name was added to several committees and he became a very active member of the House.[50] Not until December 3 was Beverley Randolph elected Governor in Edmund's place, the state meantime having had no chief executive.[51]

Despite Edmund Randolph's obvious influence, Henry could feel that he had been highly successful with his legislative program. He believed that he had earned a surcease from his labors, and he had pressing personal obligations in Prince Edward. In a letter to his daughter Betsey from Richmond on November 11, he spoke of how much he wanted to see her, but his horses had been sent home and even if they had not he did not have a moment to spare. His sister, the widowed Mrs. Christian, had come from Kentucky in poor health and was waiting to see him, he expected, with great impatience. His own "dear little Family," as he called it with some understatement, was also waiting; and there were all the commitments of his large plantation and renewed law practice. On November 19 he obtained a leave of absence from the House and did not return during the remainder of the session.[52]

The receding of the anti-Federalist tide, perceptible before Henry left the Assembly, became more evident during the winter. "There is a general calm in politicks," Edmund Randolph wrote Madison from Williamsburg on March 27, 1789. Even the "discontented" seemed "willing to wait with temper" until Congress should "open their views." "With much pleasure" Randolph had read a letter by Madison showing an appreciation of the need for constitutional amendments and "a disposition" to procure them. Although Randolph was convinced nothing would "soften the rancour of some men," he believed that "moderate and conciliatory conduct" by the federal rulers would "detach from their virulence" those who had been opposed to them on principle.[53] Certainly, most Virginia Federalists were still careful not to crow over their victory in the Convention.

Moreover, the state Federalists had benefited from events in connection with the inauguration of the new government. By a consensus of the American people, George Washington's name was brought forward for the presidency. When elected, he had to face "the agonizing question" as to whether he was duty bound to accept the demanding position. Ever the country gentleman, Washington preferred the peace and quiet of Mount Vernon, even though he did find that mansion like "a well resorted tavern," where scarcely a passing stranger did not stop over for a day or two. However, making what he called "the sacrifice of my fondest wishes, so far as to enter again upon the stage of Public Life," Washington was on April 30, 1789, inaugurated at New York as the first American president.[54]

Meantime, Henry's name had bobbed up several times in the presidential and vice-presidential campaign. Much to the disgust of a Federalist newspaper, the *North Carolina State Gazette* of January 15, 1789, he was mentioned as a presidential candidate. A Philadelphia dispatch of December 13, 1788, to the *State Gazette* asserted that the anti-Federal parties of Pennsylvania, New York, and elsewhere had secretly combined to oppose the election of Washington as

President and "to fill it with a man better calculated to stir their purposes."

> Every whig in America will execrate the men who would pluck the laurels of our illustrious Fabius from his brow, to adorn that of a man, whose violent opposition to the federal constitution is his only recommendation. The person pitched upon is PATRICK HENRY.

"Oh ye Gods, what a worthy competitor with a WASHINGTON!" the dispatch sarcastically commented. And it spoke of the same people as having agreed to run Governor Clinton of New York for Vice-President, "instead of a Hancock or an Adams, who have been nominated by the friends of the constitution." [55]

Despite this story, there is no proof that Henry was ever approached on the subject of the presidential nomination. He was, however, chosen as presidential elector from Virginia and helped to swell the unanimous vote for Washington. John Adams, a New Englander, with Washington's approval received a majority of the ballots for Vice-President, but Henry cast his vote for George Clinton.[56]

During the Convention William Grayson had hinted at the influence of a great name in favor of the Constitution. Without Washington's strong though often indirect support, it is very doubtful that the document would have been ratified. The election of the revered General, a native Virginian, as President of the new government was now a powerful influence in its favor with the Virginia people.

The increased strength of the Federalists was further proved during the winter by Madison's election to Congress. Besides arranging Madison's congressional district so as to prevent his selection, as they hoped, the anti-Federalists secured a likable candidate in James Monroe. A principal issue was Madison's attitude toward amendments to the Constitution, and he and his supporters now stressed his advocacy of proper ones. Madison also made an active campaign in the district, receiving a battle scar from a frostbitten nose during one wintry ride. As election day, February 2, 1789, approached, a letter in which he was at pains to explain his position on the amendment issue was published in the *Independent Chronicle*. The letter was written by Madison to Thomas Mann Randolph of Goochland, an influential citizen of Madison's sprawling new district. After alluding to "many opinions" ascribed to him, Madison offered this pointed explanation:

> I have said that I think the amendments ought to be undertaken by the Congress. I prefer that mode, to a General Convention, as most expeditious, most certain (since there are States who will object to the mode of a Convention, without being averse to amendments in themselves), as most safe, and as most economical. It will not have escaped you, however, that the question concerning a General Convention does not depend on the discretion of Congress. If two thirds of the States make application, Congress cannot refuse to call one; if not, Congress have a right to take the step.[57]

Although Henry's name was invoked against Madison in the campaign, there is no evidence that he came into the disputed district during the fight. Madison was elected by a considerable majority, despite his unfavorable vote in Amherst County, the Cabell bailiwick. When Madison took his seat in the new House of Representatives at New York, he was joined by six other Virginians who could be classed as Federalists—another sign of their party's increasing strength.

In his optimistic political appraisal for Madison on March 27, 1789, Edmund Randolph noted one adverse factor: a "very injudicious" publication by one "Decius," which irritated those men who were "well affected to the object of his bitterness."[58] This object was Patrick Henry, and the series of letters, published in the Virginia *Independent Chronicle* during January–March, 1789, were significant as more than a notorious example of political calumny.

Some of Decius' venomous allegations were obviously false on the face of it: "AMBITION, AVARICE, ENVY, HATRED AND REVENGE" were "the secret promoters of all the late noise about liberty."[59] Patrick Henry (readily identified from the description) had the prudence not to risk his own life in a cause which he only meant to make the ladder to a greater height. He took advantage of his position as the head of the state to engage in monetary speculations, and he had "been among the first to exercise his influence in turning that kind of government to the destruction of every blessing of popular government. . . . Even the Spanish Inquisition," so Decius shrilly asserted, "could not afford better examples of personal abuse" than could be drawn from the Virginia Assembly, and Henry was "at the bottom of all the iniquity." [60] Such charges could not be proved, but others by Decius do require some analysis.

Had Augustus Davis, who was then publishing the *Independent Chronicle* at "The Bridge," in Richmond, run the Decius articles at the present time, he would very probably have become involved in a libel suit. Publication of the anonymous letters did not speak well for Davis' character. But he undoubtedly had some support from Henry's opponents and may not have expected such a strong outburst of disapproval. The articles are written in a pleasing style which drew praise even from a critic repelled by Decius' gross slander. The literary form is somewhat like that of Junius, the anonymous English pamphleteer, and the content is of a type that often appeals to scandal-loving newspaper readers.

Perhaps to help disguise himself, Decius stated in his first article, written on December 1, 1788, and published the following January 7, that he had "never been a violent partisan in the late dispute" over the Constitution. Also, he said that until the meeting of the present Assembly he had never felt "any dread about our liberty." By the second article he was getting more specific. He referred, without naming Henry, to his assertion in the Convention that the Constitution "squints toward monarchy," and he declared that "the most ridiculous medley of nonsensical and contradictory" arguments were used against it.

The letters continued into March, 1789, often on the front page of the *Independent Chronicle* or in some other prominent position. The "Chief magistrate," obviously Henry, was accused of having his son taught by a double dealer and of being a landmonger. Taking advantage of the fidelity of the people, he was said to have borrowed money on his credit as Governor, with the intention of paying it off in depreciated money.

Among the outraged replies which began to appear in the newspaper, "Juvenal" pointed out that Decius wrote a great deal and had not been able to prove anything. Robert Greenhow of Williamsburg,

answering a charge regarding £300 borrowed by Henry from Greenhow's father during the war, said that the whole interest then due
had been paid in 1786, along with part of the principal. The younger
Greenhow had never found that Henry had the least aversion to a
fair and honorable settlement.[61]

On February 25 Augustus Davis stated that the Decius series
would be discontinued after the next number, but that they could be
had in a short time in booklet form, with considerable additions, at a
moderate price. Actually, the final article, No. 15, written by Decius
in February, 1789, did not appear until March 25. One of the last
indignant answers published at this time was from "I.W." in Hanover, who countered Decius' charge of Henry's dubious connection
with a Scotch Tory.[62] On the other hand, no signed letters, whether
or not in the *Independent Chronicle*, appeared in defense of Decius.
James Innes wrote a letter to Henry deprecating the Decius articles,
and Edmund Randolph, in a private letter to Madison on March 27,
spoke somewhat more mildly of Decius' facts as "of a trivial cast" and
his assertions "not always correct," so that he became "vulnerable in
almost every part." [63]

As for Henry's own reaction, we have the firsthand evidence in
Spencer Roane's memory as to Henry's remarkable indifference to the
diatribes. This is largely confirmed by a letter which Henry wrote
Senator William Grayson on March 31, 1789.

"What Decius says of me, & others say for me the Gazettes have
told you. I have not seen them except a few numbers (about 5),"
Henry said. In these he was "not lucky enough to hit upon one
charge that is warranted by Truth. How lucky it is that he knows me
no better, for I know of many Deficiencys in my own conduct, that
I can easily conceive myself an unprofitable Servant— But alas! how
difficult it is for human pride to submit to that appellation from
others!" [64]

Yet, while basically undisturbed, Henry was human enough to
make some comment on the implications of the articles:

> It is not candid to characterize a system of Government from the
> men who will ever form the fag end of human society—from
> the political understrappers who ever follow the footsteps of

power and whine and fawn or snarl & bark as they are bid; who ape their Betters & are content with their Leavings, as the wages of the dirty Work assigned them, such men are found in most Govern'ts & no doubt in the American. But whether their superiors will be of a more tolerant spirit is yet to learn. That dirty scribblers will be disowned by their own party I doubt not—But that they are encouraged also is little doubt.[65]

Henry was almost certain that Decius was encouraged by Federalists, and from the content of the articles he may well have suspected that one or more of the Nicholas family was involved. Later, Henry's son John was told that the letters were the work of John Nicholas, Jr., clerk from 1792 to 1815 of Albemarle County. Nicholas was known as "Clerk John" to distinguish him from his cousin "One-eyed John" Nicholas, the brother of Wilson Cary Nicholas and of Patrick Henry's bitter opponent, George Nicholas. George, it will be recalled, had made an unsubstantiated accusation in the Convention regarding Henry's land dealings; the available evidence only indicates that Henry was becoming more preoccupied with land speculation. John Nicholas, Jr., hardly got a favorable view of Henry from his cousin George, and in any event he had his own special reason for disliking him. After rising to the rank of a Continental colonel, Nicholas had been appointed by Jefferson as a militia lieutenant colonel in charge of the troops in the Richmond area during Arnold's invasion of 1780–1781. The militia made the miserable showing which contributed to Henry's support of the legislative inquiry into Jefferson's war governorship, and Nicholas had to bear his part of the blame.

Unlike many of the scandalmongers of history, Decius did not hurt his enemy. One influential critic who had an opportunity to note this was Thomas Jefferson. He did not see the Decius letters until soon after his return from France in December, 1789. Although Jefferson found strong evidence that John Nicholas, Jr., was at least involved in their publication, he is not known to have expressed any disapproval at that time; not until 1811 did he find reason to refer to Nicholas as his "malignant neighbor" and as a "miserable scribbler."[66] When he first read the letters, along with the published replies and Nicholas' penned comment,[67] Jefferson must have seen that the net result had been in Henry's favor. And this was confirmed by the general reaction in Virginia.

Even before reading the articles, Jefferson had spoken of Henry's continued influence in the state. Ever the superlative letter writer, Jefferson had hardly got back to Virginia before he sent a long epistle to his friend, William Short, with news of everything there: from how Benjamin Harrison of Brandon had married a daughter of Mrs. Byrd, and both Molly Nicholas and Polly Stith were keeping "batchelor's house" in Williamsburg, to how the new Virginia capitol would be "an edifice of first-rate dignity," once certain corrections were made, and to the chief events on the political scene. North Carolina had acceded to the Constitution "by a great majority," Jefferson continued, but anti-Federalism was "not yet dead in this country. The gentlemen who opposed it retain a good deal of malevolence toward the new government. . . .

"Henry is it's avowed foe. He stands higher in public estimation than he ever did," Jefferson unhappily concluded.[68]

The Federalists' desire for constitutional amendments to propitiate Henry and other powerful opponents was evident from the start of the new government. In his brief inaugural speech on April 30, 1789, Washington proposed the adoption of constitutional amendments to avoid objections and "inquietude." On May 4, Madison stole the thunder of the opposition by announcing in Congress that he would bring up the issue on the fourth Monday, and his resulting action was scrutinized closely by Henry and some other anti-Federalists. Madison's timidity or sensitiveness in the face of Virginia political opinion was noticed by a fellow congressman, Fisher Ames of Massachusetts. Madison had already become known as a leader of the House, and Ames praised him as a man of sense, reading, address, and integrity and said that he could speak decently and to the point in "a very pure and perspicuous language."[69] On the other hand, Ames considered Madison "a little too much of a book politician, & too timid in his politics, for prudence & caution are opposites of timidity . . . not a little of a Virginian," he "thinks that state the land of promise but is afraid of their state politics."[70] Madison could have replied, however, that the amendments he favored did not cripple the new government and that they helped to prevent the Virginia anti-Federalists from curbing his productive political career.

During the next few years the Federalist party made some notable gains in Virginia. This was true despite their opposition from a nascent Jefferson-Madison party. A towering source of strength for the Federalists was President Washington, who continued to a remarkable degree to hold the respect and admiration of his countrymen. After North Carolina ratified the Constitution in November, 1789, Rhode Island followed the next May. In 1792 Washington was easily elected President for a second term. From late 1791 to 1794, a popular Federalist, General "Light-Horse Harry" Lee, served as Governor and became an intermediary with his friend Henry for the Washington administration. Moreover, Henry was more inclined to listen to Lee after Congress adopted ten constitutional amendments, the American Bill of Rights.

On May 5, 1789, Theodorick Bland presented to Congress the application of Virginia for a second federal convention.[71] There was already a fear on the part of the Federalists that such a convention might disrupt the fledgling national government; Madison had more reason for pushing his proposed constitutional amendments. But Congress was absorbed with the vital problem of securing revenue for the new government, and not until June 8 could he obtain even a preliminary discussion of his amendments. Omitting some which Henry had proposed, Madison offered twelve, chiefly comprising a bill of rights.

"You may be assured that nothing on my part was left undone to [secure the passage of] all the amendments proposed by our country," Lee wrote Henry on September 14. "We might as well have attempted to move Mount Atlas upon our shoulders."[72] Some congressmen wanted further amendments to protect state and individual rights; others showed no great desire for any amendments at all.[73] After various delays, Congress passed ten of Madison's twelve amendments, and they were finally ratified by the states in December, 1791.

The ten amendments seemed a drastic reduction from the forty originally proposed by Henry. But it must be remembered that the forty included the twenty articles for a bill of rights. A number of the ten finally passed contained various sections. As a whole, they represent an abridgement of—rather than a deletion from—the bill of rights which Henry offered, along with two of his other amendments. For example, the First Amendment of the Constitution provides for religious liberty, freedom of speech and of the press, and the right of the people to assemble peaceably and to petition the government for redress of grievances. These provisions are adapted from numbers 15, 16, and 20 in Henry's resolutions passed by the Virginian Convention. The Ninth Amendment provides that the enumeration in the Constitution of certain rights shall not be construed to deny or disparage others retained by the people. This article is based on the first and second articles in Henry's resolutions. Further emphasizing the anti-Federalist belief in states' rights, the Tenth Amendment provides that powers not delegated to the United States by the Constitution nor prohibited by it to the states are reserved to the states or to the people. Although this article was not included in those offered by the Convention, it is found in the preamble to the Virginia ratification resolution.

We must be careful not to minimize the work of a number of men in securing the Bill of Rights. Yet Madison had rendered an important service in deleting some amendments proposed by Henry which were unnecessary or impractical. And, under strong prodding, Madison was the congressman most responsible for pushing the ten amendments through the House of Representatives. It may well be argued, however, that no one had done as much as Henry to secure their adoption. Without the pressure from him and his party, first in the Virginia Convention and then in Congress, it is doubtful if the United States would have had a federal Bill of Rights in its present form.

It remains to note the significance of these amendments. In general, Henry, Mason, and their anti-Federalist associates had offered a negative program at the Virginia Convention. They had not presented enough satisfactory remedies for the critical weaknesses of the Confederation. But when working for a bill of rights during and after the Convention, they took a more positive stand. For them it was not sufficient to argue that fundamental liberties were already protected in the Constitution, that powers not granted the federal government remained with the states. Henry and his supporters believed that definite constitutional guarantees were needed. And in their advocacy of a bill of rights they had the backing of the American people.

Henry had spoken in the Convention of the need for "a firm and solid" union, for reaching "solid reality—the hearts and hands of the men who are to be governed." Through passage of the Bill of Rights the American people were influenced to provide the consent needed to buttress a durable central government. From such documents as the Magna Carta, the English Bill of Rights, colonial charters, and state bills of rights, the majority of American voters had developed an ingrained belief in the importance of written guarantees of personal liberties. Without the promise of amendments to be adopted by Congress, it is doubtful that the Constitution would have been ratified. Certainly, the new government, if adopted, would have been seriously weakened and might not have survived some future stresses and strains.[74]

Moreover, the principles of the Bill of Rights were strengthened to meet the exigencies of later years. While still under the impetus for amendments largely provided by the anti-Federalists, Congress in 1794–1798 proposed the later Eleventh and Twelfth Amendments respecting the judiciary and the election of the President and Vice-President.[75] In 1833 the Supreme Court held that the Bill of Rights imposed restrictions only upon the federal government. But in the Thirteenth, Fourteenth, and Fifteenth Amendments following Union victories in the Civil War, and in various civil rights acts, some during the past generation, the basis was laid for a "vast expansion" of federal power.[76]

The "remarkable pace of change in constitutional law . . . continues unabated," writes an authority. "There has been activity on a wide front, but civil rights and liberties problems predominate." [77] Indeed, some interpretations of the courts are doubtless broader than Henry ever envisaged.

When the Bill of Rights was finally ratified by the states, Henry had attended in 1789–1790 two more sessions of the legislature. During the Fall Assembly of 1789 he retained some important committee appointments, but the Federalists were much more influential than the previous year. Among their outstanding members were Edmund Randolph, John Marshall, and General "Light-Horse Harry" Lee. Although Henry was still trying to influence Congress into proposing further constitutional amendments, he was making a less strenuous effort toward that end. On November 22 Edmund Randolph reported him as quitting the House "rather in discontent," since he had found it "not so pleasant as the last" one.[78] Indicative of his changing viewpoint toward the national government was his support of a resolution by which the legislature provided ammunition for some friendly Chickasaw Indians. In an explanatory address to President Washington, proposed by Henry, the House stated, "It is incumbent on us to make this communication, lest in case of silence it might be interpreted into a design of passing the limits of State authority." [79] Henry would not have it appear that he opposed the power of Congress to control Indian affairs!

In March, 1790, Colonel William Grayson died and Henry lost one of his strongest supporters in Congress. A member of the Governor's Council wrote to ask Henry whether or not he would accept the Senate seat if appointed. During the first years of Congress there had been an unsuccessful effort to give President Washington the title of "His Highness, the President of the United States, and Protector of Their Liberties." Considerable criticism had followed of the form and ceremony in the new government, and Henry, when declining the senatorship, was reported to have said he was "too old to fall into those awkward imitations which are now become fashionable." In a letter to Washington, Colonel David Stuart voiced his suspicion that "the old patriot [Henry] has heard some extraordinary representations of the etiquette established at your levees. Those of his party no doubt think they promote themselves in his good opinion by such high coloring."

We have no further instances of Henry's adverse criticism of Washington during this period of their somewhat "strained relations." However, when Henry's friend, Colonel Martin, requested him to secure an appointment for Martin with Washington, Henry wrote him on January 25, 1790, that "I cannot with propriety write to the President on your affair." [80]

The Assembly which met the following October was the last that Henry ever attended. Some of the routine business to be disposed of was much like that in the earlier postwar years: a petition for uncollected pay from a Revolutionary veteran, another seeking improvement of the navigation at the Great Falls of the Potomac,[81] and a bill for dividing Henry County. On a matter of far greater significance—Secretary Alexander Hamilton's proposed financial measures—Henry expressed real apprehension. However, his opposition to the national government was beginning to lack something of his former zeal.

Under Hamilton's influence, Congress passed bills in 1790 providing for the establishment of a national bank, for a tariff to provide revenue and to protect American manufacturers, and for the federal government to assume the national and state debts. This brilliant program assured the fiscal stability of the new government, and Alexander Hamilton would become acclaimed as one of the great finance ministers of history. But as Henry and other anti-Federalists had feared in the Virginia Convention of 1788, his measures benefited Northern manufacturing and commercial interests at the expense of the agrarian South. Such economic differences were a primary cause for the development within the next few years of the Democratic-Republican party under the leadership of such statesmen as Jefferson and Madison.

In Virginia during the Fall, 1790, Assembly, the opposition to the Hamiltonian measures was strongest against the proposal for the federal government to pay the state and national debts. By great sacrifices, Virginia had largely reduced her state debts, yet had to provide her full share of those for all the states, including some which had made far less effort to meet their financial obligations. Moreover, many Northern speculators had purchased government securities from their original owners at a heavy discount. In 1795 federal interest payments would be $62,300 for Virginia, as compared with $309,500 for Massachusetts and $365,000 for New York.[82] Soon after Henry took his seat in the House, the Assembly approved a memorial to Congress protesting federal assumption of the state debts. The people

of Virginia had ratified the federal Constitution with the positive condition that "every power not expressly granted was retained," and
they could find no clause in the Constitution authorizing Congress to
assume the debts of the states.[83] In words reminiscent of Henry's
speeches during the 1788 Convention, they emphasized that "as the
guardians then of the rights and interests of their constituents, as sen-
tinels placed by them over the ministers of the Federal government,
to shield it from their encroachments," they could never "reconcile"
themselves to the measure.[84]

On or about November 12, 1791, Henry left the Assembly. First
entering the House of Burgesses in 1765, he had served in that body
and in the House of Delegates for nearly twenty years. During all
this time he had been an outstanding legislator associated with the
important events of that formative period. Indeed, he became, year
after year, the acknowledged leader of the House of Delegates. His
old associates in the House could well wonder if they would ever see
his like again.

After he left his seat, Henry County was divided, and a new
county, formed of the westerly section beyond Leatherwood, was
named Patrick. The following spring he declined re-election to the
House, and he never sat in another deliberative body.[85]

During the summer of 1792, Henry appears to have put a damper
on Jefferson's proposal for a convention to amend the Virginia Convention of 1776.[86] And he continued to be consulted by former political associates such as James Monroe, who had been elected to the
Senate in place of Colonel Grayson. In his reply to Monroe on
January 24, 1791, Henry gave expression to his opinion of the federal government. The form of this government still incurred Henry's
enmity, "yet as we are one & all imbarked, it is natural to care for the
crazy Machine, at least so long as we are out of Sight of a Port to
refit." As for one of Secretary Hamilton's financial proposals, of
which Monroe had sent Henry a copy, Henry said that "it seems to
be a consistent part of a system which I ever dreaded. Subserviency
of Southern to N——n Interests are written in Capitals on its very
Front; whilst Government Influence, deeply planted & widely scat-

ter'd by preceding Measures, is to receive a formidable Addition by this plan."

But Henry declared that he must suppress his feelings. He consoled himself "with hoping that the Advocates of Oppression may find the Time when the Measures of Iniquity shall give place to just & enlightened Policy." [87] He would be "sparing of Complaints" against the federal government and find fault as little as his "fixed Habits of thinking will permit. . . . Allowances ought to be made, & some Hopes indulged of future amendment." [88]

But Henry was now viewing politics from the sidelines: he had set himself another and very difficult task for the next few years.

"I am obliged to be very industrious & to take on me great Fatigue to clear myself of Debt—I hope to be able to accomplish this in a year or two if it pleases God to continue me in Health & Strength," he had written his daughter Betsey the previous October 30, 1791.[89] At a grave risk to that already diminishing health and strength, he was devoting himself to a now large and remunerative law practice, along with farming and heavy land speculation.

24

Again the Law and Other Business Interests

Fools and obstinate men make lawyers rich.——H. G. BOHN

If truth were self-evident, eloquence would not be necessary.
——CICERO

1786–1792 (circa). Henry, besides being a large planter, again becomes an outstanding lawyer and land speculator.

1789. Takes oath as attorney in Prince Edward District Court. Defends a Revolutionary commissary in suit by John Hook. Becomes active in a Georgia land company.

November 23, 1791. Qualifies for practice in U.S. District Court. Appears in *Jones v. Walker*, a leading case involving British debts.

1792–1793. Moves, December, 1792, to Long Island in Campbell County. Appears in many criminal and civil cases, including the Randolph murder case.

SOON AFTER MOVING to Prince Edward County, Patrick Henry expressed to a neighbor his anxiety about some debts which he was unable to pay. The neighbor, probably Captain Philemon Holcombe, advised him to resume the practice of law. "Your tongue will soon pay your debts," he said.

Henry took the advice. When not preoccupied with farming and politics, he began to pick up the threads of his new law practice. Judge Roane, who observed his legal work after his return to the bar, thought that he "must necessarily have been very rusty," although "acquainted with the rules and canons of property." Fortunately, however, he could easily fall back on criminal practice while perfecting himself in civil law. In the criminal field, he benefited from his prestige as a popular champion, his wide experience with country juries, and his oratory then almost *sui generis* in America for the richness and the variety of the talents displayed. "As a criminal lawyer . . . his eloquence had the fairest scope," Judge Roane would recall.

> He was perfect master of the passions of his auditory, whether in the tragic or the comic line. The tones of his voice, to say nothing of his matter and gestures, were insinuated into the feelings of his hearers in a manner that baffled all description. It seemed to operate by mere sympathy, and by his tones alone it seemed to me that he could make you cry or laugh at pleasure; yet his gesture came powerfully in aid, and if necessary would approach almost to the ridiculous.[1]

Daniel Webster, perhaps the greatest American orator of the next century, was also a "master of the passions" of his art. Like Henry, Webster was a highly successful jury lawyer. And, like him, Webster was most effective when advocating a great heartfelt theme—Webster, American unity; Henry, American liberty. But somehow the dignified, dark-haired, dark-eyed New Englander seems to have been more effective on a formal occasion; Henry, when arguing before a country jury or a popular assembly. Certainly, Henry seems to have been more the master of "the comic line." And considering his great success as a criminal lawyer, he must have developed this propensity early when in Prince Edward.

Yet, however much Henry may have swayed the rustic jurors of the area, it was several years after his arrival in the county before he appeared in any of his more celebrated criminal cases. His criminal practice continued to be a cash business, seldom recorded in his account books. We must turn elsewhere for some impressions of his life during the first Prince Edward years.

After Henry left Richmond, it was some time before he became comfortably settled in Prince Edward and longer before his plantations were on a paying basis—that is, if they ever were. By March,

1788, his account books show him charging Captain John Harvie of nearby Charlotte County £2.10 for handling a minor civil case in the General Court and three shillings for some corn and a barrel of rum.[2] On the Virginia plantations rum was used for a variety of purposes. We may imagine Henry joking over a moderate glass with fellow lawyers at a courthouse tavern. But, always of simple tastes, he had more and more in late years come to be in the crowd rather than of it. In Richmond during the Convention we have seen that he had stayed at the somewhat circumspect Swan, rather than in the hubbub of Formicola's.

Other items in the 1788 accounts tell us more than the "barrel of rum." The meager income, not more than a few hundred pounds, which he listed as making that year from his plantations does not appear as yet to have been substantially increased by his legal practice. In 1788 we find him charging a few clients for such items as a retainer fee, a trespass case, and seven cases for a Petersburg merchant. Although Captain Philemon Holcombe, Jr., was charged £14 in one case,[3] the fees were usually not more than a few pounds, the total for 1788 less than a hundred. That was the year when Henry attended not only two sessions of the Assembly but the Virginia Convention of 1788. His lengthy political career had nearly always been at a financial sacrifice, and this was especially so now that he was trying to pay off debts and establish a new law practice.

The next year, 1789, Henry took the oath as an attorney for the Prince Edward District Court. Many times during the next six years before his retirement from the bar his life would follow the familiar pattern. Packing his spare linen and legal papers into his small leather trunk, he would step into his chaise and ride through the Piedmont countryside: the great expanses of forest interspersed with tobacco and corn fields, the muddy creeks, and the occasional hamlets. He would stop over at the rude inns in the courthouse villages: Prince Edward Courthouse near Hampden-Sydney, where he often had a son or other relative attending college; Rustburg in Campbell County; New London, near Poplar Forest and the Blue Ridge Mountains, where Jefferson would come to look after his plantation and escape the swarm of guests at Monticello. One route which

Henry and other itinerant lawyers followed to New London, then the Bedford County seat, is still known as Lawyers Road. And from numerous people in the area have come marvelous stories of Henry, their patron saint, some easily proven, others requiring dissection to uncover the elements of legend and folklore.

Henry's revived fame as a lawyer began to spread to other sections of Virginia. His first case of statewide significance during this period was in August, 1789, when he had to ride to Leesburg to appear in *Carter of Shirley v. Carter of Nominy*. This was a large land suit in Loudoun court. It was significant not only for the amount of land involved—12,000 acres with rents thereon for fifty years—and the prominence of the principals but also for the insight it gives into Henry's career at the period. Both Henry's client, the defendant, Robert ("Councilor") Carter of Nominy in Westmoreland, and the plaintiff, Carter's first cousin, Charles Carter of Shirley on the James, were grandsons of "King" Carter, the landed magnate; and Charles' daughter by his second wife, a cousin of Dolly Henry's, would become the wife of "Light-Horse Harry" Lee and the mother of Robert E. Lee.

The suit was to be tried at Leesburg in the upper corner of Virginia near the Maryland border, and the litigants, among the wealthiest landholders in Virginia, could well afford to hire outstanding counsel. Charles Carter employed Edmund Randolph, and Robert Carter sought the services of Patrick Henry. Doubtless Robert Carter had heard some tirades against Henry by his uncle, Landon Carter, but they were not to be taken too seriously when a good lawyer was needed. Henry declined the case because of the labor and "fatigue" involved; he would need to charge a fee which Carter might call exorbitant. But Carter persuaded Henry to change his mind, and he set out on the 140-mile ride to Leesburg through the summer heat and dust.

Shortly after the trial, Edmund Randolph wrote an account of the "diverting scene." The case went on for three days. His client, Charles Carter, would have been defeated if a single one of four points had gone against him, "and to obtain one everything was tried in the way of assertion, defamation, and solecism." Henry lost three of the points by a unanimous vote of the judges and a fourth by a majority. "Mortified" by his defeats, so Randolph declared, "and willing to disguise them under the name of a compromise," Henry secured an agreement that his client should surrender 6,000 acres of land, or half of the claim, and £450. But Henry evidently felt that he had done as well as could be expected with the difficult case, and Randolph knew he himself was on somewhat shaky ground in event of an appeal. "I agreed [to the compromise], knowing that two of the four points were in strictness by no means in our favor," Randolph admitted.[4]

The following March, 1790, Henry was still trying to collect a 200-guinea fee from Councilor Carter. This amount, so Henry wrote him, was contingent upon whether he was "successfull" in the case. If entirely so, he would have charged Carter 400 guineas. Through the compromise settlement, he had saved Carter half of the land and nine-tenths of the rent. He had, therefore, charged Carter 200 guineas. Had he known that Carter would not pay the fee, Henry would not have undergone "that distressing Fatigue" which his strength "illy enables me" to endure. He asked Carter to spare him "the Misery of being obliged" to sue him. He realized that Carter did not see the matter with his (Henry's) eyes and believed the error was "involuntary."[5]

Henry's attitude toward the fee was firm yet reasonable. His charges in his account books for civil cases all appear modest enough; like the other lawyers on his circuit he depended mostly on the number rather than the size of his fees. There is some sketchy evidence, however, that he was none too squeamish in the criminal cases accepted and fees charged. Moreover, his respected neighbor, Richard N. Venable, who heard Henry at the September, 1791, court in Prince Edward, spoke of him as displaying "great eloquence" in one case and the jury being hung; and in another, a rape case, of his making "an ingenious" defense.[6] A few years later he would defend the tragic Richard Randolph in one of the oustanding criminal cases in Virginia history. By the early 1790's it is doubtful that any American lawyer was his superior in arguing criminal cases before country juries.

During this same period Henry's brilliant argument in *Ware v. Hylton,* an important debt case, won him fame as one of America's leading civil lawyers. To no small degree it was this case—along with some practical politics—which led President Washington to attempt to appoint Henry to the United States Supreme Court.

For Henry, *Ware v. Hylton*—the British Debts Case—was in a sense both a crowning triumph and a valedictory. Directly or indirectly, the suit involved the question of whether British merchants could collect millions of dollars from prewar American debtors. It revived highly controversial issues of public and private honor, of a state's wartime confiscatory powers, and of natural rights. The case was first heard in a packed courtroom at the September, 1791, session of the Federal District Court in Richmond. The judges, with all of whom Henry had had earlier contacts, were the District Judge, Cyrus Griffin of Virginia, and two Supreme Court Justices, John Blair of Virginia and Thomas Johnson of Maryland. After this hearing, when Henry was at the height of his powers, there was another trial of the case at the May, 1793, term of the court. The arguments were repetitive and somewhat inferior to those at the earlier trial, but Henry again won plaudits. During the next year he appeared in a number of less important cases and then retired from active practice, his high position at the bar now generally recognized.

Ware v. Hylton was the most important civil suit in which Henry ever appeared, with the possible exception of the Parson's Cause; that celebrated suit had been tried thirty years earlier, when Henry had been a callow country lawyer and, minimizing the strictly legal issues, had electrified his friendly listeners with his exposition of natural rights, thus helping to move forward the American Revolution. But as one of the defense lawyers in *Ware v. Hylton,* Henry was in the full maturity of his legal talents.

In a real sense, the British Debts Case revived—and inflamed—issues growing out of the war. The case was ideally constituted to arouse the fighting spirit of Patrick Henry. During late 1777 the hard-pressed Virginia Assembly had enacted legislation making it lawful for her citizens to rid themselves of debts owed to British subjects by paying the money in Virginia currency into the state treasury. At first many dilatory or cautious debtors did not utilize the opportunity to cancel these debts with the state notes. It could be, some reasoned, that the war would lead to the cancellation of all British debts. As the Virginia currency depreciated it became more advantageous to pay debts—especially if in sterling money—with the state notes. There was an element of calculation in the procedure; indeed, among the more careless planters, an "aristocratic and feudal" attitude toward debts in general.[7] Yet many debtors in Virginia and other states supported the sequestration acts as necessary war measures. To patriotic Americans in the critical period of Valley Forge, of Arnold's treason, and of the Camden debacle, the acts were legally and morally justifiable. As Henry would argue in *Ware v. Hylton,* the funds thus obtained were through specific legislation of an independent state and they were vitally needed to help finance the war.

Examining the voluminous, closely written accounts of the Virginia Loan Office which handled the sequestrated debts, a present-day researcher cannot but be impressed with the names of her citizens thus disposing of their British obligations. Besides many obscure but patriotic farmers, the list is studded with representatives of well-known Virginia families, outstanding for their sacrifices on behalf of the American cause. Sometimes one man would make payments at intervals as he mustered the funds. Patrick Henry is said to have been included in the list, but that record is lost or misplaced. His British debts, whether or not paid into the Loan Office, appear to have been small and all paid by late 1785.[8]

Yet among scattered entries in the surviving Loan Office records are, for the Washington family, Lawrence Washington, £201.12; Lawrence Washington, Jr., £300; "General Washington," £3,999.18 on October 20 and £1,009 on October 30, 1779. Other prominent names, some of them Henry's associates of the war period, include John Page, Jr., £3,200; John Robinson's administrators, £3,125; Edmund Pendleton, £103.4; Edmund Randolph, £210; Paul Carrington, £242.2 and later £1,000; William Byrd's trustee, £602.14;

and Theodorick Bland, £8,424.6. There are several entries for the Burwell family, including Nathaniel Burwell, £335.[9] While Governor, Patrick Henry signed a Loan Office receipt on February 27, 1779, for £972 received of John Randolph by the hands of Thomas Jefferson, Esq. The receipt stated that it was for money due from Randolph to Farrell and Jones (the British firm suing through a surviving heir in *Ware v. Hylton*).[10] Even John Blair, a judge in the case, is listed as having paid £1,005 into the Loan Office. Altogether, between March, 1778, and June, 1780, there were some 552 payments made into the state treasury. In April and May, 1778, when a pound sterling was worth about £60 in inflated Virginia currency, the total amount received was £119,522. The next month the Sequestration Act was suspended because of the "collapse" of the Virginia finances.[11]

Obviously, it would have been too burdensome for many of the debtors to pay the British accounts a second time. During the hard times of the war and early postwar period, a number of states not only passed sequestration acts but also legislation barring action to recover the British debts. Such a law preventing action for the recovery of the debts in her state courts was passed by Virginia in 1782 with Henry's support.

British debts! British debts! British debts! How often Henry, as lawyer, Governor, and legislator, had been concerned with them! Farrell and Jones, the pertinacious Bristol firm, had traded with Henry's father, half brother, and father-in-law. To be sure, John Syme had been more interested in having Farrell and Jones send him a suit "of the best Cloath of a fash[ble] Color, with two pair of breeches made very long over the knees," than in promptly paying his debts to the British company. But Henry had no doubt that under the restrictive mercantilist system the planters as a whole were more sinned against than sinning. The British debts remained a matter of grave concern, especially in Virginia and some other Southern states. Of the total owed, some six-sevenths was in the South and three-sevenths in the Old Dominion alone. As late as 1791 the British merchants were claiming a total of nearly £5,000,000, including interest of £2,000,000.[12]

While securing American independence, the Treaty of Paris provided that there was to be no legal impediment to the collection of British debts in sterling money. There were indeed reasons of sound policy for the American commissioners at Paris—Benjamin Franklin, John Adams, and even Henry Laurens, the South Carolina planter-merchant—agreeing to this concession. But the commissioners were largely representative of the commercial interests. They had not seen as closely as had Henry the problems of the Southern farmer. They did not feel as he did the burning injustice connected with payment of debts to British citizens when troops of their country had been responsible for such great losses in American lives and property—especially when many hard-pressed debtors would be repaying money already paid into the state treasuries under the sequestration acts. A last-ditch champion of the debtor interest in the 1787 legislature, he re-entered the arena as a defense attorney in the British Debts Case.

Under the American Constitution of 1787, it was provided that legal cases involving citizens of the United States and those of another country should be tried in the federal courts. After the passage of the Judiciary Act in 1789 and the opening of these courts, hundreds of suits were filed in the Federal District Court at Richmond. *Jones v. Walker*, later termed *Ware v. Hylton*, was the first of these suits to be brought to trial. William Jones, a British citizen and surviving partner of Farrell and Jones, sued Dr. Thomas Walker of Albemarle County for a pre-Revolutionary debt of £2,151.18, and Walker, a prominent planter and Jefferson's onetime guardian, offered a receipt in proof that he had paid the debt into the Virginia Loan Office.[13] Dr. Walker and the other defendants in the British Debt Cases before the court, joining in a common cause, employed an array of illustrious counsel, as did the British merchants. Patrick Henry, as a defense lawyer, again became a popular champion.

"Next fall the great question will come on as to their [the British merchants'] right to recover from our citizens," Colonel William Duval, an associate counsel for Walker, wrote Henry. "Your countrymen look up to you on that occasion."[14]

Because of the importance of the case, Henry appears to have made the most thorough preparation for any lawsuit in his career. For several days before leaving for Richmond, he buried himself in his office. His young grandson, Patrick Henry Fontaine, was sent sixty miles to obtain a copy of Vattel's *Law of Nations,* and Henry filled a notebook over an inch thick with notes from Vattel and other authorities and with headings for his argument. The grandson recalled seeing Henry walking along the locust-lined avenue in front of his office, reading aloud at intervals from his notes and gesticulating. William Wirt was so impressed by Henry's conduct of the suit that he devoted over a tenth of his entire Henry biography to it. And the more critical Jefferson stated that Henry "exerted a degree of industry in that case" which was "totally foreign to his character, and not only seemed, but had made himself really, learned on the subject." [15]

On November 23, 1791, Henry appeared in the Federal District Court at Richmond and was qualified to practice there. Soon afterward the case of *Jones v. Walker* was called to trial. Besides Henry, the counsel for the defendant included John Marshall, Alexander Campbell, and the Attorney General of Virginia, the eloquent James Innes. Henry would recall the tall, rotund Innes for his outstanding summary speech in the late Virginia Convention. It was also reassuring to be associated with John Marshall and with Alexander Campbell, another leader of the Richmond bar. On the other hand, the counsel for the British merchants were lawyers certain to test the mettle of the defense attorneys. The ablest of them was probably John Wickham. Wickham, born on Long Island, New York, and with Tory connections, was now a rising Richmond lawyer. Exalted by the Irish poet, Tom Moore, as "the only gentleman in America," Wickham was a friend and neighbor of John Marshall; Henry must have met him at the Marshalls' "lawyers' dinners" or on other social occasions in the Virginia capital. Later, Wickham would win national distinction in such cases before the United States Supreme Court or District Court (Chief Justice Marshall presiding) as *United States v. Aaron Burr,* and *Martin v. Hunter's Lessee.* Moreover, there were other outstanding lawyers for the British merchants: John Baker, John Starke, and the Scottish William Ronald.

Baker was the last lawyer to lead off for the plaintiff. Word then went the rounds that Patrick Henry would open for the defendant at 11 A.M. on November 25, 1791. There was a scene reminiscent of several of his great speeches in past years. The legislators left the Assembly to hear him and, with numerous other spectators, soon overflowed the large courtroom into the windows and even the adjoining portico. Henry's speech, as recorded by the reporter, David Robertson, shows that he had acquired a remarkable knowledge of the legal principles involved in the case, with the historical background. Yet, as at the Constitutional Convention, Robertson could not indicate in cold print Henry's full, dramatic effect.

With the other defense counsel, Henry made a principal point of the Virginia Sequestration Act of 1777 that legalized the payment of debts owed British citizens into the Loan Office. But the lawyers for Walker pled two other important laws. The first was the act of forfeiture on May 3, 1779, which provided that any property in Virginia belonging to a British subject at that time should be deemed to be invested in the Commonwealth. The second was the act of May 6, 1782, stating that no amount originally due a British subject should be recoverable in any Virginia court unless the assignment was made prior to May 1, 1777. It was likewise argued that the British King and his subjects were still alien enemies and that a state of war still continued because of various violations of the Treaty of Paris, which they listed. This was one of the weakest arguments by the defense counsel and would be recognized as such by the federal judges in a later retrial of the case.

When Henry rose to speak, there was a deep silence. He began quietly as if in a conversation. But it was soon obvious that he felt deeply about the case. Old memories of British wrongs, of the American struggle for liberty, swelled within him. As "a liberal man and a Christian," he knew that it became him "to forget and to forgive" British injustices.

> But when to the character of Christian you add the character of patriot, you are in a different situation. . . . If your enemy smite one cheek, turn the other to him. But you . . . cannot apply this to your country. . . . Observations of this nature are exceedingly unpleasant, but it is my duty to use them.[16]

Henry read "copious extracts" from Vattel and Grotius to support his contention that in revolutionary wars debts became subject to forfeiture. He admitted that men and nations have engaged in wars for the most trivial and frivolous causes, but the American war "was in opposition to the most grievous oppression—we resisted, and our resistance was approved and blessed by Heaven." [17] Impelled by "dire necessity," America was compelled "to make impresses" upon her own citizens. The laws and practices of Great Britain supported his position in this respect. He cited various instances in British history down to the rebellions of 1715 and 1745 to show that if the Americans had been conquered "the most horrid forfeitures, confiscations, and attainders, would have been pronounced against us." [18]

Here Henry might have referred to the sentence of hanging, drawing, and quartering, which had threatened him personally.

"Would not our men have shared the fate of the people of Ireland?" Henry continued.

A great part of that island was confiscated, though the *Irish* people thought themselves engaged in a laudable cause. What confiscations and punishments were inflicted in Scotland? The plains of *Culloden*, and the neighboring gibbets, would show you. I thank Heaven that the spirit of liberty, under the protection of the Almighty, saved us from experiencing so hard a destiny. But had we been subdued, would not every right have been wrested from us? What right would have been saved? . . . Would it not be absurd, to save debts, while they should burn, hang, and destroy? [19]

Had America been conquered, Henry said, he "would not wish to have lived to see the sad scenes we should have experienced. Needy avarice, and savage cruelty, would have had full scope. Hungry *Germans*, blood-thirsty *Indians*, and nations of another colour, would have been let loose upon us." [20]

Although he had stressed the right of forfeiture of the British debts, Henry was particularly effective when he took up the various "objections" made by the counsel for the plaintiff. As he made those objections, Henry took "ample" notes. If his answer was to be brief, he would make it without removing his spectacles from his nose,

Hardin Burnley, an eyewitness, recalled. "But if he was ever seen to give his spectacles a cant to the top of his wig, *it was a declaration of war*, and his adversaries must stand clear."

Was it terrible to confiscate debts when there were laws to forfeit life and to corrupt the very source of your blood? "Though every other thing dear to humanity is forfeitable, yet *debts*, it seems, must be spared!" he exclaimed. "Debts are too sacred to be touched? It is a mercantile idea that worships Mammon instead of God."[21]

It was in the course of this counterplay that Henry gave a devastating reply to William Ronald, who had been suspected of being at one time "not very warm in the American cause." Ronald had argued that at the time of the passage of the Virginia laws for confiscation and forfeiture of the debts she was no more than a colony in revolt. When Henry, in his reply to various arguments, came to this remark he gave his spectacles the "war cant." Another of the plaintiff's observations, he said, was that by the law of nations Virginia had no right to legislate on the subject of British debts. "And I thought that I heard the word—*revolt!*" he exclaimed.

We may discount some superlatives used by Wirt in describing the following scene, but there is no doubt as to Henry's effectiveness. At the word "revolt," Henry turned upon Ronald "with an expression of indignation and contempt, which seemed almost to annihilate him." Ronald shrank from the "withering look" and appeared as if "he might drop through the floor," Wirt wrote. One had to witness the effect of Henry's anger to appreciate it fully. Certainly, for a Richmond lawyer to be branded with Toryism would have been no small matter. However, Henry perceived Ronald's "suffering, and his usual good-nature immediately returned." We continue with Wirt's somewhat high-flown account:

> He raised his eyes gently toward the court, and shaking his head slowly, with an expression of regret, added, "I wish I had not heard it: for although innocently meant (and I am sure that it was so, from the character of the gentleman who mentioned it), yet the sound displeases me—it is unpleasant." Mr. Ronald breathed again, and looked up, and his generous adversary dismissed the topic, to resume it no more.[22]

Altogether, Henry spoke some three days. He had not failed to employ his oratorical arts, especially when invoking for his receptive audience the memories of the Revolution. Yet, while the case turned at times on somewhat technical points of law, the audience, "mixed as it was," followed him throughout with increasing interest and pleasure. The room continued to be full to the last; and the rapt spectators rose with a murmur of admiration that was likened to a great theatrical assembly which had just enjoyed a splendid new drama. The echoes of his speech were heard in every quarter of Richmond and, later, throughout the state.[23]

The hearings at the first trial of the debt cases had been based upon the law involved in the pleadings. With the death of William Jones *pendente lite,* and other changes, the litigants were *Ware v. Hylton,* and the pleadings, when again discussed in 1793, were somewhat revised. Also, while Judge Griffin, the District Judge, again appeared in the case, the Supreme Court Justices, Johnson and Blair, had been replaced by two recent appointees to the court. They were the new Chief Justice, John Jay, Henry's colleague in the First Continental Congress, and a dark-haired, dark-eyed North Carolinian of English birth, Judge James Iredell. As long as he lived the distinguished Judge Iredell would recall with pleasure the arguments in the suit, some made during Henry's presence: the ingenuity, the depth of investigation, the power of reasoning, the oratory surpassing anything he had heard before. But the arguments in the 1793 hearing were not deemed as forceful as those of 1791. It made all the more impressive Judge Iredell's comment after hearing Henry lead off in the case: "Gracious God! He is an orator indeed!" [24]

This remark, addressed by Judge Iredell to Judge Jay, was heard by young John Randolph, who had worked his way through the crowd. To Randolph, a candid observer, Henry presented the appearance of an old man wrapped in heavy clothing, resting his head on the bar. As he rose to speak, he complained of how "it was a hardship too great to put the laboring oar in the hands of a decrepit old man, trembling, with one foot in the grave, weak in his best days, and far inferior to the able associates by him." [25] Randolph declared that he knew "it was all put on," yet such was the power of Henry's manner

[411]

and voice that Randolph could in a moment "find himself enraged with the Court for their 'cruelty.'" He went on to give an outline of Henry's progress in his argument, comparing him to "a first-rate four-mile race-horse, sometimes displaying his old power and speed for a few leaps" and then slowing down again. At last, Randolph said, Henry got into full stride and reviewed what England would have done had she been successful in arms. What would have been our fate if we had been unsuccessful? "The color began to come and go in the face of the Chief Justice, while [Judge] Iredell sat with his mouth and eyes stretched open in perfect wonder."

It was apparently at this session of the District Court that a miniature of Henry was painted, from which Sully later drew the portrait.[26]

The judgment of the court was in favor of the plaintiff, except for the sums that the defendant paid into the State Loan Office. The suit was then appealed to the United States Supreme Court and tried in 1796, after Henry had retired from the bar. The Supreme Court reversed the decision of the District Court and held that the debtors were liable for their entire original obligations. Two principles of the law were upheld: first, that the Treaty of Paris in 1783 had enabled the British creditors to recover debts previously owed to them from American citizens, notwithstanding a payment into a state treasury under a state law of sequestration; and, second, that an individual citizen of one state could not set up the violation of the peace treaty by other contracting parties to avoid an obligation arising under such a treaty. The power to declare a treaty of war for such cause rests solely on the government, which may or may not exert its option in the premises.[27] However, much of the British debt was either paid later by the United States government or never paid.[28]

Patrick Henry's appearance as seen through the unhappy eyes of John Randolph, fresh from his brother's murder trial, is accurate enough. As a lawyer, as a brilliant orator, Henry never owed much to a striking appearance. He had no piercing eyes like George Whitefield, no impressive mien like Daniel Webster. Judge Roane could only note that his father-in-law was "not a handsome man."

Another Henry associate even contended that Henry's "great

plausibility of argument consisted entirely in manner"—gesture, voice and so on.[29] Indeed, to his mastery of voice tones is attributed much of his brilliant success as a speaker. Manifestly, Henry had not disciplined his voice by talking with pebbles in his mouth as had Demosthenes; he had no formal training in oratory as had William Pitt the Younger. His superior vocal apparatus with its helpful variety of tones was a God-given gift, a gift Henry rendered more valuable by his sharp wit and low-keyed, sometimes deadpan humor. We get an inkling of this humor in the fragment of a conversation that Henry had about 1789 with another prominent Prince Edward citizen, General Edward Lawson. The General had become involved in some serious difficulties, probably of a legal nature, and he asked Henry, with whom he had served in the Convention of 1788 and in the Assembly, just what he should do about them.

"Why faith, General, you had better run away," Henry replied. He may well have been joking but Lawson followed his advice and moved to Kentucky, with not altogether happy results.[30]

A number of traditional stories of Henry's marvelous talents as a criminal lawyer date back to his last years of practice in the Southside. In one case he defended a country client accused of aiding and abetting a wagoner to steal a turkey. During his argument Henry declared, "But, gentlemen of the jury, this plaintiff tells you that he had nothing to do with the turkey . . . not until it was *roasted*." Henry, we are told, "pronounced the word *roasted* with such rotundity of voice," such comic manner and gesture, that he "threw everyone into a fit of laughter at the plaintiff." The defendant was released "with little or no damage." [31]

One murder case had continued throughout the day, and the prosecutor had made such a strong argument that the crowd believed that the defendant was guilty and could not be saved. It was almost dusk and candles were lighted when Patrick Henry, "plain, simple, and entirely unassuming," rose to speak in the quiet manner which he frequently affected.

> "Gentlemen of the jury, I dare say we are all very much
> fatigued with this tedious trial. The prisoner at the bar has been
> well defended already; but it is my duty to offer you some further

[413]

observations in behalf of this unfortunate man. I shall aim at brevity. But should I take up more of your time than you expect, I hope you will hear me with patience when you consider that *blood is concerned*." [32]

A reliable witness, the Reverend Conrad Speece of the Augusta Church, declared that one who had never heard Henry speak could not fully conceive the impression he gave through the word "blood." Speece found everything within him responding: "Yes, since blood is concerned, in the name of all that is righteous, go on; we will hear you with patience until the rising of to-morrow's sun." [33]

All of the audience must have been affected similarly, Speece indicated, for there was "the profoundest silence . . . as if our very breath had been suspended." Under the influence of Henry's "genius, every particular of the story assumed a new aspect, and his cause became continually more bright and promising" until he dwelt upon the alleged murder itself.

Speece told how Henry handled a key point of the evidence, then said that the defendant was freed by the jury with the full approval of the numerous spectators.

What gave "such transcendent force" to Henry's eloquence? Speece asked. He spoke of Henry's reasoning powers, good but "more than equalled by those of many men"; of his "exceedingly quick" imagination, his "inexpressibly happy" voice. "But his most irresistible charm was the vivid feeling of his cause with which he spoke. Such feeling infallibly communicates itself to the breast of the hearer." [34]

Archibald Alexander, a young theological student who went out of his way to hear Henry in a murder trial, described him about as would be expected: appearance "nothing very remarkable. . . . You might readily have taken him for a common planter who cared very little about his personal appearance"; but Alexander did say that Henry's manners were "uniformly respectful and courteous." [35]

Henry was defending in the Circuit Court three men charged with murder. The reliable Alexander, later a distinguished Presbyterian minister, tells us that the trial continued throughout the day and that candles were lit before Henry had an opportunity to speak. In a few impressive words he emphasized the responsibility which rested on him to defend the lives of three fellow citizens, and he got the trial postponed until the next morning. The prosecuting attorney "opened with a clear and dignified speech" and presented what appeared to be conclusive evidence to the jury. Yet Henry won the case, largely by arousing the prejudices of the jury against the principal witness for the prosecution, "Butterwood" Tom Harvey, "this would-be constable." [36] Alexander, who made a particular study of Henry, believed that he

> owed much to his singular insight into the feelings of the common mind. In great cases, he scanned his jury and formed his mental estimate; on this basis he founded his appeals to their predilections and character. It is what other advocates do in a lesser degree. When he knew that there were conscientious or religious men among the jury, he would most solemnly address himself to their sense of right, and would adroitly bring in Scriptural citations. If this handle were not offered, he would lay bare the sensibility of patriotism. Thus it was when he succeeded in rescuing the man who had deliberately shot down a neighbor who lay under the odious suspicion of being a Tory, and who was proved to have refused supplies to a brigade of the American army. [37]

Some of Henry's most effective oratory was in cases growing out of the war to which he had devoted himself heart and soul. One of the "authenticated" Henry stories involved the well-known case of John Hook, a storekeeper at New London. Hook, a Scotch Tory, sued John Venable, a former commissary in the Continental Army, for seizing two of Hook's steers during Cornwallis' invasion. When prosecuting the case, Hook had put himself into an extremely vulnerable position, and Henry, Venable's attorney, did not fail to take advantage of it. By arousing the passions and the laughter of the audience, which must have included a number of Revolutionary veterans, he got their full sympathy. He depicted the American soldiers leaving bloody tracks as they walked barefoot over the frozen ground.

> "Where was the man," he said, "who had an American heart in his bosom, who would not have thrown open his fields, his barns,

his cellars, the doors of his house, the portals of his breast, to receive with open arms the meanest soldier in that little band of famished patriots? Where is the man? *There* he stands—but whether the heart of an American beats in his bosom, you, gentlemen, are to judge." [38]

Then Henry "carried" the jury verbally to Yorktown and the American victory. "But hark! What notes of discord are these which disturb the general joy and silence the acclamations of victory? They are the notes of *John Hook*, hoarsely bawling through the American camp, *beef! beef! beef!*" [39]

This remark, made in Henry's most ludicrous manner, "convulsed" the audience. James Steptoe, the county clerk, was unable to control himself, and rather than commit a breach of decorum he rushed out of the courthouse and rolled on the ground "in the most violent paroxysm of laughter."

As might be anticipated, the jury retired and returned immediately to report a verdict in favor of the defendant. Among the excited people there was a cry of "tar and feathers"—from which Hook escaped only by flight.[40]

In a secluded, still thinly settled countryside before the day of radio and television, Patrick Henry brought much pleasure to the spectators —and not a little to himself—through the conduct of his criminal trials. Sometimes it is difficult to distinguish between established fact and folklore in the accounts handed down to us.

One anecdote was told about Henry's having so much corn stolen from one of his corn cribs that he set a steel trap and caught the culprit. Coming to the barn early one morning, Henry found a neighbor of good reputation standing there with one arm invisible. "Good morning, sir," Henry politely greeted the thief. He inquired about the man's family, discussed weather and crops and cried out heartily, "Come in to breakfast, come on in!" and then walked away.

Another traditional story was of a girl who wanted to marry her sweetheart despite the objections of her parents. But she was under age, and the young man consulted Patrick Henry. Henry told him to get the young lady to ride to meet him on her father's horse, then mount behind her, ride to the nearest preacher, and get married. At the trial, apparently for abduction of a minor, Henry, leading the girl in her testimony, asked if her lover had run away with her. "No, sir," she replied, "I ran away with him!" "Oh," Henry said, "I see!" The crowd laughed delightedly and Henry won the case.[41]

It was a period when there was less criticism of lawyers than today. The local citizens did not think the less of their champion for having been more successful than his opponents with his tricks and stratagems.

In a life so full of high drama as Patrick Henry's, we need not be surprised to find that he was also a leading lawyer in the sensational Randolph murder trial. Richard Randolph and his sister-in-law, Nancy Randolph, were co-defendants against charges of infanticide in Cumberland court, a pitiful case which became noised about the state and must have soon aroused the interest of Patrick Henry. Only at the last, however, after an offer of a substantially increased fee, did he bestir himself to ride to Cumberland and join the distinguished attorneys for the Randolphs.

Prior to the trial Henry could hardly have had more than a slight acquaintance with Nancy Randolph and her brother-in-law, Richard. But Nancy and her sister, Judith, Richard's wife, were daughters of Thomas Mann Randolph of Tuckahoe and cousins of Thomas Jefferson. And Richard, although sprung from a "weak strain" of the influential Randolphs, was a gentleman of enough sensibility to free his slaves by his will a few years later. In burning words that would have befitted a Northern Abolitionist, Richard wrote that he would make retribution so far as he was able "to an unfortunate race of bondmen," over whom his ancestors had "usurped and exercised the most lawless and monstrous tyranny . . . in violation of every sacred law of nature."

The scene of the family tragedy was laid against a background of youthful marriage. Judith Randolph's union with her cousin, Richard Randolph, had not had the approval of her mother, now Mrs. St. George Tucker. It had been her wish, so Mrs. Tucker wrote, to keep her daughters single until they "were old enough to form a proper judgment of Mankind." At nineteen and sixteen, Richard and Judy "think everybody perfect" that "they take a fancy to; the Lady expects nothing but condescension and the Gentleman thinks his mistress an angel."

Moreover, Judith appears to have been "a rather commonplace young woman absorbed in her family cares," whereas her sister Nancy was attractive, forceful, and "infinitely courageous." It is not surprising that she and Richard were drawn to each other after she had come to live with her sister Judith. If Nancy had been a man, Dr. J. G. Eckenrode would write, she could have lived "the wild, adventurous life that she hungered for." But, being a woman in that age, she, along with the susceptible Richard, "precipitated a catastrophe."

On October 1, 1792, Nancy, Richard, and Judith Randolph went for a visit to Glenlyvar, the Randolph Harrison home. Nancy, who at least to one observer, showed signs of pregnancy, complained of being ill and retired to her room. During the night there were loud screams from this room; the Harrisons were told they were Nancy's. A person in the room asked for and was provided with laudanum. Not long afterward, steps (presumably Richard Randolph's) were heard descending the stairs, then soon returning. Also bloodstains were found on the stairs and in poor Nancy's room. Randolph Harrison was informed by Glenlyvar Negroes that a foetus had been left on a pile of shingles outside the house, and some weeks later he saw on the pile what appeared to be a suspicious stain.

Word of the tragedy spread through the countryside; considering the prominence of the persons involved, some leading Cumberland citizens showed a commendable willingness to see that justice was done, and a vociferous element in the lower class appears to have been aroused against the Randolphs.

Although both Nancy and Richard Randolph are said to have been indicted in connection with the charge of infanticide, only Richard is known to have been incarcerated in Cumberland jail. Legal assistance, the best in the state, was sought for the distraught young man; John Marshall and Alexander Campbell of Richmond were employed, and the services of Patrick Henry were sought.

Henry had recently moved to his new Long Island plantation and was recovering from an illness when the messenger arrived from Richard Randolph. Although offered the large fee of 250 guineas to defend Randolph, Henry declined on the ground that he was too unwell to make the long journey to Cumberland Courthouse. But some days later the messenger returned with an offer to double the fee, urging that the trial would soon open. Henry discussed the matter with Dolly, on whom he had come to depend more in late years.

"Dolly," he said, "Mr. Randolph seems very anxious that I should appear for him, and 500 Guineas is a large sum. Don't you think I could make the trip in the carriage?" She agreed, and the next day Henry appeared at Cumberland court. The trial was about to begin, and Henry cooperated in the defense already planned by his brother lawyers, John Marshall and Alexander Campbell.

In view of the prominence of the Randolphs and the lurid evidence in the case, it is not surprising that it aroused "intense excitement" or that Richard Randolph was refused bail. We know that Henry was selected by Marshall and Campbell for the work in which he was so skillful—examination of the witnesses. This would be no easy task in view of the law and the facts. Under the state law neither Richard Randolph nor Nancy could be forced to take the witness stand, since they might incriminate themselves. Again under the Virginia legal code, none of the Harrison slaves was permitted to testify to the incriminating evidence which they alone possessed. On the other hand, the members of the court were none too friendly to the defense. Apart from the alleged infanticide, several of the prominent Carringtons who served among the gentleman justices had had a feud with Richard Randolph. The court minutes have been lost or destroyed but notes on them have been copied, as have those on the evidence prepared by John Marshall. The defense lawyers relied on a number of contentions in the hope that at least one would bring in a favorable verdict. It had never been absolutely proved, Marshall noted, that Nancy Randolph had borne a child or that there had been an abortion on the night of October 1, 1792. Every circumstance advanced by Nancy's enemies, he added, could be explained with words that must also have represented Henry's sentiments: "Candor will not condemn or exclude from society a person who may be only unfortunate."

One incident of the trial became a part of the local folk lore; the details as handed down appear basically accurate. Among the opposing witnesses was Mrs. Carter Page, a daughter of Henry's old political enemy, Archibald Cary. This lady, a cousin of the Randolphs, had lived in Cumberland since her marriage. Sometime before October 1, 1792, she had satisfied her curiosity as to whether Nancy was pregnant. The highly connected matron testified at the trial as to Nancy's condition and thus fell into a trap laid by her wily questioner.

When in the house with Nancy, the lady had peeped through a crack in the door while Nancy was undressing.

"Which eye did you peep with?" Henry asked in the tone and manner effective with many audiences. And turning to the court, he declared, "Great God deliver us from eavesdroppers!" We need not be surprised that the witness was angered by the ensuing laughter or indeed that ill feeling aroused by the case continued for years among prominent Virginia families.

There was insufficient evidence for the court to convict the two defendants. Richard Randolph and then Nancy were freed. The story handed down to a present-day descendant of Harrison Randolph is that the baby at Glenlyvar was born dead. Thomas Jefferson was among the Virginians who took the charitable view of Nancy's conduct. Should a less tolerant one be taken in the present age, an age possessed of sophisticated knowledge which could have prevented the pathetic incident from even occurring?

Henry had ended for Richard Randolph with one of "his most masterly efforts," and the verdict of the court was greeted with acclaim by an audience which had been largely hostile to the defendants. There was no longer any doubt that Henry was one of the leading criminal lawyers in Virginia; he further confirmed in the British Debt Case that he was one of the leading civil lawyers. John Randolph of Roanoke, a younger brother of Richard, heard Henry speak on these and probably a number of other occasions. Moved to superlatives, Randolph declared in his later years that Henry was "the greatest orator that ever lived"; he was "Shakespeare and Garrick combined, and spake as never man spake." [42]

Often in fragile health, Henry was working long and hard to provide for his family against his approaching retirement. He was now making a substantial income through his law practice and was supplementing it through continued land speculation, some of it on a scale that is now difficult to envisage. This activity enabled him to become one of the greatest landowners in Virginia.

From a recent study of the tax records, we learn that in 1788 Henry was one of the hundred largest land proprietors in Virginia. A decade later he ranked with George Washington among the leading landed magnates of the state, and his holdings included enough valuable plantation lands, river bottoms, and other fertile acreage for no one to disparage him as land poor.

Not until he was almost at death's door did Henry lose the keen eye for land values which brought such impressive results. The tracts which he had bought in Kentucky during the early 1780's, while mostly in wilderness country, were acquired with a view to future development: 4,000 acres on the Kentucky River and the North Fork of the Sandy River, 500 acres on the Cumberland Trace, and 1,000 acres on Rolling Fork in Lincoln County. "Farmington," a "classic" brick mansion near Louisville, was built in 1810 by the Speed family on land which they had bought from Henry—a choice seat where he himself might have located if he had assumed fewer responsibilities in Virginia.

With his property outside of Virginia unlisted, the 1788 tax receipts show that Henry then owned 70 acres in Prince Edward County (exclusive of over 1,600 acres there for which he would soon acquire title), 8,000 acres in Henry County, and nearly 14,000 in Princess Anne and Norfolk counties. On his Leatherwood and Prince Edward properties he had 66 slaves, 38 horses, and 66 cattle; his other Virginia land must have been all, or in large part, undeveloped.

In a letter which Henry wrote in May, 1784, to John Tabb regarding some Norfolk County property, he expressed a meticulous desire to trade land of equal quality to that intended for him. But William

Wirt, in a good position to know the facts, wrote that Henry had been "censured" for an attempt to acquire land on the shores of Chesapeake Bay which had hitherto been used as a public common. There was no Virginia law at this time which prevented Henry from acquiring the land, but Wirt philosophied that "we do not claim for him a total exemption from the failures of humanity."

There appears to have been a private suit against Henry involving Norfolk County land. But Governor Harrison wrote in October, 1784, to Edmund Randolph, Attorney General of Virginia, that he was returning Henry's deed for the land to Randolph and that the Council's advice was not to intervene in the suit, since the Councilors "are altogether unacquainted with the subject and know not the quantity of land heretofore reserved nor its bounds."

Striving not to be too partial to his biographical subject, Wirt also noted that Henry was not "free from censure" on account of his interest in the Yazoo lands of what was then Georgia. Records still preserved at Prince Edward Courthouse recall the fruitless efforts of Henry and some local associates to promote the great speculation in wild Georgia land. But the Yazoo company with which Henry was identified proved not to be the fraudulent enterprise for which John Randolph of Roanoke would later excoriate on the floor of Congress the guilty and allegedly guilty participants.

In 1788, the year Henry took the oath as a lawyer before the Prince Edward District Court, his business affairs were becoming more promising. With his associates from the Southside area he cast venturesome eyes upon the great unsettled region in Georgia, including the Yazoo lands in its northwest. Henry's investments in the region were curtailed by what he deemed arbitrary action of the federal government. He owned an interest in land on the bend of the Tennessee River which had been ceded by the Creek Indians to Georgia, then ceded back by the federal government to the Creeks. In letters to Governor Telfair of Georgia and to an Augusta, Georgia, citizen, Henry complained bitterly of the interference with the sovereign right of the state and of the "Deception" on the part of the federal government: it was easy to see the fatal example which was being set.

Not long before, Henry had written that he had considered moving to North Carolina if certain measures to implement states' rights were not taken in Virginia. Now he spoke of moving some of his family to Georgia, "endeared" as he was to her by "the hope of being possessed of valuable property within her limits & where he fondly hoped to fix [his posterity]." On December 21, 1789, the Georgia legislature granted Henry's Virginia company preemptive rights to a large tract of land in northwestern Georgia. The land was subject to the Indian title and the company was to pay Georgia $93,750 within two years, including a small payment at an early date in paper money. But the Georgia legislature drastically increased the terms of payment, and the Virginia Yazoo Company was unable to make a satisfactory adjustment. Patrick Henry and David Ross, another large Virginia speculator, were appointed a committee to prosecute the claims in the United States Supreme Court. But the suit was prevented by the adoption of the Eleventh Amendment to the Constitution, which provided that the judicial power of the United States should not be extended to suits by citizens of one state against another state. We do not need to discuss the separate Yazoo "frauds" against which John Randolph would inveigh.

Henry would never live either in Georgia or in North Carolina. But besides his earlier land investments in the Tarheel State, he purchased a large tract in North Carolina shortly before his death. Once the property of the Saura Town Indians, it had been acquired by William Byrd II, who had helped to survey that beautiful border land between Virginia and North Carolina, and was sold to Henry by Byrd heirs. As usual, Henry's speculation included much undeveloped land, but the tract contained some fine low ground along the Dan River and extended north from present Eden, North Carolina, across the Virginia line. Henry acquired in early June, 1799, for five shillings and cancellation of a debt due him, an undivided fourth part of a vast tract containing over 25,000 acres.

In a codicil to his will dated February 12, 1799, Henry stated that he had agreed to purchase from General Henry Lee "two shares of the Saura Town Land, amounting to about 6,314 acres certain," and this land was given in fee simple to be divided equally in value to two of his sons by his "dear wife," Dorothea. Thus, with the Red Hill, Long Island, and Saura Town estates, he could proudly note that he had bequeathed "seats" for his six living sons by his second wife. Although it was claimed that he had already provided adequately for the children of his first wife, there would be a lawsuit after his death which involved children by the two wives and did not sweeten family relations.[43]

25

The Last Years

"Real patriotism is a virtue of that exalted nature which will
induce individuals to set aside every private advantage, when
such happens to clash with the interests of the community."
——PROBUS [1]

I decline to accept the end of man. . . . I refuse to accept this.
I believe that man will not merely endure: he will prevail. He
is immortal, not because he alone among creatures has an in-
exhaustible voice, but because he has a soul, a spirit capable of
compassion and sacrifice and endurance. The poet's, the
writer's . . . privilege is to help man endure by lifting his
heart, by reminding him of the courage and honor and hope
and pride and compassion and pity and sacrifice which have
been the glory of his past.——WILLIAM FAULKNER [2]

1795–1799. Henry in retirement at Red Hill. Declines high
government positions.

January 15, 1798. Birth of his seventeenth child.

March, 1799. Makes his last speech, at Charlotte Courthouse, a plea for American unity.

June 6, 1799. Henry's death.

DURING THE LAST decade of his life, Patrick Henry was
offered an extraordinary number of high governmental positions.
Coming particularly during the final years of George Washington's
administration, they ranged from United States Senator and Gov-

[425]

ernor to minister to Spain and to France, Chief Justice, and Secretary of State. Some of the offers were no more than tentative, but Henry, recently a Federalist bête noire, was now perhaps their most courted personage.

Henry refused all the flattering proposals, however, largely because of physical debility. In July, 1789, he at first declined, for reasons of health as we have seen, the invitation to appear in the lucrative lawsuit at Loudon Courthouse.[3] Three years later, on May 10, 1792, Richard Venable wrote in his diary, after spending the day at Henry's house, "What a weight of worldly concerns rest upon this old man's shoulders. He supports it with strength & fortitude; but nature must sink under the load ere it be long." Then on September 7 Venable noted that Henry was sick when attending New London court, and many cases were continued for him. Perhaps he was suffering from the seasonal malaria which was said to have plagued him in past years. Two weeks later he was still absent from the court. "Business much retarded by absence of P. Henry," Venable stated.[4] In 1794 Henry declined a United States senatorial post in Philadelphia as too demanding of his strength and retired from the bar, to spend a few happy years at Long Island and especially at Red Hill, his last plantation homes, on the Staunton River. But his health continued to decline, perhaps from about 1797, as the result of a fatal malady; he refused still more offers of top governmental posts. When almost at death's door, however, he would ride from Red Hill to Charlotte Courthouse to make a moving plea for national unity.

During the winter after the Venable visit, 1792–1793, the Henrys moved to a place more remote than Prince Edward. Apparently intended as his permanent residence, this plantation was situated about forty-five miles southwestward at Long Island in Campbell County. By the end of 1792 he had settled with his family in the new house, a two-story rectangular frame structure of some eight rooms, which was comfortable enough for their simple tastes.

When acquiring his various plantations, Henry continued to have an eye not only for a good buy but also for a good view. Situated on a bluff north of the Staunton River, the residence commanded a magnificent vista of the river meandering below, the long island thereon, the bottom lands, and, across the Staunton, the low hills of Pittsylvania and Halifax counties. Back of his house Henry could see his fields extending toward the overseer's house, the Quarter Place, and the roads connecting with the mill, New London, and Rustburg, the Campbell County seat. Altogether, the estate comprised 3,522 acres, with much fertile soil and dark bottom land. Many years later, after extensive cultivation, the island alone was said, not altogether expansively, to have produced enough corn to "feed all Pittsylvania County."

Henry bought the plantation from General Henry Lee. In addition to his distinguished military and political service, Lee had engaged in large land speculations. This get-rich-quick scheme, which lured so many gentlemen of the period, proved his undoing. By the 1790's the General was so hard pressed that he apparently sold not only the large Long Island property but two other tracts of land to Patrick Henry.

Fifteen miles below present Alta Vista on the Staunton River, and thirty-five miles south of Lynchburg, Long Island is a secluded spot even in the automobile age. Here Henry could hope to get away from political demands and importunities after more than a generation of strenuous public service. But such plans were chimerical in view of the difficulties of the new American government and his national influence. The passage of the Hamiltonian financial measures had revived or created enmities between the commercial interests, strong in the North, and the agrarian interests, especially influential in the South and Southwest. Successful as it was, the Hamiltonian program had nevertheless discriminated in favor of what its author termed "the rich and well born" at the expense of the mechanics, laborers, and the small farmers, particularly of the South. Indeed, many Southern tobacco growers and other farmers of the area had never recovered from the postwar depression.

More and more, Thomas Jefferson was becoming dissatisfied with the Hamiltonian legislation, and his opposition was intensified by Federalist sympathies with Great Britain in her war with revolutionary France. In 1793 Jefferson resigned as Secretary of State and, ably assisted by James Madison, worked successfully to form a new party—the Democratic-Republican, or Republicans. Opposing this party were the Federalists, led by Hamilton and John Adams, now with the more overt support of President Washington. Patrick Henry, although still retaining much sympathy with the anti-Federalist principles of states' rights and strict construction of the Constitution, was becoming more impressed with the stability of the new national government, more willing to listen to the arguments of such Federalist leaders as Henry Lee and Washington. He was no less favorable to the Federalists because of their opposition to Madison, and especially Jefferson, his long-time political opponents.

Already, in Philadelphia during February, 1793, General Lee, then the Virginia Governor, had discussed with Washington the possibility of adding Henry's great influence to the administration. Washington was in hearty agreement: a seat on the Supreme Court was deemed most suitable and likely to be accepted. Returning to Virginia, Lee discussed the matter with Henry, but Henry had been induced to believe that Washington in 1791 had described him as "a factious, seditious character" and, so Lee wrote Washington in August, 1794, had been "sorely affected" by the alleged statements. Lee made numerous attempts to assure Henry that the remarks attributed to Washington had never been made, but his efforts were "unavailing." [5]

When Washington replied to Lee on August 26, he was wrestling with the problem of the Whisky Rebellion in western Pennsylvania, an armed insurrection in opposition to the federal excise tax on domestic distilled liquors. But he spoke to Lee of his "sincere consolation" in finding that "the good people of Virginia" held the rebellion in "general detestation." As for Henry, Washington declared that a part of the plan for creating discord was "to make me say things of others, and others of me, which have no foundation in truth . . ." [6] He stated positively that he had never expressed such opinions regarding Henry as Lee said the former had been led to believe.

"I had heard . . . with very peculiar pleasure," Washington continued, that Henry "was acquiescent in his conduct, and that, though he could not give up his opinion respecting the constitution, yet unless he should be called upon by official duty, he would express no sentiment unfriendly to the exercise of the powers of a government which had been chosen by a majority of the people, or words to this effect." [7]

While these negotiations regarding the high federal post were in a preliminary state, Governor Lee had the satisfaction of writing Henry on July 11, 1794, to offer him a seat in the United States Senate. James Monroe had resigned the position in order to become minister to France, and the Governor and Council thereupon appointed Henry to fill the vacancy. It was the second effort to place him in the post. In Lee's brief letter, happily worded to persuade Henry to return to the political forum, Lee referred to their reluctance to interrupt him in his "happy retreat" but spoke of their belief in his "preferential love of country." Lee alluded in flattering terms to "concerns of the highest national magnitude [that] may engage the attention of the Senate" and the particular need for Henry's counsel. [8]

Henry replied to Lee's letter on the very morning after its receipt. With "great pain" he spoke of "existing circumstances" which compelled him to refuse an appointment, particularly honorable in view of the manner in which it was communicated. But he apologetically declined because of his "Time of life—combined with the great Distance to Philadelphia." He regretted his lack of ability for the exertion called for by "the arduous situation of affairs" [9] and believed he should undertake only the less demanding duties of his now restricted law practice and of his new plantation in lower Campbell County.

When that venturesome Pennsylvanian, John Irvine, had come a half century before to the southeastern part of what later became Campbell County, he had found a virgin forest. The wilderness stretched from thirty-five to forty miles, with few open fields and scarcely a white inhabitant. In the Staunton River Valley, at the lower end of the county, there were still traces of recent Indian habitation. Fish, partridge, duck, and wild geese abounded. Among the first order books at Campbell Courthouse were records of recent payments of £250 in tobacco to a local settler for five young wolves' heads and £600 for eleven heads to another settler. [10]

During the war, most of the local farmers were strongly Whig in sympathy. When Henry moved to Campbell County, there were a number of local citizens who, under command of Colonel Charles Lynch, had fought gallantly with General William Campbell's riflemen at Guilford Courthouse. After the countryside was threatened by Tory partisans, Lynch and several other Whig leaders of the area had used summary methods to suppress them. But the punishment meted out was chiefly flogging, not the more barbarous treatment with which "lynching" is now often associated.

Despite the war, the area continued to develop. In the 1780's Campbell County was cut off from Bedford and named for General William Campbell, Henry's brother-in-law; the town of Lynchburg was established, and a rude log courthouse was built at the present Rustburg, along with stocks and a whipping post. Henry, a criminal lawyer who defended the poor and lowly as well as the rich and highly placed, must have found much in the local scene to arouse his humanitarian sensibilities. In some respects the late eighteenth century was no more cruel than the present atomic age, but the criminal law did not err on the side of leniency. One Campbell County citizen, found guilty of contempt of court, was ordered to be committed to the stocks where he was to remain until the "COURTE BE ADJOURNED." [11] Among frequent references in the court records to flogging, we find that Jack, a Negro slave guilty of robbery, was ordered to be given "thirty-nine lashes at the publick whipping post, well laid upon his bare back"; also, to have "about ⅔" of his right ear cut off and to be burned on his right hand.[12]

When Henry lived in Campbell County, many of his fellow citizens were of the restless breed which later sought opportunities to the westward. In a list of seven otherwise qualified justices of Campbell Court during 1789, four were reported as having moved to Kentucky, among them one of the pioneer Irvines. Often whole families, with neighbors from the Piedmont region, would trek together to Kentucky and later perhaps to the Old Northwest, settling together in the same area.[13]

For the citizens who remained in Campbell County, however, there was increasing opportunity. In a petition to the Assembly during 1793, "Sundry, the Inhabitants" [14] of Campbell, Pittsylvania, and

Halifax counties complained of the steep approach road and lack of proper regulations for the ferry at Long Island.[15] But at least there was now a ferry, and bateaux were coming up the Staunton River to beyond Red Hill, where Henry would soon move. The river bottom land in particular offered some of the best soil in Virginia, and crops were being sent downstream for transshipment and ready sale in such easterly markets as Manchester and Petersburg. Henry was now obtaining enough money from his corn, cattle, and tobacco to retire from the law; while at Long Island he handled only two noteworthy cases, one only after some persuasion from his wife.

It was while Henry was engaged in one of these *causes célèbres,* the British Debts Case, that he attended a family dinner at which there was a revealing political incident. During the court session at Richmond, John Syme gave a dinner party at "Rocky Mills," his fine estate in upper Hanover County. The company, in the staid words of the day, was comprised of "respectable characters of both parties." After removing the cloth, Syme offered "very audibly" the first toast—to "The people." Henry was obviously disturbed. He pushed aside his old black wig as was his habit when greatly excited.

"What, brother! Not drink to General Washington as we used to do? For shame, brother!" he exclaimed, with arms akimbo, and after filling his glass with Thomson's Madeira, he called out "Washington!"[16]

There continued to be difficulties between Henry and his improvident half brother. In July, 1794, Syme, evidently of the Jefferson-Madison party or influenced by their persuasive arguments, wrote a blunt letter to Henry which may have ruffled his usually amiable disposition. Syme said that Henry's June letter had just reached him, and, besides some rambling remarks, he accused Henry of having "shrank from your Country, the majority of w^ch (at least) have always treated you well. I am sorry to have it trumpeted so often, in my Ears, but contract [sic] it, I will not, knowing it to be the truth."[17]

Syme's letter came that same July, 1794, when Henry declined the Senate seat offered him by Governor Lee. Two months later

Washington also tendered Henry a position as envoy plenipotentiary to Spain, where he would be in charge of negotiations to secure free navigation of the Mississippi River. A subject of vital importance at the time of Henry's fight against ratification of the Constitution, it was no less so now that the Mississippi Valley was being filled with settlers and Kentucky had already become a state.[18] The situation was further aggravated by the French Revolution, with weak Spain inevitably affected by French policy. Not many years before, the appointment as envoy there might have had special appeal for Henry. But he wrote Edmund Randolph, now Secretary of State and acting for President Washington, that while it would be "highly gratifying" to him on all occasions to further Washington's views, yet he was constrained to decline the appointment. The lengthy negotiations in a country so distant presented difficulties with which it was not easy for Henry to reconcile himself in his "time of life," and he expressed his sincere regret that he could not accept the honor extended him.

Thomas Pinckney of South Carolina, appointed in his stead, made a favorable treaty with Spain by which the United States was granted free navigation of the Mississippi River and her southern boundary fixed at the thirty-first parallel of latitude.

The conflict over foreign policy continued to accentuate the growth of American political parties. A decade after the Revolutionary War, the British had not given up their forts in the Old Northwest and were seizing American ships and impressing American seamen as callously as if they were on British merchantmen. President Washington sent Chief Justice John Jay to England to try to negotiate a treaty which would at least alleviate the causes of conflict. The resulting Jay Treaty of November 19, 1794, did remove some of the difficulties and perhaps prevented a war with England, but it led to more interparty conflict with the anti-Federalists, who violently attacked Jay and even George Washington as subservient to the British. In Henry's own Southside Virginia a brilliant but eccentric young man, John Randolph, of whom Henry would hear much more, helped to prepare for his political debut by offering "Damn George Washington" as a public toast.

The trend of events was particularly favorable to the Republicans in the South and West. And Thomas Jefferson, seeking every possible opportunity to promote the Democratic-Republican party, was even willing to overlook his differences with Henry in the effort to strengthen the new party.

"With respect to the gentleman we expect to meet [at Bedford Court]," Jefferson wrote Archibald Stuart on April 18, 1795, "satisfy him, if you please, that there is no remains of disagreeable sentiment towards him on my part. I was once sincerely affectioned towards him, and it accords with my philosophy to encourage the tranquillizing passions." [19]

In France the government had seized the church property, and by 1793 a ruthless dictatorship had intensified the bloody proscription of its political enemies. Henry, who was particularly disturbed by the French antireligious policy, voiced his opinion of their revolution in a manner which Jefferson could hardly appreciate. Hearing of Jefferson's use of French cooking at Monticello, Henry commented with provincial narrowness that he did not "approve of gentlemen abjuring their native victuals." Yet Jefferson, who felt that he had more than this to forgive, showed for some time a commendable willingness to bury the hatchet.

Meantime, the lengthy efforts of General Henry Lee to remove the misunderstanding between Henry and Washington had been successfully concluded. For Washington, Henry had the highest respect and admiration; he was far more sensitive to allegedly unfavorable criticism from the General than to other words which were more extreme. Sometime about June, 1795, Lee sent Henry the portion of Washington's long letter of the previous August which related to him. In his reply, Henry wrote that he was highly flattered to have evidence of "the esteem of that personage" most responsible for the success of the American Revolution. "The intimation now given me, that there was no ground to believe I had incurred his censure, gives very great pleasure." [20]

In the autumn of 1794 Henry wrote Betsey that he must give up the law and "plague" himself "no more with business." He would settle down with what he had, for it would be "sufficient employment to see after" his "little Flock, and the management" of his plantation. The "little flock" included eight children by his second wife, and the end was not yet. Actually, too, he had already acquired another large plantation—Red Hill, eighteen miles down the Staunton from Long Island. To Red Hill he would soon move, first for several months of the year, then from 1796 until his death. There were overseers or other assistants, however, to help look after his large farming operations; for a few years he could enjoy a retirement becoming more urgent because of his increasing physical infirmity.

With more leisure, Henry had time for reflection on men and events of his lengthy political career. One valuable legacy of his latter years was his observations on several of his leading political associates. Within a few months in 1794 Richard Henry Lee and George Mason had died, both after distressing illnesses. Thus only Henry was left of this great Virginia triumvirate. Lee, after proposing the Declaration of Independence, had continued his legislative career until 1792. As an idealistic young man he had quoted an ancient Roman precept that every man owed seven years of service to his country; Lee had given over four times seven. As for Mason, author of the Virginia Bill of Rights, his death had attracted enough attention to elicit a notice in the English *Gentleman's Magazine,* which contained an extract from his will, enjoining his sons to defend and cherish the liberties of their country.[21]

We are indebted to Spencer Roane for reminiscences which Henry gave him of Mason and Lee, along with a few more of his notable contemporaries. Henry, so Roane recalled, had "strong prejudices for and against many of his political associates, though he only expressed them to his particular friends. He had the highest opinion of George Mason's talents, patriotism, and republican principles," considering Mason "a man well acquainted with the interests of the people and warmly attached to the liberty of his country. A cordial friendship existed between them." Of Richard Henry Lee, however, Henry "did not think quite so well, and they were often opposed to each other; yet they coalesced on great questions, as that of independence, and opposition to the federal constitution." Roane also

[434]

spoke of Henry as being "very fond" of John Tyler, whom he considered "a warm hearted patriot and an honest, sensible man." [22]

Of James Madison, Henry was less complimentary, especially during his own last years. During 1783–1784, when he and Madison served together in the House of Delegates, Henry considered Madison "a man of great acquirements, but too theoretical as a politician," and Henry became more unfavorable to him in the Convention of 1788. Henry, Roane declared, "was astonished" that Madison would accept the Constitution, "admitting its defects, and in a season of perfect peace, and believed him too friendly to a strong government and too hostile to the Governments of the States." [23]

What Henry thought of the reversal of political principles by which Madison, so recently a leading Federalist, had become an outstanding anti-Federalist, we can only surmise. Nor do we know what Madison thought of Henry's increasing fondness for Federalism. To quote the old adage, "Times change and men change with them." It was a fact probably more easily understood by the middle-aged Madison than by the aging Henry.

Curiously, Spencer Roane in his lengthy memoirs of Henry for William Wirt offered no observations by Henry on Thomas Jefferson. Henry did speak with some frankness of Madison. Why not more so of Jefferson, who had opposed him so bitterly, and especially in view of Henry's "strong prejudices" regarding his political associates? Perhaps Henry did make some animadversions on Jefferson to Roane, but the Judge, an ambitious Jeffersonian, may not have thought it expedient to offer them for publication by Wirt. However, a letter of Dolly Henry's, a month after her husband met his death with Christian resignation, indicates that the attitude at the Henry home was hardly favorable toward Jefferson. She wished that "Jefferson and the other deists" could have seen the way her husband died, Dolly said.

Red Hill, which Henry reportedly described as "The Garden Spot of Virginia," is mentioned in surviving family correspondence as early as January 2, 1794. In a letter to one of her half sisters in the Tidewater, Henry's thirteen-year-old daughter Kitty indicated that she was particularly interested in the Lynchburg ball which she had attended on St. John's Day the past December. There were "50 ladies and near that number of Gentlemen" present, and Kitty, with her sister Sally, fourteen, intended to venture forth to Lynchburg again to attend the ball on George Washington's birth night. Then, after a reference to "Mama" having had "a fine son" on January 20, Kitty noted that "Papa" had bought old Dick Booker's place, for which Henry was to pay £1,700.[24] The Booker plantation was Red Hill.

Obviously, the fact that Red Hill was at least "a more public place," a little closer than Long Island to the social life of eastern Virginia, contributed to its popularity with Dolly and the young girls. "Dr Sister, Write to me & let me hear all news of Fredericksburg & Richmond as L Island affords none worth your perusal," Kitty had said in her ecstatic letter. But, of more importance, Red Hill was a fine plantation in a beautiful location—another good buy by the canny Henry. Red Hill is in Charlotte County, only a few miles across the boundary line from Campbell County. With its lush low grounds stretching for several miles along the Staunton River and its fertile tobacco lands, it is indeed a garden spot. Henry's final resting place, it is the best known of all the plantations chiefly identified with his peripatetic life.

Thanks to the efforts of a dedicated memorial foundation and of Eugene Casey, a very generous donor, the simple story-and-a-half frame house of Henry's time has been restored, along with his office and some other outbuildings. Here a visitor may speculate as to the location of the favorite tree where Henry often sat on pleasant days, quaffing from a bucket of spring water, or of the spot where he waited for the sound of the horn announcing an approaching bateau. Or again, he may wonder how the aging Henry could live placidly in a house overrun by so many children!

Midway between Red Hill and Long Island on the south side of the Staunton, near present Brookneal, Henry acquired another farm, Seven Islands. The small frame building there, known as "The House with the Three Front Doors," was long the residence of some Henry descendants. There is a story of two of the boys playing with a surviving relic of an illustrious ancestor—Patrick Henry's wig! In the early days there was much visiting between the three Henry plantations. One night, we are told, a Negro traveling from one to another ran into a bear as he was crossing over a fence. "The best man got over last." [25]

By the late 1790's Henry had not only become one of the large Southern landed proprietors but he would be able to leave valuable working plantations to several of his children. True, there were vicissitudes, more or less serious, such as when he wrote that some hogsheads of his tobacco were "duk't" [ducked], probably in the Staunton River, and when his crops were seriously damaged by the river flood. Also, much of his accumulating wealth came from speculation in land rather than from its cultivation. On the whole, however, his farming records for this period show the beneficial results of good management with a considerable capital investment.

On the three plantations Henry must have owned some hundred slaves, representing a capital of at least £4,000 to £5,000, as well as hundreds of farm animals: cattle, horses, hogs, and sheep. His inventory after his death showed that he had 88 cattle alone on Long Island and 156 at Red Hill. One Red Hill Negro man, Jesse, probably a skilled workman, was valued at £200; several men at £120 apiece; a "young wench," doubtless of childbearing value, at £100; and there were some sixty other slaves of assorted ages and generally of less value. [26] During that era of manual labor, Negroes were usually deemed essential to the operation of a large Southern plantation. Although Henry had deplored the evils of slavery, there is no evidence that he shared the strong emancipationist sentiments of his sister, Elizabeth (now become Madam Russell), and in his will Henry left Dolly full power to emancipate only "one or two" of them. But, always the good master, when offering to buy some Seven Islands land in late 1797, he had said that he would also hire the Negroes since they were "desirous to stay together & not be parted," and that he would "use them well." [27]

"No man ever vaunted less of his achievements than Mr. Henry," Spencer Roane testified; he hardly ever heard Henry "speak of those great achievements" which formed the "prominent part" of his life. [28]

As for *boasting,* he was an entire stranger to it; unless it be that in his latter days he seemed proud of the goodness of his lands, and, I believe, wished to be thought wealthy. It is my opinion that he was better pleased to be flattered as to his wealth than as to his great talents. This I have accounted for by reflecting that he had long been under narrow and difficult circumstances as to property, from which he was at length happily relieved, whereas there never was a time when his talents had not shone conspicuous, tho' he always seemed unconscious of them.[29]

There is a story of Henry standing by the Red Hill house and calling directions to his slaves in the river bottom lands a half mile below. (If so, the feat was equaled by Madam Russell when directing her field hands near Seven Mile Ford in Southwest Virginia.) Not only from family tradition but from Henry's letters and accounts we get evidence that he kept a sharp eye on his various business interests until too handicapped by illness. We have a further picture of a loving father, a generous neighbor—altogether a mild and amiable private citizen quite in contrast with the fierce fighter in court and legislative hall.

Henry took a particular interest in the education of his young children. He employed the brother of the Scottish poet, Thomas Campbell, as a tutor for them, but Campbell never reached America. With his boys and girls Henry was "on the most familiar footing," treating them as "companions and friends."[30] Visitors to his plantation sometimes found him lying on the floor with a group of little children who were "climbing over him in every direction, or dancing around him to the tune of his violin," the only contest seeming to be who could make the most noise. Now that Henry had more leisure, he appears to have revived his love of music and was fond of entertaining his wife and children with his violin, often improvising.

These incidents, so W. W. Henry says, occurred during his grandfather's "green old age." We may wonder if the relationship was so close during his last declining years. One of his daughters recalled that every morning, after rising, her father would seat himself in the dining room and read the Bible. Then, as his children passed him for the first time during the day, he would raise his eyes from his book and greet them with a "Good morrow." At least to the younger children, while at Red Hill, he became a venerated and somewhat remote old man. An exacting supervision of them seems to have been beyond his strength or inclination. A few years after her husband's death, Dolly contracted what seems to have been mostly a *mariage de convenance* with Edmund Winston. The Judge took on some problems with his ready-made family which he had hardly bargained for. It was difficult enough to see to them at Red Hill, and he was often absent on the judicial circuit. Moreover, they included the younger Henry boys, spirited lads who had their troubles at college, after Henry's death. There was the worrisome case of young Nathaniel Henry, who was suspended at New London Academy and Hampden-Sydney and even denied admission to Drury Lacy School. Not content with these misadventures, he also got into hot water at Washington College (now Washington and Lee University) by calling the soup "slop," threatening the steward, and alleging that there were "flees" [sic] in the bread. The college historian, Ollinger Crenshaw, who recounts these student misdeeds, notes that the "flees" were probably weevils.[31] In any event, it takes little imagination to picture Judge Winston as he left his judicial duties to make what were then no easy journeys to Lexington or elsewhere in the effort to extricate young Nathaniel from his difficulties. One or two of the other Henry lads also, while they would become good citizens, were not distinguished for their collegiate achievements.

Just about the time that Henry moved to Red Hill, he passed his sixtieth birthday. But until his death he retained many qualities of a distinctive personality. There was a still at Red Hill where Henry manufactured some whisky, as did many Southern plantation owners, but he remained temperate in his habits, seldom drinking anything but water. In the effort to encourage temperance he had small beer made, but there is no indication that he was able to change the drinking habits of his neighbors. Unlike so many of them, he did not even use tobacco, and tobacco smoke repelled him. Altogether, we find no reference to his having any personal vices, and "scarcely a foible"— that is, unless we agree with Judge Roane that he was "too much attached to property." [32] His manners were simple and kindly and he

[439]

had the ability, so helpful to a politician, of being able to adapt himself to any company. Somewhat surprisingly, he had a kind of humor described as "extremely amusing, without detracting from his dignity." At the risk of making him seem a paragon of virtue we should also repeat the story of his generosity to the poor people of the neighborhood, to whom he not only supplied provisions from his plantation but loans of money for food which he could not supply. Often these debts were never collected. Altogether, the story of the Red Hill years may even seem at times one of cloying sweetness—that is, if politics had not again intruded.

At first sympathetic with the French Revolution, Henry was too practical-minded to favor its extreme measures. As the French government was changed to a limited monarchy, to a bloody dictatorship, and a military despotism, he became openly hostile to its radical policies. In April, 1792, the French declared war on Austria and Prussia, and the following January, 1793, they executed Louis XVI. There was a strong effort among the Jeffersonian Republicans to bring the United States into the war on behalf of her ally in the American Revolution. But Edmund Randolph wrote in June that Henry had been "loud in reprobating the decapitation of the French king"; he was a friend to the American policies pursued to secure peace and nothing would induce him to "vote" for war but the "reprieve" of the Marquis de Lafayette, then in a French prison. Henry "grows richer every hour and thus his motives to tranquility must be multiplying every day." To these somewhat acid sentiments it should be added that the devout Henry was strongly opposed to the extreme French antireligious policy, which in 1794 even included the enthronement in Paris of a Goddess of Reason.

Among books listed in Henry's inventory after his death was the *Campaign* of Napoleon. In 1796 Napoleon Bonaparte crossed the Alps and won a series of brilliant victories over his Austrian and Italian opponents. "It won't all do!" Henry was later heard to say. And he declared that the present generation in France had become "so debased by a long despotism" that it was "incapable of forming a direct and just estimate of rational liberty. . . . I should not be surprised if the very man at whose victories you now rejoice, should, Caesar-like, subvert the liberties of his country." [33]

Following the crushing Napoleonic victories, France by the Treaty of Campo Formio in 1797 secured the Austrian (Belgian) Netherlands, and the Austrian power in Italy was greatly restricted. With only Great Britain still in arms against France, by January, 1799, Henry was convinced that her conduct had "made it the interest of the great family of mankind to wish the downfall of her present government." But while he saw the dangers that threatened America from "her intrigues and her arms," he was more alarmed that France would destroy "the great pillars of all government and of social life; . . . virtue, morality, and religion." [34]

For some time there had been signs that Henry's health was gradually declining, and this became more evident during his last two years. It was during this final period of "debility," so Spencer Roane asserted, that Henry made his "most violent complaints" against the Republicans. Roane again wrote as a strong Jeffersonian partisan, not without aspirations for high office. To differ with the Judge's political opinions was hardly a mortal sin; Henry was joined in his Federalist sympathies by some of the ablest and most lucid-minded Americans. Moreover, his surviving papers show that he retained considerable mental perspicuity until his last hours. During the Red Hill period, however, he became more conservative; he was indeed "very retired," as Roane states, and often poorly informed. [35]

In the effort to enlist Henry's help for the Federalists by offering him the high political appointments, Judge Roane stated that General Henry Lee was "the principal agent." Roane accused Lee of misrepresenting the Republicans, of flattering Henry and assailing him "on his weak side, in the trading for valuable lands" which Henry "wished to acquire for the sons of his second marriage." When visiting Mrs. Henry after her husband's death, Roane said that he referred to General Lee's activity in this respect and spoke of the injury which it had done Henry with the Republicans.

"She seemed to agree with me on the subject," Roane wrote, "but concluded, with a laugh, that Henry Lee had been a great friend to their family, for that Mr. Henry had got two fine tracts of land from him!" [36] On the whole, Roane believed that Henry "was operated upon by the artfulness and misrepresentation of artful and designing men, under circumstances of seclusion and debility arising from the infirmity of age and disease peculiarly fitting him for the operation; and that by this means he was carried to greater lengths against the measures of the Republicans than he would otherwise have gone." [37]

To what he contended were Henry's declining mental faculties in this period, Roane also attributed the fact that the aging gentleman became "more religious." Previously, Henry had been "remarkably tolerant" of other religious opinions, not intruding his own into his conversation. Now he became a perfervid Christian, anxious to convert less zealous associates. He was particularly opposed to the then current deistic thought which had influenced other Founding Fathers such as Franklin and Jefferson. He did much reading of the Bible and of such Anglican divines as Archbishop John Tillotson, Bishop Joseph Butler, and Bishop Thomas Sherlock. One of Sherlock's sermons, so Henry declared, had removed all his doubts as to the truth of Christianity. [38] Tom Paine's *Age of Reason* prompted Henry to write a treatise in defense of the Christian faith. But deciding that some other writer had made a better defense, he destroyed his own. [39]

Henry's books as listed in the inventory after his death comprise over 225 well chosen volumes relating to religion, history, law, politics, classical literature, and other topics. But there are none by such deistic writers as Voltaire and Rousseau. Among the typical titles, often incorrectly spelled in the court records, are Homer's *Ilias, Don Quck Zotte, The Compleat English Farmer* and *Modern Farmer's Guide, Essays on Slavery, Bonepartte's Camphain,* Tillotson's *Sermons,* and two volumes of *The Independant Wigg* (Whig). Henry was too occupied with political business when in Williamsburg and Richmond to absorb much of the local deistic thought, and in the secluded back country his religious influences were of the conservative—indeed, rather fundamentalist—type. While he had gone through a period of some religious questioning, by the Red Hill years his views had become decidedly orthodox.

"Amongst other strange things said of me," Henry wrote to his daughter Betsey in August, 1796, "I hear it said by the deists that I am one of their number." But to him deism was only "another name for vice and depravity." He was, however, much consoled by reflecting that the Christian religion had, "from its first appearance in the world, been attacked in vain by all the wits, philosophers, and wise ones aided by every power of man, and its triumph has been complete . . . the puny efforts of Paine are thrown in to prop their tottering fabric, whose foundations cannot stand the test of time." [40] It hurt Henry much more to have some good people think that he was not a Christian than to be given "the appellation of tory."

One of the falsehoods repeated about Henry, so General Lee wrote him, was that in declining the position of Secretary of State, Henry had advised Washington "to return home, since a man of sixty-four was unfit for the duties of his arduous station." [41] It was not a story calculated to improve Henry's relationship with the President. Yet, after the rejection of John Rutledge as Chief Justice of the United States, Lee, as Washington's intermediary, also wrote Henry on December 26, 1795, to ascertain whether he would accept the position. Lee spoke of his friendship for Henry and trusted that Henry knew he would not address him "on such a subject without good grounds." Henry could continue at home when not on duty; the salary was "excellent and the honor very great." Moreover, the vacancy had not been filled on January 11, 1796, and Washington found this and some connected vacancies "embarrassing in the extreme." The position, which Henry declined for the now obvious reasons, was one of the highest ever offered him, a notable tribute to his standing in the legal profession. [42]

There seemed to be no end to Henry's courting by the Federalists, always with negative results. As his health declined, he would not consider any political appointment except in a dire emergency. When John Adams ran for the presidency in 1796 on the Federalist ticket, there was some vain talk of offering Henry's name as Vice-President. Moreover, after the presidential electors had been chosen, several of them stated that they were willing to vote for Henry but not Jefferson for President.

"Most assiduous court is paid to Patrick Henry. He has been

[443]

offered every thing which they knew he would not accept," Jefferson wrote Monroe on flimsy evidence, July 10, 1796.[43] Jefferson did not believe that enough impression had been made on Henry but added, "If they thought they could count on him they would run him for their vice-president, their firm object being to produce a schism in this State." [44] When the Virginia legislature met that fall the members, although supporting Jefferson for the presidency, still maintained their loyalty to Henry, who was now elected Governor for the sixth one-year term. But he declined the office in a brief note.

During the summer of 1797 Henry was trying to wind up his financial affairs, including those involving distant property. He had sold his Prince Edward land and was complaining of trespassers on his Norfolk County lands, where he was being "much plundered." He was also trying to dispose of 3,500 acres of his Kentucky land, of which 1,500, so he understood, were "quite valuable," worth perhaps £20 per acre.

The following Christmas season of 1797 found the family coming in and out of Red Hill perhaps even more than usual. Henry's daughter Martha was there, as well as West Dandridge and his wife. Patrick Henry, Jr., and Johnny Christian had gone to Richmond, but Henry's daughter, Dolly Winston, was visiting at the plantation and "has a fine son." And to further crowd the simple story-and-a-half house, Henry's two teen-age daughters had just returned from Lynchburg, where they had attended another St. John's Day ball. Most of this news was in a letter which Henry wrote to Betsey. He poured out his affection to her; he spoke of the very great comfort he derived from her character and disposition. In August, 1798, his health and strength were still declining but he found consolation in that his daughter Kitty, who had married a distant Henry "cousin" from the Eastern Shore, would not be far from her sisters, Betsey and Annie.

During the last year of his life Henry was given to further religious and political retrospection. And some grave political events briefly pushed him out of his cherished retirement. In his will, written on November 20, 1798, Henry left, besides plantations to several of his sons and other large bequests, a final injunction for his "dear family." It was that "the religion of Christ" could give them a heritage which "will make them rich indeed."

Henry had also been giving a summary thought to the American Revolution. With his will was found a sealed letter which his executors were instructed to open. The letter contained a copy of his Stamp Act resolutions with his statements on the back as to his role therein: how he had ventured alone to write them; how despite the threats and abuse against him they had been carried by "a very small majority," and how the alarm had been spread.[45]

Cocksure after the Napoleonic victories, the French Directory had issued an order on March 2, 1797, drastically restricting American trade, especially with England. In the effort to avert war with France, President Adams sent General Charles Pinckney, John Marshall, and Elbridge Gerry as special American plenipotentiaries to Paris. But the emissaries were insulted by a proposal to negotiate with them in return for a large bribe. Back in America there was a cry of "Millions for defence, not a cent for tribute," and preparations were made for war with France, which was narrowly averted.

In its plans for the expected war, Congress had the support of the country, but it now enacted a classic piece of bad legislation, the infamous Alien and Sedition Acts. Under the Alien Act President Adams was authorized to evict from the country such aliens as he deemed dangerous to the safety of the United States. Under the Sedition Act fines and imprisonment were permitted for unlawful conspiracies to oppose the operation of the government, and for the publication of false and malicious writings against the President or members of the Congress. The Alien Act was not actively enforced, but the Sedition Act led to some of the most unjustifiable prosecutions in American history. Most of the two dozen men fined or imprisoned were Republican editors, but one man was convicted for persuading some Massachusetts citizens to erect a liberty pole and another for expressing his wish that wadding in a cannon used for a presidential salute would land in John Adams' backside!

These laws were criticized as a violation of fundamental principles on which the American Constitution was based. The sagacious Jefferson, unable to defeat them in Congress, secured the aid of Madison for a strong counterstroke through the medium of the state legislatures. Under the terms of resolutions which Jefferson had approved, the Kentucky legislature adopted provisions stating that the federal government was formed under a compact with the states which reserved to them all powers not specifically granted to the federal government. When this government assumed undelegated powers, its acts were "unauthoritative, void, and of no force." Jefferson also sent a copy of the Kentucky resolutions to Madison for the introduction of similar ones in the Virginia legislature. He carefully noted, however, that they were not to "be committed absolutely to push the matter to extremities, and yet may be free to push as far as events will render prudent." Madison thereupon drew up resolutions providing that, "in case of a deliberate, palpable, and dangerous exercise of other powers not granted by" the compact, the states had the right and were "in duty bound to interpose for arresting the progress of the evil." [46]

In a further resolution Virginia appealed to the other states to declare the Alien and Sedition Acts unconstitutional and to unite in proper measures to maintain the rights reserved to the states and to the people. During December, 1798, these resolutions were carried in the Virginia legislature by a large majority.

It was under such circumstances that John Marshall, urged by General Washington, ran for Congress from a district comprising Richmond and some surrounding counties, among them Hanover, where Henry still had numerous friends and relatives. Marshall, a popular Federalist with moderate opinions, actually voted against the Sedition Act. But he had a strong opponent, and the election was closely contested. On December 28, 1799, Archibald Blair wrote a letter to Henry enclosing a copy of the Virginia resolutions and seeking Henry's support in the congressional election. From his detailed reply, written from Red Hill on January 8, 1799, we learn that Henry believed most of the measures lately pursued by the opposition party would lead to "dissolving the confederacy." He paid a strong tribute, in the Blair letter, to Marshall, and the letter, circulated through his congressional district, largely contributed to Marshall's election by a small majority.

In the letter Henry said that he was "too old and infirm ever again to undertake public concerns." He lived "much retired, amidst a multiplicity of blessings from that Gracious Ruler of all things," to whom he owed "unceasing acknowledgments for his unmerited goodness" to him. If he "was permitted to add to this catalogue one other blessing, it would be" that his "countrymen should learn wisdom and virtue, and in this their day know the things that pertain to their peace." [47]

Greatly alarmed by the threat to the national government through the Virginia and Kentucky resolutions and other Republican measures, George Washington had urged Marshall to run for Congress. On January 15, 1799, Washington made an appeal to Henry to return to the political forum. When declining the political appointment which Washington offered him in early 1796, Henry had written him that if America was destined in his time "to encounter the horrors of anarchy, every power of mind and body" would be exerted to support the government. Washington felt that such a dangerous time had come and that he was justified in calling upon Henry's help on the basis of the emergency. In his confidential letter, Washington spoke of "the endeavours" of a certain party to disquiet the people with unfounded alarms and to set them in opposition to their government. He did not believe it necessary to predict to Henry what would be the inevitable consequences of this policy if it could not "be arrested." He had to state that Virginia had taken the lead in this opposition, and its principal legislative leaders were seeking help in other states, though as yet only successful in Kentucky. One reason for the influence of the Virginia Republicans in both Congress and in their state legislature was that "the most respectable and best qualified" Virginians would not come forward. Measures were being "systematically and pugnaciously pursued, which must eventually dissolve the union or produce coercion." Washington, therefore, expressed his earnest wish that Henry would be a candidate at the ensuing elections, if not for Congress, which might take him "too long from home," then as a candidate for the General Assembly. And he spoke flatteringly of what Henry could accomplish through his "character and influence." [48]

Henry now declared himself a candidate for the House of Delegates. He announced that he would address the people of Charlotte County on court day, the first Monday in the month. When word of

[447]

the announcement spread about the state, a special effort was made by the state Republicans to assure the election of their chieftains such as James Madison, George Nicholas, William Branch Giles, and John Taylor of Caroline; as on earlier forensic battlefields, Madison was to be the opposition leader in the Assembly.

There had been a time when Henry, his legal papers in his saddle-bags, would ride horseback a hundred miles in a few days on his legal circuit. Now his health was so feeble that he rode the twenty miles from Red Hill to Charlotte Courthouse in his carriage, stopping the night before his speech with a friend, Colonel Joel Watkins, who lived a few miles north of the village. Next to George Washington there was no Virginia statesman who had a greater hold on the people of his state than Henry. He was particularly revered in the Southside, and believing that this was the last time that he might ever appear before the public, a crowd of people collected from miles around to see the orator and patriot. Among them were the faculty and students of Hampden-Sydney College, who had left the class-rooms deserted to come over from adjacent Prince Edward County. One of these students has given us an excellent account of Henry's last oration.

The simple wooden courthouse where he spoke was situated a little to the eastward of the present Charlotte Courthouse building. After Henry's arrival at the village he was treated with such admira-tion by a crowd which followed him about that a Baptist minister, disturbed by the homage given to a mortal being, asked the people why they treated Henry in such a manner.

"Mr. Henry is not a god," the minister said, to which Henry, suffering from a fatal malady, gave a response which was not as affected as it may seem: "No, indeed, my friend; I am but a poor worm of the dust—as fleeting and unsubstantial as a shadow of the cloud that flies over yon fields, and is remembered no more." [49]

The hour arrived for Henry's speech. He rose from his chair with difficulty and stood somewhat bowed. His face was pale and his voice "slightly cracked and tremulous." But soon, as he warmed to his theme, there was a remarkable transformation. He drew himself erect, his eyes shone with an almost supernatural light, his face glowed, and his voice rang out like "some grand musical instrument," the notes falling pleasingly upon the ears of the large assemblage.[50]

Again we do not know the exact wording of Henry's speech but have evidence of its main thread from reliable witnesses. The late proceedings of the Virginia Assembly, he said, had filled him with apprehension and alarm—had "planted thorns upon his pillow." These proceedings had drawn him from the happy retirement which it had pleased a bountiful providence to bestow on him. Virginia, he continued, had quit the sphere in which she had been placed by the Constitution. She had dared to pronounce upon the validity of federal law, thus going out of her jurisdiction in a manner not warranted by any authority. Such opposition to the acts of the federal government must lead to their enforcement by military power and probably to civil war and foreign alliances. And these alliances must necessarily end in subjugation to the powers whose help was secured. He urged his audience to consider well before they rushed into such a desperate situation from which there could be no reprieve. Depicting General Washington at the head of a numerous army executing the national law, Henry asked, "Where are our [Virginia's] resources to meet such a conflict?"[51]

Here a comic note was introduced, not surprisingly by one of the drunkards who so often collected in the Virginia courthouse villages. "Who will dare to lift his hand," Henry asked, "against the father of his country, to point a weapon at the breast of a man who had so often led them to battle and victory?" "I dare to do it," the drunken man exclaimed.

The words, though irresponsible babbling, were for Henry an attack on the American whom he most revered, the champion of the cause for which Henry had risked his life, his fortune, and his "Sacred Honor." Weak as he was, Henry answered the drunkard with a flash of the old courage. To the threat against Washington, he answered, "You dare not do it; in such a parricidal attempt, the steel would drop from your nerveless arm!"[52]

Henry's reply, as recalled by one of the former Hampden-Sydney students present, sounds somewhat stilted. Also, it may now strain credibility to read of the overpowering effect Henry's oratory had upon the audience. Henry had to be heard to be fully appreciated.

Would Charlotte County have any authority to question the laws of Virginia? Henry cried. Virginia was to the union what Charlotte County was to the state. He denied the right of a state to decide the constitutionality of federal law. The Alien and Sedition Acts were "too deep" for him; they might be wrong. But it remained for the people who held the reins over Congress to say whether or not the acts were acceptable to Virginia. He had seen with regret the unlimited power over the purse and sword consigned to the general government, but he had been overruled, and it was now necessary to submit to the constitutional exercise of that power.[53]

"If I am asked what is to be done when a people feel themselves intolerably oppressed, my answer is ready: *Overturn the government*," Henry continued.[54] But he besought the people not to carry matters to this length unless there was some infringement on their rights which could not be otherwise redressed, "for if ever you recur to another change, you may bid adieu forever to representative government. You can never exchange the present government but for a monarchy. If the administration have done wrong, let us all go wrong together."

Here Henry clasped his hands and moved his body to the right and left, his audience unconsciously swaying with him. "Let us," he said, "trust God and our better judgment to set us right hereafter. United we stand, divided we fall. Let us not split into factions which must destroy that union upon which our existence hangs. Let us preserve our strength for the French, the English, the Germans, or whoever else shall dare invade our territory, and not exhaust it in civil commotions and intestine wars."[55]

Concluding, he spoke of his purpose to exert himself "in the endeavor to allay the heart-burnings and jealousies which had been fomented" in the Virginia legislature. He fervently prayed that, if he was deemed unworthy to effect this design, it might be "reserved to some other and abler hand to extend this blessing over the community."[56]

After Henry returned to his room in the tavern, a tall, pale-faced

[450]

young man rose to answer him before the crowd. It was John Randolph of Roanoke plantation, who was offering himself as a Republican candidate for Congress. As the audacious Randolph began to speak, the audience started to leave. "Tut! Tut! it won't do, it's nothing but the bating [sic] of an old tin pan after hearing a fine church organ," an Irishman said. But in his brief address Randolph displayed some of his budding genius, apparently with none of its cross-grained quality. Henry, when informed of Randolph's main points, did not come out to answer him but commented, "He is a young man of promise; cherish him." [57]

Although elected to the legislature by a good majority, Henry was unable to attend and to accomplish the purpose which he planned. But by mid-May his election was enough cause for another sharp attack by Jefferson. Writing Archibald Stuart on the fourteenth, Jefferson said that Henry would "have the mortification of encountering" in the legislature "such a mass of talents as he has never met before. . . . His apostacy must be unaccountable to those who do not know all the recesses of his heart." [58] However, John Tyler argued that while Henry might have been misled in forming "his opinions by misrepresentations in his aged and infirm state, . . . his principles were too well fixed" for such apostasy. Before Henry's death he sent Tyler a message in which he stated "men might differ in ways and means, and not in principles." [59]

Ill as he was, Henry found some consolation in still another flattering political appointment. He was made a member of a three-man mission to discuss and settle the controversies between the United States and France. But in his declination on April 16, 1799, he said that he had been confined for several weeks by "a severe indisposition" and indicated that he was almost too ill to write the letter. He had informed Dr. George Cabell that he was suffering from a disease "like the gravel" and asked the doctor, then in Lynchburg, to come to Red Hill and treat him. "Dear Patsy, I am very unwell, and Doctor Cabell is with me," he wrote his daughter. A number of his immediate family, with the exception of his daughter, Anne Roane, who was also ill, gathered at Red Hill. When Anne died in May, 1799, Henry was so ill that it was thought best not to inform him.

Henry was said to have been suffering from intussusception, but medical specialists today might diagnose his symptoms as those of a malignancy. Dr. Cabell, who had studied medicine at Edinburgh, was much better qualified than many physicians of the age, but with the limited medical knowledge of the time he could offer no cure. On June 6, as Henry's last hour approached, he was sitting in a large three-cornered chair where he was more comfortable than lying down. After trying various other remedies, Dr. Cabell now resorted to a final desperate expedient—a dose of liquid mercury.

"I suppose, doctor, this is your last resort," Henry said, after taking the vial of medicine in his hand.

"I am sorry to say, Governor, that it is," Dr. Cabell replied, and went on to explain that acute inflammation of the intestines had already taken place. The medicine would give Henry immediate relief or—the doctor did not finish the sentence. Upon Henry's question, he could only explain that he could live only a very short time without the medicine and it might possibly relieve him. Excusing himself, Henry drew his silken cap over his eyes and prayed a short prayer for his family, his country, and his own soul, then calmly swallowed the liquid mercury. There was time for him to say a few loving words to his family, weeping around the chair; to tell them how thankful he was that God, who had blessed him all his life, would permit him to die without any pain. Fixing his eyes tenderly on his friend, Dr. Cabell, with whom he had often argued regarding the Christian religion, he asked the doctor to observe how great was the reality and benefit of that religion to a man about to die.[60]

After some last words in favor of the religion which had never failed him, Henry died quietly. There would be a highly laudatory obituary in the *Virginia Gazette* and eulogies from some of Henry's leading contemporaries, such as John Marshall and General Henry Lee. Lee is said to have written a striking eulogy upon the "Demosthenes of modern liberty." More appropriate was the inscription on the plain slab covering his grave at Red Hill:

His fame his best epitaph.

APPENDIX I

It has been common to suppose that Patrick Henry, "the natural orator," as he is properly called, was very slightly, if at all, indebted for his wonderful eloquence to those sources of mental culture which are held in highest esteem as at once the models of taste and the instruments of learning. It seems, however, that this opinion is unfounded, and that the American Demosthenes is no exception to the great law which affirms that "the gods give nothing to men without labor." From an interesting and instructive Oration delivered by Mr. Hugh Blair Grigsby, before the students of William and Mary College, on the 4th of July last, we cite the following statement in reference to the literary style and early classical proficiency of Patrick Henry:

> One instance of the application of philology to . . . the history of Virginia is within my own experience and may not be without interest to the students of William and Mary. From a critical examination of the fragments of the speeches and writings of Patrick Henry which have come down to us, and by a careful collation of them with those of his prominent contemporaries, I was convinced that our Patriot Prophet had received a regular and [thorough] training in the Latin classics, and that he had received that training in early life. There was to be seen in his style a *"curiosa felicitas"* and a *"callida junctura,"* a purity and a tact which could not have been the result of chance, or they would have been equally apparent in the works of his rivals; and it was evident, so finely were these characteristics interwoven in the general texture of his style, that he must have studied [the] ancient authors in early life; as such results rarely appear so conspicuously in the productions of those who become acquainted with the classics at a more advanced age. This was the argument of internal evidence—an argument which was satisfactory to me, but which, without an infinitely minute exposition of details that none but a philologist could comprehend, would not be conclusive to others. It would thus be regarded rather as an opinion than a demonstration; and I must therefore, sustain

[453]

my conclusion, for the benefit of others, from the facts of Henry's early life. His father was a teacher, and a native of Scotland, and he was educated in that country when Latin was taught with substantial skill, but many years before the sun of Greek literature had risen in the Scottish horizon. Now, the Scotch teach Latin at the tenderest age. I am myself of Scottish descent on the maternal side, and was taught by Scottish teachers, and I can hardly remember a time when I could not read Latin, or at least when I was not familiar with the grammar. But the father of Henry was not only a teacher and a Scotchman, but he was an admirable Latin Scholar; for we are told in the diary of Samuel Davies, himself a fine scholar, that the father of Henry was more familiar with his Horace than with his Bible. Hence the conclusion was irresistible that, if the father of Henry taught his pupils the classics, he would, like the rest of his countrymen, teach them early and, as he was proved to have been thoroughly skilled in them, that he would teach them well; and, further, that if he taught the children of other people Latin, he would at the same time teach his own. This was the argument from probability, which I did not need to enhance my own conviction, but which might be necessary to gain the assent of others. Here, then, was a fact ascertained in the life of Patrick Henry which was not only not known, but which ran counter to the opinions and statements of all his contemporaries and biographers. But was my conclusion true after all? It was strictly true in both respects, that our great orator had learned the Latin classics, and that he had learned them in early life; for in the recently published dairy [sic] of John Adams, under the date of September, 1774, we have it from the lips of Henry himself that *before* fifteen he had read Virgil and Livy— a degree of proficiency which, even in this day, except under favorable auspices, is rarely attained at so early an age; for, between the grammar and Livy, as was observed by my venerable friend, Bishop Meade, our old teachers, even those with whom I studied, introduced nearly the entire series of classical authors.

———*Washington Intelligencer*

Hugh Blair Grigsby (1806–1881) was the author of *The Virginia Convention of 1776* and *The Virginia Federal Convention of 1788,* as well as other historical works. An alumnus of Yale College, he lived in Charlotte County, Va., during his latter years and was well acquainted with a number of Patrick Henry's relatives and associates.

APPENDIX II

(As listed in the 1802 inventory in Will Book 2, Charlotte Courthouse, Va. The clerk or assistant making the list obviously suffered from some of the educational deficiencies of the period.)

1	Vol.	Grotious on peace & War	£3.
1	"	Peire Williams' rep'ts	4.10.
2	"	Strange's rep'ts	3.
1	"	Salkil's do.	2. 8.
2	Vernon's	do.	1.16.
1	Vol.	Carthew's do.	1. 1.
5	"	Modern do.	3.
1	Equity Cases		2.
1	"	Virginia Laws	1.
5	"	Bacon's abridg'e in fol.	9.
3	"	Crock's reports	2. 8.
1	"	Cumberback's do.	1.
1	"	Parkhurst's Lexicon	1.10.
3	"	Cocke's Institutes	2.
1	"	Hardwick's reports	2. 5.
4	"	Blackston's Comm'ty	1.16.
1	"	Equity Ca. in Talbot's time	1. 4.
1	"	Centris reports	1.
1	"	Cocke's do.	1.16.
2	"	Nelson's do.	2. 8.
1	"	Hawkins's Pleas of the Cro.	3.
1	"	Swinborn on Wills	.18.
1	"	Rayman's reports	1.
1	"	Orphan's Legacy	.10.
1	"	Virginia Laws	.10.
2	"	Chalmers' Collect'n of Treats.	1. 4.
2	"	Coleman's Terance	.12.
1	"	Ward's Es. on Gram.	2.

3	"	Modern rep'ts, a brok'n sett	.18.
1	Entick's Dictionary		. 3.
1	Vol.	Uses & trust	.10.
2	"	Spirit of Laws	1.
1	"	American Negotiator	. 6.
1	Vol.	Gibson's Guide	. 4.6
7	"	Smallit's Hist'y of England	2. 2.
2	"	Watson's Horrace	.10.
1	"	Paraphrase with anotations on the Eps. to the Romans	1. 4.
3	"	Beeldfield's Erudition	2. 8.
2	"	Robertson Navega'n	.12.
1	"	Buchan's Dom. Medicine	.15.
3	"	Adams' Defence of the American Constitution	.18.
1	"	Impey's practice	.13.
1	"	Bland on Decipl'n	. 6.
2	"	Ramsey's revolution S. Carol.	1.
1	"	Milner's Greek Gram.	. 7.6
1	"	Junious's Letters	. 7.6
1	"	Life of Dr. Franklin	. 4.
1	"	Breviarin Cronologe	. 7.6
2	"	Newman's Chimistry	1.
1	"	Juvenal	.10.
1	"	Don Quck Zotte [Quixote]	. 6.
1	"	Watts' Hyms	. 3.
2	"	Blair's Sermons	.10.
1	"	Decalo dis Mortis	. 2.6
4	"	Proceed'g & debates of Parlem't	1. 4.
1	"	Munford's Poems	. 6.
1	"	Cureosities of Spain	. 7.6
2	"	Homeri Ilias	1.
1	"	D'Arsay	. 2.6
1	"	Muir's Introduction	. 3.
1	Testament		. 1.3
1	Vol.	Iradical Vocabulary	. 7.6
1	"	History of F. Eugine	. 1.6
1	"	Lord Shefield's Observa.	. 6.
1	"	Dismal Fractions	.12.
1	"	Roman Antiquities	.12.
2	"	Ovid's Metamorphoses	.12.

1	"	Selectra profanus	. 3.
1	"	Compleat Eng. Farmer	.10.
5	"	Monthly review	1.10.
1	"	Conspiracy	. 3.
1	"	Spirit of Patriotism	. 3.
1	"	Juvenalis	. 2.
1	"	Selecta Colequorum	. 1.6
1	"	History of England	. 3.
1	"	Clark to Dodwell	. 3.
1	"	Thompson's Fables	. 2.
1	"	Brooker's Gazett'r	.10.
1	"	British Youth's Instructor	. 5.
1	"	Robertson Crueso	. 1.6
1	"	Art's Treas'r of Religion	. 1.3
1	"	Gordin's Gram.	. 6.
1	Vol.	Christian's Consolation	. 2.6
2		French Prayer Books	. 3.
1	Vol.	New art of War	. 1.6
1	"	Abridgm't of the celebrated Mr. Pennett's discrip'n of the Brit. Capi'l	. 3.
1	Vol.	Elphenston on Education	. 2.6
The American Constitu'n			. 3.
1	Vol.	Es. on Slavery	. 2.
1	"	Introduction of the Gram.	. 1.6
1	"	All for the best	. 1.6
1	"	Hyman Reason	. 1.6
1	"	Debates of the Convent'n	. 6.
1	"	Munroe's review	. 6.
1	"	Bonepartte's Camphain	. 6.
1	"	The Banished Man	. 3.
1		Spelling Dictionary	. 3.
1	Vol.	Pleasing Instructor	. 3.
1	"	Infant's Lawyer	. 6.
1	"	Antiquity of Greece	. 7.6
1	"	Jacobinism	. 9.
1	"	Euclid's Elem'ts	. 7.6
1	"	Guthrie's Gram.	1. 4.
1		Pronouncing Spelling Dictionary	. 2.
2	Vol.	Leland's Demosthenes	.12.
1	"	Cocker's Arethmatick	1. 9.
1	"	Discorses on Religion	. 3.

1	"	Pope's Poems	. 2.
1	large old Bible		. 7.
1	Vol.	Page's Travels	.12.
1	"	Creden's Concordance	.18.
1	"	Glass's Cookery	. 6.
1	"	Dillon's Travels thro Spain	.12.
1	"	Modern Conveyancer	. 7.6
1	"	Es. on Establishing a Standard	. 7.6
1	"	Mottes's Philosefical Transact'gs	.18.
2	"	Danvers' abridgment	1.10.
1	"	Ward's 4 Esays	. 6.
1	"	Dr. Sydenham's Works	. 3.
1	"	Ward's Mathematics	.12.
1	"	Parlem'y register	.12.
2	"	N. Test. Grecum, Hardy	1.
1	"	Preceptor	.12.
1	"	Barkley's Greek rudem'ts	. 6.
1	"	Lex Parliment	.10.
1	"	Tyrace's directions	. 6.
1	Wallace's Gram.		. 6.
1	Vol.	Gibson's Fair'rs Guide	. 6.
1	"	Treatise on the Mathematics	. 6.
1	"	Sacred & profain history	1.10.
2	"	Johnson's dictionary	.12.
1	Vol.	Sum'y of the Crown Law	. 6.
1	"	Buller's Nise prius	.10.
1	"	Scott's Lessons	. 4.
1	"	Tisol on Phisick	. 6.
2	"	Independant Wigg	. 9.
1	"	Tillotson's Sermons	. 3.
1	"	Aneckdotes on Frederick	. 3.
1	"	Education compleat	. 3.
2	"	Nature displayed	. 6.
1	"	Junious' Letters	. 6.
1	"	Noxe's Esays	. 6.
4	"	Pope's Odysey	.12.
3	"	Contea Morlax	. 9.
1	"	Turkish Spy	. 1.6
1	"	Prophain History	. 3.
1	"	Pender's works	. 1.6

A parcel of Greek & Lattin books, in
         our estimation worth   1.16.

1 Vol.	Chimistry	. 7.6
1 "	Modern Farmer's guide	. 3.
1 "	Trials—Pais	. 3.

$$5727.19.0$$

D. Henry			J. Scott
E. Winston	} exrs.		W. Cooper
Geo. D. Winston			Joe Marshall

Memo.:   This appraisement and Inventory differs in as much as that the Inventory given by Mrs. Henry was agreeable to the number of cattle turned out in the Spring and the appraisement being only for the number shown at the time of the appraisement.

J. Scott
Joe Marshall
W. Cooper

At a Court held for Charlotte County the 6th day of September, 1802, this Inventory and appraisement of the estate of Patrick Henry, dec'd., in the County of Charlotte, was this day returned by Edmund Winston, one of the executors, and ordered to be recorded.

Teste, Thomas Read, Cl.
A Copy.
Thomas Read, Cler.

[459]

LIST OF PRINCIPAL SOURCES

MANUSCRIPTS

The chief sources for manuscript material on Patrick Henry are the Virginia State Library, the Virginia Historical Society, and the Valentine Museum, all in Richmond; the University of Virginia Library; and the Library of Congress. Other helpful sources for such data have been found in the voluminous records of some forty Virginia counties, chiefly in the Piedmont. The most valuable records are in these courthouses: Louisa, Goochland, Prince Edward, Henry, Campbell, and Charlotte. Some of the records or photostatic copies have been placed in the Virginia State Library.

NEWSPAPERS

While useful newspaper references have been found in the British Museum, in Bristol and Glasgow, the American newspapers have of course been most valuable. The American Antiquarian Society, Duke University, and the Pennsylvania Historical Society have been particularly helpful in sending me Xerox copies from newspapers outside of Virginia. In the state the various editions of the *Virginia Gazette* have been indispensable, as have the *Virginia Independent Chronicle* and the *Virginia Gazette, or American Advertiser*, both published in Richmond. *The Farmville Herald*, the *Petersburg Index-Appeal*, and the *Lynchburg News* have been among other useful Virginia newspapers.

MICROFILM AND OTHER PHOTOGRAPHIC REPRODUCTIONS

A large quantity of microfilm, Xerox, and other photographic reproductions have been supplied me by the University of Virginia Library, the Virginia Historical Society, and the Library of Congress. Microfilm from the last includes copies of a very large collection made by a photographer for the Library who photographed the Patrick Henry records in numerous Virginia counties.

PUBLISHED VOLUMES

Abernethy, T. P., *The South in the New Nation*. Baton Rouge, La., 1961.

————, *Three Virginia Frontiers*. Baton Rouge, La., 1940.

————, *Western Lands and the American Revolution*. New York, 1937.

Adams, Charles Francis, *The Works of John Adams*. 10 vols. Boston, 1850–1856.

Alden, John Richard, *General Charles Lee*. Baton Rouge, La., 1951.

————, *The South in the Revolution, 1763–1789*. Baton Rouge, La., 1957.

Alexander, James W., *The Life of Archibald Alexander*. New York, 1854.

Ambler, Charles H., *Sectionalism in Virginia from 1776 to 1851*. Chicago, 1910.

Bakeless, John Edwin, *Background to Glory: The Life of George Rogers Clark*. Philadelphia, 1957.

Ballagh, James Curtis, *The Letters of Richard Henry Lee*. 2 vols. New York, 1911–1914.

Barbarossa (pseudonym), *The Lost Principle*. Richmond, Va., 1860.

Barck, Oscar T., Jr., and Hugh T. Lefler, *Colonial America*. New York, 1958.

Barry, Richard Hayes, *Mr. Rutledge of South Carolina*. New York, 1942.

Bemis, Samuel Flagg, *A Diplomatic History of the United States*. New York, 1955.

————, *Jay's Treaty—A Study in Commerce and Diplomacy*. New York, 1924.

Beveridge, Albert J., *The Life of John Marshall*. 4 vols. Boston and New York, 1916.

Blanton, Wyndham B., *Medicine in Virginia in the Eighteenth Century*. Richmond, Va., 1931.

Boatner, Mark May III, *Encyclopedia of the American Revolution*. New York, 1966.

Bolton, Charles Knowles, *The Private Soldier Under Washington*. New York, 1902.

Boorstin, Daniel J., *The Americans: The Colonial Experience*. New York, 1958.

Borden, Morton, *The Anti-Federalist Papers*. Ann Arbor, Mich., 1965.

Bouldin, Powhatan, *The Life of John Randolph*. Richmond, Va., 1878.

Bowman, Eldon Glasco, *Patrick Henry's Political Philosophy* (Ph.D. dissertation, Claremont Cal. Graduate School), University Microfilm, Ann Arbor, Mich., 1961.

Boyd, Julian P., editor, *The Papers of Thomas Jefferson*. Princeton, N.J. 1950–.

Boyd, Thomas, *Light Horse Harry Lee*. New York, 1931.

Brant, Irving, *James Madison*. 6 vols. Indianapolis and New York, 1941.

Brigance, William Norwood, editor, *A History and Criticism of American Public Address*. 2 vols. New York, 1960.

Brock, Robert K., *Archibald Cary of Ampthill*. Richmond, Va., 1937.

Brown, Alexander, *The Cabells and Their Kin*. Richmond, Va., 1939.

Bruce, William Cabell, *John Randolph of Roanoke*. 2 vols. New York, 1922.

Brydon, George MacLaren, *Virginia's Mother Church*. Philadelphia, 1952.

Buell, Augustus C., *Paul Jones, Founder of the American Navy*. New York, 1901.

Burk, John Daly, cont'd by Skelton Jones and Louis Hue Girardin, *The History of Virginia*. Petersburg, Va., 1816.

Burgess, Louis A., *Virginia Soldiers of 1776*. 3 vols. Richmond, Va., 1927.

Burnett, Edmund C., *Continental Congress*, New York, 1964.

————, *Letters of Members of the Continental Congress*. 8 vols. Washington, 1921–1936.

Burrell, Charles Edward, *A History of Prince Edward County, Va.* Richmond, Va., 1922.

Burton, Rev. L. W., *Annals of Henrico Parish*. Richmond, Va., 1904.

Butterfield, Lyman H., editor, *Adams Family Correspondence*. Cambridge, Mass., 1963.

————, editor, *Diary and Autobiography of John Adams*. 4 vols. Cambridge, Mass., 1961.

Cabell, Margaret C., *Sketches and Recollections of Lynchburg by the Oldest Inhabitant*. Richmond, Va., 1858.

Callahan, North, *Daniel Morgan, Ranger of the Revolution*. New York, 1961.

Campbell, Charles, editor, *The Bland Papers*. Petersburg, Va., 1840.

————, *History of the Colony and Ancient Dominion of Virginia*. Philadelphia, 1860.

Campbell, T. E., *Colonial Caroline*. Richmond, Va., 1954.

Cappon, Lester J., and Stella F. Duff (comps.), *Virginia Gazette Index*. 2 vols. Williamsburg, Va., 1950.

Carrington, J. Cullen, *Charlotte County, Va.* Richmond, Va., 1907.

Carson, Jane, *James Innes and His Brothers of the F.H.C.* Williamsburg, Va., 1965.

Chapman, Charles E., *A History of Spain*. New York, 1918.

Chastellux, Marquis de, *Travels in North America in the Years 1780–1781–1782*. New York, 1828.

Clark, Thomas D., *A History of Kentucky*. Lexington, Ky., 1950.

Conway, Moncure Daniel, *Edmund Randolph*. New York, 1888.

Davis, Curtis Carroll, *The King's Chevalier; a Biography of Lewis Littlepage*. New York, 1961.

DeKoven, Mrs. Reginald, *The Life and Letters of John Paul Jones*. New York, 1913.

Dodson, E. Griffith, *The Capitol of the Commonwealth of Virginia*. Richmond, Va., 1937.

Draper, Lyman C., *King's Mountain and Its Heroes*. New York, 1929.

Early, Ruth H., *Campbell Chronicles and Family Sketches*. Lynchburg, Va., 1927.

Eaton, Clement, *A History of the Old South*. New York, 1966.

Eberlein, Harold D., and Cortlandt V. Hubbard, *Portrait of a Colonial City*. Philadelphia, 1939.

Eckenrode, Hamilton James, *The Randolphs*. Indianapolis and New York, 1946.

———, *The Revolution in Virginia*. Boston and New York, 1916.

Elliot, Jonathan, *The Debates in the Several State Conventions on the Adoption of the Federal Constitution*. 5 vols. Philadelphia, 1941.

Farrand, Max, *The Fathers of the Constitution*. New Haven, Toronto, Glasgow, London, 1921.

Faust, Albert B., *The German Element in the United States*. Boston and New York, 1909.

Ferguson, E. J., *The Power of the Purse*. Chapel Hill, N.C., 1961.

Fitzpatrick, John C., *The Diaries of George Washington*. 4 vols. Boston and New York, 1925.

———, editor, *The Writings of George Washington*. 39 vols. Washington, D.C., 1931–1944.

Fleet, Beverley, *Virginia Colonial Abstracts*. 34 vols. Baltimore, Md., 1961.

Foote, Rev. W. H., *Sketches of Virginia*. 2 vols. Philadelphia, 1850–1855.

Force, Peter, *American Archives* (in six series). Washington, D.C., 1840.

Ford, Paul Leicester, *Pamphlets on the Constitution of the United States*. Brooklyn, N.Y., 1888.

Ford, W. C., editor, *Journals of the Continental Congress*. Washington, D.C., 1904.

Freeman, Douglas Southall, cont'd by J. A. Carroll and M. W. Ashworth, *George Washington*. 7 vols. New York, 1948–1957.

Gaines, William H., Jr., *Thomas Mann Randolph*. Baton Rouge, La., 1966.

Gay, Sydney Howard, edited by John T. Morse, Jr., *James Madison*. Boston and New York, 1898.

Goolrick, John T., *The Life of General Hugh Mercer.* New York and Washington, 1906.

Grigsby, Hugh Blair, *Virginia Historical Collections: Virginia Convention of 1788.* 2 vols. Richmond, Va., 1815.

———, *The Virginia Convention of 1776.* Richmond, Va., 1855.

Gwathmey, John H., *Historical Register of Virginians.* Richmond, Va., 1938.

———, *Twelve Virginia Counties.* Richmond, Va., 1937.

Harrell, Isaac Samuel, *Loyalism in Virginia.* Durham, N.C., 1926.

Harris, Malcolm H., *History of Louisa County.* Richmond, Va., 1936.

Hart, Freeman H., *Valley of Virginia in the American Revolution.* Chapel Hill, N.C., 1942.

Haworth, Paul L., *George Washington: Being an Account of His Home Life and Agricultural Activities.* Indianapolis, 1915.

Hazeltine, Mayo W., editor, *Orations from Homer to McKinley.* 25 vols. New York, 1902.

Heitman, F. B., *Historical Register of the Continental Army.* Washington, D.C., 1893.

Hening, William Waller, *The Statutes at Large.* 13 vols. New York, Philadelphia, Richmond, 1823.

Henry, William Wirt, *Patrick Henry: Life, Correspondence and Speeches.* 3 vols. New York, 1891.

Hill, Helen Day, *George Mason, Constitutionalist.* Cambridge, Mass., 1938.

Hill, Judith P. A., *History of Henry County.* Martinsville, Va., 1925.

Howe, Henry, *Historical Collections of Virginia.* Charleston, S.C., 1856.

Hughes, Rupert, *George Washington, the Rebel and the Patriot.* 3 vols. New York, 1926, 1927.

Hunt, Gaillard, editor, *The Writings of James Madison.* 9 vols. New York, 1900–1910.

Hutchinson, William T., and William E. Rachal, editors, *The Papers of James Madison.* 5 vols. Chicago, 1965.

James, James Alton, editor, *George Rogers Clark Papers, 1771–81* (Springfield, 1912), in *Collections of the Illinois State Historical Society,* Vol. VIII, *Virginia Series,* Vol. III.

———, *The Life of George Rogers Clark.* Chicago, 1928.

Jefferson, Thomas, *Notes on Virginia.* Chapel Hill, N.C., 1955.

Jensen, Merrill, *The New Nation.* New York, 1950.

Jillson, Willard Rouse, *The Kentucky Land Grants.* Louisville, Ky., 1925.

———, *Old Kentucky Entries and Deeds.* Louisville, Ky., 1926.

Johnson, William, *Nathanael Greene.* Charleston, S.C., 1822.

Kegley, F. B., *Kegley's Virginia Frontier.* Roanoke, Va., 1938.

Kelley, Effie B., *The Slashes of Hanover County, Va.*, Richmond, Va., 1929.

Kennedy, John P., *Memoirs of the Life of William Wirt, Attorney General of the U.S.* Philadelphia, 1860.

Kercheval, Samuel, *History of the Valley*. Woodstock, Va., 1850.

Kimball, Marie, *Jefferson, The Road to Glory*. New York, 1943.

Kincaid, R. L., *The Wilderness Road*. Indianapolis, 1947.

Knollenberg, Bernhard, *Washington and the Revolution, a Reappraisal*. New York, 1940.

Knorr, Catherine L., *Marriage Bonds and Ministers' Returns of Charlotte County, Virginia, 1764–1815*. Pine Bluff, Ark., 1951 (mimeographed).

Koch, Adrienne, *Jefferson and Madison: The Great Collaboration*. New York, 1950.

Lawrence, Ruth, *The Burwell, Spotswood, Dandridge, West, and Allied Family Histories*. New York, 1948.

Lee, Cazenove G., Jr., *Lee Chronicle, Studies of the Early Generations of the Lees of Virginia*. New York, 1957.

Lee, Edmund Jennings, *Lee of Virginia*. Philadelphia, 1895.

Lee, Henry, *Memoirs of the War in the Southern Department*. New York, 1870.

Lee, Richard Henry, *Memoir of the Life of Richard Henry Lee, by His Grandson*. 2 vols. Philadelphia, 1825.

Lefler, Hugh T., and Albert R. Newsome, *The History of a Southern State: North Carolina*. Chapel Hill, N.C., 1954.

Leland, Thomas, *The Orations of Demosthenes, on Occasions of Public Deliberation*. London, 1763, and New York, 1900.

Lipscomb, Andrew A., editor, *The Writings of Thomas Jefferson*. Washington, D.C., 1903–1904.

Little, John P., *History of Richmond*. Richmond, Va., 1933.

Lossing, Benson J., *Field Book of the Revolution*. New York, 1890.

Macmillan, Margaret Burnham, *The War Governors in the American Revolution*. New York, 1943.

Main, Jackson T., *The Antifederalists: Critics of the Constitution, 1771–1778*. Chapel Hill, N.C., 1961.

Malone, Dumas, *Jefferson and His Time*. 3 vols. Boston, 1962.

————, *The Story of the Declaration of Independence*, New York, 1954.

————, and Basil Rauch, *Empire for Liberty*. 2 vols. New York, 1960.

Manahan, John Eacott, *Charlottesville Bicentennial History* (pamphlet). Charlottesville, Va., 1962.

Mason, Kathryn Harrod, *James Harrod of Kentucky*. Baton Rouge, La., 1951.

Mayo, Bernard, *Henry Clay*. Boston, 1937.

————, *Myths and Men.* Athens, Ga., 1959.

Mays, David John, *Edmund Pendleton, 1721–1803.* 2 vols. Cambridge, Mass., 1952.

————, *The Letters and Papers of Edmund Pendleton.* 2 vols. Charlottesville, Va., 1967.

McCrady, Edward, *The History of South Carolina in the Revolution.* New York, 1901.

McLaughlin, A. C., *The Confederation and the Constitution.* New York and London, 1905.

McLendon, S. G., *History of the Public Domain of Georgia.* Atlanta, Ga., 1924.

McMaster, John B., *A History of the People of the United States.* 5 vols. New York, 1901–1902.

Meade, Bishop William, *Old Churches, Ministers, and Families of Virginia.* 2 vols. Philadelphia, 1857.

Middleton, Arthur Pierce, *Tobacco Coast: A Maritime History of Chesapeake Bay in the Colonial Era.* Newport News, Va., 1953.

Mitchell, Broadus, *Alexander Hamilton.* New York, 1957.

Monaghan, Frank, *John Jay, Defender of Liberty.* New York and Indianapolis, 1935.

Montross, Lynn, *The Reluctant Rebels.* New York, 1950.

Moore, Josiah Staunton, editor, *Annals of Henrico Parish.* Richmond, Va., 1904.

Mordecai, Samuel, *Richmond in By-gone Days.* Richmond, Va., 1860.

Morgan, George, *The True Patrick Henry.* Philadelphia and London, 1907.

Morison, Samuel Eliot, *John Paul Jones.* Boston and Toronto, 1959.

————, and Henry Steele Commager, *The Growth of The American Republic.* 2 vols. New York, 1962.

Morris, Richard B., *The American Revolution.* Princeton, N.J., 1955.

Morrison, Alfred J., translator and editor, *Travels in the Confederation,* from the German of Johann David Schoepf. Philadelphia, 1911.

Morse, John T., Jr., *John Adams.* Boston and New York, 1899.

Morton, Oren F., *The Story of Winchester in Virginia.* Strasburg, Va., 1925.

Munford, Beverly B., *Virginia's Attitude Toward Slavery and Secession.* New York, 1909.

Munford, George Wythe, *The Two Parsons.* Richmond, Va., 1884.

Nevins, Allan, *The American States During and After the Revolution.* New York, 1924.

Oliver, Robert T., *History of Public Speaking in America.* Boston, 1965.

Parker, Jula Jeter, *The History of Bedford County, Va.* (pamphlet). 1911.

Parrington, Vernon L., *Main Currents in American Thought*. 3 vols. New York, 1927–1930.

Pease, Theodore Calvin, *The Story of Illinois*. Chicago, 1949.

Pedigo, Virginia G. and Lewis G., *History of Patrick and Henry Counties in Virginia*. Roanoke, Va., 1933.

Pennsylvania Magazine of History and Biography. Philadelphia, 1877–

Percy, Alfred, *Piedmont Apocalypse* (pamphlet). Madison Heights, Va., 1949.

———, *Tobacco Rolling Roads to Waterways*. Madison Heights, Va., 1963.

Peyton, Neale Clarke, *Old King William*. Louisville, Ky., 1897.

Porter, Nannie Francisco, and Catherine Fauntleroy Albertson, *The Romantic Record of Peter Francisco, A Revolutionary Soldier*. Staunton, Va., 1929.

Preston, Nelly C., *Paths of Glory* (pamphlet). Richmond, Va., 1961.

Randall, Henry S., *The Life of Thomas Jefferson*. Philadelphia, 1865.

Rawlings, Mary, *The Albemarle of Other Days*. Charlottesville, Va., 1925.

Rives, William C., *History of the Life and Times of James Madison*. 3 vols. Boston, 1868–1873.

Rossman, Kenneth R., *Thomas Mifflin and the Politics of the American Revolution*. Chapel Hill, N.C., 1952.

Rouse, Parke, *Planters and Pioneers*. New York, 1968.

Rowland, Kate Mason, *The Life of George Mason*. 2 vols. New York and London, 1892.

Rutland, Robert A., *Birth of the Bill of Rights, 1776–1791*. Chapel Hill, N.C., 1955.

———, *George Mason*. Charlottesville, Va., 1963.

Sampson, Henry Aylett, *Sonnets and Other Poems*. New York, 1920.

Scharf, J. Thomas, and Thompson Westcott, *History of Philadelphia, 1609–1884*. Philadelphia, 1884.

Scheer, George, and Hugh F. Rankin, *Rebels and Redcoats*. Cleveland and New York, 1957.

Smith, Charles Page, *James Wilson*. Chapel Hill, N.C., 1956.

Smith, Margaret, *Virginia 1492–1892—A History of the Executives*. Washington, D.C., 1893.

Smith, Page, *John Adams*. 2 vols. New York, 1962.

Smyth, Albert Henry, editor, *The Writings of Benjamin Franklin*. New York, 1907.

Sparks, Jared, *The Writings of George Washington*. 12 vols. New York, 1847.

Squires, W. H. T., *Through Centuries Three*. Portsmouth, Va., 1929.

Stanard, Mary Newton, *Richmond, Its People and Its Story*. Philadelphia and London, 1923.

Stoner, Robert Douthat, *A Seedbed of the Early Republic: Botetourt*. Roanoke, Va., 1962.

Summers, Lewis Preston, *Annals of Southwest Virginia*. Abingdon, Va., 1929.

Swem, Earl G., *Virginia Historical Index*. 2 vols. Roanoke, Va., 1934.

Thayer, Theodore, *Israel Pemberton, King of the Quakers*. Philadelphia, 1943.

Torrence, Clayton, editor, *The Winstons of Virginia, and Allied Families*. Richmond, Va., 1927.

Trenholme, Louise Irby, *The Ratification of the Federal Constitution in North Carolina*. New York, 1932.

Trevelyan, Sir George Otto, *The American Revolution*. New York and London, 1917.

Tucker, George, *The Life of Thomas Jefferson*. 2 vols. Philadelphia, 1837.

Tyler, Lyon G., *The Letters and Times of the Tylers*. 3 vols. Richmond, Va., 1884–1896.

————, *History of Virginia: The Federal Period*. Chicago, 1924.

Tyler, Moses Coit, *Patrick Henry*. Boston and New York, 1887.

Van Deusen, Glyndon G., *The Life of Henry Clay*. New York, 1937.

Van Tyne, Claude Halstead, *The American Revolution, 1776–1783*. New York and London, 1905.

Ver Steeg, Clarence L., *Robert Morris*. Philadelphia, 1954.

Virginia Magazine of History and Biography. Richmond, Va., 1893–.

Waddell, Joseph A., *Annals of Augusta County, Va*. Staunton, Va., 1902.

Wall, Joseph Barrye, *Old Homes of Prince Edward*. Farmville, Va., 1935.

Wallace, David Duncan, *South Carolina: A Short History*. Columbia, S.C., 1961.

Walz, J. and Audrey, *The Bizarre Sisters*. New York, 1950.

Ward, Christopher, *The War of the Revolution*. New York, 1952.

Warren, Charles, *A History of the American Bar*. Boston, 1911.

Waterman, Joseph M., *With Sword and Lancet: The Life of General Hugh Mercer*. Richmond, Va., 1941.

Watson, John F., and Willis P. Hazard, *Annals of Philadelphia, and Pennsylvania, in the Olden Time*. Philadelphia, 1881.

Weddell, Alexander Wilbourne, editor, *A Memorial Volume of Virginia Historical Portraiture, 1585–1830*. Richmond, Va., 1930.

William and Mary College Quarterly Historical Magazine. Williamsburg, Va., 1892–.

Wirt, William, *The Life of Patrick Henry*. New York, 1852.

NOTES

Chapter I

THE APPROACHING CONVENTION

1. Roy P. Basler, ed., *Collected Works of Abraham Lincoln*, V, 537.
2. *Pa. Gazette*, Oct. 26, 1774.
3. Charles Francis Adams, *The Works of John Adams*, II, 367 (hereafter cited as Adams, *Works*).
4. These "seditious" speeches were of course Henry's argument in the Parson's Cause, Dec., 1763, and his Stamp Act speech, May, 1765.
5. Adams, *Works*, X, 78.
6. John Adams to William Wirt, Jan. 23, 1818, in Adams, *Works*, X, 277–279. Adams also wrote Wirt in this letter: "From a personal acquaintance, perhaps I might say a friendship with Mr. Henry of more than forty years, and from all that I have heard or read of him, I have always considered him as a gentleman of deep reflection, keen sagacity, clear foresight, daring enterprise, inflexible intrepidity, and untainted integrity, with an ardent zeal for the liberties, the honor, and felicity of his country, and his species."
7. William Wirt Papers, Library of Congress.
8. Richard Frothingham, *The Rise of the Republic of the United States*, p. 337.
9. Rupert Hughes, *George Washington, the Rebel and the Patriot*, III, 59–61 (hereafter cited as Hughes, *Washington*).
10. Adams, *Works*, III, 91.
11. Washington to President of Congress, April 10, 1778. John C. Fitzpatrick, *The Writings of George Washington*, XI, 237 (hereafter cited as Fitzpatrick, *Washington's Writings*).
    On July 27, 1781, a French resident of London, found guilty of high treason for giving information on the British armies and fleets, was hauled on a sledge to Tyburn Hill. His heart was torn out and thrown into a fire. Hughes, *Washington*, III, 60, citing *The Complete Newgate Calendar*, IV, 153, 156.
12. See p. 409.
13. Nathaniel Pope, Jr., to William Wirt, Wirt Papers.

14. Pinkney's *Va. Gazette*, Nov. 14, 1774. One of Henry's in-laws listed in the express to Pinkney's *Gazette*, Nov. 10, as being wounded was Col. William Fleming; another reported as killed was a Capt. Robert M'Clenahan (McClanahan). For Henry's connection with these and other Valley of Virginia families see Robert Douthat Meade, *Patrick Henry: Patriot in the Making*, I, esp. 336–337 (hereafter cited as Meade, *Henry*). Evidence of Henry's reading of Virginia newspapers is in Day Book, *Virginia Gazette*, University of Virginia Library, and p. 388.

15. For a list of Henry's books made after his death, see p. 455. The titles and dates of publication indicate that a large proportion were obtained after the American Revolution.

16. Accounts of John Syme with Patrick Henry, Library of Congress.

17. This was an aunt of Henry's second wife.

18. Albert B. Faust, *The German Element in the United States*, I, 298–302. Also Freeman H. Hart, *Valley of Virginia in the Revolution*, p. 93; and *Virginia Magazine of History and Biography*, X, esp. 128 (hereafter cited as *Va. Magazine*).

19. For a brief sketch of this Anthony Winston, who moved from Hanover County to Buckingham County, see John H. Gwathmey, *Twelve Virginia Counties*, pp. 255–256; for more detailed information on him and other Winston relatives see Meade, *Henry*, I, and Clayton Torrence, ed., *Winstons of Virginia*.

20. Nelly C. Preston, *The Tragic Life of Elizabeth Henry*, pp. 38–40. See also Henry Howe, *Historical Collections of Virginia*, pp. 206–209, and biographies of Peter Francisco by Nannie Francisco Porter and Alma Shelley Power-Waters.

21. See note 13, above.

22. *Va. Magazine*, XLIII, 118.

23. Meade, *Henry*, I, 65–74.

24. See copy in Henry Papers, Library of Congress. Also George Morgan, *The True Patrick Henry*, p. 467 (hereafter cited as Morgan, *Henry*).

25. Leland's translation of Demosthenes' *Orations* was reprinted in 1900 by the Colonial Press, New York. See particularly the *Special Introduction*, pp. vii, viii.

26. Thomas Leland, *op. cit.*, Henry's copy.

27. *Ibid. Solicitous* is here spelled "sollitous"; someone, probably Henry, wrote "ci" after "solli" in his copy.

28. *Ibid.*

29. Pinkney's *Va. Gazette*, Oct. 27, 1774.

30. William Wirt Henry, *Patrick Henry; Life, Correspondence and Speeches*, I, 251 (hereafter cited as Henry, *Henry*).

31. Microfilm of Mutual Assurance Society policy, Virginia State Library.

32. The site of Smith's Tavern or Merry Oaks gives little indication today of an earlier fame. Situated in the gently undulating country of lower Hanover, with its prolific oak, pine, and holly, the tavern was in one of the most historic sections of the country. Only a half mile distant is Slash Church, where Henry had worshiped as a small boy, while within the radius of a few more miles are the old road from Richmond to Hanover Courthouse and the birthplaces of Henry Clay and of Thomas Sumter, "the Gamecock of the Revolution."

33. Letter of May 21, 1959, and other information from the late Judge Leon Bazile, the authority on Hanover County history; Charles Dabney Memoir in Wirt Papers; Effie B. Kelley, *The Slashes of Hanover County, Va.*, pp. 10–11.

34. W. C. Ford, ed., *Journals of the Continental Congress*, I, esp. 13 *et seq.* (hereafter cited as *Journals*).

35. Meade, *Henry*, I, 64–65.

36. Charles Dabney Memoir, Wirt Papers; Henry, *Henry*, I, 251–252.

37. For a contemporary letter illustrative of what proved to be an obvious point, see Charles Campbell, ed., *The Bland Papers*, I, 33, letter from Theodorick Bland to Farrell and Jones, merchants at Bristol, England, Dec. 1, 1774:

"I should have vested the small proceeds in goods, but the present political disputes, between these colonies and the mother country, which threaten us with a deprivation of our liberties, and every thing that is dear to us, forbid such a step, and induce us to exert every nerve to imitate the silk-worm, and spin from our own bowels, although the webb should be our winding-sheet."

38. Jan. 7, 1775.

39. Dixon and Hunter's *Va. Gazette*, Jan. 21, 1775.

40. *Ibid.*, Feb. 4, 1775.

41. Pinkney's *Va. Gazette*, Jan. 5, 1775. Anthony Winston's attitude toward Great Britain was doubtless not sweetened by a suit brought against his son, Edmund (Patrick Henry's future executor), for £914.4 sterling with interest at 10% per annum from March 15, 1774, until payment. The British debt cases, some of which dragged on for over twenty years, contain a revealing record of Anglo-American relations during the period. The Winston suit papers, which long reposed undisturbed in Box 12 of the United States Circuit Court records in Richmond, have been removed to the Virginia State Library. See *Murdock, Donald, & Co. v. Winston*, U.S. Circuit Court, Ended Cases, 1797.

[471]

42. Dixon and Hunter's *Va. Gazette*. In case of Edmund Randolph's death, Robert Carter Nicholas was empowered to convene the delegates of the Convention at such time as he judged proper. Peter Force, *American Archives*, Series 4, Vol. I, p. 688 (hereafter cited as *American Archives*).

43. *American Archives,* Ser. 4, I, 688.

44. Dixon and Hunter's *Va. Gazette,* Feb. 11, 1775.

45. This Deane letter to Henry was still in possession of a descendant of Patrick Henry, Mrs. Lucy Harrison of Red Hill, as late as Dec. 20, 1910. On this date it was sold by Stan V. Henkels of Philadelphia to Deforest Burns for $125. See published catalogue of Patrick Henry Papers auctioned by Henkels. A copy of the Deane letter is in the *New York Historical Society Publications, Deane Papers,* I, 33–42.

46. Purdie's *Va. Gazette,* Feb. 10, 1775. Information that Capt. Russell had studied under Henry's father from Ms. of the late Nelly C. Preston, Seven Mile Ford, Va. See also significant data on early Fincastle County in Robert Douthat Stoner's *A Seedbed of the Early Republic: Botetourt.*

47. Purdie's *Va. Gazette, ibid.*

48. Purdie's *Va. Gazette* for Feb. 10, 1775, states that Col. Christian arrived in town from Fincastle the previous Sunday night. Scotchtown was in a convenient location for travelers from Fincastle to Williamsburg.

49. H. R. McIlwaine, general editor, *Official Letters of the Governors of Virginia* (Richmond, Va., 1926), I (Henry), 20–27.

50. *American Archives,* Ser. 4, I, 1248.

51. *Ibid.*

Chapter 2

THE ST. JOHN'S CHURCH SPEECH, INTRODUCTORY

1. Plutarch, *Morals: Lives of the Ten Orators,* referred to by Cicero, *De Oratore,* III, 213, *Oration,* p. 55, and *Brutus,* p. 234. For a Greek version with more literal translation see Harold Fowler, *Plutarch's Moralia,* p. 415. Assistance from Robert B. Lloyd, Professor of Classics, Randolph-Macon Woman's College.

2. Meade, *Henry,* I, 337.

3. *Ibid.,* p. 338, and Nelly C. Preston, *Paths of Glory,* pp. 101–102. Miss Preston, a descendant of Henry's sister, Elizabeth, had much family data which she made available to this writer. However, it was usually not documented. She states that "none of the doctors, either at Hanover or in Williamsburg, could quiet" Sarah's mental disturbance. Many of

Henry's friends begged him to put her in the new insane asylum at Williamsburg, but Henry and his family "deemed it best that she be confined in one of the airy, sunny rooms in the half-basement. Here she was in her own home with her own loyal and faithful servants giving her every tender loving care. This was why Patrick spoke of himself at forty-four as 'a distraught old man.'"

4. Louisa County Deed Books, esp. 1774–1775. Information from Josephine Neal, Louisa, Va. For help in the Louisa County records and other valuable assistance, I am much indebted to Mrs. Neal, a descendant of the Johnson family of Louisa, Henry's influential friends and supporters. See also Meade, *Henry*, I, 128, *passim*.

5. Henry, *Henry*, I, 318.

6. Richmond *Daily Whig*, Sept. 23, 1843. From the *National Intelligencer—A descriptive view of Hanover* [in Va.]. Meade, *Henry*, loc. cit. Data from the late Judge Leon Bazile, Hanover County, Va., and from Mrs. Spencer Hamilton, Riverside, Cal., a descendant of Henry's physician, Dr. Thomas Hinde.

7. John Syme Accounts, Library of Congress.

8. Meade, *Henry*, I, 255.

9. May 19, 1774.

10. Josiah S. Moore, ed., *Annals of Henrico Parish*, p. 25; Edward M. Riley and Charles E. Hatch, eds., *James Towne in the Words of Contemporaries*, p. 12.

11. Moore, *op. cit.*, p. 21. Also I am grateful for assistance with this and Chapter 23 to Mrs. P. F. Tuck, a descendant of Patrick Henry and a member of the staff at St. John's Church; to Professors Hugh Lefler, University of North Carolina; John Graham, University of Virginia; and Daniel Boorstin, University of Chicago.

12. Hamilton J. Eckenrode, *The Randolphs*, pp. 40 *et seq.*

13. Mary Newton Stanard, *Richmond: Its People and Its Story*, p. 23. There apparently is no record of scolding women being ducked in Richmond.

14. *Ibid.*, p. 21.

15. *Ibid.*, p. 25. Henry Account Book, sections at Virginia State Library and Valentine Museum, Richmond, Va.

16. Stanard, *op. cit.*, p. 4.

17. Meade, *Henry*, I, 229.

18. Arthur P. Middleton, *Tobacco Coast*, p. 134; William Cabell Diary, microfilm copy, University of Virginia.

19. Alexander Brown, *The Cabells and Their Kin*, p. 105.

20. John C. Fitzpatrick, ed., *The Diaries of George Washington*, II, 188–189 (hereafter cited as Fitzpatrick, *Washington Diaries*).

21. William Lee to Richard Henry Lee, Jan. 20, 1775. Photostat from the Virginia Historical Society. The first session of the Convention was March 20, 1775.

22. Henry was present at the opening session of the Convention on March 20. *Proceedings of the Convention of Delegates . . . of Virginia . . . 1775*, p. 3 (hereafter cited as *Proceedings*).

23. *Ibid.* Numerous advertisements of this type are in the contemporary *Gazettes*.

24. Dixon and Hunter's *Va. Gazette*, March 18, 1775.

25. *Ibid.*

26. *Proceedings*, pp. 3–4. "New York hath been the colony on which administration have hitherto solely relied, whether they had any rational grounds for such reliance, the subsequent advices will testify." New York dispatch of March 20, 1775, in *Norwich* [England] *Mercury*, May 6, 1775. In British Museum, London.

27. Henry, *Henry*, I, 252–253. "A scene of greater confusion, misrule, and injustice, cannot be conceived, than is described in a letter of Lord Dunmore's, dated Dec. 24, as now prevailing in the province of Virginia: committees are appointed in every county, to enforce what they call the *laws* of the congress. . . ." *Gloucester* [England] *Journal*, Feb. 20, 1775, in British Museum.

28. Dixon and Hunter's *Va. Gazette*, March 18, 1775.

29. See p. 98.

30. *Ibid.*

31. *Proceedings*, pp. 3–4.

32. *Ibid.;* Freeman H. Hart, *Valley of Virginia in the Revolution*, esp. Chap. V.

33. *Proceedings*, pp. 3–4.

34. Meade, *Henry*, I, 169 *et seq.* Also numerous references in Hugh Blair Grigsby, *The Virginia Convention of 1776*; and portrait of Carrington in courtroom at Charlotte Courthouse, Virginia.

35. Meade, *Henry*, I, 124, *passim.*

36. Henry Account Book; *Journal of House of Burgesses*, 1766–1769, pp. 244–245.

37. *Proceedings*, pp. 3–4.

38. Stanard, *op. cit.*, pp. 29–30; Moore, *op. cit.*, pp. 23, *passim;* William Cabell Diary.

39. Moore, *op. cit.*, pp. 22–23; George M. Brydon, *Virginia's Mother Church*, II, 420–425.

40. *Proceedings*, p. 4.

41. *Ibid.*, pp. 4–5.

42. *Ibid.*

Chapter 3

THE ST. JOHN'S CHURCH SPEECH, CONCLUSION

1. Parke Rouse, *Planters and Pioneers*, p. 15.

2. *Proceedings*, pp. 4–5.

3. Contemporary Anglican prayerbook.

4. Meade, *Henry*, I, 263.

5. *Proceedings*, p. 5; David John Mays, *Edmund Pendleton*, I, 4 (hereafter cited as Mays, *Pendleton*); and note 8, following.

6. Henry, *Henry*, I, 256–257.

7. Mays, *Pendleton*, II, 4 *et seq.*

8. *Proceedings*, p. 7.

9. *American Archives*, Ser. 4, I, 1072–1074.

10. Mays, *Pendleton*, II, 4 *et seq.*

11. Henry, *Henry*, I, 256.

12. *Proceedings*, p. 5; Josiah S. Moore, ed., *Annals of Henrico Parish*, pp. 23–24; data from Mrs. P. F. Tuck and other members of St. John's staff.

13. *American Archives*, Ser. 4, I, 1022, 1032, 1145 *et seq.*

14. *Ibid.*, p. 1022.

15. *Ibid.*, p. 1031.

16. *Ibid.*, pp. 1145–1146.

17. *Ibid.*, pp. 1253–1254.

18. *Proceedings*, p. 5.

19. Mays, *Pendleton*, II, 5; Meade, *Henry*, I, 309–313.

20. Henry, *Henry*, I, 258.

21. *Ibid.*

22. Mays, *Pendleton*, II, 8.

23. *Ibid.*

24. Interview with John Winston Fontaine, at Wilson, N.C., Feb. 12, 1949. Then fifty-nine years old, Mr. Fontaine is a great-great-grandson of Patrick Henry through his daughter, Elizabeth Henry Aylett.

25. Henry, *Henry*, I, 264.

26. *Ibid.*, pp. 259–260.

27. *Ibid.*, p. 261.

28. William Wirt, *The Life of Patrick Henry*, pp. 120–123 (hereafter cited as Wirt, *Henry*). In view of Wirt's reconstruction of Henry's speech, it should also be noted that certain extracts supplied Wirt from later recollections of his auditors were not given as direct quotations. (The 1852 edition of Wirt is always cited in this volume.)

29. *Ibid*. I have omitted some of the "sirs" which Wirt used so copiously and divided one of his lengthy paragraphs.

30. *Ibid*., p. 268. The paper cutter was shown me in 1952 by Charles S. Borum, then of 4908 16th Road N., Arlington, Va. Mr. Borum, a Henry descendant, gave me a family account of how Henry employed the paper cutter at St. John's, and further details were added for me by another Henry descendant, the present John Fontaine, of Paces, Va. In 1861 the contemporary John Fontaine who was Henry's great-grandson showed the paper cutter to Henry A. Wise and explained Henry's use of it. *Tyler's Quarterly*, VIII, 173–175.

31. Wirt, *Henry*, pp. 141–142.

32. Edmund Randolph's essay in *Va. Magazine*, XLIII, 22.

33. *Ibid*., pp. 222–223.

34. *Ibid*., p. 223.

35. *Ibid*.

36. Meade, *Henry*, I, 175 *et seq*.

37. James Parker to Charles Steuart, *Magazine of History*, III, 158.

38. The guide was Spencer Roane, sexton at St. John's. Data from church staff. The Virginia historian's critique was written by Dr. Douglas Southall Freeman. See his *George Washington*, III, 403–405 (hereafter cited as Freeman, *Washington*).

39. Wirt, *Henry*, p. 142.

40. Henry, *Henry*, I, 270.

41. Edmund Randolph's essay in *Va. Magazine*, XLIII, 222.

42. Henry S. Randall, *The Life of Thomas Jefferson*, I, 101–102.

43. *Ibid*.

44. For instance, see Dixon and Hunter's *Va. Gazette*, March 25, 1775; also *Va. Magazine*, XLIII, 222.

45. Fitzpatrick, *Washington Diaries*, II, 189.

46. *Tyler's Quarterly*, VIII, 173–175; Grigsby, *Virginia Convention of 1776*, p. 150.

47. Freeman, *Washington*, III, 403–405.

48. William Wirt Henry Papers, Library of Congress.

49. Morgan, *Henry*, p. 187.

50. Wirt, *Henry*, pp. vii, viii.

51. *Ibid*. Wirt says Pope never accepted data except from "the purest sources; and his authority for every incident was given with the most scrupulous accuracy." Information to Wirt from numerous Henry associates is in the Wirt Papers.

52. Wirt, *Henry*, p. ix.

53. *Ibid*., pp. ix, x; Henry, *Henry*, I, 261.

54. Wirt, *Henry*, p. xi. An ardent, politically minded young Whig,

Randolph may have attended the convention of which his uncle was the presiding officer. Certainly he knew many of Henry's auditors in Williamsburg and Richmond.

55. Henry, *Henry*, I, 267–268.

56. Wirt Papers; Henry, *Henry*, I, 267. Of Jefferson's assistance, Wirt adds: "Mr. Jefferson, too, has exercised his well-known kindness and candour on this occasion; having not only favoured the author with a very full communication in the first instance; but assisted him, subsequently and repeatedly, with his able counsel, in reconciling apparent contradictions, and clearing away difficulties of fact." Wirt, *Henry*, p. x.

57. For a valuable criticism of Henry's speech, see William N. Brigance, *A History and Criticism of American Public Address*, II, with article on Henry by Louis A. Mallory, pp. 580–602.

58. *Magazine of History*, III, 158.

59. *Proceedings*, p. 5.

60. *Ibid.*, p. 6.

61. Wirt, *Henry*, p. 143. Nicholas' resolution was supported by the able William Cabell; Charles Campbell, *History of the Colony and Ancient Dominion of Virginia*, p. 627 (hereafter cited as Campbell, *Virginia*).

62. *Proceedings*, pp. 7–8.

63. *Ibid.*

64. *Ibid.*, p. 8.

65. *Ibid.*

66. *Ibid.*

67. *Magazine of History*, III, 158. I have received valuable help with this and the preceding chapter from Professors John Graham, University of Virginia, and F. M. Litto, University of Kansas.

68. *Magazine of History*, III. The statement in the *Proceedings*, p. 6 (March 25), that the plan for arming the militia was read, amended, and unanimously agreed to seems to contradict James Parker's assertion that Henry's motion to arm the soldiers was passed 65 to 60. But a number of motions was passed unanimously on March 24 and 25, and these final votes were after any preliminary discussions, votes, and amendments. The earlier 65-to-60 vote seems to allow properly for the conservative strength in the Convention.

Chapter 4

The Gunpowder Episode

1. Quoted in Nardi Reeder Campion, *Patrick Henry, Firebrand of the Revolution.*

2. Nathan C. Goodman, ed., *A Benjamin Franklin Reader,* p. 301.

3. For detailed information on the British punitive measures, see Henry, *Henry,* I, 154–173.

4. *American Archives,* Ser. 4, I, 881.

5. Wirt, *Henry,* p. 151.

6. *Ibid.,* pp. 151–152; Hamilton J. Eckenrode, *The Revolution in Virginia,* pp. 50–51.

7. Wirt, *Henry,* p. 152.

8. Dixon and Hunter's *Va. Gazette,* May 13, 1775. See also Campbell, *Virginia,* p. 610. Campbell has a detailed account of the whole gunpowder incident.

9. Mays, *Pendleton,* II, 20.

10. Wirt, *Henry,* p. 156.

11. Meade, *Henry,* I, 89.

12. Wirt, *Henry,* pp. 111 and 155.

13. Henry, *Henry,* I, 279.

14. Edmund Randolph in *Va. Magazine,* XLIII.

15. George Dabney to Wirt, May 14, 1805, in Wirt Papers, Library of Congress.

16. Nathanial Pope, Jr., Memo to William Wirt, June 23, 1806, in Wirt Papers.

17. Charles Dabney Memo of gunpowder episode, Dec. 21, 1805, in Wirt Papers; Henry, *Henry,* I, 279–280.

18. Charles Dabney, *loc. cit.;* Meade, *Henry,* I, 281; W. H. Miller, *History and Genealogies* (Lexington, Ky., 1907), Part 7, p. 637; W. B. Blanton, *Medicine in Virginia,* p. 385.

19. Charles Dabney Memo, *loc. cit.*

20. Wirt, *Henry,* pp. 156–157.

21. Meade, *Henry,* I, 71–74.

22. Wirt, *Henry,* pp. 157–158.

23. Nathanial Pope, Jr., and George Dabney Memos, Wirt Papers; Purdie's *Va. Gazette,* May 12, 1775.

24. Pope Memo, *loc. cit.;* Wirt, *Henry,* pp. 158–160; Henry, *Henry,* I, 282; Purdie's *Va. Gazette,* May 5, 1775.

25. *Ibid.*

26. This information on Corbin and his mansion is from a field trip to

Laneville, March, 1964; Works Progress Administration, *Virginia, A Guide to the Old Dominion*, p. 972; Rev. Alfred Bagby, *King and Queen County*, pp. 78–79; A. W. Weddell, ed., *A Memorial Volume of Virginia Historical Portraiture, 1585–1830*, pp. 199–200.

27. Henry, *Henry*, I, 282–284; Campbell, *Virginia*, pp. 611–614; Purdie's *Va. Gazette*, May 7, 1775.

28. *Reports of the Royal Historical Commission*, Mss. of the Earl of Dartmouth, III, quoted in *Va. Magazine*, XX, 85; Campbell, *Virginia*, pp. 612–613; *The London Chronicle*, July 4–6, 1775.

29. Henry, *Henry*, I, 286–291; William T. Hutchinson and William E. Rachal, eds., *The Papers of James Madison*, I, 146–148; Purdie's *Va. Gazette*, May 18, 1775; Lloyd Smith Papers, Morristown National Park, courtesy of Francis Ronalds.

30. Henry, *Henry*, I, 285–286.

31. *Ibid.*, pp. 284–285.

32. *Ibid.*, pp. 286–287.

33. *Ibid.*, pp. 287–289.

34. See p. 37.

35. Wirt, *Henry*, p. 159.

36. *Ibid.*, pp. 147–148.

37. Henry, *Henry*, I, 290; *American Archives*, Ser. 4, II, 541.

38. Henry, *Henry*, I, 286; George Bancroft, *History of the United States*, VII, 334–335.

Chapter 5

THE SECOND CONTINENTAL CONGRESS

1. *American Archives*, Ser. 4, II, 1517.

2. Albert Henry Smyth, editor, *The Writings of Benjamin Franklin*, VI, 408 (hereafter cited as Smyth, *Franklin Writings*).

3. Edmund C. Burnett, *Continental Congress*, p. 102.

4. *Journals*, II, 1, 55, *passim*.

5. *New York Historical Society Publications, Deane Papers*, I, 50.

6. *Pa. Gazette*, May 10, June 7, June 10, June 21, 1775.

7. *Journals*, II, 28–42.

8. Copy in possession of author.

9. Burnett, *Continental Congress*, p. 64; Mays, *Pendleton*, II, 19.

10. *Pa. Gazette*, May 17, 1775; *Connecticut Courant*, May 15, 1775; *Massachusetts Gazette*, May 19, 1775; *Pennsylvania Journal*, May 10, 1775.

11. *Essex Gazette*, May 25, 1775.

12. Edward Stabler to Pemberton, *Pemberton Papers*, Vol. 27, p. 144, quoted in Mays, *Pendleton*, II, 21.

13. Pendleton to William Woodford, Edmund C. Burnett, *Letters of Members of the Continental Congress*, I, 102, May 30, 1775 (hereafter cited as Burnett, *Letters*), quoted in Mays, *Pendleton*, II, 17.

14. Samuel Adams to James Warren, Philadelphia, June 10, 1775, in Burnett, *Letters*, I, 121.

15. Adams, *Works*, I, 175–176.

16. *Journals*, II, 80, 81 *et seq*.

17. *Ibid.*, p. 82; Burnett, *Continental Congress*, pp. 72–73.

18. *Journals*, II, 93.

19. Burnett, *Letters*, I, 28–29.

20. *Ibid.*, pp. 89–90.

21. Adams, *Works*, II, 408.

22. Lyman H. Butterfield, ed., *The Adams Papers*, III, 316–317.

23. For a good, brief account of South Carolina with Gadsden's role during this period, see David D. Wallace, *South Carolina, A Short History*.

24. Field trip to Dickinson mansion near Dover, June 6, 1964. His *Letters of a Pennsylvania Farmer*, in protest against the British Townshend duties, were published in Purdie and Dixon's *Va. Gazette*, Jan.–March, 1768.

25. W.P.A. Project, American Guide Series, *Pennsylvania, A Guide to the Keystone State*, p. 258.

26. *Journals*, II, 22, 55.

27. Burnett, *Continental Congress*, p. 75.

28. Claude H. Van Tyne, *The American Revolution*, in the American Nation Series, Vol. 9, pp. 34–35.

29. *Journals*, II, 55.

30. *Ibid.*, pp. 58, 59.

31. *Ibid.*, p. 101.

32. Burnett, *Letters*, I, 90; "Galloway is fled, as they say," Silas Deane to Mrs. Deane, May 12, 1775, *New York Historical Society Publications, Deane Papers*, I, 48.

33. There is a readable modern biography of James Wilson by Charles Page Smith.

34. Purdie's *Va. Gazette*, May 19, 1775.

35. *Ibid.*

36. *Ibid.*, June 9; Campbell, *Virginia*, p. 623.

37. George Scheer and Hugh F. Rankin, *Rebels and Redcoats*, pp. 65–66.

38. Smyth, *Franklin Writings*, VI, 409.

39. *Journals*, II, 60. The quotations from John Adams are in Butterfield, *The Adams Papers*, I, 321, or Adams, *Works*, II, 412.

40. The account of the proceedings of the Continental Congress is from the *Journals*, II, esp. for dates cited. The data on the army recruitment and pay are in *ibid.*, pp. 89–90. See also North Callahan, *Daniel Morgan*, pp. 119–120, and Oren Morton, *Winchester*, pp. 87–88.

41. *Journals*, II, 91–93; Butterfield, *The Adams Papers*, III, 321–323; Mays, *Pendleton*, II, 23–26; Freeman, *Washington*, III, 432–440; Henry, *Henry*, I, 298.

42. Butterfield, *The Adams Papers*, III, 323–324; *Journals*, II, 89–92. For a more favorable view of Lee, see John Richard Alden, *General Charles Lee*.

43. Fitzpatrick, *Washington Writings*, III, 299.

44. Freeman, *Washington*, III, 458.

45. Memorial of Dr. Benjamin Rush at American Philosophical Society, Philadelphia.

46. *Journals*, II, 102.

47. *Ibid.*, 127; Burnett, *Continental Congress*, p. 85.

48. *Journals*, II, 178–183.

49. Adams, *Works*, II, 411.

50. *New York Historical Society Publications, Deane Papers*, I, 55, 61, 72.

51. *Journals*, II, 234–235.

Chapter 6

HENRY AS COLONEL

1. Sir John Randolph to his cousin, Thomas Jefferson, Aug. 31, 1775, in Julian Boyd, ed., *The Papers of Thomas Jefferson*, I, 244 (hereafter cited as Boyd, *Jefferson Papers*).

2. Quotation from Fisher Diary in Hughes, *Washington*, III, 407.

3. *Va. Magazine*, XIX, 406. There is good data on military developments and other aspects of life in Williamsburg during the period in Jane Carson, *James Innes*, pp. 42 *et seq.*

4. Morgan, *Henry*, p. 218.

5. Andrew Lewis was a delegate to the Convention from Botetourt County. *American Archives*, Ser. 4, II, 165.

6. Morgan, *Henry*, p. 218.

7. Hughes, *Washington*, II, 135 *et seq.*

8. *American Archives*, Ser. 4, III, 375.

9. *Ibid.;* Mays, *Pendleton,* II, pp. 5 *et seq.*

10. Joseph M. Waterman, *With Sword and Lancet, the Life of General Hugh Mercer,* pp. 27 *et seq.;* W. B. Blanton, *Medicine in Virginia,* pp. 223–224; John T. Goolrick, *The Life of General Hugh Mercer.*

11. *American Archives,* Ser. 4, IV, 1519–1520.

12. *Ibid.,* III, 375.

13. Mays, *Pendleton,* II, 32–33.

14. *American Archives,* Ser. 4, IV, 1520.

15. *Ibid.,* III, 375.

16. *Ibid.,* p. 393.

17. *Ibid.,* p. 377.

18. See Convention Proceedings in *American Archives,* Ser. 4, III, 366 *et seq.*

19. *Ibid.,* 368.

20. Kate Mason Rowland, *The Life of George Mason,* I, 211 (hereafter cited as Rowland, *Mason*).

21. R. Wormley Carter to his father, Landon Carter, Aug. 5, 1775. Landon Carter Papers, University of Virginia Library.

22. *American Archives,* Ser. 4, III, 377–378.

23. *Ibid.,* p. 378.

24. *Ibid.,* p. 394.

25. *Ibid.*

26. *Ibid.,* p. 430.

27. *Ibid.,* p. 429.

28. *Ibid.,* pp. 392–393.

29. *Ibid.,* pp. 411, 418–419; Hamilton J. Eckenrode, *The Revolution in Virginia,* pp. 123–126.

30. Henry, *Henry,* I, 318.

31. L. C. Hatch, *The Administration of the American Revolutionary Army,* pp. 1–2; *American Archives,* Ser. 4, III, 398 *et seq.;* records of Va. military store, State Library.

32. Purdie's *Va. Gazette,* Sept. 29, 1775; Albert J. Beveridge, *The Life of John Marshall,* I, 70, 74; Henry, *Henry,* I, 319; Mays, *Pendleton,* II, 44.

33. Henry, *Henry,* I, 319; Philip Slaughter, *St. Mark's Parish,* pp. 107–108.

34. Richard Henry Lee, *Memoir,* II, 191–192.

35. *Ibid.*

36. Purdie's *Va. Gazette,* Sept. 10, 1775.

37. *Ibid.,* Oct. 13.

38. *Ibid.,* Oct. 6.

39. Smyth's narrative is in *Pa. Magazine*, XXXIX, 152; Parker's letter in *Magazine of History*, III (1906), 159. Parker concluded, "I am still of opinion when General Gage begins to act on the offensive the Rebellion will be immediately crushed."

40. E. C. Branchi, translator, *Memoirs of the Life and Voyages of Doctor Philip Mazzei*, first installment, *Wm. and Mary Quarterly*, Ser. II, 9, 172–173.

41. *Ibid.*

42. *Va. Magazine*, II, 216–217. Henry to General Adam Stephen.

43. Dixon and Hunter's *Va. Gazette*, Dec. 16, 1775.

44. *Ibid.*

45. *Ibid.*, Nov. 4, 1775.

46. *Council Journal* I, *passim*.

47. Nelly C. Preston, *Paths of Glory*, pp. 111–112.

48. See Thomas L. Preston, *A Sketch of Mrs. Elizabeth Russell*, pamphlet by her grandson, Nashville, 1888; Morgan, *Henry*, IX; data from the late Miss Nelly C. Preston, Seven Mile Ford, Va., including copy of a letter of Oct. 2, 1812, from her ancestress, Elizabeth Campbell Russell; article on Elizabeth Henry in *Scribner's Magazine*, June, 1928; *Christian Advocate*, Jan. 3, 1889; and Nelly C. Preston, *Paths of Glory*, *passim*. After a field trip to the Seven Mile Ford area and the Campbell graveyard, I received in March, 1967, numerous copies of legal records on General William Campbell from John A. Blakemore of Emory, Va.

49. Purdie's *Va. Gazette*, Sept. 29, 1775.

50. Mays, *Pendleton*, II, 35–56.

51. *Ibid.*, p. 55; David John Mays, *The Letters and Papers of Edmund Pendleton*, I, 124 *et seq.* (hereafter cited as Mays, *Pendleton Papers*).

52. *Ibid.*

53. Mays, *Pendleton Papers*, p. 362.

54. John Page letter, University of Virginia Library.

55. *American Archives*, Ser. 4, III, 1385.

56. *Ibid.*, pp. 1387–1388.

57. Further details of the last months of Henry's colonelcy are given in Mays, *Pendleton*, I, Chap. 4; Campbell, *Virginia*, Chap. LXXXV; and Henry, *Henry*, I, Chap. XIV. See also letters of Henry to Pendleton, Dec. 19, 1775, and Dec. 23, 1775, in the Historical Society of Pennsylvania; also Woodford to Joseph Jones, Dec. 13, 1775, in Virginia Historical Society.

58. Henry, *Henry*, I, 334–335.

59. *Ibid.*, pp. 335–336.

60. Mays, *Pendleton*, II, 70–71, citing Pendleton to Woodford, Dec. 7, 1775.

61. *Proceedings*, p. 75.

62. Henry, *Henry*, I, 341.

63. *American Archives*, Ser. 4, IV, 87.

64. Henry, *Henry*, I, 343.

65. *Ibid.*, pp. 343–344.

66. Mays, *Pendleton*, II, 80.

67. *American Archives*, Ser. 4, IV, 77–78.

68. Henry, *Henry*, I, 345.

69. *Ibid.*, p. 347.

70. *Ibid.*, p. 348. W. W. Henry notes: "The Journal of the Committee of the next day contains the following entry, which shows the careful habit of Mr. Henry in money matters:

"Patrick Henry Esquire settled his account of money laid out for contingent expenses, balance due to him £12.7.9 for which he received an order to have credit with the Commissary of Stores.' "

71. Purdie's *Va. Gazette*, March 1, 1776.

72. *Ibid.*

73. Henry, *Henry*, I, 349–350.

Chapter 7

INDEPENDENCE: THE VIRGINIA RESOLUTIONS

1. Herbert Hoover, *The Challenge to Liberty*, p. 205.

2. *American Archives*, Ser. 4, V, 1203.

3. Mays, *Pendleton*, II, 368; W. T. Hutchinson and W. E. Rachal, *Madison Papers*, I, 165–169.

4. John Page to Richard Henry Lee, Lee Papers, University of Virginia.

5. Samuel Eliot Morison and Henry Steel Commager, *Growth of the American Republic* (1950 ed.), I, 209.

6. Dixon and Hunter's *Va. Gazette*, March 23, 1776; *American Archives*, Ser. 4, III, 240–241.

7. Hugh T. Lefler and Albert R. Newsome, *The History of a Southern State: North Carolina*, p. 204.

8. Page to Richard Henry Lee, Lee Papers. For a letter of protest against the reluctant attitude of Robert C. Nicholas and William Norvell toward independence, see Purdie's *Va. Gazette Supplement*, April 26, 1776. Nicholas and Norvell were delegates from James City County to

the May Convention. In instructions signed by a "majority" of the free-holders living in the county, the two delegates were instructed "(provided no just and honorable terms are offered by the king) to exert your utmost ability, in the next Convention, towards dissolving the connexion between America and Great Britain, totally, finally, and irrevocably."

9. *Va. Magazine*, XXXIV, 185–186. (When Powhatan County was formed from Cumberland, Henry as governor appointed Fleming as county lieutenant, July 31, 1779. *Ibid.*, XXIV, 328.)

10. *American Archives*, Ser. 4, V, 1034–1035. For instructions to the delegates from nearby Buckingham, see *ibid.*, pp. 1206–1208. The instructions called for establishment of a "government" in America.

11. Henry, *Henry*, I, 378–382.

12. *American Archives*, Ser. 4, VI, 1509 *et seq.*

13. *Ibid.*, pp. 1510–1511. If the Henry party had wanted to do so, they could have prevented the election of Pendleton as President. Hugh Blair Grigsby, *Virginia Convention of 1776*, pp. 13–14.

14. Pendleton did, however, refer to the "critical" time when the "most important" subjects require the "serious attention of the Convention." *American Archives*, Ser. 4, VI, 1511.

15. For Henry's committee appointments on May 6–8, see *ibid.*, pp. 1511 and 1514.

16. These included a committee to arrange for hospitalization for the sick and wounded soldiers (May 21), another committee for Indian affairs (May 22), and still another to report the cause of the depreciation of paper money and to inquire into the pay of soldiers (June 4–5). *Ibid.*, pp. 1532, 1534, 1550.

17. *Ibid.*, pp. 1512, 1522.

18. *Ibid.*, pp. 1512, 1514, 1522.

19. For this and other connected data relating to Lee, see John Richard Alden, *General Charles Lee*, esp. pp. 113, 116; *American Archives*, Ser. 4, VI, 403–408; and Henry, *Henry*, II, 383–386.

20. Henry to R. H. Lee, May 20, 1776; Henry, *Henry*, I, 393–394; and Henry to John Adams, *ibid.*, pp. 412–413.

21. Henry, *Henry*, I, 422–423.

22. *Ibid.*, pp. 395–396.

23. *Ibid.*, p. 396; Mays, *Pendleton*, II. Meriwether Smith in *Dictionary of American Biography*; Mays, *Pendleton*, II, 106–108. W. W. Wirt indicates that the so-called Pendleton resolutions were written by him, but Pendleton's scholarly biographer is doubtful.

24. Henry, *Henry*, I, 394–395.

25. *Ibid.*, p. 395.

26. Mays, *Pendleton*, II, 109, citing Henry, *Henry*, I, 395.

27. *Ibid.*
28. Lefler and Newsome, *op. cit.*, p. 204.
29. Dixon and Hunter's *Va. Gazette*, May 18, 1776.
30. Henry, *Henry*, I, 412–413.

Chapter 8

A PILOT DECLARATION OF RIGHTS AND A STATE CONSTITUTION

1. Lord Acton, *Essays on Freedom and Power*, p. 41.
2. Quoted by Henry Steel Commager in "Should the Historian Make Moral Judgments?" *American Heritage*, Feb., 1966.
3. Henry, *Henry*, I, 410.
4. *Ibid.*, pp. 413–414.
5. *Ibid.*, p. 413.
6. The data on Mason's close election to the Convention and his initial appearance there is found in Mays, *Pendleton*, I, 368; Rowland, *Mason*, I, 228–229 *et seq.*; *American Archives*, Ser. 4, VI, 1524–1530.
7. Helen Day Hill, *George Mason, Constitutionalist*, pp. 117, 136, 138–140, *passim* (hereafter cited as Hill, *Mason*).
8. Henry, *Henry*, I, 424–425.
9. *Ibid.*, p. 425.
10. Sources for this discussion of the wording of the Virginia Declaration of Rights are: Hill, *Mason*, Chap. X; Rowland, *Mason*, I, including Appendix; *American Archives*, Ser. 4, VI, 1537, *passim*; Henry, *Henry*, I, 423–435. There is a brief readable account of Mason's role in the Convention in Robert A. Rutland, *George Mason*. Much documentary material with excellent analysis is found in Boyd, *Jefferson Papers*, I, and Hutchinson and Rachal, *Madison Papers*, I.
11. Rowland, *Mason*, I, 440.
12. Irving Brant, *James Madison*, I, 242 (hereafter cited as Brant, *Madison*).
13. Edmund Randolph Essay; Henry, *Henry*, I, 434–435.
14. Mays, *Pendleton*, II, 122, quoting Edmund Randolph, *Manuscript History*, II, 66; Henry, *Henry*, I, 435. Rutland in his *George Mason* argues that the wording of the Sixteenth Article seems to have been Mason's except for the "free exercise of religion," which Madison suggested. *Ibid.*, p. 60.
15. Henry, *Henry*, I, 418–420.
16. *Ibid.*, pp. 418–422. Braxton was one of the more influential dele-

gates, and his plans had features which appealed to members fearful of some democratic features in the Constitution.

17. *Ibid.*, p. 411.

18. *Ibid.*, p. 412.

19. *Ibid.*, p. 414.

20. *Ibid.*, p. 413.

21. *Ibid.*, p. 422.

22. Mays, *Pendleton*, II, 122.

23. *American Archives*, Ser. 4, VI, 1525.

24. *Ibid.*, pp. 1557–1558. In a similar procedure, John Goodrich, another of Dunmore's followers, was found guilty of aiding and abetting the enemy and ordered to be imprisoned in Charlottesville. *Ibid.*, pp. 1559–1560.

25. *Ibid.*, p. 1569.

26. Henry, *Henry*, I, 405–406.

27. *Ibid.*, pp. 405–407.

28. *Ibid.*

29. *American Archives*, Ser. 4, VI, 1598–1599.

30. *Ibid.*, V, 1206–1209.

31. Henry, *Henry*, I, 436.

32. Charles S. Sydnor, *Gentlemen Freeholders, Political Practices in Washington's Virginia*, *passim*.

33. *American Archives*, Ser. 4, VI, 1598–1600; Henry, *Henry*, I, 437–438.

34. Henry, *Henry*, I, 436.

35. *Ibid.*, pp. 438–439.

36. *American Archives*, Ser. 4, VI, 1599.

37. *Ibid.*, p. 1601.

Chapter 9

GOVERNOR FIRST TERM

1. Quoted in Morgan, *Henry*, p. 270.

2. *American Archives*, Ser. 4, VI, 1599; Mays, *Pendleton*, II, 124. The Speaker of the House did not become the most powerful office in the new government.

3. *Ibid.*

4. Malcolm H. Harris, *History of Louisa County*, pp. 178–179.

5. William Nelson was born at Yorktown, then (1711) the almost feudal domain of the Nelsons. As a baby, he is said to have been held up by his nurse while a brick was passed through his hands, a symbolic laying

of the cornerstone for the still surviving Nelson mansion. A. W. Weddell, ed., *A Memorial Volume of Virginia Historical Portraiture, 1585–1830,* p. 196.

With much of the vigor and influence of the Tidewater aristocracy being transplanted to the unexploited Piedmont, it was not surprising that some of the Nelson plantation interests were becoming concentrated not at York port and genteel York Hall but in up-country Hanover. One of Henry's early lawsuits had been against "Squire" Nelson's overseer in the county, and a few years later Henry had represented his own cousin, Geddes Winston, in three suits against the "Honble Wm. Nelson." On occasions, too, some of the Nelsons were among the gentlemen worshiping with Henry at Fork Church or gossiping in the churchyard, though his chief association with the family came to be at the capital, where they had been long entrenched.

An accomplished gentleman in his early sixties, Thomas, Sr., had been educated in England and at the Middle Temple before returning to Virginia. Here, as a member of one of the wealthy and prolific first families, intermarried with the Carters, the Burwells, and the Armisteads, he was soon made a member of the Council, sitting with his brother, William. The Councillors, appointed by the King, were usually conservative gentlemen, living within the convenient distance of Williamsburg and compliant to the royal regime. Thomas, while possessing many estimable qualities, never deviated too much from the accepted pattern.

Henry Account Book; W. M. Clark, compiler, *Colonial Churches in Virginia,* 2nd ed., p. 306; William Meade, *Old Churches, Ministers, and Families of Virginia* (1857 ed.), I, 202–215.

6. Edmund Randolph Essay. Quoted in H. J. Eckenrode, *The Revolution in Virginia,* p. 166. There is also much data on the Randolphs of the Revolutionary period in Eckenrode, *The Randolphs.*

7. For these Carter references, see *Wm. and Mary Quarterly,* Ser. I, 20, 175–180, 184; also, for biographical data on Carter, *ibid.,* pp. 45–46.

8. *Tyler's Quarterly,* XIII, No. 4, 246–247.

9. *American Archives,* Ser. 4, VI, 1599.

10. *Wm. and Mary Quarterly,* Ser. I, 20, 180.

11. H. J. Eckenrode, *The Revolution in Virginia,* p. 166. In a letter of July 6 to "My dear Friend" General Charles Lee, Richard Henry Lee (no relative) sent a copy of the new form of government which would show him "that this Country has in view a permanent system of liberty." Henry had been chosen governor with a privy council to assist him and a great seal adopted so that they now had "in all respects a full and free Government which this day begins the exercise of its powers." James

Curtis Ballagh, *The Letters of Richard Henry Lee*, I, 205 (hereafter cited as Ballagh, *Lee*).

12. *American Archives*, Ser. 4, VI, 1602.
13. Brant, *Madison*, I, 262.
14. Boyd, *Jefferson Papers*, XV, 576.
15. *Wm. and Mary Quarterly*, Ser. I, 20, 184.
16. *Ibid.*
17. See p. 133.
18. Boyd, *Jefferson Papers*, I, 455.
19. *American Archives*, Ser. 4, VI, 1600–1601.
20. *Ibid.*
21. *Ibid.*, pp. 1602–1603.
22. Dixon and Hunter's *Va. Gazette*, July 20, 1776.
23. *Ibid.*, Aug. 10.
24. *Ibid.*, Aug. 3, 1776.
25. Harris, *op. cit.*, esp. pp. 51–53.
26. J. A. James, *George Rogers Clark Papers*, esp. pp. 21–27 (hereafter cited as James, *Clark*); Henry, *Henry*, I, 469–473; *Council Journal*, II, 56, 57, *passim*; *Official Letters*, I, 33, 56, *passim*.

Chapter 10

REVOLUTION AT A DESPERATE STAGE

1. Quoting letter from Newark, N.J., of Nov. 23, 1776.
2. Morgan, *Henry*, p. 439.
3. There are biographical sketches of John Page in A. W. Weddell, ed., *A Memorial Volume of Virginia Historical Portraiture*, p. 330 (with portrait) and in the *Dictionary of American Biography*.
4. *Council Journal*, I, 154–163.
5. *Ibid.*, pp. 154, 163.
6. Dixon and Hunter's *Va. Gazette*, Sept. 14, 1776.
7. Fitzpatrick, *Washington's Writings*, VI, 26–33 and esp. p. 28.
8. Ballagh, *Lee*, I, 215, Sept. 15, 1776.
9. Meade, *Henry*, I, esp. 243–244.
10. See Chap. 5, Note 19. Also valuable family data through courtesy of Mrs. Spencer Hamilton, Riverside, Cal., a descendant of Dr. Hinde.
11. Henry, *Henry*, I, 329–330, *passim*.
12. *Council Journal*, I, 168.
13. *Ibid.*, p. 166 *et seq.*; *Official Letters*, I, 60.
14. Ballagh, *Lee*, I, 215.

15. Fitzpatrick, *Washington's Writings*, VI, 163–168.

16. Freeman, *Washington*, IV, 72, 73.

17. Fitzpatrick, *Washington's Writings*, VI, 163–168.

18. *Ibid.*

19. *Official Letters*, I, 155, *passim*; Henry, *Henry*, I, 477–482.

20. *Official Letters*, I, 47.

21. *Ibid.*, p. 360. March 31, 1779.

22. *Ibid.*, p. 59.

23. Freeman, *Washington*, IV, esp. 215, 252.

24. Dixon and Hunter's *Va. Gazette*, Oct. 4, 1776.

25. *Council Journal*, I, 243, 246, 247; *Official Letters*, I, 66.

26. *Council Journal*, I, 262–266.

27. *Ibid.*, pp. 267, *passim*.

28. *Official Letters*, I, 72–73; *Council Journal*, I, 298. Dec. 23, 1776.

29. *Official Letters*, I, 71.

30. *Ibid.*, p. 75. Dec. 10, 1776.

31. *Ibid.*, pp. 76, 82.

32. Dixon and Hunter's *Va. Gazette*.

33. *Ibid.*

34. *Official Letters*, I, 82–83.

35. *Ibid.*, p. 83.

36. *Ibid.*, p. 82.

37. *Ibid.*, pp. 73, 75.

38. Henry, *Henry*, I, 505.

39. *Ibid.*, pp. 506–507.

40. *Ibid.*, p. 506.

41. *Ibid.*, p. 507.

42. *Ibid.*, pp. 507–509.

43. *Council Journal*, I, 294–297.

44. *Ibid.*, p. 296.

45. *Ibid.*, p. 300.

46. There is a good general account of the Trenton and Princeton battles in Mark M. Boatner III, *Encyclopedia of the American Revolution*. See also Freeman, *Washington*, III, Chap. 13, "Audentes Fortuna Iuvat" (Fortune favors the daring).

47. Henry, *Henry*, I, 511–513.

48. Lee to Henry, Jan. 17, 1777; Henry, *Henry*, III, 40.

49. The military service of John Henry is listed on p. 151. Besides serving as a justice in Fluvanna County and sheriff during part of the war (Fluvanna Minute Books 1777–79 and 1781), William Henry, Patrick's brother, was a militia lieutenant. Brief military records of Henry's son John and of Henry's brothers-in-law, Dabney cousins, and other relatives

are given in John H. Gwathmey, *Historical Revolution,* or F. B. Heitman, *Historical Register of the Officers of the Continental Army.*

50. John Syme Account Book, Library of Congress.

Chapter 11

BITTER DISCOURAGEMENT BUT ANOTHER GUBERNATORIAL TERM

1. Freeman, *Washington,* IV, 380, quoting *The Evelyns in America,* pp. 232–233.

2. *Official Letters,* I, 129, March 28, 1777. For other Henry letters hitherto used in this chapter, see references under dates listed therein, in *Official Letters* and *Council Journal.*

3. Fitzpatrick, *Washington's Writings,* VII, 350.

4. Henry to Lee, April 7, 1778. Henry, *Henry,* I, 559–560. On April 11, 1777, Dixon and Hunter's *Va. Gazette* announced the death of the Rev. Patrick Henry, rector of St. Paul's Parish, Hanover County.

5. Henry, *Henry,* I, 521; *Senate Journal,* p. 16; *Journal of House of Delegates,* pp. 48, 49.

6. *Official Letters,* I, 155; *Senate Journal,* pp. 16, 50.

7. *Official Letters,* I, 154.

8. We have noted that Henry, like some other prominent Virginians, had been interested prior to the Revolution in western lands. William Byrd III, a well-known plunger in the field, had been offered a tract of land by the Cherokees, and some years later, in early 1774, as well as Henry remembered, he and Byrd fell into conversation on the subject. Then, as Henry stated in his deposition of June 4, 1777, Byrd, the late John Page, Sr., and Henry agreed to send a representative to the Cherokees to ascertain if they were willing to sell them some of the Indian land in Virginia; Col. William Christian was to be a partner if the scheme succeeded. Some of the Indians did decide to negotiate on the subject, but before any agreement could be concluded, difficulties with Great Britain rose to a climax, and Henry became a member of the first Virginia Convention and the First Continental Congress. *Official Letters,* I, 156–158.

9. *Ibid.,* pp. 157–159.

10. In a letter of June 10 accompanying the estimates, Henry observed that the calculation was based upon one regiment and would be increased in accordance with the number "taken into pay." The Council could not give a satisfactory estimate of hospital expenses because the number of troops was not known and the prices of almost every necessary were "so very fluctuat-

ing." He therefore annexed a list of articles containing "general heads" of expenses. *Ibid.*, p. 161.

11. *House Journal,* June, 1777.

12. Henry, *Henry,* I, 525–526, and III, 88. There is an interesting account of Jones' courtship of Dolly Dandridge in S. E. Morison, *John Paul Jones,* 27–30, 112.

13. *Official Letters,* I, 171–174.

14. *Council Journal,* I, 463–468.

15. *Ibid.,* p. 488.

16. *Ibid.,* p. 489.

17. Photostat of record of Clerk of Hanover County, Virginia Historical Society.

18. C. G. Chamberlayne, *Vestry Book of St. Paul's Parish,* p. 530.

19. Letter from the Rev. George M. Brydon, Virginia church historian, Sept. 19, 1959.

20. *Ibid.*

21. *Ibid.;* contemporary Anglican prayerbook.

22. Brydon letter.

23. Henry, *Henry,* I, 618. Family data handed down by a Henry descendant, John Fontaine, Paces, Va. There is a brooch containing reddish-brown hair of Dorothea at the John Marshall House, Richmond, Va.

24. S. E. Morison, *op. cit.,* pp. 27–30.

25. Mrs. Reginald DeKoven, *The Life and Letters of John Paul Jones,* pp. 77–79.

26. *Council Journal,* II, 9.

27. Family data in Ruth Lawrence, *The Burwell, Spotswood, Dandridge, West, and Allied Family Histories.*

28. Letter of Mrs. Nathaniel Dandridge to her sister, Mrs. Anne Thornton, June 12, 1778. Valentine Museum, Richmond, Va.

29. Henry, *Henry,* I, 618.

Chapter 12

A More Hopeful Interlude

1. *Pa. Magazine,* XXI, 53.

2. Ballagh, *Lee,* I, 325.

3. *Ibid.*

4. *Official Letters,* I, 201.

5. Charles Campbell Papers, William and Mary Library. Campbell

(1807–1876) was a great-nephew of Philip Aylett, who married Patrick Henry's daughter, Elizabeth. Letter to Lucy Henry, Sept. 26, 1843, *ibid.* During his earlier years Campbell "spent many happy days" at Montville, the Aylett place in King William County, and was "very devoted" to several of the Aylett family. Interview with John Fontaine, Wilson, N.C., Feb. 12, 1949. The "undisputed family source" from whom Campbell secured his information was very probably Elizabeth Henry Aylett, for she did not die until 1842. Data from Aylett family Bible through John Fontaine. The official records of John Henry's military service are incomplete, but on Jan. 13, 1777, the Council recommended a John Henry to be first lieutenant of artillery, and in Washington's letter of September 13, 1778, to Patrick Henry he refers to Capt. Henry, as noted. Henry, *Henry*, III, 190–191. On Nov. 3, 1778, Washington wrote Governor Henry that he had been informed about Sept. 15 that Capt. Henry was at Elizabeth, N.J., where he had been "indisposed" for some time and was "rather distressed for want of money." Washington arranged for Col. Bannister to supply needed money and otherwise help the pitiful young officer on to Virginia. Fitzpatrick, *Washington's Writings*, XIII, 199. Fitzpatrick refers to Capt. Henry as Patrick Henry's son and as captain of the First Continental Artillery. *Ibid.*

6. Meade, *Henry*, I, 299–300.

7. Letter of Robert Pleasants to Henry, March 28, 1777. From the original in possession of Mrs. E. D. Tinsley, Lynchburg, Va., a Henry descendant.

8. Dixon and Hunter's *Va. Gazette*, Dec. 26, 1777.

9. *Pa. Magazine*, LXXXII, 411–413.

10. Ballagh, *Lee*, I, 320–321; Oren F. Morton, *The Story of Winchester*, pp. 90–92; *Official Letters*, I, 194.

11. For a good treatment see Charles E. Chapman, *A History of Spain*, founded on the *Historia de España y de la civilizacion española* of Rafael Altamire, Chaps. 35, 36, 37.

12. *Official Letters*, I, 195.

13. *Ibid.*, pp. 195–196.

14. James, *Clark*, pp. 91–98.

15. *Ibid.*, p. 98.

16. *Official Letters*, I, 227–229; James, *Clark*, pp. 100–108.

17. Dumas Malone and Basil Rauch, *Empire For Liberty*, I, 169.

18. Samuel F. Bemis, *Diplomatic History of the United States*, pp. 24, 94.

19. *Ibid.*, pp. 23–24.

20. *Official Letters*, I, 251.

21. *Ibid.*, p. 207.

22. *Ibid.*, pp. 216–217n.

23. Meade, *Henry*, I, 334–335.

24. *Official Letters*, I, 242; James, *Clark*, p. 59.

25. *Official Letters*, I, 242.

26. James, *Clark*, p. 112.

27. Henry, *Henry*, I, 583–587.

28. *Council Journal*, II, 56.

29. *Ibid.*

30. *Ibid.*, p. 57.

31. John E. Bakeless, *Background to Glory, The Life of George Rogers Clark*, pp. 93–94.

32. *Illinois Historical Society Collections*, Vol. 8, p. 218.

33. *Council Journal*, II, 57–58.

34. *Official Letters*, I, 224.

35. Henry, *Henry*, I, 609.

36. James, *Clark*, p. 115.

37. *Official Letters*, I, 230.

38. James, *Clark*, pp. 115–116; John E. Bakeless, *Background to Glory*, p. 56.

Chapter 13

STILL MORE CRISES

1. Hughes, *Washington*, III, 229, quoted in *Pa. Magazine*, XXI, 305.

2. Freeman, *Washington*, IV, 562.

3. Hughes, *Washington*, III, 231.

4. *Ibid.*

5. Henry's letter to Washington of Oct. 30, 1777, is in Henry, *Henry*, III, 111–112; Washington's two replies of Nov. 13 in *ibid.*, pp. 117–122. See also Thomas Mifflin and Joseph Trumbull in the *Dictionary of American Biography* and *Encyclopedia of the American Revolution;* Fitzpatrick, *Washington's Writings*, X, 183–185, Washington to the President of Congress, Dec. 22, 1777; and the detailed study in Freeman, *Washington*, IV, 241–242 and 639–642.

6. Fitzpatrick, *Washington's Writings*, X, 192–193.

7. Henry, *Henry*, III, 132–133, 135–137; Fitzpatrick, *Washington's Writings*, X, 194–195.

8. See data on the Trumbulls in Note 5 and esp. in Freeman, *Washington*, IV (including photograph from portrait of Joseph Trumbull, opposite p. 242).

9. Thomas Mifflin in *Dictionary of American Biography*. There is a somewhat more favorable estimate of him in Kenneth Rossman, *Thomas Mifflin*.

10. Hughes, *Washington*, III, 232, quoting Henry Dearborn, *Journal*, Dec., 1777, p. 13.

11. Ballagh, *Lee*, I, 351–352.

12. *Official Letters*, I, 219.

13. *Ibid.*, p. 390.

14. *Ibid.*, pp. 219–220.

15. J. S. Bassett, *A Short History of the U.S.*, p. 238.

16. Dixon and Hunter's *Va. Gazette*, Nov. 28, 1777.

17. Ballagh, *Lee*, I, 361.

18. *Official Letters*, I, 205; Freeman, *Washington*, IV, 571–573.

19. *Official Letters*, I, 212–215; Freeman, *Washington*, IV, 534–536, 570–571.

20. Freeman, *Washington*, IV, 572.

21. Albert J. Beveridge, *The Life of John Marshall*, I, 116–117.

22. Bernhard Knollenberg, *Washington and the Revolution, A Reappraisal*, p. 76.

23. Hughes, *Washington*, III, 252–253; Freeman, *Washington*, IV, 556, 586, *passim*; Burnett, *Letters*, II, 570. Numerous Washington letters relating to the Conway Cabal are in Fitzpatrick, *Washington's Writings*, X, 29, 437–441, *passim*.

24. The anonymous letter of Feb. 19, 1778, to Henry from Valley Forge is in Fitzpatrick, *Washington's Writings*, X, 483–485. See references in Note 23 and esp. the critical reappraisal in Knollenberg, *op. cit.*; also the account of the Conway Cabal with the Washington–Henry correspondence in Henry, *Henry*, I, 544–552. I am much indebted to Mr. Knollenberg for reading this and some other chapters in the manuscript.

Although Dr. Rush was one of the outstanding physicians of the age, a leader in humanitarian activities, he has even been accused of being responsible more than any other man in America for "the great vogue of vomits, purging, and especially of bleeding, salivation, blistering, which blackened the record of medicine and afflicted the sick almost to the time of the Civil War." Such medical methods, however, which helped explain the death of many a miserable soldier in the Revolution and later of George Washington himself, were the common practice of the period. Hughes, *Washington*, III, 729n, quoting Col. P. M. Ashburn, *A History of the Medical Department of the United States Army*, p. 19. Also sketch of Dr. Rush in *Dictionary of American Biography*.

25. Hughes, *Washington*, III, 254, quoting Burnett, *Letters*, III, 56.

26. *Official Letters*, I, 231.

27. *Ibid.*

28. *Ibid.*

29. *Ibid.*, p. 232.

30. *Ibid.*, pp. 232–233.

31. *Ibid.*, p. 238.

32. *Ibid.*, p. 258.

33. *Ibid.*

34. *Ibid.*, p. 260. Letter dated Williamsburg, April 7, 1778.

35. *Official Letters*, I, 260–261; Henry, *Henry*, I, 559–560.

36. Fitzpatrick, *Washington's Writings*, XI, 278–279.

37. *Official Letters*, I, 270–273.

38. *Ibid.*, p. 275.

39. For data on Jefferson's work in the House of Delegates, 1776–1778, see Dumas Malone, *Jefferson and His Time*, I, *passim*, and the excellent sketch of Jefferson by Dr. Malone in *Dictionary of American Biography*.

40. Malone, *Jefferson*, I, 303; *Official Letters*, I, 285.

Chapter 14

HENRY AS GOVERNOR—THIRD TERM

1. Letter to Benjamin Harrison, Speaker of the House of Delegates of Virginia, Dec. 18, 1778. Fitzpatrick, *Washington's Writings*, XIII, 464.

2. Thomas A. Bailey, *The American Pageant*, pp. 116–117.

3. *Official Letters*, I, 211, Dec. 6, 1777.

4. *Ibid.*, p. 289.

5. *Ibid.*, p. 286. Actually, the payment of so-called Virginia money was to be in tobacco at the rate of $100 per hundred pounds.

6. Ballagh, *Lee*, I, 451.

7. The interesting data on the Continental volunteers is derived from Oscar T. Barck and Hugh T. Lefler, *Colonial America*, pp. 664, *passim*. Henry's letter to Lee is in *Official Letters*, I, 291–292.

8. *Official Letters*, I, 292. June 18, 1778.

9. *Ibid.*, pp. 292–293.

10. *Ibid.*, p. 295.

11. *Ibid.*, pp. 296–297.

12. *Ibid.*, p. 303.

13. *Ibid.*, pp. 301–302; Robert Douthat Stoner, *A Seedbed of the Early Republic: Botetourt*, p. 107.

14. Spotsylvania County Order Book, 1774–1782, p. 88. Virginia State Library.

15. Maude Carter Clement, *The History of Pittsylvania County*, pp. 156–157.

16. Fluvanna County Minute Book, June 4, 1778, p. 28.

17. *Official Letters*, I, 293.

18. Bellini, who probably came from Italy to Virginia with Henry's friend, Philip Mazzei, had lately been serving the state government as an interpreter and secretary. *Ibid.*, p. 255; *Council Journal*, II, 109, March 25, 1778.

19. Morgan, *Henry*, Bible entry opposite p. 406.

20. *Ibid.*, p. 402, and portrait of Dorothea on opposite page.

21. Henry, *Henry*, II, 363. George D. Winston, the son of Henry's first cousin, Judge Edmund Winston, would serve as one of Henry's executors. R. D. Meade, "Judge Edmund Winston's Memoir of Patrick Henry," in *Va. Magazine*, Jan., 1961.

22. Henry's brother-in-law, Gen. William Campbell, who died during the Yorktown campaign, also proved an outstanding military officer, at least of irregular troops.

23. *Official Letters*, I, 332–333; John Richard Alden, *The South in the Revolution*, pp. 235, *passim;* Mark M. Boatner III, *Encyclopedia of the American Revolution*, articles on Gen. Henry Clinton, the Southern Campaign, *et al.*

24. *Official Letters*, I, 313.

25. *Ibid.*, pp. 313, 318, 319–320; *Council Journal*, II, 207–208, Oct. 31, 1778.

26. *Official Letters*, I, 332–333.

27. *Ibid.*, p. 353.

28. John R. Alden, *The South in the Revolution*, p. 230.

29. Fitzpatrick, *Washington's Writings*, XIII, 462–465.

30. *Ibid.*, pp. 465–466.

31. *Ibid.*, pp. 466–467.

32. *Official Letters*, I, 280, 330.

33. *Ibid.*, p. 334.

34. *Ibid.*, p. 373.

35. F. J. Turner, "Western State Making in the Revolutionary Era," *American Historical Review*, I, 85.

36. *Official Letters*, I, 323–324; James, *Clark*. Briefer accounts are in the readable Thomas D. Clark, *History of Kentucky*, and John E. Bakeless, *Background to Glory: The Life of George Rogers Clark*. Much documentary material is printed in *Collections of the Illinois State Historical Library*.

37. *Official Letters*, I, 338.

38. *Ibid.*, pp. 338–339.

39. *Ibid.*

40. *Ibid.*, p. 339.

41. *Ibid.*, pp. 341–344.

42. *Collections of the Illinois State Historical Library*, VIII, 140.

43. *Official Letters*, I, 340–342, 347n. See also p. 220.

44. Jane Carson, *James Innes*, pp. 101–102.

45. *Council Journal*, I, 349; *Official Letters*, I, 110, 113.

46. Henry, *Henry*, II, 36–37. Data kindly supplied in Dec., 1961, by Mrs. St. G. Tucker, Lexington, Va.

47. Henry, *Henry*, II, 34.

48. *Ibid.*, p. 35.

49. *Ibid.*, pp. 37–38.

50. *Official Letters*, I, 236.

Chapter 15

War Governor—Gladly Resigning

1. Burnett, *Letters*, IV, 133.

2. *Journals*, XIII, 1201; *Official Letters*, I, 333.

3. *Official Letters*, I, 353; *Journals*, IV, 93.

4. Burnett, *Letters*, III, 467–468.

5. *Ibid.*, p. xxix.

6. Ballagh, *Lee*, II, 36.

7. *Journals*, XII, esp. 1234–1238 and, in general, 1233–1267.

8. Burnett, *Letters*, IV, 79–80.

9. *Journals*, XIII, 6, 7.

10. On June 27, 1777, the Speaker had laid before the House of Delegates a letter from Nelson declining election to the Council. Two months later, Henry, on advice of the Council, appointed the capable Nelson a brigadier general. *Official Letters*, I, 167, 179.

11. *Official Letters*, I, 250–251; Franklin to Henry, American Philosophical Society, Philadelphia.

12. *Official Letters*, I, 358; Henry, *Henry*, II, 14.

13. *Official Letters*, I, 359–360.

14. *Ibid.*, p. 360.

15. *Ibid.*, p. 363; P. H. Baskervill, *Andrew Meade of Ireland and Virginia*, pp. 31, *passim*.

16. *Official Letters*, I, 362–363.

17. *Ibid.*, p. 363.

18. David D. Wallace, *South Carolina*, p. 289.

19. *Official Letters*, I, 365.

20. *Ibid.*, pp. 364–365.

21. *Ibid.*, pp. 371–372.

22. Mark M. Boatner III, *Encyclopedia of the American Revolution*, pp. 1033–1037; Wallace, *South Carolina*, pp. 287–305.

23. Henry, *Henry*, II, 39, quoting *House Journal*, p. 29.

24. *Official Letters*, I, 377.

25. Purdie's *Va. Gazette*, Aug. 22, 1777; Henry, *Henry*, I, 618–619. I am further indebted to the late Judge Leon Bazile for copies of legal records of the property transfers for Scotchtown.

26. Henry, *Henry*, II, 39, quoting *House Journal*, p. 29.

Chapter 16

LEATHERWOOD AND THE BRITISH

1. *Calendar of Va. State Papers*, 353. Greene went on to apologize to Harrison for a mistaken criticism of Virginia military policy.

2. *Wm. and Mary Quarterly*, Ser. 2, X, 1, 8, 9.

3. Henry, *Henry*, II, 42; I, 618–621.

4. In 1774, a half century after Byrd wrote his urbane *Journey to the Dividing Line*, a British traveler found some large plantations in the rich, low grounds on Leatherwood Creek. But all the inhabitants had fled to a nearby fort because of a rumored Indian raid. For miles en route he had not found a single habitation, and he would have seen few more if he had journeyed into the adjoining foothills. Judith Hill, *A History of Henry County;* data on its early history from the county histories by Hill and Virginia and Lewis Pedigo.

5. Information, with photographic view of purported Henry house, by Mrs. Whitney Shumate, Martinsville, Va., and in 1945 from the late Rives Brown, Martinsville. Mr. Brown repeated a description of the Henry house given him about 1908 by H. C. Lester, then eighty-six. *Danville* (Va.) *Times*, July 4, 1789, clipping in Virginia Historical Society. Visit to purported site of Henry house on Ralph Hooker farm and data from Mr. Hooker. The Hooker son, Robert, spoke of an Indian tomahawk being found on the place and what he believed were Indian graves. Henry's letter of Aug., 1780, is in the New York Public Library.

6. Henry, *Henry*, II, 43; Boyd, *Jefferson Papers*, III, 293–294.

7. Henry, *Henry*, II, 43, 48, 49. Copy of family Bible entry in Morgan, *Henry*, opposite p. 406.

8. Henry County Order Book 2, pp. 33, *passim*; other miscellaneous entries in County Order Books at Martinsville; Hill, *Henry County*, p. 68. The grave of Mrs. George Hairston (née Letcher), may still be seen at Beaver Creek, the old Hairston place just north of Martinsville.

9. Henry, *Henry*, II, 48–49.

10. *Va. Magazine*, IX, 421.

11. Henry, *Henry*, II, 48–49.

12. *Ibid.*, p. 57.

13. William W. Hening, *The Statutes at Large*, X, 85–89.

14. John P. Little, *History of Richmond*, p. 65; Albert J. Beveridge, *The Life of John Marshall*, I, 165–166.

15. Hutchinson and Rachal, *Madison Papers*, II, 30.

16. *House Journal*, VI, May, June, 1788. The *Journal* for the period indicates that Richard Henry Lee was also a very active member of the House. Henry was the ranking member of the House committee which examined the ballots for Governor. *Ibid.*, pp. 31–34.

17. Henry, *Henry*, II, 50–51; Hening's *Statutes*, X, 221–222; *House Journal*, VI, 20–21, *passim*.

18. David D. Wallace, *South Carolina*, pp. 293–294.

19. Edward McCrady, *South Carolina in the Revolution*, pp. 507–511.

20. Christopher Ward, *The War of the Revolution*, II, 698.

21. *Journal*, June 6, 1780.

22. Henry, *Henry*, II, 51–52.

23. *Ibid.* See also informative letter of Joseph Jones, Nov. 5, 1780, Richmond, to Madison. Hutchinson and Rachal, *Madison Papers*, II, 161–162.

24. Henry, *Henry*, II, 52–53; *Journal*, VI, 35–37.

25. *Journal*, June 7, 1780.

26. Henry, *Henry*, II, 53–54.

27. *Ibid.*, p. 54. The quotation regarding the Continental notes is from E. J. Ferguson's *The Power of the Purse*, p. 66.

28. Henry, *Henry*, II, 61.

29. Ward, *op. cit.*, II, 724, 728.

30. Henry, *Henry*, II, 73.

31. John W. Herndon, "A Genealogy of the Herndon Family" in *Va. Magazine*, XI, 99–100.

32. Mary Newton Stanard, *Richmond*, p. 39.

33. John P. Little, *History of Richmond*, pp. 67–71, reprinted from a serial in the *Southern Literary Messenger* from Oct., 1851, to June, 1852; Josiah S. Moore, *Henrico Parish*, p. 151.

34. Malone, *Jefferson*, II, 343.

35. *Ibid.*, p. 341.

36. *Ibid.*

37. David D. Wallace, *South Carolina*, pp. 312–313; *House Journal*, Feb.–March, 1781.

38. *House Journal*, Feb.–March, 1781.

39. Henry County Order Book 2, 1778–1782, p. 165.

40. Henry, *Henry*, II, 67–68, citing *Calendar of Virginia State Papers*, I, 504.

41. *Ibid.*, pp. 68, 533.

42. Christopher Ward, *The War of the Revolution*, II, 787; Henry, *Henry*, II, 69.

43. Henry, *Henry*, II, 69.

44. *House Journal*, May, 1781.

45. *Ibid.*

46. *House Journal*, May–June, 1781.

47. Boyd, *Jefferson Papers*, XIII, 362–364; Malone, *Jefferson*, I, 445–446.

48. Henry, *Henry*, II, 128–129.

49. Information on Henry during the legislative session at Charlottesville and flight to Staunton is found in the *House Journal*, May–June, 1781; John Cook Wyllie, "New Documentary Light on Tarleton's Road" in *Va. Magazine*, LXXIV (1966), pp. 452–461; Virginius Dabney, "From Cuckoo to Monticello" in *The Iron Worker*, Summer, 1966; Henry, *Henry*, II, 128–129; and Morgan, *Henry*, 303–306.

50. Besides the *House Journal*, the Staunton episode in Henry's career is based on Boyd, *Jefferson Papers*, VI, 74–108; Henry, *Henry*, II, 141–154; clipping file and other local data kindly provided by Staunton Public Library.

Chapter 17

MR. JEFFERSON AND OTHER DIFFICULT PROBLEMS

1. George Tucker, *The Life of Thomas Jefferson*, I, 151.

2. Archibald Cary to Jefferson, June 19, 1781, in Boyd, *Jefferson Papers*, VI, 96.

3. Hening's *Statutes*, X, 413–416.

4. *Ibid.*

5. Henry, *Henry*, II, 147–148.

6. *Ibid.*, p. 148.

7. Boyd, *Jefferson Papers*, VI, 97.

8. Henry, *Henry*, II, 143–144.

9. Boyd, *Jefferson Papers*, VI, 104–106.

10. Henry, *Henry*, II, 150.

11. *Ibid.*

12. *Ibid.* See charges advanced by Nicholas with Jefferson's answers in Boyd, *Jefferson Papers*, VI, 106–108.

13. Boyd, *op. cit.*, VI, 135–136.

14. *Ibid.*

15. Lyon G. Tyler, *The Letters and Times of the Tylers*, I, 87–88.

16. Boyd, *Jefferson Papers*, VI, 184–185.

17. Henry, *Henry*, II, 144.

18. Boyd, *Jefferson Papers*, VI, 204–205.

19. *Ibid.*, pp. 32–33.

20. George Tucker, *op. cit.*, I, 146.

21. Henry, *Henry*, II, 169–170, citing *Council Journal*, p. 44, and Hening's *Statutes*, X, 501.

22. *Ibid.*, pp. 170–171.

23. *Ibid.*, p. 171, quoting *Historical Magazine for 1867*, p. 91.

24. *Ibid.*, p. 173.

25. *Ibid.*, p. 174; Hening's *Statutes*, XI, 39.

26. *Ibid.*, pp. 175–176.

27. *Ibid.*, Hening's *Statutes*, XI, 66.

28. *Calendar of State Papers*, III, 168, May 18, 1782.

29. *Ibid.*, p. 210, July 6, 1782.

30. *Ibid.*, pp. 242–243.

31. *Ibid.*, p. 321.

32. *Ibid.*, p. 372.

33. *Ibid.*, p. 374.

34. Henry, *Henry*, II, 184–185.

35. Morgan, *Henry*, p. 100. The copy of these resolutions, with Henry's inscription, is now at Colonial Williamsburg.

36. Henry, *Henry*, II, 185–187.

Chapter 18

POSTWAR LEGISLATOR

1. Alfred J. Morrison, translator and editor, *Travels in the Confederation*, from the German of Johann David Schoepf's *Reise Durch Einige Der Mittlern Und Sudlichen Vereinigten Nordamerikanischen Staaten*, II, 50–56.

2. *Ibid.*, p. 55.

3. *Ibid.*, pp. 56–57.

4. Schoepf also stated that "as in all other public and private societies there are certain men who lead the debate, and think and speak for the rest, so it is also in these Assemblies." And he continued: "Among the orators here is a certain Mr. Henry who appears to have the greatest influence over the House. He has a high-flown and bold delivery, deals more in words than in reasons. . . . Men of this stamp, either naturally eloquent or become so through their occupation, as e.g. lawyers, invariably take the most active and influential part in these Assemblies. . . ." There is a question as to how well Schoepf, who incorrectly described Henry as being a "country schoolmaster not so long ago," was able to evaluate him. *Ibid.*, p. 56.

5. Brant, *Madison*, II, 33.

6. Mays, *Pendleton*, II, 35.

7. Boyd, *Jefferson Papers*, VI, 428–430.

8. *Ibid.*, IV–VI.

9. *Ibid.*, VI, pp. 335–336.

10. Gaillard Hunt, *The Writings of James Madison*, I, xxv–xxvi (hereafter cited as Hunt, *Madison Writings*).

11. Boyd, *Jefferson Papers*, p. 266.

12. *Ibid.*

13. *Ibid.*, p. 277.

14. Brant, *Madison*, II, 251.

15. Lyon G. Tyler, *The Letters and Times of the Tylers*, III, 1–2, 7.

16. Wirt, *Henry*, p. ix.

17. Letters of John Tyler, *Tyler's Quarterly Magazine*, XIII, 2.

18. Hening's *Statutes*, XI, 195; Henry, *Henry*, II, 191.

19. Wirt, *Henry*, p. 254.

20. *Ibid.*, pp. 254–255.

21. *Ibid.*, p. 255.

22. Henry, *Henry*, II, 192, quoting *House Journal*, pp. 22, 76; and Hening's *Statutes*, XI, 324.

23. Wirt, *Henry*, p. 250.

24. *Ibid.*

25. *Ibid.*

26. *Ibid.*, p. 251.

27. *Ibid.*, p. 253.

28. *Ibid.*, p. 254.

29. *Ibid.*

30. *Ibid.*, pp. 256–257.

31. *Ibid.*, p. 258.

32. *Ibid.*, pp. 258–260.
33. Henry, *Henry*, II, 219.
34. Morgan, *Henry*, pp. 449, 444–445.
35. *Va. Gazette* or the *American Advertiser*, April 26, 1782.
36. *Calendar of State Papers*, III, 509, July 7, 1783.
37. *Ibid.*, p. 600, July 13, 1784.
38. Henry, *Henry*, II, 212.
39. *Ibid.*
40. *Ibid.*, pp. 212–213.
41. *Ibid.*, p. 213.
42. *Ibid.*, pp. 213–214.
43. *Ibid.*, p. 214.
44. Hening's *Statutes*, XI, 250–251.
45. Henry, *Henry*, II, 197; Hening's *Statutes*, XI, 250.
46. Hening's *Statutes*, pp. 164–166.
47. Henry, *Henry*, II, 198–201; Hening's *Statutes*, XI, 282–283.
48. A. C. Buell, *Paul Jones*, II, 152–154.
49. Schoepf, *Travels in the Confederation, 1783–84*, II, 64.
50. Moncure D. Conway, *Edmund Randolph*, pp. 56–57 (hereafter cited as Conway, *Randolph*).
51. Morgan, *Henry*, p. 443.
52. Brant, *Madison*, II, 316.
53. *Ibid.*
54. *Ibid.*, p. 318.
55. Rowland, *Mason*, II, 44–47.
56. George M. Brydon, *Virginia's Mother Church*, II, 420.
57. *Ibid.*, pp. 385–386.
58. *Ibid.*, p. 408.
59. *Ibid.*, p. 409.
60. Henry, *Henry*, II, 201–203.
61. *Ibid.*, p. 204.
62. *Ibid.*, pp. 205–206.

Chapter 19

GOVERNOR FOR A FOURTH AND FIFTH TERM

1. Boyd, *Jefferson Papers*, VIII, 41.
2. Hunt, *Madison Writings*, II, 89–90.
3. *Ibid.*, p. 118, Madison to Jefferson, Jan. 9, 1785.
4. *Ibid.*, p. 90.

5. *Ibid.*, p. 94; *House Journal*, fall, 1784, p. 27.

6. Hunt, *Madison Writings*, p. 97.

7. *House Journal*, fall, 1784, p. 79.

8. *Ibid.*, p. 30.

9. Jefferson to Henry; copy in Virginia Historical Society.

10. Morgan, *Henry*, p. 448; *Official Letters*, I, 88, 108.

11. Morgan, *Henry*, p. 448.

12. *Ibid.*, p. 443.

13. I am grateful to Curtis C. Davis of Baltimore for data on leading men of the Richmond area in the 1780's and especially that in his biography of Lewis Littlepage, *The King's Chevalier*.

14. *Council Journal*, III, 412.

15. Henry, *Henry*, II, 272–275; Countess of Huntingdon in *Dictionary of National Biography*.

16. Meade, *Henry*, I, 218.

17. Henry, *Henry*, II, 273.

18. *Ibid.*

19. *Ibid.*, pp. 274–275.

20. *Ibid.*, III, p. 273.

21. *Ibid.*, II, pp. 271–275.

22. *Ibid.*, p. 251.

23. *Ibid.*, p. 252.

24. *Ibid.*, pp. 464, 490, and letter from E. Demarest Peterson, Richmond, Aug. 19, 1966. The trunk was showed me by Mr. Peterson, then the owner.

25. *Ibid.*, III, p. 369.

26. *Ibid.*

27. *Ibid.*, II, pp. 286–287.

28. Personal research at Oxmoor, the Christian estate in Louisville which had descended to the William M. Bullitt family. Lee Blackwell of Louisville kindly supplied me with an illustrated article from the Louisville *Courier–General*, Sept. 8, 1968, on the small stone house in Jefferson County, Ky., where Col. Christian lived.

29. Henry, *Henry*, III, 350–355, 364.

30. *Ibid.*, p. 368.

31. *Ibid.*, pp. 381–382.

32. Henry, *Henry*, II, 246–247; Raymond Walters, Jr., *Albert Gallatin*, pp. 17, 19; Elizabeth Henry Aylett Memo in Campbell Papers, William and Mary Library. On Feb. 10, 1786, Governor Henry granted Gallatin 1,500 acres of land. In 1962 this document, on vellum, partly printed, was advertised for sale by Paul Richards of Brookline, Mass.

33. Henry, *Henry*, II, 255–261; Freeman, *Washington*, VI, 28–31.

34. Henry, *Henry*, II, 261–267.
35. Curtis C. Davis, *The King's Chevalier, passim; Council Journal*, III, 478; Henry, *Henry*, II, 267–269.
36. *Council Journal*, III, 422, 429; Henry, *Henry*, II, 269–270.
37. *Ibid.*, 270–272; and III, 286–287. The Pennsylvania Historical Society has a letter from Fitch to Henry, Nov. 27, 1786, concerning Fitch's plan to construct a steamboat. Fitch's bond to Henry in this regard is in the Valentine Museum.
38. Henry, *Henry*, II, 272; and III, 285; *Council Journal*, III, 428, *passim*.
39. For general information on Col. Campbell's movement and related disaffection, see Lewis P. Summers, *Annals of Southwest Virginia*; T. P. Abernethy, *Western Lands and the American Revolution*; Lefler and Newsome, *North Carolina*; Henry, *Henry*, II, 276–279; and the voluminous correspondence in *Calendar of State Papers*, III and IV.
40. Henry, *Henry*, II, 280–281.

Chapter 20

LIFE IN THE RICHMOND AREA

1. Boyd, *Jefferson Papers*, VIII, 344; *Official Letters*, I, 355.
2. Boyd, *Jefferson Papers*, XI, 226. Jefferson to Madame de Tessé, March 20, 1787.
3. *Ibid.*, VIII, p. 509.
4. More realistic than the marquis, a building committee in 1810 reported the house as being "too small" for the residence of the Chief Magistrate and his family, and Governor Tyler, in a message to the Assembly, declared it to be "originally badly built." Ulrich Troubetzkoy, "The Governor's Mansion," *Virginia Cavalcade*, XI, 23, 26.
5. Mary Wingfield Scott and Louise F. Catterall, *Virginia's Capitol Square*, p. 3. Data from Mrs. Catterall, then associated with the Valentine Museum.
6. *Council Journal*, III, 436–489, 500, 502.
7. Henry Account Book. Also four dozen Queen's China plates at 4 shillings per dozen, ten yards of carpeting at 4 shillings 4 pence per yard, three pair of hinges for window shutters, a counterpane, sheets, another set of china, etc.
8. Fitzpatrick, *Washington Writings*, II, 371, May 1, 1785. Roane Memo in Morgan, *Henry*, pp. 437–438; Henry, *Henry*, II, 253. Elizabeth Henry Aylett Memo in Campbell Papers, William and Mary Library.

9. A traditional account for Henry's later years has his boys living a free life on the plantation and under little paternal discipline. Legal and political business kept him away from home during much of his married life, and in his last few years he was too infirm to give adequate attention to his growing children.

10. Henry, *Henry*, II, 250. Henry Account Book. After Henry retired as Governor, Randolph published the following advertisement in the *Virginia Independent Chronicle* for March 28, 1787:

SALISBURY FOR SALE and possession given immediately. This tract of well timbered land contains 1263 acres, it lies in Chesterfield County, 3 Miles from James River, and 12 from Manchester, in the midst of a Coal Country, and the Probability is, that there is Coal on the land. . . .

11. Henry Account Book.

12. Genealogical chart in Appendix, Henry, *Henry*, II, 644.

13. Henry Account Book. There are unhappy references to Edward Henry in his father's correspondence during the early 1790's.

14. Data from Chesterfield court records, including the contemporary deed books.

15. Records of Chesterfield Baptist Church, 1773–1778, in Virginia State Library.

16. Morgan, *Henry*, p. 319.

17. Voluminous data from John Fontaine, Wilson, N.C., Feb. 12, 1949, including notes from Aylett family Bible in his possession. Mr. Fontaine's sister, Mrs. Celeste Creath of Paces, Va., showed me a table, called the Patrick Henry table, which Henry was said to have used when visiting his favorite daughter, Betsey. Also see *Virginia Independent Chronicle*, Oct. 18, 1786; J. S. Moore, *Henrico Parish*, p. 230.

18. Roane Memo in Morgan, *Henry*, pp. 435–436.

19. Copy in William Wirt Henry Papers, Virginia State Library. Also see Beverley Fleet, *Virginia Colonial Abstracts*, VI, 82–84.

20. Photograph of Roane at Virginia State Library. There is a flowery obituary of the brilliant judge in *The Richmond Enquirer*, Sept. 13, 1822, and his grave may still be seen in the cemetery at Warm Springs, Va. See likewise John H. Gwathmey, *Twelve Virginia Counties*, and Beverley Fleet, *Virginia Colonial Abstracts*. There is explanatory data on Roane's suit against Patrick Henry's executors in the letter of Judge James Keith to W. W. Henry, Jan. 15, 1898. William Wirt Henry Papers, Virginia Historical Society.

21. A revealing note on Anne's marriage was given me by Mrs. Mattie Guy Daniel, Drake's Branch, Va. The story was handed down in her family that Patrick Henry said Anne was the most unattractive of his

daughters and he was glad "to marry her off." This information came to Mrs. Daniel from her mother, Mrs. Martha Wright, of Essex County, Va., who was born in 1816.

22. Henry, *Henry*, II, 305–309.

23. William Ellery Channing, *Memoir of William E. Channing*, I, 82.

24. Meade, *Henry*, I, 300.

25. Washington County Will Book 2, pp. 58–59, July 21, 1795.

26. *Ibid.*, Sept. 20, 1793.

27. Boyd, *Jefferson Writings*, VIII, 342–343.

28. Hening's *Statutes*, XII, 182–183.

29. Letter of Judge James Keith to William Wirt Henry in William Wirt Henry Papers, Virginia Historical Society. See Note 20 above.

30. Morgan, *Henry*, p. 454.

31. From a copy of a Henry memorandum in the author's file.

Chapter 21

A New Home and a New Arena

1. Merrill Jensen, *The New Nation*, pp. 430–431.

2. Boyd, *Jefferson Papers*, XII, 557–558 (Jefferson to Smith); *ibid.*, X, p. 133 (Randolph to Jefferson).

3. Henry, *Henry*, II, 302–304. On Wednesday, Nov. 29, 1786, Henry attended his last session of the Council, a nearly full meeting with these members present in addition to His Excellency: Mathews, Wood, McClurg, Jones, Selden, and Braxton. During the routine proceedings a pension of £6 per year was granted to a disabled soldier, and a Negro slave, convicted of murder, was recommended "as a proper object of Mercy." At the next meeting of the Council on Dec. 1, 1786, Edmund Randolph, the Governor elected to succeed Henry, took his place as presiding officer. *Council Journal*, III, 598–599.

4. Henry, *Henry*, II, 304–305; III, 379–380. Morgan, *Henry*, opposite p. 406. Henry Aylett Sampson, *Sonnets and Other Poems*, p. 122.

5. This data on Henry's removal to Prince Edward and influences on him there is derived from Henry, *Henry*, II, 304–305; III, 379–380; Charles Edward Burrell, *History of Prince Edward County*; Herbert Bradshaw, *History of Prince Edward County*, and helpful correspondence with Mr. Bradshaw; Prince Edward records in the courthouse at Farmville and various field trips in the county; and Henry Account Book. In 1785 Henry sold his "chariot" for £100. During this period he also sold relatively small amounts of beef and corn. There is considerable evidence to

indicate that he ran a store on both his Leatherwood and Prince Edward plantations or resold some goods which had been transported from Richmond or elsewhere.

6. Journal of William Loughton Smith, 1790–1791, quoted in *Massachusetts Historical Society Publication*, Oct., 1917.

7. There is voluminous evidence in Henry's papers of his delays in communication, and his difficulties in this respect were hardly less serious in Prince Edward than at Leatherwood. See also Notes 8 and 9.

8. Henry, *Henry*, II, 310–311.

9. Fitzpatrick, *Washington Writings*, XXIX, 278.

10. *Virginia Independent Chronicle*, Feb. 7 and 28, 1787.

11. Morison and Commager, *The Growth of the American Republic* (1950 ed.), I, 275–276.

12. These figures are conveniently stated in Ralph Harlow, *The United States: From Wilderness to World Power*, p. 147.

13. Sydney H. Gay, *James Madison*, p. 74. On Feb. 24, 1787, Madison wrote somewhat similarly to Edmund Pendleton. Hunt, *Madison Writings*, II, 316–320.

14. Smyth, *Franklin Writings*, IX, 547–548.

15. Ralph Harlow, *op. cit.*, p. 150.

16. Merrill Jensen, *op. cit.*, pp. 304–305.

17. Boyd, *Jefferson Writings*, VII, 256–258.

18. Hunt, *Madison Writings*, II, 297.

19. Oliver P. Chitwood, *A History of Colonial America* (3rd ed.), p. 605.

20. Henry, *Henry*, II, 291–298.

21. *Ibid.*, pp. 299–300.

22. *Ibid.*, p. 302.

23. Hunt, *Madison Writings*, II, 296–297; Henry, *Henry*, II, 301.

24. Henry, *Henry*, II, 310–311.

25. *Ibid.*, pp. 311, 312.

26. *Ibid.*, p. 312.

27. *Ibid.*

28. Ballagh, *Lee*, II, 415.

29. Brant, *Madison*, III, 18, quoting Madison, *Debates on the Federal Convention* (Ms. in Library of Congress).

30. Henry, *Henry*, II, 330.

31. Lyon G. Tyler, *History of Virginia*, II, 289.

32. Allan Nevins and Henry Steele Commager, *Short History of the United States*, p. 121.

33. Henry, *Henry*, II, 318.

34. One may reasonably surmise that Henry's influence would have

been exerted in favor of a weaker central government than that adopted.

35. Jackson T. Main, *The Antifederalist*, p. 249. Like Jensen's *The New Nation*, Main's book contains valuable data on Henry's career in this period.

36. *Ibid.*, pp. 17–31.

37. *New Hampshire Spy*, Oct. 30, 1787.

38. *Ibid.*, Dec. 7, 1787.

39. Main, *op. cit.*, pp. 252–259; Lyon G. Tyler, *The Letters and Times of the Tylers*, I, 142–143.

40. Far more than most anti-Federalists, Lee saw the need of their interstate action. When writing Mason on Oct. 1, Lee tried ineffectually to have him enlist the aid of Maryland and South Carolina for a combined movement to secure another constitutional convention. Ballagh, *Lee*, II: to Mason, dated New York, Oct. 1, 1787, pp. 438–440; to Samuel Adams on Oct. 5, pp. 444–447; to Randolph on Oct. 16, pp. 450–455.

41. Washington to Madison, Oct. 22, 1787. Fitzpatrick, *Washington's Writings*, XXIX, 292.

42. Letter dated Oct. 21, 1787, in New York Public Library.

43. Henry, *Henry*, II, 322–324.

44. *Ibid.*, p. 324.

45. *Ibid.*

46. Boyd, *Jefferson Papers*, XII, 425. Jefferson says that "Washington will be for it, but it is not in his character to exert himself much in the case."

47. *Ibid.*

48. William C. Rives, *History of the Life and Times of James Madison*, II, 544–545.

49. Henry, *Henry*, II, 333.

50. Beveridge, *Marshall*, I, 366.

51. *Ibid.*

52. Hunt, *Madison Writings*, V, 114–115.

53. *Ibid.*, pp. 121–122.

54. Letter to Col. John Francis Mercer, Annapolis, Md., in Rowland, *Mason*, II, 214. Madison thought that the superiority of ability lay on the Federalist side. Among its most noteworthy delegates he named Edmund Pendleton, George Wythe, John Blair, John Marshall, George and William Nicholas, General Stephen, Archibald Stuart, and Henry Lee, Jr. For the anti-Federalist leaders he listed Patrick Henry, George Mason, Benjamin Harrison, and John Tyler. In view of Governor Randolph's temperate opposition, Madison did not believe that he could be properly classed as an enemy of the Constitution, and Richard Henry Lee had not been elected to the Convention. Letter to Thomas Jefferson, dated Virginia Orange, April 22, 1788, Hunt, *Madison Writings*, V, 120–121.

55. Max Farrand, *The Fathers of the Constitution*, pp. 148–149.
56. *Ibid.*, p. 151.
57. *Ibid.*, pp. 151–152.
58. Boyd, *Jefferson Papers*, XII, 570–571.

Chapter 22

CONVENTION OF 1788

1. General Henry Knox to Rufus King, June 19, 1788, quoted in Beveridge, *Marshall*, I, 358.
2. Microfilm copy of Cabell Diary, University of Virginia Library.
3. Hugh Blair Grigsby, *The Virginia Convention of 1778*, I, 27.
4. Mary Newton Stanard, *Richmond*, pp. 59–60.
5. Henry, *Henry*, II, 345; Rowland, *Mason*, II, 222; Jonathan Elliot, *The Debates in the Several State Conventions on the Adoption of the Federal Constitution*, III, 3–4 (hereafter cited as Elliot, *Debates*).
6. Mays, *Pendleton*, II, 229–230; Elliot, *Debates*, III, 3–4.
7. Lee spoke of the Constitution as having been the subject of public and private consideration of most persons on the continent and "the peculiar meditation of those who were deputed to the Convention." Elliot, *Debates*, III, 4.
8. *Ibid.*, pp. 4–5.
9. His cousins, John Carter Littlepage of Hanover and Judge Winston from Chestnut Hill on the James, and Thomas Roane of his new son-in-law's clan.
10. Beveridge, *Marshall*, I, 401–402. At the Philadelphia Constitutional Convention Gouverneur Morris had taken more part in the debates than even James Madison. While he favored a strong central government in the hands of the rich and well-born, he had accepted "the bundle of compromises" which made up the finished document and had done much to put it in its final polished form. Henry could hardly appreciate the special knowledge, the powers of persuasion, which the affable and lively Morris used in behalf of the Federalists, nor, indeed, those of his dignified cousin, Robert. See Gouverneur Morris in *Dictionary of American Biography*.
11. Stanard, *op. cit.*, p. 59; Hunt, *Madison Writings*, V, 179.
12. Henry, *Henry*, II, 342–343.
13. *Ibid.*, p. 343.
14. Elliot, *Debates*, III, 6.
15. Mays, *Pendleton*, II, 231.

16. *Ibid.*

17. Beveridge, *Marshall*, I, 374.

18. Brant, *Madison*, III, 201.

19. Beveridge, *Marshall*, I, 374.

20. Although Henry continued for over two hours without losing the "rapt attention" of his audience, his speech, as reported by Robertson and reprinted by Elliot, covers only thirteen and a half pages—further evidence of the incomplete stenographic accounts.

21. Henry, *Henry*, III, 431–433.

22. Elliot, *Debates*, III, 24.

23. *Ibid.*, pp. 28–29.

24. *Ibid.*, pp. 29–34.

25. Letter to John Jay, June 8, 1788. Fitzpatrick, *Washington's Writings*, XXIX, 512–514.

26. Hunt, *Madison Writings*, V, 133–137. One delegate, George Washington's nephew, Bushrod Washington, was so carried away by Madison's "force of reasoning" and display of "irressistible truths" that he said the opposition had "quitted the field." But, more soberly, Bushrod Washington declared that Madison had influenced only a few decided anti-Federalists. Any conclusion that Washington might attempt to make as to the decision of the Convention must be "founded on conjecture." Thus, his opinion as to the close final vote tended to be much like Henry's. Jared Sparks, *The Writings of George Washington*, IX, 378.

27. Elliot, *Debates*, III, 36–38.

28. *Ibid.*, p. 40.

29. *Ibid.*, pp. 40–41.

30. *Ibid.*, p. 42.

31. Henry, *Henry*, II, 351.

32. *Ibid.*, pp. 346–347.

33. Elliot, *Debates*, III, 43–44.

34. *Ibid.*, pp. 44–45.

35. *Ibid.*, p. 45.

36. *Ibid.*, p. 46.

37. *Ibid.*, p. 47.

38. See p. 347.

39. Elliot, *Debates*, III, 53–54.

40. Henry, *Henry*, II, 359.

41. *Ibid.*, pp. 359, 637.

42. Elliot, *Debates*, III, 55.

43. *Ibid.*, p. 57.

44. *Ibid.*, pp. 57–58.

45. *Ibid.*, pp. 58–59.

46. *Ibid.*, p. 62.

47. *Ibid.*, p. 63.

48. *Ibid.* Before concluding, Henry said he feared he had fatigued the Convention. He admitted that he had found his "mind hurried on from subject to subject, on this very great occasion. We have been all out of order, from the gentleman who opened to-day to myself. I did not come prepared to speak, on so multifarious a subject, in so general a manner. I trust you will indulge me another time. Before you abandon the present system, I hope you will consider not only its defects, most maturely, but likewise those of that which you are to substitute for it." Elliot, *ibid.*, p. 64.

49. Beveridge, *Marshall*, I, 392.

50. Brant, *Madison*, III, 197.

51. *Ibid.*, p. 199.

52. Elliot, *Debates*, III, 81, 82–83.

53. *Ibid.*, p. 86.

54. Hugh Blair Grigsby, *Virginia Convention of 1788*, I, 96.

55. Elliot, *Debates*, III, 86–91.

56. *Ibid.*, p. 93.

57. *Ibid.*, p. 98.

58. *Ibid.*, p. 103.

59. *Ibid.*, p. 105.

60. *Ibid.*, pp. 105–106.

61. *Ibid.*, pp. 114–119, esp. p. 119.

62. The contributions from the states to the Confederation had been decreasing instead of increasing, and from June, 1787, until June, 1788, the states had paid only $276,641 into the federal treasury to support the national government and discharge the interest on its debts. "Suggestions and strong assertions dissipate before these facts." Elliot, *Debates*, III, 136–137.

63. *Ibid.*, p. 126.

64. *Ibid.*, p. 128.

65. *Ibid.*, p. 138.

66. *Ibid.*, p. 187.

67. Morgan, *Henry*, p. 351.

68. John R. Alden, *The South in the Revolution*, p. 395.

69. John B. McMaster, quoted in *Pa. Magazine*, LVII, 27.

70. Henry, *Henry*, II, 376.

71. Hugh Blair Grigsby in *Va. Magazine*, I, 230.

72. Elliot, *Debates*, III, 326.

73. *Ibid.*

74. *Ibid.*, pp. 353, 365–367.

75. Hunt, *Madison Writings*, V, 179, 216.

76. Elliot, *Debates*, III, 500.
77. *Ibid.*, p. 486.
78. *Ibid.*, p. 103.
79. *Ibid.*, p. 97.

Chapter 23

The Battle for Amendments

1. Henry, *Henry*, II, 361–362.
2. *Ibid.*, pp. 362–363.
3. Elliot, *Debates*, III, 576.
4. *Ibid.*, pp. 580–582.
5. The motion for ratification would pass by ten votes. George Wythe's successful motion for amendments after ratification seems to have won a few votes for the Federalists. See Note 6.
6. Elliot, *Debates*, III, 586.
7. *Ibid.*, pp. 586–587.
8. *Ibid.*, pp. 587–589.
9. *Ibid.*, pp. 657–659.
10. *Ibid.*, p. 659.
11. *Ibid.*, p. 649.
12. *Ibid.*, pp. 651–652.
13. *Ibid.*, p. 652.
14. *Ibid.*, pp. 656–662.
15. *Ibid.*, p. 652.
16. Beverley Fleet, *Virginia Colonial Abstracts*, VI, King and Queen County Records Concerning 18th Century Persons, Third Collection, p. 78.
17. *Virginia Independent Chronicle*, July 14, 1788.
18. Hunt, *Madison Writings*, V, 234.
19. *Ibid.*, pp. 240–241.
20. Moses Coit Tyler, *Patrick Henry*, p. 345; Elliot, *Debates*, I, 327–331.
21. Tyler, *op. cit.*, p. 345.
22. Henry, *Henry*, II, 412–413, quoting the account by David Meade Randolph in the *Southern Literary Messenger*, I, 332. W. W. Henry surmises the Meade in question was General Richard Kidder Meade. But he was a Revolutionary colonel, and it was his brother, Everard, another Revolutionary officer, who after the war became a general of the Virginia militia.

23. Mason, in a letter dated Dec. 18, 1788, quoted in a letter from Kate Mason Rowland to William Wirt Henry, Jan. 22 (no year given). The latter letter is in William Wirt Henry Papers, Virginia Historical Society.

24. Mason in apparently the same letter as above written to his son John, then in France, quoted a letter from K. M. Rowland to W. W. Henry, Jan. 15 (no year given). In William Wirt Henry Papers, Virginia Historical Society. (The letter dated Jan. 22 appears to be Rowland's response to W. W. Henry's query about the information in Rowland's letter of Jan. 15 to him.)

25. Henry Account Book.

26. Deed filed in Henrico County, Oct. 17, 1788, between Patrick Henry and wife to James Thompson, Purchase of 214 acres in Henrico adjoining Brook Run for £700 current money. Henry Account Book.

27. Boyd, *Jefferson Papers*, XIII, 539–540.

28. *Ibid.*, pp. 497–498. Madison, New York, Aug. 10, 1788, to Jefferson.

29. Edward Carrington in a letter to Madison, Oct. 19, en route to Richmond after visiting Washington. Cited in Henry, *Henry*, II, 415.

30. Lyon G. Tyler, *History of Virginia*, II, 399.

31. Henry, *Henry*, II, 416, citing a letter of Charles Lee to Washington, Oct. 29, 1788.

32. *House Journal*, Fall, 1788, pp. 16–17.

33. *Ibid.*

34. The text of this letter, from the *House Journal* for Nov. 14, 1788, is reprinted in Henry, *Henry*, II, 423–425.

35. Wirt, *Henry*, pp. 320–321.

36. *Ibid.*, p. 322; Henry, *Henry*, II, 420.

37. Henry, *Henry*, II, 421–422.

38. *Ibid.*, p. 422.

39. Wirt, *Henry*, pp. 322–324.

40. Madison to Jefferson from Philadelphia, Dec. 8, 1788. Hunt, *Madison Writings*, V, 313.

41. *Ibid.*

42. Conway, *Randolph*, p. 120.

43. Henry, *Henry*, II, 428–429 *et seq.*

44. *Ibid.*

45. *Ibid.*, pp. 429–430.

46. *Ibid.*, pp. 430–431.

47. Sydney H. Gay, *James Madison*, p. 120.

48. Brant, *Madison*, III, 237.

49. Conway, *Randolph*, pp. 120–121.

50. *House Journal,* Fall, 1788, pp. 46 *et seq.*

51. *Ibid.,* p. 80.

52. Letter to Mrs. Aylett, Henry, *Henry,* II, 434; *House Journal,* Fall, 1788.

53. Conway, *Randolph,* p. 121.

54. Fitzpatrick, *Washington's Writings,* XXX, 288.

55. *North Carolina State Gazette,* Jan. 15, 1789. "Our correspondent assures us, that he had undoubted authority for these assertions, and then continues to remark, that it is highly necessary that the friends of the constitution, in every state, should be active in choosing federal electors only, who will undoubtedly elect THE MAN OF THE PEOPLE." *Ibid.*

56. John B. McMaster, *A History of the People of the United States,* II, 86–88; Freeman, *Washington,* VI, 157–158.

57. *Virginia Independent Chronicle,* Jan. 28, 1789.

58. Randolph to Madison, in Conway, *Randolph,* p. 121.

59. *Virginia Independent Chronicle,* Jan. 14, 1789.

60. *Ibid.,* Feb. 11, 1789.

61. *Ibid.,* Feb. 18, 1789.

62. *Ibid.,* Mar. 25, 1789.

63. Conway, *Randolph,* p. 121.

64. *Va. Magazine,* XIV, 202–204. Letter of Patrick Henry to William Grayson, Mar. 31, 1789.

65. *Ibid.*

66. Boyd, *Jefferson Papers,* XVI, 140, *passim.*

67. Nicholas asserted to Jefferson that some of the replies had been made with Henry's approval. *Ibid.,* p. 143.

68. *Ibid.,* pp. 24–28, letter dated Eppington, Dec. 14, 1789.

69. Brant, *Madison,* III, 249. Robert Scribner of the James Madison Papers, office at the Virginia Historical Society, has made helpful criticisms of this chapter.

70. *Ibid.*

71. Moses Coit Tyler, *Patrick Henry,* p. 315.

72. Ballagh, *Lee,* II, 502.

73. The attitude of Congress toward the amendments is discussed at length by Richard Henry Lee when a member of that body after the ratification of the Constitution. See Ballagh, *Lee,* II, 478 *et seq.,* including letter to Patrick Henry from New York, May 28, 1789.

74. For data on this complex and controversial subject, I am grateful for assistance by Charles P. Light, then Dean of the Law School, Washington and Lee University; Professor John Norton Moore of the University of Virginia Law School; Professors Guy Carson of Randolph-

Macon Woman's College; and Spencer Albright of the University of Richmond.

75. During this period Henry was in retirement and not actively engaged in the movement to secure the Eleventh and Twelfth Amendments.

76. Thomas E. Emerson, David Haber, and Norman Dorsen, editors, *Political and Civil Rights*, pp. 12–13. In the opinion of one authority, "the presence of the particular language of the Bill of Rights has . . . acted as a springboard for a more thoroughgoing concern with civil liberties" in our nation than any other in the world. Letter from Professor John Norton Moore, Sept. 8, 1967.

77. Letter from Dean C. P. Light, Sept. 27, 1967, quoting 1967 Supplement to Noel T. Dowling, *Cases on Constitutional Law*.

78. Henry, *Henry*, II, 449.

79. *House Journal*, Fall, 1789, p. 24.

80. Henry, *Henry*, II, 452–453.

81. *House Journal*, p. 3 *et seq.*

82. Morison and Commager, *The Growth of the American Republic*, I, 329.

83. *House Journal*, p. 80.

84. *Ibid.*

85. Henry, *Henry*, II, 459.

86. *Ibid.*, p. 463.

87. *Ibid.*, p. 460.

88. *Ibid.*, p. 461.

89. Henry to Betsey Aylett. From original in possession of their descendant, Mrs. Celeste Fontaine Creath, Paces, Va.

Chapter 24

AGAIN THE LAW AND OTHER BUSINESS INTERESTS

1. Morgan, *Henry*, p. 445.

2. Henry Account Book.

3. *Ibid.*

4. Conway, *Randolph*, p. 126.

5. Henry, *Henry*, II, 469–470.

6. *Ibid.*, p. 476. Also Venable Diary, copy in Virginia Historical Society.

7. Morison and Commager, *The Growth of the American Republic*, I, 265.

8. Copy of Henry's financial statement in possession of the writer.

9. Records of Treasurer's Office, Journal of Receipts, in Virginia State Library.

10. The author owns this original receipt, a gift from the late Beverley Fleet, Richmond, Va.

11. *Wm. and Mary Quarterly*, Ser. 2, V, 168–170.

12. Samuel F. Bemis, *Jay's Treaty*, pp. 102–103.

13. Wirt, *Henry*, pp. 332–333.

14. Henry, *Henry*, II, 472.

15. *Ibid.*

16. Wirt, *Henry*, pp. 331–339. See John Wickham in *Dictionary of American Biography*; also copious references to the British Debts Case and the opposing lawyers in Beveridge, *Marshall*, I.

17. Wirt, *Henry*, pp. 340–342.

18. *Ibid.*, pp. 359–364.

19. *Ibid.*, pp. 364–365.

20. *Ibid.*, p. 365.

21. *Ibid.*, pp. 381–382.

22. *Ibid.*, pp. 384–385.

23. *Ibid.*, p. 385.

24. Henry, *Henry*, II, 475.

25. *Ibid.*, p. 474.

26. *Ibid.*; Sully portrait in Morgan, *Henry*, p. 118.

27. Henry, *Henry*, II, 475, quoting Dallas, *Cases Ruled and Adjudged in the Supreme Court of the United States*, III, 257.

28. Bemis, *op. cit.*, Appendix IV.

29. John Campbell to James Campbell, November, 1815, giving reminiscences of George Hay. David Campbell Papers, Duke University Library. Courtesy of Professor Joseph H. Harrison, Jr., Auburn University.

30. Morgan, *Henry*, p. 449.

31. *Ibid.*, pp. 446–447.

32. *Ibid.*, pp. 378–379.

33. *Ibid.*, p. 379.

34. *Ibid.*, pp. 379–380.

35. *Ibid.*, p. 383.

36. *Ibid.*, p. 384.

37. *Ibid.*, p. 386.

38. *Ibid.*, p. 376.

39. *Ibid.*, pp. 376–377.

40. *Ibid.*, p. 377.

41. *Ibid.*, pp. 374–375.

42. My study of the locale for the Randolph murder case is based primarily on several field trips in the summer of 1963 to Cumberland

County, including a visit to Glenlyvar, about a dozen miles north of Cumberland Courthouse, near Cartersville, Virginia. Helpful data was given me by Edmund R. Harrison, who lived on Route 45, a few miles from the site of the former Glenlyvar house. Mr. Harrison is a great-great-grandson of Randolph Harrison of Glenlyvar. Other information came from Walter H. Stockman, then owner of Glenlyvar, who showed me a trace of the circle on which carriages came to the house. The site is on a raised place about four miles from the James River.

There is a "novelized" account of the trial and related proceedings in J. and Audrey Walz, *The Bizarre Sisters,* and a helpful list of the *dramatis personae.* The Walzes give an interesting account of Patrick Henry's role in the trial which cannot be fully documented; also, a valuable letter by Richard Randolph, reprinted from the *Virginia Gazette and General Advertiser* of April 3, 1793.

The records of the Randolph trial have disappeared from Cumberland Courthouse, but some twenty-five years ago I had an opportunity to read an article on the murder trial which was based on these notes. As I recall, the facts given did not differ from those in the excellent account by William Cabell Bruce in his *John Randolph of Roanoke,* esp. Vol. 1, pp. 106–123. Bruce had access to the Randolph records before they were removed from the Cumberland Courthouse. See also H. J. Eckenrode, *The Randolphs,* esp. pp. 168–187. Much related data may also be found by references cited in Swem's *Index to the Virginia Magazine of History* and the *William and Mary Quarterly,* and in Hugh A. Garland, *The Life of John Randolph of Roanoke.*

43. Jackson T. Main, an authority on the period, ranks Henry among the hundred richest Virginians in the 1780's. Main's study is based on Virginia tax records for 1787 and 1788 in the State Library. See Main, "The One Hundred," in *Wm. and Mary Quarterly,* Ser. 3, Vol. II, pp. 354–384. For a comparative evaluation of George Washington's wealth in the late 1780's see Paul L. Haworth, *George Washington: Being an Account of His Home Life and Agricultural Activities.*

Data on Henry's Kentucky land is contained in his Account Book; his will at Charlotte Courthouse; W. R. Jillson, *The Kentucky Land Grants,* p. 62, and *ibid., Old Kentucky Entries and Deeds,* p. 221; *Register of the Kentucky State Historical Society,* Vol. 28, p. 243.

Among various records of Henry's Kentucky land dealings which I examined in the William Marshall Bullitt Papers at Oxmoor, Louisville, Kentucky, was a memo of an agreement between Patrick Henry and William Christian, Mr. Bullitt's ancestor, dated March 3, 1770.

In the Kentucky surveys, Virginia State Archives, photostat No. 20,999, p. 224, we find record of 3,000 acres of land granted Henry by virtue of three Virginia state treasury warrants. The land lay in Jefferson County, Kentucky, on the southwest side of Samuel Bealle's entry of 5,000 acres on Mill Creek.

There are references to Henry's land in Botetourt County, Virginia, in the local courthouse at Fincastle, in F. B. Kegley, *Kegley's Virginia Frontier*, pp. 441–450, and in R. D. Stoner, *Botetourt County*. The Bullitt Papers contain a little data on Henry's land in Mulberry Bottom, Botetourt County. Henry's letter to John Tabb on May 2, 1784, is in the University of Virginia Library.

In return for £20 paid by Patrick Henry and several associates into the Virginia treasury, Governor Benjamin Harrison granted them 4,000 acres in Norfolk County on Feb. 19, 1779. For Henry's land in the Norfolk County area see also Wirt, *Henry* (1952 ed.), p. 419, and data secured from the state records by Willam M. E. Rachal, The Virginia Historical Society.

On June 4, 1964, M. N. Shaw, then of Leaksville, North Carolina, helped me materially with a field trip on the Henry land in that area. Near the corner of Early Avenue and North Hamilton Street, Leaksville, is a marker for the corner of William Byrd's land granted in 1733, and the Henry land stretched to the northward toward or across the Virginia boundary line. There is a Patrick and a Henry Street in Leaksville, and Mr. Shaw showed me the little brick school house on Henry Street where Patrick Henry's son, Nathaniel, and his son Patrick III taught. A. D. Ivie, a Leaksville lawyer, whom I interviewed the same day, gave me valuable information on Henry's North Carolina land including a copy of a speech which he delivered on the subject.

Since I made the field trip and examined the Henry records at Wentworth, the county seat of Rockingham County, Leaksville and nearby Spray and Draper have been combined into the city of Eden, North Carolina. For the deed by which Henry acquired his land in this section on June 3, 1799, see Deed Book F, pp. 87–89, in Rockingham Courthouse at Wentworth.

I am indebted to J. C. Bonner of Georgia State College, Milledgeville, for information on Henry's Georgia land. An authority on Georgia state history, Mr. Bonner referred me to an invaluable source of information on the Yazoo lands: S. G. McLendon, *History of the Public Domain of Georgia*, esp. pp. 35–39. See also Henry, *Henry*, II, 505–515, and H. C. Bradshaw, *History of Prince Edward County*, pp. 288, 359.

Chapter 25

THE LAST YEARS

1. In Purdie's *Va. Gazette*, March 10, 1775, Supplement. In view of this date of publication, Henry most likely read Probus' letter shortly before his Give Me Liberty speech.

2. Faulkner's speech when accepting the Nobel Prize, Dec. 10, 1950.

3. Henry, *Henry*, II, 466.

4. Venable Diary at Virginia Historical Society.

5. Henry, *Henry*, II. The foregoing information on Henry's life at Long Island is derived from data in Henry, *Henry*, II, 535 *et seq.*, and III, 422–424; Morgan, *Henry*, pp. 394 *et seq.*, including Appendix; field trips to the Long Island neighborhood and numerous conversations with the local people; and Henry Account Book.

6. Fitzpatrick, *Washington's Writings*, XXXIII, 475–476.

7. *Ibid.*, p. 477.

8. Henry, *Henry*, II, 546–547.

9. *Ibid.*, pp. 547–548.

10. Campbell County Order Book #3, Nov. 13, 1789, p. 255. Also background material in Ruth H. Early, *Campbell Chronicles*.

11. *Ibid.* Order Book #1, p. 114, Nov., 1782.

12. *Ibid.* Order Book #3, pp. 317–318.

13. One family living not very far from Red Hill, where Henry would move, was the Hanckses (or Hankses) of the early Hat Creek area. A Hanks girl, Nancy, was Abraham Lincoln's mother, and there is a persistent tradition that his maternal grandfather was one of the local gentry. There are early Hanks records at the Campbell County Courthouse in Rustburg, also voluminous family data at the Jones Memorial Library, Lynchburg, Va.

14. Juliet Fauntleroy, *Campbell County Petitions*. Copies from the Original Petitions Filed in the Archives Dept., Virginia State Library, p. 10. Jones Library.

15. *Ibid.*

16. Morgan, *Henry*, p. 417.

17. Henry Family Papers, Virginia State Archives, No. 12. Further indicative of Syme's bitterness was his comment to Henry that he was not sorry about the "hoss accident" which occurred on Dolly's return (to Long Island?). "She would not even give us a call as she pass'd by."

18. For a good general treatment see Thomas D. Clark, *A History of Kentucky*.

19. Henry, *Henry*, II, 550.

20. *Ibid.*, p. 551.

21. See portion of Henry's letter to Betsy Aylett in Morgan, *Henry*, pp. 395–396. The letter is dated from Long Island, Oct. 26, 1793; Rowland, *Mason*, II, 365–366, gives the citation from the *Gentleman's Magazine*, Jan., 1793, p. 89.

22. Henry, *Henry*, II, 517.

23. *Ibid.*, 517–518.

24. Letter from Martha Catharina Henry, Jan. 30, 1794, in Henry Family Papers, Virginia State Library. The account of Red Hill given in this chapter is based on data in the Henry biographies by W. W. Henry and George Morgan; the Henry Account Book; field trips to Red Hill and information from people who have lived in the neighborhood; Stanhope Johnson of Lynchburg, the architect of the Red Hill restoration; copies of Henry family letters supplied by descendants; and the large number of newspaper clippings about Red Hill, collected by a Henry descendant, Mrs. M. B. Harrison, and now at the Virginia Historical Society.

25. The guiding spirit of the Patrick Henry Memorial Foundation for a generation after its organization was its president, James S. Easley of Halifax, Va., who died in 1965. Among officers of the Foundation who have contributed very generously of their time and talents are D. Quinn Eggleston, the current President, and Mrs. William Page Williams, the long-time Secretary. Eugene Casey of Rockville, Md., has provided the major funds for rebuilding the Henry home and various outbuildings as well as other parts of the restoration. Stanhope Johnson of Lynchburg had, when a young architect a half century ago, taken careful drawings of the original Patrick Henry house, and he employed them in the recent reconstruction of the Red Hill house and grounds. Mrs. Mabel Bellwood has been serving as the gracious and hard-working custodian at Red Hill for many years. The writer has also benefited from a field trip to Seven Islands and from neighborhood lore. He is particularly indebted for family data supplied by Mrs. E. D. Tinsley of Lynchburg and her sister, Mrs. P. F. Tuck of Richmond, both descendants of Patrick Henry through his daughter, Sarah Butler Henry, who married Alexander Scott. The Scott family was long associated with Seven Islands.

26. Morgan, *Henry*, pp. 461–462.

27. Henry's will at Charlotte Courthouse. Copy of family letter in possession of writer.

28. Morgan, *Henry*, p. 439.

29. *Ibid.*

30. Henry, *Henry*, II, 518.

31. Robert Douthat Meade, "Judge Edmund Winston's Memoir of Patrick Henry," *Va. Magazine*, LXIX, 34.

32. Henry, *Henry*, II, 520–521.

33. *Ibid.*, p. 576.

34. *Ibid.*, pp. 591–592.

35. Morgan, *Henry*, pp. 451, 453.

36. *Ibid.*, pp. 452–453.

37. *Ibid.*, p. 453.

38. Henry, *Henry*, II, 519.

39. Morgan, *Henry*, 366n.

40. Henry, *Henry*, II, 570.

41. *Ibid.*, p. 562.

42. *Ibid.*, pp. 563–564.

43. *Ibid.*, p. 572.

44. *Ibid.*

45. Morgan, *Henry*, p. 100.

46. Hunt, *Madison Writings*, VI, 326; Andrew A. Lipscomb, editor, *The Writings of Thomas Jefferson*, X, 63.

47. Henry, *Henry*, II, 591–594.

48. Fitzpatrick, *Washington's Writings*, XXXVIII, 87–90.

49. Henry, *Henry*, II, 606.

50. *Ibid.*, p. 607.

51. *Ibid.*, p. 608.

52. *Ibid.*

53. *Ibid.*, p. 609.

54. *Ibid.*

55. *Ibid.*, pp. 609–610.

56. *Ibid.*, p. 610.

57. *Ibid.*, p. 611.

58. *Ibid.*, p. 616.

59. *Ibid.*, p. 622.

60. Moses Coit Tyler, *Patrick Henry*, p. 377.

INDEX

INDEX

INDEX

in France, 271, 273, 274, 280, 295, 317, 333, 340, 345
as Governor, 210-211, 219, 225-228, 230, 232-238, 250, 276-277, 279
on Henry's oratory, 39
personal life, 249
reaction to Decius letters, 389-390
resigns as Secretary of State, 427-428
revises Virginia legal code, 195-196
at Second Continental Congress, 63, 64, 71
on slavery, 312
at Virginia Convention, 22, 23, 35-36, 40, 42, 78
Jansen, Merrill, 317
Jenyns, Soame, 290
Jesse (slave), 437
Johnson, Dr. Samuel, 25
Johnson, Thomas, 154, 194, 203, 403, 411
Johnson, Reverend Thomas, 276
Johnson family, 133
Johnston, Joseph E., 303
Jones, Allen, 158
Jones, John Paul, 159, 163-164, 271-272
Jones, Joseph, 91, 92, 257, 273, 282, 283-284
Jones, William, 406, 411
Jones, Willie, 158
Jones v. Walker, 398, 406-411
Jouett, Jack, 236, 237, 238
Jouett's Tavern, 266
Journal (Committee of Safety), 63, 94, 154, 202
Journals of Congress, 58
Judiciary Act of 1789, 406

Kellon, R., 157
Kennedy, John F., 298
Kentucky, 173, 252, 290-291
secessionist movement in, 296-297
King's Mountain, battle of, 221, 231, 233
Knox, Henry, 342

Lafayette, Marquis de, 198, 231, 235, 236, 240-241, 243, 282, 294-296, 440
Lamb, John, 347-348
Langdon, John, 72
Laurens, Henry, 198, 200-201, 203, 406
Law of Nations (Vattel), 407
Lawson, Edward, 413
Lawson, Robert, 337
Leatherwood (plantation), 209, 220, 268-269, 282, 303, 316
British and, 221-242
location of, 221-222, 223
Lee, Arthur, 172, 215, 327
Lee, Charles, 68-69, 103-104, 130, 143, 145, 170, 191, 197, 198
Lee, Francis Lightfoot, 54, 151, 192, 214-215
Lee, Henry (cousin), 156
Lee, Henry ("Light-Horse Harry"), 156, 345, 346, 354, 355, 391, 394, 401, 423, 427-429, 433, 441-443, 452
Lee, Ludwell, 114-115
Lee, Richard Henry, 20, 80, 83, 93, 96, 102, 105-106, 125-127, 138, 141, 150-151, 154, 155, 156, 166-167, 179, 183, 185-186, 194, 199-200, 214-216, 229, 231, 258, 267, 268, 273, 275, 286, 307, 328, 333, 341, 346, 376
death of, 434
independence motion of, 110, 111
at Second Continental Congress, 59, 61, 68, 71
senatorial candidacy, 380-382
Washington conspiracy and, 191-192
at Virginia Convention, 22, 23, 35, 40, 78
Lee, Robert E., 150, 401
Lee, Thomas Ludwell, 88, 92
Lee, William, 20, 61, 172
Lee family, 126, 180, 202, 221
Leland, Thomas, 6-8
Lemaire, Captain, 171-172, 215
Leslie, Alexander, 230
Letcher, William, 225
Letcher, Mrs. William, 225
Letters of a Federal Farmer (Lee), 338, 340

Lewis, Andrew, 4, 23, 37, 40, 74, 132, 202
appointed brigadier general, 94
Lewis, Charles, 74, 154
Lewis, Fielding, 78-79
Lewis, Mrs. Fletcher, 79
Lexington, battle of, 45, 47, 50, 58, 69, 70
Liberty Hall Academy, 270, 295
Lincoln, Abraham, 1, 43
Lincoln, Mrs. Abraham, 208
Lincoln, Benjamin, 218, 323-324, 338
Lippman, Walter, 368
Littlepage, Lewis, 295-296, 298
Logan, Colonel, 291
Lomax, Thomas, 220
London Chronicle, 65
Louis XIV, King, 440
Lovell, James, 214
Lynch, Charles, 430
Lynchburg *Daily Virginian*, 453-454
Lyons, Peter, 302

McClanahan, Robert, 239
McClurg, James, 283-284, 328-329
McCrae, Christopher, 227
McDowell, James, 241, 246
McIntosh, Lachlan, 201
McMaster, John B., 364
Madison, James, 52, 85, 105, 117, 160, 242, 267, 270, 273, 274, 280-282, 287, 318, 324-330, 332, 337, 338, 376, 384, 388, 395, 428, 445-446, 448
at Constitutional Convention, 329-330
in Congress, 385-386, 390-391, 392
correspondence with Jefferson, 257-259, 279, 313, 325-326, 328, 333, 335, 339, 375
Henry on, 435
reapportionment controversy, 382
senatorial candidacy, 380-382
on slavery, 313
at Virginia Convention (1788), 344, 346, 352-354, 360-362, 364, 371, 372, 383
on Virginia Council, 182
Madison, Thomas, 12, 13-14, 132, 201, 334
Madison, Mrs. Thomas, 132
Magdalen (schooner), 45
Magna Carta, 393
Manhattan Island, battle at, 136, 140-141, 143
Manuscript History (Randolph), 116-117
Marshall, John, 83, 184-185, 265, 294, 300, 327, 334-335, 338, 346, 364, 394, 407, 418, 419, 445, 446, 452
Marshall, Thomas, 36
Martin, Joseph, 286, 394-395
Martin v. Hunter's Lessee, 407
Maryland Convention, 40, 41-42
Matthews, Sampson, 283-284
Mason, George, 77, 80, 97, 102, 119-121, 127, 138, 174, 208, 216-217, 225-226, 254, 275-276, 312, 317, 318, 327, 333, 334, 339, 341
Bill of Rights (Virginia) and, 113-117, 119
at Constitutional Convention, 330, 331
death of, 434
Fairfax resolutions, 29, 116
at Virginia Convention, 79, 113-117, 119, 344-345, 347, 348, 351-353, 355, 364-366, 370-374, 392-393
Mason, Thomson, 258
Massachusetts Constitution of 1780, 115-116
May, John, 290-291
Mayo, Joseph, 313
Mays, David, 68, 88-89
Mazzei, Philip, 84-85, 94, 222, 261
Meade, Everard, 216, 373
Memoirs (Jefferson), 250
Mercantile system, 19
Mercer, Hugh, 74-76
wounded, 150
Mercer, James, 92
Meredith, Samuel, 50, 102, 288-289
Meredith, Mrs. Samuel, 288-289
Mermaid (ship), 288
Middleton, Arthur, 62
Milton, John, 202
Mifflin, Thomas, 179, 180, 186, 189

[528]

INDEX

INDEX

DATE DUE

New Books 4-8-71		
FEB 27 1986		